01/06

THE PENGUIN DICTIONARY OF
ECONOMICS

Graham Bannock
R. E. Baxter
Evan Davis

SIXTH EDITION

PENGUIN BOOKS

PENGUIN BOOKS

Published by the Penguin Group
Penguin Books Ltd, 27 Wrights Lane, London W8 5TZ, England
Penguin Putnam Inc., 375 Hudson Street, New York, New York 10014, USA
Penguin Books Australia Ltd, Ringwood, Victoria, Australia
Penguin Books Canada Ltd, 10 Alcorn Avenue, Toronto, Ontario, Canada M4V 3B2
Penguin Books (NZ) Ltd, Private Bag 102902, NSMC, Auckland, New Zealand

Penguin Books Ltd, Registered Offices: Harmondsworth, Middlesex, England

First published 1972
Second edition 1978
Third edition 1984
Fourth edition 1987
Fifth edition 1992
Sixth edition 1998
3 5 7 9 10 8 6 4 2

Set in 8.5/10.5 Monotype Times New Roman
Typeset by Rowland Phototypesetting Ltd, Bury St Edmunds, Suffolk
Printed in England by Clays Ltd, St Ives plc

FOREWORD TO THE FIFTH EDITION

'. . . no dictionary of a living tongue can ever be perfect, since while it is hastening to publication, some words are budding, and some falling away'

Samuel Johnson, *The Dictionary of English* (1755)

'In the case of economics there are no important propositions that cannot, in fact, be stated in plain language'   J. K. G. Galbraith, *Annals of an Abiding Liberal* (1979)

Our labours in regularly improving and updating this book have been rewarded, to date, by total sales, world-wide, in excess of 500,000 copies. For this fifth edition we have continued the process of revision. Some seventy entries have been deleted and many others abbreviated to make space for over 150 new entries taking account of new developments in economic theory and practical affairs.

Both the intended readership and the scope and method of the book are unaltered. The dictionary is planned as a companion to two kinds of users of economics. First, for the general reader who wants to follow economic discussion in the press or elsewhere and for the increasing number of people who need some knowledge of economics in their daily work, in teaching, business, the civil service, representative bodies and the professions. Secondly, it is aimed at students, especially those up to the second-year university courses in the subject, but also others, for example those at business schools for whom economics is part of the curriculum.

Our distinctive approach remains unique. This approach consists of a micro-encyclopedic treatment with extensive cross-referencing, up-to-date institutional material and a level of exposition that attempts to combine a reasonable degree of academic rigour with brevity and practical relevance.

Our subject is large and growing continuously and we have had to be highly selective. Words in common usage are not normally included unless they have a specialized meaning in economics. Economic theory, including international, monetary and welfare economics, has been treated fairly comprehensively. We have also given considerable emphasis to the history of economics in keeping with our view of the subjects as a developing one. Individual economists are included only where they have made an important and definable contribution to the body of economic thought as it exists today. We have been particularly sparing in our inclusion of contemporary economists (other than Nobel prize-winners), so that many distinguished living members of the profession are left out. We have tried to include all the key terms used by econometricians and statisticians that are in general use. Our treatment of financial and business economics, public finance, international trade and development and payments has been more selective still but, institutions apart, we hope that nothing important has been omitted.

We have been helped and encouraged by the response we have received from our readers. We hope that they will continue to point out to us any errors or omissions.

G.B.
R.E.B.
May 1991   E.D.

Single and double arrows (➤ ➤➤) in the text indicate, respectively *see* and *see also*, where a point is either amplified or complemented in another entry.

FOREWORD TO THE SIXTH EDITION

This new edition has been substantially revised and updated. To make space for new terms we have removed some now dated material. In some cases, for example banking and credit control, deregulation has simplified our task. In others, for example taxation, the continued growth of complexity has, for reasons of space, obliged us to curtail what hitherto was fairly comprehensive coverage. In selecting entries, we have given priority to recent developments in economic theory and, in keeping with trends in the economics profession, we have continued to emphasize the international rather than the purely UK aspects of our subject.

We are greatly indebted to the help and support we have received from Dee Baxter and Françoise Bannock in getting the work to press.

We must also thank our many readers who have contacted us with valuable suggestions which we have endeavoured to meet. We are sure that they will understand that because of limited space not all their proposed additional entries could be accommodated but we do hope that will not deter them from writing to us with their comments and suggestions in the future. The *Dictionary of Economics* now has a web site by which readers may easily contact us at www.penguin.co.uk/economics.

G.B.
R.E.B.
E.D.

Little Bettenham,
Kent
September 1997

A

'A' shares ►share.

above the line ►below the line.

absolute cost advantage ►barriers to entry.

absorption Total expenditure on final goods and services. Domestic absorption in an economy is equal to ►consumption plus ►investment plus ►government expenditure (or C + I + G), and is equivalent to ►national income minus net exports.

abstinence theory of interest ►interest, abstinence theory of.

acceleration principle The hypothesis that the level of ►investment in an economy varies directly with the rate of change of output. Given technological conditions and the relative prices of ►capital and ►labour, a certain size of capital stock will be chosen to produce a particular level of output. If this level of output changes, then, other things being equal, the desired size of capital stock will also change. Net investment is, by definition, the amount by which the capital stock changes, so it follows that the amount of investment depends on the size of the change in output. At its simplest, the hypothesis asserts that investment will be *proportional* to the rate of change of output, at all levels of output. However, under more realistic assumptions the relationship may cease to be a simple proportional one. There may, for example, be spare capacity over some range of increasing output, so that the capital stock does not have to be increased until full capacity is reached; or the capital intensity (►capital-intensive) of production may vary as the level of output varies. In addition, the relation will be influenced by ►expectations, time lags, etc. As well as being very important in explaining the determination of investment expenditure in the economy, the acceleration principle also plays an important part in theories of the ►business cycle, e.g. the ►accelerator–multiplier model, and the theory of ►economic growth, e.g. in the ►Harrod–Domar model. ►►accelerator coefficient; Clark, J. M.

accelerator coefficient The factor which determines how much ►investment is induced by a change in output (►acceleration principle). Its value is influenced by the availability of spare capacity, the productivity of capital, the rate of ►interest and the price of labour. ►capital–output ratio; productivity.

accelerator–multiplier model A model of economic growth, incorporating the effects of the ➤acceleration principle and the ➤multiplier. An increase in government expenditure, say, raises consumers' incomes which through the multiplier leads to an increase in output which in turn, through the accelerator, raises investment. The increase in expenditure in investment, itself raises incomes and the process is repeated. The model reveals that the multiplier and the accelerator interrelate in a way that can produce a cyclical pattern to economic growth. ➤➤Harrod–Domar model; Samuelson, P. A.

accelerator theory of investment ➤acceleration principle; business cycle.

acceptance The act of accepting, i.e. agreeing to honour a ➤promissory note such as a ➤bill of exchange. By extension, the document itself.

accepting house An institution specializing in accepting or guaranteeing ➤bills of exchange. All accepting houses have taken on other functions as the use of bills of exchange has declined, returning to their original, wider, function of merchant banking (➤merchant banks). The Accepting Houses Committee is a body that ensures policy coordination between them, the ➤Treasury and the ➤Bank of England. Members of this committee are eligible for finer ➤discounts on bills bought by the Bank of England, though this privilege has recently been extended to other banks, including foreign banks, and the term accepting house is now an indication of status rather than function.

account 1. A record of financial transactions in the form of ➤stocks or flows. (➤➤balance of payments; balance sheet; current account; social accounting.) **2.** An arrangement between a seller and a buyer under which a period of ➤credit is allowed before payment; for example the period in which ➤stock exchange transactions take place and after the end of which settlement must be made. Up to the end of an account, transactions are made without payment and account dates are thus of vital importance to speculators.

account day The day on which all transactions made during the previous ➤account at the ➤stock exchange must be settled (hence, *settlement day*). On the London Stock Exchange, as in the USA, the markets use rolling accounts which are settled a fixed number of days after the transaction: at present five days, or 'T + 5'.

accounting equation, basic ➤balance sheet.

accruals ➤accrued expenses.

accrued expenses The cost of services utilized in advance of payment and written into a company's accounts as ➤liabilities.

ACP Africa, the Caribbean and the Pacific. ➤Lomé Convention

acquisition ➤take-over.

ACT Advance corporation tax ➤corporation tax.

active labour-market policies Measures taken to increase the employment prospects of the unemployed (►long-term unemployment) without creating upward pressure on wage levels. Such policies embrace almost anything from better advice and jobs counselling (job broking); to training measures; to direct job creation, through subsidies or public-sector employment. They are distinct from the passive measure of paying out state benefits to the unemployed. The distinguishing characteristic of active labour-market measures is that they do not rely on general macroeconomic growth to generate employment (and are thus not usually born of a diagnosis of ►Keynesian unemployment); nor do they include measures designed to price the unemployed into existing jobs (they are thus not an obvious choice for reducing ►classical unemployment). Active measures have been most extensively pursued in Sweden where, after 300 days, benefits for the unemployed are replaced by options for work or training. There is some debate as to whether these policies were responsible for the relatively low unemployment rate in Sweden up to the 1990s. In the UK there has been a growing interest in such measures and, in 1997, a comprehensive *welfare to work* package was introduced, for those under 25 and unemployed for over six months. This embodies a 'carrot and stick' approach, combining the threat of loss of benefit, with the opportunity of a place on a training scheme, community work, or a temporary job subsidy. Success of such schemes can be judged by a downward shift of the ►Beveridge curve. ►►workfare.

activity analysis ►linear programming.

activity rate ►labour force.

actuary Someone trained in the calculation of ►risk and ►premiums for ►assurance purposes.

ad valorem tax ►tax, ad valorem.

adaptive expectations The formulation of beliefs about the future value of variables based on their past value and direction of movement. If economic agents wanted to predict inflation next year, using adaptive expectations they would take last year's rate and adjust it. The adjustment would depend on how wrong they had been last year when predicting inflation this year – if they had underestimated inflation, they would upwardly revise their prediction for next year. Adaptive expectations are perhaps naive, in that they will respectively always under- – or overestimate a variable which is consistently rising or falling. The assumption that people hold them is crucial in allowing certain economic policies to have an effect (►policy ineffectiveness theorem) and has been criticized as ad hoc. ►►expectations; rational expectations.

ADB African Development Bank; ►Asian Development Bank.

administered prices Strictly, prices which are set by management decision rather than by negotiation between buyer and seller. True ►market prices are to be found only in the ►stock exchange and other places where prices change constantly. Most retail and industrial prices are set by management, though they will be altered in response to competition. The term administered prices is often used to refer to price-fixing by a ►monopoly firm, a ►cartel or a government body. Some economists have argued that inflexible administered prices have been an important contributory cause of ►inflation. ►►mean costs.

ADR ►American depository receipt.

advance corporation tax (ACT) ►corporation tax.

advanced countries States with the highest levels of ►national income per head, such as the member countries of the ►Organization for Economic Cooperation and Development (OECD). ►►developing countries; transition, economies in.

advances Loans (►bank loan).

adverse selection The problem that, in certain markets, the inability of one trader to assess the quality of the other makes it likely that poor-quality traders will predominate. Noted by Akerlof in 1970, adverse selection is sometimes referred to as *the lemon problem*. A popular example of the phenomenon is in the second-hand car market, where *sellers* know whether or not their car is a lemon (i.e. performs badly), but where *buyers* cannot make that judgement without running the car. Given that buyers can't tell the quality of any car, all cars of the same type will sell at the same price, regardless of whether they are lemons or not. The risk of purchasing a lemon will lower the price buyers are prepared to pay for any car and, because second-hand prices are low, people with non-lemon cars will be little inclined to put them on the market.

There are three ingredients in this problem. First, a random variation in product quality in the market; secondly, ►asymmetric information about product quality between traders in the market; and thirdly, a greater willingness for poor-quality traders to trade at low prices than for high-quality ones to. (Lemon car owners will still put their cars on the market when the prices drop; other car owners will not.) There are many important markets where adverse selection is held to be significant – notably insurance and the market for credit. ►►market failure.

advertising Paid announcements to persuade or inform members of the public. Outside the theoretical world of ►perfect competition, advertising of goods and services is necessary to ensure that potential buyers are informed and helps to make markets function efficiently. However, advertising can create or increase ►barriers to entry into an industry and enhance product differentiation (►differentiation, product) and, it has been argued, promote ►concentration. Proponents of heavy advertising expenditure argue that it provides a ►signalling mechanism whereby high-quality producers publicly demonstrate their commitment to their product, something they would do only if they genuinely believed that it had a long-term future; while others point out that consumers may have little choice in a concentrated industry but to bear the cost of unnecessary advertising which serves only to keep out new entrants. Although 'own brand' products in supermarkets (which are not advertised) have not replaced advertised brands, this could be explained by the power of advertisers to manipulate consumer psychology.

African Development Bank (ADB) A regional international bank (➤banking) established in 1964 for assisting in the economic growth of the independent African states. In 1972 an affiliated organization, the African Development Fund, was set up with a membership open, unlike that of the Bank, to non-African states. It is through this Fund that loans are made to African member states at low ➤rates of interest (➤➤soft loan). Affiliation to the Fund has enabled the Bank to broaden its sources of funds for investment. In 1982 the African members of the Bank agreed to open its membership to non-African states. In 1996 the Bank had fifty African member states and twenty-five other member states. ➤➤Asian Development Bank; Caribbean Development Bank; Colombo Plan; foreign aid; Inter-American Development Bank.

African Development Fund ➤African Development Bank.

agency costs The inefficiencies associated with employing a representative to carry out a task for you, rather than carrying it out yourself. In any situation where people are employed to perform a task, those employees – or agents – may well have their own interests, quite separate from those of the employer (often referred to as the 'principal'). Agency costs refer to the loss of efficiency in the conduct of a task from the fact that agents may let their own interests temper their behaviour. For example, a travel agent may sell a more expensive ticket than necessary, to obtain a bigger commission. Agency costs – in practice very common in all sorts of economic relationships – only prevail where the behaviour of the agent is hard to monitor directly. ➤principal–agent problem.

aggregate concentration ➤concentration.

aggregate demand The sum of all expenditure within an economy, making up ➤gross domestic product. The main categories are consumers' expenditure on goods and services; government spending (➤public expenditure); ➤investment in capital goods and stocks (➤inventories) and ➤exports of goods and services, less expenditure on ➤imports of goods and services. Since ➤J. M. Keynes, economists have debated how far the level of aggregate demand affects the total level of output and ➤economic growth. ➤➤policy ineffectiveness theorem; national income.

aggregate supply The total of all goods and services produced in an economy. Prior to ➤Keynes, it was believed that ➤national income was determined by aggregate supply. Keynes shifted the emphasis on to ➤aggregate demand, with supply meeting whatever demand existed up to a point. More recently, supply

factors have received more consideration in the determination of total output.
➤supply-side economics.

aggregated rebate ➤deferred rebate.

aggregation problem ➤Cambridge school.

aid ➤foreign aid.

AIM ➤unlisted securities market(s).

air-passenger duty A flat-rate indirect tax (➤direct taxation) levied on air departures from the UK. Introduced in 1995/96, the 1996/97 rate is £10 per person for
European and £20 for non-European flights.

Allais, Maurice (b. 1911) Educated at the École Polytechnique and the École
Nationale Supérieure des Mines in Paris, in 1944 Maurice Allais became director
of the Centre d'Analyse Économique at the École Nationale Supérieure, where
he taught notable economists like Malinvaud and ➤Debreu. He became the first
French citizen to win the ➤Nobel Prize in Economics in 1988. His main work is
his book *À la recherche d'une discipline économique* (1943), a report on ➤general
equilibrium and ➤economic efficiency without any assumption of ➤convexity. His
name is best known for the Allais paradox, an attempt to show the impact of
psychological factors on consumer decision-making in conditions of ➤risk. The
paradox is as follows: if you offer people either a certain £500 or a lottery ticket
that gives them a 10 per cent chance of winning £2500, an 89 per cent chance of
winning £500 and a 1 per cent chance of winning nothing, they often take the
certain £500. But, if you offer them a choice between two lottery tickets, one
which gives them an 11 per cent chance of winning £500 and an 89 per cent
chance of winning nothing, or another one which offers them a 10 per cent chance
of winning £2500 and a 90 per cent chance of winning nothing, they often take
the second one. Interestingly, however, the effective choice being made is the
same in both cases, and consistent consumers should pick either the first option
both times or the second option both times.

Allais paradox ➤Allais, M.

allocative efficiency ➤economic efficiency.

allotment letter A letter addressed to a subscriber to an issue of ➤shares informing
him of the number of shares that he has been allotted and, where payment was
not made with the application, the amount due.

Alternative Investment Market ➤unlisted securities market(s).

American Depository Receipt (ADR) A document issued by a US bank against
➤shares deposited with it or a bank overseas. The ADR circulates as a bearer
document, (➤bearer bonds), in effect giving title to the underlying shares.

amortization Provision for the repayment of ►debt by means of accumulating a 'sinking fund' through regular payments which, with accumulated ►interest, may be used to settle the debt in instalments over time, or in a lump sum. The term is also used as a synonym for ►depreciation.

Amsterdam Treaty ►European Union.

Andean Pact A ►customs union agreed at Cartagena in 1969 between Chile, Peru, Colombia, Bolivia and Ecuador. Venezuela joined the Pact in 1973, but Chile terminated her agreement in 1976. Free trade was established between the member states, although it was not until 1994 that a Common External Tariff regime was agreed. In 1996 the Act of Trujillo committed the member states to the setting up of an Economic Community (►European Union) by 2001. ►►Central American Common Market; Latin American Integration Association.

annual allowances ►capital allowances.

annual percentage rate (APR) A legally standardized form for presenting the ►rate of interest and all the associated costs of a loan in the UK. The idea behind the APR, which was introduced under the ►Consumer Credit Act, was to prevent lenders quoting low interest rates while in effect making the loan expensive by charging arrangement fees and demanding frequent payments. The APR is the ►compound interest you would pay if all costs associated with the loan were collected as interest. It is calculated subject to a complex formula issued by the Office of Fair Trading (►Fair Trading Act).

annuity 1. A constant annual payment. **2.** A guaranteed series of payments in the future purchased immediately for a lump sum. Annuities are described as 'certain' where payment is specified for a fixed number of years. A 'life' annuity payment continues until the death of the person for whom it was purchased. Annuities may be 'immediate', where payment commences on purchase, or 'deferred', where payment starts at a future specified date. Some annuities offer protection against the erosion of the real value of income through ►inflation. The British government sold annuities until 1962, but they are now available only from ►insurance companies (►personal pension). The price of an annuity is based on the ►present value of the stream of income payments it provides, and it varies with ►rates of interest and, in the case of life annuities, the age and sex of the person who will draw the annuity.

anti-trust (US) Legislation to control ►monopoly and restrictive practices in favour of ►competition. It applies not only to amalgamations of firms (►trust) but also to single companies. The *Sherman Act* (1890) made monopoly or the restraint of trade illegal. The *Clayton Act* (1914) clarified earlier legislation and prohibited specific activities, notably ►price discrimination, ►exclusive dealing, and ►interlocking directorates and shareholdings among competitors. The *Celler–Kefauver* Act (1950) amended the Clayton Act by prohibiting mergers which might lessen competition. The *Robinson–Patman* Act (1936) strengthened the provisions in the Clayton Act against price discrimination and made it illegal to sell goods to retailers or wholesalers at different prices unless justified by differences in the cost of supply. Anti-trust policy is overseen by the *Federal Trade Commission* (FTC), a federal government agency created in 1914 which cooperates with, but is independent of, the Anti-Trust Division of the Department of Justice. US anti-trust law is intended to be non-discretionary, in contrast to the UK approach which is more pragmatic. ➤➤competition policy; Monopolies and Mergers Commission; Restrictive Trade Practices Acts; Chicago school.

APACS Association for Payment Clearing Services. ➤clearing house.

APC ➤average propensity to consume.

appreciation Increase in the value of an ➤asset; the antonym of ➤depreciation. Appreciation may occur through rising ➤prices as a result of ➤inflation, increased scarcity or increases in earning power. ➤➤currency appreciation.

appropriation account A business account showing how net ➤profit is distributed between ➤dividends, reserves, ➤pension funds, etc.

appropriation accounts ➤public expenditure.

APR ➤annual percentage rate.

APS ➤average propensity to save.

arbitrage The exploitation of differences between the prices of financial ➤assets or ➤currency or a ➤commodity within or between markets by buying where prices are low and selling where they are higher. If wheat is cheaper in Chicago than in London after allowing for transport and dealing costs, it will pay to buy in Chicago and sell in London. If interest rates are higher on a deutschmark deposit in London than in Frankfurt, a higher return will be obtained by switching funds from one centre to the other. It will also pay to switch funds from a deutschmark deposit in Frankfurt to a sterling deposit in London if the interest rate differential is greater than the cost of covering against the risk of a fall in the exchange rate of the pound against the deutschmark (➤forward exchange market). Unlike ➤speculation, arbitrage does not normally involve significant risks, since the buying and selling operations are carried out more or less simultaneously and the profit made does not depend upon taking a view on future price changes. By eliminating price differentials, arbitrage contributes to the achievement of ➤equilibrium. ➤Price discrimination between markets is difficult or impossible where possibilities for arbitrage exist. ➤➤efficient markets hypothesis.

arbitration The process in which parties to a dispute allow a third party, who has no other direct involvement, to suggest or impose a solution. Each party will be more inclined to go to arbitration the better they think their chance is of winning, and the higher the cost of resolving the dispute by other means. The logic behind arbitration is that disputants find it easier to agree with a third party than to resolve their argument themselves. Arbitration can be binding, in which case each party agrees in advance that they will do whatever the arbiter decides, or non-binding, in which case the parties are free to reject the arbiter's advice. *Pendular arbitration* is that in which the arbiter can only accept the point of view of one side or the other, but is not allowed to advocate a compromise solution. The idea behind this is to encourage the disputants to make reasonable offers to each other before the arbiter makes a decision. (➤bargaining theory of wages; game theory.

arithmetic progression A sequence of numbers in which the differences between all adjacent numbers in the sequence are the same, e.g. 2, 4, 6, 8, 10 . . . ➤geometric progression.

Arrow, Kenneth Joseph (b. 1921) After graduation at Columbia University and a period at the Cowles Commission, Professor Arrow went to Stanford University in 1949, where he became a professor in 1953. In 1968 he accepted a Chair at Harvard University, but returned to Stanford University in 1979. He was awarded the ➤Nobel Prize for Economics in 1972 (with ➤Hicks). His publications include *Social Choice and Individual Values* (1951), *Existence of an Equilibrium for a Competitive Economy* (1954) with ➤Debreu, *Studies in Mathematical Theory of Inventory and Production* (1958), *Public Investment, the Rate of Return and Optimal Fiscal Policy* (1970), *Essays in the Theory of Risk-Bearing* (1971) and *General Competitive Analysis* (1971).

Professor Arrow showed that it was logically impossible to devise a constitution for a community that would always ensure to rank outcomes in a way that appeared desirable. (➤impossibility theorem.) He made important contributions to ➤general equilibrium analysis which placed the theory on a firmer basis after the work of ➤Walras. Professor Arrow has also made contributions to the theory of decision-making under uncertainty (➤risk) and to ➤growth theory.

articles of association ➤Memorandum of Association

Arusha Agreement ➤Lomé Convention.

ASEAN ➤Association of South East Asian Nations.

Asia–Pacific Economic Cooperation (APEC) A forum of, originally, fifteen Pacific Rim countries, formed in 1989 on the initiative of Australia. In 1992 a Secretariat was opened in Singapore and in 1994 agreement was reached for the establishment of a ➤free-trade area. The ➤advanced countries in the group should achieve the objective by 2010 and the ➤developing countries by 2020. At a meeting in Osaka in 1995 the member countries agreed to reduce import tariffs (➤tariffs, import) and liberalize services, public procurement contracts and ➤foreign investment. It was accepted that flexibility should be allowed in the implementation of measures by the ➤developing countries in the group and in relation to particularly sensitive areas, such as agriculture. The APEC countries agreed that the liberalization measures undertaken would not discriminate against third countries. The 1995 meeting also agreed that each member should present its five-year plan for liberalization at the meeting in 1996. In 1996 there were eighteen members, viz Australia, Brunei, Canada, Chile, China, Hong Kong, Indonesia, Japan, Malaysia, Mexico, New Zealand, Papua New Guinea, the Philippines, Singapore, South Korea, Taiwan, Thailand and USA. Applications to join have been received from India, Russia and Vietnam. ≫Association of South East Asian Nations; North American Free Trade Agreement.

Asian Development Bank (ADB) The Asian Development Bank, based in Manila, was established in 1966, following the recommendations of the United Nations Economic Commission for Asia and the Pacific. It was formed 'to foster economic growth and cooperation in the region of Asia and the Pacific and to contribute to the acceleration of economic development of the ►developing countries of the region'. It encourages economic and financial cooperation among the regional members. Membership carries the right to contract for projects supported by bank loans. About 60 per cent of the total subscribed ►capital of $1100 million was contributed by the nineteen countries within the United Nations commission region, which include the three developed countries of Japan, Australia and New Zealand. The remaining non-regional members include the USA, which subscribed $200 million (as did Japan), West Germany, Canada, the UK and Switzerland. The bank operates as a viable ►banking institution, charging realistic ►rates of interest and encourages a flow of capital to the region from outside sources. The Bank's affiliate, the Asian Development Fund, gives ►soft loans to the poorest nations in the region. In 1986, the People's Republic of China became a member and the authorized capital stock of the Bank was increased to SDR 15,900 million (►special drawing rights). The Bank has a membership of thirty-six countries in Asia and the Pacific and sixteen countries outside the region. ≫African Development Bank; Caribbean Development Bank; Colombo Plan; foreign aid; Inter-American Development Bank.

assessable profits The taxable ►profit of a business, normally after the deduction of ►capital allowances, interest and other business expenses. It differs, however, from accounting profit not only because of different treatment of ►depreciation, but because some business expenses, e.g. some forms of entertaining, are not allowable in computing taxable profit.

asset specificity The feature of durable or fixed ►assets which have no, or limited, alternative uses, such as a nuclear power station, and which, once built, therefore generate ►sunk costs.

assets 1. A business accounting term. On the ►balance sheet of a company, everything that the company owns and which has a money value is classified as an asset, total assets being equal to total liabilities. Assets fall into the following categories, roughly in order of the extent to which realizing their money value would disrupt the company's business: (a) *Current assets*: ➤cash, bank deposits and other items that can readily be turned into cash, e.g. bills receivable, ➤stock and work in progress, marketable ➤securities. (b) *Trade investments*: ➤investment in subsidiary or associated companies. (c) *Fixed assets*: ➤land, buildings, plant and machinery, vehicles and furniture, usually at cost less ➤depreciation written off. (d) *Intangible assets*: goodwill, patents, etc. The assets of an individual are those possessions or the liabilities of others to him, which have a positive money value. **2.** *Financial assets* are titles to cash, such as a bank ➤deposit or income and/or ➤capital gains. Financial assets may be classified according to their ➤liquidity, the protection they offer against ➤inflation (➤indexation) or changes in ➤exchange rates and the risk of default. Some financial assets are income-certain (for example ➤gilt-edged securities), while some are not (for example ➤ordinary shares). Some assets are capital-certain, for example a fixed-interest security which is redeemable at par (➤par value; redeemable securities) but ordinary shares are subject to a price risk. **3.** *Real assets* are tangible assets such as land, buildings or equipment.

assisted areas Regions in Great Britain which attract government assistance because of their persistent high levels of unemployment relative to the rest of the country. (Northern Ireland has its own forms of financial aid.) First introduced in the 1930s, they were substantially extended following the recommendations of the Hunt Committee in 1969. Legislation was revised and consolidated in the Industrial Development Act 1982. Under the 1982 Act the government is empowered to give grants and loans for investment which expand capacity and generate employment in assisted areas (➤investment incentives). Since the accession of the UK to the ➤European Union, similar grants and other forms of financial assistance are available from the European Regional Development Fund and the European Social Fund. ➤➤enterprise zones; free-trade zone.

Association of South East Asian Nations (ASEAN) An association set up in 1967 by five countries in South-East Asia: Indonesia, Malaysia, the Philippines, Singapore and Thailand. In 1976, the Association agreed to a list of industrial projects covering petrochemicals, fertilizers, steel, soda ash, newsprint and rubber, on which the group would cooperate in the construction of major plants. The Association also agreed to set up a permanent secretariat. Brunei joined the Association in 1984, Vietnam in 1995 and Burma and Laos in 1997. In 1994 it was agreed that import tariffs (➤tariffs, import) on intra-ASEAN trade should be reduced to a maximum of 5 per cent by 2003, subject to the right to exclude some sensitive traded goods or services. ➤➤Asia–Pacific Economic Cooperation; free-trade area.

assurance That branch of ➤insurance under which a contract is made to pay a ➤capital sum on a specified date or on the death of the person assured. The former contract or policy is called term or endowment assurance, and the latter whole-of-life. Both types of policy may be with or without ►profits. By paying a higher ►premium, the policyholder can receive a share of the profits earned by the life fund. Policies may also be linked in some way to ►equities so that the final payment is determined by the stock market prices current at the time (►unit trust). Life assurance is an important form of private ►savings.

asymmetric information Information concerning a transaction which is unequally shared between the two parties to the transaction. The most famous application of the problems that asymmetric information can create has been Akerlof's discussion of the second-hand car market (►adverse selection). Other important applications relate to the ►principal – agent problem and ►moral hazard. Much of economics in the 1970s and 1980s has been devoted to the discussion of mechanisms for coping with these types of problem. ►►screening; signalling.

ATM Automatic teller machines (►credit card).

auction A type of transaction in which the buyer of an item and the price that is paid for it are chosen after a number of different potential buyers has each made some declaration of their willingness to pay for the item. Auctions can be held in a variety of forms: the *English auction*, in which the bidders sequentially offer higher prices, with the last remaining bidder paying his last offered price; the *Dutch auction*, in which a list of sequentially lower prices are offered by the seller, until a potential buyer accepts one of these prices and then pays that price for the product; the *sealed-bid auction*, in which each bidder is given one chance to make an offer, in ignorance of the offers of other bidders, and in which the highest offer is accepted; and the *second-price* (or ►*Vickrey*) *auction*, which is exactly like a sealed-bid auction, except that the highest bidder has to pay only the price offered by the second-highest bidder. Economists have used ►game theory to study how auctions should be conducted, and what strategy should be adopted in each case by the bidders.

Austrian school A tradition of economic thought originating in the work of ►Menger (1840–1921), who was Professor of Economics at Vienna until 1903. Menger's principal achievement was the construction of a marginal utility theory of value (►value, theories of). He was succeeded in the Chair by von ►Wieser (1851–1926) who developed his work, and in addition, clearly formulated the important concept of ►opportunity cost. ►Böhm-Bawerk (1851–1914), who followed, made his main contributions in the fields of ►capital and interest-rate theory (►rate of interest). The Austrian tradition was followed in the work of von ►Mises and von ►Hayek, and, later, in work by ►Hicks. ►►Jevons, W. S.; Longfield, S. M.

autarky National economic self-sufficiency (i.e. exclusion from international trade) pursued as a policy by means of ►tariffs, ►exchange controls and other devices of the ►planned economy as in Fascist Germany and Italy in the 1930s (►►closed economy).

authorized capital The amount of share ➤capital fixed in the ➤memorandum of association and the articles of association of a company as required by the Companies Acts (➤company law). Also known as *nominal capital* or *registered capital*.

auto-correlation A ➤correlation, not between two different variables, but between successive values of one variable. It is used most frequently to refer to a potential problem in ➤least-squares regression, when the residual of the regression is auto-correlated, i.e. appears to have a systematic pattern, and therefore deviates from the assumption of randomness usually made. Auto-correlation, or serial correlation, requires other analytical methods to be adopted.

automatic stabilizers ➤built-in stabilizers.

autonomous investment Investment expenditure which is not induced by changes in output (➤acceleration principle). Examples of such investment are government expenditure on infrastructure and firms' expenditure on new plant to exploit an invention.

average A single number calculated to summarize and represent the values of items in a set (➤frequency distribution). The most common such measure is the *arithmetic mean*. This is calculated by adding together the values of the items in the set and dividing the total by the number of items. For example, suppose that the wages of five employees were £300 per week, £320 p.w., £380 p.w., £400 p.w. and £450 p.w. respectively. The arithmetic mean is (£300 + £320 + £380 + £400 + £450) divided by 5 = £370. There is an implied assumption in the arithmetic mean that the values from which the mean is calculated are more or less of the same order of magnitude. For instance, if another employee were included who earned £1000 p.w. the arithmetic mean would show an average wage of the six employees to be £475 p.w., which would be misleading as all but one earned less than this. ➤standard deviation.

The *median* avoids this problem of extremes by taking that value for which there is an equal number of items with values below it as above it. For instance, in the above example of five employees, the median is £380 as there are two employees with wages above and two with wages below this. If we include the sixth employee, the median is the arithmetic mean of the two middle values (as there is an even number of items), that is (£380 + £400) divided by 2 = £390. The median, therefore, is less affected by extreme values and will be less than the arithmetic mean where the items include an extreme high value and will be higher than the arithmetic mean where there is an extreme low value.

The third important measure of average is the *mode*. This is simply the 'most popular' value in a set of numbers. For instance, suppose out of a total of fifty employees, five earned £300 p.w., ten earned £320 p.w., twenty-five earned £380 p.w., five earned £400 p.w. and five earned £450 p.w. The mode would be £380 p.w. because more employees earned that sum than any other of the sums specified.

It is to be noted that unlike the other two measures the mode is totally uninfluenced by other items in the set.

A fourth measure of average is the *geometric mean*. This is calculated by multiplying the items in the set and taking the nth root, where n is the number of items in the set. For instance, the geometric mean of 3 and 12 is the square root of $(3 \times 12 = 36) = 6$. In general, the formula can be written as log (geometric mean) = $\log x_1 + \log x_2 + \log x_3 \ldots + \log x_n$ *divided by* n. In the above example of five employees' wages the geometric mean works out at £366, compared with the arithmetic mean of £370. If the additional employee, earning £1000 is added the arithmetic mean rises to £475, an increase of 28 per cent but the geometric mean rises only to £433 an increase of 18 per cent. This is a general characteristic of the geometric mean. It tends to constrict the effects of large-value items and enhance the effect of low-value items. ➤➤weighted average.

average cost Total production costs per unit of output. It is calculated by adding total ➤fixed costs to total ➤variable costs and dividing by the number of units produced. The effect of indivisibilities (➤economies of scale) is that average costs fall as output expands, spreading the fixed cost over more units. After a time, however, average variable costs may increase as, for example, workers are paid overtime to operate machinery nearer to its full capacity and more has to be spent on maintenance. This is said to give short-run average cost curves a characteristic U-shape. In the ➤long run all costs are variable because more fixed ➤assets can be acquired or surplus capacity scrapped. The shape and slope of the long-run average-cost curve, when all costs are variable, will be determined by the extent of long-run economies of scale (if any).

average-cost pricing The pricing of goods or services so as just to cover the ➤average cost of production. The firm engaging in this will neither make a profit nor loss. ➤➤marginal-cost pricing.

average propensity to consume The proportion of income, whether of individuals, households or countries, spent on goods and services, other than for ➤investment (➤➤consumption function; marginal propensity to consume; savings ratio).

average propensity to save The proportion of income, whether of individuals, households or countries, which is not spent on consumption (➤average propensity to consume; ➤➤savings ratio).

average revenue Total sales value divided by the number of units sold and equal, therefore, to average ➤price.

Averch–Johnson effect The tendency of companies, whose ➤rate of return is regulated, to engage in excessive accumulation of capital in order to expand the volume of their profits. If companies are told that they are not allowed to earn more than a 15 per cent return on capital, there is a strong incentive for them to over-invest in order to earn that 15 per cent on as large a capital base as possible, even if it would be more efficient for them to have less capital and higher ➤variable costs. ➤rate-of-return regulation; ➤➤price regulation; regulation; yardstick competition.

avoidable costs ➤prime costs.

B

backwardation 1. In a ►commodity market, the amount by which the spot ►price (including the cost of stocking over time) exceeds the forward price. ►►spot market; forward exchange market. 2. On the ►stock exchange, a sum of ►money paid by a ►bear to a ►bull for the right to delay delivery of ►securities sold forward at a fixed price. A bear will have sold securities to a bull for delivery on a certain date in the expectation that, by that date, the market price will have fallen. If it does not, in fact, fall, he may consider it worthwhile to pay a backwardation so as to defer delivery of the shares until the next account period. 3. A temporary situation in which one ►market maker has a lower offer price than another's bid price.

BACS Bankers' Automated Clearing Service (►clearing house).

'bad money drives out good' The idea that an injection of a low-quality coinage into a monetary system will dissuade holders of high-quality coins from parting with cash. Before paper ►money (►banknote) became universally accepted as a means for settling ►debts, precious metals were the most common forms of money. Gold and silver coins were struck bearing a ►face value equivalent to the value of their metal content. Debasement of the coinage occurred when the face value was kept above the value of the metal content of the coinage. The holders of the correctly valued coinage became unwilling to exchange for the debased coinage because they would obtain less metal in exchange than if they bought direct. The result was that the 'good', undebased coinage did not circulate. The process is referred to as ►Gresham's law, and is an early application of the idea of ►adverse selection.

Bagehot, Walter (1826–77) Bagehot graduated in mathematics at University College, London, and qualified as a lawyer in 1852. After a spell as a banker in his father's business he succeeded his father-in-law as editor of the *Economist* newspaper in 1860, a post he held until 1877. He was an influential commentator on current economic affairs and a prolific writer who is often quoted today. His publications include *Universal Money* (1869), *Physics and Politics* (1872), *Lombard Street. A Description of the Money Market* (1873) and *Postulates of English Political Economy* (1876).

balance of payments A tabulation of the credit and debit transactions of a country with foreign countries and international institutions during a specific period. The data is collated on the principle of ►double-entry bookkeeping, although, by convention, the figures are published in a single column with positive (credit) and negative (debit) signs. The entries in the account should, therefore, add up to zero but because of measurement problems they fail to do so in practice and recourse has to be made to a ►balancing item. Transactions are divided into two broad groups: ►current account and capital account. The *current account* is made up of trade in goods (so-called visible trade) and in services and the profits and interest earned from overseas ►assets, net of those paid abroad (invisible trade). It is the current account that is generally referred to in discussion of the state of the balance of payments. The *capital account* is made up of such items as the inward and outward flow of money for ►investment and international grants and loans.

The UK has traditionally had a ►deficit on visible trade – that is, it imports more goods than it exports. However, in the past this has been more than compensated for by the surplus which it has earned on invisible account. From the middle of the nineteenth century up to 1931 the UK's balance on current account was always in surplus (except for the period during the First World War and perhaps to a minor extent in 1926). Even after 1931, up to the Second World War, the deficits

UK Balance of Payments – 1995

Current Account	*£billion*
Export of goods	+152.3
Imports of goods	−164.0
Visible balance	−11.7
Trade in services (net balance):	
Government	−2.0
Transport	−0.5
Travel	−3.7
Financial and other services	+12.4
Total services	+6.2
Other transactions (net balance):	
Government	−9.9
Other	+12.5
Current balance	−2.9
Capital Account	
Investments overseas by UK residents	−65.9
Investment in the UK by overseas residents	+37.3
Other capital transactions	+29.0
Balancing item	+2.4

Source: *UK Balance of Payments, 1996*, Office for National Statistics, London.

were relatively small. In the 1940s the UK was forced to liquidate many of its overseas assets and to borrow substantial sums to pay for the war. Since then the current balance has varied – falling towards deficit until the ➤devaluation of the late 1960s when it recovered; that was followed by the increase in the price of oil by ➤OPEC in 1973, driving the account into deficit; only to see it move sharply into surplus with the UK's own oil discoveries. It fell into substantial deficit during the boom of the late 1980s, and recovered again in the early 1990s, even in fact when demand at home was strong. The tables show the composition of the balance of payments of the UK and the USA in 1995.

The overall deficits or surpluses in the balance of payments are brought into balance by movements in the ➤gold and foreign exchange reserves or liabilities to non-residents. The transactions between foreigners and residents are carried out, in the UK, through the ➤exchange equalization account. The balance of payments reflects many factors – first, the state of ➤aggregate demand at home and the state of demand abroad; and secondly the ➤exchange rate and the relative costs of domestic production. Governments can only really influence the balance by changing demand, or by changing the exchange rate. In the past it was felt important to avoid a deficit which implied a net demand for foreign currency. In the fixed exchange rates of the time, the central authority had to finance an imbalance by selling gold or foreign exchange for its currency. This was not sustainable for ever.

USA Balance of Payments – 1995

Current Account	$billion
Export of goods	+574.9
Imports of goods	−749.3
Visible balance	−174.5
Trade in services (net balance):	+51.7
Other transactions (net balance):	
Government	−14.1
Other	−16.0
Current balance	−152.9
Capital Account	
Investments overseas by USA residents	−270.4
Investment in the USA by overseas residents	+426.3
Other capital transactions	−9.7
Balancing item	+6.7

Source: *US Department of Commerce: OECD 'Economic Survey of United States'*, 1996.

A current account surplus can be seen as an accumulation of foreign ➤assets, and is thus equivalent to a form of national saving. It is certainly true that the balance of payments of different countries has tended to reflect savings levels. A deficit in the balance of payments is not necessarily a bad thing, any more than a surplus need be a good thing. It is a form of borrowing which could be used to enhance domestic investment to the benefit of future growth. On the other hand if a deficit is caused by an unsustainable period of excess demand, perhaps occasioned by an excessive ➤budget deficit, it will persist until the home market has reached ➤equilibrium.

Governments have grown to be increasingly relaxed about the current balance, and to assume any problem is caused by an imbalance in domestic policy. Although in principle, there are many measures that can be taken in an attempt to correct a ➤disequilibrium in the balance of payments, many, such as import ➤tariffs, import ➤quotas, ➤import deposits and ➤export incentives are now constrained by the rules of the ➤World Trade Organization, or the ➤European Union, and are generally reckoned to be ineffective in the long term. ➤➤invisible; J-curve; competitiveness.

balance of trade The difference between a nation's imports of goods and services, and its exports of them. It is the most important element of the ➤balance of payments.

balance sheet A statement of the ➤wealth of a business, other organization or individual on a given date, usually the last day of the ➤financial year; not to be confused with the profit-and-loss account (➤double-entry bookkeeping), which records changes in the company's wealth over one year. A balance sheet is in two parts: (a) on the left-hand side or at the top, ➤assets, and (b) on the right-hand side or at the bottom, ➤liabilities. The assets of the company – ➤debtors, cash, investments and property – are set out against the claims or liabilities of the persons or organizations owning them – the ➤creditors, lenders and shareholders – so that the two parts of the balance sheet are equal. This is the principle of double-entry bookkeeping. The fact that the assets and liabilities are equal does not mean that the ➤equity shareholders owe as much as they own; they are included among the claimants.

According to the *basic accounting equation*, Assets = Liabilities + Equity; therefore, Assets – Liabilities = Equity. Equity, shareholders' interest or net worth (which are all the same thing) calculated from the balance sheet in this way may not reflect its true market value, since assets are normally written into the balance sheet at historical cost (➤book value) without any adjustment for ➤appreciation (➤inflation accounting).

Until the 1981 Companies Act the law did not, in Britain, lay out requirements for financial reporting of companies in detail or to any particular format, so that the layout and content of balance sheets varied considerably. The Companies Acts now require accounts to be set out in conformity with the EEC (➤European Union) Fourth Directive (➤company law). Notes to the accounts provide breakdowns of some of the elements of the balance sheet, for example tangible assets, as well as other information required by statute, for example details of directors' and employees' remuneration.

balanced budget A situation in which the government's planned expenditure equals its expected income. In public finance it refers to a situation where current income from ➤taxation and other receipts of central government are sufficient to meet payments for goods and services, ➤transfer payments and debt interest. The UK budget is often in deficit (does not balance) on both ➤current account and ➤capital account and these deficits are financed by net borrowing and changes in the ➤money supply (➤public-sector borrowing requirement). The importance of the budget balance and how it is financed is that it may affect levels of demand and prices in the economy (➤fiscal policy; Keynes). ➤➤public-sector financial deficit.

balanced budget multiplier The effect upon the ➤national income of equal changes in government expenditure and revenues. If government expenditure is increased by £100m. and income-tax rates are increased to raise an additional £100m. in revenue, ➤aggregate demand may not, as might be expected, remain the same since, although personal ➤disposable income has been reduced by £100m., some of that income would have been saved, whereas all the increase in government expenditure results in increased demand. If the ➤savings ratio were 10 per cent then the additional demand would be £10m., which would have a ➤multiplier effect upon the national income.

balanced growth The state of an economy in which there is a constant relationship between the components of aggregate ➤national income. Consumption expenditure, ➤investment and employment grow at the same rate as national income. The model is applied to the study of equilibrium conditions in ➤growth theory. ➤➤steady-state growth.

balancing allowance ➤capital allowances.

balancing item Data for the ➤balance of payments accounts is collated on the principle of ➤double-entry bookkeeping. For example, the value of a shipment of the export from the UK of a motor vehicle to the USA will be recorded as a credit item. The payment for the motor vehicle by the US importer by, say, his depositing a sum to the account of the UK exporter in a bank in New York will be recorded as a debit item to the same amount. In principle, for every credit item there is a corresponding debit item and for every debit item a corresponding credit item, although, by convention, the figures are published in a single column with positive (credit) and negative (debit) signs. The entries in the account should, therefore, add up to zero. In practice, this is difficult to achieve for a number of reasons. For instance, the difficulty of collecting accurate information, a difference in the timing between the two sides of the balance, a change in exchange rates. Because of such measurement problems, recourse has to be made to the ➤balancing item which simply adjusts the difference between the sums of the credit and the sums of the debit entries in the balance of payments accounts so that they add to zero.

bancor The term ►Keynes applied to the ►currency which he proposed a new central international bank should create and put into circulation for the payment of ►debts between countries (►►Keynes Plan). His proposal was rejected at the 1944 ►Bretton Woods Conference, which established the ►International Monetary Fund. However, the beginning of 1970 saw the introduction of a similar international currency in the allocation of ►special drawing rights through the IMF.

bank, commercial ►commercial banks.

bank, industrial ►industrial banks.

bank, joint-stock ►commercial banks.

bank, overseas ►overseas banks.

bank, secondary ►secondary bank.

bank advances ►bank loan.

bank bill ►bill of exchange.

bank clearings ►clearing house.

bank credit ►credit.

bank deposits The amount of money standing to the ►credit of a customer of a bank. Bank deposits are ►assets of its customers and ►liabilities of the bank. Deposits may arise from the payments of ►cash or a ►cheque to a bank for credit to a customer, or by transfer into an account from another account, including a ►loan from a bank to its customer. Bank deposits are simply IOUs written in the books of the bank. They do not necessarily reflect actual holdings of cash by the bank. Since bank deposits are used in the settlement of debts, they are ►money in the economic sense, so that by creating deposits banks create money (►banking). A deposit may be on ►current account or ►deposit account. These two types of account are known as ►demand deposits and ►time deposits in the USA. Bankers' deposits are deposits by a ►commercial bank at the ►central bank.

Bank for International Settlements (BIS) An institution, with head offices in Basle, set up on the basis of a proposal by the Young Committee in 1930. The original purpose was to enable the various national ►central banks to coordinate through their own central bank the receipts and payments arising mainly from German war reparations. It was hoped, however, that it would develop beyond this, but many of the functions which it might have performed were in fact taken over by the ►International Monetary Fund after the Second World War. It has, however, in recent years played a more active part in attempting to mitigate the effects of international financial ►speculation and acts as a trustee for international government loans. In addition, the bank has carried out financial transactions for the ►Organization for Economic Cooperation and Development, ►European Coal and Steel Community and the ►IMF. From 1973 the Bank acted as Agent for the European Monetary Cooperation Fund (►►European Monetary System). In 1995 the ►European Monetary Institute took over the Bank's responsibilities in this area. Although major functions of a central bank for central banks are performed by the IMF, the meetings of the central board have been an important means of central bank cooperation, especially in the field of offsetting short-term monetary movements of a speculative kind. In 1996 the BIS had 32 members but in that year invited a further 9 financial institutions to subscribe to the Bank's equity, in Brazil, China, Hong Kong, India, Korea, Mexico, Russia, Saudi Arabia and Singapore. ►►capital adequacy.

bank loan A sum borrowed from a bank, normally for a fixed period of two to three years or more for a specific purpose, usually by a commercial concern. The phrase 'bank loan' is also loosely used to include ►overdrafts and ►personal loans. In this broader sense bank loans are more commonly known as *bank advances*, while total *bank lending* includes commercial paper (►promissory note) and ►acceptances. In Britain over 70 per cent of bank lending to UK residents by value is for business purposes, although the ►commercial banks now make ►mortgage loans for house purchase on a large scale. Bank loans are normally secured (►collateral security), repaid in regular instalments and with interest charged at rates which vary with the bank's ►base rate. British banks have been compared unfavourably with banks in other countries in the extent to which they provide long-term loans to industry. It is true that until about twenty-five years ago the bulk of bank advances were in the form of overdrafts, which are repayable on demand. This was partly because the banks in Britain have not in general been able to attract long-term deposits, and it is regarded as bad banking practice 'to borrow short and lend long'. However, commercial customers of the banks in Britain have also preferred overdraft finance, which is cheaper and more flexible than other types of borrowing, provided the banks were willing to renew overdraft facilities and allow, as they have done, much overdraft borrowing to become 'hard core'. In recent years the British banks have greatly increased contractual medium-term lending (►term loan), and this type of advance now accounts for over half the bank advances to non-personal customers. Most medium-term lending is for periods of five to seven years, and lending for longer periods than this is still less common in Britain than in some European countries. ►►business finance.

Bank of England The ►central bank of the UK. Set up in 1694 as a joint-stock company by Act of Parliament, the Bank was a private company formed by a group of London merchants to lend ►money to the state and deal with the ►national debt. The Bank of England Act of 1946 brought the Bank into public ownership. Until 1997 the Bank of England was the government's banker, for which it arranged borrowing through the issue of ►gilt-edged securities. It was also responsible for regulating the banking sector, and supervising the activities of the ►wholesale markets in sterling, ►foreign exchange and ►bullion, the gilt-edged market (►gilt-edged securities), and other financial institutions and, when necessary, supported them, to prevent the failure of any institution which might endanger public confidence and the viability of the financial system as a whole. The slump in property values in 1975, for example, created difficulties for a number of fringe ►banks and property companies, and the Bank intervened in several instances to provide financial assistance. The Bank was also the principal organ for implementing the state's financial and ►monetary policy (►banking).

In 1997, however, the arrangements changed dramatically. Debt management passed to the ►Treasury; regulation of the financial sector to the Securities and Investment Board (►Financial Services Act 1986), and the Bank was given the power, through a new ►monetary policy committee, to *set* interest rates rather than simply implement Treasury decisions on them.

It is managed by a governor, at least one deputy governor and a court (board) of sixteen directors (four full-time executive directors) appointed by the Crown for periods of five and four years.

Under the Bank Charter Act of 1844 (►banking and currency schools) the Bank of England is divided into an issue department and a banking department. The issue department is responsible for the issue of ►banknotes and coins, which it buys from the Royal Mint, against its holdings of government ►securities and a relatively small amount of gold, coin and other securities. The banking department's liabilities consist of: bankers' ►deposits, i.e. deposits of the commercial banks; deposits of government departments, including the ►Exchequer, which receives the proceeds of ►taxation; the Post Office Savings Bank (►savings bank); and the Bank's own ►capital, held by the Treasury since nationalization. The principal assets of the banking department are government securities, discounts and advances, notes and coin.

The Bank also publishes an annual report, an inflation report and a *Quarterly Bulletin*. Besides its management of the national debt, the operation of monetary policy and the other domestic activities mentioned above, the Bank manages the foreign reserves in the ►exchange equalization account and conducts transactions between Britain and the rest of the world, including other central banks and international financial institutions such as the ►International Monetary Fund. The Bank also acted as the agent of government in administering ►exchange control regulations when in force, and is a registrar for government securities.

bank overdraft ►overdraft.

bank rate A now obsolete term for the ►rate of interest at which the ►central

23

bank lends to the banking system. In October 1971 the penal rate for assistance to the ➤discount market became the minimum lending rate and the term 'bank rate' has not been used since.

banker's draft A ➤cheque drawn by a bank as opposed to a bank's customer. Banker's drafts are drawn at the request of a customer, and that customer's account is debited when it is drawn. They are regarded as ➤cash, since they cannot be returned unpaid and are used when a creditor is not willing to accept a personal cheque in payment.

banking The business of accepting ➤deposits and lending ➤money. Banking defined in this way, however, is carried out by some other ➤financial intermediaries that perform the functions of safeguarding deposits and making ➤loans. ➤building societies and ➤finance houses, for example, are not normally referred to as banks and are not regarded as being part of the banking system in the narrow, traditional sense. The *banking system* is still normally understood to include the ➤commercial banks (joint-stock banks), the secondary banks, the ➤central bank, the ➤merchant banks or ➤accepting houses and the ➤discount houses (which are not banks as such), but to exclude the ➤savings banks and ➤investment banks and other intermediaries. The deposits of some types of bank, e.g. the Post Office Savings Bank, cannot be used in the settlement of debts until they are withdrawn, but a deposit in a commercial bank can be used to settle debts by the use of ➤cheques or ➤credit transfer. When the manager of a branch of one of the ➤clearing banks opens an ➤overdraft account for a customer, the loan creates a deposit; that is to say, a book debt has been incurred to the customer in return for a promise to repay it. Whether or not the overdraft is secured by ➤collateral security, such as an ➤insurance policy, or some other ➤asset, when the customer draws upon the loan the bank has added to the total ➤money supply. In ➤balance-sheet terms, the deposit is a claim on the bank – that is, a ➤liability – while the customer's promise to repay it (or the collateral security) is an asset to the bank. In the absence of government control on lending the limitation on the bank's ability to create deposits is their obligation, if they are to remain in business, to pay out ➤current account deposits in cash on demand. Since the bank's customers meet most of their needs for money by writing cheques on their deposits, the cash holdings the banks need are only a small fraction of their total deposits. (The settlement of debts between the clearing banks is made by cheque and increasingly by electronic transfers (➤clearing house).) This ratio between their deposit liabilities and their cash holdings is called the ➤cash ratio (sometimes called the primary ratio). Banks also hold other ➤liquid assets (➤bills of exchange, loans at call and other loans to the money market) (➤liquidity ratio (secondary ratio).) The object of the banker is, of course, to keep his reserves as near as possible to the minimum, since no return at all is earned on holdings of cash and a relatively low return in the money market. The banking system is based on confidence in the system's ability to meet its obligations. In the short run, no bank is able to meet all its obligations in cash and, if demands upon it exhausted its cash reserves, the bank would be obliged to close its doors.

The prevention of bank failure and the protection of bank customers against fraud and loss is one objective of the control and regulation of the banking system which is, under proposals announced in 1997, the responsibility of the ➤Securities and Investments Board. That regulation now relies on prudential ratios (➤capital adequacy) to minimize failure and instability in the banking system. There is also increasing emphasis on assessing the adequacy of the bank's own risk management systems as an instrument of bank supervision. Until 1997, under the 1979 and 1987 ➤Banking Acts, virtually all deposit-takers had to be licensed by the ➤Bank of England, which monitored their activities through regular statistical returns and attempts to control their exposure to risk by indicative controls on capital ratios and uncovered foreign-currency positions (➤capital adequacy).

The Bank of England remains responsible for ensuring the financial system generally is secure. Since the money supply is a basic tool of economic policy, the government also wishes to exert control over the creation of credit by the banking system through its finance ministry. In Britain this function is also performed by the Bank of England (➤central bank). Direct controls on bank lending in the interests of controlling the ➤money supply were removed in 1971 in an attempt to introduce more competition into the banking system. There are now no longer any significant reserve ratios as such (➤reserve requirement). The Bank of England now relies on interest rates to influence inflation.

Recent years have seen substantial growth and change in the banking system. The main features have been an increase in the importance of ➤overseas banks operating in the UK and other non-clearing banks, the increasing use of new parallel markets as a source of funds for the banks and a decline in the number of merchant banks. At the same time, traditional distinctions between the various types of bank are breaking down as most ➤financial intermediaries diversify their activities. Building societies and merchant banks are offering high-interest cheque accounts, non-banks such as multiple retailers are entering the banking market, and some building societies are incorporating as banks (➤incorporation). The clearing banks have become major providers of ➤mortgage lending for house purchase and are increasingly providing non-banking financial services such as insurance broking, ➤equity purchases, traveller's cheques and, of course, ➤credit cards. ➤➤banknote (for the origin of banking).

banking, retail ➤commercial banks.

banking, wholesale ➤wholesale banking.

Banking Acts The (UK) Banking Act 1979 introduced recognized status by banks and deposit-taking institutions (the distinction between the two was abolished in the Banking Act 1987). The Act specified capital requirements and required the ➤Bank of England to satisfy itself that the bank had a good reputation and was able to manage its affairs with 'integrity and prudence'. The 1979 Act also created a *Depositors' Protection Fund*, to which all recognized banks contribute. At present the fund will compensate any one depositor for up to 75 per cent of a loss, subject to a maximum of £15,000. The Bank of England is responsible for ensuring that recognized banks continue to satisfy its requirements. ➤capital adequacy.

The 1979 Banking Act was made necessary by the ➤European Union's *First Banking Coordination Directive*. The Second Banking Directive allowed EU credit institutions to operate anywhere in the EU without having to seek authorization from the host state (the principle of mutual recognition).

banking and currency schools The representatives of the two sides of opinion in a controversy which centred on Sir Robert Peel's Bank Charter Act of 1844. This Act effectively limited the creation of ➤banknotes to the ➤Bank of England and regulated their issue. The *banking school* argued that, given that banknotes were convertible into gold, there was no need to regulate the note issue because the fact of convertibility would constrain any serious over-issue. Moreover, it was pointless to try to regulate the issue of banknotes because the demand for currency would be met by an expansion of ➤bank deposits, which would have the same effect as an expansion of the note issue. The *currency school*, on the other hand, argued that the check offered by convertibility would not operate in time to prevent serious commercial disruption. Banknotes should be regarded as though they were the gold specie they in fact represented, and consequently the quantity at issue should fluctuate in sympathy with the ➤balance of payments. ➤➤banking; fiduciary issue; gold standard; money supply.

Banking Directives ➤Banking Acts.

banknote A note issued by a bank undertaking to pay the bearer the ➤face value of the note on demand. Banknotes in England had their origin in the receipts issued by London goldsmiths in the seventeenth century for gold deposited with them for safe-keeping. The whole practice of ➤banking had its origin in the activities of these goldsmiths, who began lending money and whose deposit receipts came to be used as money. Later the goldsmiths issued banknotes, and so did the banks that developed later still. Today only the ➤Bank of England and the Scottish and Irish banks in the UK are allowed to issue banknotes. Since 1931, when banknotes became inconvertible to gold, the promise on a banknote to 'pay the bearer on demand' has simply been an undertaking that the note is legal tender. Thus, the Currency and Bank Notes Act of 1954, which regulates the issue of banknotes in Britain, refers to the ➤fiduciary issue. Only four denominations of notes are now issued to the general public, the largest being the £50 note. Most other developed countries issue notes of much larger denominations than this, probably because the use of ➤cheques is less developed elsewhere than in Britain. (The 10s. note was replaced by the 50p coin in 1969 and a £1 coin was introduced in 1983, entirely replacing the £1 note in 1986.) ➤➤banking and currency schools.

bankruptcy A declaration by a court of law that an individual or company is insolvent, that is, cannot meet its ➤debts on the due dates (➤insolvency). A bankruptcy petition may be filed either by the debtor or by his creditors requesting a receiving order. An inquiry into the debtor's affairs is then conducted by, in Britain, the Official Receiver, an official of the Department of Trade and Industry, who retains temporary control of the debtor's financial affairs. If he thinks fit, the receiver may call a meeting of the debtor's creditors and, if they wish it, declare the debtor bankrupt. The debtor's assets are then realized and distributed among his creditors either by the receiver or by a trustee appointed by the creditors and approved by the Department of Trade. In the case of a company it goes into ➤liquidation. Until he is discharged, i.e. has paid off his debts and has been declared a discharged bankrupt in law, a bankrupt may not incur ➤credit in excess of £10 without making it known that he is an undischarged bankrupt, nor may he serve as a director in a limited company without permission from the court.

The *Insolvency Acts 1985* and *1986* codified existing law and made the handling of the affairs of insolvent debtors the responsibility of a registered insolvency practitioner. Companies may be placed under administration rather than go into liquidation. The Act introduced a wider range of sanctions against directors who have acted negligently, as did the *Company Directors Disqualification Act 1986*.

bargaining The interaction between participants to a transaction by which they decide on an allocation of the surplus they create by entering the transaction. If a car is worth £10,000 to a potential buyer and £9000 to the owner, there is a potential welfare gain of £1000 to be made by a sale. The buyer would be willing to buy it at £9999, and the seller would sell it at £9001. Somehow, a price has to be fixed between these two *reservation prices*. In this case, once they have decided to enter the transaction, the negotiation between them can be likened to a ➤zero-sum game, or to a problem of ➤bilateral monopoly. Economists have used ➤game theory to look at the best bargaining strategies, and the potential outcomes of more complicated bargaining situations, for example one in which the surplus to be divided shrinks the longer the parties negotiate. ➤arbitration.

bargaining theory of wages A theory of wage determination based on negotiations between employers and unions. The theory has been set within a number of different assumptions. For instance, as a ➤game-theory problem in which both sides wish to divide the firm's profits but also to maximize them: an exercise in ➤cost–benefit analysis where each is aware of the costs of a strike and the risks of participating in one. These theories are complementary to those based on ➤supply and ➤demand analysis (➤price theory) in the sense that the bargaining is seen to be carried out within the framework of the conditions existing at the time in the ➤labour market (➤wage-fund theory). ➤➤arbitration; bargaining.

barriers to entry Economic or technical factors which prevent or make it difficult for firms to enter a market and compete with existing suppliers. An established firm may enjoy an *absolute cost advantage* which might arise from the possession of patent rights to certain production processes or a long-term contract for the supply of energy or the ownership of sources of raw materials. In the same way, existence of ►economies of scale might mean that a new entrant would have to invest large sums and produce on a large scale in order to compete on price. If the market were small in relation to the ►optimum scale of production, new entrants might calculate that the risk of entry would be unacceptably high because any new supplier would reduce the output of all suppliers below the optimum, so that either the new or an existing supplier would fail. Product differentiation (►differentiation, product) can also raise the cost of entry by necessitating heavy expenditure on advertising and the support of dealer outlets to overcome significant buyer preferences. Finally, ►collusion on pricing and restrictive practices, such as ►full-line forcing and ►exclusive dealing, may exclude newcomers, as may legislation, such as a requirement for licensing. Barriers to entry may allow established firms to charge prices above the level that would obtain in the absence of these barriers. ►►competition policy; contestability; monopoly; sunk costs; protection.

barriers to exit Restrictions on the ability of a producer to withdraw from an activity, or to redeploy its resources to an alternative activity. Such restrictions may be legal, designed to protect communities from the discomfort of factory closure. In this case, they often in fact act as a deterrent to new entry into a sector (which becomes more risky if exit is not an option), and as an impediment to economic transformation. However, the economics of ►industrial organization has used ►game theory as a device for analysing business behaviour, and this can demonstrate the paradoxical logic that companies may want to restrict *their own* ability to withdraw from an industry. Such a strategy might be rational, as a means of dissuading a potential competitor not to enter the industry, on the grounds that the incumbent is committed to remaining.

barter Acquiring goods or services by means of exchange for other goods or services, rather than for ►money. A form of barter has grown in recent years in the USA and Australia into a serious business activity. Corporations specializing in barter deals offer to buy surplus products in exchange for credits which the company disposing of the goods can use to buy other goods and services, such as TV advertising time, specified by the barter corporation. These corporations have sufficient financial weight to be able to obtain large discounts for the goods and services they offer for trade. ►counter trade.

base period The reference date from which an ►index number of a ►time series is calculated. For instance, the price index of commodities produced in the UK has a base period of 1990. The base year may be changed to reflect any changes over time in the composition of items making up the index. ➤Laspeyres index; weighted average.

base rate The ➤rate of interest which forms the basis for the charges for ➤bank loans and ➤overdrafts or deposit rates of the ➤commercial banks. Since 1971 the banks have fixed their base rates independently of one another, though obviously they cannot differ very much for long periods. Prior to 1971 the banks agreed on their deposit and overdraft rates, but this ➤cartel arrangement has been abandoned. Very large first-class risk companies may borrow at one percentage point above base rate or even less, but small firms and individuals will have to pay several percentage points more than this. Base rates will be generally close to short-term ➤money market rates but change less frequently, so when, as sometimes happens, rates on the ➤inter-bank market rise much above base rate, large companies have taken advantage of the interest-rate differential, borrowing on overdraft and lending in that market.

Basle Agreements ➤capital adequacy.

battle of the sexes A situation – popularly characterized in the economics of ➤game theory – in which people or institutions have a strong interest in coordinating their behaviour, but disagree over quite how to behave. An example would be in the setting of an industry standard for, say, a pipe fitting. Everybody may agree that it is overwhelmingly important that some standard fitting is agreed; but each firm may take its own view as to what that standard should be. The characterization of such situations as a 'battle of the sexes' derives from a simple analogy used in game theory to caricature them: a husband and wife want to spend the evening together, but what should they do? His first choice is to go to the ballet with her; while she wants to go and watch some boxing with him. Assuming these are the only possible activities, his ranking of different ways of spending the evening in order of preference is thus:

> Go to ballet with her
> Go to boxing with her
> Go to ballet alone
> Go to boxing alone

Her preferences are to:

> Go to boxing with him
> Go to ballet with him
> Go to boxing alone
> Go to ballet alone

It should of course be possible to agree on an evening together, but the crucial feature of these situations is the possibility that a struggle by husband and wife to get their first best option, may result in them each getting their third best option.

For example, if he insists on going to the ballet, and she insists on going to the boxing, they may end up going their own way, even though both would prefer to be together. It is generally recognized that if the situation is commonly repeated, it is easier to reach agreement than if it occurs once only (►repeated games). The game is not as commonly discussed as the ubiquitous ►prisoner's dilemma.

Baumol effect The idea that certain services become relatively more expensive as economies develop, and that some manufactured goods become relatively less expensive. It was outlined by W. J. Baumol in 1967, and was based on the following reasoning: it is increases in ►productivity in a sector which allow prices of a product to fall; it is new technology which drives increases in productivity; and new technology emerges most quickly in capital-intensive sectors – those sectors employing machines, for example, rather than just people. As manufacturing industries tend to be more capital-intensive than services, they would enjoy relatively falling prices.

It is true that in less developed countries the price of manufactured goods tends to be very high compared to the price of services; whereas in rich countries, services tend to be very expensive. But the Baumol effect should not be overstated: many non-manufacturing sectors (such as telecommunications) have enjoyed spectacular increases in productivity based on new technology. Moreover, it is argued that it is hard to measure productivity in service industries, where outputs are often hard to define precisely. (It is difficult to tell just how the productivity of a lawyer or teacher should be defined.)

The Baumol effect is partly used to explain the growth of government spending – as government primarily provides services rather than goods to the public. ►►public expenditure.

Baye's theorem A formula in ►probability theory for calculating the chance that an unknown prior event occurred, given that a known subsequent event occurred. Suppose we are trying to analyse whether a doctor prescribed the right drugs to a patient. Before the event we believe that there is a fifty-fifty chance that he makes the right prescription. When we see whether the patient recovers or not, we can make a better assessment, but not a perfect one: the patient might get better without the right medicine, and may not get better even with the right medicine. Baye's law allows us to estimate the probability that the right medicine was prescribed, by observing what happened to the patient. If one in ten patients who are wrongly prescribed recovers, and one in two patients who are correctly prescribed recovers, the observation that a patient did recover makes it five times more likely that they were rightly prescribed than wrongly prescribed.

More generally, the formula says that the probability of a prior event E having occurred, given that a subsequent event S occurred, is equal to the prior probability of E times the probability of S occurring given E occurred, all divided by the probability of S occurring one way or the other. In the above example, this is:

Probability that the *wrong* medicine
was prescribed given that
the patient got better $= \dfrac{0.5 \times 0.1}{0.05 + 0.25} = 16.6$ per cent

Probability that the *right* medicine
was prescribed given that the
patient got better $= \dfrac{0.5 \times 0.5}{0.05 + 0.25} = 83.3$ per cent

The theorem has led to considerable controversy among statisticians, who argue about the validity of ascribing a probability to a past event.

bear A ►stock exchange speculator who sells ►stocks or ►shares that he may or may not possess because he expects a fall in prices and, therefore, that he will be able to buy them (back) later on at a ►profit; the antonym of ►bull. A bear who sells ►securities that he does not possess is described as having 'sold short'. If he does possess the securities he sells, he is described as a 'covered' or 'protected' bear. A 'bear market' is one in which prices are falling.

bearer bonds ►Bonds the legal ownership of which is vested in the holder, no ►transfer deed being required since there is no central register of ownership. An endorsed ►cheque, or a cheque made payable to a bearer, or a ►banknote are similar in nature to bearer ►securities. Bearer bonds normally have dated interest ►coupons attached to them which can be presented to the issuer of the security for payment.

bearer securities ►bearer bonds.

Becker, Gary (b.1930) An idiosyncratic and controversial economist, and winner of the ►Nobel Prize for Economics in 1992. Becker has been more prominent than any other member of the profession in using economic reasoning in the analysis of social behaviour. From *The Economics of Discrimination* (1957) to *An Economic Analysis of Fertility* (1960) to A *Theory of the Allocation of Time* (1965), to *Crime and Punishment: an Economic Approach* (1968) his style has been to characterize behaviour in the language of economics, and explain behaviour according to principles of rational choice. Nowhere is this more obvious than in his analysis of the family. He discusses the allocation of work within the household, and the impact of changing household technology on, for example, female participation in the labour market, and on the level of divorce. He is also responsible for pathbreaking work in formulating and formalizing the microeconomic foundations of our understanding of investments in training and education, in the creation of human capital. Becker has been at the University of Chicago since 1970.

'beggar-my-neighbour' policy ►reciprocity.

behavioural assumption The pattern of human motivation built into any economic theory. For example, the theory of the firm (►firm, theory of the) assumes that entrepreneurs are profit-maximizers; the cobweb theory (➤cobweb model) assumes that market suppliers are motivated by price in the period preceding that in which they sell their supply. ➤➤model.

behavioural theory of the firm An approach to the study of firms which analyses how decisions are reached within them, rather than, as is more traditional, assuming that their behaviour conforms to the pursuit of some single goal. It was primarily developed by R. Cyert, J. G. March and H. A. Simon. The main tenets of the behavioural theory are: (a) that firms attempt to ➤satisfice rather than adopt maximizing behaviour; (b) that the firm is a set of individuals and groups each of which has its own aspirations; these groups, sometimes in coalitions, continuously bargain over the decisions the firm makes, leading to the pursuit of many complex goals. The theory has not displaced the traditional approach, for a number of reasons, most notably that it fails to generate any specific predictions about what firms would actually do in any particular circumstances. Its primary influence has been in reminding economists of the fact that, in practice, maximizing profits may be expensive for a firm (acquiring full and unbiased information from all departments is no easy task) and institutional factors may impede the single-minded pursuit of any one goal. ➤➤firm, theory of the; X-efficiency.

below the line Items in an account which are underneath the line at which a total is made. If *above the line*, an item is included in the total.

In the ➤balance of payments, for example, the basic balance includes the net flow of long-term capital above the line together with the current balance, i.e. the basic balance equals the current balance plus net long-term capital flows. In reported results for quoted companies (➤quotation), *extraordinary items* that arise from transactions which are outside the ordinary activities of a business (for example, the sale of an office building) may be taken below the line for the purposes of calculating ➤earnings per share, whereas *exceptional items* that do derive from the ordinary activities may be taken above the line for that purpose.

benefit–cost analysis ➤cost–benefit analysis.

Benelux The ➤customs union between Belgium and Luxembourg on the one hand and the Netherlands on the other was set up in 1948. The union abolished internal ➤tariffs, reduced import ➤quotas between the three countries and adopted a common external tariff. The aim of the union was the eventual merging of the fiscal and monetary systems of the member countries. There is free movement of ➤labour and ➤capital within the union and a common policy with other countries. In 1958 Benelux joined the then European Community. ➤European Union.

Bentham, Jeremy (1748–1832) The leading philosopher of ➤utilitarianism. Self-interest was deemed the sole stimulus to human endeavour and the pursuit of happiness an individual's prime concern. The purpose of government should be to maximize the sum of the happiness of the greatest number of individuals.

Bernoulli, Daniel (1700–82) ➤Bernoulli's hypothesis.

Bernoulli's hypothesis A proposition by Daniel Bernoulli (1700–82) that a decision as to whether or not to accept a ➤risk depended not just on money but also on ➤utility. For instance, a bet would appear to be worth accepting if, at the toss of a coin, you won £10 for every head and lost only £5 for every tail. Given the coin is unbiased, there is an equal chance of a head or a tail turning up. However, if £5 was all you had in the world, the bet would not seem so attractive. The £5 would have a high utility attached to it and Bernoulli suggested that this is what counted in such decisions. ➤➤marginal utility of money; risk aversion.

Bertrand competition A model of price competition between ➤duopoly firms in which each charges the price that would be charged under ➤perfect competition (➤marginal-cost pricing). As a model it contrasts with that of ➤Cournot, who found that price and output in a duopoly situation would be somewhere between the extremes of ➤monopoly and perfect competition. The Bertrand result can be seen as a ➤Nash Equilibrium outcome. ➤➤oligopoly.

BES ➤Enterprise Investment Scheme.

beta 1. In finance theory, the degree to which the returns on a particular financial asset track those of the rest of the market. A beta of one indicates that an asset, on average, moves with the rest of the market. A higher beta indicates that it moves in the same direction as the market, but with more extremity. A negative beta indicates that the return on an asset grows when returns elsewhere in the market are falling and vice versa. Assets with a low beta are held to be attractive, as they perform well when the market generally is doing badly. Under the ➤capital asset pricing model, it is believed that they are highly priced for this reason. **2.** The Greek letter which is commonly used in econometrics to represent the relationship between the ➤dependent variable and the ➤independent variable. If ➤regression analysis produces an estimate of a high beta, relative to the scale of the units involved, it means the relationship is strong. ➤➤null hypothesis.

Beveridge, William Henry (Lord Beveridge) (1879–1963) Director of the London School of Economics from 1919 to 1937, Lord Beveridge's work in economics arose from a continuous interest through his life in the problem of ➤unemployment. His major contribution to the subject was published in *Unemployment* (1931). He was a major influence in the setting up of labour exchanges, and his 1942 report, *Social Insurance and Allied Services,* which became known as the Beveridge Report, led to the extension of the welfare services. His definition of full employment, which he gave in *Full Employment in a Free Society* (1944) as being reached at a level of 3 per cent unemployed, became a reference point for subsequent government policy. ➤➤Sismondi, J. C. L. S. de.

Beveridge curve A graphical depiction of the relationship between the level of ➤unemployment in an economy, and the level of vacancies. It is drawn with vacancies on the vertical axis, and slopes downwards as a higher rate of unemployment tends to occur with a lower rate of vacancies. If it is observed that the curve moves outwards over time, a given level of vacancies would be associated with higher and higher levels of unemployment, and that would imply a less and less efficiently operating labour market, with an increasing mismatch between the unemployed, and the jobs available. ➤structural unemployment; long-term unemployment; active-labour-market policies.

Big Bang Term used to encapsulate the changes occurring on the London ➤stock exchange before and after 27 October 1986 when the strict segregation between jobbers (➤market maker) and ➤brokers and fixed commissions on securities, purchases and sales were abolished. In July 1983 the government agreed to exempt the Stock Exchange from the provisions of the ➤Restrictive Trade Practices Acts in return for lifting a number of restrictions on competition, including fixed commissions. In 1982 the Stock Exchange Council had raised the limit on any one outside shareholder in a Stock Exchange member firm from 10 per cent to 29.9 per cent and on 1 March 1986 this limitation on outside shareholdings was removed completely. Average commission rates fell by about 40 per cent to 0.26 per cent immediately following Big Bang, but many bargains (transactions) are now carried out at net prices, i.e. the market maker quotes a price direct to the purchaser (who may be a large ➤institutional investor) which includes his profit margin. Commission rates for small transactions have risen with the introduction of higher minimum charges. Many banks and other financial institutions, both domestic and foreign, have acquired interests in, or control of, Stock Exchange companies since March 1986 while increased competition has led to mergers, a few failures and the withdrawal of some firms from certain activities, such as dealing in ➤gilt-edged securities. Other changes associated with Big Bang have been the closure of the trading floor in March 1987, a major extension in off-the-floor electronic dealing and a major expansion in dealings in international ➤equities.

bilateral monopoly A market in which a single seller (a ➤monopoly) is confronted with a single buyer (a ➤monopsony). Under these circumstances, the theoretical determination of output and price will be uncertain and will be affected by the interdependence of the two parties. ➤bargaining.

bilateralism The agreement between two countries to extend to each other specific privileges in their ➤international trade which are not extended to others. These privileges may, for instance, take the form of generous import ➤quotas or favourable import duties (➤tariffs, import). In so far as such agreements tend to proliferate, and in that they impose artificial restraints on the free movements of goods between countries, in the long run they could have an unfavourable effect on international trade compared with ➤multilateralism, under which there is no discrimination by origin or destination. Bilateralism became widespread in the 1930s as countries tried to protect themselves from the fall in international trade during the depression.

After 1945 there was a fear that a restrictionist policy would be followed by the Commonwealth and Western European countries in order to protect themselves from the influence of the USA, which had emerged from the war in a relatively strong position. However, the ►General Agreement on Tariffs and Trade was established in 1947 on multilateral principles, and has since been pursuing a policy designed to eliminate bilateralism and other restrictions on international trade. The success of this policy has been somewhat constrained by the setting up of a number of ►common market and ►free-trade areas (►counter-trade).

bill A document giving evidence of indebtedness of one party to another. A bill may simply be a written order for goods which can be used as security for a loan to the supplier from a bank, or it may be a security such as a ►treasury bill or ►bill of exchange.

bill broker A firm or individual that deals in ►treasury bills and ►bills of exchange on the London ►money market. Normally a bill broker is a ►discount house. ►►broker.

bill of exchange An IOU used in ►international trade by which the drawer makes an unconditional undertaking to pay to the drawee a sum of ►money at a given date, usually three months ahead. In principle a bill of exchange is similar to a post-dated ►cheque, and like a cheque it can be endorsed for payment to the bearer or any named person other than the drawee. A bill of exchange has to be 'accepted' (endorsed) by the drawee before it becomes negotiable. This function is normally performed by an ►accepting house, but bills may also be accepted by a bank (it is then known as a *bank bill*) or by a trader (*trade bill*). Once accepted, the drawee does not have to wait for the bill to mature before getting his money; he can sell it on the ►money market for a small discount (►discount house). Bills of exchange, also referred to as *commercial bills*, were first developed in inland trade by merchants who wished to resell goods before making payment for them. They later became of great importance in international trade, but with the development of other means of ►credit, their use declined.

bill of sale A document that gives evidence of transfer of ownership but not of possession of goods. It is not often used nowadays, but was once a common method of raising a ►loan on the security of personal possessions, the borrower retaining possession of goods until the ►debt is repaid. ►►mortgage.

BIMBO Buy-In Management Buy-Out. ►management buy-out.

birth rate The crude birth rate is the average number of live births occurring in a year for every 1000 population. The birth rate of the UK fell steadily from about thirty-five per 1000 population in the 1870s to about twenty in the 1920s. It fell dramatically to about sixteen in the 1930s and rose equally dramatically in 1947 to nearly twenty-one. After falling back from this exceptionally high figure, it was on an upward trend from the early 1950s until the mid-1960s. From 1964 it fell every year until it reached 11.8 in 1977, the lowest ever recorded. Since increasing to 13.8 in 1988, it has been roughly stable. Other statistical measurements which are computed for the study of population trends include (a) the *fertility rate*, which measures the average number of live births per 1000 for all women between the ages of fifteen and forty-four, a statistic which has in fact exhibited trends in the UK similar to the crude birth rate (it reached a low level of 59.4 in 1977 and rose to 63.1 in 1988), and (b) the rate specific for age of mother in which the number of live births per 1000 is given for different age groups of mother. There has been growing anxiety about the social and economic consequences of the rapidly expanding size of the world population. At the present rate of growth the current world population of 5.8 billion people will double by 2042. By 2025 the ➤developing countries will account for about 85 per cent of the total compared with 80 per cent today. A major factor in growth has been the extension of life expectancy achieved by modern medicine, but high birth rates have also played an important part. Measures of family control are being taken, particularly in critical developing countries such as India, in order to try to achieve a growth in population more in line with available economic and social resources (➤Malthus T.R. population).

BIS ➤Bank for International Settlements.

black economy 'Underground' economic activity which is not declared for ➤taxation purposes. Difficult to measure accurately, the black economy is probably heavily concentrated in personal services and repair work carried out in exchange for cash. It can, however, also be generated from incomes earned overseas and repatriated in cash outside the banking system. The latter, for instance, is thought to be an important factor in inflating the black economy of the Philippines by up to about 20 per cent of ➤gross domestic product (GDP). The Statistical Office of the European Communities (SOEC) has estimated that the black economy accounts for about 10 per cent of the GDP of the ➤European Union on average and, possibly, as high as 20 per cent in Belgium, Greece and Portugal. Although estimates of the tax revenue lost through the black economy range from 3 to 5 per cent or more it cannot be assumed that such activities would remain viable if captured by the tax net. Not to be confused with *black market*, which is the illicit trade in goods contrary to government regulation.

black market ➤black economy.

Black–Scholes formula A complex equation used to establish a fair price for ➤options in financial markets. The formula, which is used to solve what had previously been considered a difficult problem was published in 1973. It was based on looking at the price of a basket of financial assets which carried the same risk and return as an option.

blue book An annual digest published by the UK Office of National Statistics containing the national income and expenditure statistics of the UK (►national income; social accounting).

blue chip A first-class ►equity share, the purchase of which (the hope is) entails little ►risk, even of sharp declines in ►earnings, in economic recessions (►depression). The term is, of course, applied as a matter of subjective judgement. In the UK, Marks & Spencer, Unilever and Shell equities, for example, are commonly regarded as blue chip.

Böhm-Bawerk, Eugen von (1851–1914) A member of the ►Austrian school who took over the Chair of Economics at Vienna from von ►Wieser. His analyses of the rate of ►interest and ►capital have had an important influence on the development of these aspects of economic theory. His major publications include *Capital and Interest* (1884) and the *Positive Theory of Capital* (1889). The nature of the rate of interest could be found, he argued, in the three propositions, (a) that people expect to be better off in the future, (b) that people put a lower valuation on future goods than on present goods 'jam today is better than jam tomorrow' – these two 'psychological' factors making people willing to pay to borrow against their future income to spend on consumption goods now (►►time preference), and (c) the proposition that goods in existence today are technically superior to goods coming into existence at some future date because today's goods could be capable of producing more goods during the interval. (►►Fisher, I.; interest, productivity theories of.) Capital is associated with roundabout methods of production. In order to reap a harvest you could send workers into the fields to pluck the ears of corn. A more efficient method is to spend capital on making scythes and then use these to cut the corn. An even more efficient method is to spend even more capital manufacturing reaping machinery and use this to harvest your corn. Progress is achieved through the use of ►labour in more roundabout methods of production; a widening of the gap between ►inputs and outputs (►►input–output analysis). Capital supplies the necessary subsistence to labour during the 'waiting time' before new consumer goods are produced (►►wage-fund theory). This waiting time is extended to yield increased productivity until, in equilibrium, productivity is equated with the ►rate of interest. This theory was later developed into a theory of the ►business cycle by members of the Austrian school (►►Hayek, F. A. von; Hicks, J. R.; Mises, L. von; Wicksell, K.).

bond 1. A form of fixed-interest ►security issued by central or local governments, companies, banks or other institutions, e.g. National Savings Income Bonds. Bonds are usually a form of long-term security but do not always carry fixed interest and may be irredeemable and may be secured or unsecured. Economists frequently make use of the term bond in theoretical analysis, for example of choices between holding cash and other financial assets, in which a bond is a proxy for a whole range of securities. *Eurobonds* have been defined by Morgan Guaranty, the investment bankers, as a 'bond underwritten by an international syndicate and sold in countries other than the country of the currency in which the issue is denominated'. There is no specific ➤stock exchange for these bonds (➤➤bearer bonds; eurocurrency). The term bond has also been given to types of non-fixed-interest security, such as property bonds, which provide the holder with a yield on funds invested in property, or 'managed bonds', in which the funds are placed in a variety of investments. In the USA the term bond includes ➤debentures. **2.** A term used to describe goods in a warehouse on which customs duty (➤tariffs, import) has not yet been paid.

bonus issue, or scrip issue, capitalization issue (US **stock dividend, stock split**) Virtually synonymous terms describing ➤shares given without charge to existing shareholders in proportion to the shares already owned. A *scrip issue* does not add to the ➤capital employed by the firm, but is made where the capital employed has been increased by withholding profits, and is therefore, out of line with the ➤issued capital. Consequently, it is a purely bookkeeping transaction. ➤Dividends, for example, will, after a scrip issue, be divided among a larger number of shares, so that the dividend per share will fall in proportion to the number of bonus shares issued. ➤➤new-issue market; rights issue.

book value The value of ➤assets in the ➤balance sheet of a firm. This is often the purchase price, and may be less than the market value. ➤➤inflation accounting.

BOTB ➤British Overseas Trade Board.

bounded rationality The idea that economic agents may not have the cognitive power to make decisions about their optimum behaviour very precisely. They thus may intend to be rational, but in practice, make choices on the basis of rules of thumb. These limits make it very hard to specify ➤contracts that cover all contingencies (➤incomplete contract) and, according to ➤Simon, who coined the phrase 'bounded rationality', this makes forms of organization such as the firm necessary. ➤➤satisficing; transaction costs.

branch banking A ➤banking system, most highly developed in the UK, in which the small number of ➤commercial banks have a large number of branches (some 12,000). Many other ➤advanced countries have a much larger number of banks with fewer branches; for example, Germany has some 246 commercial banks with 6500 branches, less than half of which are operated by the six large universal banks. A banking system in which each bank is a separate enterprise without affiliations with other banks or branches is called *unit banking*.

In the USA it was believed that branch banking led to ➤concentration of the banking system and lack of competition. Prohibitions on branch banking have been relaxed in the USA and, although branch banking is growing, of the 15,000 commercial banks 11,000 are purely local, with five or fewer branches. Branch networks have been diminishing in importance in recent years, as automated teller machines have to some extent obviated the need for personal contact with bankers; and telephone services have supplanted the face-to-face visit.

Bretton Woods An international conference held at Bretton Woods, New Hampshire, USA, in July 1944 to discuss alternative proposals relating to post-war international payments problems put forward by the US, Canadian and UK governments. The agreement resulting from this conference led to the establishment of the ➤International Monetary Fund and the ➤International Bank For Reconstruction and Development. ➤➤Keynes plan; Smithsonian Agreement.

British funds ➤stock exchange.

British Overseas Trade Board (BOTB) Export promotion agency of the UK Department of Trade and Industry. It was set up in 1972 to replace the British Export Board. The board includes representatives of business, the trade unions and government departments such as the ➤Export Credits Guarantee Department. Its main function is to ensure the best use of the government's export promotion services and to advise on education, training and other matters. Through its regional offices throughout the UK, the board provides information, assists in the organization of overseas missions and exhibitions and provides help to exporters needing overseas representation and market research.

broker An intermediary between a buyer and a seller in a highly organized market, e.g. a ➤stockbroker, commodity broker or a market operator working on his own account, e.g. a pawnbroker, ➤bill broker. On the ➤stock exchange, a broker is the intermediary between a ➤market maker and the public.

brokerage Commission or fee charged by a ➤broker. It is characteristic of the broking profession that they operate only in highly organized markets where margins are relatively small.

Buchanan, James McGill (b. 1919) Professor Buchanan studied at the University of Tennessee prior to obtaining his Ph.D. at the University of Chicago in 1948. He became Professor of Economics at the University of Virginia in 1956 and was appointed, in 1969, Director of the Center for Study of Public Choice, and is currently Professor at George Mason University, Virginia. Professor Buchanan was awarded the ➤Nobel Prize in Economics in 1986. His published work includes: *The Calculus of Consent: Logical Foundations of Constitutional Democracy* (1962); *Public Finance in a Democratic Process* (1966); *The Demand and Supply of Public Goods* (1968); *Cost and Choice. An Enquiry in Economic Theory* (1969); *Theory of Public Choice. Political Applications of Economics* (1972); *The Limits of Liberty. Between Anarchy and the Leviathan* (1975); *Freedom in Constitutional Contracts. Perspectives of a Political Economist* (1977); *Democracy in Deficit. The Political Consequences of Lord Keynes* (1977); *The Power of Tax* (1980).

Professor Buchanan established, and inspired study in, ➤public-choice theory. As 'economic man' acted in his own self-interest so government officials behaved also. Government actions, therefore, will be pursued according to the self-interest of politicians and lobbyists rather than for the public good. Unpopular, but inevitably required, corrective actions will be delayed by governments to force others into the responsibility, and political costs, of taking action. Individuals yield up their freedom of decision-making to representative government, subject to constitutional constraints. The growth and complexity of government, however, renders these constraints ineffective unless they are continually reconstituted. Professor Buchanan is anti-Keynesian (➤Keynes, J. M.) and is an advocate of the ➤balanced budget for the control it imposes on governments.

budget An estimate of ➤income and expenditure for a future period as opposed to an account which records financial transactions. Budgets are an essential element in the planning and control of the financial affairs of a nation or business, and are made necessary essentially because income and expenditure do not occur simultaneously.

In modern large-scale business the annual budget, which is normally broken down into monthly and weekly periods, is a complex document that may take several months to prepare. The starting-point will be an estimate of sales and income for the period, balanced by budgets for purchasing, administration, production, distribution and research costs. There will also be detailed budgets of ➤cash flows and ➤capital expenditure. These are often also made for periods of further than one year ahead, so that borrowing requirements and capacity requirements can be assessed (➤capital budgeting). A *flexible budget* is one based on different assumed levels of plant activity.

The UK's national budget sets out estimates of central government expenditure and revenue for the financial year, and is normally presented by the Chancellor of the ➤Exchequer to the British Parliament late in the previous financial year. The Labour government which came to power in 1997 decided to pre-release a green paper outlining the background to the budget, and certain options. The budget is formally concerned with ➤consolidated fund revenue, and not with ➤National Insurance or local government finance, although in practice all spending and revenue decisions are discussed. In his statement, the Chancellor reviews economic conditions and government expenditure for the past year, makes forecasts for the coming year and announces proposed changes in ➤taxation. These changes normally become effective immediately, but are subject to parliamentary debate and approval in the Finance Bill and Act. With the increasing importance of government expenditure in the economy, the annual budget is an important instrument in government economic policy. Fiscal changes may have more to do with decisions to modify the budget surplus or deficit in the interest of demand management (➤balanced budget) than with planned expenditure which, in any case, is essentially discussed and presented earlier in the year. ➤supply services. ➤➤public expenditure; medium-term financial strategy.

budget deficit ➤balanced budget; public-sector borrowing requirement; ➤➤Ricardian equivalence.

budget line A set of combinations of different commodities which, given a consumer's income, can just be afforded. If there were only two commodities – cornflakes and milk – the budget line could be drawn on a graph which had cornflakes on one axis and milk on the other. Given the price of each and the consumer's income, it would be a straight downward-sloping line cutting each axis at the quantity of that commodity which could be purchased if all income were devoted to it. The budget line represents the constraint facing the consumer when consumption decisions are made and is used in ▶indifference-curve analysis.

budgetary control A system of control which checks actual ▶income and expenditure against a ▶budget so that progress towards set objectives may be measured and remedial action taken if necessary. Budget-control statements comparing actual and estimated expenditure are issued weekly or monthly. These statements will be issued in considerable detail to department heads, and in less detail to higher management. Budget control statements must, if any necessary remedial action is to be taken in time, be issued as soon as possible after the close of the period to which they relate, and for this reason need not be of the same accuracy as accounting statements and may be based on estimated data. The development of computerized accounting procedures has greatly facilitated budgetary control. ▶▶resource accounting.

building society An institution that accepts ▶deposits, upon which it pays ▶interest and makes ▶loans for house purchase secured by ▶mortgages, and which is not owned by shareholders, but by its members, comprising its customers. Building societies are unique to Britain, though elsewhere similar functions are performed by ▶savings bank, for example Saving and Loan Associations in the USA. Building societies grew out of the Friendly Society movement in the late seventeenth century and are non-▶profit-making. Their activities were initially regulated by the Building Societies Act of 1874, which set up a Registrar of Building Societies. Subsequent Acts have tightened controls over the societies' financial management and the 1986 Building Societies Act (see below) initiated fundamental changes to the whole movement. The societies accept deposits which can be withdrawn on demand up to a limited amount or at one month's notice, or 'shares' which may be subject to a longer notice of withdrawal. Traditionally, the societies' deposits are fed by regular small savings and the average holdings are about £5000, though they also raise funds on the ▶money market, i.e. on a wholesale as well as a retail basis. Loans are made to persons wishing to purchase their homes, or more rarely to builders, and administrative costs are financed by the difference between the borrowing and lending rates. The loans are usually repaid on regular monthly instalments of ▶capital and interest over a period of years, usually on a ▶reducing balance basis. Sometimes loans can be repaid with an ▶assurance policy and remain outstanding until the policy matures; in these instances only interest (and the premiums on the policy) are paid during the period of the loans. Building societies' ▶rates of interest must bear a close relationship to rates charged or obtained elsewhere, since they compete with other institutions for funds. Investors in building societies may put their money into shares or into deposit. The former confer some rights of ownership but are not ▸equity shares; they are simply a form of deposit for which slightly more restrictive withdrawal terms are rewarded by a higher interest rate. Special interest-rate incentives are provided for regular savers. Originally highly localized in their operations, the building societies became increasingly to operate on a national scale. However, their numbers in Great Britain have fallen from over 500 in the late 1960s to 94 in 1995, and even further since, mainly as a result of ▸mergers and the recent process of conversion into banks. The biggest remaining building society is the Nationwide. The 1986 Act allowed the societies to widen their services from their traditional property-mortgage business to include loans to individuals for other purposes, money transmission and foreign-exchange services, personal financial planning services (acquisition and disposal of shares, insurance, pension schemes), estate agency, valuation and conveyancing services. The Act also provided for a regulatory agency, the Building Societies Commission, and an Investor Protection Scheme. ▸▸financial intermediaries.

built-in stabilizers Institutional features of the economy which without explicit government intervention automatically act to dampen down fluctuations in employment and ▸national income. Examples of these are (a) aggregate unemployment benefits and welfare payments, which automatically increase when unemployment increases and fall when unemployment falls, so that this part of government expenditure adjusts automatically in the desired directions to offset in part changes in other components of ▸aggregate demand, and (b) government taxation, which falls in total as national income falls and rises as national income rises, both because the burden of ▸income taxes changes and because, with changes in ▸consumption expenditures, sales tax revenues also change. Since an increase in taxation tends to restrain expenditure, while a fall in taxation stimulates it, we again have 'automatic' factors counteracting inflationary and deflationary pressures in the economy (▸inflation; deflation). These built-in stabilizers rarely have sufficient force to render positive corrective policies unnecessary. ▸▸fiscal drag.

bull A ▸stock exchange speculator who purchases ▸stocks and ▸shares in the belief that prices will rise and that he will be able to sell them again later at a profit (▸speculation); the opposite of ▸bear. The market is said to be *bullish* when it is generally anticipated that prices will rise.

bullion Gold, silver or other precious metal in bulk, i.e. in the form of ingots or bars rather than in coin. Gold bullion is used in international monetary transactions between ▸central banks and forms partial backing for many ▸currencies (▸gold standard). A *bullion market* is a gold market.

Bundesbank The ▸central bank of Germany, based in Frankfurt. It was formally established in 1957, although its origins can be traced to 1875. Its constitution demands that it maintains the internal and external value of the currency. To help it resist short-term political pressures, the Bank is shielded from governmental interference in the conduct of monetary policy, although the powerful Bundesbank President is effectively appointed by the government. During the life of the ➤European Monetary System, the Bundesbank was dominant in establishing monetary policy for the entire European Union, with other member states gradually converging on Germany's low ➤inflation rate. The Bundesbank will play a major role in the development of ➤European Monetary Union.

business angels ➤risk capital.

business cycle Regular fluctuations in the level of ➤national income. The business cycle is a well-observed economic phenomenon, though it often occurs on a generally upward growth path and has a variable time span, typically of the order of five years. It has been a matter of government policy in western economies to dampen the amplitude, that is, the height of the peaks and depths of the troughs, of the cycle so that the trend path of output is followed without much fluctuation (➤stabilization policy).

Several suggestions have been put forward as to the cause of cycles. The best known, developed by ➤Samuelson, ➤Hicks, Goodwin, ➤Phillips and Kalecki in the 1940s and 1950s, combines the ➤multiplier with the accelerator theory of investment (➤accelerator–mulitplier model). In certain cases, investment can be positively related to output one period back, and negatively related to output two periods back. This can cause an oscillating path for income. This account quite plausibly requires that investment is based upon companies' expectations of future growth; but rather less plausibly relies upon these expectations being drawn from a naive extrapolation of what happened in the last period. ➤Friedman, in his analysis of US monetary history, notes the correlation between money supply and economic activity and suggests that the business cycle is a monetary phenomenon. Several theories of the cycle embrace the notion of ➤rational expectations, or the idea that expectations are more forward looking. ➤New Keynesianism suggests that fluctuations in ➤aggregate demand account for the cycle. ➤New classical economics explains it in terms of *unanticipated* fluctuations in demand. More recently, attention has been paid to the effects of shocks to the economy from technology and taste changes. These 'real' phenomena can, it is suggested, account for many economic fluctuations. (➤real business cycle theory.) There has been much debate on the effectiveness of policy-makers' attempts to dampen the cycle (➤policy ineffectiveness theorem), and there is a broad consensus that governments should make strenuous efforts to avoid inflaming it. ➤Frisch, R. A. K.; Kondratieff cycle; stop–go, stabilization policy.

Business Expansion Scheme (BES) ➤Enterprise Investment Scheme.

business finance The provision of ➤money for commercial use. The ➤capital requirements of business may be divided into short and medium term, or long term. Short-term capital consists of the current ➤liabilities of a business plus medium-term capital. The main sources of short- and medium-term capital (for a company) can be further subdivided into internal and external:

Internal: ➤retained earnings, including ➤accrued expenses and tax reserves. ➤➤cash flow; corporation tax; self-financing.

External: Temporary ➤loans from sister companies, directors and others; ➤factoring; ➤bills of exchange; trade creditors and expense creditors; and short-term ➤trade investments. Short-term capital should in theory only be used for investment in relatively liquid assets (➤➤liquid) so that it is readily available to discharge the liability if necessary. Thus, these sources of short-term capital may be used for finished goods in stock and work in progress, trade debtors, prepaid expenses, cash in hand and at the bank.

Correspondingly, the main sources of long-term liabilities or capital can be subdivided in the same way.

Internal: Reserves, retained earnings and ➤depreciation provisions.

External: Share capital, i.e. ➤ordinary shares, ➤preference shares, long-term loans including ➤mortgages, ➤leaseback arrangements and ➤debentures.

Long-term capital may be used for long-term investment in fixed assets (land, buildings, plant, equipment and machinery, etc.), in goodwill, patents and trademarks and long-term trade investments.

There are important differences in the sources of capital open to large and small firms. The latter do not have access to the ➤stock exchange and rely more heavily upon family and friends for equity capital, as well as upon the ➤commercial banks. The main institutional sources of business finance are the commercial banks, the ➤merchant banks, the ➤finance houses, the ➤discount houses, factoring companies and the institutions concerned with new issues (➤new-issue market). ➤insurance companies and ➤pension funds hold a large proportion of all quoted securities (➤quotation). A number of other institutions specialize in providing ➤term loans and ➤risk capital, especially for innovation and smaller businesses.

business saving That part of the net revenue of a firm which is not paid out as interest, ➤dividends or ➤taxation, but rather is kept in the business as reserves and ➤depreciation allowances or to finance new ➤investment. Sometimes called *retentions*. ➤➤self-financing.

business taxation ➤corporation tax.

buyer's market A ➤market in which prices are falling, owing, for instance, to an excess of ➤supply of the goods or services traded compared with ➤demand. ➤➤price system.

by-product The output from a process designed for the production of some other product. It is a necessary outcome of the production process and cannot be avoided. Its ➤opportunity cost is zero. ➤economies of scope.

C

cabotage The transportation of goods or passengers wholly within one country by vehicles, ships or aircraft which are foreign-owned. Many countries prohibit or place restrictions on such operations. For instance, under the Jones Act of 1920, some US ships are given preferences in the carriage of US domestic cargo and the Merchant Marine Act of 1936 enables the US government to impose penalties on foreign vessels which have been built cheaply by means of subsidy, if they operate in US domestic trade. A number of European countries also prohibit or restrict cabotage. Road transport operated by members of the ➤European Union will be free to operate cabotage trade by mid 1998. Similarly, restrictions were removed on shipping cabotage in 1993, except for island traffic which continues to be restricted until 1999 and, for Greece, 2004. ➤➤free trade.

calculus The branch of mathematics concerned with the gradient of curves. Basic calculus consists of a set of rules which determine for any ➤function, the slope of the curve of the function at any point. Thus, if $y = x^2$, calculus reveals that, when $x = 3$, the slope of the curve depicting this function is 6 $(2x)$. The value y of the function is 9 (3^2) at this point.

The importance of calculus is that the slope of a function effectively says how much the ➤dependent variable changes for a very small unit change in the ➤independent variable. Working out the slope of a function gives us valuable information as to the responsiveness of one variable to changes in another. More specifically, the slope of a function gives the marginal value of that function. In the example above, if y is 'utility' and, x is 'number of chocolate bars eaten', we know from calculus that when three bars are eaten, the number of 'utils' gained from very small increments of chocolate bar is six; this is ➤marginal utility. ➤➤marginal analysis; integration.

calculus of variations A branch of mathematics that is concerned with tracing the optimal path of variables over time. It is to ➤dynamics what the ➤Lagrange multiplier is to static analysis. An example of the use of the calculus of variations would be to work out the path of economic growth in terms of the capital stock and ➤investment (➤optimal-growth theory).

call An unpaid portion of the price of a ➤share. This may appear when an applicant for a new share issue pays only part of the price of the share on application and the remainder on allotment or when the issued shares of a company are not fully paid up (➤paid-up capital).

call option A contract giving a right to buy ➤shares from the dealer making the contract at the price ruling at the time within a specified future period, usually three months. Call options carry a ➤commission to the dealer on the price of the shares traded. The opposite of *put option* (➤option).

Cambridge school A system of economic thought influenced by economists at the University of Cambridge, England. ➤Alfred Marshall (1842–1924) held the Chair of Political Economy until 1908 and ➤A. C. Pigou (1877–1959) until 1944, and during this period the school was characterized by the theory of late ➤classical economics. After the end of the Second World War, the school attempted to refute what became known as ➤neo-classical economics and developed ideas based on those of ➤J. M. Keynes (1883–1946), although linked also with the early ➤classical period. The leading figures in the post-war debate were ➤J. V. Robinson (1903–83) and ➤N. Kaldor (1908–86). The Cambridge school emphasized a ➤macroeconomic approach compared with the ➤microeconomic approach of the neo-classical school. The Cambridge school denied that there was a direct functional relationship between the rate of ➤profit and the capital intensity of an economy. They have demonstrated the possibility of ➤capital re-switching (➤Wicksell effect, price) and have criticized the neo-classical school for leaping to conclusions about the aggregates derived from micro-analysis. For instance, they argue that the aggregate ➤production function of the ➤Cobb–Douglas type is not compatible in practice with the micro-functions from which it is derived. The neo-classical theory of ➤distribution which relates relative factor prices (➤factors of production) to relative ➤marginal revenue productivities is deficient in throwing light on aggregate factor distributed shares of product (➤Euler, L.). *Per contra*, they themselves are criticized for neglecting ➤microeconomic theory.

Cantillon, Richard (1680–1734) An Irish international banker who wrote *Essai sur la nature du commerce en général,* which was not published until 1755 but had circulated from about 1730. This work was one of the first synoptic descriptions and analyses of the economic process. His views on the importance of agriculture, based on its receipt of pure ➤rent, and his analysis of the circulation of wealth foreshadowed the ➤Physiocrats and the ➤'tableau économique'.

CAP ➤Common Agricultural Policy.

capacity utilization rate The output of a plant, firm or a whole economy divided by its output at full capacity. ➤➤excess capacity; output gap.

capital 1. Assets which are capable of generating income and which have themselves been produced. Capital is one of the four ➤factors of production, and consists of the machines, plant and buildings that make production possible, but excludes raw materials, ➤land and ➤labour. All capital is itself, however, the product of labour and raw materials and can be seen as holding the stored value of them. If a Stone Age man spent one day producing a tool (a capital good) he gained no utility from doing so at the time. He did, however, save labour by using the tool thereafter. By building the tool he had in effect put some labour away for use at a later date. The essence of capital, therefore, is that it represents deferred consumption.   **2**. In more general usage, any asset or stock of assets – financial or physical – capable of generating income. ➤➤wealth.

capital adequacy A requirement placed on ➤financial intermediaries to maintain a minimum proportion of ➤liquid assets. Various regulatory bodies impose minimum capital requirements upon banks, ➤investment banks and ➤investment trusts. For banks (➤banking), these requirements may be used to control monetary aggregates (➤money supply; reserve requirements) but increasingly they are aimed at preventing failure and instability in the financial system (*prudential regulation*). The increasing ➤globalization of the world financial system has stimulated international agreement on capital adequacy standards. Beginning in 1975, a series of international agreements under the auspices of the ➤Bank for International Settlements have laid down, in the *Basle Agreements*, standards for bank supervision and capital adequacy. The latter include minimum ratios of capital to risk ➤assets with weights (➤weighted average) to adjust risk for the status of the borrower. For example, commercial ➤loans carry a 100 per cent risk weighting, so that banks have to allocate the full capital required under the ratios to such loans, while sovereign credits to ➤Organization for Economic Cooperation and Development member governments are given a zero risk weighting.

There are national capital adequacy requirements for banks which, within the ➤European Union, derive from various ➤Directives of the EU (➤Banking Acts). The Second Banking Directive imposes a minimum ➤equity capital requirement of ➤ECU 5 million on all credit institutions. The Own Funds Directive (1989) and the Solvency Ratio Directive (1989) are generally consistent with the Basle Agreements. The Capital Adequacy Directive (1993) relates capital requirements to trading exposures for banks and securities firms. There are other Directives affecting capital requirements and risk exposure for financial intermediaries, and also specific national requirements ➤➤derivatives; Financial Services Act; Federal Reserve System.

capital, authorized ➤authorized capital.

capital, cost of 1. The ➤rate of interest paid on the ➤capital employed in a business. Since capital will be usually drawn from a variety of sources it will be an average cost derived from weighting the cost of each source, including ➤equity capital, by its proportion of the total. There has been extensive debate about whether the cost of capital is too high in the UK, or whether indeed company executives merely think it is higher than it is. A high cost of capital is considered detrimental to ➤investment.   **2**. The cost of raising additional capital, i.e. the marginal cost. The marginal cost of capital on a ➤discounted cash flow basis may be used as the minimum level of return in assessing investment projects. ➤➤Modigliani – Miller theorem, capital asset pricing model.

capital, issued ➤issued capital.

capital, marginal efficiency of ➤internal rate of return.

capital, marginal productivity of ➤internal rate of return.

capital, nominal ➤authorized capital.

capital, registered ➤authorized capital.

capital, sources of ➤business finance.

capital, working ➤working capital.

capital account ➤balance of payments.

capital allowances Reductions in tax (➤taxation) liability which are related to a firm's ➤capital expenditure. In most countries expenditure on new capital assets is encouraged by various kinds of allowances, and annual ➤depreciation is recognized as an expense of the business in calculating tax liability. The taxation authorities' methods of depreciating an ➤asset are not necessarily the same as those used by the company in the published ➤accounts. Where a company may claim depreciation for tax purposes at will, e.g. to write off the whole of the cost of an asset against tax in a single year, or to spread it over twenty years as it chooses, this is known as *free depreciation* or *depreciation at choice*.

capital asset pricing model A model of the market for different financial assets which suggests that asset prices will adjust to ensure that the return an asset makes precisely compensates investors for the risk of that asset when held with a perfectly diversified *portfolio*. The model has dominated economists' understanding of the financial sector. Under simplifying assumptions, the following propositions hold:
(a) Everybody will hold a portfolio of assets which is as diversified as possible (➤➤diversification).
(b) This means the particular risks of each individual asset will be unimportant because the ups and downs of assets' performances will tend to cancel out (➤➤portfolio theory).
(c) There will nevertheless be some remaining market risk – the risk of factors that affect all the assets together.
(d) This risk depends on how closely the assets' performances coincide.
(e) The risk any particular asset adds to a portfolio will thus depend only on how closely its performance tracks that of the rest of the portfolio.
(f) The price of assets which closely track other assets will be low because they are unattractive – when other assets do well, they do well and vice versa (➤beta).
(g) The price of assets which hardly move at all with the market will be high, because they pay out good returns when they are needed most.

The capital asset pricing model is a development of this chain of reasoning. It can be used to calculate an expected return on any particular asset, as a function of the rate of return on riskless assets, plus a risk premium based on the degree to which the asset tracks the market. It thus provides one basis for assessing a cost of capital (►capital, cost of) for a company. ►efficient markets hypothesis; H. Markowitz; W. Sharpe.

capital budgeting The adoption of financial plans for managing and monitoring expenditure on non-recurrent expenditure. Capital is generally hard to plan for within ►cash flow accounts as, in any one period, the relationship between cost incurred and value derived is very small. ►►resource accounting.

capital charges Charges in the ►accounts of a company or individual for interest paid on ►capital, ►depreciation or repayment of ►loans.

capital consumption ►capital stock.

capital deepening ►capital widening.

capital employed The ►capital in use in a business. There is no universally agreed definition of the term. It is sometimes taken to mean ►net assets (i.e. fixed plus current assets minus current ►liabilities), but more usually ►bank loans and ►overdrafts are included and other adjustments made for purposes of calculating the return on *net capital employed* (►rate of return), such as the exclusion of intangible assets and the revaluation of ►trade investments at market prices. ►►investment appraisal.

capital expenditure The purchase of fixed ►assets (e.g. plant and equipment), expenditure on ►trade investments or acquisitions of other businesses and expenditure on current assets (e.g. stocks); to be distinguished from ►capital formation.

capital formation ►net investment in fixed ►assets, i.e. additions to the stock of real ►capital. *Gross fixed capital formation* includes ►depreciation; *net capital formation* excludes it.

capital gains A realized increase in the value of a capital ►asset, as when a share is sold for more than the price at which it was purchased. Strictly speaking, the term refers to capital appreciation outside the normal course of business. In the UK capital gains are subject to capital gains tax (CGT). The tax does not cover gains arising from the sale of personal belongings, including cars or principal dwelling houses, but it does cover gains from the sale of ►stock exchange securities (with special treatment for ►gilt-edged securities). The tax for individuals is now the same as that for other income (►income tax), while incorporated businesses pay ►corporation tax on capital gains. ►Capital losses may be set against tax liability and the first £6300 is exempt from income tax (1996/97). Capital gains arise from changes in the supply and demand for capital assets, but also from ►inflation, and for assets disposed of after the beginning of the 1982 tax year the original cost may be increased by ►indexation, i.e. the expenditure scaled up in proportion to the increase in the retail price index between, in most cases, a year after the acquisition and the date of sale. Capital gains are taxed in some countries at lower rates for short-term gains.

capital gearing ➤gearing.

capital goods ➤capital.

capital-intensive The production of a commodity in which a higher proportion of ➤capital is used in the mix of inputs compared with other factor inputs, such as labour. ➤➤factors of production.

capital loss A reduction in the ➤money value of an ➤asset; opposite of ➤capital gain.

capital market The market for long-term loanable funds as distinct from the ➤money market, which deals in short-term funds. There is no clear-cut distinction between the two ➤markets, although in principle capital-market ➤loans are used by industry and commerce mainly for fixed ➤investment. The capital market is an increasingly international one and in any country is not one institution but all those institutions that match the ➤supply and ➤demand for long-term capital and claims on capital, e.g. the ➤stock exchange, banks and ➤insurance companies. The capital market, of course, is not concerned solely with the issue of new claims on capital (the *primary* or ➤new-issue market), but also with dealings in existing claims (the ➤secondary market). The marketability of ➤securities is an important element in the efficient working of the capital market, since investors would be much more reluctant to make loans to industry if their claims could not easily be disposed of. All advanced countries have highly developed capital markets, but in ➤developing countries the absence of a capital market is often as much of an obstacle to the growth of investment as a shortage of savings, and governments and industrialists in these countries are obliged to raise capital in the international capital market, i.e. that composed of the national capital markets in the advanced countries. ➤➤business finance; public finance.

capital movements ➤foreign investment.

capital–output ratio The ratio derived by dividing the level of output into the stock of ➤capital required to produce it. The incremental capital–output ratio is a change in output divided into a change in capital stock (i.e. ➤investment). The relationship between incremental capital (investment) and output is described by the ➤acceleration principle and the incremental capital–output ratio is the ➤accelerator coefficient. The interdependence of capital and output play an important role in ➤growth theory, in which various assumptions about the ratio are explored. For example:

(a) The ratio may be assumed to be a fixed constant as the economy grows; or, as in Marxian economics (➤Marx, K.) it may be assumed to increase, implying that the rate of profit earned on investment falls (➤profit, falling rate of).

(b) Labour and capital may be substitutable depending on wages and the rate of interest.

(c) Capital-embodied technical progress may occur, meaning that new investment is more efficient than old, so that the ratio falls as old capital is replaced (►technology). ►►capital theory.

capital reserves ►company reserves.

capital re-switching A phenomenon which played an important part in the controversy over ►capital theory between a group of economists led by ►Robinson at Cambridge, England, and a group at Cambridge, Mass., USA, led by ►Samuelson and ►Solow. Specifically, it can be shown that the proposition that ►investment increases as the required ►rate of return (►internal rate of return) falls may not in fact be valid. We could imagine that, as the required rate of return falls, firms would switch from less to more ►capital-intensive methods of production, thus increasing the rate of investment. However, it is possible to show that under quite plausible circumstances the rate of return could reach a level at which firms would switch back, i.e. re-switch, from more to less capital-intensive production methods, thus causing investment to fall as the required rate of return falls. This possibility then undermines the ►neo-classical model on which the Cambridge, Mass., argument was based (►Wicksell effect, price).

capital stock The total amount of physical ►capital in the economy or, less commonly, in a firm or industry. In theory, the most important valuation of the stock is the ►present value of the ►income stream it will generate in the future and changes in the capital stock should provide a guide to changes in the productive potential of the economy. Since the different parts of the capital stock, roads, machinery and buildings, cannot be added together, in practice they have to be valued to produce an estimate of the capital stock at the prices of a given year. In the 1995 ►blue book the UK gross capital stock (at 1990 replacement values) was £2695 billion, equivalent to about four years of ►gross domestic product. *Capital consumption* is the replacement value of capital used up in the process of production, an identical concept to the ►depreciation provisions in company accounts, though not necessarily measured in the same way.

capital structure The sources of long-term ►capital of a company. A company's capital structure is determined by the numbers and types of ►shares it issues and its reliance on fixed-interest debt (►gearing). A company's choice between different sources of finance will be determined by their cost, the type of business it is, its past and expected future earnings, ►taxation and other considerations. ►►business finance; capital, cost of.

capital theory That part of economic theory concerned with analysis of the consequences of the fact that production generally involves ►inputs which have themselves been produced. The existence of these 'produced means of production', or ►capital, has profound implications for the nature of the economic system. A central element is the role of time and inter-temporal planning. The production of capital requires the sacrifice of current consumption in exchange for future, possibly uncertain, consumption, and the mechanisms by which this process is organized influence the growth and stability of the economy in important ways. The existence of capital is also central to the analysis of the ►income distribution. A major and controversial question has been: what determines the income derived by the owners of capital relative to that of the suppliers of labour, and can their share be justified in terms of their contribution to the production of output? An understanding of the nature and implications of capital is fundamental to an understanding of our economic system and, indeed, as one leading contributor to the subject has remarked, the problem in attempting to define capital theory is to do it in such a way 'as to embrace something less than the whole of economics' (C. J. Bliss, in *Capital Theory and the Distribution of Income*). ►►Böhm-Bawerk, E. von.

capital transfer tax ►inheritance tax.

capital widening Increasing the quantity of capital without altering the proportions of the other ►factors of production. This will occur where the ►capital stock and employment are both increasing. Where the capital stock is increased and the numbers employed remain constant or fall then production has become more capital-intensive and *capital deepening* has occurred.

capitalism A social and economic system in which individuals are free to own the means of production and maximize ►profits and in which resource allocation is determined by the ►price system. ►Marx argued that capitalism would be overthrown because it inevitably led to the exploitation of labour.

capitalization 1. The amount and structure of the ►capital of a company. 2. The conversion of accumulated ►profits and reserves into ►issued capital. 3. *Market capitalization* is the market value of a company's issued ►share capital, i.e. the quoted price of its shares multiplied by the number of shares outstanding.

capitalization issue ►bonus issue.

capitalized ratios Ratios which describe the ►capital structure of a company, by indicating the proportion of each type of ►security issued.

capitalized value The ►capital sum at current ►rates of interest required to yield the current earnings of an ►asset. For example, if the earnings of an asset were £5 per annum and the appropriate rate of interest were 5 per cent, its capitalized value would be £100, as an asset worth £100 yields an annual return of £5. The general formula for capitalizing the value of an asset is to divide the annual income by the annual rate of interest (all multiplied by 100). ►►annuity.

captives ►risk capital.

carbon tax ➤pollutor-pays principle.

Caribbean Basin Initiative (CBI) The Caribbean Basin Economic Recovery Act, passed by the United States Congress in 1983, granted preferential and ➤tariff-free access to the US market for a range of goods exported from twenty-three countries in the Caribbean and Central America. These privileges excluded some commodity groups such as textiles and clothing, sugar and oil. This agreement, referred to as the Caribbean Basin Initiative, was originally scheduled to end in 1995, but Congress passed an Act in 1990 which made the provisions of the 1983 Act permanent. ➤➤Caribbean Common Market.

Caribbean Community and Common Market (CARICOM) Formed in 1973, the Caribbean Community has fourteen member states: Belize, Guyana and Surinam on the American mainland and Antigua, Barbados, Dominica, Grenada, Jamaica, Montserrat, St Christopher/Nevis/Anguilla, St Lucia, St Vincent and Trinidad/Tobago in the Caribbean. The Bahamas is a also a member of the Community, although not of the Common Market. The Community has a secretariat in Georgetown, Guyana. The British Virgin Islands and the Turks and Caicos Islands are associate members. A Common External Tariff has been set up and restrictions on foreign exchange and the free movement of skilled workers have been eased. The aim is the eventual establishment of a ➤common market with monetary union. In 1996, discussions were held with a view to the setting up of a ➤free-trade area with the ➤Central American Common Market. ➤➤Caribbean Basin Initiative; Caribbean Development Bank; Lomé Convention; customs union.

Caribbean Development Bank A regional development bank, established in 1970 which channels ➤soft loans and grants for the financing of agricultural and industrial projects in the Caribbean. It has twenty regional members and five others (viz Canada, France, Germany, Italy and the UK) ➤African Development Bank; Asian Development Bank; Inter-American Development Bank; International Bank for Reconstruction and Development.

CARICOM ➤Caribbean Community and Common Market.

carry-over Postponement of settlement of ➤account on the ➤stock exchange until the following period involving payment of a ➤rate of interest on the account. Also called *contango* (➤backwardation).

cartel An association of producers to regulate ➤prices by restricting output and competition. Cartels are illegal in the USA but cartels have been promoted by governments to achieve 'rationalization', as in Germany in the 1930s. They tend to be unstable because a single member can profit by undercutting the others, while price-fixing stimulates the development of substitutes. The most prominent example of an international cartel is the ➤Organization of Petroleum Exporting Countries (OPEC). ➤➤oligopoly; prisoner's dilemma.

cascade tax ➤turnover tax.

cash 1. Coins and ➤banknotes. 2. ➤legal tender in the settlement of ➤debt.

cash flow The flow of ➤money payments to or from a firm. Expenditure is sometimes referred to as a 'negative' cash flow. The *gross cash flow* of a business is the gross ➤profit (after payment of a fixed ➤rate of interest) plus ➤depreciation provisions in any trading period, i.e. that sum of money which is available for ➤investment, ➤dividends or payment of taxes. The *net cash flow* is retained ➤earnings and depreciation provisions before or after tax (➤taxation). Net cash flows of a particular project are usually defined as those arising after taxes have been paid, expenditure on repairs and maintenance carried out, any necessary adjustments made to ➤working capital, and account is taken of any residual value of ➤assets at the end of a particular project's life or other miscellaneous income accruing to the project or business. This term is important in ➤investment appraisal. 'Cash-flow statement' is often used synonymously with 'statement of ➤sources and uses'. ➤➤budget.

cash-flow accounting ➤inflation accounting.

cash ratio 1. The ratio of a bank's ➤cash holdings to its total deposit ➤liabilities. (➤➤liquidity ratio; banking.) 2. For an individual firm, the proportion of its current liabilities that are accounted for by cash in hand, including ➤bank deposits, and sometimes payments due from customers.

Cassel, Gustav (1866–1945) ➤purchasing-power parity theory.

CBI ➤Caribbean Basin Initiative; Confederation of British Industry.

CCA Current-cost accounting (➤inflation accounting).

CD ➤certificate of deposit.

CDB ➤Caribbean Development Bank.

CDC ➤Commonwealth Development Corporation.

Celler–Kefauver Act ➤anti-trust (US).

census A statistical survey covering every member of a ➤population. ➤➤sample.

Central American Common Market (CACM) A common market of four Central American states – Guatemala, El Salvador, Honduras and Nicaragua – agreed at Managua, Nicaragua, in the General Treaty of Central American Economic Integration signed in December 1960. This treaty came into operation in June 1961, and a headquarters was established in San Salvador. Costa Rica and Panama have since also joined. ➤Free trade between the member countries was expected to be established by June 1966. In the event, although duties have been eliminated on about 95 per cent of products, duties on many of the remaining products, particularly agricultural, are likely to continue. An agreement on the Equalization of Import Duties and Charges was made in September 1959, and subsequent agreements have established a common external ➤tariff on all but a small number of products. In 1961 the Central American Bank for Economic Integration was formed to finance industrial projects, housing and hotels in the region. In 1964 the five ➤central banks agreed to establish, in the long term, a common ➤currency. The Common Market suffered a set-back by the imposition of import duties on a number of commodities by Costa Rica in 1971 and Nicaragua in 1978. Little progress has been made since for the setting up of the market structures. However, at a meeting in 1990 the members reaffirmed their determination to establish the Market as agreed at Managua. In 1996 discussions were held on a plan for the establishment of a ➤free-trade area with ➤CARICOM. ➤➤customs union; Inter-American Development bank.

central bank A bankers' bank and ➤lender of last resort (➤Bank of England). All developed and most ➤developing countries have a central bank that is responsible for exercising control of the ➤credit system, sometimes under instruction from government and, increasingly often, under its own authority. Central banks typically execute policy through their lead role in setting short-term interest rates (➤rate of interest) which they control by establishing the rate at which loans of last resort will be made. Some central banks also use other devices to control ➤money supply, such as special deposits. With an increasing consensus that ➤monetary policy plays an important part in determining ➤aggregate demand, the stability of the ➤business cycle and the rate of ➤inflation, central banks have found themselves in an increasingly central role in economic management. The success of those which operated at arm's length from political authority – notably in the USA and Germany (➤Bundesbank) – has led other nations to follow in granting independence. The premisses are that the temptation to engage in ➤overheating will be diminished if monetary authorities do not have to face an election every few years; and that ➤credibility of policy will be greater if a bank is in charge. Some independent central banks have more power than others. In Britain, New Zealand and Canada, the central bank essentially decides on the level of interest rates, but does so to aim at an ➤inflation target set by the government. In Germany, and indeed in the constitution of the European Central Bank governing ➤European Monetary Union, the bank sets its own target. The power of central banks led one commentator in 1996 to assert the western world was in the grip of *central bankism* in reference to the orthodox values most represent. Apart from their function of making broad economic judgements, central banks, such as the Bank of France, the Federal Reserve Bank and the Bank of Canada, control the note issue (➤banknote), act as the government's bank, accept ➤deposits from and make ➤loans to the ➤commercial banks and the ➤money market, and conduct transfers of ➤money and ➤bullion with central banks in other countries. ➤➤Bank for International Settlements; Federal Reserve System.

central bank of central banks ►Bank for International Settlements; International Monetary Fund; Keynes Plan.

central government ►public sector.

central government borrowing requirement ►public-sector borrowing requirement.

certificate of deposit (CD) A negotiable claim issued by a bank in return for a term ►deposit. CDs are ►securities which are purchased for less than their face value, which is the bank's promise to repay the deposit and thus offer a ►yield to maturity. The ►secondary market in CDs is made up by the ►discount houses and the banks in the ►inter-bank market. Where a depositor knows that he can, if necessary, sell his CD he will be willing to place his funds with a bank for long periods. CDs were first issued in New York in the 1960s and thus denominated in dollars. Sterling CDs followed in 1968. ►►parallel money markets.

certificate of incorporation A document issued by the Registrar of Companies certifying the legal existence of a company after certain legal requirements for registration have been met. ►►company law.

certificate of origin A certificate which specifies the country of origin of an export or import. Such a certificate would be required by a customs authority for such purposes as determining whether an import should benefit from a preferential ►tariff which may have been agreed with specific countries, such as those in a ►free-trade area or ►customs union, or whether, for instance, a product is liable to an anti- ►dumping tax. Somewhat different rules may be applied depending on the purpose for which the country of origin is required to be specified. The ►European Union, for instance, generally determines origin by the location at which the last major manufacturing activity took place but applies a somewhat less stringent definition to some imports from ►developing countries benefiting from the ►generalized system of preferences. ►Customs Cooperation Council.

CGT Capital gains tax (►capital gains).

Chamberlin, Edward Hastings (1899–1967) After a period at the University of Michigan, Professor Chamberlin joined Harvard as a tutor in 1922 and became a Professor of Economics there in 1937. His publications include *Theory of Monopolistic Competition* (1933), *Towards a More General Theory of Value* (1957) and *The Economic Analysis of Labour Union Power* (1958). In *Theory of Monopolistic Competition* he proposed a new emphasis for economic theory which broke away from the old concepts of pure or ►perfect competition or pure ►monopoly. These two cases he saw as special limiting ones. In between was 'monopolistic competition', which was the condition under which most industries, in fact, operated. Each firm pursued a policy of product ►differentiation by special packaging or advertising so that it created a 'penumbra' of monopoly around its product. He also analysed the problem of selling costs, e.g. advertising. ➤➤mono-polistic (imperfect) competition; Robinson, J. V.

chaos theory A branch of mathematics that is concerned with the time path of ➤dependent variables in systems of non-linear equations. The odd feature of these systems is that, even though the observed variable is not random in that it is governed by a perfectly simple equation, it behaves in a way that looks very chaotic and unpredictable. This is because, in these systems, very small changes in initial conditions lead to large changes in the outcomes that result. It makes accurate long-term forecasting impossible. The weather is taken as an archetypal chaotic system, and economists have questioned whether certain variables, such as stock-market prices, might not best be understood in the same way.

CHAPS Clearing House Automated Payment System (➤clearing house).

charge account (US) ➤credit account.

chartist A stock-market analyst who predicts share-price movements solely from a study of graphs on which individual ➤share prices, price indices and sometimes trading volumes are plotted. This technique is called *technical analysis*. Unlike *fundamental analysis,* which requires the study of financial accounts of companies, technical analysis is based upon the belief that all the necessary information is in the share price. In contrast to both chartists and fundamentalists the adherents of the ➤efficient-markets hypothesis believe that stock-market prices adjust rapidly and fully to all information as soon as it becomes available and that neither existing nor past price levels are of any help in predicting the future.

cheque An order written by the drawer to a ➤commercial bank or ➤central bank to pay on demand a specified sum to a bearer, a named person or corporation. Although still very important, the use of cheques is gradually giving way to other forms of ➤credit transfer, ➤credit cards and electronic payments systems.

Chicago school The free-market and monetarist (➤monetarism) economic think-ing that has been associated with the Economics Department at Chicago University, and with ➤Milton Friedman in particular. The Chicago school is most closely associated with the complementary ideas that first, in ➤microeconomics, markets allocate resources most efficiently, and that government intervention should be very limited. Secondly, in ➤macroeconomics, with the ➤monetarist thesis that, as monetary growth causes inflation, discretionary policies to manage ➤aggregate demand should be avoided. Government should stick to rules aiming at a steady, low rate of growth of money supply. Common to both beliefs is the idea that the unregulated actions of private individuals are usually socially benign. For that reason, the school has tended to argue for a 'light touch' in ➤competition policy, and has suggested that most problems of ➤monopoly are created by government regulation, rather than solved by it. The school has also suggested that ➤vertical restraints are typically harmless. ➤➤laissez-faire.

CHIPS Clearing House Interbanks Payments System (►clearing house).

c.i.f. Cost, insurance and freight, or charged in full. The seller of the goods must pay the costs of carriage to the port of destination specified in the contract of sale and must, also, insure the goods against loss or damage during transit. The UK Overseas Trade Accounts record ►imports in terms of their value c.i.f. (charged in full) and exports ►f.o.b.. (free on board) or ►f.a.s. (free alongside ship). In order to determine the goods or ►visible trade balance for the ►balance of payments accounts, the import figures are adjusted to an f.o.b. basis. The insurance and freight element, which accounts for about 10 per cent of the total import bill, is included in the balance of payments as ►services (►invisibles).

circular flow of income A simple model of the workings of an economy depicting the movement of resources between producers and consumers. A number of flows comprise the circular flow of income. First, there are the wages and salaries paid by firms to ►households. Secondly, there is the money spent by households and received by firms. Corresponding to each of these flows of cash is a flow of some resource in return – labour is provided by households to firms; goods and services are provided by firms for households. There is then a total of four flows in this highly stylized account of how economies function, and there is complete symmetry between the two sectors: households and firms. Each provides the other with some real resource and each receives cash in return; and each spends that cash on the supplies of the other. The same cash is spent by one sector and then the other continuously.

►National income can be measured by either of the two cash flows; total wages and salaries comprise the *income measure*, while total household spending comprises the *expenditure measure*. These two are different sides of the same coin and, in an economy where all income is spent domestically, will necessarily be equal to each other. In reality, there are leakages from the circular flow: ►savings (when money is received by households but not spent); ►imports (where money flows to foreign firms); and ►taxation (when money flows to the government). Each of these 'withdrawals', however, gives rise to a corresponding 'injection': ►investment, ►exports and government spending (►public expenditure) – and, if all markets are in equilibrium, each pair will balance exactly. (Other complications include transactions on the ►invisible account such as dividend income received from abroad.)

►Macroeconomics can be seen as the study of and extension to the circular-flow model, removing the unrealistic assumptions underlying it and allowing for deviations from the equilibrium. ►multiplier; 'tableau économique'.

claimant count A measure of ►unemployment based on the number of people out of work and successfully claiming benefits related to unemployment. Claimant-count measures are useful in that they are quick and cheap to calculate, they are accurate (without sample error) and can be used to obtain reliable measures of unemployment at a very local level. They are, however, inconsistent over time, in as far as they are affected by changes in benefit-entitlement rules. They do not count many people who would like to work, but for one reason or another, are not entitled to benefits. Relative to what some economists consider the real level of unemployment, they include many people who are not actively seeking work, but who are still on benefits. ➤➤Labour Force Survey.

Clark, John Bates (1847–1938) Educated at Amherst College, and Heidelberg and Zürich Universities, Clark taught at Amherst until, in 1895, he was appointed Professor of Economics at Columbia University. He held this post until his retirement in 1923. His major publications include *Philosophy of Wealth* (1885), *Distribution of Wealth* (1899), *Essentials of Economic Theory* (1907), *The Control of Trusts* (1901) and *The Problem of Monopoly* (1904). He is regarded as the founder of the marginal productivity theory of distribution in the USA (➤distribution, theory of).

Clark, John Maurice (1884–1963) The son of ➤J. B. Clark. He succeeded his father to the Chair of Economics at Columbia University in 1926. His publications include *Economics of Overhead Costs* (1923) and *Essays in Preface to Social Economics* (1963). In an article, 'Business Acceleration and the Law of Demand', in the *Journal of Political Economy* in 1917, he formulated the ➤acceleration principle, one of the basic theories upon which has been constructed modern dynamic macroeconomic theory (➤macroeconomics).

classical economics The dominant body of economic thinking, economic method and economic style in the period from ➤Adam Smith's *Wealth of Nations,* which was published in 1776, through to ➤J. S. Mill's *Principles of Political Economy* of 1848. It was dominated by the work of ➤Ricardo. The French ➤Physiocrats had laid stress on the position of agriculture in the economy, claiming that this sector was the source of all economic wealth. Smith rejected this view and drew attention to the development of manufacturing and the importance of labour ➤productivity. Ultimately ➤labour was the true measure of ➤value. Ricardo took up this idea and propounded a theory of relative prices based on costs of production in which labour cost played the dominant role, although he accepted that ➤capital costs were an additional element. Capital was important, not only by improving labour productivity, but also by enabling labour to be sustained over the period of waiting before work bore fruit in consumable output. This was the idea of the wages fund (➤wage-fund theory). Wages were dependent on two forces: (a) the demand for labour, derived from the availability of capital, or savings, to finance the wage bill; and (b) the supply of labour, which was fixed in the short run, but in the long run was dependent on the standard of living. The latter was related to the level of subsistence. This was not regarded as merely the basic necessities required to keep the workers alive and to reproduce themselves. It was determined by custom, and was accepted to be increasing as real living standards improved.

classical school

➤Malthus, in his theory of population, pointed to the need for restraint because of the presumption that there was a natural tendency for the growth of population to outstrip agricultural output. Ricardo analysed the implications of the productivity of land at the margin of cultivation. The Physiocrats and Adam Smith had attributed agricultural ➤rent to the natural fertility of the soil, but Ricardo refuted this. Rent existed because of the poor fertility of the final increment of land taken under cultivation. Because of competition, ➤profits and labour costs must be the same everywhere and, therefore, a surplus must accrue to all land that was more fertile than that on the margin. This surplus was rent. The presumption of competition was the foundation of classical thought. The classical economists believed that, although individuals were each motivated by self-interest and personal ambition, free competition ensured that the community as a whole benefited. As Adam Smith put it, 'It is not from the benevolence of the butcher that we expect our dinner, but from [his] regard to [his] own interest.' As a consequence, they concluded that government interference should be kept to a minimum. The classical economists gave little attention to macroeconomic problems (➤macroeconomics), such as the ➤business cycle. Most of the classicists accepted ➤Say's 'law of markets', the gist of which purported to maintain the impossibility of any severe economic recession (➤depression) arising from an overall deficiency in ➤aggregate demand. (Malthus disputed this. He argued that increased savings would not only lower consumption but would also increase output, through increased investment. However, his view was not accepted.) The classical economists, including Malthus, held a theory in which savings were equated with investment through changes in the ➤rate of interest (➤Turgot, A. R. J.). J. S. Mill's book was used as a school text until the end of the nineteenth century. ➤Alfred Marshall in his *Principles of Economics* of 1890 assimilated the old classical economics with the new marginalism of ➤Jevons, ➤Menger and ➤Walras. The great controversy which raged in the years of the Great Depression of the 1930s between the late classical economists and the advocates of deficit spending on public works was resolved at the time when the classical macroeconomic theory gave way to the new economic revolution set in train by ➤Keynes. Classical economics continues to influence economists, however. (➤neo-classical economics; new classical economics. ➤➤economic doctrines.)

classical school The tradition of economic thought that originated in ➤Adam Smith and developed through the work of ➤Ricardo, ➤Malthus and ➤J. S. Mill down to ➤Marshall and ➤Pigou (➤classical economics; neo-classical economics).

classical unemployment A situation in which the number of people able and willing to work at prevailing wages exceeds the number of jobs available. In short, the real wage (the price of labour) is higher than that at which the market clears. Classical unemployment is explained by any operations of the labour market that prevent the unemployed bidding down wages until it is profitable for firms to find jobs for everyone. It contrasts with ➤structural unemployment or ➤frictional unemployment which occurs when the prevailing wage is too low to attract some people into employment. Classical unemployment also contrasts with ➤Keynesian unemployment, although both represent different regimes of ➤quantity rationing. Under classical unemployment, firms are not rationed at all – they can get all the labour they want and can sell all the goods they produce. Households, however, can neither sell all the labour they wish nor obtain all the goods they would like to buy with their excessively high wages. ➤➤insider–outsider theory.

clearing house 1. Any institution that settles mutual indebtedness between a number of organizations. **2.** More specifically, in England and Wales the Cheque and Credit Clearing Company Ltd operates a bulk clearing system for ➤cheques and other paper credit items paid into banks other than those upon which they were drawn. Bankers' Automated Clearing Services (BACS) clears electronic debits and credits, and the Clearing House Automated Payments System (CHAPS) clears high-value electronic funds transfers on a same-day basis. These three clearing companies are grouped under the Association for Payment Clearing Services (APACS). These systems and others are used not only by the ➤commercial banks but also by the ➤building societies and other financial institutions as well as large corporate customers of the banks. Similar institutions exist in other countries, for example, the Clearing House Interbank Payments System (CHIPS) in New York. Similar arrangements exist to clear transactions between members of ➤commodity exchanges and other markets, for example the International Commodities Clearing House.

cliometrics The 'new' ➤economic history in which quantitative techniques including ➤econometrics are used to make interpretations and reconstructions of the past. Pioneered by Robert Fogel and Douglass North (➤Fogel, Robert W.; North, Douglass C.).

closed economy An economic system with little or no external trade, as opposed to an *open economy*, in which a high proportion of output is absorbed by exports and similarly domestic expenditure by imports. ➤➤international trade.

closed-end fund An ➤investment trust or other investment company with a fixed ➤capitalization.

closing prices Price of a ➤commodity, e.g. ➤securities on the ➤stock exchange, at the end of a day's trading in a ➤market.

Coase, Ronald (b. 1910) Ronald Coase – the winner of the Nobel Prize in Economics in 1991 – is an economist who was born and educated in Britain, but who made his home in Chicago. He graduated from the London School of Economics, then taught at Dundee (1932–4), Liverpool (1935–6) and the L S E from 1935 to 1951. His great contribution to economics during his life in Britain was an article, 'The Nature of the Firm', published in *Economica* in 1937, which had in fact been drafted as an undergraduate essay several years before. It struggled to explain why individuals group together in firms, rather than making contracts with each other for the delivery of specified pieces of work. He couched his explanation in terms of ►transaction costs, the difficulty that individuals would face in writing contracts and agreeing prices with each other. His ideas opened up a seam of literature as rich today as ever, and now commonly associated with Oliver Williamson. In the 1950s he emigrated to America, taking up posts at universities in Buffalo (1951–8) and Virginia (1958–64) before settling at Chicago Law School until 1982. It was in America that he made his second great contribution, loosely labelled the ►Coase theorem, which relates to the efficiency of property rights as a means of allocating resources. This appeared in a 1959 article in the *Journal of Law and Economics* (a journal he later edited) called 'The Federal Communications Commission', but which is more commonly associated with 'The Problem of Social Costs' that appeared in the same journal the next year.

Coase's other preoccupations were monopoly and pricing, and it was these that laid the foundation of his work on property rights. He wrote *British Broadcasting: A Study in Monopoly* (1950) and *The British Post Office and the Messenger Companies* in 1961. His output is best measured in terms of quality rather than quantity. His contribution is to have explained the underpinnings of ►market forces more successfully than anyone of his generation. He did so while countering post-war trends by looking at practical issues in non-mathematical terms.

Coase theorem A theorem stating that ►economic efficiency will be achieved as long as property rights are fully allocated and that completely free trade of all property rights is possible. The importance of the theorem is in demonstrating that it does not matter who owns what initially, but only that everything should be owned by someone. Trade will place resources in their highest-value occupation eventually.

The theorem is used to show that a solution to the problem of ►externalities is the allocation of property rights. For example, suppose someone wishes to play loud music that disturbs her neighbour. It is unfair to allow her to play the music as this ignores her neighbour's interests; equally, it is unfair to prohibit her from playing it as this ignores her interest. Social efficiency requires that she should be allowed to play the music only if the pleasure it gives her exceeds the displeasure it causes her neighbour. This efficient outcome can be achieved by giving her the right to play the music, but allowing her neighbour to bribe her not to play, an option she will exercise if the necessary bribe is large enough. Alternatively, the neighbour could have the right to enjoy silence, but could allow the music to be played for a fee. It does not matter who has the initial prerogative – both arrangements will lead to music being played only when the neighbour's displeasure is sufficiently small. The theorem stands as a classic of modern economics, but has been shown to rely on a number of strong assumptions that render it of limited practical value. ►►compensation principle; environmental economics; welfare economics.

Cobb–Douglas function A ➤production function or ➤utility function with special characteristics, proposed by ➤K. Wicksell and tested against statistical evidence by C. W. Cobb and P. H. Douglas in 1928. For production, the function is $Y = A.L^{\alpha}.C^{\beta}$, where Y = output, L = Labour input, and C = Capital input. A, α and β are constants determined by technology. If α and $\beta = 1$, the production function has constant returns to scale (➤➤economies of scale) (i.e. if L and C are increased by 10 per cent, Y increases by 10 per cent). If $\alpha + \beta$ is less than 1, returns to scale are decreasing; if greater than 1, increasing. Assuming perfect competition in markets, α and β can be shown to be labour's and capital's share, respectively, of the value of output. Cobb and Douglas were influenced by statistical evidence at the time that appeared to show that labour and capital shares of total output (i.e. ➤national income) were constant over time in ➤developed countries. They sought explanations for this by statistical fitting (➤least-squares regression) of their production function. There is doubt now whether, in fact, such constancy of shares is true. The Cobb–Douglas form can also be applied to ➤utility. Consumer satisfaction or utility is represented by $U = A X^{\alpha}{}_1 X^{\beta}{}_2$) where X_1 and X_2 are quantities of commodities or services consumed (➤Euler, I.)

cobweb model This is a simple dynamic ➤model of cyclical ➤demand and ➤supply in which there is a time lag between the responses of producers to a change in price. Farming, because of the gap between seed-time and harvest, is illustrative of such a model. Consider the diagram (above). ➤equilibrium is represented at the point of intersection of the demand and supply curves at which Q satisfies demand and supply at price P. Suppose in the following period (1), there is a very poor harvest and supply falls to Q_1. At Q_1, prices will rise to P_2 corresponding to (2) on the demand curve. Producers then initiate a new production phase influenced by this high price and in the next period supply Q_2 (point (3) on the supply curve). But prices must now fall to P_3 (point (4) on the demand curve) for all the output to be sold. The process then repeats itself. It can be seen in the diagram that the path converges to the equilibrium point Q_0, so that the system is stable. However, if the demand and supply curves were drawn such that the latter was steeper than the former (to the P axis), the fluctuations in price and quantity would get wider and wider. If the slopes were equal, the cycle would oscillate around the equilibrium point (►elasticity; rational expectations).

CoCom ►Coordinating Committee for Multilateral Export Controls.

coefficient of determination ►multiple correlation coefficient.

collateral security A second ►security (in addition to the personal surety of the borrower) for a ►loan. ►Bank loans, other than ►personal loans, are normally made against the security of ►stocks and ►shares, property or ►insurance policies.

collinearity ►correlation between two variables. ►►multicollinearity.

collusion Cooperation between independent firms so as to modify competition. Collusion may be tacit or explicit and may involve fixing prices. In *collusive oligopoly* (►oligopoly), where two or more firms produce identical or near-identical products, levels of price and output may be similar to those obtaining under ►monopoly. ►►cartel; prisoner's dilemma.

Colombo Plan for Cooperative Economic and Social Development in Asia and the Pacific A plan for economic assistance for the ►developing countries of Asia and the Pacific agreed in 1950, originally with special concern for the re-establishment of economic activity in the aftermath of the Second World War. The plan was put on a permanent basis in 1980. There are twenty-four member countries, all from the Asia and Pacific Region. The Consultative Committee publishes an annual report describing the economic progress and aims of the developing countries in the plan and the nature and level of assistance received. The secretariat is in Colombo, Sri Lanka. ►►Asian Development Bank.

Comecon ►Council for Mutual Economic Aid.

commercial banks Privately owned banks operating cheque ►current accounts, receiving ►deposits, taking in and paying out notes and coin and making ►loans, in the UK through a large number of branches (►banking; bank loan; branch banking). Sometimes referred to as *retail* (►wholesale banking) or *deposit banks*. In the USA these banks are sometimes referred to as *member banks* (►Federal Reserve System) and in Western Europe as *credit banks* to distinguish them from

➤investment banks. In most countries the commercial banks are concerned mainly with making and receiving payments, receiving deposits and making short-term loans to private individuals, companies and other organizations. The banks increasingly provide a number of other services to their customers: trustee and executor facilities, the supply of foreign currency, the purchase and sale of ➤securities, ➤insurance, ➤credit transfer, ➤personal loan and ➤credit-card facilities. The banks have also over the years diversified into other financial services in competition with the ➤finance houses and the ➤merchant banks, e.g. venture or ➤risk capital and the management of ➤unit trusts (➤universal banks). In the UK competition among the retail banks has intensified as technology has rendered the large branch network far less important in the delivery of services; and as the division between different types of financial service has broken down. In 1997, to reflect that, it was announced that a new unified regulatory structure for all types of financial institution would be created. ➤Financial Services Act 1986.

commercial bills ➤bill of exchange.

commercial paper ➤promissory note.

commission A percentage of the ➤value of a transaction taken by an intermediary as payment for his services, e.g. ➤broker's commission, estate agency's commission.

commodity 1. In economic theory, a commodity is a tangible good or service resulting from the process of production. Differences between commodities, real or imagined, will determine whether or not they are close ➤substitutes for one another. 2. In general usage, a primary product, such as coffee, copper, cotton, wool, rubber and tin (➤commodity exchange).

commodity agreements ➤international commodity agreements.

commodity control schemes ➤international commodity agreements.

commodity exchange A ➤market in which ➤commodities are bought and sold. It is not necessary for the commodities to be physically exchanged; only rights to ownership need be. The old practice of auctioning commodities from warehouses in which samples could be inspected beforehand has become less important. An efficient system of grading and modern systems of communication have enabled the practice of ➤'c.i.f. trading' to develop. A buyer can buy a commodity in the country of origin for delivery c.i.f. to a specified port at which he can off-load for direct delivery to his own premises. This method saves warehousing costs and auction charges. The market not only enables commodities to be sold 'spot' or for delivery at some specified time and place (➤spot market), but it also includes a market in ➤'futures'. This latter enables merchants to avoid the effect of price fluctuations by buying for forward delivery at an agreed price; which will not be affected by intervening changes in the 'spot' rate (➤clearing house). London has a number of important commodity and futures markets (e.g. the London Metal Exchange, the London Grain Futures Market), as do other centres, notably Chicago, Amsterdam, New York, Sydney and Singapore.

commodity stabilization agreements ➤international commodity agreements.

commodity tax A levy on the price of a good or service. ➤direct taxation.

Common Agricultural Policy (CAP) The system of agricultural support adopted by the ➤European Union. The CAP covers about 90 per cent of EU farm output. The central feature of the policy is that it raises the income of farmers by keeping agricultural prices to the consumer at an agreed level. 'Target' prices are fixed by the EU Commission for specified commodities. Import prices are kept above the target prices by the imposition of levies. 'Intervention' prices for domestic supplies are set somewhat below the 'target' prices. If sales can only be made on the market below the 'intervention' price, the Commission buys into store in order to drive the price up. The 'intervention' price may vary from place to place in the Community in order to induce 'surplus' areas to transport to 'deficit' areas and the Commission may also subsidize exports in order to keep prices above the intervention level. For some commodities there is no intervention system and the EU relies on high import ➤tariffs to keep prices high. The accumulation of large surpluses in some commodities has led to the use of direct payments to farmers. Criticism has been made of the high cost of CAP. In the early 1980s about 70 per cent of the Community budget was absorbed by agriculture. However, some reforms were introduced in 1992 including a programme for a reduction in support prices for beef, cereals and dairy products coupled with the setting aside to fallow of 15 per cent of arable land. The agricultural budget is now about 50 per cent of the total EU budget. These reforms were encouraged by the negotiations leading to the Agricultural Agreement of the ➤Uruguay round of trade negotiations in 1993. ➤green currency.

Common Fund for Commodities ➤United Nations Conference on Trade and Development.

common market ➤Andean Pact; Benelux; Caribbean Common Market; Central American Common Market; customs union; European Union; Mercosur.

Commonwealth Development Corporation (CDC) A statutory body established by the UK government originally to channel overseas aid to the ➤developing countries of the Commonwealth. Under the Overseas Resources Development Act of 1969, the CDC was able to extend its overseas assistance to developing countries outside the Commonwealth. Finance is allocated to the corporation by the UK government from the Overseas Aid ➤budget. It may invest indirectly through ➤equities or ➤debentures or directly in projects administered by its own staff. ➤foreign aid.

community charge ➤local taxation.

Company Directors Disqualification Act 1986 ➤company law.

company law The law governing the establishment and conduct of incorporated business enterprise. It originally developed from the ➤partnership, and has its origins in common law and, from the eighteenth century onwards, in a series of company and other Acts. The first companies were created by Royal Charter, and the whole basis of company law is that certain benefits are conferred (in many of these first instances, that of a ➤monopoly) in return for certain obligations. The Act of 1720 created the statutory company with ➤limited liability, making possible, for example, the establishment of the early British railway companies. By 1825 the expansion of business had made the creation of companies by separate Acts of Parliament too cumbersome, and in that year a new Act made it possible to form *joint stock companies* by registration with a Registrar of Companies. It was not until 1862, however, that limited liability was extended to certain private as well as public companies. Company law has continued to evolve under successive Acts as the needs of business have developed and altered. The 1907 Act introduced the distinction between the ➤private company and the ➤public company. Other laws such as the Prevention of Fraud Act also apply to companies (➤bankruptcy). Under present law (deriving principally from the 1948, 1967, 1976, 1980 and 1981 Companies Acts which were repealed and consolidated in the Companies Act 1985 and the Companies Act 1989) there are three classes of company: (a) limited and (b) unlimited private companies; and (c) public limited companies (plc). Compared with the two other forms of business unit, the ➤sole proprietor and the partnership, ➤incorporation confers advantages for financing and in certain circumstances ➤taxation, in addition to limited liability where appropriate. (An unlimited private company does not have limited liability, i.e. its owners are responsible for company debt to the full extent of their fortune.) However, companies, unlike individuals or partnerships, are obliged to make public certain information about their business. Both private and public limited companies are obliged to file certain information for public inspection and to circulate accounts to their shareholders. Until 1967 certain private companies, 'exempt private companies', were not obliged to comply with all of the accounting and disclosure requirements and under present legislation there are exemptions for small and medium-sized companies which are not public companies. Small and medium companies are defined in terms of turnover, assets and employment (small, 50 or fewer employees and medium, 250 or fewer employees).

The amount of information which larger companies are required to publish has increased in successive Companies Acts, and the directors' report must now cover such matters as employment, exports, employee aggregate remuneration and donations to political causes or charities. The 1976 Companies Act contained provisions to speed up the publication of accounts and covered the appointment and removal of auditors and other matters. The 1981 Companies Act allowed companies to acquire their own shares under certain circumstances and required them to publish details of such transactions. That Act also, in a major departure, laid down detailed schedules for the form and content of the ►balance sheet and profit-and-loss account (►double-entry bookkeeping) to give effect to the EC Fourth Directive harmonizing company law in the Community. All these provisions remained essentially the same in the 1985 Act. Among other provisions, the 1989 Act requires companies to disclose a holding of more than 3 per cent in another company (►Monopolies and Mergers Commission). A public company may have an unlimited number of shareholders and may offer ►shares for public subscription. The nominal value of the allocated share capital may not be less than £50,000. Quoted companies are public limited companies whose shares are listed on a recognized ►stock exchange. Private companies may place certain restrictions on the transfer of shares, but not offer shares to the public. Company law sets out other provisions dealing with the powers, appointment, terms and disqualification of directors (Company Directors Disqualification Act 1986), the protection of investors, including minorities, ownership and control, the regulation of shares, the disclosure of interest in shares, the group accounts prepared by a holding company, winding up and other matters.

company reserves ►Profits retained in the business and set aside for specified purposes. The various Companies Acts have drawn distinctions between capital and revenue reserves and undistributable and distributable reserves. Capital reserves are created when new shares are issued at a ►premium over par or when the book value of existing assets is revalued to bring it into line with replacement costs or when ►capital gains are made. These capital reserves may later be transformed into issued capital (►capitalization). Revenue, or distributable reserves, are created by transfers of undistributed profits into special accounts, out of which a dividend may be paid in a later year in which the company makes a loss. Reserves of either type may be converted into capital by a ►bonus issue. *Provisions* are not the same as reserves but arise out of ►depreciation or allowances made for ►liabilities, for example provisions for doubtful debts.

company taxation ►corporation tax.

comparative advantage The idea that economic agents are most efficiently employed in activities in which their relative efficiencies are superior to others. The importance of comparative advantage is that it suggests that, even if someone is very bad at some activity, perhaps even worse than anyone else at it, it could still be profitably efficient for him or her to pursue it, if he or she is even more inept at other activities. The idea has been seen as particularly important in explaining ►international trade. Countries should specialize in areas in which they have a comparative advantage. (►►Ricardo, D.; division of labour.)

comparative cost ►Ricardo, D; international trade.

comparative static equilibrium analysis The analysis of markets or economies in terms of their different ►equilibrium positions, without reference to the process by which adjustment between equilibria is achieved. Most non-mathematical economics is static in this sense. It consists of comparing diagrams which represent snapshots of the state of a market at a single point in time, and it aims to assess the characteristics of the equilibrium state and discover the position of a new equilibrium when some variable is changed. For example, most ►demand and ►supply analysis is of this sort. An equilibrium is noted; then, the effect of a shift in demand or supply is analysed; its impact on price and quantity sold is determined, and the effect of demand or supply curves with different slopes can be assessed.

What is missing from such analysis is any trace of the path or speed of adjustment between different equilibria. In ►perfect competition, for example, firms are assumed to have no influence on price and be unable to deviate from the going market rate at all – yet, by what process can the market price change? As there is no auctioneer telling everybody what price to set, the price-takers themselves must also be the price-setters, even though this contradicts the basic assumption of the model. (►tatonnement process.) Comparative statics simply ignores problems such as these, ►dynamics

comparative statics ►comparative static equilibrium analysis.

compensation principle The principle that total economic welfare increases from a change in the economy, if those who gain from the change could compensate those who lose from it to their mutual satisfaction. It is not necessary for money transfers actually to take place. However, the principle has been criticized in this respect because, without actual transfers, interpersonal comparisons of ►utility of money are implied. Actual transfers are required if individuals are to reveal the total worth they place on their gains and losses (►economic efficiency). ►Pareto, V. F. D.; social-welfare function; welfare economics.

compensatory finance ►United Nations Conference on Trade and Development.

competition ►perfect competition.

Competition Act 1980 An Act which extended the powers of the Office of Fair Trading (►Fair Trading Act), subject to the approval of the Secretary of State, to undertake preliminary investigations into anti-competitive practices (►vertical restraints) in any commercial firm and certain public-sector bodies, including public corporations. The OFT could therefore investigate the efficiency of nationalized industries and could be ordered by the Secretary of State to investigate prices (both these powers had hitherto been restricted to the Price Commission which was abolished in the Act). On completion of the investigation the OFT may obtain undertakings from firms to cease any anti-competitive practices identified or, with the approval of the Secretary of State, it may make a reference to the ►Monopolies and Mergers Commission. Competition in the UK is also covered by articles 85 and 86 and other provisions of the Treaty of Rome (►European Union). ►►competition policy.

competition policy The name given to any set of government measures aiming to stimulate competition and protect consumers against ►monopoly. The areas of such policy include (a) control of dominant firms by ►regulation, such as British Telecom through the Office of Telecommunications, (b) control of mergers to prevent industries becoming monopolized, and (c) control of anti-competitive acts, such as ►full-line forcing and predatory pricing. ►►Competition Act 1980; Fair Trading Act; Monopolies and Mergers Commission.

competitiveness A loose term, popularly used to reflect the ability of a nation to grow successfully, and to maintain its share of world trade. While there have been several government White Papers on the subject in the UK, a wide-ranging debate about it in Europe and the USA and, while league tables of national competitiveness are regularly produced by reputable business authorities, the term has never impressed academic economists. It is used as though it refers to the state of the productive base of the economy, yet attempts to apply a precise definition have foundered. It either reduces to a measure of how rich a country is, measured by its ►gross domestic product per head of population; or to a measure of the price of tradable goods expressed in foreign currency (primarily a reflection of the ►exchange rate). Yet, those who use the term appear to believe they are talking of a broader concept than either of these. Those who have criticized the growth in usage of the term, argue that basic economic theory of ►international trade and ►comparative advantage makes clear that we should not view the world as a group of nations competing in a ►zero-sum game.

complementary goods Pairs of goods for which consumption is interdependent, for example cars and petrol or cups and saucers, are known as *complements* or complementary goods and changes in the demand for one will have a complementary effect upon the demand for the other. Complements have a negative ►cross-price elasticity of demand: if the price of one rises the demand for both may fall. Complementary demand creates difficulties in the application of the theory of ►marginal utility since it cannot be said that the level of utility yielded by a complementary good is yielded directly by that good and in isolation. ►►substitutes.

compliance cost Expenditure of time or money in conforming with government requirements. The compliance costs of ►income tax will include the cost of record-keeping, payments to an accountant, etc. Compliance costs are additional to the costs of collection, which are borne by the government and may be lesser or greater than compliance costs. The compliance costs of ►regulation include the payment of licence fees for permission to trade and, for example, the cost of fireproof doors installed to comply with fire regulations.

compound interest The calculation of total interest due by applying the rate to the sum of the capital invested plus the interest previously earned and reinvested. In contrast, *simple interest* is calculated only on the capital invested.

concealed discount ►trade discount.

concentration The extent to which a small number of firms account for a high proportion of sales or another dimension of economic importance in an industry. Concentration is said to be high, for example, if 90 per cent of industry sales or employment is accounted for by three firms – this is the three-firm concentration ratio. *Industry concentration* is the key element in ►market structure and an important determinant of conduct and performance and hence of the nature of competition. The two extremes are: ►perfect competition, in which products are homogeneous and firms small in relation to the size of the total market so that they cannot individually influence price (concentration is low), and ►monopoly, in which there is a single seller (concentration is absolute). Most markets in the ►advanced countries have high (►oligopoly) to intermediate levels of concentration and operate under conditions of ►monopolistic competition in which prices tend to exceed marginal cost in theory and even if there is no ►collusion, ►barriers to entry may keep concentration high.

Industry concentration, measured by the ►concentration ratio generally increased in the UK from 1950 to the early 1970s, though there are a number of practical and conceptual difficulties in measuring concentration and in generalizing about trends over time. According to the census of production (►production, census of), the largest five firms accounted for an average of 65 per cent of sales at the four-digit ►Standard Industrial Classification level in some 250 UK manufacturing industries in 1975. Attitudes to concentration among economists vary according to their assessment of the relative importance of competition and the ►economies of scale. Where the ►optimum scale of output is high relative to the size of the total market, more competitors might lead to higher costs through lower-scale economies. In general, however, ►enterprise concentration in a given market is much higher than ►establishment (or plant) concentration, indicating that leading firms have a larger share of markets than would be necessary for them to operate at optimum scales of output (though there may be economies in distribution or other aspects of multi-plant operation). Larger firms also operate in more than one product market (►diversification) and this can result in high levels of *aggregate concentration* in which a small number of firms have a significant share in economic output as a whole. In fact, the share of the 100 largest manufacturing enterprises was about 41 per cent of total manufacturing net output in the UK in 1982 compared with some 27 per cent in 1953 and only 16 per cent in 1909. Since 1983 the aggregate concentration ratio has fallen to 36 per cent (1992). Although concentration appears to be relatively high in the UK compared with other, comparable, ►European Union countries and the United States, there is some controversy about how important national concentration is, at least in manufacturing, given the extent of actual and potential competition from imports. ►►Chicago school.

concentration ratio A ratio calculated to show the degree to which an industry is dominated by a small number of large firms or made up of many small firms.

confidence interval

There are many ratios that may be calculated, based on turnover, capital employed, employment, etc., for instance the ratio of the total capital employed of the top five firms as a percentage of the industries' capital employed. However, a comprehensive ratio is the Herfindahl index. This index is given by the sum of the squares of the market shares of each firm in the industry: $H = \Sigma_n f_n^2$, where f_n = the market share of firm n (i.e. the sales of firm n divided by industry sales). A pure ➤monopoly would take the value of 1. At the other extreme, if all the firms in the industry had equal market shares the value would be $1/n$. ➤➤concentration.

confidence interval A measure of the likely statistical error in the estimation of a ➤parameter. It is a term frequently used in ➤econometrics, where a sample of data is used to make a generalization of the relationship between different variables – for example, between the level of consumption and the level of income. A sample may imply, for example, that consumption is equal to 0.8 times the level of income in the economy. But the sample may naturally deviate from the exact relationship across the whole economy. The more variable the relationship in the sample, the less certain one can be about the true relationship. A confidence interval expresses the range of estimates within which it is likely the real relationship lies. For example, it may be 0.8, plus or minus 0.1.

To estimate the confidence interval, one typically assumes the sample is representative of the whole population, bar some random deviation. Given the variation within the sample, one can calculate how many times such random samples would generate estimates of the parameter outside the confidence interval. Usually, the confidence interval is expressed as the range within which only 5 per cent of samples would generate estimates lying outside the range (a 95 per cent confidence interval). For more precision, one might describe a wider confidence interval, that suggests the range outside of which only 1 per cent of random samples would generate estimates. Clearly, the bigger the sample, the more certain one can be of the estimate, and the smaller the confidence interval. For an estimate of a parameter in any very large sample, the 95 per cent confidence interval can be calculated as the estimate plus or minus 1.96 times the ➤standard deviation of the estimate.

confirming house An agency in the UK which purchases and arranges the export of goods on behalf of overseas buyers.

conglomerate (US) A business organization generally consisting of a ➤holding company and a group of subsidiary companies engaged in dissimilar activities. ➤➤downsizing.

Consolidated fund Sums standing to a particular account of the ➤Exchequer (for which it is often used synonymously) into which the proceeds of ➤taxation are paid and from which government expenditures (➤budget) are made. Prior to 1787 different funds were maintained for various purposes and taxation receipts divided among them, but after that date the various funds were consolidated, leaving, of major significance, only the *National Insurance Fund*, which receives ➤National

Insurance contributions and a grant from the Consolidated fund to meet social-security payments. *Consolidated fund standing services* is an item in the UK budget which includes expenditure authorized by specific legislation. This expenditure, such as the salaries of judges and payments to the ►National Loans Fund for service of the ►national debt, is paid out of the Consolidated fund but, unlike ►supply services, does not have to be voted annually in Parliament.

consolidated stock ►consols.

consols Abbreviation for *consolidated stock*: unredeemable government stock first issued in the eighteenth century as a consolidation of the ►national debt. Consols bear an interest of 2½ per cent and have a total nominal value of £267 million.

conspicuous consumption A term used by Thorstein Veblen (1857–1929) in his book *The Theory of the Leisure Class* (1899) to identify that ostentatious personal expenditure which satisfies no physical need but rather a psychological need for the esteem of others. Goods may be purchased not for their practical use but as 'status symbols' and to 'keep up with the Joneses'. (►giffen good.)

constant prices ►real terms.

constant returns to scale ►returns to scale.

consumer behaviour ►demand, theory of; indifference curve; indifference-curve analysis; marginal utility; Marshall, Λ.

consumer credit Short-term►loans to the public for the purchase of specific goods. Consumer credit takes the form of ►credit by shopkeepers and other suppliers, ►credit accounts, ►personal loans and►hire purchase. ►Overdrafts, money-lenders and other private sources of borrowing are not referred to as consumer credit, either because they are not tied to the purchase of specific goods or because they are long-term loans, e.g. ►mortgages. ►banking; finance; finance house.

Consumer Credit Act The Act, passed in 1974, following the recommendations of the Crowther Committee. The Act tidied up and consolidated legislation in the field of ►consumer credit, some of which had existed on the statute books since Victorian times. The Act introduced a licensing system which applied not only to credit and hire firms such as ►financing houses and banks, but to all agencies connected with consumer credit such as credit brokers and debt collectors. Licences are issued by the Office of Fair Trading if it is satisfied that the applicant has in no way infringed any of the consumer protection laws. Group licensing may be granted to cover the individual members of a professional body which has the authority and standing to discipline its members; such a licence has, for example, been issued to solicitors. Regulations may be made under the Act with respect to the content and style of advertising material or other documents relating to consumer credit, and also to the way the effective annual ➤rate of interest is calculated and explained to the consumer (➤annual percentage rate). ➤➤Fair Trading Act.

consumer durables ➤durable goods.

consumer good An ➤economic good or ➤commodity purchased by ➤households for final consumption. Consumer goods include, e.g., chocolate or draught beer consumed immediately as well as ➤durable goods which yield a flow of services over a period of time, for example a washing-machine. It is the use to which it is put which determines whether a good is a consumer good (sometimes referred to as a *consumption good* or final good), not the characteristics of the good itself. Electricity, or a computer, bought for the home is a consumer good, but the same thing bought for a factory is a ➤producer good.

consumer price index ➤retail prices index.

consumer surplus The amount by which consumers value a product over and above what they pay for it. Before the phrase was coined by ➤A. Marshall, the idea of a surplus of ➤utility over the price paid for a good or service was explored by ➤Dupuit in his study of the benefits arising from the construction of public facilities such as roads and bridges. Marshall explained consumer surplus: 'The price which a person pays for a thing can never exceed and seldom comes up to that which he would be willing to pay rather than go without it: so that the satisfaction which he gets from its purchase generally exceeds that which he gives up in paying away its price: and he thus derives from the purchase a surplus of satisfaction. The excess of the price which he would be willing to pay rather than go without the thing, over that which he actually does pay, is the economic measure of this surplus satisfaction.' Marshall's surplus is illustrated in the diagram of a ➤demand curve opposite.

The consumer buys on the market quantity Q_n at a price P_n. However, following his demand schedule, if only Q_1 were available he would be willing to pay P_1, if Q_2 to pay P_2 and so on. If the supplier had a ➤monopoly and could practise ➤price discrimination, he could extract as revenue the whole of the area under the demand curve, that is $XY0Q_n$. However, there is a market price P_n, so that the supplier only obtains P_nY0Q_n and leaves the difference XP_nY as a benefit to the consumer. A difficulty is that as the price falls along Marshall's demand curve, the real income of the consumer increases. To get a more accurate measure of the benefit of the surplus, therefore, an adjustment must be made to offset the effect of the difference in real income at the higher price (P_1) and the lower price (P_n). (➤➤Hicksian demand function; income effect.) Consumer surplus plays an important role in ➤welfare economics. ➤➤producer's surplus.

consumers' expenditure Consumers' expenditure amounts to about 60 per cent of the UK's ➤gross domestic product. It comprises expenditure by ➤households

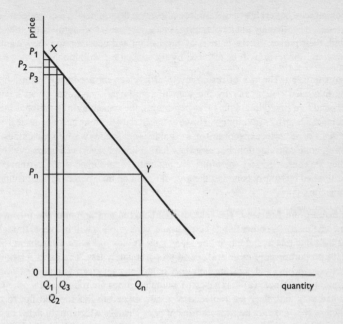

(including certain non-profit-making organizations). It excludes house purchase (including charges for services on the transfer of ownership) and major house improvements, which are regarded as capital expenditure. It includes, however, an imputed rent for owner-occupied houses and expenditure on durables such as motor vehicles.

consumers' preference Attitudes which determine consumer choice between alternative ➤commodities or groups of commodities. When good X is preferred to good Y it will have greater ➤utility to the buyer, so that the allocation of expenditure between these alternatives will, in a ➤free-market economy, be determined by consumer preference and their relative ➤prices. These preferences will, in conjunction with the ➤production function and the prices of the ➤factors of production, therefore, determine the allocation of scarce resources to the production of various goods. Consumer preferences may change independently with, say, fashion or may be influenced by ➤advertising and other forms of sales promotion as well as by the availability of new goods arising from technological progress (➤technology). Although preferences are something the economist takes as given, and makes no ➤value judgement about, at the same time preferences are assumed to be consistent and rational in certain ways (➤indifference-curve analysis; revealed preference; transitivity) (➤➤endogenous preferences).

consumers' sovereignty ➤Resource allocation determined by ➤consumers' preference rather than by ➤state planning. In a ➤free-market economy consumers vote with their purses for the pattern of production and consumption they want; the outcome, however, will be affected by the ➤income distribution.

consumption The use of resources to satisfy current needs and wants. It may be measured statistically by the sum of consumers' and government's current expenditure (including defence expenditure), the remainder of ➤national income being made up by ➤investment. However, such statistics may be inadequate in some cases. For instance, expenditure on ➤durable goods such as washing-machines, may exaggerate consumption, because they have a life of, say, seven years over which they are consumed and, therefore, are not entirely consumed in the current period as implied by simply counting the amount spent on their purchase (➤consumption function).

consumption function The relationship between consumption and income. As income increases, other things being equal, consumption will increase, though not at the same rate as income in the short term. As income rises, consumers tend to save proportionately more and spend proportionately less. The exact relationship between income and consumption only holds constant given a number of assumptions. For instance: (a) Purchases of ➤durable goods are related to income in the stated way, e.g. they are replaced at a rate related to income and not to other factors. (b) There are no expectations of price changes which might delay or bring forward consumption. (c) No change takes place in the availability or the cost of credit. (d) There is a constant level of ➤savings in real terms at any level of income. (➤Inflation could decrease the real value of savings such that consumers react by increasing their contributions to their savings stock from current income until their real value has been restored; they then revert back to the previous rate of saving.) The consumption function was introduced by ➤J. M. Keynes and applied to his analysis of income determination. ➤➤average propensity to consume; marginal propensity to consume; multiplier; ➤➤permanent-income hypothesis.

consumption good ➤consumer good.

contango Synonym for ➤carry-over.

contestability The degree of ease with which firms can enter or leave an industry. A *perfectly contestable* industry is one in which, as in ➤perfect competition, there are no barriers to entry at all. Unlike perfect competition, however, perfect contestability implies nothing about how many firms currently exist in the industry – it is possible for an efficient monopolist to exist while no barrier to entry prevents other firms from competing. Contestability theory was stimulated by ➤W. J. Baumol in the early 1980s. He showed that the attractive features of perfect competition could be achieved merely by the threat to incumbent firms that entry would occur should large profits be made.

The threat of entry should induce ➤marginal-cost pricing and efficient production. In practice, entry barriers *do* exist and, because incumbent firms can often scare potential entrants away from entering, the discipline that potential competition provides is considered less effective than that of actual competitors. ➤➤barriers to entry; competition policy; sunk costs.

contingency reserve ➤public expenditure.

contingent protection The use of anti- ➤dumping and ➤countervailing duties as insidious devices to protect domestic industry from foreign competition. Under the various international treaties since the end of the Second World War (➤➤General Agreement on Tariffs and Trade), considerable progress has been made in the freeing of ➤international trade from protectionist measures (➤➤protection). The application of ➤tariffs against products sold by foreign suppliers below their normal price or against foreign exports which have received government subsidy are generally allowed; the purpose of these tariffs being seen as correcting price distortions in the market without affecting the integrity of free-market principles. However, the considerable growth in the number of applications filed, particularly by the ➤European Union and the USA has led to the suspicion that they are being used in restraint of trade. Ambiguities can be exploited in the meaning of 'normal' price and in the difficulties of obtaining convincing data. Moreover, the need to defend a case is in itself a cost to the accused exporter. An exporter could be induced to adjust his price simply to avoid a hearing.

continuation Synonymous with ➤carry-over.

contract A statement of the rights and obligations of each party to a transaction or transactions. A contract, as familiarly envisaged, is a formal written statement of the terms of a transaction or relationship: a house purchase or a pop star's deal with a record company. But most transactions and relationships are conducted without a formal contract: the contractual terms that exist when you buy a newspaper are simple enough to obviate the need for written terms and conditions; and many business relationships are based on implicit contractual terms that are supported not by law but by the mutual interest of the involved parties. An example might be the obligation of a ➤building society to charge a reasonable rate of interest on a variable rate mortgage. While the formal contract that someone may have with an institution lending them money to buy a house may not preclude the institution raising its interest rate to above market levels, there is an implicit contract that it would not do so. It is in the interest of the building society not to abuse the implicit contract, for to do so would damage its long-term reputation. ➤➤incomplete contract; tit-for-tat.

contract curve The curve of exchange between two parties along which their ➤marginal rates of substitution are the same in relation to the commodities traded. Any bargain concluded at a rate of exchange other than one on the contract curve could be improved (that is, by making at least one party better off without making the other worse off) by moving to the contract curve. A term introduced by ➤F. Y. Edgeworth. ➤Pareto, V. F. D.; ➤➤economic efficiency.

contracting out 1. The practice by governments or firms of employing an outside agent to perform some specific task rather than perform it themselves. The practice is defended on the grounds that it stimulates competition between companies for contracts to provide services which might otherwise be run less efficiently in-house. The Local Government Act 1988 requires authorities either to contract out or to expose to competition a number of services, including refuse collection, vehicle maintenance and general catering. (➤➤vertical integration.) But it is proposed that this should be replaced by an obligation simply to ensure 'best value' is obtained. In the public sector contracts are normally awarded after a competitive *tender* in which bidders state the price and conditions under which they are prepared to supply. 2. An employee or employer may contract out of the SERPS (➤National Insurance) where alternative pension arrangements have been made.

control ➤separation of ownership from control.

control total The measure of UK public expenditure used as the basis of annual spending discussions between government departments. It comprises all ➤general government spending, except important areas where there is felt to be little policy discretion involved: most importantly, central government debt interest and the elements of ➤social security which are cyclical (determined by the general state of the economy). In 1997/98 the control total was expected to represent 83 per cent of total general government expenditure. ➤➤EDX; public expenditure.

convergence This asserts that countries become, or will continue to get closer in terms of ➤per capita income (productivity). In the eighteenth and nineteenth centuries Great Britain, followed by the USA and some other European states, widened the gap between their productivity and that of the rest of the world. Between the latter part of the nineteenth century and the mid-1930s there was some convergence in the range and variation of output per capita in these countries, although none caught up with the USA. After the Second World War, convergence was resumed, while new members joined the convergence 'club' with some reduction in the US lead. Since 1970 performance has been variable and more new members of the club have emerged, including some ➤newly industrialized countries. The convergence hypothesis is controversial and debate has been confused by differences in the period and number of countries covered, as well as by differences in what is meant by convergence. The term can be interpreted to mean a narrowing in the variation between productivity in a group of countries or the catching up of countries on the leader or leaders. If all countries, including the poorest ➤developing countries, rather than ➤Organization for Economic Cooperation and Development members, are included in the analysis, there has in fact been negative convergence in the recent past. ➤least developed countries; sow's ear effect.

The convergence hypothesis is resisted by those economists who emphasize the role of internal or ➤endogenous factors, and thus the potential role of government in economic growth, rather than external or exogenous influences (➤institutional economics; endogenous growth theory).

convergence criteria The conditions laid out in the Maastricht Treaty, that were to act as a guide to the suitability of different ➤European Union nations to enter ➤European Monetary Union. The conditions were never hard and fast. Each was drafted in a way to allow countries to avoid them; and the whole group were only indicative anyway. The criteria held that:

(a) the government deficit (➤Public Sector Borrowing Requirement) should be below 3 per cent of ➤GDP, unless any excess over that level is exceptional, temporary and small

(b) that government debt (➤national debt) should not exceed 60 per cent of GDP, or it should be approaching that level

(c) ➤inflation should not exceed the performance of the best three performing countries by more than 1.5 percentage points

(d) long-term interest rates should not exceed those of the three best countries in terms of inflation performance by more than 2 percentage points

(e) that the ➤exchange rate shall have respected the normal fluctuation margins of the European Exchange Rate Mechanism for two years, without severe tension.

conversion Issue of a new ➤stock to replace another. This may arise where a ➤debenture or ➤warrant is convertible into ➤equity shares or where holders of ➤government stock at or near redemption are offered a new stock in exchange for existing stock.

convertibility A ➤currency is said to be convertible when it may be freely exchanged for another currency or gold. All foreign ➤exchange controls were completely removed by the UK in 1979. The convertibility of US dollars into gold was abandoned in 1971. ➤exchange control; foreign-exchange market; gold standard.

convertible debenture stock ➤debentures.

convexity A characteristic of tastes or technology that a combination of commodities is preferable to any one on its own. If someone prefers a slice of bread and half a gram of butter to either a whole slice of bread or a whole gram of butter, they have convex preferences. If it is easier to make one car using ten men and ten machines than to make it using twenty men and no machines or using twenty machines and no men, the production technology is convex. Convexity implies that combinations of products are more desirable than extremes. It is itself usually implied by ➤diminishing marginal utility. It takes its name from the shape of the ➤indifference curves or ➤isoquants that convexity generates.

Coordinating Committee for Multilateral Export Controls (CoCom) An international agreement, originally signed in 1950, between the member countries (excluding Iceland) of the North Atlantic Treaty Organization (NATO), Australia and Japan, which agreed the control of the exports of specified strategic products to the member countries of the Warsaw Pact, Albania, China, North Korea, Mongolia and Vietnam. In 1990 agreement was reached for the liberalization of industrial technology exports to the USSR and East European countries. Controls were retained on munitions and atomic energy products. The agreement was terminated in 1994 and replaced by the Wassenaar Arrangement of 1995. This new group of 28 countries includes not only the original 17 members but also Russia and four other nations of the Warsaw Pact. Unlike CoCom, recommendations by the group to restrict sensitive exports to specified countries are not binding on the members.

corporate income tax (US) ➤corporation tax.

corporate planning A business function concerned with the formulation of long-term objectives and the development of plans to achieve them. Corporate planning has become more and more formalized as business units have grown larger and more diversified. ➤Galbraith argued in *The New Industrial State* that the enormously large ➤capital requirements of modern technology require that the consumer and the ➤market become subservient to the planning needs of the large corporations which have come increasingly to characterize the modern economy.

corporation tax A tax (➤taxation) levied on the assessable ➤profits of companies and unincorporated associations at the rate of 31 per cent in the UK in 1997/98. It is calculated after ➤interest and all Inland Revenue allowances (➤capital allowances; stock appreciation), but before ➤dividend distribution. In 1997/98 the corporation tax rate for companies with taxable profits of less than £300,000 was 21 per cent, with tapering relief up to the full tax rate of 31 per cent for companies with profits in excess of £1,500,000. In the USA companies are liable for *corporate income tax*, which also has a progressive element.

Corporation taxes generally can be modelled on one of a variety of forms: the *comprehensive business income tax* applies tax to all profits, allowing no deduction for interest costs. No major country has adopted this form, although American tax authorities have shown an interest in it. The *classical system* (used in the USA and the Netherlands) allows a deduction for interest payments, but charges tax on all other profits, whether distributed as dividends or not. Shareholders receiving dividends do then end up paying income tax on profits already taxed. Thirdly, there is the so-called *imputation system* in which some relief is offered to shareholders, to ensure that dividends are not subject to both income tax and corporation tax. This was the system introduced in the UK in April 1973, six years after corporation tax as such had itself been introduced. But it was in effect abolished in 1997/98. Under the old system, companies made a payment of *advance corporation tax* (ACT) of 20 per cent on their dividend payments. This piece of corporation tax was recognized as a payment of income tax on dividends by the shareholders who received them. It thus limited the degree to which profits distributed as dividends suffered both corporation tax and income tax. Now, however, ACT is set to be abolished. Companies are to pay mainstream corporation tax on all profits, and shareholders will also have to pay income tax on any dividends they receive.

The rationale for corporation tax is not entirely clear. It was originally introduced in classical form to encourage the retention of earnings by companies, in the hope that this would stimulate ►investment. The reversion to something closer to the classical system was justified on the same grounds. Some economists argue that the allocation of capital ►resources is best determined by the ►capital market, and would prefer to see a higher proportion of dividends distributed and then rechannelled back to investment via the capital market. Moreover, the possibility of ►tax avoidance by individual investors liable to high rates of tax in close companies has in the past led to the application of special rules to enforce distributions by these companies, so called *shortfall assessments*. Close company tax law is somewhat complex, and there are also special provisions regarding ►loans to participators, ►interest and salaries or fees paid to directors as well as special reliefs for small trading companies.

Companies are also liable to corporation tax on ►capital gains. *Stock relief* was available to companies or individuals between 1974/75 and 1983/84 to offset the effects of inflationary increases in the value of stocks upon assessable profits for tax purposes. Special provisions allow capital gains taxation on the sale of productive ►assets to be deferred (*roll-over*) where the proceeds are used to purchase new assets of the same type. There is also a special relief for persons of retirement age.

Individuals in business on their own (operating on own account) and members of ►partnerships pay income tax on their individual share of total profits (broadly defined in the same way as for companies). For an established business, tax is payable in any year on the profits earned in the accounting period that ended in the previous fiscal year (►financial year).

correlation A statistical measure of the closeness of the variations in the values of one ►variable to the variations in the values of another. The 'correlation coefficient' (r) is calculated by the following formula,

$$r = \frac{\Sigma(x_i - \bar{x})\,(y_i - \bar{y})}{\sqrt{[\Sigma_i(x_i - \bar{x})^2]}\sqrt{[\Sigma_i(y_i - \bar{y})^2]}}$$

in which x_i and y_i are the values of the two variables, $\bar{x}$ and $\bar{y}$ are their means (►average); r can take any value between +1 and –1, at which extremes there is perfect correspondence between the variations of the variables. At the value zero, there is no correspondence. It should be noted that a value of r close to unity does not imply a causative connection between the two variables. ►►multiple correlation coefficient; partial correlation; regression analysis; Slutsky, E.

cost ➤opportunity cost.

cost, avoidable ➤prime costs.

cost, overhead ➤fixed costs.

cost accounting, costing and cost control Procedures by which the expenditure of a firm is related to units of output. Cost accounts, while they can be directly related to financial accounts, are concerned with the detailed elements of ➤opportunity costs in identifiable output for purposes of pricing, departmental budgeting and the control of manufacturing methods, material and ➤labour usage for these products rather than the overall financial results of the firm's operations.

cost–benefit analysis The appraisal of an investment project which includes all social and financial costs and benefits accruing to the project. The techniques adopted in order to evaluate and decide whether a proposed project should proceed, whether, that is, its benefits would exceed its costs, are the same as applied in ➤investment appraisal (➤discounted cash flow; present value). However, the valuation in money terms of the social or welfare costs and benefits (➤welfare economics) presents special problems; for instance, the costing of the loss of an area of outstanding natural beauty or the valuation of the benefits arising from the reduction in road accidents due to the construction of a motorway. In other cases, the market prices prevailing may not be appropriate. For instance, the real cost of labour may be much lower than the going wage rate, because of very high unemployment. The ➤opportunity cost (which is the cost that matters in cost–benefit appraisals) is lower and, therefore, a ➤shadow price is used to represent this low opportunity cost in place of the wage rate. Similarly, the rate of interest at which the future time streams of costs and benefits are discounted has to be chosen with care. ➤interest, time preference theory of; quality-adjusted life years; risk assessment.

cost control ➤cost accounting.

cost curves The graphical representation of cost schedules, ➤average costs or ➤marginal costs, dependent on various levels of output or production.

cost of capital ➤capital, cost of.

cost-of-living index ➤retail prices index.

cost-plus A method of setting a price in which the contractor charges the actual cost of the goods he supplies or the work he carries out plus either a percentage or an agreed absolute amount for his services. Used for some government contracts, the cost-plus formula provides no incentive for the contractor to keep his costs to the minimum and, where a percentage service charge is applied, he actually has an incentive to inflate them. The justification for the cost-plus system is that for certain kinds of work, e.g. development contracts in large technical projects, it is not possible to estimate costs in advance.

Cost-plus is also often used in business as a method for calculating prices, for example in retailing, by adding a ►gross margin or mark-up to the bought-in cost of goods, where there may be no simple alternative. This is in contrast to the pricing described by traditional economic theory, which asserts competitive forces should lead ►marginal cost to be equal to ►marginal revenue. But because if one retailer charges more than another he may lose custom and be obliged to reduce his margins or go out of business, ►price theory (►►firm, theory of the) is not invalidated by the widespread use of the cost-plus method.

cost-push inflation ►Inflation induced by a rise in the costs of production of goods and services. Such cost increases may arise abroad and be transmitted through higher prices of imported raw materials. The rapid escalation in oil prices in the 1970s (►Organization of Petroleum Exporting Countries) accelerated price inflation in the period, although the rate of inflation had begun to rise before this. Cost increases may also arise within the domestic economy from firms attempting to increase profits and/or employees to increase their earnings. Success in achieving increases depends on their degree of market dominance (►monopoly) and, therefore, bargaining power. Any money gains greater than ►productivity will tend to result in price increases. Economists assert that money wage increases exceeding 4.5 per cent annually, on average, are inconsistent with an ►inflation target of 2.5 per cent. The cost-push argument for inflation is traditionally held to contrast with ►demand-pull inflation and has been associated with the different policy prescriptions. (►►prices and incomes policy.) However, cost push cannot lead to sustained inflation, in the long run, without monetary growth being sufficient to support it. ►►monetarism.

cost schedule A table showing the total costs of production at different levels of output and from which ►marginal costs and ►average costs can be calculated and cost curves drawn. A *price schedule*, in a similar way, would give information about prices at different levels of sales or output. Cost and price schedules are basic tools in economic theory, though in practice they are not easily constructed, especially over wide ranges of output where the ►production function may not be linear.

costing ►cost accounting.

costs, fixed ►fixed costs.

costs, historical or historic Actual costs at the time incurred. An ►asset in the ►balance sheet at historical cost is shown at the price actually paid for it, even though it might be worth more or cost more to replace. ►►depreciation.

costs, prime ►prime costs.

costs, selling The expenses incurred in creating or maintaining the ➤market for a product. Distribution costs are normally excluded, but ➤advertising sales staff, sales campaign costs and sales office expenses are included.

costs, supplementary ➤supplementary costs.

Council for Mutual Economic Aid (Comecon) A council set up in 1949 consisting of six East European countries, namely Bulgaria, Czechoslovakia, Hungary, Poland, Romania and the USSR, followed later by the German Democratic Republic (1950), Mongolia (1962), Cuba (1972) and Vietnam (1978). Its aim was, by means of central planning (➤planned economy) to develop the member countries' economies on a complementary basis for the purpose of achieving self-sufficiency. In 1990, agreement was reached for a fundamental change in the economic policy pursued by the Council. Multilateral cooperation between member states based on five-year plans and inconvertible roubles (➤convertibility) was to be abandoned in favour of a ➤free market, bilateral trade and convertible currencies. In 1991, Comecon was replaced by the Organization for International Economic Cooperation, which would continue to encourage international trade between the member countries on a bilateral basis and offer advice and information on regional economic problems.

council tax A tax designed to finance a proportion of UK local government spending. It was introduced as a replacement to the Community Charge or Poll Tax in 1993. It is a tax on the *occupation* of property (in contrast to the old rates, which typically taxed the ownership of property), with the amount to be paid loosely determined by the market price of the occupied property. All dwellings are put into eight bands based on their values, and all homes in each group within a council jurisdiction are charged the same amount. The banding system obviates the need for periodic revaluation of properties. Homes occupied by only one person receive a discount. Council tax is normally paid in ten monthly instalments. Business occupiers of property continue to pay rates (➤➤local taxation).

counter trade A form of ➤barter in ➤international trade in which the buyer requires the seller to accept goods (of the buyer's choosing) in lieu of currency. The seller has the task of marketing the goods. Another form of counter trade is the agreement by a seller of plant and machinery to 'buy back' the products produced by the plant and machinery in settlement of the debt.

Counter trade developed rapidly as a favoured trading method by Communist states and by ➤developing countries with non-convertible currencies. (➤convertibility) and a shortage of foreign exchange. Counter trade may take the form of the exchange of one commodity for another or the exchange of a mixed selection of commodities. Multinational firms and banks have specialist divisions to advise on counter trade and firms have been established specializing in the giving of advice on conducting counter trade.

countervailing duty An additional import duty (➤tariffs, import) imposed on a

➤commodity to offset a reduction of its price as a result of an export subsidy in the country of origin. ➤➤contingent protection; dumping; export incentives.

countervailing power The balancing of the market power of one economic group by another. The concept was advanced by ➤Galbraith in the first of his books on the domination of the modern economic system by large firms (*American Capitalism*), along with ➤economies of scale and technological development (➤technology) and the need for planning, to meet the criticism that this system of ➤monopolistic competition is inferior to ➤perfect competition. The power of large manufacturers was, he suggested, balanced by that of large retailing groups; the power of large employers by that of the trade unions.

coupon A piece of paper entitling the owner to ➤money payment (as in ➤bearer bonds), cut-price or free goods (gift coupons) or rations.

Cournot, Antoine Augustin (1801–77) Cournot was made Professor of Analysis and Mechanics at Lyons in 1834, and Rector of Grenoble University in 1835 and of Dijon University in 1854. His main economic work, *Recherches sur les principes mathématiques de la théorie des richesses*, was published in 1838. Other economic works were *Principes de la théorie des richesses* (1863) and *Revue sommaire des doctrines économiques* (1877). In *Recherches*, Cournot set out in mathematical form the basic apparatus of the theory of the firm (➤firm, theory of the) which, after being refined by ➤Marshall, appears in elementary economic textbooks today. He was the first to set out the ➤variables and functions facing a firm; ➤demand as a diminishing function of ➤price; ➤cost curves and revenue curves. By the use of calculus he demonstrated that a monopolist will maximize profit at the output at which ➤marginal cost is equal to ➤marginal revenue. Cournot traced a direct logical line from the single seller (➤monopoly) through two (➤duopoly) or many (➤oligopoly) sellers to 'unlimited competition'. He showed how, in the last case, 'the marginal cost equals the marginal revenue relationship of the monopolist' becomes 'the price equals the marginal cost relationship of the firm in ➤perfect competition'. In doing so, he analysed the situation of duopoly and showed that, given that each seller assumed the other's output was unaffected by his own, they would each adjust prices and output until a position of ➤equilibrium was reached, somewhere between that reflected by the equations for monopoly and that for unrestricted competition (➤Bertrand competition). In spite of the undoubted significance of his work, he had no influence on the mainstream of economic thought until his ideas were developed by Marshall.

cover The ratio of total to distributed ➤profit of a limited company. A ➤dividend is said to be twice covered if it represents half the earnings of the company.

covered bear ➤bear.

CPP Current purchasing power (➤inflation accounting).

crawling peg ➤exchange rate.

credibility A measure of the expectation of the population that the government, or monetary authorities, will adhere to policies delivering low ➤inflation. It is an important article of faith among macroeconomists that where people – particularly those negotiating wage deals – expect inflation to be low, it is much easier to keep inflation low. Obviously, if the monetary authorities have little credibility, and people anticipate inflation, then people will factor inflation into their behaviour. They will, for example, demand higher pay rises. Those pay rises will be inflationary, or at least make it costly for the authorities to keep inflation low. The search for credibility has led governments to tie their hands and make it difficult for themselves to generate inflation. By sticking to rules on how much money is in the economy (➤medium-term financial strategy), or by delegating authority over ➤money supply to an independent ➤central bank with no incentive to print money, credibility can to some extent be enhanced. The usual measure of credibility among economists is taken as the market ➤interest rate on long-term loans: if that rate is high, then it can be assumed the market anticipates inflation will occur in the future, and hence extra compensation is required for those who are lending. ➤➤monetary policy; inflation target.

credit The use or possession of goods and services without immediate payment. There are three types of credit: (a) *consumer credit*: credit extended formally and informally by shopkeepers, ➤finance houses and others to the ordinary public for the purchase of consumer goods (➤➤consumer credit), (b) *trade credit*: credit extended, for example, by material suppliers to manufacturers, or by manufacturers to wholesalers or retailers (➤➤trade credit) – virtually all exchange in manufacturing industry, services and commerce is conducted on credit, and firms may provide small discounts on accounts settled within, say, one month – and (c) *bank credit*: credit consisting of ➤loans and ➤overdrafts to a bank's customers (➤banking).

Credit enables a producer to bridge the gap between the production and sale of goods, and a consumer to purchase goods out of future ➤income. Bank and other kinds of credit form part of the ➤money supply and have considerable economic importance.

credit account 1. An account against which purchases may be made and paid monthly (US = charge account). 2. A form of revolving ➤instalment credit offered by some retail stores in which the consumer makes fixed regular monthly payments into an account and receives in return credit to purchase goods up to the limit of a certain multiple of the monthly payments, normally eight or twelve. A service charge, which is in effect an ➤interest charge, is normally made as a percentage of the value of each purchase. 3. Bank and agency ➤credit cards in which the consumer pays his account monthly are also a form of credit account.

credit banks ➤commercial banks.

credit card A plastic, personal magnetized card with the name and account number of the holder and the expiry date embossed. Purchases up to a prescribed limit may be credited on signature of a voucher franked by the card. The vendor recovers the cash from the issuer of the card (less ➤commission) and the purchaser pays the issuer on receipt of a monthly statement. For most cards the purchaser has the option of paying a minimum amount and settling the account in instalments plus interest. Credit-card lending accounted for over 20 per cent of UK consumer credit outstanding in 1996. A *debit card* works in the same way as a credit card, but the holder's bank account is debited immediately through electronic funds transfer at a point of sale (EFTPOS). Credit cards, popularly referred to as *plastic money*, are issued by banks, ➤building societies and other organizations, including retailers (*charge cards*). Cards issued by financial institutions often serve also as *cheque cards* and may be used to withdraw cash from an automatic teller machine (ATM). A cheque card guarantees cheques, up to a specified limit, drawn on a customer's account. The recipient of the cheque notes the cheque card number on the back of the cheque, payment of which is then guaranteed by the bank. *Smart cards* contain information about the holder in a microchip in the card and can, for example, validate the holder's Personal Identification Number, improving security compared with an ordinary credit card.

credit guarantee A type of insurance against default provided by a credit guarantee association or other institution to a lending institution. Credit guarantees enable otherwise 'sound' borrowers who lack ➤collateral security, or are unable to obtain loans for other reasons, to obtain the credit they require through banks in the normal way. A government loan guarantee scheme insuring loans to small firms by the ➤commercial banks was introduced in the UK in 1980. Under this scheme the government guarantees repayment to the bank of 70 per cent of the loan in return for an annual premium of 1.5 per cent on the guaranteed portion for variable rate loans. Loans are for a period of two to seven years. All ➤European Union member states (except Denmark), the USA, Japan and other countries have similar schemes. ➤➤Export Credits Guarantee Department.

credit sale ➤consumer credit.

credit transfer, or giro A system in which a bank or post office will transfer ➤money from one account to another on receipt of written instructions. Several accounts, e.g. ➤households or trade bills, may be included in a list which must state the location or account numbers of the payee. Standing orders for giro transfer of regular payments may be made. Credit transfers, which have been used by post offices in continental Europe for many years, were first introduced into Britain by the ➤commercial banks in 1961 and the Post Office in 1968. Benefits to the customer include the saving on stamp duty payable on ➤cheques (since abolished in Britain) and economies in accounting procedures, though banks may make a charge for each item transferred.

credit union (US) A non-profit organization accepting deposits and making loans, operated as a cooperative. Credit unions are popular in the USA and some European countries. A mutual ►savings bank (►mutual company).

creditor One to whom an amount of money is due. A firm's creditors are other firms, individuals and perhaps the government to which it owes money in return for goods supplied, services rendered and taxes for which it is liable. Antonym of ►debtor.

creditor nation A country with a ►balance of payments surplus. The ►Keynes Plan recognized that ►disequilibrium in international payments was as much the responsibility of creditor as of *debtor nations*. Under that plan the International Clearing Union or international ►central bank would have given ►overdrafts to debtor countries and by so doing would have created deposits for the creditor countries in terms of its special ►currency called ►bancor, in a similar way to normal ►banking operations. However, ►interest would be charged not only on the debtors' overdrafts, but also on the creditors' deposits. Although the Keynes Plan was not accepted at the ►Bretton Woods Conference, the principle that a surplus country had 'obligations' was accepted and a scarce-currency clause written into the ►International Monetary Fund agreement. ►►international liquidity.

CREST Electronic share settlement system introduced to the UK ►Stock Exchange in 1996. By recording title to shares electronically it will reduce the cost of the traditional system of ►share certificates sent through the post. Title will be recorded through nominee companies set up by ►stockbrokers and others. However, shareholders may continue to hold paper certificates if they wish.

critical-path analysis A method of structuring the sequence of work on a project to minimize the duration of work on the whole project. Between the start of a project and its finish there are a number of separate tasks which have to be done in particular sequence: in the construction of a house, for example, the foundations are laid before the walls. Other tasks may be carried out simultaneously, such as the fitting of window frames as the roof is being tiled. Critical-path analysis attempts to order all tasks, minimizing the time that resources are spent idly waiting for other tasks to be completed. The critical path is the sequence of tasks – mostly those that have to be finished in a particular order – that affect the overall length of the whole project. The window frames, for example, may not be on the critical path, as fitters can install them while other work goes on, and there is probably some flexibility in when the windows can be fitted. The foundation is on the critical path, because every extra day spent on the foundations, means an extra day on the whole building project. Management is probably better devoted to focusing on keeping the foundations part of the project working smoothly, rather than the window frames.

cross-price elasticity of demand The proportionate change in the quantity demanded of one good divided by the proportionate change in the price of another good. If the two goods are ►substitutes (e.g. butter and margarine), this elasticity is positive. For instance, if the price of margarine increases, the demand for butter will increase. If the goods are complementary (►complementary goods) (e.g. pot plants and flower pots), this elasticity is negative. If the price of pot plants rises, the demand for flower pots will fall. ►►elasticity of substitution.

cross-section analysis Statistical analysis of the members of a ►population at one point in time. It contrasts with ►time-series analysis, in which the population is drawn from a number of time periods (generally months, quarters or years). ►►econometrics.

cross-subsidy Financing a loss-making line of business with profits made elsewhere. This may be motivated by private business concerns (to help establish new lines of business for example), or by public policy concern (the provision of rural bus routes at the expense of urban ones). It can be an important object of public policy to prevent it where it provides the means by which ►predatory pricing can occur. ►►subsidy.

crowding-out The process by which an increase in government borrowing displaces private spending. If an increase in government borrowing has a large effect on interest rates, private spending will fall as investors slim down their plans. Therefore, overall, spending will not increase much. If the government borrowing has no effect on interest rates, however, then there will be no reduction in private spending and aggregate demand will rise by the full amount of the increase in government spending. ►►IS–LM model; Keynes, J. M.; monetarism; Ricardian equivalence.

cum dividend With ►dividend; the purchaser of a security quoted 'cum dividend' is entitled to receive the next dividend when due. The term 'cum', meaning 'with', is also used in a similar sense in relation to ►bonus issues, ►rights issue, or ►interest attached to ►securities, etc.

cumulative preference shares ►preference shares.

currency Notes and coin that are the 'current' medium of exchange in a country (►money supply). Gold and national currencies that act as ►reserve currencies, such as the dollar, are referred to as *international currency* because they are regarded as acceptable for the settlement of international ►debts. ►►banknote; exchange control; exchange rate; soft currency.

currency, trading ►trading currency.

currency appreciation The increase in the ►exchange rate of one ►currency in terms of other currencies. The term is usually applied to a currency with a floating rate of exchange; upward changes in fixed rates of exchange are called *revaluations*. For example, sterling appreciated from US$1.70 in 1977 to US$2.40 in 1980; from US$1.16 in 1984 to US$1.89 at the end of 1987 and from US$1.48 in 1993 to US$1.65 in 1997. As can be seen these short-run appreciations were against the background of a long-term depreciation of sterling against the dollar. ⟫currency depreciation; devaluation; exchange rate.

currency depreciation The fall in the ►exchange rate of one ►currency in terms of other currencies. Usually applied to floating exchange rates. Downward changes in fixed rates of exchange are called ►devaluations. Sterling has endured more depreciations than appreciations in the decades since the Second World War. In 1955 there were about 12 deutschmarks to one pound, by the mid-1980s there were about 3. The pound dropped to about 2.15 after its withdrawal from the ►European Exchange Rate Mechanism in 1992; although had risen back to 3 again in 1997. A depreciation makes imports more expensive in terms of domestic currency, and exports cheaper. However, in as far as a currency depreciation simply reflects a relatively high level of domestic inflation (e.g. if a 10 per cent rise in prices leads to a 10 per cent fall in the currency), the *real exchange rate* is said not to have changed. Indeed, if inflation occurs *without* a depreciation of the currency, in real terms the currency has *appreciated* because the price of imported goods will be relatively lower than domestic goods than before the inflation, and the price of exported goods will have risen compared to foreign ones. ⟫currency appreciation.

currency school ►banking and currency schools.

currency snake ►European currency snake.

current account 1. The most common type of bank account, on which ►deposits do not earn ►interest, but can be withdrawn by ►cheque at any time (US = *demand deposit*). The bank charges according to the number of cheques cleared through the account and the credit balance. If the average balance is high, the customer may pay no bank charges. 2. That part of the ►balance of payments accounts recording current, i.e. non-capital, transactions.

current assets ►assets.

current balance The net position on the current account of the ►balance of payments.

current-cost accounting ►inflation accounting.

current expenditure Expenditure on recurrent, i.e. non- ►capital, items in business or private accounts.

current liabilities ►liabilities.

current prices ►Prices unadjusted for changes in the purchasing power of money. Whether prices are in current or constant terms in historical series of economic statistics is of great importance at times of ►inflation or ►deflation. ⟫real terms.

current purchasing-power accounting ➤inflation accounting.

current ratio The ratio of the current ➤liabilities to the current ➤assets of a business. Current assets normally exceed current liabilities. The difference between the two is ➤working capital, which is normally financed from long-term sources. The amount of working capital required varies with the type of business and its commercial practices e.g. on the proportions of its output sold for cash and on three months' ➤credit – so that the current ratio is not a universally useful guide to the solvency of a business. ➤➤liquidity; capital.

current yield ➤yield.

Customs Cooperation Council An international council established in 1950 with a secretariat in Brussels for the development of agreed rules for the application of customs procedures and the provision of advice and assistance. The Council has established a classification of commodities for the application of customs ➤tariffs to international trade.

customs drawback The repayment of customs duties (➤tariffs, import) paid on imported goods which have been re-exported or used in the manufacture of exported goods.

customs duties ➤tariffs, import.

customs union A union established within two or more countries if all barriers (such as ➤tariffs or ➤quotas) to the free exchange of each other's goods and services are removed and, at the same time, a common external tariff is established against non-members. This contrasts with a ➤free-trade area in which each member country retains its own tariffs vis-à-vis non-members At one time it was generally accepted that customs unions unambiguously yielded economic benefits. Without the distortions imposed by tariffs, trade was directed in favour of the producer with advantageous costs (➤Ricardo, D.). It was believed that as ➤free trade was itself beneficial in that it led to the optimal allocation of world resources, so a customs union, which was a step in that direction, must also be beneficial. However, Jacob Viner in *The Customs Union Issue*, published in 1950, pointed out that the creation of a customs union could have two effects: (a) a trade-creating effect and (b) a trade-diversion effect. Although the former might be a gain, greater losses might be incurred by the latter. Take the example of two countries *A* and *B* and the rest of the world *C* producing a particular commodity for £50, £40 and £30 respectively. If the home market of *A* is protected by a £25 tariff on the item, then no one in *A* will find it economic to import from *B* or *C*. Production in *A* will occur, at £50. If Country *A* then forms a customs union with *B*, trade will be *created* because it is cheaper for *A* to obtain the commodity from *B* than to produce it itself. There is a gain in so far as *A* is £10 better off. On the other hand, if Country *A*'s original import duty had been £15, trade would then have taken place with the rest of the world *C*, despite the tariff, as this would be the least-cost source to *A*. In this example, if *A* forms a customs union with *B* it will now *switch* its trade because it can obtain the commodity for £40 from *B* compared with £30 + £15 = £45 from *C*. This trade diversion represents a move away from the optimum of ➤resource allocation, because *B* is a higher real-cost source than *C* (➤second best, theory of). Whether, therefore, a customs union will yield overall gains from shifts in the location of production will depend on the superiority of trade creation to trade diversion. However, this type of analysis covers only a part of the problem; many other factors must be taken into account in assessing whether a customs union is beneficial. In particular, the removal of tariff barriers between countries will change the ➤terms of trade and therefore the relative volumes of the different commodities demanded, because of the price changes. It will shift the commodity pattern of trade as well as the geographical origins of the commodities traded. Whether a community will finish up better off therefore depends on the price and income elasticities of demand for the commodities traded (➤elasticity). An added benefit may accrue because the increase in the size of markets may enable ➤economies of scale to be made. Finally, a protective tariff is initially imposed because home costs are high; but home costs may remain high because a protective tariff is imposed. Removal of the tariff may induce more efficient operation and lower costs. ➤Association of South East Asian Nations; Benelux; Caribbean Common Market; Central American Common Market; European Union; European Free Trade Association; Latin American Integration Association.

cycle, trade ➤business cycle.

cyclical unemployment Temporary ➤unemployment resulting from lack of ➤aggregate demand in a downswing in the ➤business cycle.

D

data-mining The practice of searching for ➤correlations in data with the purpose of generating theoretical hypotheses. The normal pattern of scientific research is for hypotheses to be produced by abstract models and then validated by ➤empirical testing. Data-mining reverses the procedure. It is not held to be a respectable mode of inquiry because, while any theories it produces will be empirically valid, it is hard to tell whether they are the result of coincidence or not. All data are bound to wrap up some coincidences, and the data-miner is likely to have unearthed these. For example, a theory that people whose names start with the letter H tend to be richer than average would not be remarkable if discovered in data, as at least one letter group must have higher than average income. The theory would be convincing only if it had been thought up before being substantiated by data analysis. ➤➤null hypothesis; regression analysis.

dated securities ➤bonds, ➤bills of exchange or other ➤securities which have a stated date for redemption (repayment) of their nominal value. *Short-dated securities* are those for which the ➤redemption date is near; *long-dated securities* are those for which it is a long time ahead.

DCE ➤domestic credit expansion.

d.c.f. Discounted cash flow (➤present value).

deadweight debt A ➤debt incurred to meet ➤current expenditure, or which for any other reason is not covered by a real ➤asset. Most of the ➤national debt is deadweight debt since it was incurred to finance war and other current ➤public expenditure.

deadweight loss 1. A loss in ➤social welfare deriving from a policy or action that has no corresponding gain. Deadweight losses represent economic inefficiency (➤economic efficiency) and usually result when there is some flaw in the price-setting mechanism. For example, congestion on roads imposes costs on road users, and these costs are deadweight losses, because the inconvenience of congestion to one driver is not matched by a reduction in inconvenience to another. If road space were allocated by setting high prices for road access, the costs that would be borne by the drivers that pay them would be matched by an increase in government revenues to the benefit of everybody else. Society often finds it worth bearing certain deadweight losses in order to promote social objectives. 2. The part of the cost of a particular policy that has to be incurred, but that does not further the objective of the policy. For example, the cost of subsidizing those in ►long-term unemployment back to work includes some element of subsidy to people who would have returned to work regardless of the subsidy.

death rate The number of deaths occurring in any year for every 1000 of the population (the crude death rate). It may be quoted for each sex and each age group. The rapid growth in UK population in the early nineteenth century is attributed more to the decline in the death rate than to an increase in ►birth rate. A similar effect is to be observed in the highly populated ►developing countries. The UK death rate of male children under five years of age was 57 in 1900, compared to 2.5 at the present time. The *expectation of life at birth* in the UK has risen from about 50 years for babies born in 1900 to 74 years for males and 79 years for females born in 1996. An alternative measure is that which estimates the number of years a new-born baby may expect to have a healthy life; that is a life in which there is no illness severe enough to limit physical or mental mobility. In the UK the current expectation of such a healthy life is 60 years for males and 62 years for females. ►►poverty; demographic time bomb; dependency ratio; *qualys*.

debentures, debenture stock Fixed-interest ►securities issued by limited companies in return for long-term ►loans. The former term is sometimes also used to refer to any title on a secured interest-bearing loan. Debentures are dated for redemption (i.e. repayment of their nominal value by the borrower to the holder) between ten to forty years ahead (►redemption date) but occasionally may be irredeemable. Debentures are usually secured. There are two main types of secured debenture: (a) *mortgage debentures*, which are secured by a ►mortgage on specific ►assets of the company; and (b) *floating-charge debentures*, where its assets are not suitable for a fixed charge (►floating debentures). Debenture interest must be paid whether the company makes a ►profit or not. In the event of non-payment, debenture holders can force ►liquidation and rank ahead of all shareholders in their claims on the company's assets. The interest which debentures bear depends partly on long-term ►rates of interest prevailing at the time and partly on the type of debenture, but will in any case, because of the lower risk involved, be less than that borne by ►preference shares. Debenture shares are most appropriate for financing companies whose profits are stable and which have substantial fixed assets, such as property companies.

Convertible debentures carry an option at a fixed future date to convert the ►stock into ordinary ►shares at a fixed price. This option is compensated for by a lower rate of interest than an ordinary debenture, but convertible debentures are attractive since they offer the investor, without sacrificing his security, the prospect of purchasing ►equity shares cheaply in the future. For this reason, convertible debentures are issued at times when it is difficult to raise ►capital either by equity or fixed-interest securities. ►►new-issue market.

Debreu, Gérard (b. 1921) A graduate in mathematics at the University of Paris,

Debreu joined the Cowles Commission in 1950. In 1960 he was appointed to the Chair of Economics and Mathematics at the University of California. His published works include *Existence of an Equilibrium for a Competitive Economy* (1954) with ➤Arrow and *Theory of Value, an Axiomatic Analysis of Economic Equilibrium* (1959). Professor Debreu, who was awarded the ➤Nobel Prize in Economics in 1983, has applied the mathematical theory of sets and topology to economic analysis and advanced the study of the conditions under which markets attain ➤equilibrium.

debt A sum of ➤money or other property owed by one person or organization to another. Debt comes into being through the granting of ➤credit or through raising ➤loan capital. *Debt servicing* consists of paying interest on a debt. Debt is an essential part of all modern, capitalist economies (➤capitalism). ➤➤national debt.

debt conversion ➤conversion.

debt management The process of administering debt, for example the ➤national debt, i.e. providing for the payment of ➤interest, and arranging the refinancing of maturing ➤bonds.

debt neutrality The idea that financing spending by borrowing money will have exactly the same effects as financing it through other means. It has been applied in various forms, notably to government spending (➤Ricardian equivalence) and to corporate investment (➤Modigliani–Miller theorem).

debt ratio ➤gearing.

debtor One who owes money to another. A firm's debtors, for example, are those to whom invoices have been sent for goods or services supplied and which remain unpaid. Antonym of ➤creditor.

decentralized decision-taking ➤free-market economy.

decile ➤percentile.

decreasing returns ➤diseconomies of scale; returns to scale.

deemed disposal The assumed realization of an ➤asset in the calculation of liability for ➤capital gains taxation or ➤inheritance tax. Shares in a company, for example, might be valued and tax charged on the difference between that value and the price originally paid for them, even where the shares did not change hands.

deep discounted bonds ➤Bonds which are issued at a price much lower than that at which they can be redeemed (➤redeemable securities) at the specified date. The intention is to provide large ➤capital gains for the holders and to pay a correspondingly low interest rate. In some countries and especially for higher-rate taxpayers, less tax may be payable on a gain than upon interest income; however, the 'capital gain' on deep discounted bonds is liable to be treated as income by the tax authorities.

deferred rebate A rebate or discount on a purchase which is accumulated for a specified period to encourage customers to remain with a particular supplier. Also called *aggregated rebate.* ⤵Monopolies and Mergers Commission.

deferred shares A ►share issued where ►ordinary shares have a fixed ►dividend and which entitle the holders to all ►profits after prior charges have been met. Now virtually unknown.

deficit An excess of an expenditure flow over an income flow, e.g. ►budget deficit, ►balance of payments deficit, or an excess of ►liabilities over ►assets.

deficit financing The use of borrowing to finance an excess of expenditure over ►income. Most often, it refers to governments, who often spend more than they can raise in taxation. The term is normally used in economics to refer to a planned budget deficit (►balanced budget) incurred in the interests of expanding ►aggregate demand by relaxing ►fiscal policy and thus injecting purchasing power into the economy, a policy advocated by Keynes to increase employment in the 1930s. ⤵crowding-out; fiscal policy; public-sector borrowing requirement.

defined-benefit pension A pension policy, such as most employer-run occupational pension schemes, in which the individual's entitlement to pension receipt is tied to the individual's earnings, rather than individual's contribution to the scheme. ►pension funds.

defined-contribution pension A pension policy, such as a *personal pension,* in which the individual's entitlement to pension receipt is specifically tied to the individual's own contributions to the fund. These have grown in popularity with legislative changes in the 1980s, and the increasing job turnover of employees who required more portability of pension entitlements between different employers. Defined-contribution schemes carry no ►cross-subsidy between different categories of investor, and simply act as a personal savings account. ►pension funds.

deflation 1. A sustained reduction in the general level of prices. Deflation is often, though not inevitably, accompanied by declines in output and employment and is distinct from 'disinflation' which refers to a reduction in the rate of inflation. Deflation can be brought about by either internal or external forces in an ►open economy. 2. A deliberate policy of reducing ►aggregate demand and output so as to reduce the rate of ►inflation and the quantity of imports and lower the ►exchange rate, thus improving export performance and the ►balance of payments. Aggregate demand may be reduced by ►fiscal policy (increasing taxes or reducing government expenditure) or ►monetary policy (increases in the ►rate of interest and slower growth or contraction in the ►money supply). 3. In economic statistics, the adjustment of index numbers or economic aggregates to eliminate the effects of price changes, as in dividing an index of the ►gross domestic product (GDP) at ►current prices by a price index (►index number) to give an index of GDP in ►real terms. In estimating changes in net output in real terms there are two alternative methods. One is to deflate the series of the value of net output at ►current prices by a single index of output prices, the other is to deflate separately each particular input by its own appropriate price index, and to subtract the sum of these adjustments from the value of gross output deflated in the same way by indices of output prices. The second method is called *double deflation*, which has the advantage of capturing changes in the ratio of net to gross outputs in real terms. This may be important where, for example, profit margins are being squeezed by faster increases in input than in output prices. To deflate net output directly by output prices in these circumstances would lead to an overstatement of the real rise in net output.

deflationary gap A state of the economy in which there are unemployed resources and there is no inflationary pressure. It is a state first highlighted by ►Keynes and in more modern literature identified as ►Keynesian unemployment, characterized by a chronic shortage of ►aggregate demand. More recently, the concept has been revived in mainstream economic policy-making, as the existence of a gap between actual ►GDP, and the economy's potential GDP (►output gap). ►►inflationary gap; Keynesian economics.

deflator ►GDP deflator.

de-industrialization A decline in the share of manufacturing in ►national income. In the UK the contribution of manufacturing to the ►gross domestic product fell from 28 per cent in 1979 to 24 per cent in 1985 and 22 per cent in 1991, with little change since then. Although a decline in the manufacturing ratio is common to most of the ►advanced countries, reflecting the growth of ►services, fears have been expressed that since manufactures constitute the bulk of exports, the process of decline could continue to the point where a large imbalance on ►visible trade could not be offset by the growth of ►invisible exports without a decline in ►real income. However, it has been argued that the exceptional weakness in British manufacturing exports in the 1980s reflected the strength of sterling buoyed up by the effects of North Sea oil and that now that oil production has peaked, the growth of manufacturing output can be expected to continue. Moreover, the decline of manufacturing is to some extent a statistical illusion, reflecting the growth of ►productivity in manufacturing compared with slower growth in output per person in the rest of the economy (►Baumol effect).

demand The desire for a particular good or ►service supported by the possession of the necessary means of exchange to effect ownership. ►►demand, theory of; demand curve; Marshall, A.; money.

demand, theory of The area of economics concerned with the allocation of limited resources to different commodities in the purchasing decisions of rational consumers. Together with the theory of the ➤firm (which is really a theory of supply), it forms the basis of ➤microeconomics.

There are several different approaches to consumer behaviour: the first is the cardinal ➤utility approach associated with ➤Marshall and other economists of the nineteenth century. This was superseded by ➤indifference-curve analysis (➤ordinal utility), which dispensed with the need for an absolute measure of utility. A third approach, ➤revealed preference, is largely a re-expression of indifference-curve analysis, in which no explicit notion of utility is used at all. All these approaches give rise to the same qualitative analysis of consumer behaviour and support the laws of demand and supply, such as that price rises lead to cuts in demand. ➤➤demand function.

demand curve The graphical representation of a schedule listing the quantities of a commodity a consumer would be willing to buy at various prices. The schedule is drawn up on the assumption that other economic factors remain the same between the consideration of one price and another. Such factors are income, prices of ➤substitutes or ➤complementary goods, consumer preferences or ➤expectations. In most cases, the curve would slope downwards from left to right, reflecting the fact that the higher the price of a commodity the lower the demand for it. However, the response of demand to a change in price (➤➤elasticity) will influence the slope and shape of the demand curve in specific cases. ➤➤demand, theory of; endogenous preferences; excess demand; income effect; indifference-curve analysis; substitution effect; supply curve.

demand deposit (US) Money on ➤current account, i.e. a ➤bank deposit that can be withdrawn without notice.

demand for labour ➤labour, demand for.

demand function A mathematical expression of the relationship between the quantity of a good or service that is demanded and changes in a number of economic factors such as its own price, the prices of ➤substitutes and ➤complementary goods, income, credit terms, etc. The quantity demanded is the ➤dependent variable and the other factors are ➤independent variables. The effect of each independent variable on the dependent variable may be estimated statistically by ➤time-series analysis or ➤cross-section analysis of ➤household expenditure data. Also known as the Marshallian demand function. ➤➤demand, theory of; demand curve; elasticity; Hicksian demand function.

demand management ➤fiscal policy.

demand-pull inflation ➤Inflation induced by a persistence of an excess of ➤aggregate demand in the economy over ➤aggregate supply. The balance of aggregate supply and demand does not reach ➤equilibrium because supply reaches a capacity limit at the ➤full-employment level (➤➤output gap). The excess demand probably persists because there is a growth in the quantity of ►money either through the creation of money by government to finance the budgetary gap between its expenditure and income or because the quantity of money is allowed to expand to accommodate the rise in prices. ►►cost-push inflation; Friedman, M.; inflationary gap; Keynes, J. M.; quantity theory of money.

demand schedule A list showing the quantities of a good or service a consumer would be willing to buy at various prices. ►►demand curve.

demographic time bomb The idea that western societies face a crisis in the next few decades, caused by the ageing of their populations. Increased life expectancy, a declining ►birth rate, both sometimes allied with a trend towards earlier retirement, has meant that the proportion of the population of retirement age is expected to rise (►dependency ratio). On reliable demographic projections, the trend is least evident in the case of the United Kingdom and the United States, and most evident in Japan – but is to some extent evident everywhere. The problem has given rise to the suggestion that pensions should increasingly be provided on a ►funded basis, rather than on a ►pay-as-you-go basis. The potential for public finances to hit crisis point has also led governments to look more closely at private pensions to take the burden off government schemes. But these measures do not mean the workers of tomorrow avoid supporting the elderly; it simply means they support them by generating returns to savings rather than extra tax revenue. Those who are not working in a society, always will be dependent for their income on those who are working. Workers will only find relief if the size of the working population can be increased (through, say, later retirement); or the incomes of elderly dependants are lowered.

demography ►population.

dependency culture The phenomenon by which the granting of some kind of help or aid to those in adverse circumstances, increases the likelihood of the recipients being in adverse circumstances. The phenomenon has become a fashionable diagnosis of the increase in recipients of benefits subject to a ►means test (from under 1 million in 1948 to nearly 6 million in 1996). As such benefits are withdrawn from those whose incomes rise, they are held to penalize those who make an effort to earn their way out of them, and are blamed for fostering a reliance on benefits. This analysis has been responsible for the introduction of more ►active labour-market policies, but the analysis does not simply have to apply to the impact of the benefit system. It can be used as a description of any perverse response by private agents to a well-intentioned government intervention aimed at helping them. Dependency culture can be seen as the application of the ►Lucas critique to an area of ►microeconomics, in that it suggests the existence of a policy towards a problem affects the relationship between the problem and its causes. ►poverty trap.

dependency ratio The number of people of non-working age in an economy, relative to those who are of working age. The term is used flexibly, sometimes referring to dependants of old age only, and sometimes to those either too old or too young to work. It is calculated by taking the ratio of non-working to working-age groups, and multiplying by 100 to give a percentage. In practice, people often turn the ratio upside down, and refer to the inverse, more strictly known as the *support ratio*. In Britain, in 1996, the old-age dependency ratio was 27 per cent; but it is projected to grow to 45 per cent by the year 2050. Of course, the need to support a growing number of elderly people provides a problem for pensions systems. ➤demographic time bomb.

dependent variable A ➤variable whose value is conditional on the value of another variable. For instance, if the amount of butter a person buys falls or rises as the price of butter rises or falls, the quantity of butter is a variable depending on the movements in the variable price. ➤econometrics; endogenous variable; independent variable.

depletion theory The branch of economics concerned with the rate at which natural resources are consumed over time. For example, what determines the speed at which the world does (or ought to) use up its stock of oil? In general, economists view abstinence from using up a resource as a form of investment: by not using oil up now, we forgo some current consumption, and leave ourselves more to consume in the future, just as we invest in machines today that will produce consumer goods tomorrow. People who own resources and keep them in the ground earn a return on so doing worth only the increase in the price of their asset over the period. If an oil company believes the price of oil will rise by 10 per cent over the next year, and the market rate of interest is 5 per cent, it will keep its oil in the ground. If the oil price is expected to rise by 5 per cent and the interest rate is 10 per cent, the oil company will do better by selling the oil now and investing the proceeds, earning 10 per cent. If all oil companies behave like this, they will push the oil price down by supplying so much that it will quickly become expected that the price *will* rise by 10 per cent over the next year.

Thus the fundamental principle of depletion theory is that consumption should occur at a rate which ensures that profits to be made from not depleting stocks of the resource are equal to those on other forms of investment. In reality, extraction costs and many other factors throw into question whether the principle explains either how quickly stocks of resources do get depleted, or how quickly they ought to. ➤environmental economics; natural resources.

deposit Money placed in an account at a bank and constituting a claim on the bank. The term 'bank deposit' includes deposits on all types of account, including ➤current accounts. ➤banking.

deposit account An account with a bank, ➤building society or other financial institution in which ➤deposits earn ➤interest, and withdrawals from which may require notice. Until 1971 interest was paid by the bank at a rate fixed by agreement between the clearing banks and normally 2 per cent below ➤bank rate. Since that date banks have been obliged to fix their rates individually and now offer a range of deposit accounts to compete with the remaining ➤building societies and other ➤financial intermediaries. Deposit accounts are called *time deposits* in the USA and *savings accounts* in France and other continental European countries. ➤➤banking.

deposit bank ➤commercial bank.

depreciation 1. The reduction in ➤value of an ➤asset through wear and tear. An allowance for the depreciation on a company's assets is always made before the calculation of ➤profit, on the grounds that the consumption of ➤capital assets is one of the costs of earning the revenues of the business and is allowed as such, according to special rules, by the tax authorities. Since depreciation can be accurately measured only at the end of the life of an asset (i.e. ➤ex post), depreciation provisions in company accounts require an estimate of both the total amount of depreciation and the asset life. Annual depreciation provisions are normally calculated according to two methods: (a) the 'straight-line method', where the estimated residual (e.g. scrap) value of an asset is deducted from its original cost and the balance divided by the number of years of estimated life to arrive at an annual depreciation expense to set against revenue; and (b) the 'reducing-balance method'. In this case the actual depreciation expense is set at a constant proportion of the depreciated value of the asset, i.e. a diminishing annual absolute amount. There are other methods of calculating depreciation and also of dealing with the fact that, in periods of rising prices, the replacement cost of an asset may be very much greater than its original cost. This latter problem is dealt with by revaluing assets at intervals, or even annually, using special capital-cost indices and adjusting depreciation charges accordingly. This is called *replacement-cost depreciation* as opposed to *historic-cost depreciation* (➤inflation accounting; costs, historical) when the original cost of purchase is retained throughout the period. It should be noted that ➤obsolescence is distinct from depreciation, in that the former is an unforeseen change in the value of an asset for technological or economic reasons. If an asset becomes obsolescent its undepreciated value is usually written off (depreciated) completely in the year of replacement. In some cases the life of an asset may be very difficult to determine because it is specific to the production of a product the demand for which is subject to rapid changes in taste or fashion, i.e. there is a high risk of product obsolescence. In these cases the life of the asset is written off over a very short period. The purpose of depreciation provisions in accounting is to ensure that the cost of the flow of services provided by capital assets is met in the price of the company's products; it is not to build up funds for the replacement of these assets to be available at a certain date. In practice, depreciation provisions are treated as part of the net ➤cash flow of a business and are used to repay ➤loans, to purchase other fixed assets or to invest in other businesses; that is, they are put to the use that will give the highest possible return. Much confusion is caused by this point, since what happens to depreciation provisions – which are, in effect, transfers of funds from fixed assets to current assets and sometimes back again – is not often clear from the ►balance sheet. ►►amortization; sources and uses of funds.

Depreciation is accepted for tax purposes as a charge against profits, but this depreciation has to be calculated according to certain rules and does not necessarily bear any relation to the depreciation actually charged by the business in its accounts. ►►capital allowances.

2. A reduction in the value of a ►currency in terms of gold or other currencies under ►free-market conditions and coming about through a decline in the ►demand for that currency in relation to the supply. ►currency depreciation.

depreciation at choice ►capital allowances.

depression A downturn in the ►business cycle in which there is a sustained high level of ►unemployment. The three or four years following 1929 experienced the last major depression in the world economy. ►►recession.

deregulation The process of invigorating activity in a sector of the economy by reducing the burden of government controls, particularly those that have the effect of creating ►barriers to entry. The goal of deregulation initiatives – which have been particularly important in the last decade – is generally to promote competition, in areas previously considered to be ►natural monopoly, or in areas in which regulation appeared to have long outlived its original rationale. Deregulation in any of a variety of forms has affected a substantial area of economic life in much of the developed world: from financial services, to those manufacturing sectors subject to international competition (in Europe, in particular as a result of the ►Single European Act, but globally with the promotion of world trade); to sectors primarily under government ownership. Apparent success in sectors such as telecommunications world-wide, and inter-city coach travel in the UK, has not been matched in every area. British local bus services have proved a more controversial area; and even though in the case of the deregulated US airline sector, prices are low and activity high, the impact has been marred by a constant flow of bankruptcies and some safety concerns. More recently, there has been a concern that global deregulation has led producers to operate under such tight competitive constraints, that normal social obligations are being neglected, and that jobs are insecure as obsolescent workers are made redundant as soon as they are no longer useful (►downsizing). Nevertheless, many economists believe that, although deregulation was seen as a policy complementary to ►privatization, it was the more important of the pair. ►regulation.

derivatives A generic term for ►futures, ►options and ►swaps, i.e. instruments derived from conventional direct dealings in securities, currencies and commodities. Trade in derivatives increased substantially in the 1990s, given their usefulness to company treasurers and fund managers as a ►hedge against security price changes and currency fluctuations, particularly in the disturbed currency markets of the period. In the 10 years to 1993 18 derivatives exchanges were created in Europe, trading 98 different contracts. The market, which had come to be dominated by trade in swaps and to be handled chiefly by a relatively small number of banks, was estimated to have reached a total value of some $4 bn by 1992. This figure was questioned by some commentators, who held that the true measure was not the total value of the instruments traded but the level of risk involved, a figure around a tenth of the total value. Moreover, many, including the Group of 30 in a report published in July 1993, pointed out that the derivatives market was small in comparison with total bond, equity or foreign exchange transactions ($900 bn).

In the same report the Group of 30, while suggesting guidelines for the proper conduct of business, concluded that further regulation was unnecessary. However, central banks in particular remained unconvinced, noting that most business was outside official ▶stock exchanges, that the instruments were complex and not universally understood, and that the potential for undercapitalization, faulty systems, inadequate supervision and human error was greater than in other markets.

derived demand The demand for a ▶factor of production where the demand for the factor is derived indirectly from the demand for the finished product to which the factor has contributed in production. ▶▶labour, demand for.

destination principle ▶value-added tax.

devaluation The reduction of the fixed official rate at which one ▶currency is exchanged for another (▶currency depreciation) in a fixed exchange rate regime. Currencies have been in such regimes for much of the post-war period – first under the arrangements agreed at the ▶Bretton Woods conference; more recently in Europe under the ▶European Monetary System. There are three basic situations in which the authorities find themselves calling for a devaluation. First, most commonly under Bretton Woods, governments regarded devaluation as a means of correcting a ▶balance-of-payments deficit. Secondly, under the ▶European Exchange Rate Mechanism, pressure for devaluations has often been sparked by a period of high ▶inflation. In either of these two cases, the devaluation serves to help the exporting sector of the economy, at the expense of the non-tradable sector. For example, it works to reduce a deficit, because devaluation makes the foreign currency price of exports cheaper, and the domestic price of imports more expensive. (The immediate effect is similar to an unfavourable change in the ▶terms of trade (▶J-curve)). Or, if inflation is high, the foreign price of exports tends to rise and exports become uncompetitive – unless the exchange rate falls to make the prices competitive again. The third reason countries sometimes need a devaluation is when events in their domestic economy call for different economic policies to those in the rest of the fixed-rate area. For example, if one country is ▶overheating, while another is enduring ▶deflation, then a looser monetary policy is required in the former. But under fixed exchange rates, it is not possible for monetary authorities to fix both the ▶rate of interest and the ▶exchange rate independently – fixing one tends to imply some rate of the other. The country requiring a looser policy needs either to devalue, or repeatedly devalue, or devalue and then revalue later as policy converges. In effect, all three causes of devaluation are the same: a need to restore domestic balance (neither overheating – nor deflation) while also maintaining a reasonable balance between the exporting and non-exporting sector. Governments really have only monetary policy and ►fiscal policy to adjust these two in the short term, and a fixed exchange rate is often too much to bear.

developing country A country that has not yet reached the stage of ►economic development characterized by the growth of industrialization, nor a level of ►national income sufficient to yield the domestic ►savings required to finance the ►investment necessary for further growth (►Rostow, W. W.). Also referred to as Third World Countries. The attempt by developing countries to obtain significant increases in their ►real incomes has been frustrated by the deterioration in their ►terms of trade and the rapid expansion of their populations. Many developing countries are primary producers, so their economies are vulnerable to movements in commodity prices. Over 20 per cent of the ►gross domestic product of many developing countries is derived from their exports of primary commodities. African and Latin American countries depended at the end of the 1980s on these commodity exports for over 70 per cent of their ►foreign exchange earnings. However, commodity prices fell in ►real terms – by about 10 per cent in the 1980s, although there has been some improvement since. As a result, many developing countries have accumulated large foreign debts. The interest payments on this debt and the repayment of capital as it comes due takes up about 50 per cent of their export earnings. Many ideas have been put forward to assist these countries bridge the gap between themselves and the developed countries. (►United Nations Conference on Trade and Development.) Some developing countries, particularly in Asia have successfully embarked on economic development and attracted a substantial growth in private capital investment in the 1990s which has more than offset static or declining official ►foreign aid. (►emerging markets; newly industrialized country.) ►►Asian Development Bank; Association of South East Asian Nations; Colombo Plan for Cooperative Economic and Social Development in Asia and the Pacific; Convergence; General Agreement on Tariffs and Trade; International Bank for Reconstruction and Development; international commodity agreements; least-developed country; transition, economies in.

development areas ►assisted areas.

development economics ►economic development.

differentiation, product Distinguishing essentially the same products from one another by real or illusory means, as in petrol, washing powder, cigarettes. The significance of product differentiation in economic theory is that by relaxing the assumption of product homogeneity under ►perfect competition, each supplier may create an opportunity to depart from the market price, charge a premium for his product and make greater ►profits. Under perfect competition this supplier would sell nothing if he raised the price above market levels (he faces a horizontal ►demand curve); with product differentiation he may be able to build up some loyalty from his customers (and introduce a downward slope to the demand curve, which is a characteristic of ►monopolistic competition). The means by which suppliers differentiate their products may involve improved product performance and ►innovation, for example, radial-ply tyres which though more expensive initially than conventional tyres have a longer life, or they may be restricted to ►advertising and packaging. In business economics, differentiation is seen as one of two important strategic directions, the other being leadership through volume sales and low cost.

diminishing marginal product ►diminishing returns, law of.

diminishing marginal utility The psychological law that as extra units of a commodity are consumed by an individual, the satisfaction gained from each unit will fall. For example, although for every extra Mars bar someone eats they derive extra pleasure, the more Mars that are eaten, the less the pleasure gained from each incremental one. Eventually, as sickness strikes, subsequently consumed Mars bars will yield disutility.

The approach to consumer theory which uses the notion of diminishing marginal utility is flawed, as there is no single unit or scale by which the utility derived from a wide range of items can be measured (►►ordinal utility). Nevertheless, the concept remains relevant to many issues, especially when applied to consumption in general. For example, it provides a case against a poll tax (►local taxation) which, it shows, cuts the utility of the poor (who treasure their every possession) more than the rich (who hardly notice small losses). It also explains why people may like to avoid risk: the utility lost from a £100 cut in income is greater than the utility gained by a £100 increase in income and, consequently, most consumers would reject a fair bet in which they were faced with a 50 per cent chance of either, despite the fact that on average they would lose nothing in cash terms. ►►marginal utility; risk aversion; endogenous preferences.

diminishing returns, law of A law that states that as extra units of one ►factor of production are employed, with all others held constant, the output generated by each additional unit will eventually fall. In effect, that the ►marginal product of factors declines when they are employed in increasing quantities. For example, a farm owner with one field might find that one man could produce two tons of grain; two men five tons of grain – more than twice as much; but three men only seven tons of grain. The extra production gained from adding a worker started at two, rose to three, then fell back to two.

Diminishing returns should not be confused with negative returns. Successively adding workers to a factory can increase its total output but at a falling rate; only when the factory becomes very overcrowded would the presence of an extra worker actually cause production to fall. ➤➤diseconomies of scale; returns to scale; short-run cost curves; Turgot, A. R. J.

direct costs ➤variable costs.

direct investment ➤Investment in the foreign operations of a company through acquisition of a foreign operation, or establishment of a new ('greenfield') site. It is often referred to as foreign direct investment (FDI). Direct investment implies control and managerial and perhaps technical input and is generally preferred by the host country to ➤portfolio investment. After falling in the early 1990s, the total world flow of foreign direct investment has grown from about US$153 billion in 1992 to US$315 billion in 1995. Moreover, this investment has been a major source of finance for the ➤developing countries at a time when ➤foreign aid has fallen. Foreign direct investment into the developing countries doubled between 1992 and 1995 to US$100 billion. ➤➤foreign investment; multinational corporation; globalization.

direct taxation ➤Taxation on the income and resources of individuals or organizations. In general, direct taxation (➤income tax, corporation tax, inheritance tax, local taxation; National Insurance contributions) is levied on ➤wealth or ➤income and is in contrast to *indirect taxation* (➤value-added tax, ➤excise duties, betting duties, vehicle-licence duties, ➤stamp duty) which is levied on expenditure. Direct taxation accounts for over two-thirds of UK general government tax receipts. It was argued that a shift in favour of indirect taxation would improve incentives for higher earnings and capital accumulation; however, that process, which occurred substantially in the UK in the 1980s and 1990s, can make the tax system more regressive (➤regressive tax) and may also distort ➤resource allocation. The categorization of direct and indirect taxation is not as precise as it may appear because it tells us nothing about the incidence of taxation (➤taxation, incidence of). ➤➤expenditure tax; fiscal neutrality; marginal tax rate.

Directives of the European Union Legislation of the ➤European Union. Directives can be aimed at one or more members of the Community and are not effective until they are passed into the national law of the member state to which they are addressed. Directives, therefore, differ from Regulations which are imposed directly on to all member states and do not require further legislation. ➤➤Banking Acts; company law; Investment Services Directive.

dirty float ➤managed currency.

disclosure requirements ➤private company.

discount Generally meaning a deduction from ➤face value, i.e. the opposite of ➤premium. Discount has a number of specific applications in economics and commerce: (a) A *discount for cash* is a percentage deductible from an invoice as an incentive for the debtor to pay within a defined period. (b) A deduction from the retail price of a good allowed to a wholesaler, retailer or other agent. (c) A charge made for cashing a ►bill of exchange or other promissory note before its maturity date (►discount house; factor). (d) The difference, where negative, between the present price of a ►security and its issue price. ►►discounting; present value.

discount house 1. An institution in the London ►discount market that purchases promissory notes and resells them or holds them until maturity. Essentially a ►bill broker. The discount houses finance their purchases of securities mainly by borrowing at short term from banks and other financial institutions. These borrowings are secured against their holdings of securities. From March 1997, on a phased basis, the term *discount house* will cease to be used and the present institutions bearing that name will become banks or other ►financial intermediaries. Discount houses, as separately capitalized and regulated institutions will no longer exist. These changes result from the new policy of the ►Bank of England to influence interest rates via ►gilt repos. (►lender of last resort.) 2. A 'cut-price' retail store selling goods at a ►discount.

discount market The market dealing in ►treasury bills, ►bills of exchange and short-dated ►bonds and consisting of the ►banking system, the ►accepting houses and the ►discount houses. Although the existence of discount houses as such will cease in the City of London, a ►money market of some kind is a feature of all financial centres. The discount houses originally dealt mainly in bills of exchange accepted by the ►merchant banks, but over half of their assets now consist of government (including local government) securities, and negotiable ►certificates of deposit. The discount houses purchase these securities from the government and the ►private sector with ►money borrowed from the banking system, including overseas banks in London, and to a lesser extent from industrial and commercial companies, supplemented by their own ►capital. Their profit is made by borrowing at very short term (normally twenty-four-hour call-loans) and lending by ►discounting securities at slightly higher ►rates of interest. In this way the discount houses take up the surplus ►liquidity of the banking system and lend it to the government and those issuing bills of exchange. The discount houses retain some bills to maturity; others are sold to the banking system as they near maturity. The discount houses perform a useful function in providing a flexible and smooth ►market in short-term securities, and used to play an important part in the mechanism by which the authorities exert control over the monetary system. ►discount.

discount rate ►bank rate; discounting.

discounted cash flow (**d.c.f.**) ►present value.

discounting 1. The application of a discount or ►rate of interest to a ►capital sum or title to such a sum. Calculations of ►present value or the price of a bill before maturity are made by discounting at the current appropriate rate of interest. 2. The future effects of an anticipated decline or increase in ►profits or some other event on ▸security prices, commodity prices, or ▸exchange rates. These are said to be discounted if buying or selling leads to an adjustment of present prices in line with expected future changes in these prices. **3**. (US) The pledging of accounts receivable, i.e. sums owed by debtors, as ▸collateral security against a ▸loan. ▸▸discount.

discriminating duty An import duty (▸tariffs, import) imposed at a level different from other comparable import duties such as to favour (or discourage) the importation of a particular commodity or imports from a particular country of origin. ▸▸customs union; General Agreement on Tariffs and Trade; most-favoured nation clause.

discriminating monopoly A company with some degree of ▸market power, and able to charge different prices for its output in the different markets. ▸▸price discrimination.

diseconomies of scale Increase in long-run ▸average costs which may set in as the scale of production increases. Although the unit cost of production may fall as plant size increases (▸economies of scale), there are several reasons why this process is eventually reversed:
(a) The different processes within a plant will probably not have the same ▸optimum scale. For example, a car-body press might be at its most efficient at 150,000 units a year, while an engine transfer machining line may be optimal at 100,000 units a year. When 150,000 cars are produced it will be necessary either to have a suboptimal engine line with a capacity of 50,000 in addition or to run a second line at 50 per cent capacity.
(b) As firm size increases, problems of administration and coordination increase and there is a growth of bureaucracy.
(c) If output for a national or international market is concentrated at one large plant in a single location, transport costs of raw materials and finished goods to and from distant markets may offset scale economies of production at the large plant.
    These are *internal diseconomies*. *External diseconomies* are said to arise as a geographic region sees larger-scale production – these might include traffic congestion or pollution, for example (▸externalities). Diseconomies of scale are not to be confused with diminishing returns (▸diminishing returns, law of). ▸▸returns to scale.

disequilibrium A state in which the forces influencing a system are not in balance and there is a tendency for one or more ▸variables in the system to change. The operation of some mechanism or process is central to the concept of disequilibrium, as it is this that drives the system variables to move. The direction of movement caused by a process in most applications is towards a state of equilibrium, but this need not be the case. The ▸cobweb model provides an example of a mechanism that can take either form. ▸▸dynamics; equilibrium; stability analysis.

disguised unemployment A situation in which more people are available for work than is shown in the ➤unemployment statistics. Married women, some students or prematurely retired persons may register for work only if they believe opportunities are available to them. Also referred to as *concealed unemployment* and the 'discouraged worker effect'. Disguised unemployment will be revealed in an unusually low ➤participation rate. In some countries, for example the USA, unemployment is measured by surveys rather than numbers registered as available for work (unemployed) as in the UK, and this term is less relevant. ➤➤claimant count; Labour Force Survey.

dishoarding The reduction of stocks of goods or money previously accumulated by ➤hoarding.

disinflation The reduction or elimination of ➤inflation. ➤➤deflation.

disintermediation Flows of funds between borrowers and lenders avoiding the direct use of ➤financial intermediaries. Companies, for example, may lend surplus funds to each other without the use of the banking system or may issue bills guaranteed (accepted) by the banks but sold to non-banks. Disintermediation may make it more difficult to measure and control the ➤money supply since the authorities' measures to do so are focused upon financial intermediaries which can avoid controls based upon deposits by lending through ➤parallel money markets (➤special deposits). The use of financial intermediaries for lending and borrowing activities previously carried out outside them, i.e. the opposite of disintermediation, is called *re-intermediation*. ➤➤securitization.

disinvestment Negative investment which occurs where part of the capital stock is destroyed or where gross ➤investment is less than ➤capital consumption, i.e. capital equipment is not replaced as it wears out. Antonym for investment. ➤➤divestment.

disposable income Total ➤income of households less ➤income tax and employee ➤National Insurance contributions.

dissaving Negative ➤saving, i.e. ➤consumption in excess of ➤income. Dissaving is financed either by the running down of ➤assets or by borrowing, and results in a reduction in *net worth*. ➤balance sheet; ➤➤public-sector financial deficit.

distribution, theory of Explanation of the determination of the ➤incomes of the ➤factors of production. The theory of distribution is actually part of the more comprehensive theory of production and distribution (➤production, theory of), since in their determination output and factor prices are interdependent. It is one of the oldest branches of economic theory (➤Marx, K.; Ricardo, D.) but today is still dominated by the basic theoretical structure of ➤neo-classical economics. Under this theory, the incomes of ➤land, ➤labour and ➤capital are determined by the ➤supply and ➤demand for them, which in turn is a ➤derived demand for

➤commodities. In the market for the factors of production, the owners of the factors will seek to maximize their incomes and the purchasers (firms) will seek to maximize their ➤profit from the use of the factors in the production process. Firms will adjust their output and their employment of each factor to the point where the ➤marginal cost and ➤marginal revenue of each additional unit of the factor are equal. This equilibrium quantity and equilibrium price will be determined by supply and demand. For instance, shortages of computer programmers will tend to push up their incomes. On the other hand, if there are more programmers than jobs, their wages will fall. The theory does not state, it should be noted, that a computer programmer will receive his marginal product (the amount he personally adds to his employer's revenue), but the increase in output that would arise from the employment of one additional programmer if inputs of all other factors of production were held constant. Profit maximization and competition between them should, in theory, ensure that factor incomes equate to their marginal products. ➤marginal productivity theory of wages. This is how the first part of the theory explains the reward to the factors of production.

The second part of the theory describes the share of total output accruing to different groups, for example the amount going to workers equals the wage rate multiplied by the number of workers employed. When the number of workers increases, the ➤marginal product of labour is assumed to fall and the wage level will fall, but as the total number of workers has risen, the share of output going to labour may not fall.

The third part of the theory holds that with total output divided up in this way between the different groups, there will be nothing short and nothing over. This is, in fact, true in conditions of perfect competition with constant returns to scale or zero profits (➤Euler, L.).

For these reasons, alternative theories to replace each part of the traditional account have been developed. On the first part, wage bargaining is viewed as occurring outside perfectly competitive markets with collective bargaining by trade unions. On the second part, shares of national income have been explained in terms of the distribution necessary to maintain ➤balanced growth in a macroeconomic approach associated with ➤Kaldor. On the third part, the existence of monopoly profits suggests that some portion of total output does not accrue to workers, investors or property owners, but to those fortunate enough to be in monopoly industries. ➤bargaining theory of wages ➤➤Cobb–Douglas function.

diversification 1. Extending the range of goods and services in a firm or geographic region. The motives for diversification will include declining profitability or growth in traditional markets, surplus capital or management resources and a desire to spread risks and reduce dependence upon cyclical activities. Diversification has accounted for a significant proportion of the growth of ➤multinational corporations, though more recently competitive pressures have encouraged large corporations to return to core businesses and dispose of unwanted subsidiaries. This process has been called ►downsizing (US) or ►divestment. The means of diversification are either internal growth or ►merger. By definition a ►conglomerate is a diversified firm. **2.** The holding of shares in a range of firms in a ►portfolio in order to spread the risk. ►►capital asset pricing model; portfolio theory; risk.

divestment The liquidation or sale of parts of a firm. Divestment is, in effect, the opposite of acquisition or ►merger.

dividend The amount of a company's ►profits that the board of directors decides to distribute to ordinary shareholders. It is usually expressed either as a percentage of the ►nominal value of the ►ordinary share capital, or as an absolute amount per ►share. For example, if a company has an issued ►capital of £100,000 in 400,000 25p ordinary shares and the directors decide to distribute £10,000, then they would declare a dividend of 10 per cent or 2½p per share. A dividend is only the same as a ►yield if the shares stand at their nominal value. Some shareholders may not have bought their shares at ►par value and might have paid, say, 50p each for them, in which case the yield would not be 10 but 5 per cent.

Dividends are declared at general meetings of the shareholders. Interim dividends are part payments of the annual dividend made during the year. Dividends are paid out of profits for the current year or, if profits are inadequate but the directors consider that a dividend is justified, out of reserves from profits of previous years. The profits after tax from which dividends are paid are those after payments to holders of ►preference shares and ►debentures have been allowed for, the balance being split between dividends and reserves.

There has been much discussion of whether the rate of ►investment could be raised if companies paid out fewer dividends, as that would leave more cash to invest.

dividend cover The number of times the net ►profits available for distribution exceed the ►dividend actually paid or declared. For example, if a company's net profits are £100,000 and the dividend was £5000, the dividend cover would be 20. It is the inverse of the payout ratio.

dividend warrant The ►cheque by which companies pay ►dividends to shareholders.

dividend yield ►yield.

divisia money ►money supply.

division of labour The allocation of labour such that each worker specializes in one or a few functions in the production process. ►Adam Smith illustrated the principle in the different stages of pin-making: drawing the wire, cutting, head-fitting, sharpening. The division improved labour productivity (a) by the more efficient acquiring of specialist skills and (b) through the saving of time because workers did not have to move from one operation to another. Through the division of labour ➤economies of scale could be achieved. The exchange economy was essential to its operation. Each worker could so specialize as long as he was assured that he could exchange his output for others to satisfy his needs. The principle applies to firms and countries also: similar benefits may be achieved by the specialization in those activities in which the firm or country has a ➤comparative advantage. ➤➤Ricardo, D.

dollar certificate of deposit ➤Eurocurrency.

domestic credit expansion (DCE) A measure of monetary growth that allows for changes in the ➤balance of payments. It is equal to the ➤public-sector borrowing requirement minus public-sector borrowing from the domestic non-bank private sector plus the increase in bank lending to the private sector in domestic currency at home and overseas. The significance of the DCE, a measure favoured by the ➤International Monetary Fund, is that it nets out changes in the ➤money supply created by overseas capital flows on capital and current account of the balance of payments. ➤➤monetary policy.

dominant strategy A course of action that is best pursued whatever it is that other agents choose to do. It is a concept of ➤game theory, applied to situations in which players choose from a selection of strategies, taking into account the response and behaviour of fellow players. The best-known dominant strategy is to 'confess' in the ➤prisoner's dilemma game. The strategy to 'not confess' is *dominated*. In most situations, there are no dominant or dominated strategies; the best strategy will depend on what the other side chooses to do. ➤➤tit-for-tat.

dominated strategy A course of action which would not make sense whatever other agents chose to do. ➤➤dominant strategy.

double deflation ➤deflation.

double-entry bookkeeping The accounting system in which every business transaction, whether a receipt or a payment of ➤money, sale or purchase of goods or ➤services, gives rise to two entries, a debit and a corresponding credit, traditionally on opposite pages of a ledger. The credit entries record the sources of finance, e.g. shareholders' ➤capital, funds acquired from third parties or generated through current operations; the debit entries record the use to which that finance is put, e.g. acquisition of fixed ➤assets, ➤stocks, financing of debtors and current operating expenses, etc. Since every debit entry has an equal and corresponding credit entry, it follows that if the debit and credit entries are added up they will (or should) come to the same figure, i.e. balance (➤balance sheet). Confusion is caused by identifying credits and debits with gains or losses. While this is basically true in the very long run, the profit or loss over a short period of time is measured by selecting from ledger balances items of income and expenditure which are then used to produce a *profit-and-loss account* (US *income and earned surplus statement*). ➤➤business finance; balance of payments.

double option ►option.

double taxation The situation in which the same ►tax base is taxed more than once. Double-taxation agreements between two countries are designed to avoid, for example, ►incomes of non-residents being taxed both in the country they are living in and in their country of origin. Many proponents of an ►expenditure tax argue that its main advantage is to avoid double taxation of savings.

Dow–Jones Industrial average A daily index (►index number) of prices on the principal ►stock exchange in New York. It is an ►average of the prices of thirty industrial stocks accounting for about 25 per cent of the market ►capitilization of the shares quoted on the New York Stock Exchange and is calculated and published every day the exchange is open. In its present form the index dates from 1928.

downsizing Large-scale shedding of employees by major corporations, sometimes also used to refer to the disposal of subsidiaries and other unwanted activities. Downsizing is generally a response to pressures from competition, or investors, to reduce costs and may in some cases reflect long-delayed reaction to technological change which allows output to be maintained with fewer employees. In a dynamic and changing economy some firms will be reducing and others gaining employment, but redundancies by large firms attract more attention than widespread employment gains among smaller firms. Downsizing in the USA – for example, an announcement by AT & T in 1996 that it would reduce its employment by 40,000 persons over a period of time – has created concern and a sense of insecurity on the part of many employees. Over the past decade, however, US employment has risen substantially and studies suggest that the average length of job tenure has changed little. Critics point out that the quality of jobs lost in large corporations, in terms of salaries, pensions and other benefits, is superior to that in employment gained in smaller firms, but this might suggest the existence of ►economic rent.

drawback ►customs drawback.

duality An area of mathematics, sometimes used in economics, in which essentially the same optimization problem can be framed in two different ways. For example, the problem of maximizing ►utility given prices and income can also be seen as a problem of minimizing the cost of obtaining the level of utility that would be achieved. This can be useful for the economist trying to observe consumer behaviour, if the cost-minimizing problem is easier to frame than the utility-maximizing one. ►►envelope theorem.

dummy variable A variable in ►regression analysis that takes a value of one or zero depending on whether some particular characteristic applies to the observation. For example, in a regression that measured the relationship between weight and height, there might be a sex dummy which takes a value of one for men, and zero for women. This would take account of the possible fact that on average a man of the same height as a woman may weigh more.

dumping Strictly, the sale of a ➤commodity on a foreign ➤market at a ➤price below ➤marginal cost. An exporting country may support the short-run losses of this policy in order to eliminate competition and thereby gain a ➤monopoly in the foreign market. Alternatively, it may dump in order to dispose of temporary surpluses in order to avoid a reduction in home prices and therefore producers' ➤incomes. The ➤General Agreements on Tariffs and Trade approves the imposition of special import duties (➤tariffs, import) to counteract such a policy if it can be established that dumping is taking place and is harming a domestic industry. Under GATT regulations if products are sold in a foreign market below the price at which they are sold on the home market, dumping is deemed to take place. The practice of dumping is prohibited under the terms of the ➤European Union's Treaty of Rome. Rules to be followed by governments were agreed as part of the GATT Kennedy round of trade negotiations concluded in 1967 by the European Union, North America and the ➤European Free Trade Association. The review of the rules for determining anti-dumping measures was also part of the negotiations of the ➤Uruguay round of trade negotiations. Market economies are more open to the making of comparisons of the prices and input costs of products in different markets in order to judge whether dumping is taking place. For planned economies, the EU compares the price of the product exported with that produced in a free-market non-EU country in order to decide whether the product is being dumped. If such a free-market price cannot be found, the EU judges a fair price on the basis of its own calculations of the costs of production. In the USA, the government must obtain the approval of the ➤International Trade Commission before imposing anti-dumping duties on an import and decisions may be overruled by the US Court of International Trade. ➤➤contingent protection; protection; free trade; reciprocity.

duopoly Two sellers only of a good or service in a market. A feature of this situation is that any decision by one seller, such as the raising or lowering of his price, will stimulate a response from the other which, in turn, will affect the market response to the first seller's initial decision. Depending on assumptions made about the market and each seller's responses, price ➤equilibrium may exist at any point between that of a ➤monopolist and that of ➤perfect competition (➤Cournot, A. A.; Bertrand competition). ➤➤game theory; oligopoly.

duopsony Two buyers only of a good or service in a market.

Dupuit, Arsène Jules Étienne Juvénal (1804–66) A French civil engineer, whose main works relating to economics were *De la mesure de l'utilité des travaux publics* (1844) and *De l'influence des péages sur l'utilité des voies de communication* (1849). His studies of the pricing policy for public services such as roads and bridges led him to the concepts of ➤consumer surplus and ➤producer's surplus. These terms were, in fact, invented by ➤Marshall, but the ideas were clearly brought out by Dupuit. He realized that the prices were not the maximum users would be willing to pay for services, except those users at the very margin who found it just worth while to pay. Consumers, therefore, benefited by the difference. Similarly, the producer selling the service obtains a surplus in so far as his fixed charge is related to his cost at the margin (►marginal cost) and this is greater than his ►average cost.

durable goods Consumer goods like washing-machines, motor cars and TV sets, which yield ►services or ►utility over time rather than being completely used up at the moment of ►consumption. Most consumer goods are in fact durable to some degree, and the term is often used in a more restricted sense to denote relatively expensive, technologically sophisticated goods – 'consumer durables' – such as the examples given above. The significance of the durability of these goods is that the conventional apparatus of demand analysis must be supplemented by the modes of analysis developed in ►capital theory (►demand, theory of).

dynamic peg ►exchange rate.

dynamics Analysis which aims to trace and study the behaviour of variables through time, and determine whether these variables tend to move towards ►equilibrium. Although the word 'dynamic' is used rather loosely, it safely describes any analysis which gives an account of the process by which equilibrium is achieved, or disequilibrium sustained. An example of dynamic analysis is ►optimal-growth theory, which traces the path an economy should follow to maximize the ►present value of consumption over time. In contrast to ►comparative static equilibrium analysis, dynamics does not just specify the conditions that prevail when the economy is in equilibrium, or whether it is in a satisfactory equilibrium or unsatisfactory one. It traces the optimal path towards an equilibrium.

E

earnings 1. The return for human effort, as in the earnings of ➤labour and the earnings of management. In labour economics, wage earnings are distinguished from wage rates; the former include overtime, the latter relate only to earnings per hour or standard working week. Earnings may be quoted as pre- or post-tax (gross or net) and other deductions and in ➤real terms or money terms. 2. The ➤income of a business, part of which may be retained in the business and part distributed to the shareholders (➤retained earnings). Earnings per ➤share (post-tax), which is a measure of the total return earned by a company on its ➤ordinary share capital, are calculated by taking gross income after ➤depreciation, ➤interest, ➤preference shares and minority interests, deducting tax and dividing the resulting figure by the number of ordinary shares. Note that earnings per share are normally higher than the ➤dividend per share. For example, a firm may earn 10p per share but may only pay a 5p or 20 per cent dividend on its 25p ordinary shares.

earnings yield ➤yield.

EASDAQ ➤European Association of Securities Dealers Automated Quotation System.

East African Community ➤Lomé Convention.

ECA ➤Economic Cooperation Administration.

ECGD ➤Export Credits Guarantee Department.

econometric models The representation of a relationship between economic variables as an equation or set of equations in which statistical precision can be attributed to the ➤parameters linking the variables. ➤➤econometrics; model.

econometrics The setting up of mathematical ➤models describing economic relationships (such as that the quantity demanded of a good is dependent positively on income and negatively on price), testing the validity of such hypotheses (➤statistical inference) and estimating the ➤parameters in order to obtain a measure of the strengths of the influences of the different independent ➤variables. Econometricians most commonly use the techniques of ➤regression analysis (➤➤least-squares regression), in which the relationship between a ➤dependent variable and an ➤independent variable is analysed, based on the ➤correlation in the variation of the two. The more they move together, the more likely it is there is a relationship between them. If the variation analysed is variation over time, then it is referred to as ►time-series analysis; if the variation is across a sample of different subjects, it is known as ►cross-section analysis. Sets of such models are used to make ►macroeconomic forecasts (e.g. by the UK ►Treasury). Although econometrics has dominated all ►empirical testing in economics, it has nevertheless had its critics, who point to problems in interpreting causation between variables that are correlated; and in separating out statistical fluke from underlying cause (►data-mining; confidence interval). ►►Frisch, R. A. K.

economic activity rate ►participation rate.

Economic Community of West African States (ECOWAS) The sixteen members of ECOWAS agreed, by the Treaty of Lagos in 1975, to develop a ►customs union, and in 1981, at Freetown, Sierra Leone, concluded a plan for the elimination of trade restrictions. The Treaty was revised in 1993. The aim is for the gradual elimination of all barriers to trade in goods and services, the free movement of people between member states and the improvement in inter-regional transport and telecommunications. A Fund for Cooperation, Compensation and Development has been established to finance projects and to compensate for losses derived from the implementation of the Treaty. A Secretariat operates from Abuja, Nigeria. ►►Lomé Convention.

Economic Cooperation Administration (ECA) An authority for transmitting US funds overseas. An Act for the appropriation of $6098m. for foreign aid was signed by President Truman in 1948 and the ECA was set up under Paul G. Hoffman, President of the Studebaker Corporation, to administer the fund. Under the programme the UK received $2694m. The ECA was superseded by the *Mutual Security Agency* in 1951, the *Foreign Operations Administration* in 1953 and the *International Cooperation Administration* in 1955. ►►European Recovery Programme.

economic development The growth of ►national income per capita of ►developing countries. Such countries need to generate sufficient ►saving and ►investment in order to diversify their economies from agriculture to industry, with the necessary supporting infrastructure such as roads and seaports (►►economic growth, stages of). In recent years, several countries primarily considered to be in the developing stage, notably Singapore and Hong Kong, have overtaken some western economies in per capita ►GDP. But for remaining developing countries, especially in Africa, problems remain severe. Growth has been constrained because of a fall in their export prices compared with the prices they have been able to obtain for their imports; and at the same time, developing countries have experienced a rapid growth in ►population. As a result their ►balance of payments has run into substantial deficit on current account and a high burden of debt financing has been incurred. Loans and grants are channelled to developing countries through such institutions as the ►International Bank for Reconstruction and Development, the ►International Finance Corporation and the ►International Development

Association. The theory and practice of *development economics* which deals with the problem of growth in developing countries, has undergone considerable change in recent years. On the theoretical side the relevance of ►neo-classical economics to developing countries has been questioned and there has been increasing emphasis upon institutions (►institutional economics) and controversy about the role of government. In the practice of donor agencies, early emphasis on the need to promote large-scale industry has given way to ►►deregulation, sound ►public finance, education (►sow's ear effect) and the promotion of ►small business (►convergence; emerging markets; endogenous growth theory; transition, economies in).

economic doctrines Sets of beliefs about how economies function and their corresponding policy implications. The most interesting modern means of truly defining different mainstream doctrines, is in their view of the importance of ►aggregate demand in determining output and employment in the economy, and in whether policy to influence demand has any effect (►policy ineffectiveness theorem). (a) ►classical economics was not much concerned with macroeconomics, but generally held ►Say's law, that anything supplied would create a demand – as the earnings paid to the supplier would be spent, equating overall demand and supply. Investment and saving would be equated, through the interest rate. Almost by assumption, therefore, the economy was in ►equilibrium. (b) Keynesian disequilibrium economics (►►Keynesian economics; quantity rationing) holds that the economy can get stuck in ►disequilibrium as the overall level of saving may not be absorbed by the level of investment, and hence not all output will necessarily be bought by anyone; hence government *can* influence the economy by increasing demand, most effectively by borrowing (►►fiscal policy). (c) Neo-Keynesian/ ►neo-classical economics holds that the Keynesian view is broadly right in the short term, but that over long periods of time, the economy *did* have a natural tendency to find an equilibrium. Policy could be effective in the medium term. (d) Monetarist economics (►►monetarism; quantity theory of money) holds that it is money, rather than aggregate demand which matters, and that policies to increase demand using money-supply growth would only be effective in the short term, and then at the cost of increasing rates of inflation. (e) ►New classical economics holds that policy won't even work in the short run if private agents anticipate its effect. A policy to increase money supply will simply increase prices immediately if agents spot it coming, and have ►rational expectations. ►New Keynesians revert to the idea that anticipated policy can have short- to medium-term effects, on the grounds that prices are sticky, and therefore that equilibrium is not immediately restored after a shock, by a change in prices.

The doctrines also fall into categories dependent on how far they use the analysis of ►microeconomics. Classical economists almost only used microeconomic analysis; the Keynesians, and indeed the monetarists, almost only use ►macroeconomics in their analysis. Neo-classicists blend the two, while the new classical and new

Keynesian economists have attempted microeconomic rationales for all their macroeconomic findings.

economic efficiency The state of an economy in which no one can be made better off without someone being made worse off. For this to be the case, three types of efficiency must hold. The first is *productive efficiency*, in which the output of the economy is being produced at the lowest cost. The second is *allocative efficiency*, in which resources are being allocated to the production of the goods and services the society most values. The third is *distributional efficiency*, in which output is distributed in such a way that consumers would not wish, given their ▸disposable income and market ▸prices, to spend these incomes in any different way.

In a two-person, two-product economy with two factors of production, these three types of efficiency are achieved when three conditions hold: productive efficiency demands that the ▸rate of technical substitution for the two products must be equal, to ensure a unit of one factor of production is worth the same amount in terms of the other factor whichever product it is used in. Otherwise, factors could be swapped between products and extra output gained. Second, that the ▸marginal rate of substitution must be equal for both consumers; otherwise, the consumers could swap commodities to their mutual benefit. Third, allocative efficiency requires that the marginal rate of transformation must equal the marginal rate of substitution: if consumers feel one banana is worth two apples, and producers can make one extra banana at the sacrifice of only one apple, it will pay society for them to produce one apple less and one extra banana, and to go on making that switch, until eventually consumers tire of bananas and value apples more highly than they did; and land suitable for banana production will be so marginal that for every bit of land removed from apples, hardly any bananas will be produced. At this stage, the two rates of substitution will be equal.

Economic efficiency on these criteria will exist in an economy in which perfect competition characterizes every sector. ▸▸compensation principle; marginal-cost pricing; Pareto, V. F. D.; perfect competition; price system; Ricardo, D.; welfare economics.

economic good Any physical object, natural or man-made, or service rendered, which could command a price in a market.

economic growth The increase in a country's ▸national income, or sometimes, its per capita national income. Growth is taken as the basis of advancing human welfare, although in fact there are problems in the measurement of national income (some activities – such as do-it-yourself car maintenance rather than buying the services of a garage mechanic, or transactions in the ▸black economy – may not take place in a ▸market, or not in a market for which statistics are collected). Moreover, growth in national income should not be equated necessarily with growth in welfare (▸▸welfare economics, environmental accounting). The processes of growth, such as industrialization, the expansion of the motorway network, the construction of airports, yield disbenefits such as pollution, noise and the destruction of countryside amenity, all of which are costs that are not subtracted from the statistical measures of the national income. Nevertheless, explaining the factors behind economic growth, in order that more of it can be generated, is an important area of economics (►growth theory). Most important is not the growth associated with the ►business cycle, which tends to vary to some extent with ►aggregate demand, but instead ►trend growth, or the growth in the long-term productive potential of the economy. The dominant interest in growth theory is the degree to which the accumulation of ►capital through ►investment explains economic performance. Clearly, more capital, like more of any ►input, should lead to more output (eventually). But does it lead to enough output to justify the sacrifice of saving for it? And how much extra output does it yield? ►endogenous growth theory. ►►economic development; economic growth, stages of.

economic growth, stages of The five stages of economic growth through which all economies are considered to pass in their development from fairly poor agricultural societies to highly industrialized mass-consumption economies. These five stages were defined and analysed by ►Rostow in his book *The Stages of Economic Growth*, namely:
(a) The traditional society, in which adherence to long-lived economic and social systems and customs means that output per head is low and tends not to rise.
(b) The stage of the establishment of the pre-conditions for 'take-off' (see (c)). This stage is a period of transition, in which the traditional systems are overcome, and the economy is made capable of exploiting the fruits of modern science and technology.
(c) The take-off stage. 'Take-off' represents the point at which the 'old blocks and the resistances to steady growth are finally overcome', and growth becomes the normal condition of the economy. The economy begins to generate its own ►investment and technological improvement at sufficiently high rates so as to make growth virtually self-sustaining.
(d) The 'drive to maturity', which is the stage of increasing sophistication of the economy. Against the background of steady growth, new industries are developed, there is less reliance on ►imports and more exporting activity, and the economy 'demonstrates' its capacity to move beyond the original industries which powered its take-off, and to absorb and to apply efficiently the most advanced fruits of modern technology.
(e) The fourth stage ends in the attainment of the fifth stage, which is the age of high mass consumption, where there is an affluent population and durable and sophisticated consumer goods (►economic good) and ►services are the leading sectors of production.

As a broad and imaginative description of the process of economic growth, this characterization of the stages of growth is interesting and possibly useful, having much the same flavour as ►Marx's famous theory of the evolution of society from economic rent

feudalism to bourgeois ➤capitalism and finally to communism. It also leads directly to a policy conclusion which was already favoured by many: aid should be given to the economies at the pre-take-off stages, in an attempt to get them to the take-off stage. Once this is achieved, these economies will have their own dynamic and momentum, and hence aid becomes much less necessary. The theory has had only limited impact among professional economists concerned with the problem of ➤economic development. Partly this is because Rostow's analysis of exactly what factors were responsible for take-off and subsequent self-generating growth tended to be vague, ambiguous and incomplete. Also the theory is framed in such general terms that it can be made consistent with virtually any past growth situation. Partly also perhaps, the broad sweep of the historian's vision, with the implication of the inexorability of the historical processes, is not of very much help in trying to solve the particular development problems of particular economies. ➤➤economic growth.

economic history The study of the subject matter of economics in a historical context. Economic history was originally part of political economy, the antecedent of modern ➤economics, and taught in faculties of history and moral philosophy In the late nineteenth century economic history began to separate off from history and economics and is now a more or less distinct discipline. The first chair in economic history was established at Harvard in 1892 and occupied by an Englishman, William Ashley. A chair at Manchester in Britain followed in 1910, the first incumbent being George Unwin. ➤cliometrics.

economic imperialism The exploitation of ➤developing countries by ➤advanced countries. ➤Marx held that the capitalist classes were inexorably driven to overseas economic expansion by falling profit opportunities at home. The export of high ➤value-added goods and the import of raw materials developed with exported capital buttressed by ➤tariffs and other restrictions on imports of cheap manufactured goods, such as textiles, are the continuing essential features of economic imperialism even after the granting of political independence, according to critics of advanced countries.

economic rent The difference between the return made by a factor of production and the return necessary to keep the factor in its current occupation. Examples of economic rent: (a) For a brain surgeon earning £60,000 whose only other possible occupation is nursing on £6000, the economic rent is £54,000. The surgeon would remain in his current job even if it paid only £6100. (b) A firm making excess profits (➤profits) is earning economic rent.

In ➤perfect competition, no rents are made by any factor, because changes in supply bid prices of inputs and labour down to the level just necessary to keep them employed. In general, economic rents accrue where changes in supply of this sort are not possible: to a brain surgeon with rare skills, difficult to emulate; or to a ➤monopoly protected by ➤barriers to entry. True economic rents are among the few returns that can be taxed (►taxation) without distorting production decisions. ►►quasi-rent.

economic sanction A measure, taken in respect of some economic activity, which has the intention of damaging another country's economy. Examples would be a complete embargo on trade between countries, or refusal to permit ►bank deposits held in the country imposing the sanction to be drawn upon by the government and residents of another. Examples are the banning by the USA of exports of grain to the USSR following the Afghan crisis, the embargo on trade with Argentina imposed by the EC at the time of the UK conflict with Argentina; the ban placed by the United Nations on foreign trade with Iraq following the latter's invasion of Kuwait in 1990; and sanctions imposed by the United Nations in 1992 on Libya for its failure to extradite suspects in the bombing of Pan-Am flight 103 over Scotland.

economics The study of the production, distribution and consumption of wealth in human society. Economists have never been wholly satisfied with any definition of their subject. This one is as good as any. It should not be interpreted to restrict the subject-matter of economics to the positive aspects of material welfare alone. ►Robbins criticized this limitation by pointing out, for example, that the economy of war, which may destroy material welfare, is an aspect of choice in the use of resources and therefore a proper subject for economic inquiry. His definition was: 'Economics is the science which studies human behaviour as a relationship between ends and scarce means which have alternative uses.' In fact, no short definition can convey to the beginner the scope and flavour of the whole subject as it has evolved. The reader will gain a good notion of the scope of economics by examining the coverage of this dictionary, but the borderlines between such other disciplines as psychology, sociology, accounting and geography are not easily defined and it is, perhaps, not particularly productive to attempt to do so. *Political economy*, an early title for the subject, now sounds old-fashioned but usefully emphasizes the importance of choice between alternatives in economics which remains, despite continuing scientific progress, as much of an art as a science. ►economic history.

economies in transition ►transition, economies in.

economies of scale Factors which cause the average cost of producing a commodity to fall as output of the commodity rises. For instance, a firm or industry which would less than double its costs, if it doubled its output, enjoys economies of scale.

There are two types of such economies. The first – called *internal* – accrue to the individual firm regardless of the size of its industry. They generally result from technological factors which ensure the optimal size of production is large: (a) With high fixed costs in plant and machinery, the larger its production, the lower the cost per unit of the fixed inputs. For example, producing steel without a blast furnace is possible but very expensive; once a blast furnace is built, it is inefficient only to make small quantities of steel with it: hence, steel companies tend to be large. (b) Large firms can also arrange for the specialization of labour and machines – as in the techniques of the production line which can increase productivity. (➤Smith, A.) (c) Only large firms can afford the high costs of research and development. Non-technological factors are important, too, however. For example, by buying inputs in bulk, large firms can get discounts from their suppliers (who grant them because of economies of scale in distributing the supplies). There are also economies of scale in ➤business finance.

The second type – *external* economies – arise because the development of an industry can lead to the development of ancillary services of benefit to all firms: a labour force skilled in the crafts of the industry; a components industry equipped to supply precisely the right parts; or a trade magazine in which all firms can advertise cheaply. These can at least partially explain the much observed tendency for firms to cluster geographically more often than would be predicted from random location decisions. ➤industrial districts.

The existence of economies of scale in most industries is used to explain the predominance of large firms in the world economy, but recently there has been some reassessment of the relative importance of technological economies of scale as such. ➤➤diseconomies of scale; economies of scope; minimum efficient scale; returns to scale.

economies of scope Factors which make it cheaper to produce a range of related products than to produce each of the individual products on their own. Economies of scope can provide a base for corporate ➤diversification. ➤➤economies of scale.

Économistes, les ➤Physiocrats.

ECOWAS ➤Economic Community of West African States.

ECSC ➤European Coal and Steel Community.

ECU ➤European Currency Unit.

EDF European Development Fund (➤Lomé Convention).

Edgeworth, Francis Ysidro (1845–1926) Edgeworth held the Chair of Political Economy at Oxford University from 1891 to 1922 and edited the *Economic Journal* from 1891 to 1926. His published work includes *Mathematical Physics* (1881), *Theory of Monopoly* (1897), *Theory of Distribution* (1904) and *Papers Relating to Political Economy* (1925). The last includes the two reports of 1887 and 1889 of the committee on the study of ➤index numbers set up by the British Association for the Advancement of Science, for which Edgeworth acted as secretary. Apart from economics, he made valuable contributions to statistics, and statistical method. In showing the inadequacy of the ➤value theory of ➤W. S. Jevons, Edgeworth invented the analytical tools of ➤indifference curves and ➤contract curves. ➤➤Pareto, V. F. D.

EDX Name given to the UK Cabinet committee charged with agreeing the allocation of the overall ►public expenditure, or more precisely, the ►control total. It meets during the round of spending negotiations between departments and the Treasury, during the autumn.

effective exchange rate The ►exchange rate of a country's currency measured by reference to a ►weighted average of the exchange rates of the currencies of the country's trading partners. The weights are chosen to correspond to the relative importance of each trading partner in the country's domestic as well as overseas markets. The ►International Monetary Fund calculates effective exchange rate indices for a number of countries. The Bank of England publishes indices for sterling with weights based on the currencies of the ►European Union, the US dollar and the Japanese yen. The weights are recalculated from time to time to take into account relative changes in international trade.

efficiency-wage hypothesis The hypothesis that it may benefit employers to pay their workers wages that are higher than their ►marginal revenue product (►marginal productivity theory of wages). The idea behind the theory is that the value of a worker may depend on how much he or she is paid. This may be because richer workers are healthier and more productive, or better motivated, or keener to avoid unemployment. The theory can be used to explain why it is that the ►price system may not work in the ►labour market, and that wages do not get bid down until there is no unemployment. ►►tournament theory.

efficient markets hypothesis The idea that the prices prevailing in a market make it impossible to earn abnormal economic profits by trading in that market on some specified amount of information. The hypothesis is invariably applied to financial markets. Here, it says that if the price of an asset is expected to rise tomorrow, traders, anticipating this, will buy the asset today. This will drive the price of the asset up until it is no longer expected that it will rise further tomorrow. Thus no quick capital gain could be expected to be made. If the market were not efficient, the possibility of making ►arbitrage profits would exist, and a clever trader could make quick speculative gains. ►►capital-asset pricing model; chartist; random walk; rational expectations.

EFTA ►European Free Trade Association.

EFTPOS Electronic funds transfer at a point of sale ►credit card.

EIB ►European Investment Bank.

EIS ►Enterprise Investment Scheme.

elasticity The proportionate change in a ►dependent variable of a ►function, divided by the proportionate change in an ►independent variable at a given value of the independent variable. It is a measure of the sensitivity of one thing, such as demand for a commodity, to another, say the price of it. In practice, you can have elasticities of anything, with respect to anything else (➤cross-price elasticity of demand; elasticity of substitution; income elasticity of demand) and not just in the area of consumer demand theory. Government, for example, estimates the elasticity of its tax revenues with respect to economic growth.

Elasticity, being the product of ratios, is independent of the units in which the variables are measured. The formula is:

$$e = \frac{\% \text{ change in } y}{\% \text{ change in } x}$$

In the case of price elasticity, y would be quantity demanded, and x would be price. One might have observed market behaviour in order to calculate an elasticity; alternatively, it can be derived from an ➤econometric model expressing demand as a ➤function of price in equation form. If an elasticity has an absolute magnitude numerically smaller than unity, the quantity demanded is price inelastic; that means that if the price is increased (marginally) the quantity demanded will not fall proportionately as much and, therefore, the total expenditure on the good will increase. If the good is price elastic, that is, elasticity is numerically greater than unity, demand will be reduced more than price, and therefore, less will be spent on the good than before the price was increased. The term elasticity was invented by ➤Marshall.

elasticity of substitution Roughly speaking, the proportionate change in the relative use of a commodity over the proportionate change in its relative price. It is used to measure the degree to which two commodities can substitute for each other in consumer demand (➤demand, theory of) or in the production of other commodities. If labour and capital are two inputs in the production of something (➤factors of production), we would say they have a high elasticity of substitution if a small increase in the relative price of labour would lead firms to switch in large measure to the use of capital. If the elasticity is zero, the two commodities are used in fixed proportions no matter how expensive one of them becomes. If the elasticity is infinity, the two are perfect substitutes. The formula for the elasticity of substitution between two inputs, x and y, with prices p_1 and p_2 respectively, is

$$\frac{\% \text{ change in } x/y}{\% \text{ change in } p_2/p_1}$$

➤➤technical substitution, rate of.

eligible liabilities ➤credit control.

emerging markets 1. Markets in ➤securities in ➤newly industrialized countries and in countries in Central and Eastern Europe and elsewhere, in transition from ➤planned economies to ➤free-market economies (➤transition, economies in) and in ➤developing countries with ➤capital markets at an early stage of development. Examples are the ►stock exchanges in Mexico, Thailand and Malaysia. **2**. Although originally used to refer to securities markets, the term now commonly refers to the countries themselves. The economies of these countries have been growing rapidly at rates several times greater than those of members of the ►Organization for Economic Cooperation and Development. How this has been achieved and, in particular, what the role of national governments has been in the process is controversial. However, common factors have included high rates of savings, the devotion of considerable resources to education (►sow's ear effect), high levels of ►exports and shifts in the labour force from agriculture to industry and services.

empirical testing Checking theories against facts. In contrast to the physical sciences, it is rarely possible to conduct controlled experiments in economics, for example to see what would happen to exports if the ►exchange rate were reduced and all other variables in the international economy remained unchanged. It is possible, however, to test hypothesis with facts, for example to verify historically the extent to which changes in the exchange rate have been associated with changes in exports (►econometrics). In fact, experiments can be and are carried out in economics, for example laboratory simulations of market behaviour, and there is a growing interest in *experimental economics* as an adjunct to historical empiricism and theoretical work. ►►stylized fact.

Employee Share Ownership Plan (UK), Employee Stock Ownership Plan (US) ►employee share-ownership schemes.

employee share-ownership schemes Schemes to allow employees to acquire ►shares in the company in which they work. These and ►profit-sharing are promoted in some countries by various forms of tax relief, for example the Employee Share Ownership Plan (ESOP) in the UK and Employees Stock Ownership Plan (ESOP) in the USA. Tax relief under the UK Profit Related Pay (PRP) scheme is to be phased out by the year 2000. The effectiveness of these schemes in improving business performance is controversial.

employment, full A situation in which everyone in the ►labour force who is willing to work at the market rate for his type of labour has a job, except for those who are switching from one job to another, i.e. it excludes ►frictional unemployment. Under full employment there is no ►structural unemployment nor any unemployment arising from a deficiency in ►aggregate demand. It does not imply anything about the rate of ►inflation (►labour force; unemployment; unemployment, natural rate of) but the term does normally apply to a situation in which the ►capital stock and the labour force are in balance, i.e. the full employment level of ►gross domestic product is one in which capacity is fully utilized.

EMS ►European Monetary System.

endogenous growth theory A set of economic models and ideas that attempt to explain the rate of ➤economic growth without recourse to the assumption that technological progress is simply given, and cannot be accounted for. Traditional growth models did tend to assume that technology – which they interpreted very widely to include everything from new machines, to a better understanding of efficient production methods or improved marketing techniques – is exogenous (➤exogenous variable); that for all intents and purposes it is predetermined. Models of endogenous growth attempt to explain that technology. The earlier ones simply outlined a more important role for ➤investment – in physical and human capital – than had until then been common. In particular, they questioned the assumption of diminishing returns to investment (➤diminishing returns, law of). As much investment has appeared to be subject to diminishing returns, these models have been superseded by others which have tended to focus far more narrowly on 'knowledge-based' investment in education and in research in particular. They have stressed the need for institutions which nurture innovation, and provide incentives for individuals to be inventive. Indeed, ➤competition policy, industrial relations and the trade regime in place could all be said to be important. In general, these models have supported the conclusion that it may be sensible to subsidize education and research and development. They have also demonstrated that a far wider set of factors can affect growth than was traditionally supposed. But beyond that, they have not yielded a precision sufficient to offer useful prescriptions for policy. ➤sow's ear effect; supply-side economics.

endogenous preferences Consumer tastes that are not fixed as a matter of personal character, but which are to some extent dependent upon the experiences of the consumer. The most clear example of endogenous preferences follow from addiction – obviously an individual's taste for cigarettes is very much affected by whether the individual happens to have smoked many cigarettes or not. Acquired tastes, habits, the desire to justify to oneself one's past consumption – all provide examples of ways in which yesterday's purchase affects our preferences today. The notion is destructive of much traditional economics, because once the assumption of exogenous (➤exogenous variable) preferences is removed, life is far more complicated than normal demand theory (➤demand, theory of) would imply. A cut in the price of a product, may lead to a shift of the demand curve. The notion of ➤diminishing marginal utility may be turned upside down. Unfortunately, it is hard to provide a very constructive and precise theory of endogenous preferences, although study of the subject has fruitfully introduced an element of psychology into economics.

endogenous variable A ➤variable whose value is determined by other variables within a system. The quantity of a good that is demanded is seen as endogenous within the normal framework of demand theory (➤demand, theory of) because it is affected by price, while consumer tastes are not usually seen as endogenous. However, in the real world, it can be argued that almost everything is endogenous eventually. Even the weather – always taken as the prime example of a non-endogenous variable, is said to be affected, through climate change, by economic behaviour. Several recent developments in economics have simply attempted to explain factors that were considered fixed. ➤endogenous growth theory, endogenous preferences; ➤dependent variable; exogenous variable; parameter.

Engel, Ernst (1821–96) ➤Engel's law.

Engel's law A law of economics stating that, with given tastes or preferences, the proportion of income spent on food diminishes as incomes increase. The law was formulated by Ernst Engel, the director of the Bureau of Statistics in Prussia, in a paper published by him in 1857.

enterprise One or more firms under common ownership or control. A term used in the ➤census of production to distinguish the reporting unit (➤establishment) from the firm or unit of control.

Enterprise Investment Scheme A scheme which provides income-tax relief to individuals investing in ➤small business. Qualifying individuals may be a director but not an employee, or control more than 30 per cent of the capital of the firm, and many types of non-manufacturing companies are excluded. EIS was introduced on 1 January 1994 to replace the *Business Expansion Scheme* (BES) and tax relief is given only at 20 per cent rather than at the investor's marginal rate, as under the BES.

enterprise zones (UK) A designated zone in a depressed, generally inner-urban area, in which firms located in the zone are given favourable ➤taxation concessions and freedom from a number of planning constraints. Eleven zones (with a maximum size of about 200 hectares) were adopted when such zones were introduced in Great Britain in 1981. Firms were granted a ten-year exemption from ➤rates and a 100 per cent taxation allowance on new building. The UK government announced in 1989 that no further enterprise zones would be created, by which time twenty-seven had been established.

entrepôt A centre at which goods are received for subsequent distribution. An entrepôt port has facilities for the transhipment of imported goods or their storage prior to their re-export, without the need to pass through customs control. ➤free-trade zone; freeport.

entrepreneur An economic agent who perceives market opportunities and assembles the ➤factors of production to exploit them in a firm. As the prime mover in economic activity the entrepreneur has received attention from the beginnings of economics (for example, by ➤Cantillon and ➤Say) but, as Mark Casson has recently pointed out, he has never been fully integrated into modern economic theory. In the static ➤neo-classical economics of ➤perfect competition there is no place for the entrepreneur since it is assumed that there is perfect information and perfect freedom of entry. After ►Knight the pure function of the entrepreneur is to deal with uncertainty in the dynamic, imperfect, real world in which ►profit is a return to uncertainty and entrepreneurship is inseparable from control of the firm in which he operates. The essence of the entrepreneur, therefore, is that he is alert to gaps in the market which others do not see and is able to raise the finance and other resources required by a firm to exploit the market that he initiates. If successful he will make a super-normal ►profit that will later reduce to a normal profit as new competitors are attracted into the market. In this conception, the pure function of the entrepreneur is as a fourth factor of production. Other functions than risk-taking have been attributed by economists to the entrepreneur: invention, the provision of ►risk capital and management, for example. Though not part of the pure entrepreneurial function which is remunerated by profit, all these functions may be embodied in the owner–manager of a ►small business. His remuneration may be made up of ►rent as an owner of ►land, ►interest as a return on ►capital, a wage or salary for his management function and therefore as a return for his ►labour, and profit as a return for his entrepreneurship. In the large firm the entrepreneur is a theoretical abstraction whose functions are divided between the management (the board of directors and senior executives) and the shareholders. Many economists have argued that the ►separation of ownership from control has important implications for the behaviour of managers and market performance.

entry ►barriers to entry; freedom of entry.

envelope theorem A proposition with numerous applications in the economics and mathematics of ►utility and of production (►production, theory of) that uses the assumption of optimizing behaviour to simplify the mathematical relationship between different variables. It is best explained by example. Imagine a firm produces widgets, using only skilled labour and unskilled labour, and that to some extent it can ►substitute one type of labour for the other. Now imagine the firm wants to know how the total cost of producing 100 widgets changes, if the cost of skilled labour rises by £1 an hour. The answer is that there is a direct effect and an indirect effect. The direct effect is that the cost rises by £1 for every hour of skilled labour employed. The indirect effect emerges because the firm will, in light of the change in relative prices, choose to alter the mix of skilled and unskilled labour it employs. (It will want to replace skilled workers with unskilled ones as far as is possible.) The envelope theorem says that if the firm is optimizing the mix of skilled and unskilled labour, then for small changes in costs, the indirect effect is effectively zero. Thus, the theorem dramatically simplifies the calculation needed. It does so because the firm could only be optimizing when it mixes inputs such that small changes in how much of each is used, have no effect on profit. (After all, if changing the product mix could increase profits, then the firm could not have been optimizing in the first place.) If the effect of changes in the quantity of the different types of labour can be ignored, so can the indirect effects of the cost change. Thus, the change in total cost resulting in a unit change to the price of an input, is simply the amount of the input employed. Of course, if the firm were not optimizing, it would not be possible to make the assumption that small changes in the input mix were irrelevant. The theorem is central to ➤duality theory – the relationship between the ➤production function and the related function describing the firm's costs, given an optimal input mix. It asserts that the ➤demand function for inputs, is effectively derivable from the firm's cost function. Similarly, in demand theory (➤demand, theory of), it can be used as a means of obtaining the demand function, from observation of the consumers' expenditure at different prices. The theorem is also known as Shepherd's lemma.

environmental accounting The attempt to apply numerical magnitudes to un-costed environmental factors, and to include these in conventional accounts. The goal is to improve those conventional accounts as a measure of overall well-being. For example, at the national level, an environmental disaster – such as an oil-spill – has the perverse effect of enhancing national income, spawning as it does extensive, fully costed, clear-up activity. Obviously though, the economy is no richer as a result of an oil-spill. Environmental accounting can reflect this. It can also introduce rational treatment of depletable resources, deducting their consumption as a cost, rather than adding it as a benefit. Changing the national accounts on this basis would make little difference to international rankings of economic success. Those who propound it do so in the hope that a greater emphasis on environment in the headline measures of success would lead to changes in policy. Attempts have been made to produce accounts reflecting this argument. Herman Daly and Richard Cobb's index of sustainable economic welfare (ISEW), devised in 1989, appears to have grown at 0.9 per cent a year, in contrast to conventional GDP growth of about 2 per cent a year. James Tobin (➤Tobin, James) and Bill Nordhaus, constructed a measure of economic welfare (MEW) with more limited environmental accounting, (but still with a large number of welfare effects included – such as the negative cost of time spent travelling to work) and found an annual per capita growth rate of about 1.1 per cent, over a long time period in which GDP had grown at about 1.7 per cent. ➤➤environmental economics, depletion theory, social accounting, cost–benefit analysis.

environmental economics The area of economics concerned with issues relating to man's use and abuse of ➤natural resources. Environmental problems are frequently characterized by the existence of ➤externalities and ➤public goods. In these areas, it is hard for the ➤price system to operate in such a way as to allocate scarce resources – such as clean air and the ozone layer – in an efficient way (➤economic efficiency). Many of the problems that are faced in this area derive from the lack of clearly defined property rights over natural resources, which makes environmental abuse likely in the absence of governmental control (➤➤Coase theorem). Much of environmental economics has concerned the relative merits of different policy responses to the various flaws of the market mechanism in these areas. For example, should emissions be stopped by regulation, or should they be equities

taxed (►polluter pays principle)? There are also problems that derive from the depletable nature of some resources (►depletion theory).

equation of international demand The law of comparative cost (►Ricardo, D.) sets out the limits of the ►terms of trade within which one country will exchange commodities with another. ►J. S. Mill realized that the point at which exchange actually took place within these limits set by costs would depend on the reciprocal ►demand of each country for the other's commodities. The ratio at which one country's commodities exchange for another country's commodities (the ►terms of trade) will be in equilibrium when the quantity the importer will accept at this ratio equals the quantity the exporter will be willing to deliver. It will depend, inter alia, on the ►elasticities of demand and ►supply of the goods traded. ►►Marshall–Lerner criterion.

equilibrium A situation in which the forces that determine the behaviour of some variable are in balance and thus exert no pressure on that variable to change. It is a situation in which the actions of all economic agents are mutually consistent. It is a concept meaningfully applied to any variable whose level is determined by the outcome of the operation of at least one mechanism or process acting on countervailing forces. For example, equilibrium price is affected by a process which drives suppliers to increase prices when demand is in excess and to undercut each other when supply is in excess – the mechanism thus regulates the forces of supply and demand.

It is possible for a short-run equilibrium to exist, when some quickly adjusting processes are in balance, while other longer-term forces are still causing change to occur. For example, in ►perfect competition, in the short run firms' profit-maximizing behaviour can lead to a market equilibrium with price equal to marginal cost; yet if abnormal ►profits exist at that price new firms might enter the industry – a process quite separate from the price-setting behaviour of those already in it – that will change the long-term equilibrium price.

A distinction can be drawn between a static equilibrium, when the value of the relevant variable is unchanging, and a dynamic equilibrium, when the value of the variable is changing but in a regular way. Equilibrium growth, for example, might manifest itself in a steady 2.25 per cent rise in GDP.

The concept of an equilibrium has developed in recent decades with the advance of ►game theory. An equilibrium in a game is, loosely, a set of mutually compatible strategies such that given the strategies of other players, each player will be content with their own strategy.

Finally, equilibrium should not be confused with efficiency. Although the efficient level of a variable is sometimes likely to be an equilibrium, there is no guarantee that equilibria are efficient. ►►disequilibrium; Nash equilibrium; tatonnement process.

equities ►shares in companies.

equity The residual ►value of a company's ►assets after all outside ►liabilities (other than to shareholders) have been allowed for. In a ►mortgage, or ►hire-purchase contract, equity is the amount left for the borrower if the asset concerned is sold and the lender repaid. The equity in a company under ►liquidation is the property of holders of ►ordinary shares, hence these shares are popularly called *equities*. Equity yields and prices, although fluctuating, have historically delivered returns about 8 per cent higher than risk-free ►stocks (►capital-asset pricing model).

equity/efficiency trade-off The conflict that is traditionally held to arise between maximizing average consumption and making that consumption equal across the population. Under certain conditions, a ►free-market economy is generally recognized as exhibiting ►economic efficiency, but would have no tendency to result in equality of earnings. To achieve an alternative income distribution, a ►progressive tax system is required. However, it is possible that high taxes have a negative effect on the incentives people have to work, or create other distortions, and thus depress output. In so far as there is a trade-off, however, a ►social-welfare function must be defined to derive the optimal combination. ►►welfare economics.

equity gearing ►gearing.

equity-linked assurance ►assurance.

ERDF European Regional Development Fund (►European Union).

ERM ►European Exchange Rate Mechanism.

escalator The policy of the UK government to raise the specific duties (►tax, specific) on petrol and tobacco by more than the rate of inflation each year. In 1997 the escalators were set at 6 per cent and 5 per cent respectively.

ESOP Employee Share Ownership Plan; Employee Stock Ownership Plan (►employee share-ownership schemes).

establishment An operating unit of a business, to be distinguished from a firm or ►enterprise which is a controlling unit. In British censuses an establishment is a reporting unit; thus a large firm may have several factories, each of which will complete a census form but all of which will be owned or controlled by the firm itself.

estate duty (UK) ►inheritance tax.

ethical investing The attempt by lenders or shareholders to influence company behaviour by investing only in companies that observe certain standards of behaviour. The goal – apart from satisfying the conscience of the investors concerned – is to increase the cost of capital (►capital, cost of) to firms whose ethical standards are low, and in doing so make capital less available. Where a capital market is dominated by non-ethical investors, however, it is not clear that any small cluster of individuals has the power to affect any company's cost of capital. In as far as they do, the less ethical can pick up investment bargains. Ethical investment funds – and those that do research on their behalf – have influenced corporate behaviour through the publicity they bring to company actions.

Euler, Leonhard (1707–83) Economists have found that certain propositions in pure mathematics developed by Leonhard Euler, a Swiss mathematician, can be usefully applied to problems in economic theory. The most notable application concerns a theory of distribution based on ►marginal productivity. This theory states that ►factors of production (i.e. ►land, ►labour and ►capital) will each earn an ►income corresponding to the ►value of ►output produced by the last unit of the factor employed. For instance, if a firm employs nineteen workers at an average wage of £200 per week, it will be willing to employ an additional worker as long as his output is worth more than £200. Moreover, if the twentieth worker yields, say, £210 per week it will be worth while to pay him more than £200 to attract him. The firm cannot, however, pay its workers different wages if they have the same skill, and therefore must pay all of them more than £200 per week. The earnings of each worker are therefore made equal to that at which it is just worth while to the firm to employ one more worker. A similar argument is applied to other factors of production and for the total national output as well as for a single firm. However, total output must, by definition, equal total income (►national income). National output is distributed among the three basic factors of production: land, labour and capital. No arithmetical reasons, however, could be thought of how the different factor incomes, derived from marginal productivities, could necessarily add up to the same as total output. Euler's theorem resolved the problem by showing what assumptions about the nature of the ►production function (which describes how the factors of production are combined to produce outputs) had to be made in order for the equality between the sum of incomes and the sum of outputs to be achieved. ►►Cambridge school; distribution, theory of; neo-classical economics.

Euler's theorem ►Euler, L.

Euro ►European Monetary Union.

Eurobond ►bond; eurocurrency.

eurocurrency ►Currency held by individuals and institutions outside the country of issue. The ►Bank for International Settlements has described Eurodollars as the dollars acquired 'by banks located outside the United States, mostly through the taking of ►deposits, but also to some extent through swapping other currencies into dollars, and the relending of these dollars, often after redepositing with other banks, to non-bank borrowers anywhere in the world'. It should be noted, therefore, that the market for Eurocurrencies is not confined to Europe. In terms of a simple example, what happens is as follows. A London bank, as a result of a commercial transaction of one of its customers, has, say, a ►credit balance with an American bank in New York. A Belgian businessman asks his bank for dollars to finance imports from the United States. In order to meet this request the Brussels bank accepts the dollar deposit transferred by the London bank from its account in New York. The essential point about this operation is that it creates credit. The London bank still has a claim, on Brussels instead of New York, whereas the Brussels bank now has a claim on New York which its customer can use to finance his trade. The questions are naturally raised as to why London should be willing to transfer its deposit and why Brussels should finance its requirements in this way. The US ►balance of payments deficits and *dollar certificates of deposit* issued by overseas branches of US banks generate a supply of Eurodollars and interest-rate ►arbitrage (New York versus Brussels) enable a ►profit to be made. Relative ►rates of interest are a factor in these transactions, but, in addition, the existence of national ►exchange controls and credit controls may encourage the practice. For instance, the Brussels bank avoids the need to exchange francs for dollars. In practice, of course, there can be many relending transactions between banks in response to differentials in interest rates and in many different currencies.

Eurodollars ►Eurocurrency.

European Association of Securities Dealers Automated Quotation System (EASDAQ) A pan-European market for trading ►shares in growth companies and modelled on NASDAQ (►over-the-countermarket) in the USA. EASDAQ, which opened in 1986, is a for-profit company based in Brussels. Its shareholders include venture capital companies (►risk capital), ►investment banks and NASDAQ.

European Bank for Reconstruction and Development An international bank set up in 1991 to 'promote private and entrepreneurial initiative in the Central and Eastern European countries committed to and applying the principles of multi-party democracy, pluralism and market economics'. It was established to help the previously ►planned economies of Central and Eastern Europe to develop free markets which would have a minimum of government intervention and whose governments would be freely elected on a multi-party basis. Fifty-nine countries and institutions are members of the Bank, including the ►European Union and the ►European Investment Bank. The European Union, including EU institutions, holds 59.8 per cent of the Bank's voting rights, of which France, Germany, Italy and the UK hold 8.97 per cent each. Japan holds 9.0 per cent, the USA 8.3 per cent, the Russian Federation 4.2 per cent and Canada 3.6 per cent. In 1996 the shareholders agreed to double the Bank's total capital ECU20 billion but the increase was to be spread over the years from 1998 to 2010. The Bank is authorized to lend up to 60 per cent of its funds, overall and to any individual country, for private-sector projects and 40 per cent for public projects. It may lend at market

rates of ►interest or invest in ►equities. The Bank is located in London, UK.
►►International Bank for Reconstruction and Development; Marshall Aid.

European Coal and Steel Community (ECSC) The conception of the Schuman
Plan (named after the then French foreign minister) for the establishment of a
common European market in coal and steel. It was embodied in the Treaty of
Paris, of 1951, ratified by the member countries – Germany, France, Italy and
►Benelux – in 1952. All import duties and ►quota restrictions on coal, iron ore,
steel and scrap were eliminated on intracommunity trade. The treaty also provided
for the control of restrictive practices and ►mergers considered contrary to the
maintenance of free competition. The ECSC merged with the then European
Economic Community and Euratom in 1967 to form the European Community
(►European Union). ►customs union.

European Community ►European Union.

European currency snake Precursor to the ►European Monetary System. The
countries of the then European Community (►European Union) agreed in 1972
to manage their currencies so that their ►exchange rates moved in relation to one
another, and, within certain narrow bands, in relation to the dollar. It was considered
that the management of the currencies of the Community in this way was the
necessary first step to monetary union and, eventually, to the ideal of a common
currency. The fluctuations in the rates of each currency were confined within a
margin of ±2.25 per cent. In addition, the group as a whole was also managed in
respect to the dollar, with fluctuations confined within a range of ±4.45 per cent.
Initially the arrangement was referred to as the 'snake in the tunnel'. After 1973,
however, the 'snake' was left to float against the dollar, and the 'tunnel' vanished.
This method of managing European currencies was replaced in 1979 by the
►European Monetary System.

European Currency Unit (ECU) Notional currency introduced as a unit of
account (►money) of the then European Community (EC) (►European Union) on
the formation of the ►European Monetary System in 1970. By 1981 the ECU
had replaced all other units of accounts that had been used in the EC for accounting
purposes, e.g. the ►Common Agricultural Policy, European Development Fund
(►Lomé Convention) and budgeting. As with the previous units of account, the
ECU is a ►weighted average of the currencies of the member countries of the
European Union. The weight given to each currency reflects the relative size of
each country's ►gross national product and of each country's intra-Community
trade. In the development of plans for ►European Monetary Union, the ECU will
be converted to the *Euro*, the new single European currency, at the rate of one
for one.

European Development Fund ►Lomé Convention.

European Economic Area ►European Free Trade Association.

European Economic Community ➤European Union.

European Exchange Rate Mechanism (ERM) The fixed exchange-rate regime established by the then European Community (➤European Union) in 1979. It replaced the existing ➤European currency snake for the control of ➤exchange rates. The system was designed to keep the member countries' exchange-rates within specified bands in relation to each other. Each currency in the system was allowed to fluctuate between ±2.25 per cent against any other currency. This applied to the German deutschmark, the French franc, the Belgian franc, the Danish krone, the Dutch guilder, the Irish punt and the Italian lira. Spain joined in 1989, the UK in 1990, and the Portuguese escudo in 1992 but at a margin of fluctuation of ±6 per cent. The purpose of the ERM was to stabilize exchange rates, foster intra-European trade and control inflation through the link with a strong deutschmark. Finally, it came to be seen as a precursor to ➤European Monetary Union (with membership implicitly representing a condition of entry to EMU according to the Maastricht Treaty). However, after German unification, the system became strained by the different ➤monetary policy needs of different members. The pound and the lira left the system in 1992. In 1993 the fluctuation bands widened to ±15 per cent (except for the deutschmark and the guilder). The Austrian schilling joined the system in 1995. In 1996 the Finnish markka also joined and the Italian lira re-entered at 15 per cent. ➤➤devaluation.

European Free Trade Association (EFTA) The Stockholm Agreement of 1959 established a ➤free-trade area between the United Kingdom, Norway, Sweden, Denmark, Austria, Portugal and Switzerland. The Association was later joined by Finland, Iceland and Liechtenstein. While retaining their own individual tariffs on imports from non-members, they agreed to eliminate import duties on goods originating in any member country. Denmark and the United Kingdom left the association on becoming members of the then European Community (➤European Union) in 1973. Similarly, Portugal left in 1986 and Austria, Finland and Sweden in 1995. An agreement for the setting up of a European Economic Area (EEA) throughout the EFTA and EC countries for the free movement of goods, ➤services, ➤capital and people came into effect in 1994. The EEA agreement excludes Switzerland. EFTA has since continued a policy of setting up free-trade agreements with other countries and by 1997 these covered countries in Central and Eastern Europe, Turkey, Israel and Morocco. ➤➤General Agreement on Tariffs and Trade.

European Investment Bank (EIB) A bank established in 1958 by the then European Community (➤European Union) whose board of governors comprises the ministers of finance of the Community. It is a non-profit-making institution whose function is to make loans and give guarantees with respect to (a) projects in the underdeveloped areas of the Community and associated countries (➤Lomé Convention), (b) projects of modernization, conversion or development that are regarded as necessary for the establishment of the Common Market and (c) projects in which member countries of the Community have a common interest. The loans, which are generally not more than 50 per cent of the capital cost of the project, are for terms of from seven to twelve years and are made in a mix of foreign currencies. They have to be repaid in the currencies in which they were granted. Under the EIB's charter, loans and outstanding guarantees cannot exceed two-and-a-half times its subscribed capital of ECU 62 billion in 1996.

European Monetary Cooperation Fund ➤European Monetary System.

European Monetary Fund ➤European Monetary System.

European Monetary Institute The Institute established in 1994, under the Maastricht Treaty, as a forerunner of the European Central Bank of ➤European Monetary Union. Its shareholders are the fifteen central banks of the European Union. It is responsible for the ➤European Currency Unit (ECU), the managing of the foreign exchange reserves (➤reserve currency) of the European Union and of the ➤European Monetary System. Its main function, however, is to help progress towards a single European currency and a single monetary policy for the Community.

European Monetary System (EMS) The European Monetary System is the name given to the common international financial structures adopted by the member countries of the ➤European Union in advance of ➤European Monetary Union. The major elements in this structure have been the ➤European Exchange Rate Mechanism (ERM), the ➤European Currency Unit (ECU) and the European Monetary Cooperation Fund. The last has been the ➤clearing house for the ➤central banks in the EMS, although, in practice, the day-to-day running of the system is carried out by the ➤Bank for International Settlements. The central banks of the member countries in the EMS deposit 20 per cent of their ➤gold and foreign exchange reserves with the Fund on a short-term basis in exchange for ECUs. ➤➤European Monetary Union.

European Monetary Union (EMU) A programme for the establishment of monetary union was agreed under the terms of the ➤Maastricht Treaty, to establish a single European currency (the Euro) by the late 1990s. States judged to have 'converged' sufficiently with the rest of the continent, by reference to a number of conditions, are entitled to join (➤convergance criteria). The currency is to be managed by an independent ➤central bank, modelled on the ➤Bundesbank. Countries inside are to be subject to rules on government borrowing and will be subject to fines if they borrow more than 3 per cent of GDP in circumstances other than recession. ➤stability and growth pact.

A major effect of the project has been to instil discipline in ➤fiscal policy and ➤monetary policy in countries seeking membership, while yielding those countries the benefits of ➤credibility in financial markets, which they could gain through the influence of the good reputation of the ➤Bundesbank. Once inside, however, member nations are not able to exert an independent monetary policy. A level of interest rate would be set for all members. If each member tends to follow the others, and absorb similar shocks to demand and supply, this need not be a problem. But, if member states endure divergent patterns of economic performance, the burden of adjustment will have to fall on domestic prices and employment, rather than interest rates or exchange rates. For example, if Germany is ►overheating, and Austria is in the grip of ►deflation, Austria will have to endure the high interest rates suited to calm the German economy down. To boost ►aggregate demand in Austria, the government will be proscribed from borrowing very much by the stability and growth pact. It will have to wait for recession to cause domestic prices to fall, which should lead to extra demand for Austrian products, and thus stimulate higher output and employment.

It is worth nothing that on the basis of ►Keynesian economics – which regards control of aggregate demand to be central to good economic management – monetary union looks risky. On the basis of ►new classical economics, which believes in the ►neutrality of money, the single currency should not make much difference to the conduct of European economies.

European Recovery Programme The Marshall Plan. In June 1947 the US Secretary of State, General George C. Marshall, offered the assistance of the United States to countries whose productive ►assets had been destroyed in the Second World War. This offer did not exclude the USSR and the Eastern European countries but was never accepted by them. The resultant European Recovery Programme became known as ►Marshall Aid. Sixteen West European countries attended a conference in Paris in 1947, which led to the establishment of the Organization for European Economic Cooperation (►Organization for Economic Cooperation and Development) in 1948, to coordinate the recovery programme in conjunction with the US Economic Cooperation Administration. It was established on the basis of a four-year commitment to provide Western Europe with between $15 billion and $17 billion.

European Regional Development Fund (ERDF) ►European Union.

European Social Fund ►European Union.

European Union Six countries of Western Europe – France, West Germany, Italy, Belgium, the Netherlands and Luxembourg signed the Treaty of Rome in 1957 for the creation between them of a ►customs union or common market. By this treaty the European Economic Community (EEC) came into force on 1 January 1958. The Treaty of Rome was subsequently amended by the Treaties of Maastricht and Amsterdam. The primary aims of the Treaty of Rome were the elimination of all obstacles to the free movement of goods, ►services, ►capital and ►labour between the member countries and the setting up of a common external commercial policy, a common agricultural policy and a common transport policy. The treaty foresaw the prohibition of most industrial ►subsidies and

➤dumping and the supranational control of public ➤monopolies and the vetting of ➤mergers. The EEC merged with the ➤European Coal and Steel Community and Euratom in 1967 to form the European Community, subsequently referred to as the European Union (EU). The executive management of the EU is vested in a commission whose members are appointed for periods of four years. Problems of policy are the concern of the Council of Ministers, to which the commission's proposals are submitted. Each member country is represented by one minister in the Council. Decisions can be taken by unanimity (each country has a veto) or by *qualified majority voting*, in which each nation has votes partially weighted by its size, and a majority of about two-thirds of total votes is needed to carry a provision. Considerable legislative influence, but less ultimate power, also resides in the European Parliament. The European Court of Justice has ultimate authority to interpret the Treaty, and acts as a kind of supreme court. It is supported by a Court of Auditors, and a Court of First Instance. The treaty also established a parliamentary assembly and a court of justice. Decisions of the EU are transmitted either through the member countries' governments by means of Directives or directly through Regulations. Consultative institutions include an economic and social committee and a monetary committee. The ➤European Investment Bank has been formed and a European Regional Development Fund established with powers to lend and grant money for the development of backward regions of the EU. In addition, a European Social Fund has been set up to assist the redeployment of workers thrown out of work, particularly if caused by the creation of the EU, and a European Development Fund established to provide aid to countries of the ➤Lomé Convention. A European Environment Agency was set up in 1990. All internal import duties were abolished and a common external tariff established by 1 July 1968. For agricultural products, the ➤Common Agricultural Policy became effective in 1968. Workers and their families can move from one country to another without a permit, and foreign workers from within the community have the same rights to social security and are subject to the same taxation as nationals. As from 1 January 1973 the Republic of Ireland and two members of the ➤European Free Trade Association – the United Kingdom and Denmark – became full members of the EU. The elimination of tariffs between the original six and the new members and the adoption by them of the common external tariff was completed on 1 January 1977. Greece became a member of the community in 1981, Portugal and Spain in 1986, Austria, Finland and Sweden in 1995. The Commission has association agreements with Turkey and former communist states of East Europe. The German Democratic Republic (East Germany) became a member of the Community in 1990 following its merger with the Federal Republic of Germany (West Germany).

The EU is not a complete single ➤market because there exist restrictions which prevent free trade, such as national differences in technical standards within the Community and differential qualification requirements for the professions (➤barriers to entry). A programme was initiated and embodied in the Single

European Act in 1986 for the abolition of such restrictions and the creation of a Single European Market. The programme involved the abolition of exchange controls, the recognition of qualifications, the abolition of restrictions on internal transport (►cabotage), liberalization of the market in air services, public procurement tendering, life insurance and banking services, and the abolition of frontier controls (►Schengen Treaty). The Act also widened the application of qualified majority decision-making in the EU. The Commission monitors competition to ensure that no enterprise acts in such a way as to restrict the free movement of goods and services in the EU or to exploit a dominant market position (►competition policy). A number of areas, such as taxation, still required a unanimous decision from member states for any policy changes to be made. With the signing of the Maastricht Treaty, providing for ►European Monetary Union, and extending coordination in the area of employment conditions (►Social Charter), the Union emerged in the form it holds today. A programme for the establishment of a full economic and monetary union, including the setting-up of a European Central Bank and the replacement of individual national currencies with a single European currency in all transactions throughout the EU and the coordination of employment conditions (►Social Charter), was agreed at Maastricht, the Netherlands and came into force in 1993. The Amsterdam Treaty of 1997 made provisions regarding the membership of the Commission after further enlargement. Freedom of movement throughout the Union was endorsed, exception being granted to the UK and the Republic of Ireland. ►►Directives of the European Union; European Monetary System; free-trade area.

ex ante Expected or intended before the event, as distinct from *ex post*, which is the result after the event. Since the future is largely unpredictable, expectations and outcomes will often be different. The concepts of ex ante and ex post are particularly useful in economics because the nature of expectations may help either to realize or to falsify expectations in the process of moving towards ►equilibrium. For example, if investors expect security prices to rise today ex ante, this will increase demand for them and their price now, so that ex post and ex ante prices may be similar. If intended aggregate ►savings (ex ante) are larger than intended ►investment, this will set in train forces, via lower incomes, to reduce savings so that ex post savings and investment will be equal (►income determination, theory of). ►►Myrdal, G. K.

ex post ►ex ante.

exceptional items ►below the line.

excess capacity 1. The difference between the amount produced by a firm or group of firms and the higher amount that could most efficiently be produced. If a firm produces 1000 cars at a cost of £5000 each, but the lowest cost output would be 1300 cars at £4000 each, there is said to be excess capacity of 300 cars. It will exist at any point on an ►average-cost curve to the left of the lowest point.

Sustained excess capacity is a feature of firms in ►monopolistic competition. In ►perfect competition, it will exist only in the short term. **2.** The difference between actual output and maximum possible output in a firm, industry or economy. Excess capacity exists when there are unemployed resources; for a national economy it implies the existence of a ►deflationary gap. ►output gap.

excess demand The state of a market for a commodity in which consumers would choose to buy more of the commodity than is available at the prevailing price. Excess demand will be equal to zero at the ►equilibrium price; it will be negative (i.e. ►excess supply will exist) when the price is higher and will be positive when the price is lower. If price does not ration the available supply, something else must; usually it will be state-organized rationing or a queuing system coupled with a first-come first-served distribution. The situation can result from price control in which suppliers are legally prevented from raising their prices in response to high consumer demand. ►►repressed inflation.

excess profit ►profit.

excess supply The state of the market for a commodity in which more of the commodity is available for purchase than consumers choose to buy at the prevailing price. Usually, such a situation leads to a price fall and excess supply disappears. In a market in which minimum price control is applied it can, however, persist; if, for example, trade unions prevent wages from falling enough, some argue that there can be an excess supply of labour (or unemployment) at the prevailing wage. ►►excess demand; Keynesian unemployment.

exchange control The control by the state through the ►banking system of dealings in gold and foreign ►currencies. Exchange control is concerned with controlling the purchase and sale of currencies by residents alone, since governments do not have complete powers to control the activities of non-residents. This must be done through the ►market and is a matter of exchange management (►exchange equalization account). Exchange control is required only where a country wishes to influence the international value of its currency. It is not willing to leave the value of its currency in terms of other currencies or gold to be determined in the ►free market, as it would be under a system of floating ►exchange rates, or to allow the fixed external value of its currency to be the determinant of the domestic price level. In its most extreme form, a country facing a balance-of-payments deficit may use exchange control to restrict imports to the amount earned in ►foreign exchange by its nationals. All forms of exchange control are discouraged by the ►Organization for Economic Cooperation and Development and other international organizations concerned with encouraging ►international trade. It should be noted that a currency is not fully convertible (►convertibility) when exchange control is operated. Exchange controls were introduced in the UK at the beginning of the Second World War and embodied in the Exchange Control Act of 1947. These controls were abolished in 1979. Within the ►European Union exchange controls were made generally illegal by the ➤Single European Act. ➤➤European Monetary Union; counter trade; mobility of capital.

exchange economy An economy which has progressed beyond the point which each household produces goods solely for its own consumption. Exchange, whether by ➤barter or by the use of ➤money, enables the benefits of the specialization (➤division of labour) and the ➤economies of scale to be realized. ➤➤economic growth.

exchange equalization account (UK) An account controlled by the ➤Treasury and managed by the ➤Bank of England which buys and sells sterling for gold and foreign ➤currencies with the potential object of offsetting major fluctuations in the exchange value of the pound and keeping the ➤spot market price for the pound around some required rate. The account was set up by the 1932 Finance Act after the abandonment of the ➤gold standard in the previous year. The ➤assets of the account include the ➤gold and foreign exchange reserves and sterling, provided by the ➤Exchequer, invested in ➤treasury bills. Similar funds or stabilization accounts are operated by other countries. ➤➤exchange rate; International Monetary Fund.

exchange equation ➤Fisher, I.

exchange of shares A means of business combination which can take two forms. In form (a) the companies retain their separate identities, but exchange a quantity of ➤shares so that each company holds shares in the other and normally some directors will sit on both boards (➤interlocking directorates). In form (b) two companies will merge, shares of one company being exchanged with or without a cash adjustment, for the whole of the issued share ➤capital of the other. ➤➤merger; reverse take-over.

exchange rate The price (rate) at which one ➤currency is exchanged for another currency. Transactions in foreign exchange occur spot or forward (➤spot market and forward market) in the ➤foreign-exchange markets. The actual rate at any one time is determined by ➤supply and ➤demand conditions for the relevant currencies in the market. However, probably the best way of viewing the exchange rate is as the economy's device for altering the relative prices of domestic produce, which does not trade internationally; and international produce, subject to import and export. Take an example. Oil is priced internationally, with prices set in dollars. Competitive forces ensure the UK price of oil is the same as the global price. Haircuts, on the other hand, cannot be imported and are priced locally. If the pound devalues (➤devaluation), the price of oil remains constant in dollar terms, so automatically rises in pound terms. The price of haircuts remains constant in pound terms, so the relative price of haircuts has fallen. Hairdressing will now be relatively less profitable compared to oil production. The signal sent by the exchange rate eases adjustments in the economy between the domestic and international sectors. Often when the economy receives a 'shock', the relative size and profitability of the two sectors has to adjust, and the exchange rate is one means by which the price changes needed to induce the adjustment can be transmitted to the two sectors. For instance, a shock might include a big rise in domestic savings, without a rise in domestic investment. In this event, consumption at home falls, and exports logically need to rise to offset this. The exchange rate falls, increasing demand for exports through lower prices. The exchange rate is simply a component of the ►price mechanism, albeit an important one, responding to the pressures set by preferences for domestic and foreign goods, and the flows of savings and investment funds across currencies. It follows that the value of the currency is obviously also determined by domestic ►monetary policy – more inflation tends to mean a lower exchange rate as, without a depreciation, inflation hits the tradable sector more harshly than the non-tradable. (The tradable sector gets squeezed, as it has to hold its prices constant in world markets, while the domestic sector can raise its local prices in an inflationary environment more easily.) Representing such an important economic variable, governments have often sought to control exchange rates. It may be seen as the most effective means of stabilizing monetary policy, especially in smaller countries. (►European Exchange Rate Mechanism.) It may be to promote trade or international cooperation.

In the absence of government controls, there would be an entirely *free* or *floating exchange rate* in operation. With a freely floating system, no ►gold and foreign exchange reserves would be required as the exchange rate would adjust itself until the supply and demand for the currencies were brought into balance. There are merits in fixing exchange rates, or in adopting one of many hybrid systems which lie between these extremes. Fluctuations in the rate may be inconvenient for trading, and these fluctuations could be volatile if left to move freely. Moreover, because of the pressure of short-term ►capital movements or ►speculation, the exchange rate could move in a direction different from that justified by conditions in the domestic economy (►exchange-rate overshooting). The system of fixed rates has been criticized on the grounds of its inflexibility and the fact that it places too much of the adjustment burden on the domestic economy. A middle course has been proposed in the 'moving parity', 'sliding parity', 'dynamic' or 'crawling peg' idea. In the *moving parity*, the par rate is automatically adjusted according to a moving average of past rates taken over a number of months. Under the *sliding parity*, instead of the whole amount of a revaluation or devaluation taking place at once, it is spread in small percentages over a number of months, e.g. a 10 per cent devaluation may be achieved by a monthly 0.2 per cent reduction for fifty months. This system has the advantage that it is known and certain, while the monthly adjustment is too small to cause excessive speculative flows. Under the *crawling peg*, the gradual adjustments in the exchange rate are linked to the level of a country's reserves rather than past exchange rates. Portugal followed a 'crawling peg' policy for the escudo for a period until 1990 during which it was devalued by 0.25 per cent per month. The fixed exchange-rate regime that truly combines flexibility with stability has proved elusive. ⟩⟩currency appreciation; effective exchange rate; real exchange rate; European currency snake; European Monetary System; international liquidity.

exchange rate overshooting The idea, promulgated by Rudiger Dornbusch, that when governments make a domestic monetary policy shift, for a short time the exchange rate will adjust further than the changed monetary stance merits. Under plausible assumptions about the ⟩mobility of capital, if the ⟩rate of interest in the UK is to be higher than that of Germany, investors must expect the pound to devalue against the deutschmark: this depreciation would reduce the value of their sterling assets, offsetting the higher interest rate. If they did *not* believe that the pound was to devalue, they would put all their money in pounds, earning a higher rate of return. As a result, if a government orchestrates a rise in interest rates, money will flow into its currency from other lower-interest-rate jurisdictions. This will lead the currency to appreciate in value, and it will go on appreciating until it has gone up so far that it is now expected to fall again. ⟩⟩exchange rate; law of one price.

Exchequer The account of the central government kept at the ⟩Bank of England. ⟩⟩Consolidated fund.

excise duties Indirect taxes levied upon goods (e.g. beer) produced for home consumption as distinct from customs duties (⟩tariffs, import), which are levied on goods entering or leaving the country (⟩⟩taxation). Both excise duties and tariffs in the UK are administered by HM Customs and Excise.

exclusive dealing A 'tie' under which a retailer or wholesaler contracts to purchase from a supplier on the understanding that no other distributor will be appointed or receive supplies in a given area. Examples are tied petrol-filling stations and public houses. Where the sales outlets are owned by the supplier, as is frequently the case with public houses, exclusive dealing is an instance of ⟩vertical integration, but where the outlets are independently owned it is, in principle, illegal under the ⟩Restrictive Trade Practices Act, though if registered and approved it is allowed. Exclusive dealing may be a ⟩barrier to entry, but it can be defended on grounds of benefits to the consumer, such as after-sales service. ⟩⟩competition policy; Fair Trading Act; vertical restraints.

ex-dividend Without ⟩dividend. The purchaser of a ⟩security quoted ex-dividend does not have the right to the next dividend when due. The term 'ex-', meaning excluding, is also used in a similar sense in relation to ⟩rights issue, capitalization issue (⟩bonus issue), etc.

exempt company ⟩private company.

exogenous variable A ⟩variable whose value is not determined within the set of equations, or ➤models, established to make predictions or test a hypothesis. ➤➤endogenous variable; parameter.

expectation of life ➤death rate.

expectations The views held by economic agents as to the future behaviour of relevant economic variables. Although expectations have some role in the theory of ➤microeconomics (in particular, the ➤cobweb model and in pricing behaviour in ➤oligopoly) their primary importance is in ➤macroeconomics. In almost all models of the economy, in-built assumptions are made as to what views individuals hold about the future: when future rates of return in asset markets are uncertain, for example, the expectations of investors will determine the prevailing rate of interest more than the actual return made on any asset; when wage bargainers target a ➤real wage, they must have a view of expected inflation to know what money wage to seek; under the ➤acceleration principle of investment, it is the expectations of firms about future demand that determines their investment behaviour. In any model where uncertainty is prevalent, the expectation-forming process of individuals will be important.

There are various different assumptions that can be made about expectations. First, they could be an ➤exogenous variable; in this case they are not influenced by any events in the model, but are just imposed from outside. Secondly, they could be *backward-looking*, made by economic agents on the basis of past values of the variables in question (➤adaptive expectations). Thirdly, they can be ➤rational expectations, in which case agents are assumed not to make systematic errors in their forecasting of variables. In certain economic models, by assuming rational expectations, very strong conclusions can be reached about how the economy should be controlled. ➤➤Lucas critique; policy ineffectiveness theorem.

expected utility A measure of the welfare accruing to a consumer from an asset which yields an uncertain flow of benefits. Suppose, for example, a consumer takes part in a lottery, in which there is a 50 per cent chance of winning £10 and a 50 per cent chance of winning nothing. The consumer's expected ➤utility will be 50 per cent of the utility of winning £10 and 50 per cent of the utility of winning nothing. An important distinction should be made between the expected utility of a lottery and the utility of the expected outcome. In the example above, the expected utility of £5 may not be the same as the average of the utility of £10 and the utility of zero pounds. ➤➤diminishing marginal utility; risk; risk aversion.

expenditure tax A form of ➤direct taxation on spending. Advocated by ➤Kaldor and ➤Meade and others on the grounds that it would eliminate the necessity to define ➤income, which is a source of complexity and, many would argue, inequity in the common form of ➤income tax. In practice an expenditure tax would be just like income tax, either with full tax deductibility of all income that is saved; or with a zero rate of tax on all income from savings. Each of the two systems involves removing ➤double taxation from income that is invested. With so many forms of savings now subject to generous tax treatment, we in fact already have a rather complex hybrid income/expenditure tax mix. Among the advantages claimed for a full expenditure tax are that it would encourage saving and would not discriminate between alternative savings media (eliminating one set of distortions in ➤capital markets) and would close loopholes in the present system which allow the avoidance of income tax by converting income into ➤capital. It should be understood that indirect taxes such as ➤value-added tax, although taxes on expenditure, are quite different from the proposed expenditure tax both in the method of collection and in their inability to take the individual financial circumstances of the spender into account.

experimental economics ➤empirical testing.

export credit insurance The granting of ➤insurance to cover the commercial and political risks of selling in overseas markets. There has been increasing international concern about the use of export credit subsidies to capture export markets of the ➤developing countries. The member countries of the ➤Organization for Economic Cooperation and Development have concluded agreements setting up guidelines which fix the minimum ➤rate of interest and maximum repayment periods for specified categories of borrower. These guidelines were revised in 1991 following concern about the growth of the use of a mix of credits with direct aid tied to a requirement that the developing country must buy the goods and services of the donor country. ➤➤Export Credits Guarantee Department; Export–Import Bank; Multilateral Investment Guarantee Agency.

Export Credits Guarantee Department (ECGD) A UK government department (set up in 1930 as an independent department, although it had operated in another form from 1919), responsible to the Secretary of State for Trade and Industry, that has the authority, under ➤Treasury control, to issue ➤insurance policies to cover risks met by exporters. Its powers were revised by the Export and Investment Guarantees Act (1991). The Department can give insurance cover to firms selling overseas and to their banks in the UK for credit extending for two years or over. It can also insure against political risk in overseas markets. ➤➤export credit insurance; Export–Import Bank; Multilateral Investment Guarantee Agency.

Export–Import Bank A US government agency, established in 1934 for the purpose of encouraging US trade by supplying ➤credit at subsidized rates of interest and financial guarantees to customers of US exporters. It also gives US exporters ➤insurance cover (➤➤export credit insurance; Export Credits Guarantee Department; Multilateral Investment Guarantee Agency).

export incentives Preferential treatment for firms that sell their products abroad, compared with firms that sell to the home market. They may take the form of direct ➤subsidies, special ➤credit facilities, grants, concessions in the field of

➤direct taxation, benefits arising from the administration of indirect taxation, and ➤export credit insurance on exceptionally favourable terms (➤Export Credits Guarantee Department). Various international associations discourage the practice of artificially stimulating exports by any of these methods. The ➤General Agreement on Tariffs and Trade lays down special provisions relating to export subsidies, direct or indirect, in an attempt to limit them. The Treaty of Rome, which established the ➤European Union, discourages the granting of privileged aid to any economic sectors. In the field of '*tied aid*' (➤foreign aid) the OECD rules insist that a minimum proportion of the finance must be grant aid where the finance is conditional on the donor country receiving the contract for the project being financed.

export multiplier The ratio of the total increase in a country's ➤national income to the increment in export revenue generating the increase. The size of the multiplier depends on the propensities to save (➤average propensity to save; marginal propensity to save) of the recipients of the increases in incomes derived from the increase in export revenue and the country's ➤propensity to import. The export multiplier can be regarded as a special case of the general ➤multiplier.

export processing zone ➤free-trade zone.

export rebates ➤customs drawback; export incentives.

export surplus ➤balance of payments.

exports The goods and ➤services produced by one country which are sold to another in exchange for the second country's own goods and services, for gold and ➤foreign exchange or in settlement of ➤debt. Countries tend to specialize in the production of those goods and services in which they can be relatively most efficient, because of their indigenous factor endowments (➤factors of production). Countries devote home resources to exports because they can obtain more goods and services by international exchange than they would from the same resources devoted to direct home production. The UK's exports of goods amount to about 28 per cent of its ➤gross national income, compared with about 11 per cent in the USA. ➤➤balance of payments; international trade; mercantilism.

external deficit A synonym for ➤balance of payments deficit.

external diseconomies ➤diseconomies of scale.

external effects ➤externalities.

externalities Consequences for welfare or ➤opportunity costs not fully accounted for in the ➤price and ➤market system. *External diseconomies* of production include traffic congestion and pollution created by a manufacturing plant. These cause reductions in the welfare of people living near the factory and perhaps increased costs to adjacent factories which might need to purify water taken from a river bordering both plants. Because the third parties receive no compensation (do not charge) for these external diseconomies there are costs of production not accounted for in the price system. External diseconomies also arise in ►consumption, for example where people eating ice-cream leave paper on the pavement or cigarette smokers pollute the air in a public building. Both production and consumption externalities can occur simultaneously where, for example, a restaurant creates noise, congestion and smell.

External economies of production may arise where the existence of several factories stimulates the availability of skilled labour, shopping facilities or component supplies. External economies of consumption include a garden at the front of a house which gives pleasure to passers-by as well as to the occupants and increases the value of adjoining property. Defence or other public expenditure on research and development is sometimes justified on the additional grounds that it stimulates the development of new ►technology which may become freely available to all. This is usually called a *spillover effect*, an alternative term for externality.

Externalities are important in determining the efficient allocation of resources. In a ►free-market economy individuals typically only attempt to maximize their own private utility or profit, and external costs and benefits will not be reflected in the prices of things. A firm may make perfumes very cheaply, but nevertheless be polluting the atmosphere in the process, to the detriment of non-perfume buyers. Unless the cost of this pollution is reflected in the price of the perfume, people will buy more of it than they would choose to if they had to pay for the entire cost to society of its production. In short it is full *social* costs which are important in determining an efficient resource allocation, and *private* costs which determine prices.

There are two means of dealing with externalities. First, a structure of taxes and subsidies can be designed to *internalize* the externalities and ensure that the full costs or benefits of production are reflected in the prices charged. In this case, even if a factory causes pollution, it can carry on producing as long as it properly compensates society for the damage caused. A second approach is to put restrictions on certain unsocial activities and make other beneficial activities compulsory. This will, however, usually not be as efficient as the optimal taxes or subsidies could be, because you may restrict activity that, despite its negative external effects, still benefits the performer more than its restriction helps society. ►social welfare; ►►Coase theorem; environmental economics; polluter pays principle.

extraordinary items ►below the line.

F

face value Nominal as distinct from ►market value. The face value of a ►security is the price at which it will be redeemed; of an ►ordinary share its ►par value or issued price; of a coin the amount stamped on it, which might for a silver or gold coin be less than its market value.

factor 1. ►factors of production. 2. ►factoring. 3. An agent who buys and sells goods on behalf of others for a ►commission called *factorage*.

factor cost A term used in the national accounts (►social accounting) to describe the valuation of output at market prices less taxes on expenditure plus subsidies.

factor endowment The relative availability of the different ►factors of production in a country. An important determinant of the pattern of international trade. ►Heckscher–Ohlin principle; ►►comparative advantage.

factor markets The ►labour market, the ►capital market and other ►markets in which the ►factors of production are bought and sold. The theory of distribution (►distribution, theory of) attempts to explain how the ►prices of factors are determined and how they are allocated between alternative uses.

factor payments Payments made to the owners of the ►factors of production in return for their use in the production process.

factor price equalization theorem ►Samuelson, P. A.

factoring The business activity in which a company takes over the responsibility for the collecting of the ►debts of another. It is a service primarily intended to meet the needs of small and medium-size firms. Typically, the client debits all his sales to the factor and receives immediate payment from him less a charge of about 2–3 per cent and interest for the period of ►trade credit given to the customer, thus improving the client's cash flow considerably. There are a number of different types of factoring; the simplest is known as invoice discounting. In its most elaborate form the factor maintains the company's sales ledger and other accounting functions, and does not seek recourse to its client if unable to obtain payment from that client's customers (non-recourse factoring). The customer need not know that a factor is being used. The factor generally has some control over sales either by imposing a maximum ►credit limit which he is willing to meet or by vetting specific prospective clients. Through international factoring companies, the factor can offer a service to exporters by protecting his customers from bad debts overseas and by giving, for instance, expert advice on ►foreign exchange transactions (►Export Credits Guarantee Department).

factors of production The inputs or resources used in the process of production. ►land, ►labour and ►capital are the three main headings used in analysis of the factors, with entrepreneurship (►entrepreneur) often counted as a fourth. ►►factor endowment; natural resources; Say, J.-B.

fair trade policy ►reciprocity.

Fair Trading Act The Act of 1973 which in the UK replaced the Monopolies and Restrictive Practices (Inquiry and Control) Act of 1948 and the Monopolies and Mergers Act of 1965, but generally consolidated this previous legislation. The Act established the office of the Director-General of Fair Trading and gave him wide powers, enabling him to monitor and investigate trading activities and to refer monopoly situations to the Monopolies and Mergers Commission, a power previously confined to the appropriate minister. The Director-General cannot refer a merger but may be called upon to act as adviser to the minister. (The powers of the Office of Fair Trading were extended by the ►Competition Act of 1980, the ►Financial Services Act of 1986 and the Broadcasting Act of 1990.) Some larger mergers fall within the competence of the Competition Directorate of the European Commission (►European Union). A monopoly is now deemed to exist when the market share is one-quarter, compared with one-third in the 1948 Act; although, as before, a monopoly need not necessarily be considered to be against the public interest. Further, the monopoly may now be in relation to a local market, whereas previously the UK or a large part of it was deemed to be the market in question. Finally, the Fair Trading Act extended the monopoly legislation to nationalized industries and other statutory undertakings, which had previously been exempted. As for collective restrictive agreements which were placed under the jurisdiction of the Restrictive Practices Court by the ►Restrictive Trade Practices Act of 1956, the Director-General of Fair Trading has taken over the responsibilities of the Registrar of Restrictive Practices. The Fair Trading Act extended the coverage of the restrictive practices legislation to include restrictive agreements and information agreements affecting the supply of commercial services. These covered almost all commercial services such as hairdressers, travel agencies, hotels, passenger transport organizations, etc. The Director-General has a duty to keep under review and identify any commercial practices which might be against consumers' interest, that, for instance, might mislead or confuse, and on the basis of his investigations can recommend a course of action to the Secretary of State for Trade and Industry (►Competition Act). He may also seek an undertaking from individuals or firms that any unfair trading practices they have committed will be discontinued. The Act enables the Secretary of State to act moderately quickly against new forms of unwelcome trade practices by issuing Statutory Orders which obviate the need for the cumbersome procedure of progressing Bills through Parliament. The Office of Fair Trading also has the duty to supervise and grant licences under the ➤Consumer Credit Act. However, the Financial Services Act 1986 governs most competition policy considerations in the financial services industry. ➤➤competition policy; Monopolies and Mergers Commission; resale price maintenance.

FAO ➤Food and Agriculture Organization.

farm subsidies ➤Common Agricultural Policy.

f.a.s. Free alongside ship. The term in a contract by which the seller is required to deliver the goods to a quay or to lighters alongside the vessel at the seaport of shipment specified in the contract of sale. The seller is not obliged to obtain ➤insurance cover. ➤➤c.i.f.; f.o.b.

FDI Foreign direct investment (➤direct investment).

Fed ➤Federal Reserve System.

federal reserve banks ➤Federal Reserve System.

Federal Reserve Board ➤Federal Reserve System.

Federal Reserve System (Fed) The central banking system of the United States, established by the Federal Reserve Act of 1913 and modified by the Banking Act 1935. It differs from that of most other countries' ➤central banks in that it consists not of one bank but of twelve regional banks, twenty-five branches and eleven offices under the control of the Federal Reserve Board in Washington. The Board approves the discount and other ➤rates of interest of the system, supervises foreign business and generally regulates the operation of the banking system including the review of applications for mergers. It has proved a formidable force in controlling ➤inflation through tight ➤monetary policy, and its independence of decision-making has been much admired, and indeed, partly copied in the reforms of the Bank of England announced in 1997. The Federal Reserve Board consists of governors appointed for a term of fourteen years by the US President with Senate approval. The Fed Chairman has a term of only four years, allowing each President to appoint his own chairman. It is the Federal Open Market Committee, a subcommittee of the Board, which has control of purchases of government ➤securities by the reserve banks, and which thus effectively holds the key to the conduct of monetary policy. The considerable surpluses that the reserve system earns mostly go to the US internal revenue. The regional reserve banks act as central banks for their members, act as ➤lenders of last resort by rediscounting bills (➤discounting), hold their ➤cash requirements and provide clearing facilities. The commercial banks are required to hold reserves in the Federal Reserve. The US commercial ➤banking system is a unit rather than a ➤branch banking system; three-quarters of the banks in the USA have very few or no branches. Until recently, in many states branches were not allowed by law, although through the development of amalgamations and holding companies the US commercial banking system is not as fragmented as it appears. Some 176 banks account for over 60 per cent of all ►commercial bank liabilities. Since the Monetary Control Act 1980 all US banks are members of the Federal Reserve System.

Federal Trade Commission ►anti-trust.

fertility rate ►birth rate.

fiat money Currency which is legally decreed a valid means of financing trans-actions. It is, in short, legal tender, in contrast to other forms of paper, such as cheques, which carry credibility but no legal support. ►►fiduciary issue; monetary base.

fiduciary issue Paper ►money (►banknote) not backed by gold or silver. The term has its origins in the Bank Charter Act of 1844 in Britain, which fixed the fiduciary issue limit at £14 million. Any notes issued in excess of this amount had to be fully backed by gold. The fiduciary limit has been successively raised and the monetary authorities are now free to alter the note issue as they wish; effectively the note issue is now entirely fiduciary. ►►banking and currency schools.

final consumption ►final goods.

final expenditure ►final goods.

final goods Goods which are produced for ►consumption rather than as an ►intermediate product used in the process of production. *Final consumption*, i.e. consumption of final goods alone, is included in the totals of national output in ►social accounting; if intermediate goods were also included there would be double counting of output. Only government final consumption (which excludes ►transfer payments), consumers' expenditure (all of which, by definition, is final) and investment goods enter into *final expenditure* and thus into the ►gross domestic product.

finance The provision of ►money when and where required. Finance may be short-term (usually up to one year), medium-term (usually over one year and up to five to seven years) and long-term. Finance may be required for ►consumption or for ►investment. For the latter when provided it becomes ►capital. ►►business finance; consumer credit; public finance.

finance company An imprecise term covering a wide range of ►financial inter-mediaries, most commonly a synonym for ►finance house.

finance house A financial institution engaged in the provision of ►hire purchase and other forms of instalment credit. Also called finance companies, hire-purchase finance companies and ►industrial banks. There are several hundred finance houses in the UK, which together with ►credit card companies account for the bulk of ►instalment credit debt, the remainder being owed to retailers. Some of the hire-purchase debt of retailers is purchased by the finance houses under what are known as 'block discounts'. The funds of the finance houses come from interest-bearing deposits, not only from the general public, but from industrial and commercial companies and other financial institutions including the ►commercial banks (the interest paid is generally higher than that offered by the commercial banks); other sources of funds are capital reserves, ►bills discounted and bank overdrafts. The largest source of the finance houses' funds is in fact the commercial banks, and most of the larger finance houses are subsidiaries of the banks. Similarly, several finance houses are subsidiaries of manufacturing companies and advance instalment credit only for their parent company's products, e.g. Ford Motor Credit Co. Although advances for cars and other consumer durables represent a major proportion of their business, a huge proportion of the outstanding balances of the finance houses is for business purposes. Hire purchase is not the sole, although it is the main, activity of the finance houses; they also make loans for other purposes, including bridging finance, leasing and ►factoring, stocking loans for motor dealers and second mortgages.

financial assets ►assets.

financial intermediaries Institutions which hold ►money balances of, or which borrow from, individuals and other institutions, in order to make loans or other ►investments. Hence, they serve the purpose of channelling funds from lenders to borrowers. In standing between lenders and borrowers, intermediaries provide services to each, often at little or no cost compared with direct investment. By virtue of their size and expertise, financial intermediaries are able to reduce risks for lenders by enabling them to spread their investments widely, for example through ►assurance or ►investment trusts. They also provide *maturity transformation*. ►Building societies, for example, allow depositors to withdraw their money on demand but provide long-term funds for ►mortgage lending. It is usual to distinguish between banks in the banking sector and so-called non-bank financial intermediaries. The importance of this distinction arises from the fact that the ►liabilities of banks are part of the ►money supply, and this may not be true of the non-bank financial intermediaries. (►banking.) The most important of the non-bank financial intermediaries are the building societies, ►hire-purchase companies, ►insurance companies, ►savings banks, ►pension funds and investment trusts.

financial ratios 1. Specifically, measures of creditworthiness. The principal measures are the ►current ratio, the ►debt or *net worth* ratio (long-term debt to net worth), ►dividend cover, ►interest cover and the net tangible ►assets ratio (total tangible assets less current ►liabilities and minority interests to long-term debt). All these ratios are measures of the asset or income cover available to the suppliers of ►capital to the business. 2. Generally calculations based on company accounts and other sources, such as ►stock exchange share prices, designed to indicate the profitability or other financial aspects of a business, e.g. return on net assets, ►price–earnings ratio and stock sales ratio (►inventories). ►►rate of return.

Financial Services Act 1986 (FSA) (UK) Legislation enacted in November 1986 but coming into force on 29 April 1988 to regulate the investment business in the UK. The Act followed a report on investor protection commissioned in 1981 from Professor Gower and completed in 1984. The Gower Report recommended that the new regulatory system should cover life assurance, ►unit trusts and other forms of investment in business in addition to ►stock exchange investments. The Act set up a Securities and Investments Board (SIB), to oversee financial regulation, paid for by investment professionals, but with statutory powers and reporting to the Department of Trade and Industry. Investment businesses were registered with the SIB directly or with one of four *self-regulating organizations* (SROs). The original SROs were: the Financial Intermediaries', Managers' and Brokers' Regulatory Association (FIMBRA), which covered independent intermediaries such as ►brokers dealing in ►insurance; the Securities Association (TSA), for ►securities dealing such as by ►market makers; the Association of Futures Brokers and Dealers (AFBD), for dealings in ►futures and ►options (these last two bodies were merged to form the Securities and Futures Authority Ltd (SFA) in 1991; the Investment Managers' Regulatory Organization (IMRO), for investment management such as pension funds; and the Life Assurance and Unit Trust Regulatory Organization (LAUTRO). FIMBRA and LAUTRO were replaced by the Personal Investment Authority (PIA) in 1994. Certain investment markets were also approved by the SIB or via the appropriate SRO; these markets are *recognized investment exchanges* (RIEs), e.g. the *International Stock Exchange* (►stock exchange) and the Baltic Exchange. Lawyers and accountants for whom the provision of investment advice is only a minor part of their business are self-regulated by their own professional bodies. *Recognized professional bodies* (RPBs) have been approved by the SIB, including the Institute of Chartered Accountants of England and Wales.

By the mid-1990s the regulatory system was deemed to be failing – burdening firms with a large compliance burden, but not protecting consumers very adequately. In 1997 it was announced by the new Labour government that a new unified regulator would take over all the functions of SIB and the SROs, and indeed, some functions of the DTI and ►Bank of England, including bank supervision. The New Regulatory Organization (NEWRO), which is the SIB renamed and extended, is expected to be fully operational in the autumn of 1999.

***Financial Times* share indices** The standard measures of general stock market performance in London. The *FTO (Financial Times (Industrial) Ordinary)* or *FT30 Share Index*, an unweighted (►weighted average) *geometric* ►average of 30 leading ►blue chips quoted on the London ►Stock Exchange, was introduced in 1935 and calculated hourly. The FT 30 has been superseded by the *FT/SE*

100 'Footsie 100' Index, a ►market capitalization weighted average calculated minute by minute (real time). The base period for the FT 100 is 3 January 1984 = 1000, and its constituents are the 100 largest quoted industrial and commercial companies by capitalization, reviewed quarterly (►investment trusts are excluded). The *FT/SE Mid-250 Index*, also calculated minute by minute, covers the next 250 companies, ranked by market value; and the *FT/SE/Actuaries 350 Index* includes all the constituents of the 100 and 250 indices. The 350 Index covers about 92 per cent of total market value and the 100 Index about 72 per cent. The *FT/Actuaries All-Share Index* has been published daily since 10 April 1962; it now covers some 800 shares and fixed-interest ►stocks and covers some 98 per cent of total market value, and has indices for industry *baskets* and subsections. The *FT/SE Small Cap Index*, introduced in 1993 and calculated daily, covers those shares within the FT/A All-Share Index but not within the 350. In 1987 the *FT/Actuaries World Share Index* was introduced, based on a weighted sample of 2400 share prices, initially from twenty-four countries. The *FT/Actuaries Fixed Interest Indices* measure the prices and ►yields of UK gilts (►gilt-edged securities), index-linked (►indexation), ►debentures and ►loans. Total return figures are calculated for all the UK indices and published daily. These figures, which are gross of tax, take account of both price performance and income received from ►dividends. ►► index number.

financial trusts ►trust.

financial year The period of account used for financial purposes. These often do not coincide with calendar years, and are hence referred to as financial years. A financial year 1997/98, for example, might run from 31 August 1997 to 1 September 1998. The British government fiscal or tax year runs from 6 April of one year to 5 April in the following year. In the United States, the fiscal year runs from 1 July to 30 June.

firm, theory of the The study of the behaviour of firms with respect to: the inputs they buy; the production techniques they adopt; the quantity they produce; and the price at which they sell their output. Two basic approaches to the theory can be identified: (a) The traditional approach assumes that producers aim to maximize profits; whether they are monopolists or perfect competitors, they produce at a point where ►marginal cost equals ►marginal revenue and employ inputs to a point at which their ►marginal revenue product is equal to the cost of employing them (►labour, demand for; perfect competition). (b) Other theories attempt to represent the complications of the large institutions which characterize society today, especially the ►separation of ownership from control of firms, which, it is suggested, may lead to objectives other than profit maximization. These alternative theories postulate the aim as being: the maximization of sales; growth; or management utility – with profit merely held to some minimum level (►satisficing). The ►behavioural theory of the firm postulates the existence of a multiplicity of conflicting objectives. It is not clear whether the alternative theories actually contradict the claim of the traditional approach that firms maximize profits because in the long run the maximization of, for example, sales growth might merely amount to the maximization of profit. Moreover, as a single goal, profit maximization perhaps better and more simply approximates to the behaviour of firms than any other single objective. It is thus usually accepted that the insights of traditional theory are useful despite their dependence on apparently unrealistic assumptions. (c) More recently, ➤game theory has been influential in analysis of firms, with concepts like the principal–agent problem increasingly deployed to explain behaviour. ➤➤Cournot, A. A.; Galbraith, J. K.; Simon, H. A.

first-mover advantage The notion that countries or firms which create new industries or products first may establish a competitive advantage that makes it hard or impossible for other countries to follow in the same area. The advantage is most likely to prevail in sectors of large ➤economies of scale, and especially in cases where the most efficient scale represents a high proportion of the global market. It would certainly be difficult for, say, China or Japan to enter wide-bodied aircraft manufacture in competition with Boeing and Airbus. The frequency with which airframe manufacture is quoted as an example of potential first-mover advantage, suggests it may be one of very few special cases requiring a large supplier chain and technological depth. It is not difficult to think of examples of other first movers – for example, motor cycles in the UK – which have failed to sustain an early advantage. The argument is not new; it is a variant of the ➤infant-industry argument for protection against imports. But it re-emerged in the late 1980s, under the guise of *strategic trade theory*, associated with Paul Krugman. He suggested the traditional arguments for nations to allow ➤free trade were undermined. In practice, however, he has argued so few industries meet the right conditions to justify strategic trade policy, and the gains are so small, that a presumption in favour of free trade is justified.

fiscal drag The effect of inflation upon effective tax rates, or sometimes, the effect of growth in ➤nominal gross domestic product on tax revenues. Under progressive ➤income tax systems, increases in earnings may push taxpayers into higher tax brackets. In a tax system that is not indexed for inflation (➤indexation), this has the result that simply increasing earnings to keep pace with inflation will generate higher tax revenues. With the decline in inflation rates across the west since the 1980s, the term fiscal drag has loosely been used to refer to the fact that, even in an indexed tax system, if earnings grow more quickly than prices (and indeed, they typically do), then the government again ends up with extra revenues without having to raise tax rates in explicit policy changes. Fiscal drag could result in an unintended shift in ➤fiscal policy, with a depressing effect upon the growth of demand and output. A similar process can work in reverse and under conditions of ➤deflation; for example, if prices fall tax rates will also fall even though real incomes have increased. Fiscal drag therefore can have the effect of a ➤built-in stabilizer. It appears to have declined in the UK in the last ten years, as the progressivity of the tax system has fallen. Indeed, in the years of the early 1990s government appeared to face a general decline in tax revenues as a proportion of GDP, necessitating discretionary tax increases to compensate. ➤fiscal illusion.

fiscal federalism The system of sharing tax revenues and public expenditure between central and regional government (➤public sector). Revenue may be raised by the upper level of government and grants given to lower levels on the basis of population or other criteria, or revenues from specific national taxes may be shared in agreed proportions, for example a small proportion of national ➤value-added tax revenues in the ➤European Union go to help finance community institutions. Another possibility is that certain ➤tax bases, for example property in the UK, may be reserved for local government, with or without freedom on the part of local authorities to determine their own tax rates. For the division of expenditure between central and regional government the main principle is that local governments should confine their expenditure to uses which have limited spillovers outside their areas, such as roads and schools. ➤externalities. ➤subsidiarity.

fiscal illusion The lack of transparency in taxation that allows governments to raise extra revenue without the population fully understanding the extent of the tax burden. Fiscal illusion is often a consequence of ➤fiscal drag. Some economists in the area of ➤public-choice theory have worried that governments have found it too easy to grow as a result of public ignorance, and have advocated constitutional limits on the size of western governments' spending. However, the need has diminished with popular resistance to unlimited growth in tax revenues. ➤tax tolerance; Buchanan, James McGill; hypothecation.

fiscal neutrality The idea that the tax system should be designed so that as few distortions are caused to economic behaviour as possible. It is not fiscally neutral, for example, to apply ➤value-added tax to some items but not others, for this causes consumers to switch spending from taxed items to untaxed ones. This distortion of behaviour is economically inefficient. Despite the ➤economic efficiency of applying the principle of fiscal neutrality, it is often argued that distributional or other objectives are served by manipulating different taxes. For this reason, ➤lump-sum taxes, which are the most neutral, are rarely applied in practice and fiscal neutrality is seen as only one of a number of desirable features of a tax system. ➤deadweight loss, double taxation.

fiscal policy The budgetary stance of central government. Decisions to lower taxation or increase ➤public expenditure in the interests of stimulating ➤aggregate demand are referred to as loosening fiscal policy. Higher tax rates or reductions in public expenditure will tighten fiscal policy. There is considerable controversy about the appropriate weight of fiscal policy in economic management, relative to ➤monetary policy. In 1997 it was estimated that a one percentage point rise in interest rates has the same affect on demand, as a tax rise of about 9 billion pounds. Few economists think fiscal policy should be used as an instrument of fine-tuning. Most believe policy should primarily be directed towards maintaining a prudent level of borrowing (►structural deficit), preferably according to certain rules (►golden rule). ►►balanced budget; Keynesian economics; medium-term financial strategy; policy ineffectiveness theorem; public-sector borrowing requirement; quantity theory of money; reflation.

fiscal year ►financial year.

Fisher, Irving (1867–1947) A mathematician by professional training, Fisher was Professor of Political Economy at Yale University from 1898 to 1935. His main works on economics were *Mathematical Investigations in the Theory of Value and Prices* (1892), *Nature of Capital and Income* (1906), *Rate of Interest* (1907), *Purchasing Power of Money* (1911), *The Making of Index Numbers* (1922) and *Theory of Interest* (1930). *The Rate of Interest*, which was substantially revised in 1930, developed the theory of ►interest from ►Böhm-Bawerk towards the modern theory of ►investment appraisal. The ►rate of interest is governed by the interaction of two forces: (a) the 'willingness or impatience' of individuals with respect to the giving up of ►income now compared with income in the future (Fisher invented the term ►time preference); and (b) the 'investment opportunity principle', the technological ability to convert income now into income in the future. He called the latter the 'rate of return over cost', which ►Keynes said was the same as his 'marginal efficiency of capital' (►internal rate of return). He defined this 'rate of return over cost' as that discount rate (►discounting) which equalized the ►present value of the possible alternative investment choices open. He showed how the ranking of investment choices depended on the rate of interest used. He clarified economists' ideas on the nature of ►capital, distinguishing between a stock and a flow of ►wealth. A house is capital stock, but its use is a flow of income. He was the author of the 'quantity of money' (exchange) equation $MV = PT$, in which M = the stock of money, V = the ►velocity of circulation, P = the ►price level and T = the output of goods and ►services (►quantity theory of money).

Fisher developed the theory of ►index numbers and established a set of conditions which an ideal index should satisfy.

fisher equation ►Fisher, Irving; quantity theory of money.

fixed asset ►assets.

fixed capital ►business finance; capital.

fixed charge ►floating charge.

fixed costs ►Costs which do not vary with output, for example the ►rent on a factory ►lease. Also called *overhead,* although in accounting terminology all costs except direct labour and materials are usually regarded as overheads and some of these overhead costs, for example electricity and postage, may vary with output. In the ►long run all costs are variable and the short run is defined as the period of time in which all the ►factors of production cannot be varied. ►►average costs; sunk costs.

fixed debenture ►floating debentures.

fixed exchange rate ►exchange rate.

fixed interest ►securities.

fixed-point theorem A theorem stating that for certain types of functions, $y = f(x)$, there is at least one value of x such that $y = x$. That is, that x maps on to itself; or x is a fixed point. These theorems are used in ►equilibrium analysis to help prove the existence of a ►general equilibrium. If a simple economy can be modelled as a system of functions that conform to the types described in a fixed-point theorem, the fact that a fixed point must exist can be turned into proof that a market equilibrium exists.

fixed trust ►flexible trust.

flags of convenience An expression relating to the practice of shipowners of registering their vessels with countries other than those of their own home ports in order to avoid taxes, or stringent safety or crewing regulations. The extent of the movement can be seen from the growth of the merchant fleets of such small countries as Panama and Liberia.

flat yield A ►yield on a fixed-interest ►security calculated by expressing the annual ►interest payable as a proportion of the purchase price of the security. It omits any allowance for the difference between purchase price and redemption price. ►►redeemable securities.

flexible exchange rate ►exchange rate.

flexible trust The most common form of ►unit trust, in which the ►portfolio of ►securities purchased by the trust can be varied at the discretion of the managers. Also called a 'managed' trust. Flexible trusts were developed in the 1930s to overcome the problems raised by the inflexibility of *fixed trusts*, in which the investment ►portfolio is fixed in the trust deed.

floating asset ►floating capital.

floating capital ►Capital which is not invested in fixed ►assets, such as machinery, but in work in progress, wages paid, etc. Synonymous with ►working capital. ►►current ratio.

floating charge An assignment of the total ►assets of a company or individual as ►collateral security for a ►debt, as opposed to particular assets, when such an assignment is called a *fixed charge*.

floating debentures A type of ►debenture in which the ►loan is secured by a charge on the assets of a firm generally. Where specific assets secure a debenture ►loan, it is known as a *fixed debenture*.

floating debt 1. Generally, any short-term ►debt as opposed to ►funded debt. 2. Specifically, that part of the UK ►national debt that consists of short-term borrowing, i.e. ►treasury bills. Treasury bills form an important part of the ►liquid assets of the money market, so that the size of the floating debt has considerable influence over the total ►money supply.

floating exchange rate ►exchange rate.

flotation Raising new ►capital by public subscription. A private company issuing ►shares to the public for the first time is said to be 'going public' or making an *Initial Public Offering* (IPO). ►►stock exchange; unlisted securities market.

f.o.b. free on board The term in a contract in which the seller is required to deliver and load the goods on board a ship in the seaport of shipment specified in the contract of sale. The seller is not obliged to obtain ►insurance cover. UK imports are entered by HM Customs in the overseas trade accounts as c.i.f., and exports as f.o.b. For the ►balance of payments accounts, the ►import figures are adjusted to an f.o.b. basis to make them comparable with exports, the revenues or costs represented by the difference between c.i.f. and f.o.b. being included in ►invisibles. ►►c.i.f.; f.a.s.

Fogel, Robert W. (b. 1926) A joint winner of the ►Nobel Prize in 1993, an economic historian, and director of the Center for Population Economics at the University of Chicago, Robert Fogel has been a pioneer in the area of 'new economic history'. This attempts to analyse the past on the basis of new, or reconstructed databases. Fogel has applied this approach in controversial ways, for example to argue that slavery was an economically efficient social order, that ultimately collapsed on account of political decisions. He has also reassessed the role of the railways in American economic development, in *Railroads and American Economic Growth,* arguing that the sum of many changes rather than a few great innovations, determines economic advance. ►cliometrics; North, Douglass.

Food and Agricultural Organization (FAO). An organization set up in 1945, with headquarters in Rome, within the framework of the United Nations, It conducts research and offers technical assistance with the aim of improving the standards of living of agricultural areas. It is concerned with the improvement of ►productivity and distribution networks for the agricultural, forestry and fishing industries. It conducts surveys, issues statistics, produces forecasts of the world food situation and sets minimum nutritional standards.

forced saving A situation in which expenditure falls short of ►disposable income because goods are not available for ►consumption, rather than because consumers have voluntarily decided to accumulate ►saving. Under these circumstances, ►prices of goods would rise and supply would increase in a ►free-market economy so that forced saving would be a temporary symptom or ►disequilibrium. If for any reason there were ►long-run constraints on the increase in output the increase in prices would reduce demand and stimulate the development of ►substitutes. Forced saving does occur in ►planned economies and, at a ►macroeconomic level democratic governments can enforce saving by increasing ►taxation while holding ►public expenditure constant. ►►quantity rationing; repressed inflation.

foreign aid The administered transfer of resources from the ►advanced countries for the purpose of encouraging economic growth in the ►developing countries (►economic growth, stages of). Funds transferred to the developing countries from governments and international institutions (►►International Bank for Reconstruction and Development) in the form of official aid account for one-third of the total transfer of funds to the developing countries (the rest is accounted for by loans through the ►commercial banks and ►direct investment). Official aid from the advanced countries represented in the ►Organization for Economic Cooperation and Development's Development Assistance Committee accounts for about 0.27 per cent of their ►gross domestic product. UK foreign aid is administered by the Department for International Development (formerly the Overseas Development Administration (ODA)). ►►European Union; export credit insurance; export incentives; foreign investment; generalized system of preferences.

foreign balance ►balance of payments.

foreign bill of exchange ►foreign-exchange market.

foreign exchange Claims on another country held in the form of the currency of that country or interest-bearing ►bonds. ►►exchange control; foreign-exchange market; gold and foreign-exchange reserves.

foreign-exchange market The ►market in which transactions are conducted to effect the transfer of the ►currency of one country into that of another. The need to settle accounts with foreigners gave rise to the *foreign bill of exchange*, which was accepted by banks or other institutions of international standing (►accepting house). These bills were traded at discount, and in this way the foreign-exchange market was established, the bills reflecting actual international trade flows. However, the market has developed in modern times and is now dominated by financial institutions which buy and sell foreign currencies, making their ►profit from the divergences between the ►exchange rates and ►rates of interest in the various financial centres. In April 1995 the ►Bank for International Settlements estimated that average daily turnover in foreign-exchange dealing in London, the world leading market, was $464 billion, (of which $186 billion was 'spot' (►spot market) and $278 billion was 'forward') (►forward-exchange market); followed by New York $244 billion, Tokyo $161 billion, Singapore $105 billion, Hong Kong $90 billion and Zürich $86 billion. ►convertibility; Tobin tax.

foreign investment The acquisition by governments, institutions or individuals in one country of ►assets in another. Foreign investment covers both ►direct investment and ►portfolio investment and includes public authorities, private firms and individuals. For a country in which ►savings are insufficient relative to the potential demand for ►investment, foreign capital can be a fruitful means of stimulating rapid growth. In addition, direct investment may be a means of financing a ►balance of payments deficit. Direct investment often involves the setting up of subsidiary companies for the domestic production of goods which previously were imported from the parent company.

Foreign Operations Administration ►European Recovery Programme.

forward-exchange market A ►market in which contracts are made to supply ►currencies at fixed dates in the future at fixed ►prices. Currencies may be bought and sold in the ►foreign-exchange market either 'spot' or 'forward' (►spot market and forward market). In the former case the transaction takes place immediately, and it is in this market that ►exchange rates are kept at their managed levels by government intervention. In the forward-exchange market, currencies are bought and sold for transacting at some future date, i.e. in three months' or six months' time. The difference between the 'spot' rate of exchange and the 'forward' rate is determined by the ►rate of interest and the exchange risk; that is, the possibility of ►appreciation or ►depreciation of the currencies transacted. Therefore, the size of the ►premium or ►discount of, for instance, forward sterling compared with spot sterling indicates the strength of the market's expectation of an appreciation or depreciation of sterling and its extent. ►exchange rate overshooting.

forward market Any ►market in ►futures; that is to say, a market in which promises to buy or to sell ►securities or ►commodities at some future date at fixed ►prices are bought and sold. An example of a forward market is the ►forward-exchange market.

franchising A contractual arrangement under which an independent franchisee produces or sells a product or service under the brand name of the franchiser and to his specifications and with marketing and other support. The franchisee pays a royalty to the franchiser and may purchase supplies from him. The franchisee provides his own ►capital and is legally an independent ►enterprise which is none the less highly dependent upon the franchiser, though, as Curran and Stanworth have pointed out, many ►small businesses, say with a high proportion of sales to a single customer, may enjoy no greater degree of independence than many franchised enterprises. Franchising is growing rapidly in the UK but is less important than in the USA, where it accounts for over one-third of retail turnover. Examples of franchised operations are filling-stations and various fast-food outlets.

franked investment income ➤Income, normally of a company, on which ➤taxation has already been paid at source, i.e. income received as a ➤dividend by one company from another (➤corporation tax).

free depreciation ➤capital allowances.

free-enterprise economy ➤free-market economy.

free exchange rate ➤exchange rate.

free goods ➤Commodities that have no ➤price because they are not scarce and do not require the use of scarce ➤factors of production to create them, for example, fresh air and sunshine (in certain parts of the world). Things which are given away without charge, for example book matches or government services, are not free goods, because they have ➤opportunity costs.

free market A ➤market in which ➤supply and ➤demand are not subject to ➤regulation other than normal ➤competition policy, but in which property rights are allocated, and upheld so that trade can occur. The definition of a free market becomes blurred in cases where free trade and competition are incompatible. Most economists would be loath to describe the world diamond market as completely free, given its dominance by an international cartel arrangement. ➤➤Coase theorem, Chicago school.

free-market economy Strictly, an economic system in which the allocation of ➤resources is determined solely by ➤supply and ➤demand in ➤free markets, though in practice there are some limitations on market freedoms in all countries. Moreover, in some countries governments intervene in free markets to promote competition that might otherwise disappear. Usually used as synonymous with ➤capitalism.

free reserves ➤company reserves.

free-rider problem The problem, arising in many situations, that no individual is willing to contribute towards the cost of something when he hopes that someone else will bear the cost instead. The problem arises whenever there is a ➤public good. Everybody in a block of flats may want a faulty light repaired, but no one wants to bear the cost of organizing the repair themselves. They would each rather free-ride on the effort of someone else. Examples of the problem abound: shareholders take little interest in the management of their companies, hoping someone else will monitor what the executives are doing (➤separation of ownership from control); rude taxi drivers free-ride on the reputation of the profession as a whole; nations who contribute nothing to disaster relief efforts are said to free-ride on the efforts of others. Obtaining satisfactory levels of managerial monitoring, politeness or disaster relief in these situations is difficult in the absence of compulsory enforcement measures.

free trade The condition in which the free flow of goods (►economic good) and ►services in international exchange is neither restricted nor encouraged by direct government intervention. In practice all governments are involved in regulating overseas trade in some way. The most common means of affecting the distribution and levels of international trade are import ►tariffs, import ►quotas and export subsidies (►export incentives). It has been broadly accepted among economists that an international free-trade policy is desirable to optimize world output and ►income levels in the long run. The ►Organization for European Cooperation and Development and the United Nations (►►World Trade Organization) are committed to freeing world trade, but most economists would agree that under present conditions complete freedom of trade would not be desirable. In any case, it is clear that individual countries could gain from protectionism (►customs union; first-mover advantage; infant industry argument; protection). Towards the end of the eighteenth century there was a reaction against ►mercantilism, which had advocated government intervention to obtain surpluses on ►visible trade. This reaction was consolidated in a new economic liberalism and the doctrine of ►laissez-faire. The ►classical economists' support of a free-trade policy was not so much based on specific economic analyses of international trade as simply part of their general belief in what ►Adam Smith called the 'hidden hand': the greatest good is achieved if each individual is left to seek his own ►profit. The free-trade era lasted in England for almost a century. After the First World War economic nationalism reached its peak and free trade was abandoned for protectionism. However, since the end of the Second World War there has been a general acceptance internationally of the dangers of protectionism and some reduction in ►international trade barriers, especially for manufactured goods. Progress has been slow, and has paradoxically been associated with the growth of regional ►customs union. Some economists have advocated unilateral free trade (countries can help themselves by freeing up imports, regardless of other countries' behaviour). Other economists have seen the problem as that of the ►prisoner's dilemma – with individual incentives for nations to restrict trade, but a collective interest that all nations should pursue it. In practice, the latter view is reflected in the many set-piece negotiations through the ►General Agreement on Tariffs and Trade and culminating in the setting up of the World Trade Organization. ►►European Union; European Free Trade Association; first mover advantage; Free-Trade Area; General Agreement on Tariffs and Trade.

free-trade area An association of a number of countries between which all import ►tariffs and ►quotas and export subsidies and other similar government measures to influence trade (►export incentives) have been removed. Each country, however, continues to retain its own international trade measures vis-à-vis countries outside the association. There has been an increase in recent years in the number of trading areas being formed worldwide. In 1996 discussions took place in Cartagena, Colombia between representatives from thirty-four countries with a view to setting up a free-trade area for the Americas by 2005. ➤Andean Pact; Asia–Pacific Economic Cooperation; Customs Union; Economic Community of West African States; Latin American Integration Association; Mercosur; North American Free Trade Agreement; structural impediments initiative.

free-trade zone A customs-defined area in which goods or services may be processed or transacted without attracting taxes or duties or being subjected to certain government regulations. A special case is the ➤freeport, into which goods are imported free of customs ➤tariffs or taxes. ➤enterprise zones.

freedom of entry Absence of ➤barriers to entry preventing new suppliers entering a ➤market. One of the assumptions of ➤perfect competition. ➤contestability.

freeport A seaport or airport which is able to accept cargo without the imposition of any import ➤tariff or some specified ➤taxes. In addition, freeports may be granted special dispensation regarding legislation affecting businesses in the domestic market outside the port, such as employment conditions, health and safety regulations and development planning. There are several hundred such ports throughout the world. In 1984 the UK government gave approval for the setting up of freeports, in which imports were free of customs tariffs, ➤excise duties and ➤value-added tax. Goods become liable to these taxes only when they pass from the freeport zone into the domestic market. In 1990, the government extended the scheme for a further ten years. ➤free-trade zone.

frequency distribution A tabulation showing a statistical ➤population allocated numerically into subcategories of a specified classification. (➤income, distribution of.) For instance, the following frequency distribution shows how the total population of the UK was divided into different age groups in 1995.

Age group	Number (thousands)
0 to 14 years	11,362
15 to 64 years	38,019
65 and over	9,225
	58,606

Source: *UK Digest of Statistics*, HMSO, 1996.

frictional unemployment The ➤unemployment that inevitably results from the process of job-seeking. It will exist under conditions of generally so-called full-employment conditions (➤employment, full), but it is not precisely clear what proportion of total unemployment can be called frictional. Frictional unemployment arises because of time lags in the functioning of ►labour markets which are inevitable in a ►free-market economy; there are search delays involved, for example in moving from one job to another. Frictional unemployment is conceptually distinct from ►structural unemployment, which results in heavy local concentrations of unemployment and, of course, from unemployment arising from a deficiency of demand. ►►classical unemployment; labour, mobility of.

Friedman, Milton (b. 1912) Professor of Economics at the University of Chicago and leading member of the Chicago school. After a short period with the Natural Resources Commission in Washington, Professor Friedman joined the research staff of the National Bureau of Economic Research in 1937 and, apart from a short period, has maintained a close association with this important research organization. During the Second World War he served in the Tax Research Division of the US Treasury. In 1946 he was appointed Associate Professor of Economics and Statistics at the University of Chicago, becoming Professor of Economics there from 1948 until he retired in 1979. In 1976 he was awarded the ►Nobel Prize in Economics by the Royal Swedish Academy of Science. His main published works in economics include *Taxing to Prevent Inflation* (1943), *Essays in Positive Economics* (1953), *A Theory of the Consumption Function* (1957), *A Program for Monetary Stability* (1960), *Price Theory* (1962), *A Monetary History of the United States 1867–1960* (1963), *Inflation: Causes and Consequences* (1963), *The Great Contraction* (1965), *The Optimum Quantity of Money* (1969), *A Theoretical Framework for Monetary Analysis* (1971), *An Economist's Protest: Columns in Political Economy* (1975), *Free to Choose. A Personal Statement* (1980) and *Monetary Trends in the United States and the United Kingdom* (1982).

Friedman has made contributions to the ►theory of distribution, arguing for an approach in which high incomes are regarded as a reward for taking risks. He has also been a leading defender of the Marshallian tradition in ►microeconomics (►Marshall, A.) and made a methodological defence of classical economics that stimulated controversy for a decade. His ►permanent-income hypothesis was also an important contribution to the theory of the ►consumption function. His main work, however, has been on the development of the ►quantity theory of money and its empirical testing. He has extended the Fisher equation (►Fisher, I.) to include other ►variables such as ►wealth and ►rates of interest, and has made statistical tests to attempt to measure the factors determining the demand for money to hold. Friedman has advocated strict control of the ►money supply – preferably in accordance with a simple rule as to how much growth will be allowed year by year – as a means for controlling ►inflation. His view that it is not desirable to fine-tune the economy using ►stabilization policy (an early adherent to the ►policy ineffectiveness theorem) has to a large extent been accepted, but in the world of economic theory Friedman's findings have been overshadowed by the more elegant route to similar conclusions based on ►rational expectations, and associated with ►new classical economics. ►►economic doctrines, Chicago school; liquidity preference; unemployment, natural rate of.

friendly society A mutual organization, often an ➤insurance association (➤mutual company). There are several thousand friendly societies in Britain, including working-men's clubs, set up voluntarily to provide benefits and assistance during sickness, unemployment, retirement or death. The tax advantages enjoyed by the friendly societies have been reduced in recent years, and are limited in respect of life or endowment business to premiums of not exceeding £270 a year.

fringe benefits Non-wage or salary rewards provided for employees, for example pensions and company cars. Some fringe benefits, within certain limits, such as pension arrangements, luncheon vouchers or subsidized canteens are not assessed for ➤income tax, while others, such as cars and low-interest loans, are. Holidays (in excess of any legal minimum requirement), private health insurance, 'free' coal or other products and discounts on goods purchased through the employer are other examples of fringe benefits. In England a series of laws from 1749 onwards culminating in the Truck Acts in the nineteenth century made it illegal to pay workers wholly in kind, because of abuse by employers of rights given, for example, in 'company stores'.

Frisch, Ragnar A. K. (1895–1973) Born in Norway, Professor Frisch graduated in economics at the University of Oslo. He was appointed to the Chair of Economics at that university in 1931, a post he held until he retired in 1965. His published works include *Statistical Confluence Analysis by Means of Complete Regression Systems* (1943), *Planning for India* (1960), *Theory of Production* (1965), *Maxima and Minima* (1966) and *Economic Planning Studies: A Collection of Essays* (1976). He won the ➤Nobel Prize in Economics (jointly with J. Tinbergen) in 1969. Professor Frisch pioneered work in the application of mathematics and statistics in the testing of hypotheses in economics. He invented the word ➤econometrics and founded the Econometric Society. He contributed to the analysis of the dynamics of ➤trade cycles and the application of econometrics to economic planning.

'front door' ➤'back door'.

FTC Federal Trade Commission (➤anti-trust).

FT/SE 100 Share Index (Footsie) ➤*Financial Times* share indices.

full employment ➤employment, full.

full-line forcing The exercise of market power to oblige a buyer to take a whole range of products rather than only one of them. Also known as ➤tie-in sales, which more strictly means that sale of a product carries with it a condition that some other item will be purchased at the same time. ➤➤vertical restraints.

function A description of the relationship which governs the behaviour of two or more related ➤variables. Functions can be expressed in different ways. If consumption (C) is $0.9 \times$ income (Y), we can represent this information as: an fundamental analysis

equation ($C = 0.9Y$); a graph (C on one axis, Y on the other); or a tabulation (with certain values of C in one column and the corresponding values of Y in the other). The function is an important feature of many different areas of economics: the ►utility *function* maps the quantities of different goods consumed on to levels of consumer utility. A ►demand function maps different price levels on to the corresponding quantities demanded. ►►production function.

fundamental analysis ►chartist.

funded ►pension funds.

funded debt Generally, short-term ►debt that has been converted into long-term debt (►funding). Specifically, the funded debt was originally that consisting of ►consols, the ►interest on which was paid out of the ►Consolidated fund. Then it came to mean all government perpetual ►loans where there is no obligation on the part of the government to repay, such as consols 3½ per cent war loan, but it is sometimes taken to include all government ►securities quoted on the ►stock exchange.

funding The process of converting short-term to long-term ►debt by the sale of long-term ►securities and using the funds raised to pay off short-term debt. Funding may be carried out by a company because its ►capital structure is inappropriate, i.e. to take advantage of the fact that long-term ►capital is normally cheaper and less likely to be withdrawn than short-term capital. Companies or governments may also take advantage of a period of low ►rates of interest to repay long-term ►stocks at the earliest possible date and replace them with new stocks at lower rates of interest. Funding has also been used as an instrument of ►monetary policy by the government as well as for ►national debt management. By selling long-dated securities and purchasing ►treasury bills (which are treated as part of the ►cash reserves of the ►commercials banks), the ►liquidity of the ►banking system is reduced. *Overfunding* occurs when the government is selling more debt to the non-bank sector than is necessary to meet the ►public-sector borrowing requirement. ►►pension funds.

funding operations The conversion of short-term fixed-interest ►debt (►floating debt) to long-term fixed-interest debt (►funded debt). It is normally used in relation to the work of the ►national debt commissioners, but the ►Bank of England's operations in ►treasury bills and government ►bonds approaching maturity are also covered by the term. Private companies with bank ►overdrafts or other short-term sources of ►capital may also decide to convert them to long-term debt by funding operations. ►►funding.

futures Contracts made in a 'future ►market' for the purchase or sale of ►commodities or financial ►assets, on a specified future date. Futures are negotiable instruments, that is they may be bought and sold. Many commodity exchanges, e.g. wool, cotton and wheat, have established futures markets which permit manufacturers and traders to ➤hedge against changes in ➤price of the raw materials they use or deal in. ➤➤forward exchange market; London International Financial Futures Exchange; options; speculation.)

G

G7 Forum of the world's largest seven industrial economies: the US, Japan, Germany, France, Italy, the UK and Canada. The first G7 summit was in Rambouillet in November 1975 (although Canada was not yet a member) and from there the institution has developed from an informal gathering of leaders to a huge international annual summit. Russia has been admitted to the certain parts of the G7 summits, which have thus been retitled the Summit of Eight. G7 Finance Ministers meet several times a year and on, some notable occasions (such as the *Plaza agreement* in September 1985, which talked the dollar down; *the Louvre agreement* in February 1987 which set out a sophisticated package of exchange-rate coordination; and, to a lesser extent, the Washington meeting in April 1995, which set out the beliefs of the G7 that the dollar was too low) the ministers have successfully managed to engineer changes in the direction of the ➤foreign-exchange market.

Galbraith, John Kenneth (b. 1908) A leading American political economist, he was born in Canada and, after graduating at Toronto in agriculture, took a Ph.D. at the University of California. In 1949 he became Professor of Economics at Harvard University and was, from 1961 to 1963, US ambassador to India. His major books include *A Theory of Price Control* (1952), *American Capitalism* (1952), *The Great Crash 1929* (1955), *The Affluent Society* (1958), *The Economic Discipline* (1967), *The New Industrial State* (1967), *Economics, Peace and Laughter* (1971), *Economics and the Public Purpose* (1974) and *The Nature of Mass Poverty* (1979). He has been a sharp critic of current economic theory because of its preoccupation with growth (➤growth theory). He has accused advanced societies of producing waste simply to satisfy the need for growth for its own sake. He has argued that in modern advanced economies the problems of the distribution of the total product to the different sectors of society should be given more attention. At the same time, he believes that academic theoretical economics is too bound by its old tradition of the efficacy of competition to the extent of losing touch with the real world. In *American Capitalism* he showed how modern society breeds monopolistic power systems. ➤monopoly in industry induces a countervailing monopoly or ➤monopsony in distribution, in ➤labour and even in government purchasing agencies.

In *The New Industrial State* he argued that the 'technostructure' (managers) of the largest corporations in modern industrial society is motivated primarily by a desire to remain secure and to expand its corporation rather than to maximize

►profits. The highly capitalized nature of the industrial system has required a considerable extension of planning and control, notably of the ►capital supply, through ►self-financing, and of demand, through advertising and distribution techniques. Under these conditions the assumption of ►consumers' sovereignty that underlies modern microeconomic theory (►microeconomics) is invalid and the theory no longer relevant to much of the economic system. Galbraith's views have been challenged by many economists as an overstatement of monopolistic power but are none the less sometimes accepted as an accurate statement of tendency in the modern economy. He has been critical of the advocates of the strict control of the supply of ►money as a means of reducing ►inflation. ►►consumption; countervailing power; firm, theory of the; Keynes, J. M.; Mill, J. S.; oligopoly; quantity theory of money.

Galiani, Ferdinando (1728–87) A Neapolitan priest who wrote a number of treatises on economic subjects, in particular *Della moneta* (1751) on ►money and exchange, and *Dialogues sur le commerce des blés* (1770) on ►free trade in cereals. He resolved the so-called paradox of value, e.g. water is useful but cheap, whereas diamonds are useless but expensive, by analysing the ►price of a ►commodity in terms of its ►scarcity on the one hand and its ►utility on the other; utility being not only a reflection of a commodity's usefulness, but also its pleasure-giving potential. He explained how price both influences and is influenced by ►demand. Much of his work in ►value theory was original, though part of a long tradition of ecclesiastical thought. However, he was not familiar to English economists of the early nineteenth century, and much of the ground covered by Galiani was gone over again by them. ►►marginal utility.

galloping inflation ►hyperinflation.

game theory The branch of economics concerned with representing economic interactions in a highly stylized form, with players, pay-offs and strategies. Much of economic theory is concerned with the processes and conditions under which individuals or firms maximize their own benefits or minimize their own costs in markets in which their individual actions do not materially influence others (►►perfect competition). There are, however, many cases in which economic decisions are made – often in situations of conflict – where one party's action induces a material reaction from others. An example is wage bargaining between employers and unions. A more simple case is that of ►duopoly, in which the price set by one seller will be based on his view of that set by the other in reply. The mathematical theory of games has been applied to economics to help elucidate problems of this kind. The theory of games is concerned with the study of the optimal strategies to maximize pay-offs, given the risks involved in judging the responses of adversaries, and also the conditions under which there is a unique solution (i.e. that the optimum strategy for X and that of Y are both possible and not inconsistent). Games may be classified into ►zero-sum games, in which one player's gain is another player's loss; *non-zero-sum games*, in which one player's decision may benefit (or hurt) all players; *cooperative games*, in which collusion between players is possible; and *non-cooperative games*, when it is not. The application of the theory of games to economics was first introduced by J. von Neumann and O. Morgenstern in *Theory of Games and Economic Behaviour* (1944). It has since risen to become perhaps the most important source of new ideas in ►microeconomics, and the mindset of game theory now dominates almost any analysis of interactions between economic agents. ►►auction; bargaining; mixed strategy; Nash equilibrium; prisoner's dilemma; repeated game; tit-for-tat.

GATT ►General Agreement on Tariffs and Trade.

GDP ►gross domestic product.

GDP deflator An index of prices (►index number) which can be applied to the value estimates of the ►gross domestic product over a time period in order to remove the effects of changes in the general level of prices. The resultant revised estimates give a more accurate picture of movements during the period in the physical or real output of goods and services. In practice, the components of GDP are deflated (►deflation) separately to constant prices and then added together to give an estimate for a given year in ►real terms. The advantage of the GDP deflator as a measure of domestic ►inflation, is that it strips out the effect on prices of a change in the price of ►imports, on account of, say, a change in the ►exchange rate. It is argued that it represents the best measure of ►underlying inflation. It is not used as the basis for the ►inflation target, as publication of the deflator is less frequent than the ►retail prices index, and often subject to late revision.

gearing The relative importance of ►loans in the ►capital structure of a firm. Also called the *debt ratio* and, in the USA, *leverage*. There are several ways of measuring gearing. The usual way is the ratio of fixed-interest ►debt to share-holder's interest plus the debt (►net worth). *Equity gearing* is the ratio of borrowings to ►equity or risk capital. *Capital gearing* may be defined as bank borrowings and other debt as a percentage of *net tangible assets* (►assets; financial ratios). A corporation may borrow ►capital at fixed interest, and if it can earn more on that capital than it has to pay for it in interest, then the additional earnings accrue to the ►equity shareholders. A firm with high gearing will be able to pay higher ►dividends per ►share than a firm with lower gearing earning exactly the same return on its total capital, provided that return is higher than the rate it pays for ►loan capital. However, the contrary is also true, so that the higher the gearing, the greater the risk to the equity shareholder. Roughly speaking, if a firm's initial capital consists of £7000 subscribed by ordinary shareholders and £3000 borrowed at fixed interest, for example through ►debentures, it would be said to have a gearing of 30 per cent. ►►Modigliani–Miller theorem.

General Agreement on Tariffs and Trade (GATT) An international organization which came into operation in January 1948 as a result of an agreement made at an international conference the previous year, which also included plans for an ▶International Trade Organization. Nothing came of the latter, but GATT proved a useful body for international ▶tariff bargaining. Its Articles of Agreement pledged its member countries (contracting parties), to the expansion of multilateral trade (▶multilateralism) with the minimum of barriers to trade, reduction in import tariffs and ▶quotas and the abolition of preferential trade agreements. There have been successive negotiations between the contracting parties, aimed at reducing the levels of tariffs, from the first meeting in Geneva in 1947, up to the eighth, the so-called ▶Uruguay round of trade negotiations which began in 1986 and was concluded in 1993. Members were required to give details of any subsidies, and if these were liable to prejudice the interests of any other member they were required to discuss the possibility of reduction or elimination. On export subsidies, in particular, member governments 'should seek to avoid' the use of subsidies on the export of primary products. For exports of other products, subsidies, whether direct or indirect, should cease 'as soon as practicable' if they resulted in export prices lower than the home prices of the product. In 1965 a revision came into force which laid emphasis on the special problems of the ▶developing nations and a committee on trade and development was given the responsibility for progress on the elimination of barriers on the trade in products of particular interest to the developing nations. This enabled the ▶most-favoured nation principle to be waived in relation to agreements entered into with developing countries (▶generalized system of preferences). There had been a growing tendency for countries to become more protectionist (▶protection) through the imposition of non-tariff barriers and for economic blocs to make preferential trade agreements with other countries. Examples of the latter are the ▶European Union in respect of countries in the Mediterranean and the USA in respect of Latin America. ▶free-trade area.

A ministerial meeting of GATT was held in 1982 to reaffirm the free-trade principles upon which GATT was founded. The ministers affirmed that they would 'make determined efforts to resist protectionist measures and refrain from taking or maintaining any measures inconsistent with GATT'. Studies were initiated to examine farm export subsidies, financial support for domestic industries, a formula by which a country may impose import restrictions to protect its domestic industry, textiles, tropical products and trade in ▶services. Agreement was eventually reached, at a meeting of delegates at Punta del Este, Uruguay, in 1986 on an agenda for the Uruguay round of trade negotiations. This round considered aspects such as agricultural export subsidies, restrictions on trade in services (e.g. banking, insurance, transport, etc.) and restrictions on direct ▶foreign investment. GATT was replaced by the ▶World Trade Organization from 1 January 1995. ▶Tokyo round of trade negotiations; voluntary export restraints.

general arrangements to borrow ▶International Monetary Fund.

general equilibrium The state of a set of interrelated markets when there is no

➤excess demand or supply in any market. In a world of two commodities, increase in demand for one must lead to a decrease in demand for the other if all consumers spend what they have and no more. Given this interrelation, it is not as obvious that equilibrium can prevail in all markets simultaneously as it is that it can prevail in one market at a time. ➤➤general equilibrium analysis.

general equilibrium analysis 1. The study of the behaviour of economic variables taking full account of the interaction between those variables and the rest of the economy. For example, a general equilibrium approach to the study of waiters' wages would concentrate both on demand and supply in the market for waiters *and* the effects of wages or unemployment in other markets more generally. In this it contrasts with ➤partial equilibrium analysis. 2. The study of simultaneous equilibria in a group of related markets. The prime focus is whether there is a set of prices that would ensure that equilibrium exists in each market. If so, is such an equilibrium stable – if disruptions occurred, would there be a tendency to return to equilibrium? And is such an equilibrium unique, or are there any sets of prices at which all markets clear? The analysis is attributable to ➤Walras, who limited his consideration to a theoretical economic system in which all consumers were utility-maximizers and firms perfectly competitive. A unique, stable equilibrium can exist in such an economy. ➤➤Leontief, W. W.

general government Term used as an overall heading for the central and local government sectors, but which excludes public corporations. General government is thus a more restrictive notion of the state than that defined as the ➤public sector.

generalized system of preferences The elimination or reduction of import ➤tariffs by the ➤advanced countries on specified products exported by approved ➤developing countries. The scheme was first introduced in 1971. The intention is to encourage the development and diversification of developing countries' exports. However, the value of such tariff preference has been eroded by the reduction of import tariffs on international trade generally under the various tariff rounds of negotiations of the ➤General Agreement on Tariffs and Trade and specific trade agreements such as the ➤Lomé Agreement. ➤➤most-favoured nation clause.

geometric progression A sequence of numbers in which the ratio of each number to the preceding one is a constant, e.g. 2, 4, 8, 16 . . . ➤➤arithmetic progression.

GFCF Gross fixed capital formation (➤capital formation).

GGE(X) General government expenditure, excluding (a) payments made out of the proceeds of the National Lottery, (b) the negative effects of ➤privatization receipts. It also nets government receipts of interest and dividends off its payments of them.

giffen good A commodity for which demand increases at higher prices and falls at lower prices. This odd feature – that price rises cause demand to increase – was observed by Sir Robert Giffen (1837–1910) of basic commodities in the budgets of the nineteenth-century poor. As the price of bread rose, the poor, who always relied on it as their staple diet, could simply no longer afford to buy other relatively more luxurious food items, which they had to replace with increased purchases of bread. Similarly, because bread constituted the bulk of their spending, when its price fell, they enjoyed such a large increase in their ►real income that they could then afford to substitute for bread in their diet other more palatable food.

The 'giffen paradox' is explained within the normal framework of demand and supply analysis. When the price of any good rises, it has two effects: it changes the relative attractiveness of other goods, increasing the desire of consumers to buy more of items whose price has not risen – the ►substitution effect. It also has an effect on the spending power of consumers, who can do less with their money than they could before prices rose, as though their income had fallen and no prices had changed. This is called the ►income effect. Two features explain the characteristics of a giffen good. First, demand for it rises as the income of consumers falls (it is always ►inferior). But secondly, what essentially accounts for its perverse behaviour is the fact that this income effect on the demand for the giffen good outweighs the substitution effect which for all commodities causes consumers to switch purchases from items whose prices rise.

The giffen good, usually considered too much of a freak to be of anything except theoretical interest, should not be confused with items that enjoy 'snob value'. These too can enjoy simultaneously rising prices and demand, accounted for by the fact that some consumers delight in paying for the knowledge that certain of their possessions are expensive. Such behaviour can be explained as a form of ►signalling. The usual way of viewing this 'snob effect' is to treat a change in price of an item to which it applies as a change in the fundamental characteristics of the product sold, making it wholly incomparable to the same physical object sold at a different price and not therefore an item for which a single demand curve can be constructed.

gift tax (US) A levy on the ►value of certain property given away to others and paid by the donor. The gift tax is graduated and levied by the Federal Government and also by some states. In Britain, prior to the introduction of capital transfer tax (►inheritance tax) there was no tax on gifts as such, although they were added back into the estate of the donor for duty purposes if made within seven years of the donor's death.

gilt-edged securities Fixed-interest British ►government securities traded on the ►stock exchange. They are called gilt-edged because it is certain that ►interest will be paid and that they will be redeemed (where appropriate) on the due date. For individuals, no ►capital gains tax arises on disposal of gilts. Some gilt-edged securities are ►dated securities, some are ►undated securities and some are index-linked (►indexation). Gilt-edged securities are not, of course, a risk-free investment,

because of fluctuations in their market value. Gilt-edged securities do not include
➤treasury bills. ➤➤yield.

gilt repos The market in agreed sales and repurchase of ➤gilt-edged securities
(➤repo) introduced by the ➤Bank of England in January 1996. Within two months
of launch, the open gilt repo market was already much larger than the ➤bill market
(➤money market), the restricted size of which has recently hampered ➤open-market
operations. The gilt repo market was launched to increase the attractiveness of
gilts to foreign investors and to reduce the cost of funding the government ➤deficit,
but may be used by the Bank of England for open-market operations as repos are
used by the ➤Bundesbank and the ➤Federal Reserve System.

gilt stripping The creation of two tradable financial securities, out of a single
➤gilt-edged security, with one security taking the ➤interest, and the other left with
the ➤principal. The facility for strippable gilts was introduced by the Bank of
England in 1997, but has long been available in the USA for US Treasury and
other securities.

gini coefficient A coefficient, based on the ➤Lorenz curve, showing the degree
of inequality in a ➤frequency distribution such as personal incomes. It is measured
as:

$$G = \frac{\text{area between Lorenz curve and } 45° \text{ line}}{\text{area above the } 45° \text{ line}}$$

If the frequency distribution is equal, the Lorenz curve coincides with the 45° line,
and $G = 0$. ➤➤concentration ratio.

giro system ➤credit transfer.

global corporation ➤multinational cooperation.

globalization Geographical shifts in domestic economic activity around the world
and away from nation states. The ➤Organization for Economic Cooperation and
Development defines globalization as 'the geographic dispersion of industrial and
service activities (for example ➤research and development, sourcing of inputs,
production and distribution) and the cross-border networking of companies (for
example through ➤joint ventures and the sharing of assets)'. The most obvious
manifestations of this process are the facts that the annual rate of growth in
international trade has been consistently higher than that of world production,
while ➤multinational corporations have continued to extend their operations.
However, globalization no longer necessarily requires a physical presence in other
countries, or even ➤exports and ➤imports; for instance, activity can be shifted
abroad by licensing, which only needs information and finance to cross borders.
Although not new, the pace of globalization has accelerated in the post-Second
World War period, facilitated by improvements in transport and communications,
the promotion of ➤deregulation in different sectors, the removal of trade restrictions

and ➤exchange controls. (➤convertibility; General Agreement on Tariffs and Trade.) The motives for globalization include lower labour costs and other favourable ➤factor endowments abroad and the circumvention of remaining ➤tariff and ➤non-tariff barriers to trade. Concern has been expressed that economic activity and employment in the ➤advanced countries will drain away to the ➤developing countries, but the theory of ➤international trade and past experience suggest that all nations in the globalization process will gain in the long run.

That has not allayed concerns that certain sections of the population in richer countries – notably relatively unskilled workers – will lose as an abundance of unskilled labour makes itself available to the world's companies. ➤weightlessness.

GNP ➤gross national product.

gold and foreign exchange reserves The stock of gold and foreign ➤currencies held by a country to finance any calls that may be made from its creditors for the settlement of ➤debt. Reserves used to be held primarily to finance the ➤balance of payments. Pressure on the reserves, therefore, tended to reflect underlying trading problems of the country in question, or sometimes the expectation of a fall in the ➤exchange rate which led people to sell their holdings in the currency. Today, however, currencies are more freely traded than they used to be (➤convertibility) and the national reserves are not relied upon to finance private transactions. As a result, the reserves are primarily seen as a tool for influencing the ➤exchange rate. The authorities can use them to influence supply and demand on the ➤foreign-exchange market. Such intervention is bound to be of limited duration, but can serve a role as a ➤signalling device, letting the markets know what the intention of the authorities is. The official published figures of reserves, however, do not necessarily reflect the total amount of gold and foreign currency which could be used to meet obligations, any more than does an individual's ➤current account at the bank. The reserves exclude, for instance, the ➤credit facilities available through the ➤International Monetary Fund and ➤portfolio foreign investments. ➤➤foreign investment; reserve currency.

gold exchange standard A special form of the ➤gold standard. In this system the ➤central bank will not exchange its ➤currency for gold on demand (as is the case under the gold standard), but will exchange it for a currency which is itself on the gold standard. The central bank holds the parent country's currency in its reserves along with gold itself. The Scandinavian countries adopted this system in respect of sterling up until 1931, when the UK came off the gold standard.

gold points ➤specie points.

gold standard A country is said to be on the gold standard when its ➤central bank is obliged to give gold in exchange for any of its ➤currency presented to it. When the UK was on the gold standard before 1914, anybody could go to the ➤Bank of England and demand gold in exchange for ➤banknotes. The gold standard was central to the ►classical economists' view of the equilibrating processes in ►international trade. The fact that each currency was freely convertible into gold fixed the ►exchange rates between currencies (►specie points), and all international debts were settled in gold. A ►balance of payments surplus caused an inflow of gold into the central bank's reserves. This enabled the central bank to expand the ►money supply without fear of having insufficient gold to meet its ►liabilities. The increase in the quantity of money raised prices, resulting in a fall in the demand for ►exports and therefore a reduction in the balance-of-payments surplus. The reverse happened in the event of a ►deficit. The UK came off the gold standard in 1914, partly returned to it in 1925, but was forced to abandon gold finally in 1931. The USA was on the gold standard from 1879 to 1933, although gold was officially required in bank deposits to support a percentage of the currency in circulation until 1968. For overseas monetary authorities only, the dollar was convertible into gold until 1971. Switzerland, which abandoned gold convertibility in 1954, still requires a percentage of its currency to be supported by gold.

golden rule **1**. The idea that government should borrow each year only to finance ►investment, not to finance ►current expenditure. Meeting the golden rule across the economic cycle became official UK government policy in 1997. At that time net ►public-sector investment spending represented a little under 1 per cent of GDP; the government's rule could be interpreted as saying there should be a ►structural budget deficit no higher than that in any year. **2**. The level of savings and investment that an economy enjoying ►balanced growth would need to support, in order to maximize the long-term value of consumption per head. (►optimal growth theory.) The rule holds, under a number of restrictive assumptions, that the growth rate of population, output and capital stock should equal the real ►rate of interest. This is sometimes referred to as the *biological interest-rate rule*, as it stipulates projects should be discounted (►discounting) at the rate of population growth. It implies that share of profits in the economy should equal the share of savings and investment. *Note*: the first and second definitions of the rule are clearly related. If the rule in version two holds, it will in fact be the case that a government subscribing to the rule in version one will have interest payments on its debt, equal to the value of its borrowing. So, such a government would be in a sustainable and balanced position. It will be borrowing to invest, and the returns it makes on investment will just finance its debt. Conduct of government in version one, is therefore consistent with the golden rule in version two.

good ►economic good.

goodwill The value of a business to a purchaser over and above its ►net asset value. It is normal practice to show goodwill in the ►balance sheet but to write it down for ►depreciation.

Gossen, Hermann Heinrich (1810–58) Born in Düren, near Aachen, in Germany, Gossen studied law and went into government service in deference to his father's wishes. It was not until after his father's death in 1847 that he dedicated himself to the study of economics. His major economic work is *Entwicklung der Gesetze des menschlichen Verkehrs und der daraus fliessenden Regeln für menschliches Handeln* (1854). In this book, Gossen set out a theory of consumer behaviour based on theories which were subsequently to be independently rediscovered and enshrined in the theory of ➤marginal utility by ➤Jevons, ➤Menger and ➤Walras. The first edition of his book was completely ignored, and Gossen's recognition had to wait until after his death. It was Jevons who, in the preface to his own *Theory of Political Economy* (1871), drew attention to the significance of Gossen's achievement, admitting that Gossen had 'completely anticipated him as regards the general principles and methods of economics'. Gossen's first law states that the pleasure obtained from each additional amount consumed of the same ➤commodity diminishes until satiety is reached. Gossen's second law states that once a person had spent his entire ➤income, he would have maximized his total pleasure from it only if the satisfaction gained from the last item of each commodity bought was the same for each commodity. Gossen's third law, derived from the first two, states that a commodity has a subjective ➤value, and the subjective value of each additional unit owned diminishes and eventually reaches zero. ➤Bernoulli's hypothesis.

government expenditure ➤public expenditure.

government securities All government fixed-interest paper, including ➤funded debt and ➤treasury bills. The government does not, of course, issue ➤equity capital. ➤gilt-edged securities.

government stocks Fixed-interest ➤securities issued by the government, often known as ➤'gilt-edged'. ➤funded debt.

Granger causality A means for determining whether a variable *A* can be said to have a causal influence on a variable *B*. If we observe that money-supply increases are followed by inflation we cannot say that increases in money supply *cause* inflation. It may be that both money-supply increases and inflation are caused by something else. Under the Granger test of causation, a ➤time series of both money supply and inflation is taken, and each is stripped of any independent long-term trends they may exhibit. Then the values of money supply and inflation are regressed against each other. (➤regression analysis.) Money-supply changes can be said to cause inflation if in such analysis (a) values of inflation are explained by previous values of money supply, *and* (b) values of money supply are explained by future values of inflation.

green currency A currency adjustment mechanism for agricultural trade within the ➤European Union which fixes farm prices according to the ➤Common Agricultural Policy. The prices of agricultural products subject to the CAP are set in terms of ➤European Currency Units, so that in principle the price of each product is the same throughout the community. Within each country, however, these ECU prices have, of course, to be translated into national currencies according to some ►exchange rate. This would mean that farm prices would alter more or less continuously if the values of national exchange rates were used. The EC decided, therefore, to use a fixed rate of exchange specifically for the CAP agricultural prices. However, because this 'green' currency rate of exchange differs from the market rate, prices in terms of national currencies in the various EC countries may fall out of line. For instance, suppose that the ECU price of wheat on conversion by 'green' rates of exchange gives a price of £100 per tonne in the UK and 1000 fr. in France. If the rate of exchange for sterling rises from 10 fr. to 12 fr., it would pay a trader to buy a tonne of wheat in France for 1000 fr. and sell it in the UK for £100, because this revenue of £100 may be converted on the exchanges into 1200 fr., so giving a profit of 200 fr. This process can then, of course, be repeated by the trader ad infinitum to make a profit of 200 fr. on each transaction, the reason being that the price of wheat is fixed by the CAP and will not adjust to market forces, which would otherwise have caused the UK price of wheat to fall.

In order to prevent such a trade practice, *monetary compensatory amounts* are calculated by the EU on a continuing basis in line with the movements of the various intra-EU exchange rates. These amounts are taxes and subsidies which are imposed on trade within the EU of CAP products to offset the gap between the fixed 'green' currency rate and the exchange rates of the national currencies. In the above example, the MCA would have taken the form of a tax on the export of wheat from France to the UK, equivalent in effect to the profit of 200 fr. per tonne. The application of 'green' rates were revised in 1995. 'Green' rates for aid paid directly to farmers were fixed for three years to 1998.

green pound ►green currency.

Gresham's law The law states that if two coins are in circulation whose relative ►face values differ from their relative ►bullion content, the 'dearer' coin will be extracted from circulation for melting down. ('►bad money drives out good'.) The law is named after Sir Thomas Gresham (1519–79), a leading Elizabethan businessman and financial adviser to Queen Elizabeth I.

gross cash flow ►cash flow.

gross domestic product (GDP) A measure of the total flow of goods and ►services produced by the economy over a specified time period, normally a year or a quarter. It is obtained by valuing outputs of goods and services at ►market prices, and then aggregating. Note that all ►intermediate goods are excluded, and only goods used for final ►consumption or investment goods (►capital) or changes in ►stocks are included. This is because the ►values of intermediate goods are implicitly included in the ►prices of the final goods. The word 'gross' means that no deduction for the value of expenditure on capital goods for replacement purposes is made. Because ►income arising from ►investments and possessions owned abroad is not included, only the value of the flow of goods and services produced in the country is estimated; hence the word 'domestic' to distinguish it from the ►gross national product. Since no adjustment is made for indirect taxes (►direct taxation) and ►subsidies, the measure here defined is often referred to as 'gross domestic product at market prices'. ►►gross domestic product at factor cost.

gross domestic product at factor cost The measure of ►gross domestic product, that makes an adjustment for the impact of taxes and subsidies. In the measure of 'GDP at market prices', the prices used to value outputs and aggregate them, include indirect taxes, i.e. ►value-added tax, and ►subsidies. As a result, the ►value of output will not equal the value of ►incomes paid out to ►factors of production. This is because it is the revenue received by firms after indirect taxes (►direct taxation) which is distributed as factor incomes. So, by subtracting the total of indirect taxes (and, since subsidies have the opposite effect of taxes, by adding in subsidies) from the GDP we arrive at the estimate of the GDP at factor cost, which is consistent with the value of incomes paid to factors of production. This is the measure of GDP from which growth rates are conventionally drawn.

gross fixed capital formation (GFCF) ►capital formation.

gross investment ►Investment expenditure inclusive of replacement of worn-out and obsolescent equipment, i.e. inclusive of ►depreciation. ►►net investment.

gross margin In a retail business, the margin on a sale which is the difference between the purchase ►price of a good and the price paid by the retailer, i.e. it makes no allowance for ►fixed costs, ►stock appreciation or ►tax. The gross margin is sometimes loosely referred to as *gross profit*, but this term has a different, strictly defined, meaning in accounting (►profit).

gross national expenditure ►national income.

gross national product (GNP) ►gross domestic product plus the ►income accruing to domestic residents arising from ►investment abroad less income earned in the domestic market accruing to foreigners abroad.

gross national product at factor cost ►gross national product at ►market prices minus all indirect taxes (►direct taxation) and ►subsidies. ►►gross domestic product at factor cost.

gross national product at market prices ►gross national product with all flows valued at ►market prices. Since market prices include indirect taxes (►direct taxation) and ►subsidies and since taxes and subsidies are regarded simply as ►transfer payments, it is often preferable to measure national output excluding these. This gives the measure of national output, net of ►taxation and subsidies, known as ►gross national product at factor cost.

gross profit

gross profit ➤profit.

gross trading profit Gross ➤profit before allowing for ➤depreciation, ➤interest and stock ➤appreciation.

Group of Ten ➤International Monetary Fund.

growth theory The area of economics concerned with the development of models which explain the rate of ➤economic growth in an economy. The most important questions in growth theory are about (a) the optimal level of growth (➤optimal-growth theory), and (b) whether the economic system has a natural tendency to achieve ➤balanced growth, a position in which all variables grow at the same rate. If growth in the economy is balanced, it can be shown that $n = s/v$ where n is the rate of growth of the labour force, s the ➤average propensity to save and v the ratio of capital in the economy to output produced (➤capital–output ratio). For balanced growth to be sustained with ➤investment equal to savings and with constant full employment, some mechanism has to exist to cause one of these three factors to change when one of the other two moves out of balance. In the neo-classical (➤neo-classical economics) approach to growth, it is the capital–output ratio, v, which alters. If, for example, the labour force was growing too fast to maintain full employment with the given level of savings and stock of capital, the capital–output ratio would fall as entrepreneurs switched from employing capital to labour in response to the lower wages that the excess supply of labour caused. The fixed relationship between the three factors would thus still hold.

In the ➤Harrod–Domar model, none of the three variables is endogenous (➤endogenous variable) and thus there is no tendency for balanced growth to occur at all. The capital–output ratio is assumed to be fixed by technological factors or by sticky interest rates (➤liquidity trap). In models associated with the ➤Cambridge school, it is the propensity to save which is the endogenous variable; in particular, if there is a difference between the inclination for profit-earners and wage-earners to save, growth can lead to redistributions from one group to the other in such a way as to alter the savings necessary to maintain a full-employment steady-state growth path. ➤optimal growth theory.

H

Haavelmo, Trygve (b. 1911) Norwegian economist and ►Nobel Prize winner in 1989, Haavelmo's contribution to the subject was made during the Second World War in the United States. His most important paper, 'The Probability Approach to Econometrics', was path-breaking in introducing the ideas of ►probability theory into ►econometrics. He pointed out, for example, that statements of the kind that 'National income next year will be £x' are futile, and almost certainly wrong. In essence statements should be of the form 'National income next year will be approximately £x', allowing for uncertainty both in the world and in the economist's view of it.

hard currency A ►currency traded in a ►foreign-exchange market for which ►demand is persistently high relative to the ►supply. ►►soft currency.

harmonized indices of consumer prices A standardized measure of inflation introduced in 1997 by the ►European Union. The measure excludes housing, ►council tax, and National Health Service prescription charges. It includes a number of items which are not in the ►retail prices index in the UK. It is also calculated using a geometric mean, as opposed to the arithmetic mean in use in the UK. ►►average.

Harnsanyi, John C (b. 1920) Hungarian-born, John Harnsanyi made a major contribution to ►game theory in 1967–8 with his paper 'Games with Incomplete Information Played by Bayesian Players'. He was a joint winner of the ►Nobel Prize for Economics in 1994. He extended an understanding of game theory to situations where players had incomplete and differing amounts of information. He showed that for every game characterizing such a situation, there was an equivalent game that could be defined, with complete information. Those equivalent games could be studied using conventional methods. ►►Nash, John F., Selten R.

Harrod, Sir Roy Forbes (1900–78) Educated at New College, Oxford, he began his career in 1922 as lecturer at Christ Church, Oxford, and continued teaching there until 1952. From 1940 until 1942 Professor Harrod served under Lord Cherwell and in the Prime Minister's office and then held the post of Statistical Adviser to the Admiralty until 1945. In 1952 he was appointed Nuffield Reader of International Economics. His publications include *The Trade Cycle* (1936), *Essay in Dynamic Theory* (1939), *Towards a Dynamic Economics* (1948), *The Life of John Maynard Keynes* (1951), *Policy Against Inflation* (1958), *The British Economy* (1963), *Reforming the World's Money* (1965), *Towards a New Economic*

Policy (1967), *Dollar – Sterling Collaboration* (1968), *Money* (1969) and *Economic Dynamics* (1973).

His *Essay in Dynamic Theory* brought together in a mathematical framework the accelerator and the ►multiplier (►►accelerator – multiplier model). Professor Harrod shifted economic theory away from its preoccupation with the conditions of stationary ►equilibrium towards the analysis of the problems of growth (►►growth theory). He investigated the implications for growth of the interactions of the ►acceleration principle and the multiplier (►►Harrod – Domar model).

Harrod – Domar model A theory of economic growth (►growth theory) which suggests that there is no natural tendency for an economy to enjoy ►balanced growth. In the model, developed by ►R. F. Harrod in 1939 and independently by E. D. Domar, shortly afterwards, there are three concepts of growth. The first is *warranted* growth: the rate of output growth at which firms believe they have the right amount of capital and don't feel it necessary to increase or decrease investment, given their expectations of future demand (►capital – output ratio). The second is the *natural rate of growth*, which corresponds to the increase in the labour force: if the labour force rises, growth must rise to maintain full ►employment. The third is *actual* growth: the change in aggregate output that finally materializes.

In the model, two problems are seen to arise in the growth pattern of an economy. The first concerns the relationship between actual and natural growth; the second concerns the relationship between actual and warranted growth. The first is that the factors determining actual growth are quite independent of the factors determining natural growth, and so there is no reason that an economy will achieve a level of growth necessary to maintain full employment. The natural rate of growth is determined by factors such as attitudes to birth control, and the tastes of the population with respect to family size. Actual growth, however, is affected by the propensity to save (the more ►saving, the more ►investment, and the more growth) and the increase in output caused by each pound's worth of investment. Neither the capital – output ratio nor the propensity to save will adjust to meet the requirements of the labour market, however.

The second problem is that, in the model, if entrepreneurs expect output to grow they will increase their investment to meet the anticipated demand. If the increase in demand is forthcoming, the aspirations of firms will be met and warranted growth will be equal to actual growth and no problem arises. If, however, actual growth exceeds expectations, then entrepreneurs will discover they have not invested as much as they would have wanted to if they had known what was coming. In response, they will increase their investment to the level warranted by actual growth; *but this increase in investment will cause actual growth to rise even more.* A reverse story can be told when actual growth falls short of warranted growth: entrepreneurs, in the model, set up a vicious circle, by which any discrepancy between their expected growth and actual growth magnifies as they attempt to change the level of their investment to the level warranted. The result is instability.

The conclusion of the Harrod–Domar model – that the economy does not naturally find a full-employment, stable-growth rate – is analogous to the Keynesian (➤Keynes, J. M.) belief that it need not find a full-employment equilibrium level of output. However, the model's results can be criticized because of the severity of the assumptions built into it. The first problem suggested by the model – that there is no reason for growth to equal the level necessary to maintain full employment – is largely because it assumes that the relative price of labour and capital is fixed, and that they are always employed in equal proportions. It is quite possible, however, that increases in labour supply might drive down wages and lead to an increase in the amount of labour used relative to capital. Secondly, the model naively assumes that investors are influenced by only one thing: the level of output. This is the ➤acceleration principle. This explains the way in which discrepancies between warranted and actual growth may lead to spiralling increases or decreases in growth. ➤➤economic growth; optimal-growth theory; steady-state growth; trend growth.

Hawtrey, Sir Ralph George (1879–1975) After a long career in the ➤Treasury, which lasted from 1904 to 1945, Sir Ralph Hawtrey was appointed Professor at the Royal Institute of International Affairs. He held his post until his retirement in 1952. Hawtrey's publications include *Currency and Credit* (1919), *The Gold Standard in Theory and Practice* (1927), *The Art of Central Banking* (1937), *Capital and Employment* (1937), *A Century of Bank Rate* (1938), *The Balance of Payments and the Standard of Living* (1950), *Cross-Purposes in Wages Policy* (1955), *The Pound at Home and Abroad* (1961) and *Incomes and Money* (1967).

His theory of the ➤business cycle emphasizes monetary factors. The amount which consumers and investors were willing to save or spend depended on the level of ➤rates of interest. Fluctuations in economic activity arose through variations in the quantity of money (➤➤money supply), especially bank ➤credit, because these variations alter the level of the rate of interest (➤Mises, L. E. von). He criticized the Radcliffe Committee (➤Radcliffe Report) because he felt that it had not given sufficient attention to the possibility that the rate of interest had a significant influence on a firm's willingness to hold stocks of commodities (➤inventories).

Hayek, Friedrich August von (1899–1992) Born in Vienna, Hayek was director of the Austrian Institute for Economic Research from 1927 to 1931 and lectured at Vienna University. In 1931 he was appointed Tooke Professor of Economic Science and Statistics at the London School of Economics, a post he held until 1950. From 1950 until 1962 he was Professor of Social and Moral Science at Chicago University. He was Professor of Economics at the University of Freiburg until 1969, when he was appointed Visiting Professor of Economics at the University of Salzburg. In 1974 he received the Alfred Nobel Memorial Prize (➤Nobel Prize) in Economics jointly with ➤Myrdal. His published works include *Monetary Theory and the Trade Cycle* (1929), *Prices and Production* (1931), *Profits, Interest, Investment* (1939), *The Pure Theory of Capital* (1941), *Road to Serfdom* (1944),

Individualism and Economic Order (1948), *The Constitution of Liberty* (1961), *Studies in Philosophy, Politics and Economics* (1967), *Law, Legislation and Liberty* (3 volumes, 1973–9), *Denationalisation of Money* (1976), *New Studies in Philosophy, Politics, Economics and the History of Ideas* (1978) and *The Fatal Conceit: The Errors of Socialism* (1988).

A member of the ►Austrian school, Hayek elaborated the ►business-cycle theory of von ►Mises by integrating it with von ►Böhm-Bawerk's theory of ►capital. In a boom, ►real wages fall because of the rise in prices, and so firms switch to less 'roundabout' (►capital-intensive) methods of production. In consequence, ►investment in total is reduced. In ►recession the reverse situation induces 'roundabout' production methods, and investment is stimulated. Professor Hayek believed that a very severe restriction on the growth of the ►money supply was necessary in order to control the growth of ►inflation, even if such a policy lead to very high levels of ►unemployment. Hayek criticized socialist planning (►planned economy), advocating free markets which, he argued, were more accommodating to the propagation and dissemination of the knowledge required for efficient economic systems. Open markets gave proper opportunities to the expression of personal incentives and the freedom to work and save. ►►acceleration principle; Keynes, J. M.; Ricardo effect.

Heckscher–Ohlin principle The law that a country will export those commodities that are intensive (►capital-intensive; labour-intensive) in the factor in which it is most well endowed. The law of ►comparative advantage (►►Ricardo, D.) had been established by economists as an explanation for the existence and pattern of international trade based on the relative ►opportunity-cost advantages between different countries of producing different commodities. The law says nothing about why or how a comparative advantage exists. The Heckscher–Ohlin principle states that advantage arises from the different relative factor endowments of the countries trading. The principle was first put forward by Eli F. Heckscher (1879–1952) in an article published in 1919 and reprinted in *Readings in the Theory of International Trade* (1949). It was refined by ►Ohlin in his *Interregional and International Trade* (1933). The principle has been developed further by ►Samuelson in his factor price equalization theorem.

hedge Action taken by a buyer or seller to protect his business or assets against a change in ►prices. A flour miller who has a contract to supply flour at a fixed price in two months' time can hedge against the possibility of a rise in the price of wheat in two months' time by buying the necessary wheat now and selling a two months' ►future in wheat for the same quantity. If the price of wheat should fall, then the loss he will have sustained by buying it now will be offset by the gain he can make by buying in the wheat at the future price and supplying the futures contract at higher than this price, and vice versa. In practice, perfect hedging may not be possible because spot (►spot markets) and future prices will not balance one another out after the event, but a significant reduction in risk is normally possible. Hedging in this form is, in effect, shifting risk on to specialized futures operators. The purchase of ►equities, or other things for which prices are expected to move at least in line with the general price level, is often referred to as a 'hedge' against ►inflation.

hedonism The theory that all human action is motivated by pleasure and the avoidance of pain or the ethic that it should be so motivated.

Herfindahl index ►concentration ratio.

heteroscedasticity The problem encountered in ►regression analysis when the ►variance of the error term in a regression is not constant for every observation. It may be in ►time-series analysis, for example, that while the relationship between the ►dependent variable and the ►independent variable remains constant on average, it becomes more and more variable around that average as time progresses. In this case, ►least-squares regression will not be the most efficient method of measuring that relationship; instead it is better to give more weight to those observations which have the smallest expected error. ►►econometrics.

Hicks, Sir John Richard (1904–89) Educated at Balliol College, Oxford, Hicks lectured at the London School of Economics from 1926 until 1935, when he became a Fellow of Gonville and Caius College, Cambridge. In 1938 he was appointed to the Chair of Political Economy at the University of Manchester. In 1946 he was made Official Fellow of Nuffield College, Oxford, and in 1952 Drummond Professor of Political Economy at Oxford, a post he held until 1965. In 1972 he was awarded the ►Nobel Prize in Economics jointly with Professor ►K. J. Arrow. His major published works include *The Theory of Wages* (1932), *Value and Capital* (1939), *The Social Framework* (1942), *A Contribution to the Theory of the Trade Cycle* (1950), *A Revision of Demand Theory* (1956), *Capital and Growth* (1965), *Critical Essays in Monetary Theory* (1967), *A Theory of Economic History* (1969), *The Crisis in Keynesian Economics* (1974), *Capital and Time: A Neo-Austrian Theory* (1976), *Economic Perspectives: Further Essays on Money and Growth* (1977), *Causality in Economics* (1979) and *A Market Theory of Money* (1989).

In an article in *Economica* in 1934 Hicks and Professor R. G. D. Allen showed how the ►indifference curve could be used to analyse consumer behaviour on the basis of ►ordinal utility. Their exposition gave an important impetus to the development of this tool of analysis in economic theory (►►Slutsky, E.). In his work on the ►business cycle, Hicks demonstrated by means of mathematical ►models how the *accelerator* could induce several types of fluctuation in total output. In an article in *Econometrica* in 1937, 'Mr Keynes and the Classics', he expounded the analytical tool of the ►IS–LM model, which he had invented in order to explore the assumptions relating to the equilibrium between the supply and demand for ►money, ►savings and ►investment, the rate of ►interest and ►income. ►►Harrod, R. F.; Keynes, J. M.

Hicksian demand function The relationship between the consumer's demand for a commodity and the price of that commodity, when the total level of consumer ►utility is held constant. Hicksian demand curves are also known as compensated demand curves as, when the price of a product changes, it is assumed that the consumer is compensated so that he feels no less satisfied than before. They contrast with Marshallian (►Marshall, A.) demand functions (►demand function). ►►substitution effect.

hidden economy ►black economy.

hidden hand ►'invisible hand'; Smith, A.

hire purchase (HP) (UK) A form of ►consumer credit in which the purchaser pays a deposit on an article and pays the balance of the purchase price plus ►interest in regular instalments over periods of six months to two years or more; hence the US name ►'instalment credit'. The credit is usually arranged by the vendor, at least for consumer purchases such as motor cars. In a hire-purchase contract, unlike a credit sale, ownership of the goods does not pass from the seller to the buyer until the final payment is made, i.e. the goods are ►security for the ►loan. Until that time the seller is entitled to repossess the goods under law. Abuse of the right, extortionate ►rates of interest and the practices of certain salesmen, who persuaded customers to buy more than they could afford, led to a series of Hire Purchase Acts from 1938 onwards to give protection to the buyer. Because interest charges are calculated on the total loan and not the amount outstanding, hire purchase is a more expensive form of ►credit than it often seems to be. Private purchases now account for less than one-half of HP sales, and it is an important source of credit for certain types of machinery and equipment (►finance house). Hire purchase originated with retailers in the USA during the nineteenth century but is now supplemented for consumers by forms of non-vendor credit such as ►personal loans, credit cards and store cards.

historical costs ►costs, historical.

hoarding The accumulation of idle ►money balances, ►inactive money. ►►liquidity preference.

holding company A company that controls one or more other companies, normally by holding a majority of the ►shares of these ►subsidiaries A holding company is concerned with control, and not with ►investment, and may be economically justifiable where one holding company can perform financial, managerial or marketing functions for a number of subsidiaries; ICI is a very good example of this, and, indeed, most large companies in Britain are holding companies exercising a greater or lesser degree of control over their subsidiaries. The holding-company form of organization also has a number of practical advantages, e.g. it is a simpler and less expensive way of acquiring control of another company than by purchasing its ►assets, and the original company can retain its name and goodwill. It is possible for a holding company to control a large number of companies with a combined ➤capital very much greater than its own, since it needs to hold only half or even less of the shares of its subsidiaries. Abuse of this possibility of 'pyramiding', as it is sometimes called, is now limited by company legislation (➤company law). Diversified holding companies or ➤conglomerates are tending to become less important than they once were. ➤downsizing.

homogeneous in degree *n* The characteristic of a function that when all the ➤independent variables are multiplied by λ, the ➤dependent variable gets raised by λ to the power *n*. It is commonly referred to in describing the characteristics of a ➤production function, for example,

$y = f(x,z)$

where *y* is output and *x* and *z* are inputs to production. For instance, this function would be homogeneous of degree two if

$f(2x,2z) = 4f(x,z)$

(➤Cobb–Douglas function.)

homogeneous products Goods and services purchased by consumers which the latter consider to be perfect substitutes (➤perfect competition). It is mostly ➤commodity markets in which homogeneity can be assumed and, indeed, the characterization of something as a commodity frequently simply means different producers are selling more or less homogeneous outputs. In some markets, the tendency for producers to differentiate their products (➤product differentiation) is criticized as wasteful; at other times the tendency for markets to generate uniform products (➤Hotelling's law) is seen as a potential form of market weakness.

horizontal integration ➤merger.

hot money Funds which flow into a country to take advantage of favourable ➤rates of interest in that country. They influence the ➤balance of payments and strengthen the ➤exchange rate of the recipient country. These funds are highly volatile and will be shifted to another ➤foreign-exchange market when relative interest rates favour the move. ➤arbitrage; Bank for International Settlements.

Hotelling, Harold (1895–1973) Associate Professor of Mathematics at Stanford University from 1927, Hotelling became Professor of Economics at Columbia University in 1931. He held this post until 1946, when he was appointed Professor of Mathematical Statistics of the University of North Carolina. In an article in the *Economic Journal* in 1929, 'Stability in Competition', he showed how profit maximization can lead retail outlets or competing companies to locate close to each other (➤Hotelling's law). His article 'The General Welfare in Relation to Problems of Taxation and of Railway and Utility Rates', published in *Econometrica* in 1938, put forward the case for ➤marginal-cost pricing by public utilities. He argued that even if by so doing such industries ran at a loss which had to be financed by lump-sum payments by the state, total economic welfare would be increased by such a pricing policy (➤welfare economics).

Hotelling's law The observation by Hotelling that in many markets it is rational for all the producers to make their products as similar as possible. Suppose, for example, there are two newsagents in a street, each of which wanted to maximize its share of local business by locating its shop so that it is the nearest newsagent for as much of the trade visiting the street as possible. In this situation, both newsagents will position themselves in the middle of the street guaranteeing themselves half the market. It would be socially more desirable for them to separate themselves, and sit a third of the way along the street from different ends. Unfortunately, if one newsagent did this, the other could position himself so as to capture more than half the total market. Too little variety results from the process. Hotelling's law manifests itself in numerous markets – competing bus operators scheduling their buses to run at the same times for example. ➤➤Nash equilibrium.

household An economic unit which is defined for the purpose of the ➤census of population as a single person living alone or a family or group voluntarily living together, having meals prepared together and benefiting from housekeeping shared in common. Because of the fact of shared use, which is a household's characteristic, it is an important economic statistic when considering the ➤market potential for certain consumer products. The percentage of households owning certain consumer durables such as computers, washing-machines, television sets, refrigerators and video recorders is critical to the growth of the future sales of these products. In the initial introductory period sales grow fast as households buy for the first time, but they slow down rapidly when a high proportion of the households own the product (➤logistic curve). Thereafter, sales can only be for replacement. The number of households in the UK in 1996 was about 24 million.

HP ➤hire purchase.

human capital The skills and knowledge embodied in the ➤labour force. A metallurgist can expect to earn more than a laboratory assistant because he has invested more in education and training and these higher earnings are a return on the investment he (or his parents, or the state) have made in school fees and forgone earnings. Investment in human ➤capital should increase labour ➤productivity in the same way as investment in machinery. ➤➤Becker, G.; sow's ear effect.

Hume, David (1711–76) Scottish philosopher whose systematic treatment of economics is contained in several chapters of his *Political Discourses* (1752). He exposed as unwarranted the mercantilist fear (➤mercantilism) of a chronic imbalance of trade and loss of gold. He argued that the international movement in ➤bullion responded to the rise and fall of prices and in so doing kept national price differences within limits and prevented permanent ►balance of payments surpluses or deficits. He also foresaw how this mechanism could be distorted by the growth of domestic ►banking and of paper money. He accepted a ►quantity theory of money but distinguished between ►short-run and ►long-run effects. By tracing the course of the effects of a rise in the quantity of ►money, he came to the conclusion that ►money was not neutral (►neutrality of money) but could affect employment, although only in the short run. His belief that the level of the ►rate of interest depended on the rate of business profits became the basis of ►Adam Smith's interest-rate theory. ►►interest, classical theory of.

Hutcheson, Francis (1694–1746) The teacher of ►Adam Smith at Glasgow University. Smith succeeded him to the Chair of Moral Philosophy.

hyperinflation Very rapid growth in the rate of ►inflation in which ►money loses its value to the point where alternative mediums of exchange – such as ►barter or foreign currency – are commonly used. An earlier term for the same phenomenon is *galloping inflation*.

hypothecation Earmarking of particular sources of finance to particular uses. The idea of hypothecating tax to particular forms of spending has been much discussed – although in the UK, the Treasury has tended to oppose the idea on the grounds that it introduces an element of inflexibility into spending, and sometimes makes it hard to cut programmes once they are underway. Nevertheless, the principle was adopted with respect to the revenues of the National Lottery and, with decreasing ►tax tolerance, many believe it is a good way of ensuring revenue for popular programmes, and overcoming public mistrust of the way politicians use their tax revenue.

hypothesis A theoretical explanation of the behaviour of phenomena which can be tested against the facts. A hypothesis can be refuted, unlike a tautology, which is true by definition, but it may not be possible to prove that it is correct. An example of a hypothesis is that ►saving is a function of ►disposable income such that when disposable income doubles, savings will also double (the ►savings ratio is a constant). The statement that saving equals income minus expenditure, however, is a tautology. ►►empirical testing.

hysteresis A term derived from more common use in the physical sciences, to describe a lag between the behaviour of a variable, and a change in the factors that influence the variable. It is a characteristic of viscous liquids, for example, that when tipped out of a jar, they do not pour out immediately. In economics, hysteresis has acquired a life of its own, to describe the idea that the history of a variable – the path it has followed over time – can have an effect on where it settles. In its most common manifestation, hysteresis is the idea that a high level of unemployment is self-reinforcing, because the unemployed become less and less suited to work as they stay out of work longer. A burst of high unemployment tends to solidify into a permanently high level of unemployment, notwithstanding the removal of the original cause of the high unemployment. It enjoyed preponderance as a possible explanation of the rising levels of unemployment in the 1980s across western Europe. Hysteresis has also been taken as having broader implications for economic method. It holds that the ►equilibrium of a variable is dependent on the path which it follows, so conventional analysis explaining the equilibrium entirely in terms of the factors that normally influence things is impoverished. ►unemployment, natural rate of; long-term unemployment.

I

IADB ➤Inter-American Development Bank.

IBMBR Inter-bank market bid rate (➤inter-bank market).

IBOR Inter-bank offered rate (➤inter-bank market).

IBRD ➤International Bank for Reconstruction and Development.

IDA ➤International Development Association.

idle money ➤inactive money.

IEA ➤International Energy Agency.

IFC ➤International Finance Corporation.

illiquidity A situation in which ➤assets cannot easily and quickly be turned into ➤money. Antonym of ➤liquidity.

ILO ➤International Labour Organization.

IMF ➤International Monetary Fund.

impact effect The first effect of a change in a variable, before any secondary responses can be made to the change. It amounts to the very short-run effect. For example, when demand in a market increases, because output is fixed in the short period involved, price rises by more than it does once producers have had time to respond to the increases in demand.

imperfect competition ➤monopolistic competition.

imperfect market A market in which the forces that tend to ensure productive and allocative efficiency are thwarted (➤economic efficiency). In a perfect market, three characteristics predominate: price equals ➤marginal cost (or ➤marginal revenue equals marginal cost); there are no abnormal ➤profits (i.e. ➤average cost equals ➤average revenue); and production takes place at the minimum cost (that is at the bottom of the average-cost curve, where average cost equals marginal cost). Although price acceptance by consumers and firms, and free entry and exit of firms, are the important features to ensure these hold, underlying them are a number of other conditions. These include: rational consumers; profit-maximizing firms; ➤homogeneous products made without ➤economies of scale; a smooth pattern of ➤demand without peaks; a smooth pattern of ➤supply where the quantity of output is easily adjusted; no collusion between producers; and the existence of complete and costless market information. In the absence of any of these, imperfect markets exist and the efficiency result no longer necessarily holds. The most important developments in economics in recent years have concerned the role of information in accounting for deviations from perfect markets (►asymmetric information, screening, signalling). ►Pareto, V. F. D.; ►►perfect competition.

implicit contract ►contract.

import deposits A system of ►import restriction under which importers are required to deposit, with a government-nominated institution, a percentage of the value of their ►imports. This ►deposit is held for a period of time, after which it is repaid to the importer. The system restricts imports because it reduces the ►liquidity of importers and also imposes an extra charge on them, inasmuch as they are, in effect, forced to give an interest-free loan to the government. However, the impact of import deposits may be weakened if there is sufficient liquidity generally in the economy to enable importers to obtain loans at favourable ►rates of interest against the ►collateral security of their import-deposit receipts. Again, foreign exporting companies may be willing to finance the deposits themselves rather than lose their market position, especially if it is expected that the scheme is only a temporary one. ►►General Agreement on Tariffs and Trade.

import duties ►tariffs, import.

import licence A document which gives the importer authority to import the commodity to which the licence applies. It is a device to enable the government to regulate and supervise the flow of ►imports, for instance under its import ►quota regulations.

import quota ►quotas.

import restrictions Restrictions on the importation of products into a country may be effected by means of ►tariffs, ►quotas or ►import deposits, and are generally imposed to correct a ►balance of payments deficit. Their purpose, as with ►devaluation, is to divert expenditure away from foreign-produced goods in favour of goods produced at home. The magnitude of this diversionary effect will depend on the ►elasticity of demand for the ►imports in question; that is to say, the degree to which acceptable ►substitutes are available on the home market. In addition, import restrictions could be used to increase a country's economic welfare (►welfare economics) at the expense of foreign countries to the extent that it has power to exploit its foreign suppliers, e.g. as a monopolist (►monopoly), without fear of retaliation. Finally, import duties may be applied to protect the market of a domestic industry while it is being established (►free trade; infant-industry argument; protection). Non-tariff barriers to trade include revenue duties, such as value-added tax, which, being imposed as a percentage on landed, i.e. duty-paid, ►value, increase the cost of imported goods more than locally produced goods and thus discriminate in favour of the latter. Other examples are domestic taxes applied according to the technical characteristics of goods, e.g. on engine capacity, which may subtly discriminate against imports. ➤General Agreements on Tariffs and Trade.

import surcharge A temporary increase in import tariffs (➤tariffs, import) designed to correct a short-term ➤balance of payments deficit and to stabilize the ➤exchange rate.

import tariffs ➤tariffs, import.

imports The flow of goods and ➤services which enter for sale into one country and which are the products of another country. In the UK goods accounted for 81 per cent of the total in 1995. About 33 per cent of total domestic expenditure in the UK was spent on imports in 1995 compared with, for instance, the USA, where the proportion was about 12 per cent. One of the features of UK trade in recent years has been the acceleration in imports of goods which compete with domestic production. In 1975 about 23 per cent of UK demand for manufactures was met by imports, compared with a current level of 44 per cent. ➤balance of payments; exports; international trade; invisible; parallel imports.

impossibility theorem A proof that it is impossible to devise a constitution or voting system, complying with certain reasonable conditions, which can guarantee to produce a consistent set of preferences for a group from the preferences of the individuals making up the group. Suppose, for example, that a society wants to vote on whether to spend the proceeds of a national lottery on education and health, the arts, or sport. If resources are to be efficiently allocated, it would be desirable that individual rankings of the three options could be aggregated by some voting system to produce a ranking to determine which option was the choice of the society as a whole. ➤Arrow showed in the impossibility theorem that no system could be found that was both rational and egalitarian. For example, a simple majority voting system, although giving equal weight to everybody's opinion, gives rise to the ➤paradox of voting, allowing the possibility of an inconsistent ordering of preferences. A system that may be consistent would be to allow one individual – a dictator – always to determine what choice to make, but this lacks the feature of equality. It has since been shown that a democratic system can at least meet a weaker rationality condition, but only by abandoning a third desirable property of a voting system – decisiveness. Such a system would allow every individual a personal veto over any decision so that society would simply be unable to do anything unless there was no one opposed to it. ➤social-welfare function.

imputation system ➤corporation tax.

imputed cost The cost attributed to using an asset which is owned by the user. The ➤opportunity cost of not putting an asset to its best alternative use. For instance, a shopkeeper who owns his own shop forgoes rent which he could earn if he did not use the shop for his own business. This loss of income is an imputed cost, which he would compare against the revenue from his business when considering whether it were truly profitable. Similarly, an imputed income is the amount an owner would pay not to put his asset to an alternative use. If the shopkeeper had to pay £10 a day to rent an alternative to his own shop, he would willingly forgo £10 to keep it, and he thus enjoys an imputed income of £10 from his shop. ➤➤income.

imputed income ➤imputed cost.

'in the bank' A description of the state of the ➤money market, when ➤discount houses need to borrow ➤Money from the ➤Bank of England. ➤➤lender of last resort.

inactive money ➤Money which is not in circulation, i.e. not on ➤deposit or invested in other financial ➤assets or being used for transactions. Inactive money is also referred to as *idle money* or idle balances. According to ➤Keynes's theory of ➤liquidity preference the amount of idle balances will depend, among other things, upon the ➤rate of interest. ➤➤velocity of circulation.

incentive compatibility A system of behaviour in which each individual has a personal incentive to act in accordance with some overall interest. A classic example of an incentive-compatible system is that used by parents to divide a cake between two hungry children, in which one is allowed to slice the cake in two and the other is allowed to choose which slice to take. The first child then has the incentive to split the cake into two equal halves, which is the fairest division. Incentive compatibility is important throughout economics, but has more recently risen as a preoccupation, because it is an ingredient in the economics of ➤screening and ➤signalling, where there are types of behaviour (for example, the giving of an engagement ring) that are used to distinguish certain types of individual from certain other types (for example, people who are serious about getting married from those that are not). These systems work only if the types of individuals being distinguished do not have the incentive to behave like the other type (for example, it must not be the case that the benefits of pretending you were going to marry someone were so large that you would be willing to buy them an engagement ring even if you were not intending to wed). This condition is known as the incentive-compatibility condition. The same notion is important in the areas of ➤public-choice theory, where voting systems are designed to obtain true indications of people's preferences, undistorted by tactical considerations. Another example is the ➤Vickrey auction (➤auction), in which participants have the incentive to bid their true valuation of an item. ➤➤moral hazard.

incidence of taxation ➤taxation, incidence of.

income A flow of money, goods or services to any economic agent or unit. Such flows can take a variety of forms. At the level of individuals, income is usually a return to a ►factor of production. ►Labour yields wages; ►capital yields ►interest; land yields ►rent; and entrepreneurship yields ►profit. Otherwise, income can be a ►transfer payment in the form of a state benefit or receipt from a private-sector source such as alimony payments. At the level of the firm, income can be seen as either total sales receipts (turnover) or receipts minus costs. For a country, ►national income is taken as the sum of all incomes.

Economists do not view income in conventional ways. First, their concept of income extends more widely than a cash receipt: the person who lives in his own house effectively derives an income in the form of housing consumption worth the rental values of his property. Secondly, great importance is attached to the concept of 'permanent income': the flow of resources that is sustainable in the long term. For example, North Sea oil provides Britain with sale receipts but these will expire when the oil runs out. The permanent income deriving from the oil is therefore the money that would be earned from investing these receipts and making a return on them that lasts for ever. This would be lower than the actual flow of receipts while the oil is still being tapped, but it would provide a flow of income after the oil had gone. ►income, distribution of; permanent-income hypothesis.

income and earned surplus statement (US) ►double-entry bookkeeping.

income, circular flow of ►circular flow of income.

income determination, theory of The body of theory which describes the factors affecting ►national income. The term is usually used to describe specifically Keynesian models of the economy, in which ►aggregate demand is the primary factor explaining output and employment. ►►Keynesian economics.

income, distribution of A ►frequency distribution showing numbers of persons, taxpayers or households classified by levels of annual income. A feature of this distribution is that it is skewed: a greater number appear in the low-income classifications than in the high-income classifications. ►►inequality; poverty; Gini coefficient; Lorenz curve; Pareto, V. F. D.

income effect The change in demand for a product caused by the impact of a change in its price on the spending power of consumers. The change in price of a product leads to a change in the ►real income of individuals, who either can no longer afford the 'basket' of goods that they previously bought or who can afford the old basket with cash over to spend on extra items. The *income effect* is the impact of this change in spending power on the demand for the product whose price has changed. It is equivalent to some change in income with all prices remaining constant. It can be added to the ►substitution effect to derive the total effect of the price change on the demand for the product.

The main factor in determining the size of the income effect of a product is the proportion of total spending that item comprises. The effect on total spending of a change in the price of matches, for example, is trivial, but it is large for a change in the price of food. Unlike the substitution effect, the income effect can move in either direction. If a product is demanded more as incomes fall, for example second-hand clothes, it is called an ➤inferior good. If, as is more usual, it is demanded more as income rises, it is called *normal*. ➤➤giffen good; income elasticity of demand.

income elasticity of demand The proportionate change in the quantity of a commodity demanded after a unit proportionate change in the income of consumers with prices held constant. For example, a product which has an income ➤elasticity of 2 will enjoy demand growth of 2 per cent for every 1 per cent growth in consumer income. Commodities can be grouped by their income elasticities. First, luxury items which comprise a high proportion of the spending of the rich have income elasticities in excess of 1 and enjoy growth in demand above that of average incomes. Secondly, basic items such as food enjoy some increased demand when the economy grows, but proportionately not as much as the growth in average incomes. Thirdly, ➤inferior goods have negative income elasticities: as soon as people can afford to stop buying them they do – examples are second-hand clothes and certain cheap but unsavoury foods.

Income elasticities can be measured at the level of individual consumers or the economy as a whole, and can be assessed for individual commodities or groups of commodities taken together. In the most general case, the income elasticity of all spending in the long term must be equal to 1, that is, spending must rise in the same proportion as income, otherwise savings would have to be unsustainably growing or contracting. The income elasticity is of practical importance to business and policy-makers because any product which has an income elasticity below 1 in a growing economy will have a falling share of total spending and countries which export commodities with low-income elasticities will suffer worsening ➤terms of trade problems in the long term if world economic growth occurs. The income elasticity is equal to the negative of the sum of the elasticity of demand of a commodity with respect to its own price and all other prices.

income tax A ➤tax on ➤income. In the UK individuals are taxed on the full amount of their income from employment or ➤investment in the ➤fiscal year. (including some ➤fringe benefits but not including gifts: ➤inheritance tax; ➤capital gains are taxed separately). Deductions, such as single and married personal allowances, dependant's allowance and mortgage interest paid, are allowed by the Tax Act in arriving at taxable income. Income tax is progressive in its effect, and successive slices of assessable income are taxed (1997/98) at 20 per cent (lower rate) 23 per cent (basic rate) and 40 per cent (higher rate). Married couples may opt for taxation as individuals. Persons in employment are normally taxed under the ➤pay-as-you-earn system under the so-called Schedule E. The self-employed, including those in ➤partnerships, are taxed under the so-called Schedule D, Cases I and II. Under this schedule, the assessment was formerly made on the ➤profits of a continuing trade or profession for the year preceding the year of assessment, but from 1996/97 this system was changed. (►self-assessment.) (Other schedules deal with investment income (where tax is not deducted at source), income from abroad and other sources of income.) Company income is taxed under a different system (►corporation tax). There is some disagreement amongst economists on the effects of income tax on incentives to work and save and these effects are difficult to verify empirically. On equity grounds a progressive income tax places a higher burden on those with the means to bear it, but this may discourage effort through the ►substitution effect or encourage people to work harder (and encourage sophisticated tax avoidance) to make up their income (►income effect). The system of income-tax reliefs for particular types of saving (for example, pension contributions) distorts savings decisions and this is one of the reasons why many economists advocate an ►expenditure tax in place of income tax. ►►supply-side economics.

income velocity of circulation ►velocity of circulation.

incomes policy ►prices and incomes policy.

incomplete contract A formal or written ►contract which fails to outline the rights and duties of each party in all situations. The difficulty of framing complete contracts – even in quite straightforward situations – is increasingly seen as an economic problem in that it can inhibit individuals from trading with each other. A builder may not wish to enter a contract to build a wall for someone at a given price in a given time unless he knows exactly what will happen if the ground transpires to be hard to build on, or if the weather is bad. It is very costly to draw up a contract that specifies every eventuality, and this may force the builder to charge a high price to cover the risks. Or it may be that certain features of the best contract would be unenforceable. ►►principal–agent problem; transaction costs.

incorporation The action of forming a company by carrying out the necessary legal formalities. ►►company law.

increasing returns ►economies of scale.

independent commodity ►complementary goods.

independent variable A ►variable from which the values of other variables are derived. (►►dependent variable.)

indexation The introduction of automatic linkage between monetary obligations and the price level. It can apply to wages, prices, or government tax charges. In practice it should mean that the money value of a long-term loan would be increased in line with the ►retail prices index so that the borrower would have to repay the loan in ►real terms. In the absence of indexation, unanticipated ►inflation, by eroding the real value of loans, shifts resources from lenders to borrowers and therefore disrupts the credit mechanism and the ►capital market. While indexation reduces the costs of inflation, some economists believe it entrenches inflationary expectations, and makes it harder to get inflation down. General indexation has been used in some countries, for example Brazil, to help cope with inflation in the past. The UK government introduced an index-linked ➤gilt-edged security in 1981 for financial institutions and has subsequently issued others for private investors as well as institutions, for example, 2½ per cent Index-linked Treasury Stock 2011. Some ➤National Savings Certificates are also *index-linked*.

index-linked ➤indexation.

index number A ➤weighted average of a number of statistical observations of some economic attribute, as a percentage of a similar weighted average calculated for the attribute at an earlier, or base, period. Typical economic attributes for which index numbers are calculated are prices and production, the most familiar being the ➤retail prices index, or cost-of-living index. In principle, the method of indexation is the same for all indices and, therefore, can be explained by reference to this price index. The price of each commodity or service included in the index is recorded in the current period (say 1997) and divided by its price in the base period (say 1990), to obtain a *price relative* for each item. Each price relative is then multiplied by a weight and all the items summed and averaged. The weights used may be either the amount spent on each item in the current period (1997) – a *current-weighted* index or ➤Paasche index or the amount spent on each item in the base period (1990) – a *base-weighted* index or Laspeyres index. ➤➤index-number problem.

index-number problem This problem arises from the use of ➤index numbers, which are summary single numbers encapsulating a range of values and used to describe succinctly changes in the range of values over time. The ➤retail prices index, for instance, could equally rationally, for the above purpose, be calculated as a *base-weighted* or a *current-weighted* index, but the two types of index do not necessarily give the same answer. For instance, consider a simple example of two goods X and Y which have the following prices and quantities purchased in the base year 1 and the current year 2:

	Year 1		*Year 2*	
	Price	*Quantity*	*Price*	*Quantity*
X	10p	5	8p	6
Y	20p	5	25p	1

The current-weighted index is given by:

$$\text{Year } 2 = \frac{(8p \times 6) + (25p \times 1)}{(10p \times 6) + (20p \times 1)} = \frac{73}{80} = 0.91 \,(\text{Year } 1 = 100)$$

The base-weighted index is given by:

$$\text{Year } 2 = \frac{(8p \times 5) + (25p \times 5)}{(10p \times 5) + (20p \times 5)} = \frac{165}{150} = 1.10 \ (\text{Year } 1 = 100)$$

According to the base-weighted index, the general level of prices rose in year 2 compared with year 1 (by 10 per cent), but according to the current-weighted index, prices fell in year 2 (by 9 per cent). The problem of choice is that if base weights are not updated, items will continue to be included that are no longer relevant in household expenditure. On the other hand, changing weights in order to keep them current could lead to the index being influenced by changes in quantities and therefore not be properly representative of price movements only. Moreover, a consumer price index may fail to reflect in its weights technological changes enhancing product quality. The new model of a car launched in 1997 could have benefits unknown to its five-year-older predecessor which are not reflected in its price.

indexed ►indexation.

indifference curve A graphical representation of sets of different combinations of commodities which each yield to the consumer the same level of satisfaction. Indifference curves can be plotted on graphs called indifference maps, on each axis of which is represented the quantity of some commodity. To produce such a curve, any point can be taken to start with, representing a basket of two goods (though the analysis can be extended to more than two very easily). One unit of the first commodity, books say, could be removed from the basket and units of the second commodity, CDs for example, added until a point was found at which the consumer felt that the new CDs exactly compensated for the loss of the book. This new basket, with perhaps two more CDs in it but one less book, is the second point on the same indifference curve as the first. The exercise can be repeated with steadily fewer books and increasing numbers of CDs and then again with increasing numbers of books and correspondingly falling numbers of CDs. A new indifference curve altogether could be derived by taking a starting-point with both more CDs and books than the previous basket and repeating the whole process again.

Indifference curves can never intersect. If a point A lies on two intersecting indifference curves then all the points on each curve must have the same utility as point A, and the two curves must both represent bundles of goods of equal utility. It is then logically impossible for them to be separate indifference curves. As a result of this, every point on the indifference map lies on one and only one indifference curve. Normally, various assumptions are made about consumers and their tastes, with the result that indifference curves have the following properties. First, they slope downwards. As the consumer loses some of one commodity, he must receive more of another if he is to remain as satisfied as he was. Similarly, a consumer should always prefer a basket with more of both commodities than another.

Secondly, they are convex to (that is, bulge towards) the origin (►convexity). This is because, as units of the first commodity are removed from the basket, increasing amounts of the second commodity will be required to compensate. A consumer may start off valuing CDs and books equally, but after he has piled up a basket of books with only a tiny selection of CDs remaining, he will want a large number of extra books in return for one CD.

Various extreme forms of indifference curve can be drawn without the usual properties described above. Perfect ►substitutes (two identical brands of washing powder, for example) have indifference curves which are straight downward-sloping lines. At no stage will the consumer change the rate at which he swaps one item for the other. Perfect complements (►complementary goods) on the other hand, have L-shaped indifference curves; increasing quantities of a left shoe will derive for a consumer no extra utility at all unless extra right shoes are found to match. If a consumer actively hates one commodity, his indifference curves will slope upwards. Indifference maps are used extensively in theoretical economics. By plotting money against any commodity, the individual's demand curve for that commodity can be derived. If leisure is compared to money on an indifference map, analysis of the decision of individuals on how much to work (and earn) and how much to relax can be analysed. ►►convexity; demand, theory of; indifference-curve analysis; marginal rate of substitution; ordinal utility.

indifference-curve analysis The study of consumer demand in terms of ranked combinations of commodities consumed subject to the constraints of price and income. Under this approach, there is no need for an absolute measure of utility or satisfaction; consumers merely need to be able to choose between different bundles of goods (►►ordinal utility). One can view the basic task of the consumer as ranking all the combinations of items that can be bought with the income available and choosing the bundle at the top of the resulting list. The tools for this analysis are the *indifference map* (built of ►indifference curves), which expresses the consumers' tastes; and the ►budget line, which shows the combinations of items that can be bought for a given income and set of prices.

Indifference-curve analysis suggests that people should consume items such that the rate at which they are prepared to swap them with complete indifference equals the ratio of the prices of the two items. For example, if two glasses of milk cost the same as one glass of wine and a consumer values one glass of each equally, he can enhance his utility by reducing his wine consumption by a glass and increasing his milk consumption by two glasses, without an extra cost. This process can go on until the consumer has so much milk and so little wine that he would actually enjoy a single glass of the one rather than two glasses of the other. On the indifference map, this corresponds to the point at which the budget line is tangential to the indifference curve. ►►marginal rate of substitution.

indirect taxation ➤direct taxation.

indirect utility function The relationship between the total ➤utility of a consumer on the one hand, and the price of different commodities and the income of the consumer on the other. In ➤demand theory, a *direct* utility function maps the *quantity of different commodities consumed* to the *utility of the consumer*. However, for any level of income and set of prices, rational consumers will select their purchases to maximize their utility subject to what the price of goods and their total income will allow. Thus, given prices and income, we can derive the *quantities of the commodities consumed*, and from that, we can derive total utility. ➤ordinal utility.

individual savings account (ISA) A tax-free savings scheme announced in the ➤budget of 1998 and scheduled to come into operation in April 1999. ISAs will replace ➤personal equity plans. Savers will be able to invest up to £7000 in the first year, with a maximum of £3000 in cash and a maximum of £1000 in life assurance, the remainder in ➤equities. Thereafter, the limit will be £5000 in each year, with a maximum of £1000 in cash and £1000 in life assurance. Savings in these accounts will be exempt from ➤capital gains and ➤income taxes. Dividends from UK equities will receive a 10 per cent tax credit.

induced investment That part of ➤investment which is determined by changes in output, as opposed to *autonomous investment* such as government expenditure on infrastructure capital (➤acceleration principle).

industrial bank Another name for a ➤finance house.

industrial democracy The participation of employees in decision-taking in industrial organizations. The concept reached its peak in 1974–9, when the Labour government was committed to introducing legislation to facilitate industrial democracy and the Bullock Committee, which was set up to examine how this might be done, recommended in its report of February 1977 that a single-tier board system be set up with equal representation of workers and shareholders. Since then, there has been more emphasis on the notion of works councils and consultation, rather than democracy as such. It has been promoted at the ➤European Union level ➤Social Charter.

industrial districts Geographical clusters of firms in the same and related activities. Examples are Silicon Valley near San Francisco and Route 128 near Boston in the United States, and Cambridge in the UK. In these three instances the firms are predominantly in new ➤technology-based industries that are ➤research-and-development-intensive. There are many other examples of industrial districts in traditional sectors, for example ceramic goods in Sassuolo, Emilia Romagna, Italy. The existence of industrial districts has long been noted by economists – indeed, they are sometimes referred to as 'Marshallian districts' after ➤Marshall, Alfred, who first gave them extended analysis. Firms in industrial districts benefit from

➤externalities in the availability of suppliers, reserves of skilled labour, specialized distribution, training facilities and information which seems to promote ➤innovation. It has been suggested that industrial clusters allow ➤small businesses to enjoy some of the ➤economies of scale (via market coordination under conditions of low ➤transactions costs) available to large firms within their own organizations. The origin of industrial districts cannot be attributed to similar causes. In Cambridge and on Route 128 proximity to centres of academic scientific research have played a major role. In some traditional industries the origin of clusters can be traced to putting-out systems, trade routes, markets and other factors.

industrial organization Branch of applied ➤microeconomics dealing with the performance of business enterprises and especially with the effects of ➤market structures on market conduct (pricing policy, restrictive practices, ➤innovation, for example) and how firms are organized, owned and managed. ➤➤concentration; firm, theory of the; game theory.

industry concentration ➤concentration.

inequality The degree to which the distribution of economic welfare generated in an economy differs from that of equal shares among its inhabitants. In practice, the measure most commonly adopted is that of the distribution of income (➤➤income, distribution of) but other measures also employed include expenditure and wealth. The distribution may relate to all income earners or to ➤households. The inequality in the distribution of income in the UK grew substantially from the end of the 1970s, after a period of stability. The incomes of people in the lowest 5th ➤percentile fell by 11 per cent in the 1980s whereas those in the 95th percentile grew by 60 per cent. The top 30 per cent of income earners increased their share of total income from 47 per cent to 54 per cent. A similar increase in the inequality of incomes was experienced by the USA, whereas in other countries, such as Continental Europe, a similar change has not been seen. A number of causes have been suggested for the UK's shift in income distribution. These are the reduction in the higher rates of income tax, the increase in one-parent households, unemployment, reduced trade unionism and the linkage of benefits payments to prices rather than incomes. However, a more important cause has been the relative reduction in the earnings of unskilled as compared to skilled workers possibly attributable to changes in technology and increased competition from ➤international trade. It should be remembered that the use of ➤time series for analysing inequality does not imply that the people or households which made up the specific groups in one year stayed in those groups throughout the period. People are, in practice, mobile through the different income groups as they progress through their lives. Moreover, inequality does not necessarily equate with ➤poverty. The ➤World Bank has estimated that 40 per cent of the world ➤labour force has income of less than $1600, compared with an average income of unskilled labour in the richest countries of $17,000. ➤weightlessness.

infant-industry argument An argument in support of the retention of a protective import ►tariff to promote the creation of a local industry. It is held to apply in cases where an industry cannot operate at an optimum least-cost output until it has reached a sufficient size to obtain significant ►economies of scale. A new industry, therefore, in, say, a ►developing country, will always be in a competitively vulnerable position vis-à-vis an established industry in an advanced country. It follows that the stage of growth at which the industry (or country) can 'take off' (►Rostow, W. W.) industrially will be postponed indefinitely. The argument concludes that protection is necessary until the industry has reached its optimum size (►first-mover advantage) (►protection).

inferior good A good the demand for which falls as income rises; that is, its ►income elasticity of demand is negative. An example would be the demand of married couples for small apartments. A good which is not inferior is called a *normal good.* ►►giffen good; income effect.

inflation Persistent increases in the general level of prices. It can be seen as a devaluing of the worth of money. Inflation is a recurring but only intermittent historical phenomenon. Its most serious recent appearance occurred during the 1970s in the wake of the quadrupling of oil prices in 1973, when annual inflation rates in the developed world rose as high as 25 per cent, but for the rest of the post-war period it has not been unusual for the inflation rate to be exceeded by the real growth rate. A crucial feature of inflation is that price rises are sustained. A once-only increase in the rate of ►value-added tax will immediately put up prices, but this does not represent inflation, unless the indirect effects of the VAT rise have repercussions on prices in periods after the direct effects.

Accounts of the causes of inflation are numerous. The most popular arguments are that it is caused by ►excess demand in the economy (►demand-pull inflation), that it is caused by high costs (►cost-push inflation) and that it results from excessive increases in the money supply (►monetarism). These causes often amount to the same thing. The mechanism by which the increase in money supply causes inflation is by creating excess demand, making monetarism compatible with the demand-pull argument. The demand-pull and cost-push theories are also linked. An excess of demand causes producers to raise their prices – but this leads workers to demand higher wages to maintain their living standard; this causes higher demand and the process begins again. Similarly, if under the cost-push argument the cost increases stimulating price rises are wage costs (which represents most of the total net costs of the economy), firms can still only raise their prices if the demand is there for their goods to sell – if not, high costs merely bankrupt them. All three of these causes amount to an attempt by a nation to live beyond its means, or to enjoy a living standard higher than that allowed by its output and borrowing. This implies that inflation can rarely be cured by a measure which does not suppress attempts at maintaining high living standards and explains why the reduction of inflation is associated with austerity measures. When oil prices rose in the 1970s, countries without oil suffered a loss of their ►real income and should have accepted a cut in living standards; unable to impose a cut, however, governments attempted to maintain higher levels of income than were merited by the products to be bought by that income. Too much money chasing too few goods inevitably caused inflation. Controlling inflation by restricting demand (either through tight control of the money supply through high ►rates of interest, or through cuts in government borrowing) has costs, however. If wages are growing rapidly, and the government squeezes demand in the economy, unemployment may result because employers will not be able to afford to pay their staff if they cannot raise their sales prices because of low demand. In other words, if wages are high, but aggregate demand is restricted, firms will have high costs but will not be able to pass these on in higher prices because sales will be too low, and many will go out of business or sack some of their employees. In the short term, it appears that by allowing higher demand, inflation occurs, but unemployment can be lower than otherwise.

That inverse relationship between money wages and unemployment was described by the *Phillips curve* (►Phillips, A. W. H.). However, the Phillips relationship did not hold through the 1960s and the role of ►expectations in pre-empting rises in prices was stressed, mainly on account of the work of ►Friedman. Inflation could not act as a break on real wages, it was asserted, unless it outstripped the expectations of wage bargainers. If, in the longer term, inflation rates could be anticipated, inflation would have no effect on unemployment (►unemployment, natural rate of). The Friedman view that the inflation– unemployment trade-off was only short term was superseded in theoretical eco- nomics by ►new classical economics, which held that there was no trade-off even in the short term (►policy ineffectiveness theorem). Now, policy-makers tend to accept the idea that there is no trade-off, but equally, they tend to believe policy can have a positive effect on demand without necessarily provoking inflation. They act on the assumption that if the economy is operating below its potential (►output gap), inflation will tend to fall; if the economy is above its potential, inflation will tend to rise. The task is simply to manage ►aggregate demand to ensure demand is neither too high, nor too low. In its effects, inflation probably disrupts investment, by causing interest rates to rise, shortening pay-back periods, and affecting company cash flow. It arbitrarily distributes wealth away from those whose incomes are fixed in money terms or rise more slowly than inflation. It generates ►menu costs. To allow inflation to develop carries the risk of incurring rates high enough to disrupt economic life (►►hyperinflation; indexation; prices and incomes policy; superneutrality of money).

inflation accounting Methods of keeping a record of financial transactions and analysing them in a way which allows for changes in the purchasing power of money over time. Until recently, solely *historic-cost accounting* methods have been used, that is to say, accounts were derived more or less directly from bookkeeping records of actual expenditures and receipts. Fixed ►assets, for example, such as buildings, were recorded in the balance sheet at their actual (depreciated) cost (►depreciation). In a period of rapidly rising prices the replacement cost of these assets is likely to be much higher than their recorded cost, and historic-cost accounting, therefore, may understate depreciation and costs in ►real terms and overstate profits. Over a period of time this may lead to a situation where ►capital is not being maintained in real terms at all but distributed as 'illusory' money profit in dividends and tax payments.

Among the various ways of coping with inflation, is the practice of recording net assets in accounts by reference to their value rather than their cost. Among the different approaches to asset valuation (which include ►present value), the Sandilands Committee of Inquiry in 1975 adopted a form of *replacement-cost accounting* which involves revaluing assets from historic costs to current costs. The main features of the system which is called *current-cost accounting* (CCA) are that money is retained as the unit of measurement, that both 'assets and liabilities are shown in the balance sheet at a valuation' and that ►operating profit 'is struck after charging the "value to the business" of assets consumed during the period thus excluding holding gains from profit and showing them separately'.

inflation target The adoption of an explicit level of inflation to which ►monetary policy is geared towards steering the economy. Inflation targets rose to prominence in the early 1990s as national authorities grew disenchanted with the effectiveness of targeting growth of ►money supply, and the main fixed exchange rate regime (the ►European Exchange Rate Mechanism) began to break down. The UK's inflation target was introduced in 1992 as a range of 1 to 4 per cent, subsequently to fall to 'below two and a half per cent'. In 1997 the target was set at 2.5 per cent precisely for RPIX (►underlying inflation), with policy *ex post* (►ex ante) considered satisfactory if it actually delivers inflation within one percentage point either side. The recent 'point target' is a more useful guide to policy – if inflation is heading above the target, policy should be tightened, and vice versa if it is below. The range around the target is more useful for judging whether the authorities have succeeded or failed reasonably to control inflation. In New Zealand, Canada and the UK inflation targets came to have an explicit role in setting the relationship between national government and the ►central banks, who were given responsibility for setting monetary policy. The objective of policy – the target – is then an explicit political choice, while the operation of policy is delegated. ►►monetary policy.

inflation tax A form of incomes policy (►prices and incomes policy) under which firms granting pay rises above a set level are taxed on those pay rises.

inflationary gap A situation in which aggregate demand is at an equilibrium level in excess of the full-employment level of output. If it exists, all resources in the economy are fully utilized and prices have to rise to eliminate the excess demand. Based on Keynesian models of the economy, the inflationary gap leads to a ►demand-pull inflation which can be removed by ►deflation. Because persistent inflation was combined with high unemployment (something that should not occur in the inflationary gap view of the world) the concept faded from view. In recent years, however, it has been revived in all but name with the growth in popularity of the ►output gap as a basis for analysing economic policy. ►►inflation; stagflation.

infrastructure Roads, airports, sewage and water systems, railways, the telephone and other public utilities. Also called *social overhead capital*, infrastructure is basic to economic development and improvements in it can be used to help attract industry to a disadvantaged area.

inheritance tax (UK) A tax on the transmission of wealth on death and on gifts made in the seven years before death. Cumulative transfers in excess of £215,000 (1997/98) are taxed at a flat rate of 40 per cent, with tapering relief on gifts made between three and seven years of death. All transfers to a spouse living in Britain are exempt. Business property qualifies for relief of up to 50 per cent. This tax is not a true inheritance tax because it is levied on the donor or his estate, not on the recipient. The tax replaced *capital transfer tax* in 1986, which in turn replaced *Estate Duty*, first introduced in 1894.

initial allowances ►capital allowances.

initial public offering ►flotation.

innovation Putting new products and services on to the market or new means for producing them. Innovation is preceded by research that may lead to an invention which is then developed for the market (►research and development). Innovation is an important source of economic expansion and ►productivity. It is central to the new theories of economic growth (►endogenous growth theory) although it has long been taken as important – ►Schumpeter gave a central role to it in his theory of economic growth. Recent economics has been preoccupied with the incentives for innovation, in a world where the benefits of it are inevitably shared: a company that invents a new drug obtains some profit, on account of the patent system. Even that is limited in duration. But there are many innovations that cannot be patented. The idea of telephone banking, for example, has been widely copied. That replication is an important development for the benefit of consumers, but does it diminish the likelihood that such ideas will flow in future? The existence of a ►first-mover advantage is clearly important; allowing the innovator to capture profits from an early start in an industry is important. ►weightlessness.

input ►factors of production.

input–output analysis The analysis of an economy in terms of the relationship between all ►inputs and outputs. The output of a good or service in an economy is either used in the production of goods and services (including itself) or it goes into final consumption (e.g. households, exports, government). Each output in an economy can be represented by an equation, with output equal to its final consumption plus the sum of its inputs used in all production activity throughout the economy. The amounts used in production will depend on the ➤production functions for each. Consider the simplified ➤model of two commodities, Y_1 and Y_2:

$$Y_1 = C_1 + a_{11}Y_1 + a_{12}Y_2$$
$$Y_2 = C_2 + a_{21}Y_1 + a_{22}Y_2$$

Y_1 and Y_2 are total outputs, C_1 and C_2 are the final consumptions for each and a_{11}, a_{12}, a_{21} and a_{22} are the input–output coefficients representing the amounts of Y_1 and Y_2 required to produce one unit of Y_1 and Y_2. These equations may be put in ➤matrix form:

$$Y = C + AY \text{ or } Y = (1 - A)^{-1}C$$

where Y is the ➤vector Y_1Y_2, C the vector C_1C_2 and A the matrix

$$a_{11}\ a_{12}$$
$$a_{21}\ a_{22}$$

AY is the total of intermediate demands and A is the matrix of input–output coefficients or *technology matrix*. By structuring the production functions of an economy in this way, it is possible to trace the effects of a change in final demand, or change in output, of one good or service, throughout its inter-industry linked relationships, so that the knock-on effects on other industries may be measured. ➤Leontief, W. W.; ➤non-substitution theorem.

input–output matrix ➤input–output analysis; Leontief, W. W.

insider–outsider theory The division of participants in a market – usually it is the labour market – into a privileged core with a certain amount of market power; and a less privileged periphery with almost no market power. For example, there might be insiders who have good, union jobs, with full employment rights; and outsiders who find it difficult to get any job at all. The crucial feature of this kind of segmentation is that the outsiders are not in a position to influence the market conditions of the insiders – they cannot credibly offer themselves as alternative employees at a lower wage for example. As a result, the mechanism normally assumed to bring about increased employment – a falling wage reducing the cost of taking more people on – simply doesn't work. The gap between the two types of worker of course has to be explained to be meaningful. It may result from a difference in the perceived employability or skills of the different types; or from powerful unions, who can use industrial muscle to prevent non-union labour from displacing union labour. The idea has been seen both as a cause and an effect of ➤long-term unemployment. ➤hysteresis, unemployment.

insolvency The state of a firm when its ➤liabilities, excluding ➤equity capital, exceed its total ►assets. (►►bankruptcy.) A less stringent definition would be that a firm is insolvent if it is unable to meet its obligations when due for payment.

Insolvency Act 1985 ►bankruptcy.

instalment credit (US) Term for ►hire purchase, though sometimes used generally to refer to a credit sale when payment is made in instalments (►consumer credit).

institutional economics A school of economic thought which flourished in the 1920s in the USA. Economists holding institutional views criticize orthodox economists for relying on theoretical and mathematical models which not only distort and oversimplify even strictly economic phenomena, but, more important, ignore their non-economic, institutional environment. The political and social structure of a country may block or distort the normal economic processes. Institutionalists believe that there is a need for economists to recognize the relevance of other disciplines, e.g. sociology, politics, law, to the solution of economic problems. ►T. B. Veblen (1857–1929), ►W. C. Mitchell (1874–1948) and ►G. K. Myrdal (1898–1987) have been the leading economists sympathetic to institutionalism. ►least-developed country.

institutional investor An organization, as opposed to an individual, which invests funds arising from its receipts from the sale of ►securities, from ►deposits and other sources, i.e. ►insurance companies, ►investment trusts, ►unit trusts, ►pension funds and trustees. Institutional investors own three-quarters of all quoted securities.

insurance A contract to pay a ►premium in return for which the insurer will pay compensation in certain eventualities, e.g. fire, theft, motor accident. The premiums are so calculated that, on average in total, they are sufficient to pay compensation for the policy-holders who will make a claim together with a margin to cover administration costs and profit (►actuary; underwriting). In effect insurance spreads risk, so that loss by an individual is compensated for at the expense of all those who insure against it, and as such it has an important economic function. The traditional forms of insurance are *general insurance*, i.e. marine and other property insurance against theft, fire and accident, and *life insurance*, the last-named strictly being ►assurance, because the cover is given against the occurrence of an event which is inevitable. There are also many other kinds of insurance, including public or professional liability, sickness and unemployment insurance, some of which, like ►National Insurance and the BUPA insurance for private medical treatment, are not carried out by the traditional insurance companies. Traditional insurance is carried out in Britain by several hundred companies. The UK is an important centre for the world insurance industry and about half of the premium income of British insurance companies is derived from their overseas operations. The bulk of their ►assets consist of ►investments made out of premium income against their ►liabilities to 'pay out' on life policies; only about 10 per cent of their assets are in respect of general funds. Life insurance is a popular way of providing for old age and purchasing a house or even ►equity shares, as well as protecting the financial position of dependants. ►►adverse selection; Lloyd's; moral hazard; pension funds; unit trust.

insurance premium tax An indirect tax (►direct taxation) on certain ►insurance premiums (►premium) administered by HM Customs and Excise. The tax applies to motor and household insurance, but not to long-term insurance such as life and pensions. Introduced on 1 October 1994 at a rate of 2.5 per cent, the current rate (1997/98) is 4 per cent.

intangible assets ►assets.

integration ►merger; vertical integration.

Inter-American Development Bank (IADB) The Bank was established in 1959 to give financial assistance for the encouragement of economic and social development to the ►developing countries of Latin America and the Caribbean. The head office is in Washington. Membership now covers twenty-eight countries in Latin America and the Caribbean and eighteen countries in Europe, the United States, Canada, Israel and Japan. In 1994 the authorized capital of the Bank was increased to $101 billion and shares of the member countries readjusted. The main effect was an increase to 5 per cent for Japan and reductions for USA down to 30 per cent and of the Latin American and Caribbean countries to 50 per cent. Bank lending was set at about $6 billion per year and the Bank was given authority for the first time to lend to the private sector. ►Asian Development Bank.

inter-bank market The ►money market in which banks (►banking) borrow or lend among themselves for fixed periods either to accommodate short-term ►liquidity problems or for lending on. The interest rate at which funds on loan are offered to first-class banks is called the *inter-bank offered rate* (IBOR) or, in London, the *London inter-bank offered rate* (LIBOR). The corresponding rate for deposits is known as the *inter-bank market bid rate* (IBMBR).

interest 1. A charge made for the use of borrowed money, levied as a percentage of the amount of the ►debt (►rate of interest). 2. More generally, a right, privilege or share in something, as in common grazing land or in shareholders' interest (►balance sheet).

interest, abstinence theory of An explanation of ►rates of interest in terms of a reward for choosing to abstain from consumption. ►►interest, classical theory of; Senior, N. W.; time preference.

interest, classical theory of In the early tradition of classical theory, e.g. that of ►Adam Smith and ►Ricardo, interest was regarded as simply the ►rate of return on ►capital invested. It was considered to be an ►income to capital rather like

➤rent to land. With the subsequent development of the classical system, the nature and the determinants of the rate of interest came to be regarded in terms of a more complex pattern. The rate was arrived at by the interaction of two forces operating on the supply of, and the demand for, funds. On the one hand, the strength of demand was related to businessmen's expectations regarding ➤profits. This was connected with the marginal productivity of ➤investment. On the other hand, the supply was dependent upon the willingness to save. This willingness was in turn related to the marginal rate of ➤time preference. People judge how much a pound is worth to them today compared with a pound in the future. They make their decision whether to save by comparing this 'rate of exchange' between now and the future with the current rate of interest. In the classical system, therefore, it was the rate of interest which brought ➤savings into balance with investment. ➤Keynes attacked this assumption in his *General Theory of Employment, Interest and Money*. The balance was brought about, he argued, by means of changes in income and output. The rate of interest was itself more closely identified with monetary factors. ➤➤Hume, D.; liquidity preference; loanable funds.

interest cover The number of times the fixed-interest payments made by a company to service its ➤loan capital are exceeded by ➤earnings. This ratio shows the decline in earnings that could take place before interest payments could not be met out of current income and is therefore a useful guide for the prospective fixed-interest investor.

interest, natural rate of The ➤rate of interest at which economic activity is neither driving prices higher, nor lower. One of the conditions put forward by ➤Wicksell for monetary ➤equilibrium – i.e. a situation in which there are no forces tending to make ➤prices rise or fall – was that the money ➤rate of interest should be equal to the 'natural rate'. The owner of a forest has a choice between two alternatives in any one year. He can either cut down his trees and lend out the money obtained from them, or let the trees grow another year. The ➤rate of return he gets from lending is the 'money rate'; the return he gets from letting his trees grow heavier is the 'natural rate'. Wicksell thought of the natural rate, therefore, in terms of a physical investment. However, ➤Myrdal in developing this theme pointed out that the natural rate should also take into account the price at which the timber was expected to sell. ➤➤Fisher, I.; Keynes, J. M.

interest, productivity theories of Theories which place the emphasis of the explanation for the existence of a ➤rate of interest on the ➤yield from ➤investment. ➤Böhm-Bawerk, in particular, developed this theory as one of his reasons for the existence of a positive interest rate. It was built upon his theory of 'roundabout' production methods. A direct method of obtaining drinking water, for example, is to go to a stream and drink. A more roundabout method is to manufacture a bucket and use it to fetch water. An even more roundabout method is to build a water-pipe, pump and tap. Each stage involves more ➤capital, and also more time, but nevertheless yields increased product. Goods available today, therefore, have more value than goods available tomorrow, for two reasons. First, goods today can be used in a time-consuming roundabout process to yield benefits tomorrow which are greater than could be obtained by the same goods applied to direct production tomorrow. Secondly, they also yield greater benefits over the same goods applied to roundabout production tomorrow. This is because there are ►diminishing returns to the extension of roundabout methods. Present goods are, therefore, always technically superior to future goods, and it follows that there must exist a positive rate of interest by which future goods are equated to present goods. ►►interest, classical theory of; interest, natural rate of; Keynes, J. M.

interest rate ►rate of interest.

interest, time preference theory of A psychological theory of the existence of ►rates of interest. An individual prefers consumption now to consumption in the future for two reasons. First, he is aware of the possibility that he may be dead before he can derive the benefits from postponing consumption. Second, and less rationally, there exists a tendency for people to undervalue future benefits – a 'deficiency of the telescopic faculty'. ►►Böhm-Bawerk, E. von; Fisher, I.; interest, classical theory of; interest, natural rate of; interest, productivity theories of; time preference.

interim dividend ►dividend.

interlocking directorate The holding by an individual of directorships in two or more separate companies.

intermediate goods, intermediate products Something which is used in the production of other goods; for example sheet steel used in the production of car bodies. Also called producer goods.

intermediate products ►intermediate goods.

intermediate technology The use of simple, labour-intensive means of production, utilizing non-traditional techniques incorporating modern science and technology. Intermediate technology was advocated notably by Ernst Friederich Schumacher (1911–1977), in a number of publications including the popular book of essays '*Small is Beautiful': A Study of Economics as if People Mattered* (1973). Schumacher founded the Intermediate Technology Development Group, a non-governmental organization which works in ►developing countries. His ideas were based on the belief that modern large-scale ►capital-intensive industry is not an appropriate vehicle for economic development in backward societies which lack capital and skilled personnel, but have a surplus of labour. Intermediate technology is moreover less environmentally intrusive, is consistent with ►sustainable development and minimizes dependence on external assistance allowing citizens in developing countries more control over their lives.

internal markets The adoption of market-like mechanisms as a reform strategy in public services. Central to the principle of internal markets is the idea that there should be a division between those who deliver services (for example, hospitals) and those who purchase them (such as GPs, or health authorities). Reforms in the National Health Service, and at the BBC did appear to deliver productive efficiency, as cost-conscious purchasers applied pressure to the service providers to keep prices low. But the reforms were criticized as generating a great deal of extra bureaucracy – inevitable in a world where all output is measured and accounted for. And they were also criticized for failing to deliver the benefits of genuine market mechanisms – providers have not been subject to the real budget constraints of private firms, and have been cushioned by long-term contracts ensuring comfortable levels of business. ➤private finance initiative; resource accounting; privatization.

internal rate of return That ➤rate of interest which you would have to use in discounting the flow over time of net revenue generated by an investment such that the ➤present value of the net revenue flows is equal to the capital sum invested. The internal rate of return, therefore, is the discount rate at which the net present value of a project is zero. It may be used in ➤investment appraisal to determine whether a prospective investment is viable. For instance, if the internal rate of return is higher than the rate of interest at which a firm can borrow, the investment would be worth pursuing. However, the internal rate of return has two disadvantages. First, if the period (e.g. annual, quarterly) costs and revenues of the project being considered change sign more than once (costs exceeding revenues give negative flows and revenues exceeding costs give positive flows) during the life of the project, a solution cannot be found giving a unique internal rate of return. Secondly, in ranking alternative investment proposals in priority order, the internal rate of return procedure could give a different ranking from that of net present value. For instance, consider the following two investment projects:

	(1)	(2)
Capital cost	£100	£300
Net revenue per year	£ 40	£ 40
Project life (years)	3	12
Net present value at 5 per cent	£ 8.9	£ 54.5
Internal rate of return (per cent)	9.7	8

According to the ranking by net present value, (2) is preferable to (1), whereas by ranking according to the internal rates of return (1) is preferred to (2). The net present value calculation always gives the correct answer because it shows the absolute amount of profit to be made on the investment. The internal rate of return is also the *marginal efficiency of capital* and *investor's yield*.

International Bank for Reconstruction and Development (IBRD) A part of the World Bank Group (►International Development Association; International Finance Corporation; Multilateral Investment Guarantee Agency). The establishment of the IBRD, like the ►International Monetary Fund was agreed by the representatives of forty-four countries at the UN Monetary and Financial Conference at ►Bretton Woods in July 1944. It began operations in June 1946, and has its head office in Washington, DC. The purpose of the Bank is to encourage ►capital investment for the reconstruction and development of its member countries, either by channelling the necessary private funds or by making ►loans from its own resources. Originally, 20 per cent of each member's subscription was paid into the Bank's funds in ►currency and gold, but this has been progressively reduced to 4.4 per cent; the remainder is retained but available for call to meet any of the Bank's ►liabilities if required. The Bank also raises money by selling ►bonds on the world market. Generally speaking, the Bank makes loans either direct to governments or with governments as the guarantor. Contributions of member countries to its capital are made in proportion to that member's share of world trade. Members' voting rights are allocated in the same way. In 1995 the Bank had an authorized capital of $184 billion. In 1995 there were 179 member countries and gross disbursements of the Bank were $12.7 billion.

International Clearing Union ►Keynes Plan.

international commodity agreements Several international commodity agreements have been signed in the past. They have included cocoa, coffee, olive oil, rubber, sultanas, sugar, timber wheat and tin. It has been a feature of the ►markets in primary commodities that imbalance between ►supply and ►demand gives rise to wide fluctuations in ►prices. Primary commodities often have long production cycles which are difficult to adjust to bring into ►equilibrium with relatively short-run fluctuations in demand. At the same time, the development of the economies of the primary producing countries can depend heavily on the export earnings of these commodities, with the result that, in response to a fall in demand, there can be a tendency to increase supply to maintain total earnings in the face of intensified competition, thereby forcing prices down even further. There are two features, therefore, of commodity agreements. They may be concluded (a) for the stabilization of prices, or (b) for the raising or maintenance of prices. The first Coffee Agreement signed in 1962, covering the five years to 1968, was designed to halt the long decline in prices by fixing export ►quotas for each producing country. The agreement has since been regularly renewed. The last agreement expired in 1989 and was replaced by the Association of Coffee-Producing Countries which operates an export quota system to maintain prices. The International Tin Agreement was an example of a 'price stabilization' agreement. The first operated for five years from July 1956. A 'buffer' stock of tin was created and a manager appointed who had the responsibility of buying and selling tin such as to keep the price within a 'ceiling' at which point he sold, and a 'floor' when he bought, tin. However, the sixth agreement failed in 1985 when the resources of the International Tin Council were insufficient to halt the fall in prices. It has been replaced by the Association of Tin-Producing Countries which operate an export quota system. In 1973 an International Cocoa Agreement was concluded which continued until 1988. A revised agreement was reached in 1993 aimed at controlling the production of cocoa and encouraging its consumption.

At the end of 1976 an agreement was concluded among producers for the stabilization of the prices of natural rubber by means of a buffer stock and controls on production. An International Natural Rubber Council was set up. The International Rubber Agreement was renewed in 1995 with thirty-one member countries, both producers and consumers of rubber. It is now the sole agreement that regulates price by selling and buying from a buffer stock. ➤developing country; multi-fibre arrangement; Organization of Petroleum Exporting Countries; United Nations Conference on Trade and Development.

International Development Association (IDA) Part of the World Bank group (➤International Bank for Reconstruction and Development; International Finance Cooporation; Multilateral Investment Guarantee Agency), established in 1960. It gives long-term ➤loans to governments at little or no interest for projects in the poorer of the ➤developing countries. It is intended for ➤investments for which finance cannot be obtained through other channels without bearing uneconomically high interest charges and is mainly for items of infrastructure, e.g. roads or power supply. The repayment period for the loan may be up to fifty years with repayments being delayed by up to ten years. The total funding of the IDA in 1995 was $101 billion.

International Energy Agency (IEA) An organization established in 1974 by the ➤Organization for Economic Cooperation and Development. Its aims are to (a) reduce the member countries' dependence on oil supplies, (b) maintain an information system relating to the international oil markets, (c) develop a stable international energy trade and (d) through cooperative sharing, prepare and protect member countries against a disruption of oil supplies. Member countries agree to hold a particular level of oil stocks. ➤Organization of Petroleum Exporting Countries.

International Finance Corporation (IFC) A part of the World Bank Group (➤International Bank for Reconstruction and Development; International Development Association; Multilateral Investment Guarantee Agency). In the early 1950s it was recognized that the requirement that IBRD loans should have a government guarantee was a significant handicap to the attraction of private ➤investment to ➤developing countries. The IFC was created in 1956 so that greater advantage could be taken of private initiative in the launching of new ➤capital projects. Until 1961, when its charter was amended, its activities were restricted because it had few resources and could not participate itself in ➤equity holdings. Since that time its activities have been able to develop rapidly. The Corporation can invest directly and give ➤loans and guarantees for private investors. It can hold equity interests in private companies, although its interest in any one company is generally restricted to below 25 per cent. The IFC is empowered to borrow from the IBRD to relend to private investors without government guarantee. It is financed by subscriptions from the 165 countries that make up its membership. It has an authorized capital of $2.5 billion.

international investment ➤foreign investment.

International Labour Organization (ILO) An organization established in 1919 under the Treaty of Versailles that became affiliated to the United Nations in 1946. Its aims are the improvement of working conditions throughout the world, the spread of social security and the maintenance of standards of social justice. It has drawn up a labour code based on these aims. The ILO offers technical assistance to ➤developing countries, especially in the field of training. Its budget is financed by contributions from its 173 member countries. The organization was awarded the Nobel peace prize in 1969.

International liquidity The amount of gold, ➤reserve currencies and ➤special drawing rights available for the finance of international trade. Broadly, if sufficient reserves were not available, a fall in prices and world trade could follow. (➤quantity theory of money.) Gold has lost some of its appeal as a reserve asset in a world of comparatively low inflation. Preference is given to the holding of interest-bearing assets denominated in stable reserve currencies such as the US dollar, the ➤European Currency Unit, German deutschmark, Japanese yen and sterling. ➤Creditor nation; Eurocurrency: United Nations Conference on Trade and Development.

International Monetary Fund (IMF) The organization set up by the ➤Bretton Woods Agreement of 1944 which came into operation in March 1947. The fund was established to encourage international cooperation in the monetary field and the removal of ➤foreign exchange restrictions, to stabilize exchange rates and to facilitate a multilateral (➤multilaterism) payments system between member countries. In 1995 the fund had 181 members. Under the IMF's articles of agreement, member countries were required to observe an ➤exchange rate, fluctuations in which should be confined to 1 per cent around its par value. This par value was quoted in terms of the US dollar, which was in turn linked to gold. In December 1971 the 'Group of Ten' (see below), meeting at the Smithsonian Institute, Washington, agreed on new 'central values' of currencies in order to achieve a dollar devaluation of 10 per cent with a permissible margin of ±2.25 per cent. Member countries finance the IMF through quotas depending on their economic standing. In 1994 quotas were increased and totalled SDR 145.3 billion. (➤special drawing rights.) This fund is used to tide members over temporary ➤balance of payments difficulties and thus to help stabilize exchange rates. Borrowing ability and voting rights are determined by this quota. A member in temporary balance of payments deficit obtains foreign exchange from the fund in exchange for its own currency, which it is required to repurchase within three to five years. Members in deficit with the fund are obliged by the terms of the agreement to consult with the IMF on the procedures being taken to improve their balance of payments.

During the early 1960s it became evident that there was a strong case for increasing the size of the fund, and in 1962 the General Arrangements to Borrow was signed by ten countries, namely the United States, the United Kingdom, West Germany, France, Belgium, the Netherlands, Italy, Sweden, Canada and Japan – called the 'Group of Ten' or the 'Paris Club' – Switzerland and Saudi Arabia, under which SDR 6.7 billion credit was made available to the IMF should it be required. This agreement has been regularly renewed and in 1993 the credit limit was raised to SDR 18.5 billion. Countries in difficulty can also negotiate standby credit on which they can draw as necessary. The IMF cannot, however, make use of any of the currency in this scheme without the prior consent of the lending country. In September 1967, at the IMF meeting in Rio de Janeiro, the creation of an international unit of account was agreed in principle, and ratified in July 1969. The system proposed was that annual increases in international credit would be distributed to IMF members by means of ►special drawing rights (SDRs). These credits are distributed among member countries in proportion to their quotas and may be included in their official reserves; the first, $3.5 billion, was distributed in this way on 1 January 1970. Total SDRs are now about $21.4 billion. There is a limit on the acceptability for payment in SDRs, in that no country need hold more than twice its SDR quota. In 1976 an agreement reached in Jamaica led to a major revision of the fund's articles. First, it was no longer required for member countries to subscribe 25 per cent of their quotas in gold, and gold was no longer the unit of account of the SDR. The IMF was authorized to sell its gold holding. Second, the commitment to fixed par values contained in the original articles was abolished. ►gold standard.

International Settlements, Bank for (BIS) ►Bank for International Settlements.

International Standard Industrial Classification (ISIC) ►Standard Industrial Classification.

international trade The exchange of goods and services between one country and another. This exchange takes place because of differences in costs of production between countries, and because it increases the economic welfare of each country by widening the range of goods and services available for ►consumption. ►Ricardo showed by the law of comparative advantage that it was not necessary for one country to have an absolute cost advantage in the production of a commodity for it to find a partner willing to trade. Even if a country produced all commodities more expensively than any other, trade to the benefit of all could take place provided only that the relative costs of production of the different commodities were favourable. Differences in costs of production exist because countries are differently endowed with the resources required. Countries differ as to the type and quantity of raw materials within their borders, their climate, the skill and size of their labour force, their stock of physical ►capital and their institutions (►institutional economics). Countries will tend to export (►exports) those commodities whose production requires relatively more than other commodities of those resources (►factors of production) of which it has most (►Heckscher–Ohlin principle). By increasing the scope for the specialization of labour (►►division of labour) and for achieving ►economies of scale by the enlargement of ►markets, there is a presumption that international trade should be free from restrictions (►►free trade). The classical economists (►►classical economics) condemned ►mercantilism for its advocacy of government control over trade in order to achieve export surpluses, and from the nineteenth to the early twentieth century there was a presumption in favour of free trade. This philosophy gave place to economic protectionism (►protection) in the 1930s but it was revived again in the ►General Agreement on Tariffs and Trade in 1948. The latter has had some success in reducing tariffs (►tariffs, import) on ►imports, culminating in the creation of the ►World Trade Organization. However, many trade restrictions still remain (►protection). At the same time there has been an increase in the number of ►customs unions and ►free-trade areas. While these agreements do establish free trade between member countries, they discriminate against outsiders. World trade has expanded faster than world output. Over the past fifty years, trade has grown on average at about 6 per cent per annum, about 50 per cent more than world output.

International Trade Commission (ITC) A United States government agency set up by the Trade Act 1974; it replaced the United States International Trade Organization (ITO) which had previously operated since 1916. The ITC has judicial powers to investigate cases in which ►imports are alleged to damage materially domestic industry and to make recommendations to the President. Such damage need not be due to unfair trading practices, such as ►dumping, although the ITC does carry out studies to determine whether dumping has taken place. It has the power to overturn anti-dumping duties imposed by the US Department of Commerce if it finds that no injury is caused to the USA from the imports under suspicion. The Commission also investigates cases in which imports might be undermining US agriculture-support schemes. It collects and disseminates information and statistics on US international trade and domestic production. It has prepared reports on the effects on the US economy of the further economic integration of the ►European Union, of the ►generalized system of preferences and of the ►Uruguay round of trade negotiations. (►►international trade.)

International Trade Organization (ITO) A proposed organization to foster trade, in the aftermath of the Second World War. At the UN conference held at Geneva in 1947 at which the ►General Agreement on Tariffs and Trade was signed, a charter was put forward for the setting up, within the UN Organization, of the new ITO. Fifty nations signed the charter in Havana the following year, but it was never subsequently ratified by the required number of countries. In practice, GATT and the ►United Nations Conference on Trade and Development (UNCTAD) have carried out most of the functions envisaged for the ITO. ►►World Trade Organization.

intervention Any form of government interference with ►market forces to achieve economic ends. Intervention may be in the area of ►macroeconomics (►►policy ineffectiveness theorem), or may be applied to one sector or market. In the latter case, it may take the form of ►regulation, ►taxation (e.g. a tax on environmentally destructive behaviour, ►pollutor-pays principle) or ►subsidy. There are numerous problems with interventions. They may have *unforeseen costs* (for example, a regulation designed to improve food hygiene in restaurants may result in the closure of many local restaurants); they may have *side-effects* (e.g. the provision of subsidized child care may undermine the provision of informal, unpaid child care); they may have *revenge effects* (in which they achieve the opposite of the intended result, e.g. the building of a road to reduce traffic congestion may create extra traffic and increase congestion); they may create ►deadweight costs (the intervention ends up affecting many more people than it needed to, to achieve its end, e.g. a job subsidy for those in ►long-term unemployment may go to many people who would have found jobs anyway); they may create *perverse incentives* (e.g. a job subsidy to help the long-term unemployed, gives the short-term unemployed an incentive to become long-term unemployed). ►►cost–benefit analysis, risk assessment.

inventories Term for ►stocks of raw materials, work in progress and finished goods. Inventories represent ►capital tied up in unsold goods and require storage space, insurance and other incurred costs, but are an inevitable part of the process of production and distribution. This is because: (a) in most cases, customers are not willing to wait while goods are produced, but expect delivery off the shelf; (b) it is not possible to forecast sales accurately and sales might be lost if stocks were not held, while it may be uneconomic to interrupt production to match short-term fluctuations in sales because of loss of ►economies of scale; (c) while production may be continuous, deliveries of components and raw materials arrive in batches; (d) transport arrangements may be such that finished goods also need to be dispatched in batches, for example by the lorry-load. *Inventory investment* may be intentional, for example where stocks are built up to meet an anticipated seasonal peak in demand, or unintentional, when demand falls sharply. Since increasing the level of stocks is an ►investment, running them down is ►disinvestment. The management of inventories, in particular the goal of minimizing the capital tied up in them, is seen as an important task (►just-in-time). As a result, the volume of inventories, as a proportion of annual GDP, fell by 23 per cent between 1975 and 1996. Nevertheless, as the change in inventories each year varies so much, and GDP so little, inventories can affect ➤aggregate demand significantly. ➤➤inventory investment cycle.

inventory investment ➤inventories.

inventory investment cycle Fluctuations in economic activity caused by changes in ➤inventories. Although firms may increase or run down stocks to maintain a steady rate of production, there will be upper and lower limits to inventory accumulation determined by the need to hold a minimum stock and the cost of excessive stocks. For these reasons, many firms will try to keep stocks at so many days' sales or output. Since production will increase faster than sales when inventories are increasing (and vice versa) changes in inventories tend to accelerate the effect upon production of changes in sales, thus contributing to ➤business cycles. ➤➤acceleration principle.

inverse elasticity rule The rule that, if prices are to deviate from marginal cost (➤marginal-cost pricing), it is best for the mark-ups to be highest for those products which have the most inelastic demand. By this argument, first articulated by Frank Ramsey and also known as *Ramsey pricing*, if we were to tax certain goods, the tax should be highest on goods which people will continue to buy anyway and low on those items which are very price-sensitive. Keeping to these rules will minimize the distorting effect of the tax, because it means that consumers will behave very much as they would have without the tax. The same principle can also be applied to allocating fixed costs to different consumers when ➤marginal cost is below ➤average cost in a particular industry. Although this idea has achieved wide currency, it does not stand up to ➤general equilibrium analysis. If all commodities are going to be taxed, for example, the inverse elasticity rule will not apply.

investment 1. Real ➤capital formation, such as the production or maintenance of machinery or the construction of dwellings, that will produce a stream of goods and services for future consumption. Investment involves the sacrifice of current ➤consumption and the production of investment goods which are used to produce ➤commodities (➤producer goods) and includes the accumulation of ➤inventories. In the national accounts (➤social accounting) investment is the sum of gross fixed ➤capital formation and the physical change in stocks and work in progress. Investment contributes to higher output. Investment may be stimulated by changes in ➤demand or ➤technology, by high ➤profits or by low interest rates (since much *investment expenditure* is financed by borrowing). The theory of ➤income determination shows how ➤savings and investment are brought into equilibrium. (➤➤capital; depletion theory; gross investment; net investment.) 2. In common usage, expenditure on the acquisition of financial or real ➤assets. To the economist this is not investment, but simply a shift of savings from one form (cash) to another.

investment, inward ➤foreign investment.

investment allowances ➤capital allowances.

investment appraisal The evaluation of the prospective costs and revenues generated by an investment in a capital project over its expected life. Such appraisal includes the assessment of the risks of, and the sensitivity of the project's viability to, forecasting errors. The appraisal enables a judgement to be made whether to commit resources to the project. ➤➤internal rate of return; present value.

investment bank (US) A financial intermediary which purchases new issues and places them in smaller parcels among investors. In Britain, the alternative terms ➤merchant bank or ➤issuing house are still occasionally used. Investment banks are often subsidiaries of banks and other financial institutions; they provide advice on ➤mergers and acquisitions and deal in ➤securities.

investment function ➤acceleration principle.

investment goods ➤investment.

investment incentives Government assistance designed to encourage firms to invest in physical ➤assets in total, in particular industries or in particular locations. The incentives may take the form of ➤capital allowances for tax relief (for example, temporary allowances of 100 per cent were given to small firms by the UK government in the 1997 budget). Or, they may be in the form of special regional incentives. ➤➤enterprise zones; free-trade zone; regional policy.

Investment Services Directive (ISD) A ➤European Union directive coming into force in 1996 which provides for securities dealers and ➤investment banks, including portfolio managers and underwriters authorized in one member state to operate directly or via branches in any other EU state without further authorization. The Capital Adequacy Directive (CAD) sets out minimum ➤capital adequacy requirements with which ISD firms must comply. ➤➤Directives of the European Union.

investment trust A company whose sole object is to invest its ➤capital in a wide range of other companies. An investment trust issues ➤shares and uses its capital to buy shares in other companies. A ➤unit trust, on the other hand, issues units that represent holdings of shares. Unit holders thus do not share in the ➤profits of the company managing the trust. Although sharing the advantages of widespread investment with unit trusts, investment trusts pay their management expenses out of taxed ➤income and not out of shareholders' incomes. The total funds managed by investment trusts are twice as great as those of unit trusts. Investment trusts can also raise part of their capital by fixed-interest ➤securities, and the ➤yield on ➤ordinary shares can thus benefit from ➤gearing. There are some 250 investment-trust companies in Britain, and like most ➤institutional investors they have been investing an increasing proportion of their funds in ➤equities. Some investment trusts underwrite new issues (➤new-issue market; open-ended investment company).

investor's yield ►internal rate of return.

invisible A term used to describe those items, such as financial services, included in the current ►balance of payments accounts, as distinct from physically visible ►imports and ►exports of goods. Invisibles account for about 25 per cent of total ►international trade and are increasing at a faster rate than visible merchandise. Invisible trade is, however, generally less free from ►protectionism than visible trade. Examples of protective policies are (a) the exclusion of foreign ►insurance companies from some domestic markets, (b) restrictions on foreign-owned banks (►banking) setting up branches, (c) that some countries allow only a limited percentage of their visible trade to be carried on foreign-flag ships, and (d) ►exchange controls. Invisibles include government grants to overseas countries and subscriptions to international organizations, payments for shipping services, travel, royalties, commissions for banking and other services, transfers to or from overseas residents, ►interest, ►profits and ►dividends received by or from overseas residents.

The surplus earned by the UK on invisibles increased from £1.7 billion in 1975 to a peak of £8.7 billion in 1986 from which year it declined to £3.5 billion in 1995. The UK Office of National Statistics decided in 1996 to drop the group term 'invisible' in favour of specifying individual items.

invisible balance ►invisibles; balance of payments.

'invisible hand' The idea, promoted by ►Adam Smith, that society is best served by individuals being free to pursue their own self-interest. Smith said that each individual was 'led by an invisible hand to promote an end which was no part of his intention'. ►Mandeville, B. de; price system; resources.

involuntary saving ►forced saving.

inward investment ►foreign investment.

IRR ►internal rate of return.

irredeemable security A ►security which does not bear a date at which the ►capital sum will be paid off or redeemed, e.g. 2½ per cent ►consols or certain ►debentures. Sometimes called undated securities. Possession of an irredeemable security entitles the owner to ►interest payments but not to repayment of face-value capital. This affects the price at which the security is marketable. For example, 2½ per cent consols, which are irredeemable £100 stock bearing 2½ per cent interest, might, depending on prevailing interest rates, fetch only about £50, i.e. the price at which they will give a 5 per cent yield. If this stock were redeemable in one year's time, their price would obviously be very much higher.

ISD ►Investment Services Directive.

ISIC International Standard Industrial Classification (►Standard Industrial Classification).

IS–LM model A model developed by ►Hicks shortly after the publication of ►Keynes's *General Theory*, providing a framework for analysing the factors determining the level of demand in an economy. It became the standard framework for studying ►macroeconomics, primarily because it appeared to be able to encompass widely differing views of how the economy works. The strength of the model is that it combines events in the financial market with events in the market for goods and services to establish an equilibrium level of overall demand. Two variables – aggregate expenditure and the ►interest rate adjust to ensure that the demand for ►investment goods matches the supply of ►savings, and the demand for cash (or liquid assets) matches the supply. On a graph with the interest rate on the vertical axis and the level of spending on the horizontal axis, two curves can be plotted. The I–S (investment–savings) curve slopes down from left to right depicting the set of combinations of interest rate and spending which ensure equilibrium in the investment and savings market. For each level of the interest rate, there is a unique level of spending which ensures that planned investment equals planned saving. The second curve, L–M (liquidity–money supply), plots combinations of interest rates and income levels which ensure the demand for money (►►liquidity preference) is equal to the supply. A high interest rate suppresses the demand for cash and thus may be combined with a high level of national income (which stimulates the demand for cash) if equilibrium is to be maintained. This curve usually thus slopes upwards. Where the two curves intersect there is an equilibrium level of both ►aggregate demand and the interest rate.

Much of the dispute between ►Keynesian economics and ►monetarism can be interpreted as arguments over the relative slopes of the I–S and L–M curves. However, the IS–LM model says nothing of the factors determining the ►aggregate supply of goods and services, and in recent years more attention has been paid to this area of analysis rather than the level of demand. ►supply-side economics; ►►economics doctrines; transmission mechanism.

isocost line A graphical representation of combinations of inputs each of which may be purchased for a given cost. It may be that by spending £1000 per week a firm could hire ten men or ten robots or any combination between. In this case, the isocost line could be plotted on a graph with a quantity of robots on one axis and a quantity of men on the other. It would be a straight, downward-sloping line passing from the point of ten robots and no men to ten men and no robots. Every point on such a graph would represent a combination of inputs costing a certain level and each point would be on one and only one isocost line.

The isocost line, which is analogous to the ►budget line in consumer theory, is useful for analysing the optimal combination of inputs firms should employ. ►►isoquant.

isoproduct curve ►isoquant.

isoquant A graphical representation of combinations of inputs each of which produces the same output. A farmer, for example, might be able to produce fifty tons of grain either with five men and five combine harvesters, or with ten men and four combine harvesters. If so, an isoquant could be plotted on a graph on one axis of which was the number of combine harvesters and, on the other, the number of men employed. Each point on such a graph would represent a combination of inputs and each would thus produce some level of output. Each would be on one, but only one, isoquant. Normally, economists allow for two inputs – capital and labour – but the analysis can be extended.

Isoquants have the following properties: first, they are downward sloping because, as one factor is removed (and we move down one axis), more of another factor must be added to maintain the old level of output (moving up the other axis). Second, they are convex to (i.e. bulge towards) the origin, because increasing amounts of a second factor are required to compensate for unit decreases in the first (►diminishing returns, law of). The isoquant is analogous to the ►indifference curve in the theory of consumer demand. ►►convexity; isocost line; rate of technical substitution.

issued capital That part of a company's ►capital that has been subscribed to by shareholders. It may or may not be paid up (►paid-up capital).

issuing broker A ►broker acting as an agent for a new issue of ►securities.

issuing house An ►investment bank, ►merchant bank or ►stockbroker, that organizes the raising of ►capital by new issues of ►securities on behalf of clients. The issuing house will advise the client on the timing and form of the issue, and investment banks, in return for a commission, will underwrite all or part of the issue. The sponsorship of an issue by an established issuing house greatly affects the confidence of the investor and success of the issue. Increasingly, and especially in ►unlisted securities markets, other securities dealers and firms of accountants are sponsoring new issues while other financial institutions will underwrite issues. ►►new-issue market; underwriting.

J

J-curve The immediate effect of a depreciation or devaluation of the ►exchange rate is to raise import prices and reduce export prices. In the short run, therefore, the ►balance of payments could worsen. Eventually, the effects of the change in the relative price of exports, as compared with imports, induce the expansion of exports and a cut in imports which would improve the balance of payments. The J-curve traces the initial worsening in the balance of payments followed by a recovery. ►►international trade; 'leads and lags'.

Jamaica Agreement ►International Monetary Fund.

Jevons, William Stanley (1835–82) Jevons studied natural science, and worked as an assayer to the Australian Mint from 1853 to 1859. He became Professor of Logic at Owens College, Manchester, in 1866 and in 1876 at University College, London. His main theoretical economic work is *Theory of Political Economy* (1871). Other aspects of his work are collected together in *Investigations in Currency and Finance* (1884). He was one of the three economists to put forward a ►marginal utility theory in the 1870s. He argued that one ►commodity will exchange for another such that the ratio of the ►prices of the two commodities traded equals the ratio of their marginal utilities. ►Edgeworth criticized the way Jevons developed these ideas, and in so doing invented the ►indifference curve. Jevons also made an important contribution to the theory of ►capital, many aspects of which were, in fact, taken up by the ►Austrian school. He superimposed on the ►classical economic theory the idea that capital should be measured in terms of time as well as quantity. An increase in the amount invested is the same as an increase in the time period in which it is being employed. Output can be increased by extending the period in which the investment is available by, for instance, reinvesting the output instead of consuming it at the end of the production period. With given levels of ►labour and capital, output becomes a function of time only. He derived from this a definition of the ►rate of interest as the ratio of the output gained, by an increase in the time capital remains invested divided by the amount invested (►Böhm-Bawerk, E. von; internal rate of return). Jevons was also one of the founders of ►econometrics: he invented ►moving averages. He also propounded a theory of the ►business cycle based on sunspots, but this is of little importance except for the stimulus it gave to the study of statistics for economic empirical work. ►►Gossen, H. H.; Menger, C.; Walras, M. E. L.

jobber ►market maker.

jobseekers' allowance The main ►social security benefit in the UK, for those out of work but looking for a job. It replaced *unemployment benefit* (which was available to anyone who had paid sufficient ►National Insurance for twelve months), and *income support* for the unemployed (which was available on a ►means-test basis thereafter). Jobseekers' allowance is available on a non-means-tested basis for only six months. When it was introduced in October 1996, it was designed to encourage the unemployed to search for work. It was, in many cases, a little harder to claim, and it has had an effect on the ►claimant count of the unemployed. ►►unemployment.

joint costs ►Costs arising simultaneously in the production of two or more ►commodities that cannot be precisely allocated to each product. ►►economies of scope.

joint demand ►Demand for two or more ►commodities or ►factors of production which are used together so that a change in demand for one will sooner or later be reflected in a change in demand for the other; for example, cloth and thread. Another term for complementary demand (►complementary goods).

joint products ►Commodities which are produced in such a way that a change in the output of one of them necessarily involves a change in the output of the other. For example, in refining crude oil into petrol, fuel oil and other heavier oils, limits are set to the relative proportions of each product that can be achieved. Leather and beef are joint products. Under conditions of joint production, the allocation of costs between the products will be arbitrary. ►►economics of scope.

joint supply ►joint products.

joint venture A business arrangement in which two companies invest in a project over which both have partial control. It is a common way for companies to collaborate – especially on risky high-technology ventures – without engaging in full-scale ►merger. The growth of international joint ventures has been striking in the past two decades and raises many public policy issues analogous to those raised by acquisitions, for which joint ventures may often be a strategic substitute.

Juglar cycle A ►business cycle identified by Clément Juglar (1819–1905) of about nine or ten years in length. Juglar was one of the first analysts to use ►time-series data effectively to elucidate an economic problem. His work was published in 1862 in *Les Crises Commerciales et leur retour périodique en France, en Angleterre et aux États Unis*. Through his work, he came to the conclusion that 'The only cause of depression is prosperity'. ►Kondratieff cycle; Kuznets, S. S.

just-in-time A form of production management, originating in Japan, in which companies do not obtain stocks of components until they are actually needed. Traditionally, companies kept large quantities of parts ready for use in production.

just-in-time

Just-in-time management can cause the production process to be held up if a certain part is short; but, as this exposes which parts of the production process are going wrong most often, this is not seen as a disadvantage. It also lowers the costs of maintaining stocks of parts. ➤inventories.

K

Kaldor, Nicholas (1908–86) Born in Budapest, Kaldor graduated at the London School of Economics in 1930 and lectured there until 1947. Between 1943 and 1945 he was a Research Associate at the National Institute of Economic and Social Research, and in 1947 was appointed Director of the Research and Planning Division of the Economic Commission for Europe, a post he held for two years. He was a member of the UK Royal Commission on Taxation of Profits and Incomes from 1951 to 1955. In 1952 he moved to Cambridge University as Reader, and in 1966 was appointed Professor of Economics. From 1964 to 1968, and from 1974 to 1976, he was special adviser to the Chancellor of the ►Exchequer on economic and social aspects of ►taxation policy. His published works include 'The Quantitative Aspects of the Full Employment Problem in Britain', Appendix to *Full Employment in a Free Society* by ►Beveridge (1944), reprinted in *Essays in Economic Policy* (1964), *An Expenditure Tax* (1955), *Essays on Economic Stability and Growth* (1960), *Essays on Value and Distribution* (1960), *Capital Accumulation and Economic Growth* (1961), *Causes of the Slow Rate of Growth of the UK* (1966), *Conflicts in Policy Objectives* (1971), *Collected Economic Essays* (1978) and *Economics Without Equilibrium: The Okun Memorial Lectures* (1985). In his capacity as government adviser, Professor Kaldor was an advocate of the long-term ►capital gains tax and the selective employment tax and he put forward the idea of the ►compensation principle in ►welfare economics. ►►Cambridge school; distribution, theory of.

Kantorovich, Leonid (1912–86) An economist of the Soviet Union, and joint winner of the ►Nobel Prize in Economics in 1975. Based at the Academy of Sciences in Moscow, Kantorovich's subject was the optimal allocation of resources. He was keen to improve the planning system adopted by his country, and developed mathematical techniques – notably ►linear programming and the use of ►shadow prices – as a means to that end. His work was concerned with the decentralization of planning, and the need for a rational price system to make decentralization work. His book, *The Best Use of Economic Resources*, was published in 1965.

Keynes, John Maynard (1883–1946) Educated at Eton, Keynes won prizes there in mathematics as well as in English and Classics before going up to King's College, Cambridge. At university he graduated with a first in mathematics. During his stay at Cambridge he studied philosophy under Alfred Whitehead and economics under ►Marshall and ►Pigou. After a period in the Civil Service, he accepted a lectureship in economics at King's College, Cambridge. In 1911 he became editor of the *Economic Journal*. During the First World War he held a post in the ➤Treasury, but resigned because he believed that the figure for German war reparations was set too high (*The Economic Consequences of the Peace* (1919)). He was also a severe critic of the decision of the government to return to the ➤gold standard and at the pre-war ➤exchange rate (*The Economic Consequences of Mr Churchill*). In 1930 he published *A Treatise on Money*, and in the same year was appointed a member of the ➤Macmillan Committee on Finance and Industry. His major work, *The General Theory of Employment, Interest and Money*, appeared in 1936. He served a second spell in the Treasury during the Second World War, and was responsible for negotiating with the USA on Lend–Lease. He took a leading part in the discussions at ➤Bretton Woods in 1944 which established the ➤International Monetary Fund.

➤Unemployment during the inter-war period persisted in the UK at high levels, never falling below 5 per cent, and at its worst reaching 20 per cent of the total ➤labour force. The failure of the economy to recover from such a long depression was unprecedented in the economic history of industrial society. Fluctuations in activity were well known, and had received much attention from theorists on the ➤business cycle in the past. The classical economists (➤classical economics) held that in the downturn of the business cycle both wage rates (➤earnings) and the ➤rate of interest fell. Eventually, they reached levels low enough for businessmen to see a significant improvement in the profitability of new ➤investments. The investment so induced generated employment and new ➤incomes and the economy expanded again until rising prices in the boom brought the next phase in the cycle. The classical economists therefore concluded that the failure of the economy to expand was because wages were inflexible. Their policy recommendations were that the unions should be persuaded to accept a wage cut. Keynes argued that, although this policy might make sense for a particular industry, a general cut would lower ➤consumption, income and ➤aggregate demand, and this would offset the encouragement to employment by the lowering of the ➤'price' of labour relative to the price of ➤capital, e.g. plant and machinery. Pigou countered Keynes's argument by pointing out that, by lowering wages, the general price level would be lowered; therefore, liquid balances which people owned would have a higher spending value (➤Pigou effect). The upturn, it was agreed, was stimulated by businessmen responding to lower wages with increased investment expenditure. Why, said Keynes, should not the government take over the businessman's function and spend money on public works? Current opinion upheld the belief that government budget-deficit financing would bring more hardship than already existed. The ➤balanced budget was regarded as equally correct accounting practice for the government as it was for a private household. Most economists of the period accepted that public-works expenditure would reduce unemployment, even given the need to keep the budget in balance. Pigou showed the mechanism by which this could be brought about. However, the Treasury view was that public works would merely divert ➤savings and labour from the private sector and, as the former was less productive, the net effect would be a worsening of the situation (➤crowding out). It was not until after Keynes had written his *General Theory* and crystallized his arguments into a coherent theoretical framework that his views were accepted.

Keynes did not deny the classical theory. He agreed that a reduction in wage rates could be beneficial, but it would operate only through the ➤liquidity preference schedule. A fall in prices would increase the value of the stock of money in people's hands in real terms. This would make available an increase in the amount that people were willing to lend, with a consequent drop in the rate of interest to the benefit of investment. However, if this is so, why not operate directly on the rate of interest or the quantity of money in the economy? Moreover, Keynes argued that there exists a level of interest rate below which further increases in ➤money supply are simply added to idle balances (➤inactive money) rather than being used to finance investment. Wage cuts or not, the economy would stick at this point with chronic unemployment. In the classical system, the national product (➤➤national income) was determined by the level of employment and the latter by the level of ➤real wages. The quantity of money determined the level of prices. Savings and investment were brought into balance by means of the rate of interest. In Keynes's system, the equality of savings and investment was achieved by adjustments in the level of national income or output working through the ➤multiplier. The rate of interest was determined by the quantity of money people desired to hold in relation to the money supply. The level of output at which savings equals investment does not necessarily correspond to full employment. The innovation in the Keynesian system was that the rate of interest was determined by the quantity of money and not the level of output, as in the classical system. In the Keynesian model, if you increased the propensity to invest or consume, you did not simply raise the rate of interest, you raised output and employment (➤consumption function). Keynes's study of monetary aggregates of investment, savings, etc., led to the development of national accounts. Keynes's *general theory of employment* is now criticized for its reliance on special cases (wage rigidity, the insensitivity of investment to the rate of interest, and the idea of a minimum rate of interest at which the demand for money became infinitely elastic), its preoccupation with ➤equilibrium and the fact that, despite its presentation as a radical new departure, it nevertheless embodies many of the analytical limitations of the ➤classical school of economics. However, the transformation which Keynes brought about, in both theory and policy, was considerable. In effect, he laid the foundations for what is now ➤macroeconomics. ➤➤Keynesian economics; Keynesian unemployment; new Keynesian economics.

Keynes Plan Proposals by the UK ➤Treasury submitted for the establishment of an International Clearing Union for discussion at the ➤Bretton Woods Conference in 1944. These proposals were primarily the work of ➤Keynes, and became known as the Keynes Plan. The International Clearing Union would have basically the same functions as a domestic ➤bank and ➤clearing house. International ➤debts would be cleared on a multilateral basis between its members. It would give ➤overdraft facilities to a member running a temporary ➤balance of payments deficit and would create its own unit of ➤currency, called ➤Bancor, in which the overdraft facility would be made available. Bancor would have a gold ➤exchange rate in the initial phases of the scheme, though it was expected that it would eventually break its gold connection and replace gold in international finance. Each member would have a quota which determined the limits of its credit facilities with the International Clearing Union. There was a set of suggested safeguards and penalties to encourage the elimination not only of deficits but also of persistent surpluses. The plan did not win approval at Bretton Woods and the less radical ➤International Monetary Fund was established, which was more in line with the ideas put forward by the USA.

Keynesian economics The branch of economic theory, and the doctrines, associated with ➤Keynes. In general, Keynesian economics tends to support the following propositions:
(a) ➤Aggregate demand plays a decisive role in determining the level of real output.
(b) There is no automatic tendency for the level of ➤savings and ➤investment to be equal, as the level of investment is not primarily determined by the ➤rate of interest.
(c) As a result, economies can settle at positions with high unemployment and exhibit no natural tendency for unemployment to fall.
(d) Governments, primarily through fiscal policy, can influence aggregate demand to cut unemployment.

It would be wrong, however, to consider Keynesian economists to be a single, united body of theorists. Since 1945 two predominant Keynesian schools have emerged. First the *Neo-Keynesians* reached a consensus view with more classically oriented economists. Under what is known as the *neo-classical synthesis* (neo-classical economics), it was largely accepted that the practical conclusions of Keynes were correct, but that, at least in theory, the market *did* have a natural tendency towards full employment. It was on account of price rigidities and institutional inflexibility that unemployment could persist. This Neo-Keynesian view used the ➤IS – LM model to describe the determination of aggregate demand and the ➤Phillips curve acted as a description of the behaviour of ➤aggregate supply. The synthesis dominated ➤macroeconomics until it was challenged by ➤Friedman and ➤monetarism.

At the same time, a second strand of Keynesian thought emerged. This held that economists were mistaken in considering the behaviour of an economy only in ➤equilibrium. It was possible that because of interactions between different sectors of the economy, a state of ➤disequilibrium could persist. When the economy left an equilibrium state, no amount of price flexibility could guarantee its return to full employment. This branch of disequilibrium economics is associated with Robert Clower, Axel Leijonhufvud and E. Malinvaud. (➤Keynesian unemployment; quantity rationing.)

More recently, another variant, ➤new Keynesian economics, has been concerned to find foundations for Keynesian findings in ➤microeconomics. It arrives at certain Keynesian implications, using the assumption of ➤rational expectations.

Keynesian unemployment A situation in which the number of people able and willing to work at prevailing wages exceeds the number of jobs available, and, at the same time, firms are unable to sell all the goods they would like. ➤Excess supply thus exists in both the labour and goods markets. Keynesian unemployment is one of four possible regimes in an economy in which ➤quantity rationing exists, i.e. that markets are not in equilibrium. Its important distinguishing feature is in its possible cures. For ➤classical unemployment, a cut in wages should make it profitable for employers to take on new workers. In the Keynesian case, however, firms are already unable to sell all their output. This induces them to cut their prices at the same time that workers will be trying to price themselves into jobs by accepting lower wages. When both prices and wages fall ➤real wages remain constant, and it is real wages which determine the level of employment. Thus, when both the labour market and goods market are in excess supply, even if prices and wages are flexible, there will be no natural tendency for the economy to lift itself out of recession. In this case, the most obvious solution is for the government to inject some demand through higher borrowing. ➤Keynesian economics; unemployment.

Klein, Lawrence R. (b. 1920) Professor Klein studied at Berkeley, the University of California, and obtained his Ph.D. at the Massachusetts Institute of Technology. After working for the Cowles Commission, he was at Michigan University from 1949 to 1954 and at Oxford University until 1958. Professor Klein was then appointed Professor of Economics and Finance at the Wharton School of Finance, University of Pennsylvania. He was awarded the ➤Nobel Prize in Economics in 1980. His major publications include *The Keynesian Revolution* (1947), *Economic Fluctuations, 1921–1941* (1950), *Econometric Model of the United States, 1929–1952* (1955), *An Essay in the Theory of Economic Prediction* (1971) and *The Economics of Supply and Demand* (1983).

Professor Klein pioneered the design, construction and application of large-scale ➤econometric models for forecasting GNP and its components in the 1950s and 1960s, capitalizing on the emergent computer technology of the time. His work has contributed to the development of applied ➤econometrics and stimulated the development of statistical information about ➤macroeconomic fluctuations.

Knight, Frank Hyneman (1885–1973) Appointed Associate Professor of Economics at the University of Iowa in 1919 and Professor in 1922; after studying at Cornell and Chicago Universities, Knight returned to Chicago as Professor of

Economics in 1928. His major published works include *The Economic Organisation* (1933), *The Ethics of Competition and Other Essays* (1935), *The Economic Order and Religion* (1945), *Freedom and Reform* (1947), *Essays on the History and Method of Economics* (1956) and *Intelligence and Democratic Action* (1960). His most influential work has been *Risk, Uncertainty and Profit*, published in 1921. In this work, he made a clear distinction between insurable ►risk and uninsurable uncertainty. It was the latter which gave rise to ►profit. A businessman must guess future demand and selling prices and pay in advance his ►factors of production amounts based on his guesses. The accuracy of his guesses is reflected in the profit he makes. It follows that profits are related to uncertainty, the speed of economic change and business ability.

Kondratieff cycle A ►business cycle of very long duration – ►Schumpeter applied the term to a cycle of fifty-six years. Named after the Russian economist N. D. Kondratieff, who made important contributions in the 1920s to the study of long-term fluctuations. Kondratieff studied US, UK and French wholesale prices and interest rates from the eighteenth century through the 1920s and found peaks and troughs at regular intervals. Similar work has been carried out at Harvard, confirming a fifty-four-year cycle in UK wheat prices since the thirteenth century. ►►Juglar, C.; Kuznets, S. S.

Koopmans, Tjalling C. (1910–86) Professor Koopmans was born in the Netherlands and studied physics and mathematics at the Universities of Utrecht and Leiden. After four years with the League of Nations in Geneva, he went to the USA in 1940 to take up a post as Statistician with the Allied Combined Shipping Adjustment Board. He moved to the Cowles Commission at Chicago in 1944, where he was appointed Director in 1961. He was a Professor of Economics at Yale University from 1955 until his retirement in 1981. Professor Koopmans was awarded, in 1975, the ►Nobel Prize in Economics (jointly with L. V. Kantorovich). His publications include *Linear Regression and Activity Analysis of Economic Time Series* (1937), *Statistical Inference in Dynamic Economic Models* (1950), *Analysis of Production as an Efficient Combination of Activities* (1951), *Three Essays on the State of Economic Science* (1957) and *The Scientific Papers of Tjalling C. Koopmans* (1970). Professor Koopmans introduced the mathematical procedures of ►linear programming (or *activity analysis*) to economics. He demonstrated the application of linear programming to the solution of transportation problems, to general ►equilibrium analysis and to problems in ►investment appraisal. He has made important contributions to the theory of ►econometrics.

Kuznets, Simon S. (1901–85) Professor Kuznets, who was born in Russia, went to the USA in 1922 where he studied economics at Columbia University, receiving his Ph.D. in 1926. After a number of years at the National Bureau of Economic Research, he went in 1930 to the University of Pennsylvania where he was later to be appointed Professor of Economics, a post he held until 1954. There followed a period as Professor of Economics at Johns Hopkins University until 1960 when he accepted a Chair in Economics at Harvard, where he remained until his retirement in 1971. Professor Kuznets was awarded the ➤Nobel Prize in Economics in 1971. His publications include *Secular Movements in Production and Prices* (1930), *National Income, 1929–1932* (1934), *National Income and Its Composition, 1919–1938* (1941), *National Product since 1869* (1946), *Six Lectures on Economic Growth* (1959), *Economic Growth and Structure* (1965), *Modern Economic Growth: Rate, Structure and Spread* (1965), *Economic Growth of Nations* (1971) and *Population, Capital and Growth* (1979). Professor Kuznets made important contributions to the development of applied ➤econometrics through the compilation of macroeconomic statistics. His analysis and statistical identification of fifteen-to-twenty-year fluctuations in time series of production and prices initiated a continuing debate in the analysis of ➤trade cycles. He completed major studies in income distribution, exploring the relationship between growth in income per head and the distribution of income. ➤Juglar cycle; Kondratieff cycle.

L

labour A ►factor of production. The term not only includes the numbers of people available for or engaged in the production of goods or services but also their physical and intellectual skills and effort. ►►employment, full; human capital; labour force; sow's ear effect; unemployment.

labour, demand for The amount of labour that firms will employ at different wage levels. In a simple model of the structure of the ►labour market, firms employ labour as long as it is profitable for them to do so. It will be profitable as long as the selling price of the output of the marginal worker is greater than the cost of that worker. To maximize profits, therefore, firms employ additional workers until the ►marginal revenue product (that is, the marginal revenue of the firm's output times the number of extra units produced by taking on one more worker) is equal to the wage costs. In this situation: (a) when the price of the firm's output rises, its demand for labour rises; (b) when the physical output of workers rises (from more developed skills or harder work), the demand for labour rises; (c) when the wage rate falls, the demand for labour rises; (d) when the amount of capital employed increases, the demand for labour will either increase, as the capital enhances the productivity of each worker, or it will fall, if the capital displaces workers.

This account, in which all workers are assumed to be identical, has been developed in many directions. First, complications can be added – for example, trade unions and industries where there is only one employer (►monopoly). Secondly, alternative models have been developed to account for the stickiness of wages and to describe alternatives to fixed-wage contracts (►profit-sharing; efficiency-wage hypothesis). Finally, the whole subject can be viewed in a ►macroeconomic perspective, in which the demand for labour is viewed as a function of ►aggregate demand only. In this case high wages can be portrayed as stimulating employment through their effect on maintaining high aggregate demand. ►►marginal productivity theory of wages.

labour, division of ►division of labour.

labour force The total number of people in a country who are either in work or unemployed but looking for work. The labour force in Great Britain is estimated by the Office of National Statistics to have reached a peak of 28.2 million in 1990 from which it fell to 27.8 million in 1996. Within this total, however, there has been a growth in the number of women. The proportion of women in the labour force has risen from 37.5 per cent in 1971 to 44 per cent in 1996 and is expected to continue to increase in the future. This change is due to changes in the *activity rates* for women, which unlike those for men, has moved upwards in line with population growth. *Activity rate (or participation rate)* is defined as the proportion of the labour force of a specified group in the total population of that group. In 1971 the activity rate for men was 81 per cent and for women it was 44 per cent. In 1996 the activity rate for men had fallen to 72 per cent but for women it had risen to 54 per cent. The British labour force is also getting older. In 1985 46 per cent of the labour force was in the age group 16 to 34 years, this had fallen to 43 per cent by 1996 and is expected to fall further in the future, returning to the proportions which existed in the early 1970s.

Labour Force Survey A regular public survey designed to elicit accurate information about the state of the labour market. It is used to derive a measure of unemployment on the basis of the ➤International Labour Organization definition in contrast to the ➤claimant count measure. It counts everyone who wishes to work, and has looked for work in the previous four weeks, as unemployed, whether or not they are eligible for benefits. It includes many unemployed people who live with working partners and are thus excluded from obtaining benefit. It excludes people who are on benefits but admit to not having looked for work in the previous four weeks. The net effect is that the LFS measure of unemployment has followed the same trend as the claimant count, but is higher. ➤unemployment.

labour, mobility of The degree to which workers are able and willing to move between jobs in different occupations and areas. A lack of ➤labour mobility may manifest itself in high ➤frictional unemployment or high ➤structural unemployment and it has been an object of policy to encourage workers to move to areas where jobs are available and to take on jobs in new occupations requiring skills different from those in which they were first trained. Policies to this end could include a faster rate of house-building, making it easier for people to find homes in different areas; the removal of taxes like ➤stamp duty on house transfer; the provision of full information on what jobs are available and where; the provision of training courses for the unemployed; and the abolition of restrictions on entry to different jobs. In practice, it has been found that, for a multitude of social and economic reasons, labour may be geographically and occupationally immobile. Moreover, it is recognized that social costs could be incurred by an itinerant population, from regional overcrowding or depopulation. These factors have been used to justify ➤subsidies to jobs in regions of high unemployment. The Treaty of Rome of the ➤European Union guarantees the free movement of labour throughout the Community. Such movements are, however, additionally constrained in Europe by the lack of a common language. ➤active labour market policies.

labour, specialization of ➤division of labour.

labour-intensive A production technology for which relatively more labour value labour market

is required as input per unit of output than other ►factors of production. ►►capital-intensive; production function; productivity.

labour market The ►market in which wages, salaries and conditions of employment are determined in the context of the supply of labour (►labour force) and the demand for ►labour. ►►labour, demand for; labour, mobility of.

labour theory of value ►value, theories of.

labour turnover The number of employees who leave a firm in a year as a percentage of the firm's total employment.

Laffer curve A graphical illustration of the argument that there exists an optimum rate of tax at which government tax revenue is maximized. If tax rates are low, revenues will be increased if tax rates are increased; however, if rates are raised beyond the optimum point, the loss of incentives caused by the resultant low net incomes discourages production and tax revenues fall. The curve is named after the American economist Professor Arthur Laffer, who argued that the economy could be expanded without government budget deficits. Lower taxes lead to lower prices, higher output and, therefore, higher government revenues. This argument has yet to find full empirical justification. ►►supply-side economics.

LAFTA Latin American Free Trade Association (►Latin American Integration Association).

Lagrange multiplier A technique, devised by the French mathematician Joseph Louis Lagrange (1736–1813), for calculating the optimal value of a variable subject to some constraint, in order to maximize or minimize another variable. It is a technique pervasive in economics, where so many problems relate to the best use of scarce resources. In demand theory (►demand, theory of), for example, the consumer is assumed to maximize utility subject to prevailing prices and income by choosing the right combination of goods to buy. Firms are assumed to maximize profits subject to the constraints of technology and the ►production function by setting their output and price at the right levels. The Lagrangian technique allows the method of maximizing a ►function *without* a constraint – using ►calculus to set the derivative of the function with respect to the variable that can be controlled equal to zero – to be used in those cases where there is a constraint. It does this by expanding the function to be maximized – the *objective function* – to include the constraint, multiplying the constraint by a new parameter, the Lagrange multiplier, and then setting the derivatives of the new function equal to zero. For example, suppose we wish to set X and Z at a level that maximizes Y, where the objective function is:

$$Y = X \times Z$$

and is subject to the constraint that $(X + Z)$ is equal to 10, or:

$$X + Z - 10 = 0.$$

We construct a new, artificial objective function of this form:

$$L = X \times Z + \lambda(X + Z - 10).$$

This is, in fact, the same as the old one, but it has had the constraint added on. It has been added on, however, in such a way that it equals zero, if it holds. We could have just as well have subtracted it. The constraint is also multiplied by λ, called the Lagrange multiplier.

Maximizing this new objective function is the same as maximizing the old one subject to the constraint. So we then maximize L by controlling X, Z and λ in the normal way. We set the partial derivatives of these three equal to zero and solve them as a system of simultaneous equations. The resulting values of X and Z are the values we want. Note that the partial derivative of the equation with respect to λ is in fact the constraint itself, thus ensuring that it will hold when the solution is found. We can also interpret λ as the value by which the objective can be advanced for a one-unit relaxation of the constraint. It can thus be seen as the ➤shadow price of the constrained variables. In this case, the values of X and Z will each be 5, and the value of λ will be -5. ➤➤calculus of variations.

LAIA ➤Latin American Integration Association.

'laissez-faire' *'Laissez-faire, laissez-passer'* was the term originally used by the ➤Physiocrats. They believed that only agriculture yielded wealth. Consequently they condemned any interference with industry by government agencies as being inappropriate and harmful, except in so far as it was necessary to break up private ➤monopoly. The principle of the non-intervention of government in economic affairs was given full support by the classical economists (➤classical economics), who inherited the theme from ➤Adam Smith: 'The Statesman, who should attempt to direct private people in what manner they ought to employ their capitals, would not only load himself with a most unnecessary attention, but assume an authority which could safely be trusted, not only to no single person, but to no council or senate whatever, and which would nowhere be so dangerous as in the hands of a man who had folly and presumption enough to fancy himself fit to exercise it' – *Wealth of Nations*, Book IV, chapter 2. More recently, laissez-faire economics has been associated with the ➤Chicago school, who not only believe in ➤free-market economics, but have also promoted the idea that some privately imposed restrictions on trade are socially efficient. ➤➤Manchester school; Mandeville, B. de; Sismondi, J. C. L. S. de.

land Taken to include, in economics, all ➤natural resources, including the sea and outer space. One of the ➤factors of production, land is distinguished from the others in that its supply is more or less fixed. Since the productive power of land is conceptually distinct from that of ➤capital, land is a factor of production only in its natural, unimproved state. ➤➤depletion theory.

Laspeyres index An ➤index number whose weights (➤weighted average) are derived from values obtaining in a base-year. For instance, in 1996 the UK producer price index of home sales was calculated on weights reflecting the pattern of sales of the different industries making up the index in 1990. Because the weights are constant from one year to another, indices can be constructed to give a consistent time series. On the other hand, the weights do get significantly out of date eventually and have to be revised. The above index was previously based on 1985 weights. A base-weighted index formula was first published in 1864, by Étienne Laspeyres. ➤➤index-number problem; Paasche index.

latent variables A variable in ➤regression analysis which is, in principle, unmeasurable. Examples of variables which might be wanted for inclusion in a ➤model would be intelligence or permanent income (➤permanent-income hypothesis). These cannot be measured directly, and have to be replaced by proxy variables.

Latin American Free Trade Association (LAFTA) ➤Latin American Integration Association.

Latin American Integration Association (LAIA) A successor to the Latin American Free Trade Association (LAFTA), signed in 1960 under which Argentina, Brazil, Chile, Mexico, Paraguay, Peru and Uruguay agreed to establish a ➤free-trade area. Ecuador and Colombia joined the following year and Venezuela in 1966. Significant reductions in internal ➤tariffs were achieved. However, in 1969 Chile and Peru joined Bolivia, Colombia and Ecuador in forming a new economic grouping (➤Andean Pact), and in 1981 the Free Trade Association was replaced by the Latin American Integration Association. The member countries of this are Bolivia, Chile, Colombia, Ecuador, Paraguay, Peru, Uruguay and Venezuela. The intention of LAIA is to reduce tariffs between member countries but on a pragmatic industry-by-industry approach, rather than by across-the-board tariff reductions following a fixed timetable, which was attempted by LAFTA. ➤➤Mercosur.

Lausanne school The Chair of Economics in the Faculty of Law at Lausanne was founded in 1870 with ➤Walras as the first incumbent. He retired in 1892 and was succeeded by ➤Pareto. The school was noted for the development of a ➤general equilibrium theory.

Law, John (1671–1729) A Scottish financier who put his monetary theories into practice in France through such institutions as the Banque Royale and the Compagnie des Indes. His most significant publication appeared in 1705 under the title *Money and Trade Considered, with a Proposal for Supplying the Nation with Money*. He was in favour of the replacement of specie coin by paper money (➤banknote). Not only would this save expensive precious metals, but it would enable the state to manage the ➤currency more effectively by making it independent of the ➤market for precious metals. Moreover, it would facilitate increasing the quantity of money in circulation and therefore the stimulation of economic activity. ➤➤Hume, D.; quantity theory of money.

'law of demand' ➤demand curve.

law of diminishing returns ➤diminishing returns, law of.

law of large numbers ➤probability.

law of one price The law, articulated by ➤Jevons, stating that 'In the same open market, at any moment, there cannot be two prices for the same kind of article.' The reason is that, if they did exist, ➤arbitrage should occur until the prices converge. ➤➤price system.

'leads and lags' The differences in timing in the settlement of ➤debts in ➤international trade. These differences could cause a deficit or surplus for a short period in the ➤balance of payments, even though the underlying trade was in balance. The effect may be particularly acute when there is an expectation of a change in the ➤exchange rate. Importing countries will delay payment to their supplying country if it is expected that the latter's rate of exchange will fall. ➤➤devaluation; J-curve.

lease An agreement between the owner of property (lessor) to grant use of it to another party (lessee) for a specified period at a specified ➤rent payable annually, quarterly or monthly. The rental may be subject to review, say, every five years. It is possible to lease cars, office equipment, machinery, etc., as well as buildings or ➤land, and a recent development has been the rapid growth of leasing arrangements for business requirements. In most cases these include servicing and maintenance. In some cases the title of the property passes to the lessee at the end of the lease for a nominal charge. In effect, this is a form of ➤hire purchase without a down payment, and is subject to differences in tax treatment which may be advantageous.

leaseback An agreement in which the owner of property sells that property to a person or institution and then leases it back again for an agreed period and rental. Leaseback is often used by companies that want to free for other uses ➤capital tied up in buildings.

least-developed country In 1971 the General Assembly of UNCTAD (➤United Nations Conference on Trade and Development) drew up a list of twenty-four countries, which it defined as least-developed, having a per capita ➤gross domestic product of $100 (at 1968 prices) or less, a share of manufacturing of 10 per cent or less of GDP and a literacy rate of 20 per cent or less. By 1980 thirty-one countries were classified as least-developed, by 1990 forty-one and by 1995 forty-eight countries, of which, thirty-three were in Africa, nine in Asia, five in the Pacific and one in the Caribbean. In 1993 their average per capita income was

$300, compared with $906 for all ➤developing countries and $21,598 for the ➤advanced countries. LDC growth rates have persistently fallen behind the rest of the world since the 1970s. They depend heavily on primary agricultural products such as cotton, tea and coffee and are, therefore, vulnerable to falling commodity prices. ➤Recessions in the advanced countries not only lead to reduced demand for their products but also to a drop in private remittances from abroad and ➤foreign investment. There have also been failures in their institutions to protect and sustain a viable economic structure for the promotion of growth. ➤➤convergence; institutional economics; poverty.

least-squares regression A statistical technique for estimating the relationship between a ➤dependent variable and ➤independent variables. The method derives estimates for the ➤parameters and constants in the equation postulated as representing the nature of the relationship between the variables (➤model). For example, a ➤demand function may take the form $D = a + bP$, in which D is the quantity demanded of a good and P its price. The observed values of D and P, that is, how much was actually demanded at each of a number of price levels, may be plotted on a graph, with D on the x-axis (horizontal) and P on the y-axis (perpendicular) (called a 'scatter' diagram). We would expect in this case that the points on the graph would be grouped such as generally to slope downwards from left to right (the lower the price, the higher the demand). The least-squares regression finds that line such that the difference between the actual observations and those traced by the line along its length is at a minimum. The slope and position of the line yields the estimates for b and a respectively. ➤➤beta; dummy variable; heteroscedasticity; latent variable.

legal tender That which must be accepted in legal settlement of a money ➤debt. In Britain ➤Bank of England notes and £1 coins are legal tender up to any amount. Cheques and postal orders are not legal tender. ➤➤fiat money.

lemon problem ➤adverse selection.

lender of last resort The essential function of a ➤central bank, in its willingness to lend to the ➤banking system at all times. (➤bank rate.) Because it can do so on its own terms, it is this function which permits the bank, first to influence the level of ➤rates of interest and the ➤money supply and, second, as providing a basis of confidence for the banking system, since it stands ready to lend to solvent but illiquid banks. In Britain the ➤Bank of England traditionally acted as a lender of last resort only to the ➤discount houses, and would not lend to the ➤commercial banks, as part of its exercise of monetary policy (the first function). Since March 1997 the Bank uses ➤gilt repos as a means of influencing the interest rate structure and deals directly with counterparties which include commercial banks. One of the motives for these changes was to prepare the way for ➤European Monetary Union and it has brought the UK into line with other countries where the central bank deals directly with the commercial banks.

Leontief, Wassily W. (b. 1906) Born in Leningrad, Leontief obtained a post at the University of Kiel in Germany in 1927. In 1931 he moved to Harvard and was appointed Professor of Economics there in 1946. In 1973 he was awarded the ►Nobel Prize in Economics. Apart from the works mentioned below, his publications include *Studies in the Structure of the American Economy* (1953), *Input–Output Economics, Collected Essays* (1966) and *The Future of the World Economy* (1977). The interdependence of the various sectors of a country's economy has long been appreciated by economists. The theme can be traced from ►Cantillon and ►Quesnay and the ►'*tableau économique*' through ►Marx and ►Walras. The sheer complexity of the interactions and interrelationships between the different sectors of a modern economy was a Gordian knot which had to be cut before the theoretical structure could be translated into a practical reflection of an actual economy and serve as the basis for policy recommendations. Leontief's achievement was to see the solution of this problem in ►matrix algebra, and modern computers have made ►input–output analysis a practical proposition. His book *The Structure of the American Economy, 1919–1929* was first published in 1941, and a second edition, *1919–1939*, appeared in 1951. In these studies he attempted, with the limited statistical facts available to him, to establish a '*tableau économique*' of the USA. The economy was described as an integrated system of flows or transfers from each activity of production, ►consumption or ►distribution to each other activity. Each sector absorbs the outputs from other sectors and itself produces ►commodities or ►services which are in turn used up by other sectors, either for further processing or for final consumption. All these flows or transfers were set out in a rectangular table – an input–output matrix. The way in which the outputs of any industry spread out through the rest of the economy could be seen from the elements making up the rows. Similarly, the origins of its ►inputs could be seen directly from the elements of the appropriate column. Given such a structure, the implications of a specific change in one part of the economy could be traced through to all the elements in the system. ►►social accounting.

Lerner, Abba Ptachya (1903–82) ►Marshall–Lerner criterion.

letter of credit A non-negotiable order from a bank to a bank abroad authorizing payment to a person named in the letter of a particular sum of ►money or up to a limit of a certain sum. Letters of ►credit are often required by exporters who wish to have proof that they will be paid before they ship goods, or who wish to minimize delay in payment for the goods. Letters of credit, unlike ►bills of exchange, are not negotiable, but being cashable at a known bank, are immediately acceptable to the seller in the exporting country. A confirmed letter of credit is one that has been recognized by the paying bank. Letters of credit may be irredeemable or revocable, depending on whether or not they can be cancelled at any time.

leverage ►gearing.

Lewis, Sir William Arthur (1915–91) Professor Lewis was born in St Lucia in the Caribbean. He received his university education at the London School of Economics and the University of Manchester. He was appointed to a Chair of Economics at Manchester University in 1948 where he remained until he took up the post of Principal of the University College of the West Indies in 1959. He was subsequently appointed Professor of Public and International Affairs at Princeton University in 1963. Professor Lewis was awarded (jointly with ➤Schultz) the ➤Nobel Prize for Economics in 1979. His published works include *Overhead Costs* (1949), *Economic Survey, 1918–1939* (1949), *The Principles of Economic Planning* (1950), *The Theory of Economic Growth* (1955), *Development Planning* (1966), *Some Aspects of Economic Development* (1969), *Tropical Development, 1880–1913* (1971), *The Evolution of the International Economic Order* (1977) and *Growth and Fluctuations, 1870–1913* (1978). Professor Lewis has made fundamental contributions to the theory and application of economics in the context of the problems of growth of ➤developing countries. Developing countries were characterized by dual economies of urban growth centres within large areas of traditional agriculture in which the latter was the source of a supply of labour that kept urban wages low. Wages remained low until urban industrialization had absorbed the surplus labour from the agricultural sector.

liabilities Sums of ➤money for which account has to be made. The liabilities of a company include its ➤bank loans and ➤overdraft, short-term ➤debts for goods and ➤services received (*current liabilities*) and its ➤loan capital and the ➤capital subscribed by shareholders. ➤➤balance sheet.

life-cycle hypothesis A theory which suggests that consumers during their lifetime will save when their income is high and spend more than they earn when their income is low. In this way, they smooth their consumption flow, despite the fact that income varies over a lifetime. The theory, attributable to ➤Modigliani, complements the ➤permanent-income hypothesis. ➤➤consumption function.

LIFFE ➤London International Financial Futures Exchange.

limited liability The restriction of an owner's loss in a business to the amount of ➤capital that he has invested in it. If a limited public company is put into ➤liquidation because it is unable to pay its ➤debts, for example, the individual shareholders are liable only for the nominal ➤value of the ➤shares they hold (unless they have provided personal guarantees to the bank or other ➤creditors). Before the principle of limited liability was recognized, investors could be made liable for the whole of their personal possessions in the event of ➤insolvency. The extension of limited liability to private as well as public companies that wished to register for it in the second half of the nineteenth century greatly increased the flow of capital, and today the limited-liability company is the predominant form of business organization. ➤➤company law.

linear programming A mathematical technique for the solution of problems in which a maximum or minimum of a function is to be determined, subject to a set of constraints. Examples of such problems are:

(a) Stocks of a commodity are located at a number of ports and need to be shipped to meet a demand for specific quantities at a number of other ports. The cost per tonne for shipping differs between the various ports of loading and discharge. The problem is to find the minimum cost of shipment, subject to the constraints that no more than the stock available can be loaded at a port and the total amount discharged at a port should equal the demand at that port.

(b) A firm able to produce a range of commodities, each of which would require a different mix of inputs (►factors of production). Given the selling prices of the commodities and the costs per unit of the various inputs, the firm chooses the mix of output which maximizes profits, subject to the technical constraints of its ►production function and restrictions on the availability of the different inputs.

As its name implies, the technique is applicable only to problems in which all the relationships are linear (►linear relationship). In problems of resource allocation of the firm and the economy as a whole (►input–output analysis), linear programming is also synonymous with *activity analysis*.

linear relationship A mathematical ►function which traces a straight line on a graph. The ►independent variables, of which there may be one or more, are additive. The simplest example is $y = ax + b$, in which x is the independent variable, a and b are constants. These functions are such that any given absolute increase in an independent variable (e.g. x), will give an absolute increase in the ►dependent variable (e.g. y), which will always be the same whatever the size of x on which it is based. Many non-linear relationships can be transformed into linear ones, by converting the values of the variables into logarithmic form.

liquid In economics, the description of an ►asset which can easily be converted into ►money. In practice, it applies to ►cash or anything that can be quickly converted into cash at little loss. Assets are said to possess degrees of ►liquidity which are their nearness to cash. Highly liquid assets other than cash and bank deposits are Post Office ►savings, ►treasury bills, ►money at call ►►liquidity preference.

liquidation The termination, dissolution or winding up of a limited company (►limited liability). Liquidation of a company may be initiated by the shareholders, the directors (voluntary liquidation) or by its creditors, or by a court order if the company is insolvent (►insolvency). Where initiated by the creditors, a liquidator is appointed to realize the company's ►assets and to pay the creditors. In case of insolvency, these functions are performed, initially at least, by the Official Receiver. If the company is solvent, the ordinary shareholders will receive any surplus after the company's liabilities have been met. ►►bankruptcy.

liquidity 1. The degree to which an ►asset can be quickly and cheaply turned into ►money which, by definition, is completely liquid. A ►current account bank deposit is a liquid asset because it can be withdrawn immediately at little cost; an office building by contrast will take a considerable time to dispose of and estate agent's fees and other costs will be incurred. A company or individual is said to be liquid if a high proportion of its or his assets are held in the form of cash or readily marketable securities. **2.** ▶International liquidity consists of the total of ▶gold and foreign-exchange reserves and ▶special drawing rights of all countries.

liquidity preference The desire to hold ▶money rather than other forms of ▶wealth, e.g. ▶stocks and ▶bonds. It can be thought of as stemming from the ▶transactions motive, ▶speculative motive and ▶precautionary motive for holding money, and so will be influenced by the levels of ▶income and wealth, ▶rates of interest, ▶expectations and the institutional features of the economy. A high degree of liquidity preference implies that a given supply of money flows relatively slowly through the economy, resulting in a low ▶velocity of circulation. ▶▶Keynes, J. M.

liquidity ratio 1. The proportion of the total ▶assets of a bank which are held in the form of ▶cash and ▶liquid assets. These assets consist, in general, of money lent out to the ▶money market at call and short notice, short-term ▶bonds issued by the government and other borrowers and balances at the ▶Bank of England. There is no longer a mandatory liquidity ratio, although all larger banks are now required to deposit 0.45 per cent of eligible liabilities with the Bank of England. This *cash-ratio deposit* earns no interest and is effectively a tax to provide income for the bank; it has no significance for credit control or ▶monetary policy. The Bank of England now monitors the adequacy of liquidity and its composition for each individual bank, but does not make public what it regards as satisfactory liquidity ratios. (▶▶reserve requirement.) **2.** The ratio of liquid assets to the current ▶liabilities of a business. Also called the ▶cash ratio, it is a very crude test of solvency.

liquidity trap A situation in which the ▶rate of interest is so low that no one wants to hold interest-bearing assets (i.e. ▶bonds), and people only want to hold cash. The interest rate can fall far enough for everybody to expect it to rise. Bond prices fall when interest rates rise and, because no one wants to hold an asset whose price will fall, everyone will hold cash rather than bonds. In this situation, the interest rate can fall no further – ▶liquidity preference is absolute. If the government expands the money supply, instead of the usual fall in interest rates occurring, there is no effect at all. There is no need for the interest rate to drop to entice people to hold the extra cash available. Although best described in terms of the simplifying assumptions of the ▶IS – LM model, the liquidity trap can also be applied to a world where wealth is stored in forms other than merely cash or bonds. It was first described by ▶Keynes as an example of a case where, at least theoretically, changes in the money supply did not affect ▶aggregate demand. ▶▶transmission mechanism.

listed company A company the shares of which are listed on the main market of the ▶stock exchange.

listed security A ►security listed and tradable on the ►stock exchange. ►►quotation.

Lloyd's An incorporated society of private insurers established by Act of Parliament in 1871. Capital is provided by a large number of individual members or 'names', organized into syndicates, each led by a full-time underwriter (►underwriting) who writes policies on behalf of the members, each of whom bears unlimited liability. Clients are dealt with through ►brokers. The Lloyd's insurance market deals with almost any kind of insurance but has traditionally specialized in the marine market and provides a comprehensive system of shipping intelligence. As a result of severe losses incurred in 1989/91, the market has recently been reorganized.

loan The borrowing of a sum of ►money by one person, company, government or other organization from another. Loans may be secured or unsecured (►securities), ►interest-bearing or interest-free, long-term or short-term, redeemable or irredeemable. Loans may be made by individuals and companies, banks, ►insurance and ►hire-purchase companies, ► building societies and other ►financial intermediaries, ►pawnbrokers, or by the issue of ►securities. ►►bank loan; finance; term loans.

loan capital Fixed-interest borrowed funds. Alternative term for ►debentures.

loan guarantee scheme ►credit guarantee.

loan stock Synonym for ►debenture.

loanable funds Money available for lending in financial markets. It consists of current ►saving, ►dishoarding and any increase in the ►money supply, for example credit creation by the banks. The *loanable funds theory* holds that the rate of interest (like any other ►price) is determined by the supply and demand for loanable funds in the capital market. This theory has its origins in classical theory (►interest, classical theory of) but was developed by ►Wicksell.

local taxation ►Taxation levied by (or for) local rather than central government. The design of local tax systems is not straightforward. ►Income tax is not easy to administer, at least in small jurisdictions where people may work and live separately. In any event, in the UK at least, governments have been reluctant to let local authorities determine a variable as important as the basic rate of income tax. Corporate taxes do not work well at all, given the extensive nature of most large companies. ►Sales taxes fail, in that varying rates of tax encourage cross-boundary shopping, and distort trade. As a result, in the UK, local taxes have for the most part been property taxes – with the advantage that at least property can't move between jurisdictions. Until 1990 *domestic rates* were proportional to the estimated rentable value of business and domestic properties (though not farms, which were exempt). They were criticized as being unrelated to income, and there were many anomalies in the valuations which had not, in any case, been re-estimated since 1973. In 1990 (in England, earlier in Scotland) rates were replaced by the *community charge*, a flat-rate tax levied on all adults, with some exemptions and rebates for those with limited means. This tax, the poll tax (➤lump-sum tax) required costly compilation of new registers of residents and massive changes to billing systems, since under rates there was only one bill to each household while under the new system all eligible individuals had to be billed separately. The new tax aroused such widespread hostility that in 1991 the government reverted to property tax, with the ➤council tax. Local government finance still has two major problems, however. The varying nature of property prices in different authorities means that central government subsidy to poorer authorities is necessary, to equalize the effective tax base. At the same time, even in the rich authorities, as government has been reluctant to see council taxes rise to very high levels, a substantial proportion of local authority spending has to be financed nationally. This undermines the relationship and accountability that should exist between voters and their local politicians. Business rates have been retained in the UK, but are now set by the government on a uniform basis across the whole country, though the amount paid will reflect the local value of commercial property.

Internationally there are greater differences in the forms of local than national taxation. In the USA the states levy a ➤sales tax. In France the principal local tax on business is based on the rentable value of buildings and equipment but also includes a ➤payroll tax. In Germany, regional government levies local business profits, assets and property taxes.

location theory The area of economics concerned with the factors that determine where producers choose to locate and the effects of the location of a piece of land on the use made of it. The starting-point of this area of theory was developed by ➤Thünen in 1826. Thünen held that farmers near a market would tend to grow things that would be relatively expensive to transport, while those further away from towns would produce lighter items that were cheap to carry. Thus, the location of land would have a significant effect on the ➤economic rent it could derive. A second important theory, of industrial location, attributable to A. Weber, established that firms producing goods less bulky than the raw materials used in their production would settle near to the raw-material source. Firms producing heavier goods would settle near their market. The firm minimizes the weight it has to transport and, thus, its transport costs. These two theories primarily treated transport costs as the main factor in influencing location. However, many other factors have been identified as having an important role:
(a) Being able to capture monopoly power in the local market.
(b) The possibility of gaining external ➤economies of scale, by settling in an area where firms requiring similar inputs have settled.
(c) The influence of non-profit-maximizing behaviour – notably the ➤behavioural theory of the firm – suggests that location could be dependent on where a firm's management considers it pleasant to live.

(d) The possibility of attracting public assistance in the form of grants or subsidies paid out as part of a country's regional policy.

(e) The influence of local taxation and provision of ►public goods. An area which has good roads, efficient refuse collection or low business taxation will be more attractive than a high-tax or low-service area. Firms will choose the combination of service provision and taxation that most suits their needs. Those producing a lot of refuse will perhaps value refuse-collection services more highly than low taxes, while the reverse might be true for a firm requiring no refuse collection at all.

(f) The location and cost of labour. Because workers are geographically quite immobile, especially across international borders on account of, for instance, immigration controls, wages are not equal across countries. This makes it attractive for some labour-intensive firms to settle in areas where wages are low. This has particularly manifested itself in the high investment that has occurred in South-East Asia. ►labour, mobility of.

(g) Other international influences. Political and social factors have a particularly strong effect on the expectations multinational firms have as to the profits they can make. Local tariff regimes can also induce firms to produce domestically where otherwise they would be unable to sell in the local market at all. ►multinational corporation; globalization.

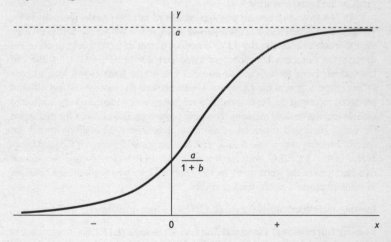

logistic curve A curve traced on a graph by the function, $y = a/(1 + be^{-cx})$, in which a, b and c are constants (►parameters), x is the ►independent variable, $e =$ approximately 2.71828, which is a constant with many applications in the analysis of growth (e can be defined as follows: if £1 were invested at 100 per cent per annum, its worth at the end of the year would get closer and closer to £e, the more frequently interest was added and compounded (►compound interest) for shorter and shorter periods during the year). The logistic function takes the following values: if $x = 0$, $y = a/(1 + b)$; if $x \rightarrow + \infty$, $y \rightarrow a$; and if $x \rightarrow - \infty$, $y \rightarrow 0$; as can be seen by substituting these values in the above equation. The curve is illustrated above. It is often used to describe the sales growth of a new product – an initial learning period when sales are low, rising rapidly as sales spread through the population and then slowing down as new demand for the product reaches ►saturation point.

Lomé Convention A convention signed in 1975 at Lomé, the capital of Togo, by the members of the then European Economic Community (EC) (►European Union) and forty-six ►developing countries in Africa, the Caribbean and the Pacific (ACP states). It replaced previous association agreements made by the original six members of the EC with former colonies (Yaoundé Convention) and the East African Community (Arusha Agreement). (The East African Community was a common market of Uganda, Kenya and Tanzania.) Under the Lomé Convention all ACP industrial exports, and most agricultural exports, to the EC are free of duty. Financial and technical aid – including an export income stabilization scheme, called Stabex, for agricultural exports – was also agreed upon, and the European Development Fund was set up by the EC to administer and channel aid funds to the Lomé countries.

In 1979 a second agreement was signed, a third in 1984 and the fourth in 1990. The Lomé IV agreement was for a period of ten years. Within the first five years, the EC made available to the ACP countries a total of ECU 10.8 billion of aid through the European Development Fund and a total of ECU 1.2 billion of low-interest loans through the ►European Investment Bank (►soft loan). Lomé IV improved access to the European Union markets for some ACP agricultural products, increased the funds available for Stabex and widened its application to include exports to third markets. The new agreement also allowed for assistance for broad economic structural adjustment programmes, in addition to aid for specific investment projects. A mid-term Review in 1995 increased the total funds available for ACP/EC cooperation to ECU 14.6 billion during the second five-year term of the Agreement. In 1997 South Africa was negotiating admission as the convention's eighty-sixth member.

London inter-bank offered rate (LIBOR) ►inter-bank market.

London International Financial Futures Exchange (LIFFE) A ►market to trade in financial ►futures and ►options. Set up on 30 September 1982. Futures traded include an equity index contract based on the *FT/SE 100 Share Index* (►*Financial Times* stock indices).

London Stock Exchange ►stock exchange.

long-dated securities ►dated securities.

long-end of the market That part of the market for ►bonds which is concerned with dealings in long-term issues.

Longfield, Samuel Mountifort (1802–84) An Irish lawyer who became the first incumbent of the Chair of Political Economy at Trinity College, Dublin. His most important work in economics was *Lectures on Political Economy*, which was published in 1834. He argued convincingly against the labour theory of value (►value, theories of) and developed a marginal revenue productivity theory (►marginal revenue product) of ►labour and ►capital. Some of his ideas on capital and ►interest foreshadowed the work of the ►Austrian school.

long rate The ►rate of interest on long-term ►bonds. Because purchasers of bonds take a risk that ►inflation may erode the value of their investment over a long time period, the market rate which is observed is often held to be a good indicator of inflationary expectations. Long rates tend to drop when the authorities gain ►credibility, and appear to be more committed to low inflation.

long run A period of time in which all variables are able to settle at their equilibrium or final disequilibrium levels and all economic processes have time to work in full. Its most common application is in the theory of the firm (►firm, theory of the), in which it is the period of time in which the quantities of all ►factors of production employed are allowed to vary and all entry and exit that can occur into or from an industry has occurred. The duration of the 'long term' will clearly vary with the context in which the term is applied, depending on the speed with which the variables spoken of change. ►►short run.

long-term capital ►business finance.

long-term unemployment Joblessness for a period in excess of six months, a year or two years. In Britain, in 1997 those out of work for more than a year represented about 3 per cent of the labour force. In much of the European Continent, the figure was higher than this, yet in the United States (in 1996) it represented about half of one per cent. There has been increasing concern that long-term unemployment is a different problem from that of unemployment generally. It has a self-reinforcing character – the longer a period of unemployment, the harder it is to find work. This may be explained by demotivation on the part of the unemployed, or by lack of trust on the part of potential employers. The existence of long-term unemployment may be associated with the protection afforded by the benefit system, particularly the indefinite persistence of unconditional benefits. Policy-makers have started to give increasing attention to ►active labour-market policies. These concentrate on ensuring the unemployed are trained and motivated and may involve a temporary employment subsidy. In the UK employers have been offered temporary rebates of ►National Insurance. Long-term unemployment is usually a form of ►structural unemployment. ►►insider–outsider theory; hysteresis.

Lorenz curve

Lorenz curve A graphical representation showing the degree of inequality of a
➤frequency distribution in which the cumulative percentages of a population (e.g.
taxpayers, firms) are plotted against the cumulative percentage of the variable
under study (e.g. incomes, employment). A straight line rising at an angle of 45°
from the start on the graph will indicate perfect equality; for instance, if 10 per
cent of firms employ 10 per cent of the total labour force, 20 per cent of firms
employ 20 per cent of the total labour force and so on (➤linear relationship).
However, if there are a large number of small firms which employ few people
and a small number of large firms employing many people, the distribution will
be unequal. When such a distribution is plotted, a curve will be traced below the
45° line (see diagram) and the degree of curvature will be greater, the greater the
inequality (➤Gini coefficient).

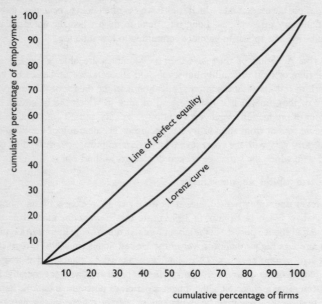

cumulative percentage of firms

Lucas, Robert E. (b. 1937) Economist from the University of Chicago, Robert
Lucas has probably had more influence than anyone else in recent decades on
research in ➤macroeconomics. He was the man who took ➤rational expectations,
first devised as an assumption by John Muth in 1961, and investigated their rich
implications for economic policy. He also did more to promote the rational
expectations hypothesis than anyone else. His name was put to the ➤Lucas critique,
the argument that relationships which appeared to characterize the fundamental
features of an economy could not be relied upon to last, were policy to change.

In particular, the Phillips curve (►Phillips, A. W. H.) would break down as soon as you attempted to exploit that apparent trade-off between inflation and unemployment. It is now virtually taken for granted that in assessing a change in policy, the authorities must take into account any change in expectations and behaviour consequent upon the policy change. For these contributions, Lucas won the ►Nobel Prize for Economics in 1995. ►policy ineffectiveness theorem; new classical economics.

Lucas critique An argument put forward by Robert ►Lucas in the 1970s that economists were mistakenly assuming that relationships they observed to hold would continue to hold even when conditions changed. The critique was an important component of the move towards accepting ►rational expectations as a significant development in ►macroeconomics. In essence, Lucas argued that, although economic agents may act in a certain way, you should not assume that they would continue to act in that way if you changed economic policy. For example, if consumers believed that inflation was to be 5 per cent next year, they might only demand 5 per cent wage increases. Suppose, knowing this, the government expands the money supply, causing inflation to be 10 per cent. The ►real income of consumers would fall, and firms would find it cheaper to employ new staff to make high-priced goods. This would increase output by effectively exploiting people's expectation that inflation would be 5 per cent and cutting their real wage. Lucas claimed that such policies may work once or twice, but that, if a government tried to exploit that, people would come to expect higher inflation and the policy would not work at all. Exploiting the trade-off between unemployment and inflation, is rather like employers getting two minutes' extra work out of their employees, by setting the clocks two minutes slow, and fooling them into staying a little longer than they wanted to stay. Observing that the workers do work more when the clocks are slow, would not imply at all that, by setting the clocks ten minutes, or an hour slow, you would get ten minutes' or an hour's more work from them. ►►new classical economics.

lump-sum tax A tax that must be paid irrespective of the behaviour of an economic agent – for instance, a tax of £100 on blue-eyed people that bore no relation to their income or spending. While usually considered impractical on political grounds, economists see lump-sum taxes as efficient in that they do not have any tendency to affect the incentives of individuals to work, save, purchase goods or services, etc. These are all things which other taxes will necessarily distort. ►►fiscal neutrality; local taxation; marginal tax rate.

M

Maastricht Treaty Treaty signed in Maastricht, the Netherlands in February 1992, more formally entitled *Treaty on European Union*. The Maastricht Treaty was simply a large package of amendments to the Treaty of Rome, with the effect of creating the ►European Union, out of the European Community; it plotted the path towards ►European Monetary Union; it enshrined for the first time the principle of ►subsidiarity into the Union's affairs; it contained the ►Social Charter. It also built the foundations of intergovernmental cooperation on foreign policy, and on certain domestic policy matters.

Macmillan Committee The Committee on Finance and Industry, set up in 1929, which published its report in 1931. It was under the chairmanship of Lord Macmillan, and ►Keynes was a member. The committee carried out its task against an economic background in which the ►gross domestic product had reached, after sixteen years, a level only 5 per cent above pre-war. Unemployment was 10 per cent in 1929, and was to rise to over 20 per cent by the time the committee published its report. The committee took the evidence from many leading economists of the day, such as ►Pigou, D. H. Robertson and ►Robbins on the subject of ►unemployment policy (►classical school). It decided in favour of the so-called ►Treasury view that expenditure on public works was not the answer, in spite of the signing of Addendum I by some of its leading members which advocated a programme of public works and ►import restrictions. However, the committee insisted that monetary policy should be concerned with 'the maintenance of the parity of the foreign exchanges before the avoidance of the credit cycle and the stability of the price level'. The maintenance of the ►exchange rate was agreed to be the first priority by all, including the signatories of Addendum I. (Two months after the report was published, the UK came off the ►gold standard and the exchange rate depreciated immediately by 2 per cent and continued downwards for twelve months.) The committee expressed concern that small companies found it difficult to raise long-term capital (►business finance) by the usual means of placing issues through the ►issuing houses; this has become known as the *Macmillan Gap*. It recommended the setting up of an institution which would 'provide adequate machinery for raising long-dated capital in amounts not sufficiently large for a public issue, i.e. amounts ranging from small sums up to say £200,000 or more'. This recommendation was eventually met in 1945, when the ►clearing banks and Scottish banks with the support of the ►Bank of England combined to finance the creation of the Industrial and Commercial Finance Corporation (ICFC). ►Radcliffe Report.

Macmillan Gap ➤Macmillan Committee.

macroeconomics The study of whole economic systems aggregating over the functioning of individual economic units. It is primarily concerned with ➤variables which follow systematic and predictable paths of behaviour and can be analysed independently of the decisions of the many agents who determine their level. More specifically, it is a study of national economies and the determination of ➤national income. It focuses on sectors of the economy but not those that function as separate units, like the 'car-production sector'; instead, those which run across the entire economy: the industrial sector; the personal sector; the financial sector; the government and the overseas sector. In classical macroeconomics (➤➤classical economics) lay a presumption of the efficiency and effectiveness of free markets, and all macroeconomic variables were seen as the sum of the variables as they applied to individual firms or consumers. Macroeconomic mechanisms were largely embedded in the theory of ➤microeconomics. Since ➤Keynes, however, economists have allowed for ➤disequilibrium in macroeconomic variables as such, and, therefore, collective outcomes distinct from those implied by individual behaviour (➤➤paradox of thrift).

The main topics covered by macroeconomics are: the determination of national income (➤➤income determination, theory of), prices (➤➤inflation) and ➤employment; the role of ➤fiscal and ➤monetary policy, analysed through different ➤models, each containing its own assumptions and emphasis; the determination of ➤consumption and ➤investment; the ➤balance of payments; and ➤economic growth. In recent years, the tendency in academic economics has been for macroeconomic models to be laid on ➤microeconomic foundations. ➤circular flow of income; economic doctrines.

mainstream corporation tax ➤corporation tax.

Malthus, Thomas Robert (1766–1834) Educated at St John's College, Cambridge, Malthus became a Fellow there after studying mathematics and philosophy. He was ordained and became a country parson. He was subsequently Professor of History and Political Economy at the East India Company's Haileybury College. His *Essay on the Principle of Population as It Affects the Future Improvement of Society* was published in 1798, with a revised edition in 1803. His other works include *An Inquiry into the Nature and Progress of Rent* (1815), *The Poor Law* (1817), *Principles of Political Economy* (1820), and *Definitions of Political Economy* (1827). Malthus is remembered for his essays on ➤population. Population had a natural growth rate described by a ➤geometric progression, whereas the natural resources necessary to support the population grew at a rate similar to an ➤arithmetic progression. Without restraints, therefore, there would be a continued pressure on living standards, both in terms of room and of output. He advocated moral restraint on the size of families. Malthus also carried on a long argument with ➤Ricardo against Say's law (➤Say, J.-B.). Briefly, Say's law stated that there could be no general overproduction or underproduction of ►commodities on the grounds that whatever was bought by somebody must have been sold by somebody else. (►Keynes found some affinity between Malthus's conclusions and his own in his *General Theory*.) Malthus, however, was arguing strictly within the basic assumption of the equality of planned ►savings and ►investment in ►classical economics, and was a long way away from Keynes's revolutionary assumption that they are made equal only by movements in total ►income. Saving to Malthus was investment. His argument for under-consumption was simply that an increase in savings necessarily diminished consumption on the one hand, and on the other increased the output of consumer's goods through increased investment. At the same time, because the ►labour supply was inelastic (►elasticity), wages rose and, therefore, so did costs. ►►Sismondi, J. C. L. S. de.

Malynes, Gerald (1586–1641) An English merchant and government official and a leading exponent of ►mercantilism. His publications include *A Treatise of the Canker of England's Commonwealth* (1601), *Saint George for England, Allegorically Described* (1601), *England's View in the Unmasking of Two Paradoxes* (1603), *The Maintenance of Free Trade* (1622) and *The Centre of the Circle of Commerce* (1623). He showed how an outflow of precious metals could lead to a fall in ►prices at home and a rise in prices abroad. This was an important clarification of the economic thought of the time. He suggested that higher import ►tariffs should be levied and ►exports of ►bullion prohibited, because he believed that a country's growth was related to the accumulation of precious metals. He thought that exchange control should be used to improve the UK ►terms of trade, supporting his policy on the belief that the UK's exports were price inelastic (►elasticity). ►►quantity theory of money.

managed bond ►bond.

managed currency A ►currency is said to be managed if the ►exchange rate is not fixed by ►free-market forces, i.e. if the government influences the rate by buying and selling its own ►money or by other means. Most currencies are managed in some sense today, even when they are allowed to float. ►►European Exchange Rate Mechanism; exchange control; International Monetary Fund.

managed trade ►protection.

management accountancy Business accounting practice concerned with the provision of information to management for policy-making purposes as opposed to that required for the preparation of ►balance sheets and other information required by law. In so far as the two sets of information overlap, the phrase is imprecise, but it usefully emphasizes the recent aspects of the development of accounting, notably in cost control (►cost accounting) and ►investment appraisal.

management buy-in ►management buy-out.

management buy-out (MBO) The acquisition of all or part of the ►equity capital of a company by its directors and senior executives, usually with the assistance of a financial institution. (►risk capital.) Competitive pressures upon large companies in the 1980s led to the disposal of many weak or peripheral subsidiaries in this way. In a *management buy-in* an outside team of managers acquires a company in the same way. In a ►BIMBO, some existing management is retained. Developing in the early 1970s in the USA, buy-outs were virtually unknown in the UK before 1980.

Manchester school 'Manchesterism' was an epithet applied in Germany to those who subscribed to a political-economic philosophy of ►'*laissez-faire*'. It was applied, in particular, to the movement in England from 1820 to 1850 which was inspired by the propaganda of the Anti-Corn Law League. This was headed by Cobden and Bright, and supported by the economics of ►Ricardo. The 'school' believed in ►free trade and political and economic freedom with the minimum of government restraint.

Mandeville, Bernard de (1670–1733) Born at Dort in Holland, Mandeville obtained an MD at Leyden and established himself in London as a general practitioner. In 1705 he published a poem called *The Grumbling Hive*, which was reissued in 1714 and 1729 under the title of *The Fable of the Bees or Private Vices, Public Benefits*. In this pamphlet he showed how, although individuals indulge in unholy vices in their private behaviour, nevertheless in the aggregate they contributed to the public good and therefore could be excused. ►Adam Smith was severely critical of the satirical nature of the work (►'invisible hand').

marginal analysis The study of ►variables in terms of the effects that would occur if they were changed by a small amount. For example, rather than analyse whether or not it is in the interest of an individual to spend money on food at all, attention can sensibly be focused on whether or not welfare could be enhanced by spending slightly more or less on food. Nothing better demonstrates the concept than the ►paradox of value: although water is more necessary to man than diamonds, it has a much lower price. This is because man usually has so much of it that extra water is worthless. This is not true of diamonds. (►►marginal utility.) The marginal value of a variable is equivalent to its rate of change: or mathematically, its first derivative (►calculus). For example, a firm's sales revenue rises as sales increase and this can be plotted on a graph as total revenue. By taking the gradient of the total revenue curve, ►marginal revenue can be derived, depicting how much extra revenue is gained, from an extra sale, at each different level of total sales. If the marginal revenue is plotted on a graph, total revenue can be derived by finding the area under the marginal-revenue curve up to a given level of sales. The marginal value of a variable lies below the average value of that variable if the average is falling. The marginal value lies above it if the average is rising.

The margin is important in economics as it is the impact of small changes in variables rather than their level per se that determines whether rational economic agents change them. It is the average level of utility, costs or revenues that tends to determine whether things are consumed or produced at all, but the marginal utility, costs or revenues that determine how much is consumed or produced once a decision to do so at all has been taken. ≫Gossen, H. H.; Jevons, W. S.; marginal cost; marginal-cost pricing; marginal product; Menger, C.; Thünen, J. H. von; Walras, M. E. L.

marginal cost The increase in the total costs of a firm caused by increasing its output by one extra unit. If all costs are fixed, the marginal cost of the first unit of output will be very high, but all subsequent units can be made for nothing. Economists normally assume firms to be producing at a point at which marginal costs are positive and rising. ≫firm, theory of the.

marginal-cost pricing The setting of the price of an item equal to the cost of producing one extra unit of the item. ➤Marginal cost represents the ➤opportunity cost, or the total sacrifice to society from producing an item. The price represents the cost to consumers of buying a unit of it, and they will ensure therefore that they will buy it if and only if they value it at least as much as the money it sells for. If price is below marginal cost consumers will be happy to buy an item even if they perhaps value it less than the goods that could have been made if it had not been produced. If, on the other hand, price is greater than marginal cost, some consumers who value the item more than it costs to make will still be deterred from buying it. For an efficient allocation of ➤resources (➤economic efficiency), therefore, marginal-cost pricing is considered essential.

There are, however, factors which undermine the case for marginal-cost pricing. Primarily, any company enjoying ➤economies of scale will have average costs in excess of marginal costs (➤marginal analysis), and with marginal-cost pricing, average costs will exceed price. A company in such a position will therefore make a loss. Only if production is at a point at which marginal and average costs are equal will marginal-cost pricing be sustainable. Marginal-cost pricing provides a major advantage of ➤perfect competition over ➤monopoly or ➤monopolistic competition, and attempts to impose it on firms outside competitive markets – especially ➤nationalized industries – have been made, with limited success. ≫Hotelling, H.; peak pricing.

marginal efficiency of capital ➤internal rate of return.

marginal efficiency of investment ➤internal rate of return.

marginal product The output created by the employment of one additional unit of a ➤factor of production. In general, it is believed that the marginal product of a factor rises when the factor is employed in small quantities, but eventually falls as the amount of the factor employed increases. Marginal product is measured in the physical units of the output produced and it is thus sometimes called *marginal physical product.* ≫diminishing returns, law of.

marginal product of labour The output created by the employment of one extra worker with all other ➤factors of production held constant. It is a measure of the physical increase in output that occurs in a firm or in the economy as a whole when one extra person starts work. It is generally assumed that the marginal product of ➤labour rises initially, and then diminishes. In a hypothetical factory manned by a single worker, at first adding helpers would allow for specialization and the ➤division of labour. Eventually, however, all such gains would be realized and the gains from employing additional staff would diminish. ➤➤diminishing returns, law of.

marginal productivity of capital The value of the output that would be created by the employment of one extra unit of capital. As a major part of the cost of capital is the interest that has to be paid to buy the capital, the marginal productivity of capital can be measured by the ➤internal rate of return, the interest rate at which the marginal productivity has a ➤present value of zero.

marginal productivity theory of wages The doctrine that the demand for labour is determined by the value of the output created by the employment of an extra worker. In this account of the determination of wages, firms employ workers as long as the revenue generated by the output of the marginal worker exceeds the cost of that worker; that is, until the worker's ➤marginal revenue product is equal to the market wage rate. From this account of firm's behaviour, a curve depicting the demand for labour at different wage levels can be derived, and the wage rate is determined by the interaction of this curve with that of the supply of labour at different wage levels. As more workers are employed at a given level of capital stock the ➤marginal product of labour will decline and the wage of all workers will fall (➤diminishing returns, law of). This fall in wages occurs because any new workers entering the labour market cannot profitably be employed at the going wage rate as the value of their output would be less than that of the workers already employed. If they are keen for work, therefore, they will offer themselves to employers at lower rates of pay than the current employees, and all wages will be bid down. At the new lower wage level, all workers can profitably be employed.

The theory is part of the *neo-classical theory of distribution* (➤distribution, theory of) which attempted to explain the share of total output accruing to labour, investors and landowners (➤bargaining theory of wages; efficiency-wage hypothesis; neo-classical economics).

marginal propensity to consume (MPC) The proportion of a small increase in income which would be spent rather than saved. The most important variable determining expenditure on consumption is income (➤➤consumption function). The *average propensity to consume* is the proportion of total income which is spent, rather than saved. In principle, the MPC should really depend on whether the income is assumed to be permanent, or a temporary windfall. ➤permanent-income hypothesis; ➤➤Keynes, J. M.; multiplier.

marginal propensity to save (MPS) The proportion of a small increase in income which is saved. It is equal to $1 - MPC$ (➤marginal propensity to consume). ➤➤savings ratio.

marginal rate of substitution (MRS) The rate at which a consumer needs to substitute one commodity for another in order to maintain constant total ➤utility from the commodities taken together. If a consumer values two boxes of Daz equally to one of Persil, the marginal rate of substitution between them is two, because if one box of Persil were taken away from the consumer, two boxes of Daz would have to be provided to compensate. The marginal rate of substitution between commodity A and commodity B usually diminishes as consumption of commodity A increases. If at consumption of twenty apples and twenty bananas the consumer is indifferent between one of either, at consumption of thirty apples and ten bananas the consumer is likely to start demanding more than a mere one apple before giving up a scarce banana. Graphically, the MRS is the slope of an ➤indifference curve and it is in ➤indifference-curve analysis that the concept is important. Mathematically, it is the ratio of the ➤marginal utilities of two items. As long as the MRS declines with increased consumption of an item, the indifference curves are convex (➤convexity) to the origin of an indifference map. ➤➤rate of technical substitution.

marginal revenue The increase in the total revenue received by a firm from the sale of one extra unit of its output. For a small firm which cannot influence market price (➤➤perfect competition), the extra revenue gained is equal to the price of the sale. For a firm with a large share of the total market (➤monopoly), however, putting an extra item on sale drives down the market price slightly, so that the revenue gain equals the cash gained on the new sale *minus* the loss that occurs on all the sales that would otherwise have been made at the previously higher price. ➤➤market power.

marginal revenue product The revenue gained by a firm when it sells the output generated by the employment of one additional unit of a ➤factor of production. It is influenced by three factors: (a) the physical output of the extra factor; (b) the sale price of the product made; (c) the rate at which that price falls when the extra supply of the new factor is put on to the market. To calculate it, ➤marginal product must be multiplied by ➤marginal revenue (➤marginal productivity theory of wages; marginal value product).

marginal social product The effect on ➤social welfare of employing one additional unit of a ➤factor of production. When new workers are taken on, for example, the physical output which they build has a private value to their employer, measured as the ➤marginal value product, or the price at which the output is sold. However, to measure the value of their output to society, two other factors must be taken into account. The first is ➤consumer surplus: the amount by which consumers value something in excess of what they pay for it. The second factor is any ►externality which is present: a benefit (or cost) which accrues to those other than the purchaser of the item.

marginal tax rate The rate of tax paid on extra units of income. An individual may pay no tax on the first £1000 of income, and 50 per cent tax on all pounds earned thereafter. Those individuals earning more than £1000 will thus face a marginal tax rate of 50 per cent even though their overall tax rate will be less than 50 per cent. Someone earning £1001, for example, will only pay 50p of tax – a tiny proportion of his total income. The marginal tax rates facing economic agents are often considered important in determining how far taxation impinges on incentives to work, save or spend money. They are of only limited importance in determining whether a tax is progressive or not (►progressive tax). The fact that poor people may lose 80 per cent of any marginal earnings (►►poverty trap) and the rich only 60 per cent is irrelevant in assessing whether the tax system is borne more heavily by either group – an assessment which depends not on the tax paid on incremental pounds of earnings, but on tax paid on all actual earnings. ►►lump-sum taxes; taxation.

marginal utility The extra satisfaction gained by a consumer from a small increment in the consumption of a commodity. More formally, it is the partial derivative of the ►utility function with respect to the quantity of some commodity consumed (►calculus). It is a concept of central importance to demand theory (►demand, theory of), one approach to which holds that marginal utility diminishes as consumption of an item increases (►marginal utility, diminishing). Rational consumers will equalize the marginal utility gained from a unit of spending on all the different things they consume, because not to do so would imply that costless extra utility could be derived by switching spending from items yielding low marginal utility to those where it is higher. Such a theory can explain why a price rise causes consumers to cut demand of an item. As consumers, however, do not possess an objective scale of utility measurement (►ordinal utility), in more modern theory (►indifference-curve analysis) no meaning is attached to the numerical magnitude of the marginal utilities themselves, but only to their ratios and signs. ►►demand, theory of.

marginal utility, diminishing ►diminishing marginal utility.

marginal utility of money The pleasure or satisfaction gained by a consumer from an extra unit of money. The rational consumer should ensure that the marginal ►utility of money with respect to the different things he consumes is the same: if someone would get more utility from spending an extra pound on clothes than they would get from spending it on books, by transferring some of their budget from books to clothes they would costlessly increase their utility. They should go on transferring until they have so many clothes that they no longer value them, pound for pound, more than books. The marginal utility of money diminishes the greater the quantity of money available to a consumer. ⇒demand, theory of; marginal utility; Marshall, A.; ordinal utility.

marginal value product The market value of the output generated by the employment of one additional unit of a ➤factor of production. It is equal to the ➤marginal product of a factor multiplied by the unit selling price of the extra output produced. It is thus comparable to the ➤marginal revenue product, which is marginal product multiplied by ➤marginal revenue; in ➤perfect competition, where price is equal to marginal revenue, the two are identical.

market A collection of homogeneous transactions. A market is created whenever potential sellers of a good or service are brought into contact with potential buyers and a means of exchange is available. The medium of exchange may be ➤money or ➤barter. Exchange agreements are reached through the operation of the laws of ➤supply and ➤demand. In traditional economics (➤Marshall, A.) a market is characterized by a single prevailing price for commodities of uniform quality (➤law of one price). This is not necessarily the same as the business view – the market is a collection of selling opportunities; or the legal view; where the market is a trading zone free of artificial restrictions on transactions. ⇒price system; single market.

market capitalization ➤capitalization.

market economy ➤free-market economy.

market failure An outcome deriving from the self-interested behaviour of individuals in the context of ➤free trade, in which ➤economic efficiency does not result. Market failures provide a ubiquitous argument for ➤intervention of some form or other. But they have two main sources. First, they derive from the fact that many transactions which would need to occur for the sake of economic efficiency simply do not occur. This may be on account of ➤transaction costs. Or, there may be a deficiency of information to the parties involved, or there may be ➤asymmetric information (with its corresponding problems of ➤adverse selection, ➤moral hazard and ➤agency costs). Or, the necessary transaction may be deterred by the fact that the efficient price is not set – on account of ➤menu costs. Or, there may be *strategic behaviour* by the individuals involved, who fail to engage in a trade, in the hope that they might extract a better deal from their adversary if they 'play it tough'. A large number of 'missing trades' are those involving the many resources over which no properly defined ➤property rights exist (such as clean air) and thus over which no trade can occur. (⇒Coase theorem.) The second main category of market failures derive from the fact that there are sometimes collective interests that are unable to be served by self-interested, individual behaviour. There are goods or services that have to be consumed collectively (➤public goods like defence); there can be ➤free-rider problems in which, for example, citizens hope to avoid paying for a service on the grounds that someone else will pay (why should I invest in ➤innovation, if someone else will do it for me?); there can be ➤prisoner's dilemma-type situations, in which selfish behaviour leads to sub-optimal outcomes (particularly apt in areas where ➤utility is a function of relative position, rather than absolute position). There can be industries subject to ➤increasing returns to scale, in which ➤monopoly is inevitable, which carries large efficiency costs unless there is a collective effort to regulate. This provides an almost comprehensive list of the sources of market failure. Some of the conventionally discussed forms of failure are derivable from this list. For example, ➤externalities are a combination of lack of allocation of property rights, and a lack of trade in the externality itself. The deviation from ➤marginal cost pricing tends to occur as a result of increasing returns to scale.

market forces The application of self-interested, individual behaviour in a ➤free-market economy which, through ➤supply and ➤demand in different ➤markets, determine ➤price and the allocation of resources.

market maker A ➤broker–dealer who is prepared to quote buy and sell (bid-and offer) prices and to buy and sell specified ➤securities at all times at these prices and is thus 'making a market' in them. Prior to the ➤Big Bang this function was carried out by the ➤jobbers, who were not allowed to deal with the public. Since the Big Bang all members of the ➤stock exchange have been able to deal with the public as broker–dealers, some of whom specialize as market makers and others as ➤stockbrokers. Market makers help to provide ➤liquidity on the stock market, particularly for less frequently traded ➤shares.

market power The degree to which a firm exercises influence over the price and output in a particular market. Under ➤perfect competition, all firms are assumed to have zero market power: they have to take the going price, and cannot hope to alter it on their own. Wherever firms represent a non-negligible portion of the whole market, however, instead of facing a flat ➤demand curve, they will face a downward-sloping one. This means that, in contrast to the perfect competitor, if they raise their price they do not lose all their sales. It also means, however, that if they wish to increase their sales they have to lower their price. The stronger this relationship, the greater the market power. Where market power exists, the producer has such influence on the market that the amount he decides to produce affects the market price, and so price is not equivalent to ➤marginal revenue. Market power is related to the availability of substitute items. Those items which are highly differentiated from those of competitors will give more market power to the producer than those which are standard. ➤➤monopoly.

market share Either (a) the sales of the product or products of a firm as a proportion of the sales of the product or products of the ➤market as a whole, e.g. sales of Ford motor cars compared with total UK motor-car sales; or (b) the sales of a particular ➤commodity compared with the total sales for the class of commodity of which the particular commodity is a member, e.g. sales of mobile telephones compared with sales of all telephones. The presumption is that the firm's product in (a) and the particular commodity in (b) are faced with competitive ►substitutes in their respective markets.

Market shares may also be calculated in terms of the proportion of the product in the total existing stock of that class of products, as opposed to its share of the flow of new sales. ►►saturation point.

market structure The organizational and other characteristics of a ►market and in particular those which affect the nature of competition and pricing. Traditionally, the most important features of market structure are the number and size distribution of buyers and sellers, which reflect the extent of ►monopoly or ►monopsony; this, in turn, will be affected by the existence or absence of ►barriers to entry. ►►concentration.

marketable securities ►Securities dealt in on the ►stock exchange.

marketing Broadly, the functions of sales, distribution, ►advertising and sales promotion, product planning and market research. That is, those functions in a business that directly involve contact with the consumer and assessment of his needs, and the translation of this information into outputs for sale consistent with the firm's objectives.

Markowitz, Harry M. (b. 1927) Harry Markowitz, from the City University of New York and a joint winner of the 1990 ►Nobel Prize for Economics, is credited with the pioneering contribution in the field of financial economics. His insight was to recognize that the risk of an asset that was relevant to assessing its price, was its risk relative to the market generally. Other risks, more specific to particular assets can be diversified away in a moderately sized ►portfolio. With his contribution, the massive problem of designing the optimal portfolio, with maximum expected return for minimum risk, could be seen to be reduced to a two-dimensional problem, of looking at the mean and the variance of the portfolio returns. That laid the foundation to the ►capital-asset pricing model.

Marshall, Alfred (1842–1924) Educated at Merchant Taylors' School, Marshall graduated in mathematics at St John's College, Cambridge. In 1868 he was appointed to a lectureship in moral science at Cambridge, and it was during this period that he began to study economics. In 1882 he moved to the Chair of Political Economy at Bristol. In 1885 he returned to Cambridge as Professor of Political Economy, a post he retained until his retirement in 1908. His most important works include *The Pure Theory of Foreign Trade* (1879), *The Principles of Economics* (1890), *Industry and Trade* (1919) and *Money, Credit and Commerce* (1923). Marshall was in the long tradition of the English ►classical school, which was founded by ►Adam Smith and ►Ricardo, and his influence on succeeding generations of economists has been very great. His achievement was to refine and develop ►microeconomic theory to such a degree that much of what he wrote is still familiar to readers of the elementary economic textbooks today. His theory of ►value brought together the diverse elements of previous theories. On the one hand, he showed how the demand for a ►commodity is dependent on a consumer's ►utility or welfare. The more of a commodity a consumer has the less extra utility or benefit accrues to him from an additional purchase (►Gossen, H. H.). He will not go on buying a commodity until this extra benefit falls to zero. Rather, he will stop buying extra when he finds that the ►money he has to pay for it is worth more to him than the gain from having an extra unit of the commodity. At this point of ►equilibrium a fall in the ►price, therefore, will mean that it becomes worth while to him to exchange his money for more of the commodity. In general, therefore, a fall in price will increase the quantity of the commodity demanded, and in theory a schedule could be drawn up which shows how much would be demanded at each price. The resultant graph would show a downward-sloping ►demand curve. Marshall invented the expression ►elasticity to describe his measure of the response of demand to small changes in price. Similarly, on the supply side, higher prices are necessary to bring forward increased outputs and a supply schedule with its corresponding supply curve can be drawn up. The price of the commodity is determined at the point where the two curves intersect. These work like a pair of scissors, neither blade of which cuts without the presence of the other.

Marshall recognized that his consumer utility theory was in some ways an oversimplification. It does not take account of complementary or competitive goods (►complementary goods), and assumes that the ►marginal utility of money is constant. However, he argued that his analysis applied to small price changes and to goods upon which only an insignificant proportion of income was spent. It was within this framework that Marshall discussed the idea of ►consumer surplus (►Dupuit, A. J. E. J.). For a given quantity of a commodity purchased on a competitive market, the price will be the same for each unit of the commodity sold. However, for any individual purchaser the price is equal to the utility to him of the last unit of the total quantity purchased; the last but one being worth more, the last but two worth more again, and so on. These utilities can be added up and the extra, over the price and quantity paid out, is the consumer's surplus. He was aware of the shortcomings of the 'stationary state' of the typical classical analysis and emphasized the importance of the production period. He recognized the element of time as the chief difficulty of almost every economic problem. He considered (a) a market period in which supplies are all fixed, (b) a short period in which supplies can be increased, but only to the extent possible by better use of current capacity, and (c) a long period in which capacity itself can be increased. The classical economists had shown how ►rent is received by landowners as a surplus. As land was a ►factor of production in fixed supply, it differed from other factors of production in that its returns were not related to work done. Marshall extended the concept by pointing out that, in the short run, man-made ►capital was in fixed supply also, and during the period which it took to manufacture, it earned a ►quasi-rent. ►►Cournot, A. A.; Marshall–Lerner criterion; Mill, J. S.

Marshall Aid At the end of the Second World War, only the USA had the necessary productive capacity to make good the losses experienced by other countries. European countries had heavy ►balance of payments deficits vis-à-vis the USA. In 1946, in order to alleviate the resultant shortage of dollars, the USA and Canada made substantial ►loans, including £1 billion to the UK. It was expected that these loans would be sufficient to cover requirements over the short period which was all that was expected to be necessary for the world economies to recover. However, in 1948 a general ►liquidity crisis was avoided only by further loans made under the ►European Recovery Programme, through which the UK received loans amounting to £1.5 billion between 1948 and 1950. This programme was called Marshall Aid, after the then US Secretary of State, General George C. Marshall. The loans were allocated under the direction of the Organization for European Economic Cooperation (►Organization for Economic Corporation and Development) set up for this purpose.

Marshall–Lerner criterion A rule which states the ►elasticity conditions under which a change in a country's ►exchange rate would improve its ►balance of trade. A. P. Lerner set out the appropriate formulae in his book *Economics of Control* on the basis of the elasticity concepts developed by ►Marshall. In its simplest form, the rule states that the price elasticities of demand for ►imports and ►exports must sum to greater than unity for an improvement to be effected. The volume of exports increases and the volume of imports decreases in response to a fall in the ►price of the former and rise in the price of the latter when a ►currency is devalued (assuming, for the sake of the argument, that there are no other factors influencing the ►market, such as ►supply restrictions). There would, therefore, be an improvement in the balance of trade in volume terms, i.e. in terms of the prices ruling prior to ►devaluation. However, what is important for the ►balance of payments is the impact of devaluation on the value of trade. If the price elasticity of exports plus the price elasticity of imports is less than unity, it means that the increased cost of imports in terms of the domestic currency outweighs the value of the growth in exports. Putting it another way, the improvement in the volume of the balance of trade is not sufficient to offset the fall in the value of the balance of trade occasioned by the devaluation. ►►J-curve; terms of trade.

Marx, Karl (1818–83) Born in Trier, Marx studied philosophy at Bonn University and at the Hegelian Centre at Berlin University, and took a doctorate at Jena. For a time, he was editor of *Rheinische Zeitung*, but the paper was suppressed, and in 1843 he fled to Paris. There he began his friendship and close association with Friedrich Engels, who encouraged in him an interest in political economy. After a brief return to Germany he was banished, and in 1849 he settled in London where he remained until his death in 1883. The *Communist Manifesto*, written jointly by Marx and Engels, was published in 1848. In 1859 the first fruits of his long, painstaking research at the British Museum appeared: the *Critique of Political Economy*. The first volume of *Das Kapital* appeared in 1867. The remaining volumes, edited by Engels, were published posthumously in 1885 and 1894.

Marx's economics was essentially that of the ►classical school, especially of ►Ricardo, to whom he owed a great debt. However, he shifted economics away from its preoccupation with agriculture and stationary states. For Marx, ►capitalism was a stage in the process of evolution, removed from the primitive agricultural economy and moving towards the inevitable elimination of private property and the class structure. Marx attempted a synoptic view of the development of the whole structure of human society. His economics was only a part, though a fundamental part, of his all-embracing sociological and political theories. Marx postulated that the class structures of societies, their political systems and, indeed, their culture were determined by the way in which societies produced their goods and ►services. Moreover, the whole structure was evolutionary. The class structure of a capitalist state was a reflection of the split between owners and non-owners of ►capital, which division characterized the manner in which production was carried out, and which already had within it the necessary ingredients of change.

Marx developed from ►Adam Smith and Ricardo their labour theory of value (►value, theories of), which held the central place in his economic theory. For Ricardo, the amount of ►labour used in the production of ►commodities was a rough determinant of relative prices in the long run. For Marx, however, the quantity of labour used up in the manufacture of a product determined value, and this value was fundamental and immutable. He did not satisfactorily explain any connection with relative prices. Labour consumption determined exchange value, which differed from use value. The distinction between the two in the case of labour, regarded in itself as a commodity, was a vital one in Marx's analysis. The capitalist pays wages which are determined by the exchange value of workers. This exchange value is, in turn, determined by the socially necessary labour time required to 'produce' the worker, that is, the labour inputs required to rear, feed, clothe and educate him. However, in return the capitalist receives the labourer's use value. The value of the labourer to the capitalist who uses him is greater than the value the capitalist paid in exchange for his services. This difference Marx called 'surplus value' (s). Only labour yields surplus value. Other ►factors of production, such as plant and machinery and raw materials, reproduce only themselves in the productive process. (These ideas have some affinity with the ►Physiocrats' *'produit net'*, although in their case it was ►land which was the only factor which produced a surplus.) The amount of capital required to pay wages Marx called variable (v) (►wage-fund theory), and the remainder he called constant (c). ►Gross national product in the Marxian system therefore is given by $c + v + s$. The ratio of constant capital in total capital $c/(c + v)$ he called the organic composition of capital. The 'exploitation rate' was s/v. The rate of profit was $s/(c + v)$. The desire for further wealth, coupled with competition and technical change, induced capitalists to invest from the surplus (which they expropriated matrix

from the workers) and in labour-saving machinery. The organic composition of capital, therefore, rose over time as more was spent on plant and machinery (c) compared with wages (v), with the result that, as only variable capital produced a surplus (and assuming that the exploitation rate remained constant), the rate of profit tended downwards (➤profit, falling rate of). On the one hand, diminishing profits and stronger competition would lead to ➤monopoly and the concentration of ➤wealth in a few hands, and on the other hand there would be an increasing squeeze on the ➤real incomes of workers by the capitalists in their attempt to maintain ➤profits and the emergence of a large 'reserve army of unemployed' arising from mechanization (➤Ricardo, D.). The class conflict would become increasingly acute until the environment was such that the change inherent in the economic structure would be made manifest by the overthrow of capitalism.

matrix An array of numbers displayed in rows and columns. For instance:

$$
\begin{array}{cc}
2 & 1 \\
7 & 3
\end{array}
$$

The numbers are called the *elements* of the matrix and are generally denoted by a_{ij} in which i refers to the row and j to the column. In the example above $a_{21} = 7$. The order of a matrix is given by the product of the number of rows times the number of columns. The above matrix is of order 4. An algebra exists for the manipulation of matrices, with rules for addition, subtraction, multiplication and division. Matrix algebra has found many useful applications in ➤econometrics, and in particular in ➤input–output analysis and ➤linear programming.

maturity The date upon which the principal of a redeemable security becomes repayable. ➤redeemable securities; securities.

maturity transformation ➤financial intermediaries.

maximin strategy A decision rule in the theory of games (➤➤game theory). The rule states that a 'player' with a number of optional strategies to choose considers first the minimum pay-offs that could be gained from each depending on the reaction of his 'opponent'. The 'player' should then choose that strategy which corresponds to the maximum of all the minimum pay-offs to him that are possible. In other words, it is a selection of the best possible worst-case scenario. For instance, consider a decision-maker faced with two optional strategies, each of which could have two pay-offs. They can be summarized in a ➤matrix:

$$
\begin{array}{ccc}
(1) & 2 & 5 \\
(2) & 4 & 3
\end{array}
$$

Strategy (1) could have a pay-off of 2 or 5, strategy (2) a pay-off of 4 or 3. The minimum pay-off of strategy (1) is 2 and that of strategy (2) is 3. The maximum minimum pay-off is therefore 3 and strategy (2) would be chosen under the rule. There is no obvious rationale for choosing a maximin rule. Most of us would focus attention on likely outcomes, not just worst-case outcomes. However, since ➤Rawls, J., the rule has almost developed into a political philosophy, with the argument that it justifies increased attention to the poor in society. (➤➤prisoner's dilemma.)

maximum-likelihood estimation Estimation of a ➤parameter by choosing the value which is statistically most likely, given observed data. In ➤regression analysis, under certain assumptions, it can be shown that ➤least-squares regression yields the maximum-likelihood estimate of the ➤beta coefficient in an equation. Once the simple assumptions are removed, maximum-likelihood approaches may diverge from other statistically plausible methods.

MBO ➤management buy-out.

MCA Monetary compensatory amounts (➤green currency).

Meade, Sir James Edward (1907–95) Educated at both Oxford and Cambridge Universities, Professor Meade was appointed Professor of Commerce at the London School of Economics in 1947. He was appointed to the Chair of Political Economy at Cambridge University in 1957, a post he held until 1969. Professor Meade was awarded the ➤Nobel Prize in Economics (jointly with ➤Ohlin) in 1977. His published works include *The Theory of International Economic Policy* (1951), *A Geometry of International Trade* (1953), *The Theory of Customs Unions* (1955), *A Neo-Classical Theory of Economic Growth* (1961), *Efficiency, Equality and the Ownership of Property* (1964), *Principles of Political Economy* (1965/76), *The Inheritance of Inequalities* (1974), *The Intelligent Radical's Guide to Economic Policy* (1975) and *Stagflation* (1981/3). Professor Meade made important advances in the theory of international trade, in the study of equilibrium conditions in domestic and external economies. In his work on the welfare effects (➤➤welfare economics) of tariffs and customs unions (➤customs union), he introduced the concepts of the theory of the ➤second best. Professor Meade contributed much to the analysis of income distribution and in the field of ➤growth theory, being an advocate of a ➤prices and incomes policy. ➤➤nominal gross domestic product.

mean ➤average.

means test The assessment of wealth or income as, for example, when determining the eligibility of a claimant for welfare benefits. Means-tested benefits contrast with those such as child benefit which are *universal* – given to all families irrespective of income. ➤➤dependency culture; marginal tax rate; poverty trap.

measure of economic welfare (MEW) ➤➤environmental accounting.

median ➤average.

medium of exchange ➤money.

medium-term financial strategy (MTFS) A statement of the ➤monetary policy and ➤fiscal policy of the British government, set out in the ➤budget each year during the 1980s. It traced the target path of ➤money supply, ➤gross domestic product and the ➤public-sector borrowing requirement for the following three or four years. When introduced in 1980, it was believed it would add ➤credibility to the government's anti-inflation strategy, and most attention focused on the targeting of growth of ➤money supply. In 1982 the MTFS started down a path of increasingly focusing on targets of nominal GDP growth; and in 1984 another measure of money supply M0 (➤money supply), was added. After 1987 the MTFS existed in name only. Monetary policy shifted, first into the targeting of the ➤exchange rate. Then into targeting of ➤inflation directly (➤inflation target). The MTFS was formally dropped in 1997.

member banks (US) ➤commercial banks.

Memorandum of Association The document which forms the basis of registration of a company. As required by the Companies Acts, the Memorandum of Association must list the subscribers to the ➤capital of the company and the number of ➤shares they have agreed to take, the name and address of the company and, where appropriate, the powers and objects of the company, and that the ➤liability of its members is limited (➤company law). The *Articles of Association* set out the rules by which the company will be administered, e.g. the voting of directors, the calling of meetings.

Menger, Carl (1840–1921) Professor of Economics in the Faculty of Law at Vienna University from 1873 to 1903. His major work, in which he develops his marginal-utility theory, *Grundsätze der Volkswirtschaftslehre*, was published in 1871. He was one of the three economists in the 1870s who independently put forward the theory of ➤value based on ➤marginal utility and whose work had a profound influence on the subsequent evolution of economic thought (➤Gossen, H. H.; Jevons, W. S.; Walras, M. E. L.). Exchange takes place, he argued, because individuals have different subjective valuations of the same ➤commodity. Menger saw commodities in terms of their reverse order in the productive process, i.e. bread is prior to flour and flour prior to wheat. The ➤price of the first-order commodities, which is determined by their exchange for ➤consumption, is imputed back through to the higher-ordered commodities. The theory of diminishing ➤utility was the catalyst which eventually unified the theories of production and consumption. Menger himself, however, overemphasized consumption demand in the theory of value, just as the ➤classical economists had overemphasized production supply (➤Marshall, A.).

menu costs The practical costs that are incurred by producers in having to change their prices – costs of relabelling products, or re-entering prices into computer systems. Menu costs are one factor in support of keeping ►inflation relatively low. They also explain why prices may move in moderate-sized jumps, rather than in smooth, small increments. The existence of menu costs can explain why money may not be neutral (►neutrality of money). ►►new Keynesianism.

mercantilism The growth of ►international trade and the establishment of the power of the merchant after the medieval era led to the emergence of a body of thought, between the mid sixteenth and late seventeenth centuries, which was primarily concerned with the relationship between a nation's wealth and its balance of foreign trade. The mercantilists recognized the growing power of the national economy and were in favour of the intervention of the state in economic activity to maximize national ►wealth. Partly because the monetary system was very primitive in relation to the growing needs of economic expansion, mercantilist writing was often overburdened with the identification of national wealth with precious metals. But its leading writers did make important progress in developing economic thought and made significant contributions to the analysis of ►international trade problems. ►►Malynes, G.; Misselden, E.; Mun, T.; Serra, A.

merchant banks Institutions that carry out a variety of financial services, including the acceptance of ►bills of exchange, the issue and placing of ►loans and ►securities, ►portfolio and ►unit trust management and some ►banking services. Several houses, often through subsidiaries, also provide ►risk capital for small firms, deal in gold ►bullion, insurance banking and ►hire purchase and are active in the market for ►Eurocurrency. Historically, the merchant bankers were merchants dealing in overseas trade who used their knowledge of traders to accept bills of exchange and who developed other banking services connected with foreign trade, e.g. dealing in gold and foreign ►currency and assisting foreign borrowers to raise money in London. Their most prominent function has been that of advising the government on ►privatization and the ►private finance initiative and firms on ►mergers and ►take-overs and other financial matters. Many merchant banks are well known, e.g. Rothschilds, Barclays de Zoete Wedd (BZW), Lazards and Schroders. Merchant banks are also referred to as ►issuing houses, ►accepting houses or ►investment trusts in exercising particular functions. The merchant banks are relatively small institutions which pride themselves on their personal, flexible management. There has been a recent trend, especially following the ►Big Bang, for merchant banks to join financial ►conglomerates, so as to be able to offer a full range of financial services, including retail services, and many of these banks in London are foreign-owned. ►►investment banks.

Mercosur A ►customs union of Argentina, Brazil, Paraguay and Uruguay. By the Treaty of Asunción in 1991 and a final Protocol signed in 1994, they agreed to establish the Mercosur or Southern Cone common market between their four countries from January 1995. Tariffs were abolished on about 90 per cent of intra-Mercosur trade. Tariffs, retained on specified exemptions, are to be removed by 1999. At the same time a Common External Tariff (CET) ranging from zero to 20 per cent was levied against about 90 per cent of goods imported from outside the Union. Particular exemptions to this CET regime were to be lifted by 2001. In 1996 Bolivia and Chile became Associate Members. Most non-agricultural trade between Chile and Mercosur would be free of tariff protection by 2004 and on agricultural products by 2014. ➤Andean Pact; free-trade area; Latin American Integration Association.

merger The fusion of two or more separate companies into one. In current usage merger is a special case of combination, where both the merging companies wish to join together and do so on roughly equal terms, as distinct from a ➤take-over, which occurs against the wishes of one company. However, merger, take-over, amalgamation, absorption and fusion are sometimes all used as synonyms. Where two firms in the same business, i.e. competitors, merge, this is known as horizontal integration. Where two firms that are suppliers or customers of one another merge, this is known as ➤vertical integration. Acquisitions and mergers have been an important cause of increasing ➤concentration and some economists have argued that major mergers should be more closely controlled by the authorities, even where they do not threaten to reduce competition directly (➤Monopolies and Mergers Commission; Take-over Panel). This is because pressures to maintain high short-term earnings and hence share prices to avoid the risk of a take-over bid may inhibit investment in research and development. Against this it is argued that mergers are the only way of transferring assets to more capable hands when existing management has proved deficient. The value of merger activity has fluctuated roughly in line with stock-market prices. Not all acquisitions involve take-overs of independent companies. In recent years between one-fifth and one-third of total expenditure has been accounted for by sales of subsidiaries between company groups. ➤Management buy-outs have also been growing. ➤➤conglomerate; holding company; reverse take-over.

merit goods A ➤commodity the consumption of which is regarded as socially desirable irrespective of ➤consumers' preference. Governments are readily prepared to suspend ➤consumers' sovereignty by subsidizing the provision of certain goods and services, for example education.

MFA ➤Multi-Fibre Arrangement.

microeconomics The study of economics at the level of individual consumers, groups of consumers or firms. No very sharp boundary can be drawn between microeconomics and the other main area of the subject, ➤macroeconomics, but its broad distinguishing feature is to focus on the choices facing, and the reasoning of, individual economic decision-makers. It is a long-standing requirement of microeconomics, that it can justify the behaviour it ascribes to individuals as being logical, given their preferences or objectives. The general concern of microeconomics is the efficient allocation of scarce resources between alternative uses (➤resource allocation) but more specifically it involves the determination of ➤price through the optimizing behaviour of economic agents, with consumers maximizing ➤utility and firms maximizing ➤profit. It covers both the behaviour of individual sectors and the way the sectors interact in ➤equilibrium and disequilibrium in individual markets. The main areas of microeconomics are: demand theory (➤demand, theory of); the theory of the firm (➤firm, theory of the); the demand for labour (➤labour, demand for), and other ➤factors of production; ➤welfare economics; and the study of the interactions between markets in ➤general equilibrium analysis.

Mill, John Stuart (1806–73) John Stuart Mill's childhood was subjected to a regime of severe educational discipline by his father, James Mill. He was acquainted with the major works of economics of the day by the age of twelve, and was correcting the proofs of his father's book, *Elements of Political Economy*, when he was thirteen. He learnt Ricardian economics and Benthamite ➤utilitarianism from his father. In 1823 he joined the East India Company, where he remained for thirty-five years. For three years, before moving to France to spend his retirement, he was a Member of Parliament. He was an extraordinarily prolific writer, especially when it is remembered that he had a full-time job. His reputation was made by his *A System of Logic, Ratiocinative and Inductive, Being a Connected View of the Principles of Evidence and the Methods of Scientific Investigation*, which was published in 1843. His essay *On Liberty* appeared in 1859, and his *Examination of Sir William Hamilton's Philosophy* in 1865. His two most important works on economics are *Essays on Some Unsettled Questions of Political Economy* (which came out in 1844, though he actually wrote it in 1829 when he was only twenty-three) and *Principles of Political Economy with Some of Their Applications to Social Philosophy* (1848). The latter was intended to be a comprehensive review of the field of economic theory at the time, and was, in fact, an up-to-date version of ➤Adam Smith's *Wealth of Nations*. It succeeded so well that it remained the basic textbook for students of economics until the end of the century. The work is regarded as the apogee of the ➤classical school of Adam Smith, ➤Ricardo, ➤Malthus and ➤Say. Mill himself said the book had nothing in it that was original, and indeed it is basically an eclectic work, intended simply to bring together the works of others. However, it is not true to say that Mill lacked originality altogether. He analysed the forces which lead to increasing ➤returns to scale, arguing that as a result there will be a tendency for industries to become more and more concentrated in a few firms. The advantages this gave should be set against the disadvantages that will accrue in the form of higher prices from the loss of competition. Recognition of this tendency led him to support strike action by trade unions. Trade unions were a necessary counterweight to the powerful employer (➤Galbraith, J. K.). In his exposition of the theory of ➤value, Mill showed how ➤price is determined by the equality of ➤demand and ➤supply, although he did not demonstrate the relationship by means of graphs or schedules. Mill recognized as a distinct problem the case of ➤commodities with ➤joint costs. He showed also how reciprocal demand for each other's products affected countries' ➤terms of trade. Mill brought in the idea of ➤elasticity of demand (though the actual expression was invented later by ➤Marshall) to analyse various alternative trading possibilities. His father had suggested that ➤rent, being a surplus according to Ricardian theory, was ideally suited to ➤taxation. John Stuart took up this idea, and it became quite popular. Mill proposed that all future increases in unearned rents should be taxed.

Miller, Merton H. (b. 1923) An economist from the University of Chicago, and joint ➤Nobel Prize winner in 1990. Miller's great contribution was in the theory of finance, with ➤Modigliani, F. (➤Modigliani–Miller theorem). Even though the pair's findings were based on a large number of simplifying assumptions, Miller has been pre-eminent in analysing the effect of taxation and bankruptcy costs on optimal company financial structure.

minimum efficient scale (m.e.s.) The scale of production at which further increases in scale would not lead to lower unit costs (➤average costs). ➤Economies of scale are measured in terms of unit costs versus plant size or output. The resulting long-run cost curve is generally thought to be L-shaped. The m.e.s. is the point on this curve where it flattens out. Where the m.e.s. is large and requires large ➤capital expenditure it may act as a ➤barrier to entry, especially where the m.e.s. is large in relation to total market size. Often, however, a number of firms may operate profitably below m.e.s. because the cost disadvantage of doing so is small, or because of product differentiation (➤differentiation, product), or other departures from the theoretical conditions of ➤perfect competition. It should also be remembered that technological economies of scale revealed in plant size are only one of the forces determining the efficiency of firms. ➤transaction costs; X efficiency.

minimum wage Legislation prohibiting the paying of wages below some specified level. The aim of such a prohibition is to boost the incomes of the low paid, or, primarily in the UK, to prevent employers exploiting the existence of government benefits for the low paid, by cutting wages. As a means of helping the poor, minimum wages are of limited efficiency – many poor households have no worker in them and are thus not affected. Many reasonably well-off households have a second earner on low pay, and they are affected. A minimum wage can price labour out of the workforce, and create unemployment. It is at least very difficult to set a national minimum wage that is high enough to help, say, someone supporting a family of three children; while also giving employers sufficient incentive to employ single 18 year olds. In defence of such laws, it has been argued that the demand for labour is in practice very inelastic (➤elasticity) and that minimum-wage laws do not give rise to the problem of the ➤poverty trap. Moreover, they encourage employers to nurture their staff more carefully, and make them more productive (➤efficiency-wage theory).

minorities, minority interest Elements shown in the consolidated accounts of groups of companies where one or more of the ►subsidiaries is not wholly owned by the parent. Where a company owns 95 per cent of the ordinary ►capital of a subsidiary, for example, and its accounts are consolidated, then the whole of the assets and income of the subsidiary will be included in the consolidated accounts. In showing net assets attributable to shareholders of the parent company, 5 per cent in this case belongs to the minority shareholders and must be deducted. Similarly, in calculating ►net income attributable to the same shareholders, earnings will be shown after minority interest.

Mirlees, James A. (b. 1936) A Scottish-born economist, James Mirlees has been a Professor at both Oxford and Cambridge Universities, at the latter since 1995. He received the joint ►Nobel Prize in Economics in 1996. His main area of study has been in the economics of taxation. His achievement has been to analyse the trade-off between equity and efficiency in a tax system, and to derive rules and conditions to govern the imposition of efficient taxes. For example, he is credited with the finding that, under certain assumptions, it is inefficient to impose any tax that affects business production decisions. It is always better to levy taxes on final consumption, and to maintain efficient production. He also investigated the role of marginal tax rates, and the idea that it is better to have higher marginal rates lower down the income spectrum, in order that the rich pay more tax on that middle slice of their income, but themselves face a low marginal rate. He found that that particular advantage was outweighed by the fact that more people were affected by marginal rates in the middle-income spectrum than at that top. He also posited the problem of designing an income tax in terms of ►asymmetric information, in that the government does not know how hard people could work in the absence of a tax.

Mises, Ludwig Edler von (1881–1973) Professor at Vienna University from 1913 until he joined the Graduate Institute of International Studies at Geneva in 1934. In 1940 he left Europe for the USA and was appointed five years later to a professorial chair at New York University, where he stayed until 1969. His published works include *The Theory of Money and Credit* (1912), *The Free and Prosperous Commonwealth* (1927), *Geldwertstabilisierung und Konjunkturpolitik* (1928), *Bureaucracy* (1944), *Omnipotent Government* (1944), *Human Action* (1949), *Theory and History: An Interpretation of Social and Economic Evaluation* (1957) and *The Ultimate Foundation of Economic Science* (1962). Von Mises argued in favour of the ►price system as the most efficient basis of ►resource allocation. A ►planned economy must be wasteful, because it lacks a price system and cannot institute such a system without destroying its political principle. He applied the ►marginal utility theory of the ►Austrian school to develop a new theory of ►money, and pointed out that ►utility could be measured ordinally only and not cardinally (►Hicks, J. R.). He also outlined a ►purchasing-power parity theory comparable to that of Gustav Cassel. His ►business-cycle theory explained fluctuations in terms of an expansion of bank credit in the upturn which caused a fall in the ►rate of interest and surplus ►investment with a consequent reversal when the ►money supply was reduced. ►►Hawtrey, R. G.; Hayek, F. A. von.

Misselden, Edward (1608–54) A leading member of the merchant adventurers and a member of the group of writers referred to as ►mercantilists. He argued that international movements of specie and fluctuations in the ►exchange rate depended on international trade flows and not the manipulations of bankers, which was the popular view. He suggested that trading returns should be established for purposes of statistical analysis, so that the state could regulate trade with a view to obtaining ►export surpluses.

Mitchell, Wesley Clair (1874–1948) ►institutional economics.

mixed economy A market economy in which both private and ►public enterprise participate in economic activity, though not necessarily in all sectors, some of which may be reserved for public ►monopoly. Mixed ownership of the means of production is, in fact, characteristic of all contemporary economic systems. ►►free-market economy; planned economy.

mixed strategy A means of selecting one choice from a set of options, by random selection, on the basis of pre-assigned probabilities attached to each option. It is a concept used in ►game theory, where in certain situations, in order to prevent an opponent guessing your behaviour, your best strategy is behave unpredictably. It is the opposite of a *pure strategy*, in which there is no random element. A mixed strategy is beneficial when, given your opponent's action, you are indifferent between two pure strategies, and when your opponent can benefit from knowing what your next move is. It is best to adopt a mixed strategy in the game tic-tac-toe (sometimes referred to as paper-scissors-stone) for example. An important finding in game theory is that anyone facing a mixed strategy will always find a pure strategy to be among the best responses.

MNC ►multinational corporation.

mobility of capital The ability of investment funds to flow across international borders. Impediments to capital mobility may take the form of restrictions on the inflow of investment funds to a country (restrictions on the rights of foreigners to buy property or companies, for example) or ►exchange control, limiting the ability of domestic citizens to invest overseas. If capital is mobile, investors can lend money to those borrowers who are willing to pay the highest rate of return (after taking into account any expected changes in exchange rates). If they do this enough, and if the ►purchasing-power parity theory holds, real interest rates should converge across countries. In practice they deviate, but not by very much. ►►exchange rate overshooting.

mobility of labour ►labour, mobility of.

mode ➤average.

model A representation of an economic system, relationship or state, that takes any of a variety of forms. At its most informal, a model can be said to consist of a *verbal description* or *analogy* of some real-world phenomenon. It may take the form of a *diagram* (for example, the graph of the ➤cobweb model), or a *set of equations* setting out the relationship between ➤variables (➤consumption as a ➤function of income, for example). In applied economics, a model is likely to be expressed in a computer program or *spreadsheet* in which data (the 'input') are processed and manipulated to produce results (the 'output'). Model-building usually consists of two main stages. The first stage, inspired by economic reasoning, is to develop the structure of the model – setting out what factors affect which variables. Often, this is as far as construction goes. The second stage, often using ➤econometrics, is to estimate the actual strength (➤parameters) of the relationship postulated.

Models have a variety of uses. First, they can illuminate and describe systems clearly by stripping them of all unnecessary complications. Second, computer models in particular are useful for ➤simulation. A variable, such as ➤unemployment, is defined in terms of the values of a set of other variables and, by simulating a change in these, the effect of different policies on unemployment can be estimated. Third, forecasts of the behaviour of variables can be made, based on past observations. Finally, the specification of models is a prerequisite to the testing of different theories. ➤➤empirical testing; hypothesis.

Modigliani, Franco (b. 1918) Born in Rome, Professor Modigliani studied at the University of Rome. Moving to the USA, he obtained his Ph.D. at the School of Social Research in New York in 1944. He was appointed to a Chair of Economics at the University of Illinois in 1949 and in 1952 to the Chair of Industrial Administration at the Carnegie Institute. Since 1962 he has held the post of Professor of Economics and Finance at the Massachusetts Institute of Technology. Professor Modigliani was awarded the ➤Nobel Prize for Economics in 1985. His many published articles in the professional journals have been assembled in *Collected Papers of Franco Modigliani* (1980). He has put forward an explanation of the constancy of the aggregate ➤average propensity to save, in the face of rising incomes in the economy, in terms of the balance between the high savings of the employed workforce and the dissavings of the retired population (➤life-cycle hypothesis). He has also contributed to financial economics. ➤➤Modigliani–Miller theorem.

Modigliani–Miller theorem The proposition that the market value of a firm is independent of the way it chooses to finance its investment or distribute ➤dividends. If a firm wants to expand, it can choose between three methods of financing its investment: borrowing, issuing shares and spending profits rather than giving them to shareholders in the form of dividends. ➤Modigliani and ➤M. H. Miller showed that under a number of assumptions (such as an absence of taxes) in a perfectly functioning capital market the method of financing which a firm chooses will ultimately not affect the cost of capital (➤➤capital, cost of) or the value of the firm. It is the risk and expected rate of return of the expanded firm that will determine how attractive investors find it, not the way the firm raises the money. Any attempt to attract low-cost capital, will probably have the effect of raising the cost of other capital in the company. ➤➤investment appraisal; Ricardian equivalence.

monetarism The name applied to a theory of ➤macroeconomics which holds that increases in the ➤money supply are a necessary and sufficient condition for ➤inflation. Two strands of thought underlie this doctrine and distinguish it from its main theoretical antagonist, ➤Keynesian economics (➤➤Keynes, J. M.):
(a) The first is that changes in the money supply have a substantial effect on ➤aggregate demand. Two separate reasons are given for this. The first is that the demand for money is stable and insensitive to the ➤rate of interest. The second is that the demand for goods in the economy, particularly ➤investment, is sensitive to the interest rate. Together, these determine the monetarists' ➤transmission mechanism, the way in which increases in the money stock affect spending in the economy. Under the monetarist account, if the authorities printed some crisp ten-pound notes and dropped them over the country from a helicopter, people would find they had more cash in this liquid form (➤➤liquidity; liquidity preference) than they wanted. They would therefore spend much of the cash on goods and services, increasing aggregate demand. The rest might be invested in interest-bearing ➤securities; the increase in demand for these, would drive the price up, and the interest rate down. Under the monetarist account, even the smallest cut in interest rate would cause a large increase in investment, again boosting aggregate demand. The contrary account holds that the helicopter money would not be spent at all, but invested in financial assets. The interest rate would fall a great deal, but that investment is insensitive to interest rates, so this would have no effect on the demand for investment goods. In effect, all that happens from expanding the money supply is that interest rates drop, and people hold more cash, without spending it, implying that the speed with which cash circulates has slowed down to offset the extra cash (➤velocity of circulation).
(b) The second tenet of monetarism is that any change in aggregate demand the government succeeds in bringing about will manifest itself (in the long run at least) in higher prices and not higher output. The economy will tend to an equilibrium position with all markets clearing: all that money can do is raise all prices equally, leaving all relative prices constant (➤neutrality of money). Increases in the stock of money can, however, have a short-term effect on the economy, but only as long as the inflation created outstrips people's expectations of inflation. Once inflation is built into people's expectations, increases in the money supply only result in increases in the level of prices.

In terms of the ➤quantity theory of money, of which monetarism can be seen as a revival, the above propositions are equivalent to holding that the velocity of circulation of money and the level of output are ►exogenous, and fixed independently of the money stock.

Monetarists advocate ►supply-side economics; and deny a role for ►stabilization policy. Instead, greatest stability can be achieved by adhering to a rule for money-supply growth in line with the growth of real output (►real terms). The emergence of monetarism in the 1960s and among policy-makers in the 1970s can mainly be attributed to ►M. Friedman. (►►economic doctrines.) The doctrine has been somewhat superseded by the theoretically more elegant theory deriving similar results, from ►new classical economics. ►policy ineffectiveness theorem.

monetary base The stock of an economy's most liquid financial assets (►liquidity). The monetary base is usually taken as the stock of notes and coins, and the banks' own deposits at the ►central bank. It has often been suggested that the ►money supply as a whole could be controlled by strict rationing of the monetary base. However, the base is very small relative to the total money supply, so rather sensitive changes to the base could lead to instability in the money supply as a whole.

monetary compensatory amounts ►green currency.

monetary policy Central government policy with respect to the quantity of money (►quantity theory of money) in the economy, the ►rate of interest and the ►exchange rate. Monetary policy is now broadly accepted as having the predominant role in the control of ►aggregate demand, and therefore of ►inflation. This owes much to the rise of the doctrine of ►monetarism and to the defeat of the popular interpretation of ►Keynes, who was held to believe that ►fiscal policy was more important, and that monetary policy matters only in as far as it affects fiscal variables, like the ►public-sector borrowing requirement.

In deciding on how to conduct monetary policy, the authorities must make a number of decisions. The first is whether to adopt a monetary rule, or not. This might involve targeting growth in ►money supply (broad or narrow money), or stability of the ►exchange rate. If no such target is chosen, monetary policy becomes a matter of daily judgement about the manipulation of several variables. A second issue, following from the first, is which variable to target: it is not possible to set up targets individually for the money supply, the exchange rate and interest rates because the three are simultaneously determined. If the money supply is increased, for example, the exchange rate tends to fall unless interest rates are raised. To target or stabilize one variable implies at least one other must be an instrument by which the first can be controlled. Exchange-rate targets, such as those that existed for members of the ►European Exchange Rate Mechanism, encourage trade by reducing the risk of exchange-rate fluctuations, while targeting money supply, it is argued, can have an impact on ►credibility, and hence (somewhat implausibly) on wage demands; plus, money-supply targeting can better reflect domestic economic needs. The third decision – or set of decisions – is how to conduct policy in the absence of a rule. Should there be an ➤inflation target, to guide the daily implementation of policy. Should control be in the hands of elected politicians, or an independent ➤central bank? Should policy be conducted through the power of the authorities to determine market interest rates, or should there be other forms of monetary control (➤credit control)?

While monetarists appear to have essentially won the battle over the importance and objectives of monetary policy, they lost the battle over the conduct of policy. They supported the use of simple money supply growth rules, yet the experiences of the UK and USA in following such rules were unhappy. Even the ➤Bundesbank, which does target money supply, applies its policies with discretion.

monetary policy committee The nine-person committee of the ➤Bank of England, charged with setting interest rates in the UK. The committee consists of the Bank's governor, the two deputy-governors, two other officials of the Bank, plus four economists nominated by the government. It is accountable to the Court of the Bank of England, and to MPs through the House of Commons Treasury and Civil Service Select Committee. It meets monthly, and the minutes of its proceedings are published. The committee is charged with setting interest rates to meet the government's explicit ➤inflation target. ➤➤credibility, monetary policy.

monetary sector (UK) Defined by the ➤Bank of England to include its own banking department, the ➤retail banks, ➤accepting houses, other British and foreign banks and the ➤discount houses. Other ➤financial intermediaries such as the ➤building societies, insurance companies and ➤pension funds are not counted as part of the monetary sector.

money Something which is widely accepted in payment for goods and services and in settling ➤debts. In primitive economies, goods and services were exchanged wholly through ➤barter. Exchanging goods for one another or using property (cows, sheep) as money was cumbersome and inconvenient and inhibited the ➤division of labour. Later, coins made of valuable metals came into use as intermediate commodities, but in the modern economy ➤banknotes and coins have little or no intrinsic value, while ➤bank deposits are simply book entries (➤banking): their use as money depends upon confidence that they can be exchanged for things of value. In addition to its use as a medium of exchange, money acts as a store of value, making ➤saving convenient, a measure of value (or unit of account) and as a standard of deferred payments which facilitates the granting of ➤credit, though all these functions can be threatened by ➤inflation. ➤➤money supply; transactions motive.

money, demand for ➤liquidity preference.

money, inactive ➤inactive money.

money, neutrality of ➤neutrality of money.

money, superneutrality of ►superneutrality of money.

money at call and short notice In Britain, ►money loaned to the ►discount houses, i.e. to the ►money market, on a short-term basis by the ►commercial banks. These ►loans are regarded as part of the ►liquid assets of the banks because they can be withdrawn immediately or at periods of notice of up to fourteen days. They also include overnight loans. The terms of the loans vary, and in practice the money may not be called in for long periods. The discount houses use the money to purchase ►treasury bills and other short-term paper, so that the call-money rate is normally always below the treasury bills' rate. If the banks do call in their loans, then the discount houses may be forced to borrow from the ►Bank of England. The commercial banks are willing to loan their liquid funds to the money market in this way, because they know that the Bank of England will act as a ►lender of last resort. In most other countries the major commercial banks invest directly in short-term paper and have direct access to the ►central bank for loans (e.g. ►Federal Reserve System).

money illusion The confusion of changes in money values and changes in real values. If someone's salary is increased by 10 per cent over a period when consumer prices have risen by 20 per cent, he is suffering from money illusion if he thinks he is better off in ►real terms.

money in circulation ►Money in use to finance current transactions as distinct from idle money (►inactive money).

money market The financial institutions that deal in short-term ►securities and ►loans, gold and ►foreign exchange. ►Money has a 'time value', and therefore the use of it is bought and sold against payment of ►interest. Short-term money is bought and sold on the money market, and long-term money on the ►capital market. Neither the money market nor the capital market exists in one physical location. In the money market most transactions are, in fact, made by telephone or electronically. In Britain the money market sometimes refers only to the ►discount houses and the ►commercial banks dealing in ►treasury bills, ►bills of exchange and ►money at call, with the ►Bank of England acting as ►lender of last resort (►discount market). In a wider context, the money market also includes ►parallel money markets, the ►foreign-exchange market and the ►bullion market.

money supply The stock of liquid assets in an economy which can freely be exchanged for goods or services. Money supply is a phrase that can describe anything from notes and coins alone (►monetary base), to the sum of all cash plus bank deposits, because by writing cheques, individuals exchange bank deposits for goods or services. There is a spectrum of assets of differing ►liquidity in the economy, and any degree of liquidity may be chosen to define an asset as money. A set of very liquid assets is known as narrow money. A set includes also less liquid assets, known as *broad money*. In general, the wider the definition, the harder it is for the authorities to control the money supply, but the more direct the relationship between money supply and other economic variables. For example, the quantity of notes and coins in the economy, a narrow definition, is easy to control, but is of little importance in influencing the spending of individuals.

In the UK several definitions of money supply are used for monitoring the money supply. 'M0' is the stock of sterling notes and coins in circulation, plus the banks' deposits at the Bank of England. 'M4' is a much broader definition, embracing notes and coins, plus the value of all UK sterling bank (►banking) and building society accounts held by private citizens and companies. Because some of these are not really used to support transactions, they are more a form of savings. Since 1993 the Bank of England has also published an index of growth in *divisia money*. This simply takes the elements of M4, and weights them by the degree to which they are used for financing transactions. It is, in essence, a measure of M4, adjusted to give more importance to the more liquid part. At times of rapid financial innovation or change, particular definitions can exhibit rather erratic behaviour, compounding the problems of control and interpretation of the money supply. ►credit control; domestic credit expansion; monetary policy.

money terms ►real terms.

Monopolies and Mergers Commission A UK commission set up by the Monopolies and Restrictive Practices (Inquiry and Control) Act of 1948. Under this Act the Commission was given the necessary powers to obtain any information it needed to investigate monopolies referred to it by the Board of Trade. ►monopoly was defined in a broad way to include any firm which controlled more than one-third (later, one-quarter) of the ►market, and the Commission was required to judge them in the light of the public interest. The Commission's report in 1955, *Collective Discrimination: A Report on Exclusive Dealing, Aggregated Rebates and Other Discriminatory Trade Practices*, was the basis for the ►Restrictive Trade Practices Act of 1956, which set up a register for collective agreements and a Restrictive Practices Court. The Commission's powers were widened by the Monopolies and Mergers Act of 1965. ►mergers between firms in a monopoly situation or over a certain size could be referred to the Commission by the Board of Trade (later the Department of Trade and Industry) and also firms in the service industries which had previously been exempt. The Acts of 1948 and 1965 were repealed by the ►Fair Trading Act of 1973. Under this the Director-General of Fair Trading was empowered to make references, in addition to the Minister. The powers of the Office of Fair Trading (OFT) were widened by the ►Competition Act (1980). As a result, any activity considered by the OFT to be anti-competitive could be referred to the Commission. A review of merger policy published in 1988 reaffirmed that reference of mergers for investigation by the Commission would continue to be made primarily, though not exclusively, on competition grounds. The regulation of the take-over process itself has been left to voluntary arrangements (►Take-Over Panel). The Companies Act 1989 (►company law) requires the disclosure of holdings in other companies and a voluntary procedure for pre-notification of proposed mergers to the OFT. ►monopolistic (imperfect) competition.

monopolistic (imperfect) competition Competition in an industry in which there are many firms each producing products that are close, but not perfect, ►substitutes. Three features characterize such an industry. First, the firms make products between which consumers slightly differentiate (they may have different-coloured packets, for example) and consequently, the demand for any individual firm's product is not perfectly elastic (►►elasticity). Some consumers will prefer one product to those of its competitors, sufficiently to exhibit a limited amount of loyalty to that brand when its price rises. This means that each firm has a small amount of ►market power (►monopoly) and is thus not a price-taker in the market for its own product. In this regard it is similar to a monopoly, but not a perfect competitor (►perfect competition). The second feature is that firms are able to enter the industry if the level of ►profits is attractive. This is a feature shared with the perfectly competitive industry, but not the monopoly. Thirdly, like both perfectly competitive and monopolistic firms, producers in monopolistic competition are assumed to maximize profits.

In monopolistic competition, firms set output to equate ►marginal cost and ►marginal revenue. Price at the specified output is determined by demand. Profits are zero in the long term, on account of entry occurring whenever they are positive, driving up ►supply in the industry and cutting the ►demand for each company's product. While it shares this with perfect competition, its output will be rather lower than it would be under perfect competition, and its price above marginal cost and thus rather higher. Moreover, production will not take place at the lowest cost point as it does under perfect competition. Each firm operates with some ►excess capacity. The theory of such markets, which lie between monopoly and perfect competition, was simultaneously developed by ►Chamberlin in the USA and ►Robinson in Britain.

monopoly A market in which there is only one supplier. Three features characterize a monopoly market. First, the firm in it is motivated by ►profits. Secondly, it stands alone and barriers prevent new firms from entering the industry (►barriers to entry); and thirdly, the actions of the monopolist itself affect the market price of its output (►marginal revenue) – it is not a price-taker. The *output* of the monopolist will be set at the point at which marginal revenue is equated with ►marginal cost. If marginal revenue were any higher it would pay the monopolist to increase production because the additional costs generated would be lower than the revenue, and profits would rise. The reverse would be true if marginal revenue were any lower than marginal cost. (►►marginal-cost pricing.) The price of the monopolist is determined by ►demand as the firm cannot set both output and price. For its chosen output, the monopolist can read price off a market ►demand curve, which will lie above the marginal revenue curve.

The monopoly will make profits in excess of those merely necessary to keep in business, and no pressure exists for price to fall and reduce these. Theory suggests that, under monopoly, prices are higher and output lower than they would be under ►perfect competition. The power of the monopolist derives from the fact that demand for his product is not perfectly elastic (➤➤elasticity) so that, when price rises, sales largely hold up. This is not so for a perfect competitor, who will sell nothing if he raises his price even a fraction above the going rate. The degree of *monopoly power* a firm enjoys can be measured by how inelastic demand for its product is. The more inelastic demand is, the more the monopoly can raise its prices without losing sales.

Monopoly is held to be inefficient because, under it, price will be higher than marginal cost so that, even if some consumers value an item more than it costs to make, they may not choose to buy it (➤➤marginal-cost pricing). Moreover, in the long term there is no tendency for costs to be at their lowest possible level, because the pressure of more efficient, incoming competitors does not exist. It is not surprising given these results that most nations choose to control monopolies, which are usually defined as any firm dominant in a particular industry (for example, with a market share in excess of 25 per cent). However, in some industries, efficient production requires a single dominant supplier (►economies of scale; natural monopoly; regulation). Moreover, a distinction has to be made between a monopoly that has earned its dominance, and one which has not. It is possible that consumers benefit from monopoly in the long run, if the profits generated act as a spur to ►innovation. (►Schumpeter, J. A.) And in any event, defining monopoly is a more subtle process than it looks – almost no company really has a monopoly. Even what appears to be a monopoly gas company faces some competition from electricity suppliers. ➤➤bilateral monopoly; contestability.

monopoly, discriminating A ►monopoly that charges different prices for the same product to different consumers. ➤➤price discrimination.

monopsony A market in which there is only one buyer of the item sold. Unlike individual consumers in most markets, a monopsonist will have an impact on the market price. When he purchases an extra unit of the item, market demand perceptibly increases and the market price rises. This means that to buy one extra item costs the monopsonist not only the price of that item, but also the extra price that has to be paid for all the items that were previously being bought at the lower price. ➤➤bilateral monopoly.

Monte Carlo method A technique for estimating ►probabilities. The method involves the construction of a ►model and the ►simulation of the outcome of an activity a large number of times. Probabilities are then estimated from an analysis of the range of outcomes from the model.

moral hazard The presence of incentives for individuals to act in ways that incur costs that they do not have to bear. A typical case is that of insurance, because once someone has insured their house against burglary they do not have the incentive to be as careful as they otherwise would be to protect their property. Another example would be the incentive to find a job – perhaps a rather less than satisfying one – given the existence of state benefits for the out of work (►job seeker's allowance). Moral hazard is one of those important market distortions based upon imperfect information, as it is the inability of, say, the insurer to distinguish the well-behaved claimant from the badly behaved one that creates the problem. ►dependency culture; incentive compatibility; principal – agent problem.

mortgage A legal agreement conveying conditional ownership of ►assets as ►security for a ►loan and becoming void when the ►debt is repaid. ►Building societies, banks (►banking) and ►insurance companies (*mortgagees*) loan a proportion of the purchase ►price of houses to individuals or companies (*mortgagors*), the property being mortgaged to the lender until the loan is repaid.

mortgage debenture ►debenture.

most-favoured nation clause The clause in an international trade treaty under which the signatories promise to extend to each other any favourable trading terms offered in agreements with third parties. ►General Agreement on Tariffs and Trade; generalized system of preferences.

moving average A ►time series derived from another by the calculation of a sequence of ►averages. The averages are calculated in sequence from a consecutive group in the series; for each average, the next value in the series is added and the earliest value in the group is dropped. The number of values in the group to be averaged may be two or more, depending on the time series from which they are to be derived. Moving averages are calculated to eliminate seasonal variations from a series and to highlight the longer-term trends.

MPC ►marginal propensity to consume.

MPS ►marginal propensity to save.

MRS ►marginal rate of substitution.

MTFS ►medium-term financial strategy.

multicollinearity ►correlation between the ►independent variables in a regression (►regression analysis) equation. If such correlation exists, the application of ►least-squares regression for estimation of the parameters in an equation is difficult, because it is hard to determine which of several correlated variables is truly influential.

Multi-Fibre Arrangement (MFA) An international arrangement within which individual importing and exporting countries agreed that specified textile and clothing goods would be subject to ►import quotas. The aim was to protect the textile industries in high-wage countries from being overwhelmed by imports from low-wage countries. The first MFA was put in place in 1974, and renewed in 1978, 1982 and 1986. The fourth expired in 1991. Under the terms of the ►Uruguay round of trade negotiations initiated by the ►General Agreement on Tariffs and Trade the MFA is being phased out. Quotas should be abolished in stages, between 1995 and 2005. ►►developing country; international commodity agreements.

Multilateral Investment Guarantee Agency An agency of the World Bank (►International Bank for Reconstruction and Development) which was established in 1988 and is open to all members of the World Bank. The Agency gives guarantees and ►insurance cover for private direct ►investment in ►developing countries against non-commercial risks such as the imposition of►foreign exchange restrictions, war and the expropriation of assets. The Agency is financed from incomes received from insurance premiums and financial contributions made available by member countries, amounting to US$1 billion. ►export credit insurance.

multilateralism ►international trade and exchange between more than two countries without discrimination between those involved. In contrast to ►bilateralism. ►►General Agreement on Tariffs and Trade; most-favoured nation clause.

multinational corporation, multinational enterprise (MNC, MNE) A company, or more correctly an ►enterprise, operating in a number of countries and having production or service facilities outside the country of its origin. A commonly accepted definition of an MNE is an enterprise producing at least 25 per cent of its world output outside its country of origin. There are, according to United Nations estimates, 35,000 corporations with direct investments outside their headquarters country, with over 170,000 affiliates over which they have effective control. The 100 largest MNEs account for about 40 per cent of cross-border assets. The multinational corporation takes its principal decisions in a global context and thus often outside the countries in which it has particular operations. The rapid growth of these corporations since the Second World War and the possibility that conflicts might arise between their interests and those of the individual countries in which they operate has provoked much discussion among economists. MNEs possibly account for over one-quarter of world trade, but earlier fears that they would come to dominate the world economy now seem misplaced. Bartlett and Ghoshal make distinctions between three types of international company which are widely accepted as useful. They argue that neither the decentralized types of business with strong local presence (*multinational*), nor the more centralized types of business which builds cost advantages through centralized production (*global*) or exploit the parent company's ►research and development and systems capability (*international*) are now sufficient to maximize competitiveness. These authors claim that the *transnational* company which somehow blends these approaches by differentiating contributions by national units to a none the less highly integrated world-wide operation has the most successful approach.

multi-plant operations Firms which produce at more than one plant or location. Most small firms operate from a single establishment. Large firms serving a national market, for example in the brewing industry, may find that lower transport costs to the final consumer from multiple plants outweigh the ►economies of scale in a single large plant. ►►enterprise.

multiple correlation coefficient A statistical measure of the accuracy by which a known ►variable is estimated by an equation, or ►model, containing two or more ►independent variables (►►correlation). It can take values between zero and one. At zero, there is no correspondence at all between the predicted and actual variable, and at unity the coefficient indicates a perfect correspondence. Also called the *coefficient of determination* and R-squared (►partial correlation; regression analysis).

multiplier An increase in ► national income divided by the increase in expenditure generating that increase in income. In simple models, the size of the multiplier depends on the ►marginal propensity to consume. For example, if the government increased its investment expenditure by £100, this sum would be paid out in wages, salaries and profits of the suppliers. The households and firms receiving these incomes and profits will, in turn, save a proportion and spend the remainder. These expenditures will in turn again generate further incomes and profits and so on. At each round, therefore, a proportion of receipts will be paid and a proportion spent, the latter being the marginal propensity to consume, denoted, say, by c. We have, therefore:

	Expenditure	*Saving*
Round 1	£100	
2	£100c	£100$(1 - c)$
3	£100c^2	£100$(1 - c)^2$
.	.	.
.	.	.
.	.	.
n	£100c^n	£100$(1 - c)^n$

and, therefore, the total increase in national income generated by the £100 is the sum of the infinite number of expenditures:

$$£100 + £100c + £100c^2 + £100c^3 + \ldots £100c^n$$
$$= £100(1 + c + c^2 + c^3 + \ldots c^n)$$

multi-product firm

This series is the sum of a ►geometric progression whose sum can be shown to be equal to £100[(1 − c^n) (1 − c)]. The marginal propensity to consume is less than unity, so that as n gets larger, c^n becomes smaller. Therefore, the series converges to £100/(1 − c) and the multiplier is, therefore, equal to 1/(1 − c) or 1/s, where s is the marginal propensity to save. ►►accelerator–multiplier model; Keynes, J. M.

multi-product firm A business producing two or more different ►commodities or products. Most large firms produce more than one product and are often engaged in more than one industry (►diversification), although for simplicity the basic theory of the firm (►firm, theory of the) is couched in terms of a single-product firm.

Mun, Sir Thomas (1571–1641) An English mercantilist (►mercantilism) and a director of the East India Company. His publications include *Discourse of Trade from England unto the East Indies* (1621) and *England's Treasure of Forraign Trade* (1664). He attacked the idea that ►exports of ►bullion should be completely prohibited and other restrictions put on trade, pointing out that restrictions on trade invited retaliation in foreign ►markets and raised domestic ►prices. He did emphasize, however, that an export surplus should be sought in the ►balance of trade for the country as a whole, although it was unnecessary to seek to achieve this with each trading partner.

mutual company A company without issued ►capital stock owned by those members that do business with it. The ►profits of a mutual company, after deductions for reserves, are shared out among members. Some ►savings banks and ►insurance companies, e.g. Standard Life, are mutual companies. In the USA the term 'mutual' is also used to refer to open-ended ►trusts or *mutual funds*, which correspond to ►unit trusts in the UK. ►Building societies in the UK are mutual organizations, but recently some have demutualized and incorporated and sought ►flotation so as to facilitate ►mergers and capital-raising. Since mutual companies are owned by their members (e.g. depositors) in these cases members have received ►shares in the newly floated enterprises.

mutual funds ►mutual company.

Myrdal, Gunnar Karl (1898–1987) Born in Sweden, Professor Myrdal graduated in law at Stockholm University in 1923. After a period in private practice, he obtained a degree in economics in 1927 and took a post as lecturer in political economy at Stockholm University, eventually succeeding ►Cassel to the Chair of Political Economy and Financial Science in 1933. From 1936 to 1938 he was a Member of Parliament as a Social Democrat. After a period as Economic Adviser to the Swedish legation in the USA, he was appointed Minister of Commerce in the Swedish government, a post he held from 1945 to 1947. He resigned from this post to become Secretary-General of the UN Economic Commission for

Europe at Geneva, where he stayed until 1957. In 1957 he was appointed Professor at the Institute for International Economic Studies of Stockholm University and in 1974 was awarded the ►Nobel Prize in Economics jointly with von ►Hayek. His published work includes *Price Formation under Changeability* (1927), *Vetenskap och Politik i Nationalekonomin* (1929), *Om Penningteoretisk Jamvikt* (1931), *An American Dilemma* (1944), *Economic Theory and Underdeveloped Regions* (1957), *Value in Social Theory* (1958), *Beyond the Welfare State* (1960), *Challenge to Affluence* (1963), *Asian Drama: An Inquiry into the Poverty of Nations* (1968), *Objectivity in Social Research* (1969), *The Challenge of World Poverty* (1970) and *Against the Stream – Critical Essays in Economics* (1973). Professor Myrdal invented the terms and formulated the distinction between ►ex ante and ►ex post, in particular in relation to the equality of aggregate savings and investment in equilibrium. He emphasized the need to study the dynamics of ►macroeconomic processes. His book, *Monetary Equilibrium*, published in 1931, which developed the economics of ►Wicksell, foreshadowed many aspects of ►Keynes's *General Theory*. In recent years, he argued that economists should accept the need to make explicit value judgements, without which their theoretical structures are unrealistic. He became an advocate of ►institutional economics. Professor Myrdal believed that such a framework was necessary in any economic studies of the ►developing countries.

N

NACE ➤Standard Industrial Classification.

NAIRU Non-accelerating inflation rate of unemployment (➤unemployment, natural rate of).

NASDAQ National Association of Securities Dealers Automated Quotations system (➤over-the-counter market).

Nash, John F. (b. 1928) A mathematician from Princeton University in New Jersey, John Nash has put his name to the most important concept of ➤equilibrium as applied to ➤game theory. He jointly won the ➤Nobel Prize for Economics in 1994 (with ➤John Harsanyi and ➤Reinhard Selten) for the achievement. He drew the important distinction between *cooperative games* and *non-cooperative games,* where players have incompatible interests and are unable to make binding agreements to maximize joint welfare. He outlined the equilibrium notion, in which all players' expectations are fulfilled, and all players' strategies are optimal. While this notion remains the foundation of most discussion in game theory, it is not sufficiently limiting to be universally interesting as a tool of analysis. Moreover, it relies on each player having complete information about the other players' options. More refined equilibrium concepts have been developed by Harsanyi and Selten.

Nash equilibrium A concept central to ➤game theory, which characterizes any situation where all the participants in a game are pursuing their best possible strategy given the strategies of all the other participants. A game is any situation in which there are participants, rules of conduct and pay-offs. One might imagine a simple game in a two-person country where both the people have to decide the side of the road on which to drive. The pay-offs are either 'no crash' (when both drive on the left or right) or 'crash' (when one drives on the left and the other on the right). In this situation, two possible Nash equilibria exist: either both driving on the left, or both driving on the right. If one drives on the left and the other on the right, it is not a Nash equilibrium because, given the choice of the other, each would change their own policy. Popular examples of Nash equilibria arise in ➤Hotelling's law and the ➤prisoner's dilemma. (➤➤equilibrium.) The Nash equilibria are considered a rather weak basis for determining the likely outcome of a game, as in some cases Nash equilibria can involve players choosing ➤dominated strategies – strategies that can easily be bettered. In other cases, the Nash equilibria can be upheld by the use of implausible threats by one player. Even though the threat would not be likely to be carried out, it can influence a Nash equilibrium. For these reasons, economists have searched for other notions of 'solving' games. Nash nevertheless represents the starting-point for all discussion on the subject. ➤Selten, R.

national accounts ➤social accounting.

National Association of Securities Dealers Automated Quotations system (NASDAQ) (US) ➤over-the-counter market.

national debt The total outstanding borrowings of the central government ➤Exchequer. It represents the stock of borrowing, as opposed to the annual increase in total borrowing, represented by the government deficit (➤public sector borrowing requirement). In the UK in 1997 it was announced that an explicit goal of ➤fiscal policy, would be to stabilize the ratio of debt to GDP. Under the provisions of the Maastricht Treaty, countries entering ➤European Monetary Union are expected to keep debt below, or falling towards, 60 per cent of GDP.

Two different definitions of the debt are in common use. *Net public sector debt* measures the ➤public sector financial liabilities to the private sector and abroad, net of short-term financial assets. *Gross general government debt* – the variable used in the Maastricht Treaty – excludes ➤nationalized industries and measures total financial liabilities, before netting off short-term financial assets.

Until 1968 the debt was transacted through the ➤Consolidated fund but it now appears in the ➤National Loans Fund. The National Debt Commissioners and the National Investment and Loans Office have certain responsibilities towards the debt.

The UK national debt as a proportion of the ➤gross domestic product declined almost continuously from 1945 until 1990. In the 1970s it did not rise despite high levels of government borrowing, as ➤inflation eroded the value of the debt; unaided by any such luck in the 1990s, the ratio of gross debt to GDP jumped from under 34 per cent in 1990/91, to 55 per cent in 1996/97. The nominal (➤nominal value) amount outstanding in 1996 was some £392 billion. The bulk of sterling market holdings of the national debt consists of government and government-guaranteed stock and most of the remainder consists of national savings (➤National Savings, Department for). Some of the debt is held by government agencies, so that the net national debt, which excludes debt held by government, is lower than the gross debt.

The national debt can be divided into three categories: (a) ➤funded debt, that is, ➤irredeemable securities. This is now only a very small part of the total. (b) ➤floating debt, which in this context refers to short-term borrowings such as ➤treasury bills and ➤ways and means advances. (c) Other unfunded debt. This is the largest item of all, accounting for about three-quarters of the total. It includes principally ➤dated securities, some of which are repayable in external currencies such as dollar liabilities, but also non-marketable securities such as National

Savings Certificates and premium savings bonds. The national debt is of great importance in the financial system of the private sector and plays quite an important role in the interdepartmental accounting of government. Government securities provide convenient investments for ►insurance companies, for example, and these securities form an important part of the reserve assets of banks and other financial institutions. Although it is spoken of as a burden, the interest paid on the national debt held by UK residents is not a burden on the nation as a whole since the interest payments are actually transfers between those residents who pay taxation and those who also receive the interest.

national income The total incomes of residents of an economy in a given period after providing for ►capital consumption. Also referred to as *net national product at factor cost* (►factor cost). Incomes in this calculation include all payments for the use of the ►factors of production, i.e. wages, salaries, ►profits (i.e. ►dividends and retained profits), ►rents and net income from abroad but excluding ►transfer payments. The national income may be calculated in this way, or as the sum of ►value added in all sectors of the economy at factor cost, or as the sum of expenditure on final consumption and ►investment goods, plus ►exports and minus ►imports. These three methods should, in theory, yield the same figure since all incomes should equal total expenditure plus net ►saving or ►investment, which in turn should also equal the value of output (provided output is defined as value added, i.e. intermediate expenditure is excluded). In practice, each of the three methods involves estimation and the totals can significantly diverge, so an averaging procedure is often used. Comparisons of output and expenditure will be affected, among other things, by the extent of evasion (►black economy). National income before capital consumption is equal to the gross national product and, if net income from abroad is also excluded, it is equal to the gross domestic product. Comparisons between the national incomes of various countries are subject to many qualifications: the distribution of income will differ and so too may methods of estimation; moreover, the exchange rates used may not reflect purchasing-power parities (►purchasing-power parity theory).

National income or other aggregates from the national accounts are regarded as an indicator of national welfare in the market economy but they are not unambiguous in this respect. One reason is that some activities which contribute to national welfare are not included because they are not valued in markets, for example the work done by mothers in bringing up their own children. Environmental costs, such as pollution, and the depletion of natural resources are not included in the accounts (►►environmental accounting).

National Insurance (NI) A social security scheme in the UK which provides ►jobseeker's allowance, sickness benefit, flat-rate pensions, maternity benefits and other grants or benefits on widowhood or incapacity in return for regular contributions paid by employees, employers and others. National Insurance made provision for benefits not on the basis of a ►means test, but on the basis of defined causes of hardship, for those who had paid NI contributions. National Insurance has faced serious challenges. It was always necessary to have a means-tested safety-net system for those in hardship, who had not made contributions. That is the *income support* system, with other related benefits like family credit and housing benefit. Since National Insurance was introduced, the growth of contingencies (such as lone-parenthood) affecting people not covered by NI has been such that the size of the safety-net scheme approaches that of the NI.

NI started out with flat-rate contributions, and flat-rate benefits. In 1961 income-related contributions were levied and, to maintain an actuarial connection between contribution and benefit, income-related pensions were introduced and earnings-related premiums to unemployment and sickness insurance in 1966. In the 1970s and 1980s these were dropped, by which time NI was entirely based on earnings-related contributions, and flat-rate benefits. The actuarial principle had been all but abandoned.

The NI system, however, passes one important test in relation to pensions. Under NI, there is a flat-rate pension, and a top-up pension scheme, the State Earnings-Related Pension Scheme, SERPS. This was introduced in 1978. However, it became apparent that SERPS was unaffordable in the long term, and the government took measures to encourage people to 'contract out' of SERPS, and put money into an ►occupational pension or a ►personal pension instead. This has reduced SERPS to little more than a fall-back top-up pension scheme, for those on incomes too low to make it worth contributing to a private scheme. As a result of these reforms, and the fact that the flat-rate pension has been indexed to prices rather than earnings, the NI scheme will, somewhat exceptionally for western world pension systems, be affordable in the mid-2000s, even though the population will have aged, and the NI scheme is not funded. ►demographic time bomb; pension funds.

National Insurance Fund ►Consolidated fund.

National Loans Fund A government account opened in 1968 for the domestic lending of government and all the transactions relating to the ►national debt. The *payments* of the Fund include interest, management and expenses of the national debt, deficit on the ►Consolidated fund and loans to the nationalized industries and public corporations, local authorities and the private sector. *Receipts* include interest on loans, profits of the Issue Department of the ►Bank of England, interest transfer from the Consolidated fund and borrowings.

national product ►national income.

National Savings Bank (NSB) A ►savings bank administered by the Department for National Savings and operating through the post office network. The NSB has some 16 million accounts. It was formerly called the Post Office Savings Bank (POSB).

National Savings certificates A ►bond issued by the government. There have been over 50 different issues of these certificates on which interest, an index-linked increase (►indexation) or a bonus is payable on ►maturity or earlier. The certificates can be encashed at any time and interest is tax-free.

nationalized industries State-owned enterprises in the market sector of an economy, such as a post office, as distinct from state activity in ►public goods such as defence. In Britain most nationalized industry was literally private industry that was taken into public ownership, i.e. nationalized; for example, British Steel, British Leyland (now the Rover Group) and Rolls-Royce. In the UK as in other European countries most of the public utilities, electricity, water, coal, transport and communications undertakings are, or were, in state ownership, although several countries, led by Britain, have engaged in a programme of denationalization (►privatization). The growth of nationalization largely began after the Second World War and has always been a subject of controversy in Britain: the steel industry was nationalized in 1951, denationalized in 1953 and renationalized in 1967. The heads of these industries have often complained of political interference, for example in the interests of broader ►macroeconomic objectives. Whatever the relative merits of state versus private enterprise, some form of ►regulation in many nationalized industries is inevitable given their economic importance and ►monopoly powers.

natural monopoly An industry in which technical factors preclude the efficient existence of more than one producer (►monopoly). Examples are the public utilities such as water, gas and electricity, where there is a requirement for a network of pipes or cables. In order to derive the efficient (►economic efficiency) results of ►perfect competition from a market which is necessarily monopolistic various suggestions of control have been made: notably, government regulation if the firm is in private ownership, ►public ownership and ►franchising. Under any of these, control is enhanced if the monopoly can be regionally divided, allowing performance comparison between different regions (►yardstick competition). Alternatively, licensing arrangements can be set up so that a dominant supplier runs a network (e.g. pipes or cables), but is obliged to lease the use of it to competing suppliers. ►►privatization; regulation.

natural rate of growth ►growth theory; Harrod–Domar model.

natural resources Commodities or assets with some economic ►value which exist without any effort of mankind. The value they have is usually only realized, however, when they are exploited, that is, dug out of the ground, processed or refined. Natural resources are a necessary ingredient of all economic activity. Natural resources can be of three types. The first is *non-renewable*, like oil and coal, stocks of which will eventually run out (►depletion theory). The second is *renewable*, like water and fish, which are reproducible. The third is *non-expendable*: it is not used up in the consumption process. An example is a landscape of outstanding beauty, which yields ➤utility for those that see it, and tourist income for the owner. ➤➤environmental economics.

near money An ➤asset which like ➤money acts as a store of value but which is not immediately acceptable as a medium of exchange, for example a ➤building society deposit. What constitutes money and what does not, however, is controversial and important for defining the ➤money supply. ➤divisia money.

neo-classical economics The dominant school of economic thought since ➤Marshall, characterized by ➤microeconomic theoretical systems constructed to explore conditions of ➤static equilibrium (➤comparative static equilibrium analysis). Neoclassical models are based around maximizing behaviour of individual firms and consumers, with decisions at the margin (➤marginal analysis) often most important. Statements about macro-events are often derived from the aggregation of micro-relationships, and this has led to criticism, particularly from the ➤Cambridge school. In contrast to ➤Keynes, the neo-classical economists consider that savings determine investment (rather than the other way around). Equilibrium is achieved at full employment by changes in ➤factor prices. Essentially, the neo-classical school has been concerned with the problems of equilibrium and growth at full employment, again in contrast to Keynes, who was primarily concerned with the underemployment of resources. ➤➤Keynesian economics; Samuelson, P. A.

neo-classical synthesis Description given to the dominant economic consensus in ➤macroeconomics during the 1960s, between those supporting ➤Keynesian economics, and those based on ➤neo-classical economics. The compromise doctrine essentially held that, in principle, the economy did have natural mechanisms to ensure full employment, but that, in practice, ➤Keynes's analysis of the potential persistence of unemployment without government action, was well-founded. ➤economic doctrines.

net assets The ➤capital employed in a business. It is calculated from the ➤balance sheet by taking fixed ➤assets plus current assets less current ➤liabilities. Often used as a basis for calculating ➤rate of return on ➤capital.

net capital employed ➤capital employed.

net capital formation ➤capital formation.

net cash flow ➤cash flow.

net domestic product ➤gross domestic product less capital consumption.

net income Net ➤profit on earnings after tax and, where appropriate, after ➤minority interest.

net investment The addition to the ➤capital stock after gross expenditure on ➤capital formation and ➤capital consumption has been deducted. Corresponds to capital expenditure minus ➤depreciation in accounting terms.

net national product ➤national income.

net output ➤value added.

net present value ➤present value.

net profit ➤profit.

net tangible asset ratio ➤financial ratios.

net tangible assets (NTA) Fixed ➤assets plus current assets minus intangible assets such as goodwill and minus current ➤liabilities.

net worth ➤balance sheet.

net worth ratio ➤financial ratios.

neutrality of money The inability of changes in the stock of ➤money in an economy to affect anything except the general level of prices. If money is neutral, an increase in the ➤money supply causes ➤inflation, but stimulates no growth in the real level of output. The issue of whether money is neutral or not is central to debates in ➤macroeconomics. In ➤classical economics and under ➤monetarism, money *is* held to be neutral. ➤Keynes and his followers, however, have had a more complicated attitude to monetary neutrality. On the one hand, they have downgraded the importance of money in influencing ➤aggregate demand; on the other hand, they have argued that aggregate demand has an important role in influencing real ➤variables; because of this latter belief, modern Keynesian economics is associated with asserting that money is *not* neutral. It would be more accurate, however, to say that it asserts aggregate demand is not neutral.

The degree to which money can have some real impact on the economy depends on the degree to which certain prices or wages are fixed in nominal terms. For example, if the money supply authorities drop freshly printed £10 notes over the countryside (an increase in money supply), people will have high money balances which they may attempt to spend at, say, Harrods. Under neo-classical economics, this represents a shift in the ➤demand curve for Harrods products. That leads the price up immediately. It should induce Harrods to supply more. But, at the same time as this was all happening, prices were going up throughout the economy in exactly the same way, leading Harrods' costs to rise, causing a shift in Harrods' ➤supply curve – a reduction in supply. That increases prices as well – and takes the quantity sold back to where it started. The story ends up with higher prices, and the same output, money is neutral. How might this story be thwarted? Suppose Harrods suppliers are contractually obliged to provide goods at pre-set prices. In response to extra demand, Harrods this time *can* supply more at existing prices – there is no shift of Harrods' supply curve. Harrods order more, and get it from the supplier. Even without the pre-set prices, money could have a real effect if the effect of the extra demand only dawns on the shops and suppliers very slowly. They might have found themselves selling more, before they realized demand was rising everywhere. Or, the extra money could have had an effect if there is ➤money illusion. If all prices and wages went up, but people nevertheless mistakenly *felt* richer as a result, then they might have increased the supply of labour, sending costs down and Harrods' supply curve up. The view that money is neutral stems from a belief that market forces function reasonably effectively and fast (i.e. that Harrods' suppliers do not fix their prices in advance), and that economic agents are rational (suffer no ➤money illusion). ➤➤economic doctrines; monetarism; policy ineffectiveness theorem; rational expectations; superneutrality of money; supply-side economics.

new classical economics A theory of ➤macroeconomics which emphasizes the role of ➤rational expectations in decision-making and the natural rate of unemployment (➤➤unemployment, natural rate of) in ➤equilibrium growth. The central view of new classical economists is the ➤policy ineffectiveness theorem that argues governments can only have an impact on the economy in as far as their policies are unanticipated. Unlike the monetarists, therefore, proponents of this view argue that government demand-management intervention is ineffective even in the short run. Growth can only be enhanced by influencing ➤supply. This has been by far the most influential doctrine in ➤macroeconomics in the last two decades. Its prime advantage over other accounts of the economy is that it is well founded in ➤microeconomics, using the economic tradition of assuming individuals are rational. This means that, unlike other approaches, its principal conclusions do not rely on the assumption that people are systematically fooled into behaviour counter to their own true desires. Contrast it with, for example, the notion that prices are sticky, accounting for money having some effect on real output (➤neutrality of money). While the assumption of rational expectations may appear extreme, it is perhaps best to think of new classical economics as arguing that, although policy may have a short-term effect, in the long term, the short term becomes very short indeed, as people see the way policy operates. ➤➤economic doctrines; Lucas critique; supply-side economics.

New Deal The US Federal government under President Roosevelt began, in 1933, a number of projects designed to give financial assistance and work to the large number of people thrown out of employment by the great ➤depression, which followed the stock-market collapse on Wall Street in 1929. This change of policy was called the New Deal. It met with a certain amount of opposition, because it led to budget deficits (➤balanced budget). ➤➤Keynes, J. M.

New Forum ➤Coordinating Committee for Multilateral Controls.

new-issue market That part of the ➤capital market serving as the market for new long-term ➤capital. Those institutions needing capital (industrial, commercial and financial companies and public authorities) offer ➤shares and ➤securities which are then purchased by each other and the general public. Internally generated funds provide about 70 per cent or more of the capital required by business and the new-issue market is not large, accounting on average for about 5 per cent, although it is of some importance. The new-issue market does not include certain other sources of new long-term external finance, such as ►mortgages and other ►loans from financial institutions. Borrowers in the new-issue market may be raising capital for new ►investment, or they may be converting private capital into public capital; this is known as 'going public' (►flotation).

The largest concerns are able to issue stocks and shares direct to the public. These stocks and shares will normally be quoted on the ►stock exchange. Other concerns will raise their new capital through an ►issuing house that will either underwrite the issue or first purchase the securities and then offer them for sale to the public (►unlisted securities markets). In all cases the issues will actually be handled by an ►issuing broker. A full prospectus describing the company and its prospects as well as public advertising are necessary, and, for smaller issues, costs can be reduced by private placing, that is by selling the shares to ►insurance companies or other investors. Quoted companies may issue unquoted shares in this way. Rather larger amounts are raised by private placing by other ►public companies which have no quoted securities, but ►private companies have no access to the new-issue markets, since they cannot achieve quotations while retaining their private status. Well-established companies can greatly reduce the cost of raising new capital by offering shares to their existing shareholders by what are known as 'rights issues'. Rights issues save the cost of advertising, issuing brokers and underwriting commissions, although the shares will normally have to be offered at well below market price to ensure the issue is fully taken up. The difficulty that smaller quoted and unquoted companies experience in raising new long-term capital was noted in the 1931 Macmillan Report (►Macmillan Committee), although unlisted securities markets have developed further and a number of new institutions have since emerged to meet this need outside the new-issue market. The ►commercial banks have also greatly increased their lending to ►small business.

The new-issue market, sometimes called *primary market* (►secondary market), like the rest of the capital market, is increasingly becoming an international one and public companies and the public sector raise money in overseas capital markets.

new Keynesianism The economics of those who combine the assumption of ►rational expectations with the stickiness of prices and wages much discussed in ►Keynesian economics. New Keynesians stress the existence of insititutions which may quite rationally lead to sticky prices, such as ►menu costs, or long-term contracts in which prices are fixed well in advance, and cannot thus be changed in response to economic events. They do not believe that money is neutral (►neutrality of money) and believe that the ►business cycle can partially be explained by changes in ►aggregate demand. The sticky nature of prices means any change in demand does not lead to an automatic or rapid change in prices; it can lead to a change in output or employment. This position is distinct from the

➤new classical economics, which shares the rational expectations assumption, but assumes prices adjust more quickly and as a result that only *unanticipated* changes in aggregate demand have a real effect. ➤economic doctrines; policy ineffectiveness theorem.

New Regulatory Organization (NEWRO) ➤Financial Services Act 1986.

NEWRO New Regulatory Organization (➤Financial Services Act 1986).

New York Stock Exchange (NYSE) The leading New York stock exchange and largest in the world in terms of ➤market capitalization. The second US exchange, also in New York, is the American Stock Exchange (Amex). The NYSE is also referred to as the *Big Board* and as *Wall Street*.

newly industrialized country (NIC) A country which is not a ➤developing country but has not yet achieved the status of the ➤advanced countries. Malaysia and Mexico, for example, are usually counted as NICs, but some earlier examples, e.g. Singapore, have ➤per capita income similar to the levels of members of the ➤Organization for Economic Cooperation and Development.

NIC ➤newly industrialized country.

NNP Net national product (➤national income).

Nobel Prize The sixth Nobel Prize, for Economics, in memory of Alfred Nobel (1833–96), the Swedish chemist, was introduced in 1969 and is financed by the Swedish National Bank. The following economists have been awarded this prize in each year: 1969, J. Tinbergen and ➤R. Frisch; 1970, ➤Paul Anthony Samuelson; 1971, ➤Simon Kuznets; 1972, ➤Sir John Richard Hicks and ➤Kenneth J. Arrow; 1973, ➤Wassily W. Leontief; 1974, ➤Friedrich August von Hayek and ➤Gunnar Karl Myrdal; 1975, L. V. Kantorovich and ➤Tjalling C. Koopmans; 1976, ➤Milton Friedman; 1977, ➤J. E. Meade and ➤Bertil Ohlin; 1978, ➤Herbert A. Simon; 1979, ➤Theodore W. Schultz and ➤Sir W. A. Lewis; 1980, ➤Laurence Klein; 1981, ➤James Tobin; 1982, ➤George J. Stigler; 1983, ➤Gérard Debreu; 1984, ➤Sir Richard Stone; 1985, ➤Franco Modigliani; 1986, ➤James McGill Buchanan; 1987, ➤Robert M. Solow; 1988, ➤Maurice Allais; 1989, ➤Trygve Haavelmo. In 1990 the prize was won by three American finance economists, ➤Harry Markowitz and ➤William Sharpe for their development of the ➤capital asset pricing model, and ➤Merton Miller (➤Modigliani–Miller theorem). Since then the prize has been dominated by the University of Chicago (➤Chicago school). ➤Ronald Coase of Chicago won the prize in 1991. ➤Gary Becker of Chicago won it in 1992. ➤Robert Fogel of Chicago, and ➤Douglass North, collected it jointly in 1993. Three ➤game-theory pioneers won it in 1994: ➤John Harnsanyi, ➤Reinhard Selten and ➤John Nash. ➤Robert Lucas of Chicago won it 1995. And in 1996 the British economist ➤James Mirlees and American ➤William Vickrey won it.

nominal gross domestic product The value of the ➤gross domestic product at

➤current prices. Many economists, notably ➤Meade, have suggested that the government should set a target for nominal GDP; if workers take low pay rises, this target will be reached by real output increases; if workers take high pay rises, then the nominal GDP rise will almost entirely consist of ➤inflation.

nominal value The ➤face value of a ➤share or ➤bond, which may be more or less than its market price. ➤➤par value.

nominal yield The return or ➤yield on a ➤security in which ➤dividend or ➤interest is expressed as a percentage of the ➤nominal value of the security as opposed to its market price.

non-accelerating inflation rate of unemployment (NAIRU) ➤unemployment, natural rate of.

non-price competition Attracting or attempting to attract business from rivals by means other than selling at lower prices, for example by the use of ➤advertising or product differentiation (➤differentiation, product). Non-price competition is commonly found under conditions of ➤oligopoly, where price-cutting could lead to a damaging price war, thus the use of free gifts, coupons and special offers.

non-substitution theorem A theorem which states that, if there are no economies or diseconomies of scale in an economy, if there are no ➤joint products and if all inputs which are not themselves produced are used equiproportionately in production of everything, then competitive prices will reflect only technology and cost, and demand will have no impact on them.

non-tariff barriers (NTBs) Obstacles to imports other than ➤quotas or ➤tariffs. Examples include safety or construction and use regulations which favour domestic over imported products; legal requirements that providers of insurance services should be domiciled within national boundaries; and deliberate delay or obstruction at customs facilities. ➤➤barriers to entry; protection; voluntary export restraints.

normal good ➤inferior good.

normal profit ➤profit.

normative economics Economics concerned with judgements about 'what ought to be' in contrast to ➤positive economics, which is concerned with 'what is'. A normative statement would be that 'industry should be more concentrated'. Such a statement should rest upon a positive assertion about the existing level of ➤concentration and a ➤value judgement that fewer firms would lead to greater efficiency or some other benefit.

North American Free Trade Agreement A ➤free-trade area set up from 1994 comprising Canada, the USA and Mexico. ➤Import tariffs, ➤quotas and other trade barriers (➤non-tariff barriers) between the member countries are to be phased out over a period of up to fifteen years. The agreement also includes environmental provisions relating to the use of renewable resources, health and pollution.

North, Douglass C. (b. 1920) Economic historian, at Washington University, St Louis, Missouri, and a joint winner of the ➤Nobel Prize for Economics in 1993. North, like his fellow winner, ➤Robert Fogel, has been important in promoting the importance of, and explaining, the institutions in which an economy operates. He maintains that new institutions are created when groups see an opportunity for profit that cannot be realized under prevailing conditions. Attaching some weight to the context in which economic mechanisms operate, as much as to the mechanisms themselves, became fashionable in the context of former East-bloc nations (➤transition, economies in) and their attempts to emulate western nations. North himself was an adviser to the government of the Czech Republic.

NSB ➤National Savings Bank.

NTA ➤net tangible asset.

NTB ➤non-tariff barrier.

null hypothesis A proposition that is being subject to precise statistical verification. A common null hypothesis used in ➤econometrics is that some ➤parameter value is equal to zero. The results of ➤regression analysis can be tested statistically to determine whether the data confirm or deny the null within acceptable bounds of statistical likelihood, given that it is usually based on only a sample of data. ➤beta; confidence interval.

NYSE ➤New York Stock Exchange.

O

objective function ➤Lagrange multiplier.

obsolescence A reduction in the useful life of a ➤capital good or consumer ➤durable good through economic or technological change or any other external changes, as distinct from physical deterioration in use (➤depreciation). For example, a new process or machine may be developed which renders existing equipment uneconomic, because a firm could significantly reduce its costs by scrapping its existing machinery even though it might still have many years of physical life. Then the old equipment has become obsolescent.

occupational pension schemes ➤personal pension.

OECD ➤Organization for Economic Cooperation and Development.

OEEC Organization for European Economic Cooperation (➤Organization for Economic Cooperation and Development).

Office of Fair Trading ➤Fair Trading Act.

OFT Office of Fair Trading (➤Fair Trading Act).

Ohlin, Bertil (1899–1979) Born in Sweden, Professor Ohlin studied at the University of Lund and the Stockholm School of Economics. He was appointed to a Chair of Economics at Copenhagen University in 1925. In 1930 Professor Ohlin moved to the Stockholm School of Economics where he remained until his retirement in 1965. He was a Member of Parliament from 1938 until 1970 and Chairman of the Swedish Liberal Party for many years. He was awarded the ➤Nobel Prize in Economics in 1977 (jointly with ➤Meade). His major contribution, to ➤international trade theory, was published in *Interregional and International Trade* (1933). Professor Ohlin refined the theory of ➤comparative advantage by building upon the work of Eli Heckscher (➤Heckscher–Ohlin principle). He also made important contributions to ➤macroeconomic theory, in many ways anticipating in the 1930s the work of ➤Keynes.

Okun, Arthur M. (1928–80) Professor Okun graduated from Columbia University in 1956 and became Professor of Economics at Yale in 1963. From 1969 until his death he was Senior Fellow at the Brookings Institute. His major publications include *The Political Economy of Prosperity* (1970) and *Prices and Quantities: A Macro-Economic Analysis* (1981). Professor Okun argued that ➤supply and ➤demand are not necessarily brought into ➤equilibrium by lowering prices but they are by adjusting output. Excess capacity may not lead to lower prices in an economy. In *Potential GNP, Its Measurement and Significance* (1968), he analysed US gross national product through the 1950s and 1960s. He discovered that a 1 per cent increase in unemployment was associated with a 3 per cent drop in the ratio of actual GNP to full-capacity GNP. This relationship has become known as Okun's law.

Okun's law ➤Okun, A. M.

oligopoly A market which is dominated by a few large suppliers (➤concentration). Oligopolistic markets are often characterized by heavy ➤product differentiation through advertising and other marketing ploys, with long periods of price stability intermittently disrupted by keen price competition. Petrol sales and soap powder are notable oligopoly industries in the UK in which free offers, competitions and advertising are more heavily used than price competition for attracting custom.

There is no single theory of oligopoly equivalent to that of ➤perfect competition or ➤monopoly because the behaviour of oligopolistic firms is determined by the reaction and behaviour of their rivals, and the assumptions they make about those reactions. Instead, there is a number of alternative theories. The first was developed by ➤Cournot and assumed that each firm sets its price and output on the assumption that its rival does not react at all. In such a situation, each firm will leap-frog past the other, lowering price and increasing output to gain a higher market share. The result is nevertheless a market in which prices are higher and output lower than they would be if the firms behaved as perfect competitors. A second approach is that of ➤Bertrand competition, in which keen price competition drives firms to the perfectly competitive outcome. The third theory is that firms recognize their interdependence, and one among them leads in price setting with others following. In this case, the leader enjoys higher profits than any followers, but all firms benefit from the stability and predictability of the industry. A fourth case is that in which all firms attempt to act as leader; then they all earn lower profits than they would under Cournot's solution (➤➤prisoner's dilemma). A fifth case is that firms assume their rivals will follow their prices down but not follow their price if it rises; in this situation, firms will be very reluctant to change their price. It could account for the fact that prices are often stable in oligopolistic industries despite large changes in costs. A sixth case is that in which firms collude and between them achieve the outcome that would occur if a ➤monopoly existed in the industry. However, if one firm colludes, it always pays another to cheat and sell more than agreed, so that maintaining collusive agreements may be difficult in situations where firms cannot monitor each other's behaviour. Otherwise, hefty state penalties for collusion can deter oligopolists from making agreements that have negative effects on consumers.

Other approaches to oligopoly exist; notably ➤game theory has been used to simulate the reactions of firms to each other's behaviour. ➤➤anti-trust; Nash equilibrium; Organization of Petroleum Exporting Countries.

on cost The contribution of the ➤cost of ➤overheads added to the direct costs of production.

OPEC ➤Organization for Petroleum Exporting Countries.

open economy A situation in which foreign trade (➤exports and ➤imports) and payments and movements of labour and capital into and out of a country are unrestricted. The term is also used to refer to countries for which foreign trade is a large percentage of the ➤gross domestic product. The degree of openness of an economy may act as a constraint on the freedom of governments to pursue particular types of economic policy, for example the reduction of interest rates to stimulate expansion may in an open economy lead to a flight of capital to other countries, depressing the ➤exchange rate with adverse consequences for ➤inflation.

open-ended fund An investment company in which units may be purchased from or sold to the fund manager, as in a ➤unit trust. The fund is open in the sense that its size continuously depends upon its success in selling units, in contrast to a ➤closed-end fund like an ➤investment trust.

open-ended investment company (OEIC) An ➤open-ended fund listed on a ➤stock exchange at a single unit price; like an ➤investment trust, but it can issue or redeem (➤redemption) ➤shares to match demand in a similar way to a ➤unit trust. Common in Continental European countries and the United States, and permitted in the UK from 1995.

open-market operation The purchase or sale of ➤securities by the ➤central bank to influence the supply of funds in the ➤capital market, and so interest rates and the volume of credit.

operating cost (US) A term for prime or ➤variable costs.

operating profit 1. Profit on current activities. 2. The difference between total revenue and total operating costs (or ➤variable costs) and before deduction of ➤fixed costs. ➤➤profit; inflation accounting.

operating ratios Various measures of the efficiency of a business, e.g. the operating rate or ➤capacity utilization rate, the stock-sales ratio, ➤labour turnover ratio, the creditor–debtor ratio and other ➤financial ratios.

operations research (OR) A multidisciplinary approach to the solution of quantifiable business or administrative problems, for example the determination of ➤optimum levels of ➤inventories, quality control and vehicle routeing. OR usually involves the use of computer models to test alternative solutions and the basic discipline of OR personnel may be mathematics, engineering or economics. A number of techniques used in economics are of this type, for example ➤critical-path analysis, discounted cash flow (➤present value) and ➤linear programming.

opportunity cost The value of that which must be given up to acquire or achieve something. Economists attempt to take a comprehensive view of the cost of an activity. If a firm invests undistributed ➤profits to spend £1000 on new machinery which requires less electricity to run than the equipment it replaces, the cost of that machinery is not the *outlay* of £1000 alone: what could be earned from the best alternative use of the money also has to be taken into account. If, for example, the firm is paying 12 per cent interest on an overdraft and the saving in electricity is less than £120 a year, it would be better for the firm to pay off its overdraft than to invest in the new machinery. If a self-employed person makes a ➤profit of £8000 a year but pays himself no wage, he needs to consider the alternative use to which his time could be put. He might, for example, be able to earn £10,000 a year working for someone else: this is the *opportunity cost* of his time. Accounting costs, as in these examples, normally allow only for cash outlays, but cash outlays will only approximate to opportunity costs where competition ensures that the prices of all ➤factors of production are equal to those for their best alternative use (➤Wieser, F. von). (Under the assumptions of ➤perfect competition, the self-employed person would be aware that he could earn more in employment and, since we assume profit maximization, he would do so.) Economists also distinguish between private costs and ➤social costs and costs in ➤real terms and money terms. ➤➤average cost; imputed cost; prime costs; shadow price.

optimal-growth theory The area of economics concerned with analysing the level of economic growth which maximizes social welfare. The starting-point is known as the *golden rule of capital accumulation* (➤golden rule) which, under a large number of assumptions, suggests that the optimal-growth path will be the one which maximizes consumption per worker over time. To vary consumption per worker, society can vary its stock of capital per worker: if there is too much capital, maintaining the capital labour ratio will require such high levels of investment that workers would have to save a lot and refrain from consumption. If there is too little capital, however, while it is easy to maintain the stock, the product of workers is low because they are poorly equipped. The rule suggests that the optimal position is one in which the rate of growth of population equals the ➤marginal productivity of capital, or which, in a perfectly competitive economy, equals the rate of profit. An alternative way of expressing the same rule is to say that the rate of saving should equal the rate of profit. The golden rule is limited in its application to a society where ➤balanced growth is achieved from an ideal starting-point. It does not suggest how growth should proceed in the absence of an optimal starting-point nor whether balanced growth is itself desirable.

Alternative rules and principles have been developed, notably that of F. P. Ramsey in 1928 that the ➤marginal productivity of capital should equal the proportionate decline in the marginal utility of consumption. Other theoreticians have attempted to show that it is sometimes optimal to adopt the maximum or near maximum possible balanced growth path; this allows an economy to move from an unsatisfactory state to a more satisfactory one very quickly even if consumption is lower in the interim than it is at either the starting- or finishing-point. Known as *turnpike theorems* (turnpike being an American term for motorway), such theorems imply that the quickest route between two states of the economy may not be the shortest in distance terms, as is the case with many motorway journeys. Optimal-growth theory is an area of economics grounded in complicated mathematics, in contrast to the more popular debate which has raged about whether growth is desirable at all. ➤economic growth theory.

optimum A position in which the aim of any economic unit is being served as effectively as it possibly can be, within the constraints applying. Where a situation is not optimal, gains in welfare (➤welfare economics) can be made for some without any sacrifice by others. Essential to the meaningful application of the concept of an optimum is the existence of some *objective* (such as the maximization of ➤utility) and some *constraint* on the pursuit of that objective (such as a specified set of prices and a given income). While it is possible to have two conflicting objectives (for example, money and leisure), an optimum can only be attained with respect to both of them if some desired trade-off between them can be expressed; this is roughly equivalent to finding a single criterion by which both can be judged and optimizing with respect to that criterion. Individuals, trade unions, firms and countries are generally assumed to be rational in economic theory and thus exhibit optimizing behaviour. ➤economic efficiency; linear programming; Lagrange multiplier.

option An agreement with a seller or buyer permitting the holder to buy or sell, if he chooses to do so, a financial instrument or ➤commodity at a given ➤price within a given period. In the ➤stock exchange, an option may be purchased from a dealer, giving the right to purchase a certain number of ➤shares at a certain price within a certain time, e.g. a three-month option. If, in the meantime, the price falls by more than the cost of the option, then the dealer will lose and the purchaser gain, and vice versa. An option to buy is a ➤'call option', an option to sell is a *put option*, and one to buy or sell is a *double option*. Trade in option contracts (hence *traded options*) in ➤securities markets, ➤money markets and commodity exchanges has expanded enormously in recent years. (➤London International Financial Futures Exchange (LIFFE).) There are major options markets in Chicago and other financial centres. ➤Black–Scholes formula; derivatives.

OR ➤operations research.

ordinal utility A measure of consumer satisfaction expressed in terms of rankings of preferred combinations of commodities rather than through the assignment of values of some absolute ➤utility measure to them. (➤Marshall, A.) Until the turn of the nineteenth century, economists assumed that individuals possessed a cardinal measure of utility, with the consumer able to give a mark to each basket of products to reflect the pleasure it generates, rather as an examiner does to a multiple-choice paper. It came to be realized, however, that no sensible meaning could be given to statements of the form, 'This apple provides me with twice as much utility as it provides you.' Fortunately, no such scale was necessary for a consumer theory to be derived. All that is required is that consumers list bundles of commodities in order of preference and group bundles between which they have no preference. The difference between the two approaches can be highlighted by contrasting the way in which they show that a rise in the price of a product leads consumers to ▸demand less of it. The cardinal approach holds that rational consumers will equalize the utility derived from the marginal unit of cash spent on each item. A rise in the price of eggs thus requires that consumers raise the marginal utility they derive from eggs. Given the assumption of ▸diminishing marginal utility, the only way to effect such an increase is to cut consumption to a point at which eggs are more appreciated than they were and their marginal utility rises. The ordinal approach is only concerned with the *relative* attractiveness of items. It is the ratio of marginal utilities that is important and neither the consumer nor the economist needs to rely on a concept of utilities of some absolute value. In this approach, consumers will ensure that the ratio of prices of items equals the ratio at which the consumer would choose to swap the items with indifference. ▸indifference-curve analysis; marginal rate of substitution; Pareto, V. F. D.; Pigou, A. C., Slutsky, E.; social-welfare function.

ordinary least-squares estimation ▸least-squares regression.

ordinary share Shares in the ▸equity capital of a business entitling the holders to all distributed ▸profits after the holders of ▸debentures and ▸preference shares have been paid.

Organization for Economic Cooperation and Development (OECD) The organization that came into being in September 1961, renaming and extending the Organization for European Economic Cooperation. It was based on the convention signed in Paris in December 1960 by the sixteen original European member countries of the OEEC, plus Spain, the USA and Canada. Later Australia, Finland, Japan and New Zealand also became members and more recently the Czech Republic, Hungary, Mexico and Turkey. The aims of the OECD are (a) to encourage economic growth and high employment with financial stability among member countries, and (b) to contribute to the economic development of the less advanced member and non-member countries and the expansion of world multilateral trade (▸multilateralism). The Organization carries out its functions through a number of committees – namely, the Economic Policy Committee, the Committee for Scientific Research, the Trade Committee and the Development Assistance Committee – serviced by a secretariat. It publishes regular statistical bulletins covering the main economic statistics of member countries and regular reviews of the economic prospects of individual members. It also publishes ad hoc reports of special studies covering a wide range of subjects, e.g. world ▸population growth, agricultural surpluses, etc. The OECD has been particularly important as a forum for the industrial countries to discuss international monetary problems and in promoting aid and technical assistance for ►developing countries. ►►International Energy Agency; International Monetary Fund.

Organization for International Economic Cooperation ►Council for Mutual Economic Aid.

Organization of Petroleum Exporting Countries (OPEC) A group of thirteen countries which are major producers and exporters of crude petroleum. The organization, set up in 1960, acts as a forum for discussion of and agreement on the level at which the member countries should fix the price of their crude petroleum ►exports by production quotas. The organization also acts as a coordinator for determining the level of aid to ►developing countries granted by the members. In 1996 there were twelve member countries, viz Algeria, Gabon, Indonesia, Iran, Iraq, Kuwait, Libya, Nigeria, Qatar, Saudi Arabia, the United Arab Emirates and Venezuela, Ecuador having left the organization. These countries accounted for about 60 per cent of total world crude-oil production and about 90 per cent of total world exports in the early 1970s. However, their high oil prices led to substitution by other fuels, and by the expansion of supplies from non-OPEC producers. As a result, OPEC share of world exports fell to below 40 per cent in the 1990s. ►►international commodity agreements; International Energy Agency.

origin ►certificate of origin; European Free Trade Association.

origin principle ►value-added tax.

OTC ►over-the-counter market.

output budgeting ►programme, planning, budgeting system.

output gap The difference between the actual level of activity in an economy, and the sustainable amount of activity given the capacity of the economy. An output gap is measured as a percentage. It may be negative (equivalent to a ►deflationary gap) or it may be positive, implying that the economy was operating unsustainably fast – that it was ►overheating (in an ►inflationary gap). The output gap is expressed as a percentage of the *level* of GDP. Note that GDP may grow very quickly for several years; but, if the growth commenced at a time of a large negative gap, GDP may still be below its potential. Unfortunately, it is not possible to observe potential activity; it is only the actual activity we can record. So, proponents of output-gap analysis typically have to estimate potential output. This is usually extrapolated as follows: find a year in the past when the economy was neither booming nor in recession. Assume that the output gap then was zero – and that, in that year, potential GDP was the same as actual GDP. Secondly, to derive potential GDP in subsequent years, assume that it grows from the base year by a constant rate. That constant rate is ►trend growth. In any subsequent year, actual GDP can then be compared to the extrapolated potential GDP measure, to derive the gap. Proponents of the output gap make one additional plausible assumption: that, when companies operate in excess of their capacity, they attempt to raise their real prices; and, when they operate below their capacity, they tend to cut their real prices. The inflation rate tends to rise when actual output is above potential. It tends to fall when actual output is below potential. The gap is useful in assessing ►monetary policy, because it assumes that any increase in ►aggregate demand in the economy will generate extra output if actual GDP is below potential; and will generate inflation, if actual output exceeds potential. The gap is also useful in assessing how much a government can reasonably borrow.

Borrowing tends to go up or down across the ►business cycle (►built-in stabilizers). Estimating the output gap can give a clue as to the ►structural budget deficit. Estimates of the output gap for all main developed economies are produced by the ►Organization of Economic Cooperation and Development. ►►unemployment, natural rate of.

overdraft A ►loan facility on a customer's ►current account at a bank permitting him to overdraw up to a certain agreed limit for an agreed period. ►Interest is payable on the amount of the loan facility actually taken up, and it may, therefore, be a relatively inexpensive way of financing a fluctuating requirement. The terms of the loan are normally that it is repayable on demand, or at the expiration of the agreement, and it is thus distinct from a ►term loan.

overfunding ►funding.

overheads ►fixed costs.

overheating A situation in which ►aggregate demand in the economy is growing at a rate liable to lead to ►inflation. It refers to a situation in which the ►output gap is close to zero, or is positive. ►►stabilization policy; recession.

overseas banks 1. Banks operating in, say, the UK but which are not UK-controlled. There are 319 banks incorporated outside the UK represented in Britain, of which 155 were incorporated outside the ►European Economic Area. 2. Banks from, say, the UK which conduct their business mainly abroad. Many of these banks are subsidiaries of the ►commercial banks.

overseas investment ►foreign investment.

over-subscription Where a new issue of ►shares is made and the demand for the shares exceeds the number on offer, the issue is said to be over-subscribed. It is, of course, extremely difficult for the ►issuing house to estimate precisely the price at which a share issue will be fully taken up, and new issues are usually either over- or under-subscribed. It is very common for an attractive issue to be ten times or more over-subscribed, especially because of purchases by *stags* – speculators who subscribe to new issues in the expectation that they will be over-subscribed and that dealings will begin at a ►premium. Very often new issues that start at a premium fall back to below the issue price as a result of ➤profit-taking by stags.

over-the-counter (OTC) market A group of licensed dealers who provide two-way trading facilities in company ➤securities outside the ➤stock exchange. The term originated in the United States in the 1870s when stocks were first purchased across bank counters. Today the OTC in the United States is an elaborate electronic dealing system, with ➤market makers across the country, called NASDAQ (the National Association of Securities Dealers Automated Quotations system), which trades in ➤equities in over 4000 companies through 500 broker-dealers. ➤➤unlisted securities markets.

overtrading A firm is said to be overtrading when it has insufficient ➤working capital to meet the needs of its present level of business. For example, a firm which doubled its production, and then found that it could not meet all its current expenditure because too much ➤capital was tied up in stocks and work in progress, would be overtrading, even though it had correctly forecast the demands for its products. In such circumstances, the firm's ➤current ratio would probably be less than unity.

overvalued currency ➤undervalued currency.

ownership ➤Coase theorem; separation of ownership from control.

P

Paasche index An ➤index number which employs weights (➤➤weighted average) derived from current statistics rather than from those of some past period (➤Laspeyres index). As an example, an annual Paasche price index would calculate the price change (the *price relative*) of each commodity or service included in the index, between the current year and a base year, and then derive the weighted average of these *price relatives*; each weight being the amount spent on each commodity in the current year.

paid-up capital That part of the ➤issued capital of a company that has been paid up by the shareholders. Except for partly paid ➤privatization issues, it is rare among shares dealt with on the London ➤Stock Exchange for the issued capital not to be paid up, and the phrase is sometimes used loosely as a synonym for issued capital to distinguish it from ➤authorized capital.

panel data Data which consists of both ➤time series and cross-section values (➤cross-section analysis), e.g. a data set that consists of spending by a large sample of households for several years. ➤➤econometrics; regression analysis.

paper profit An unrealized ➤money increase in the ➤value of an ➤asset or assets. An individual, for example, will have made a paper profit on his house if it is worth more now than it was when he bought it.

par value The ➤price at which a ➤share or other ➤security is issued, i.e. the ➤face value of the ➤investment. A share is said to be standing above par if its quoted price on the ➤stock exchange is greater than that at which the share was issued. The term was also used to describe the official fixed ➤exchange rate of currencies in terms of gold and US dollars, as declared to the ➤International Monetary Fund.

paradox of thrift The phenomenon that can arise in an economy that, as people increase their saving, national income can fall and lower everybody's living standard. The paradox can apply under conditions of ➤Keynesian unemployment, where increased saving represents a leak from the ➤circular flow of income. It can provide a justification for an active ➤fiscal policy.

paradox of value The paradox that certain items that are very valuable to mankind (such as water) are very cheap to buy; while other less useful items (such as diamonds) are expensive. The supposed paradox is a widely used illustration of some key principles in economics. The reason that prices do not reflect our intuitive notion of value is that they are set by conditions of supply as well as demand:

water may be very important, but there is an awful lot of it, so it does not have to be highly priced. This is to repeat the conclusion that prices are set by the *marginal* value of an item – the value of consuming yet more of it – not by the value of consuming it at all. If we had to give up all consumption of either diamonds or water, we would clearly choose to give up diamonds.

paradox of voting The paradox (also referred to as 'Condorcet's paradox', after the eighteenth-century French philosopher) that a majority voting system can produce a set of inconsistent social preferences from a set of individually consistent preferences. Suppose electors Anne, Bill and Caroline rank three options, defence, education and social security, as follows:

	Anne	*Bill*	*Caroline*
Defence	1	2	3
Education	2	3	1
Social security	3	1	2

When the options, taken in pairs, are voted on, defence beats education; education beats social security but social security beats defence. In each case two of the voters rank the winning option higher than its opponent, thus ensuring its victory. As a result, the electors could either never determine which of the three options to put first, or their choice will merely depend on the order in which voting takes place – the social ranking does not possess ➤transitivity. As transitive preferences are a pre-condition for the meaningful derivation of ➤indifference curves, the paradox is one indication that the theory of optimal behaviour for individuals cannot easily be extended to 'democratic' societies. ➤➤impossibility theorem; social-welfare function.

parallel imports A flow of ➤imports into a high-price country additional to the normal flow of imports generated by the manufacturers and traders. If retail prices in one country are sufficiently lower than in another, people will travel to the low-price country from the high-price country to shop. This ➤arbitrage would eventually reduce the differences in prices between countries, unless there were technical, legal or other obstacles to this trade.

parallel money markets Markets in short-term securities other than ➤treasury bills, ➤bills of exchange and ➤bonds dealt with on the ➤discount market. Until the mid-1950s the discount market alone provided the main market for short-term money. Since 1955, when local authorities were no longer allowed to borrow at will from the Public Works Loan Board, a large market in short-term loans to local authorities has developed. Other markets have developed in ➤Eurocurrency, ➤certificates of deposit, finance-house deposits and inter-company and inter-bank loans. ⟫inter-bank market; inter-company loans market; unlisted securities markets.

parameter The values in a mathematical function which remain constant against movements in the *variables* of the function. For instance, in the demand equation, $d - aY + bp + c$, d (quantity demanded), Y (disposable income) and p (price) are all *variables, a, b, c are parameters* (constants). ⟩beta; ⟫regression analysis.

Pareto, Vilfredo Federico Damaso (1848–1923) An Italian born in Paris, Pareto was trained as, and practised as, an engineer. He succeeded his father to a post in the Italian Railways, and in 1874 was appointed Superintendent of Mines for the Banca Nazionale, Florence. He succeeded ⟩Walras to the Chair of Economics in the Faculty of Law at Lausanne University in 1892. His publications include *Cours d'économie politique* (1896–7) and *Manuale di economica politica* (1906). He retired in 1907. He developed analytical economics from the foundation laid by Walras. He pointed out the shortcomings of any theory of ⟩value in so far as it rested upon assumptions of measurable or 'cardinal' rather than ⟩ordinal utility. He demonstrated that an effective theory of consumer behaviour and exchange could be constructed on assumptions of ordinal utility alone. Exchange would take place in a competitive ⟩market between individuals such that the ratios of the ⟩marginal utilities of the goods traded equalled the ratio of their prices. An optimum point of exchange could be defined without the need to compare one individual's total ⟩utility with another's. He defined an increase in total welfare as occurring in those conditions in which some people are better off as a result of the change, without at the same time anybody being worse off (⟩compensation principle). Pareto's work in this field, coupled with the development of ⟩indifference-curve analysis, invented by ⟩Edgeworth, became the foundation upon which modern ⟩welfare economics is based. A study of the distribution of personal incomes in an economy led him to postulate what became known as *Pareto's law*, that whatever the political or ⟩taxation conditions, ⟩income will be distributed in the same way in all countries. He noted that the distribution of the number of incomes is heavily concentrated among the lower income groups, and asserted that the number of incomes fell proportionately with the size of income. Pareto's law has not, in fact, proved valid in its strict sense. ⟫economic efficiency; income, distribution of; Slutsky, E.

Pareto-optimal ⟩economic efficiency.

Pareto's law ⟩Pareto, V. F. D.

Paris Club ⟩International Monetary Fund.

partial correlation The ⟩correlation between two variables, after having adjusted for any correlation either or both the variables may have with a third variable. For instance, observations of the quantity of a commodity sold over a number of years may be highly correlated with consumers' disposable income over the period. A simple correlation between the two would be misleading if, during the same period, there was a substantial fall in price; so that there was also a strong simple correlation between quantity and price. The correlation between income and quantity is calculated, after having deducted the correlation between quantity and price, to obtain the *partial correlation*.

partial-equilibrium analysis The study of the behaviour of ►variables which ignores the indirect effects that changes in the variables have on themselves through the impact they have on the rest of the economy. When we study, for example, the market for pet dogs, we do not consider the impact that a change in the number of dogs sold has on the profits of pet-food manufacturers. This and other effects, will have an impact on prices, income and taxation and, through these, have a feedback effect on the demand for dogs. The usual partial-equilibrium approach is considered adequate for the study of most markets because such feedback effects are swamped by the direct effects of events in any individual market and are considered negligible. This approach contrasts with ►general equilibrium analysis. ►►Marshall, A.

participation rate ►labour force.

partnership An unincorporated business formed by the association of two or more persons who share ►risks and ►profits. Except in a limited partnership, which, although a legal institution since 1907, is relatively unusual in Britain, each partner is liable for the ►debts and the business actions of the others, to the full extent of his own ►resources (although he is taxed as an individual). Partnerships are a common form of organization in the professions, and in businesses where ►capital requirements are relatively small, e.g. retail shops and other service trades. Partnerships, with sole traders (►sole proprietorship), i.e. self-employed persons working on their own, account for about 85 per cent of the total number of businesses. For the tax treatment of partnerships, ►corporation tax.

pay-as-you-earn (PAYE) System of collecting ►income tax in the UK through regular deduction by the employer from weekly or monthly earnings. Confidentiality of the taxpayer's private circumstances is preserved through the use of code numbers, which, in conjunction with tax tables, enable the employer to calculate the amount of tax he has to deduct. The system was introduced in 1944 and had been recommended by ►Keynes. It is thought to be a stabilizing factor in the economy, since the tax yield automatically varies directly and rapidly with ►income and employment, whereby the government tends to spend proportionately more tax yield in recession (►depression) and less in time of high demand and employment. ►►built-in stabilizers; self-assessment.

pay-as-you-go ►pension funds.

pay-back The period over which the cumulative net revenue from an ►investment project equals the original investment. It is a commonly used but crude method for analysing ►capital projects. Its main defects are that it takes no account of the ►profits over the whole life of the investment, nor of the time profile of the ►cash flow. ►►investment appraisal.

PAYE ►pay-as-you-earn.

payment in kind Payment in goods or services instead of money ►wages; made illegal by the Truck Acts. ►►fringe benefits.

payments, balance of ►balance of payments.

payroll tax A ►tax levied on employers' ►wage bills. It is now regarded by many economists in developed economies as a means of encouraging capital intensiveness (►capital-intensive) at the expense of employment. This type of tax as such is not used in the UK, although ►National Insurance contributions are a form of payroll tax. A flat-rate employment tax (*selective employment tax*) was introduced in 1966 and abolished in 1973 on the introduction of ►value-added tax.

peak pricing The setting of higher prices than average when supplying services during a period of peak demand. For instance, enough electricity capacity must be installed to satisfy demand at peak times, because electricity cannot be stored. At off-peak times the cost of electricity is lower at the margin than at the peak, at which less efficient power stations have to be switched in to meet the demand. ►marginal-cost pricing.

peg ►exchange rate.

pendular arbitration ►arbitration.

pension funds Sums of money laid aside and normally invested to provide a regular ►income on retirement, or in compensation for disablement, for the remainder of a person's life. Nearly all developed countries have state pension schemes, e.g. the British ►National Insurance Scheme. Unlike these schemes, which operate on a *pay as you go* basis with contributions from those in employment paying for the pensions of the retired, private pension schemes for which contributions receive favourable tax treatment are usually *funded*, i.e. placed in managed invested funds. Many private pension schemes are based upon ►assurance. Occupational pension schemes may be contributory or non-contributory by the employee; the benefits of private schemes are normally related to the length of service of the employee and the level of his salary or contributions: that is to say, they are *defined pension benefits*, for example 50 per cent of final salary. In *defined pension contribution* schemes, employers and/or employees pay regular contributions, but the pension finally paid is determined by the performance of the fund in which contributions are invested. On maturity these funds are used to purchase an ►annuity. Since annuity rates vary from time to time, this introduces further uncertainty about the amount of the pension.

PEP ➤personal equity plan.

per capita income Income per head, normally defined as the ➤national income divided by the total population. International comparisons of per capita income at current exchange rates need to be interpreted with caution. ➤purchasing-power parity; real exchange rate.

percentile The *x*th percentile is that value of a distribution of numbers below which are *x* per cent of the number of observations. For instance, the 50th percentile is the value below which there are 50 per cent of the observations (this is called the *median*) (➤average). The *quartiles* are at 25 per cent and 75 per cent. Similarly, *deciles* subdivide the distribution into 10ths.

perfect competition A model of industrial structure in which many small firms compete in the supply of a single product. Three primary features characterize a perfectly competitive industry: (i) There is a multitude of firms (buyers as well as sellers) all too small to have any individual impact on market price; therefore, ➤marginal revenue and ➤price are equal. (ii) All firms aim to maximize ➤profit. (iii) Firms can costlessly enter and exit the industry. Also, it is assumed that the outputs traded are homogeneous.

Perfect competition is economically efficient in three ways (➤➤economic efficiency):
(a) In the ➤short run, profit maximization ensures that each firm will set its output so that its ➤marginal cost is equal to its ➤marginal revenue (➤firm, theory of the). To produce when marginal cost exceeds marginal revenue implies that cutting back production would save more than the revenue lost; and to produce when marginal revenue exceeds marginal cost implies that expanding production would increase revenue more than costs. Thus, marginal revenue will equal marginal cost. Moreover, under the price-taking assumption, the effect is that marginal cost equals price. This is efficient for the allocation of resources, because it ensures that no consumer will be deterred from buying something which he values more than it cost to make.
(b) In the long run, freer entry and exit ensures new entrants will be attracted into any industry where high profits are made. The effect of these new entrants is to increase supply and bid down price until no profit is made (apart from a normal entrepreneurial return), that is, when average revenue equals average cost. The zero profit result means that no entrepreneur or factor of production earns more than it just needs to be persuaded into an industry.
(c) Again, in the long run, as average revenue equals marginal cost (from the profit maximization assumption) and average revenue equals average cost (from the free entry and exit assumption), we can deduce that average cost equals marginal cost. The only point on the average cost curve for which this is true is at the bottom of it: that is, at the lowest cost point. Finally, therefore, perfect competition ensures minimum-cost production.

Although the features of perfect competition make it look a poor description of modern industry, it is a realistic description of world commodity markets where many traders deal in a homogeneous product. Moreover, its very powerful results indicate that the achievement of even a partially competitive market can be advantageous. Thus, the simple perfect competition model provides a good starting-point for illuminating the forces underlying the real behaviour of firms. ➤➤ contestability; imperfect market; marginal-cost pricing; monopoly.

peril point A term used by the US Tariff Commission to describe the point beyond which tariff reductions would threaten the existence of domestic industry.

permanent-income hypothesis The theory proposed by ➤Friedman which suggests that, however variable their income, consumers will attempt to smooth out the pattern of their consumption (➤consumption function). If, for example, someone's income varies between zero and £20,000 p.a., averaging £10,000, he will spend at a rate equivalent to a constant £10,000 p.a. Given that the ➤marginal utility of money declines with the increasing amounts of spending, it is sensible to transfer spending from bountiful times to times when one is poor. By saving in some periods and 'dissaving' in others, this can be achieved. The theory has several implications: first, the ➤marginal propensity to consume will equal the ➤average propensity to consume: any extra pound a consumer gets will be treated not as a cause for a quick spending spree, but as a temporary bonus that should raise lifetime consumption by the value of the pound spread over a lifetime. Secondly, a large increase in short-run ➤incomes will not lead to corresponding increases in consumption.

personal disposable income ➤disposable income.

personal equity plan (PEP) A scheme introduced in the UK Finance Act 1986 to provide tax relief on the proceeds of personal investments in the ➤ordinary shares of companies listed on the ➤stock exchange. A maximum of £9000 per annum could be invested (£3000 of which had to be in a Single Company PEP). Gains from selling the shares were free of ➤capital gains tax, and ➤dividends free of ➤income tax. From April 1999 PEPs will be replaced by ➤Individual Savings Accounts (ISA) and no further investments in PEPs will be permissible.

personal loan A ➤bank loan made without ➤collateral security to a private customer for specific purposes.

personal pension 1. A regular income after a certain age and usually after retirement from work, provided by a state or private scheme. The flat-rate state *retirement pension* is paid to men over 65 and women over 60 who have paid appropriate ➤National Insurance contributions. There is also the State Earnings Related Pension Scheme (SERPS, ➤National Insurance) and an Old Age Pension, the latter for those who have not participated in the National Insurance Scheme. There are two broad types of private pension schemes:

(a) *occupational pension schemes*, provided by employers, which usually involve 'contracting out' of SERPS and provided a guaranteed minimum pension (GMP). These schemes, which are known as *defined benefit schemes* (➤pension funds), are either contributory or non-contributory; in the latter the employee pays no pension contributions. The schemes are based on trust funds in which contributions are invested either directly or through ➤financial intermediaries such as life ➤insurance companies.

(b) *personal annuity schemes*, for the ➤self-employed or others who are not members of an occupational scheme.

2. A private pension scheme of the personal ➤annuity kind. Under these schemes, individuals pay contributions into a fund managed by an ➤insurance company or other ➤institutional investor which provides a cash lump sum at retirement age, part of which, if it is to qualify for tax relief on the premiums, must be used to purchase an annuity. The 1986 Social Security Act, which initiated a run-down of SERPS, also introduced *portable pensions*. After 6 April 1988 employers were no longer able to make membership of a contributory occupational pension scheme a condition of employment. All employees have the option of paying premiums into a personal private-sector scheme of their own choice in much the same way as for the personal-annuity schemes for the self-employed. This means that the employee will be able to take his pension scheme with him if he changes employment. These schemes are known as *defined contribution schemes* (➤pension funds).

Up to stated limits, pension contributions by individuals and employers qualify for ➤income tax and ➤corporation tax relief. ➤Pension funds also receive favourable tax treatment. Pension schemes may be *funded* (a capital-reserve system), in which contributions are paid into a fund that is invested in ➤securities and other ➤assets and from which pensions are ultimately paid, or *unfunded*, as in the National Insurance scheme, where pensions for retirees are paid out of the contributions of those in work (pay-as-you-go system).

personal sector Households and individuals. In the national accounts this sector includes unincorporated businesses. ➤➤private sector.

PESC Public Expenditure Survey Committee (➤public expenditure).

Petty, Sir William (1623–87) The pioneer of numerical economics. His main interest lay in public finance, and he made important contributions to monetary theory and ➤fiscal policy. His approach to these subjects contributed to the development of ➤classical economics, and from his work in the field of comparative statistics is the direct line of descent to the work of modern economists in the field of economic statistics. His best-known work is *Political Arithmetic*, published in 1691. The so-called *Petty's law* was a remarkably far-sighted statement of the tendency for the proportion of the working population engaged in ➤services to increase as an economy develops.

Petty's law ➤Petty, Sir William.

Phillips, Alban William Housego (1914–75) After a number of jobs in electrical engineering, and after serving in the RAF during the Second World War, Phillips began lecturing in economics at the London School of Economics in 1950. From 1958 until 1967 he was Tooke Professor of Economics, Science and Statistics in the University of London. In 1968 he accepted the Chair of Economics at the Australian National University. Professor Phillips published many articles exploring the relationships between the ➤multiplier and accelerator in mathematical ➤models (➤accelerator–multiplier model) with various time lags, and applied the engineering technique of closed-loop control systems to the analysis of ➤macroeconomic relationships.

In an article in *Economica* in 1958, Professor Phillips set out empirical evidence to support the view that there was a significant relation between the percentage change of money wages and the level of ➤unemployment – the lower unemployment, the higher the rate of change of wages. This relationship, which became known as the *Phillips curve*, has attracted considerable theoretical and empirical analysis. Its main implication is that, since a particular level of unemployment in the economy will imply a particular rate of wage increase, the aims of low unemployment and a low rate of ➤inflation may be inconsistent. The government must then choose between the feasible combinations of unemployment and inflation, as shown by the estimated Phillips curve, e.g. 3 per cent unemployment and no inflation, or 1½ per cent unemployment and 8 per cent inflation, etc. Alternatively, it may attempt to bring about basic changes in the workings of the economy, e.g. a ➤prices and incomes policy, in order to reduce the rate of inflation consistent with low unemployment. However, the relation between unemployment and inflation has not been sufficiently stable in practice to permit exact judgements to be made.

Phillips curve ➤Phillips, A. W. H.

physical controls Direct controls on production and ➤consumption, licensing of buildings or ➤imports, and the rationing of goods are examples of physical controls. These controls are alternatives to the use of monetary or fiscal measures (➤fiscal policy), which control production and consumption through the price mechanism (➤price system). ➤➤quotas.

Physiocrats A group of eighteenth-century French economists, led by ➤Quesnay, who later became known as the Physiocrats or '*les Économistes*'. They believed in the existence of a natural order and regarded the state's role as simply that of preserving property and upholding the natural order. They held that agriculture was the only source of ➤wealth and therefore this sector should be taxed by *l'impôt unique*. In this, and in their advocacy of free trade, their views were directly opposed to those of the mercantilists (➤mercantilism). In their belief in ➤*laissez-faire*, they had much in common with, and certainly influenced, British ➤classical economics, and especially ➤Adam Smith. Quesnay's *Tableau économique*, published in 1758, has in it the origins of modern ideas on the circulation of wealth and the nature of interrelationships in the economy. ➤➤Cantillon, R.; Leontief, W. W.; Mill, J. S.

Pigou, Arthur Cecil (1877–1959) A pupil of ➤Marshall, whom he succeeded to the Chair of Political Economy at Cambridge in 1908, Pigou continued in this chair until he retired in 1944. His major publications include *Principles and Methods of Industrial Peace* (1905), *Wealth and Welfare* (1912), *Unemployment* (1914), *Economics of Welfare* (1919), *Essays in Applied Economics* (1923), *Industrial Fluctuations* (1927), *The Theory of Unemployment* (1933) and *Employment and Equilibrium* (1941). His work on monetary theory, employment and the ➤national income, which was in the tradition of the ➤classical school, led him into controversy with ➤Keynes. He was the first to enunciate clearly the concept of the real balance effect, which as a consequence became known as the *Pigou effect*. The Pigou effect is a stimulation of employment brought about by the rise in the real value of ➤liquid balances as a consequence of a decline in prices – as the real ➤value of ➤wealth increases, so ➤consumption will increase, thus increasing income and employment. This was one of the processes by which the classical ➤model envisaged that full-employment ➤equilibrium could be obtained as a result of a reduction in real wages. Although his work on ➤macroeconomics was partly superseded by Keynes, he made a lasting contribution with his original work in ➤welfare economics. He strongly resisted the belief that practical policies based on propositions from welfare economics were impossible, because interpersonal comparisons of ➤utility cannot be made. He argued that, though this may be true for individuals, it was possible to make meaningful comparisons between groups. His distinction between private and social product now plays an important role in the formation of government economic policy in the field of ➤public expenditure.

Pigou effect ➤Pigou, A. C.

Pink Book Informal name for the annual publication, *United Kingdom Balance of Payments*. The Pink Book appears in the late summer each year, and gives estimates of the ➤balance of payments in detail over the previous ten years and in summary for the previous twenty-one years. Quarterly and more recent estimates of the balance of payments appear in the *Monthly Digest of Statistics*.

placing The sale of a new issue of ➤shares or ➤stock (➤new-issue market), usually to ➤institutional investors, by a financial intermediary, such as a firm of stockbrokers, acting on behalf of the company issuing the shares. This method of 'private placing' of shares minimizes the cost of a new issue, since it does not involve the advertising and other costs associated with an offer for sale or subscription. For shares which are to be quoted on the ➤stock exchange there are limitations on the total market ➤capitalization of shares which can be issued by this method.

planned economy An economy in which state authorities rather than market forces directly determine prices, output and production. Although planned economies can take a variety of forms, their most important features usually include: (a) production targets for different sectors of the economy, that determine the ➤supply of different commodities; (b) rationing of certain commodities, to determine ➤demand for them; (c) price- and wage-fixing by state bodies; (d) (sometimes), a conscripted ➤labour market in which workers take jobs assigned to them.

When all or nearly all economic activity is governed by the state, two advantages can prevail. First, the external costs and benefits of all activities which are not reflected in prices and are ignored by the market economy can be taken into account by the authorities (➤externalities). Secondly, a distribution of income (➤income distribution) nearer to many people's view of that which is just can be achieved. There are, however, disadvantages of planning. The first is the practical problem of setting optimal prices in all markets (➤➤price system). Too often, the authorities set excessively low prices causing goods to be rationed by queues. The second is the lack of worker and management motivation that attends a system in which earnings are not performance-related and ➤profits not retained by the companies making them. The third is the fact that, when wages and prices differ from their market levels, substantial control of individual activities is required. For these reasons, many planned economies do allow flexibility in pay and the operation of the price mechanism in inessential goods markets and performance-related wage bonuses. ➤➤free-market economy; state planning; transition, economies in.

ploughing back ➤self-financing.

poison pill A damaging action, such as sales of ➤assets, which a company threatens to inflict upon itself in the event of ➤take-over by another firm. A poison pill serves to deter other firms from attempting an acquisition in the first place, because to do so would immediately lower the value of the company they are attempting to buy. ➤merger.

policy ineffectiveness theorem The idea that if there are flexible prices and wages, and if the public hold ➤rational expectations, then any government policies to stimulate ➤aggregate demand can have no real effect on output or employment unless the policy measures are unanticipated by the public. Increasing demand only generates extra ➤inflation. The theorem is the basis of ➤new classical economics and can be thought of as saying that money is neutral in its effects (➤neutrality of money) *when a change in money supply is anticipated*. Academic economists are divided on whether monetary and fiscal policies are ineffective, or whether they have some effect in the short or long term. Economists are almost unanimous in believing that *unanticipated* injections of demand can increase output and employment in at least the short term. ➤➤economic doctrines; new Keynesianism.

political economy ➤economics.

poll tax ➤local taxation.

polluter-pays principle The idea that polluting emissions should be taxed in order that those who create them bear the costs of their actions. The principle of allowing pollution to occur, but taxing it, derives from ►Pigou in 1932. It is an approach which contrasts with banning pollution outright or allowing it within certain limits. The advantage of taxing it is that if the tax rate covers the damage or suffering caused by the pollution, it will pay firms to pollute only if the benefits of them so doing outweigh the costs. The tax will also generate revenue that can be used to compensate those who suffer most. An example of a pollution tax would be a tax on the carbon content of fossil fuels to offset the atmospheric warming effect of the carbon dioxide they produce, a carbon tax. While, under perfect information, pollution taxes can produce ►economic efficiency, it may be difficult to set the tax level correctly, and the cost of making mistakes, of allowing too much pollution, for example, may be very high.

population (a) The number of people living in any defined area, such as New York or India. (b) In statistics, a term applied to any class of data of which counts are made or samples taken, e.g. a car population. The study of the characteristics of human populations is called *demography*. According to the United Nations, the total world population in 1995 was 5.3 billion. Although the rate of growth has fallen, the UN expects that world population will reach about 10 billion by 2050. The fall in growth is a reflection of the drop in *fertility rates* (►►birth rate) throughout the world. The growth in population varies considerably, with the highest rate being experienced by Africa with a rate of just under 3 per cent per annum. The nearly doubling of world population not only raises the issue of the ability of agriculture to continue to meet the demand for food (►Malthus, T. R.) but also the effect of increasing pressure on other resources such as water and unpolluted air. These pressures arise from economic growth itself as well as population numbers.

The population of the UK is expected by the Office for National Statistics to rise from 58.8 million in 1996 to 61.3 million in 2011 and to peak at 62.2 million in 2031. Along with other ►advanced countries, such as France, Germany, Japan and the USA, the population of the UK is getting older. In 1961 about 12 per cent of the population was over 65 years of age, in 1991 16 per cent and, by 2031, it is expected to rise to 22 per cent. The *dependency ratio* is defined as the ratio of the total of children (0 to 14 years of age) and pensioners to the working population. This ratio is forecast to increase from 63 in 1991 to 79 in 2031. Population ageing raises questions about the likely effects on economic growth in these advanced countries through, for instance, changes in the propensity to save (►►average propensity to save), the financing of pensions and ability to compete with newly industrializing countries, such as China, which will retain a young age profile. ►labour force; population, census of.

population, census of In the UK, a count of the number of inhabitants that has been taken every ten years since 1801 (except in 1941). The next decennial census of the UK will be in 2001. Enumerators visit every house in areas assigned to them, leave census forms, which they later collect, and check on the accuracy of the answers. Information is collected on place of residence, age, sex, marital condition, occupation and certain supplementary information on living conditions, education and occasionally other matters. All advanced countries have regular censuses, but many ►developing countries are now in the process of organizing them for the first time. It is not possible to obtain information accurately by other means. Calculations based on births, deaths and migrations have not proved, in the past, to be very precise means of estimating, except as a means of interpolation between censuses. ►►population.

portable pensions ►personal pension.

portfolio The collection of ►securities held by an investor.

portfolio theory A branch of financial economics which analyses the most efficient amounts of different assets an investor should hold. Underlying portfolio theory is the assumption that investors like high returns and dislike risk (►►risk aversion). Risk represents a likelihood of the actual return on an asset deviating from the expected return. In general, therefore, investors will have to expect a higher return from a risky asset than a safe one in order to be persuaded to hold it, although, of course, a risky asset may actually deliver a return either higher or lower than it was expected to yield in advance.

An *efficient* ►portfolio is one which delivers the highest expected possible return for a given amount of risk, or the smallest possible risk for a given expected return. In general, by holding a variety of assets, the risk of a portfolio can be reduced, because when one asset happens to perform badly, it may be that others will be doing well. Thus, ►diversification does pay, and this explains the popularity of ►unit trusts. However, diversification can succeed in reducing risk only if the performances of the assets in a portfolio do not coincide: in as far as the assets' returns move together (because, for example, they are all affected by the state of the national economy) there will always be some systematic risk remaining that cannot be diversified away. It is the development of these basic principles which is the concern of portfolio theory. ►►capital asset pricing model.

positional goods Goods that are necessarily scarce and whose scarcity cannot be reduced by increased productivity. They were described by Fred Hirsch in his book *The Social Limits to Growth* (1977). He distinguished those positional goods whose value derived from their intrinsic usefulness, but which are limited in their supply (like holiday homes in beautiful places), and those which do not yield pleasure from their absolute qualities, but from their scarcity (like original paintings by famous artists). Allocation of these goods is a ►zero-sum game. Their importance is in explaining the observation that, as people become richer, their levels of material frustration do not appear to diminish.

positive economics The study of economic propositions which can, at least in principle, be verified by observation of events or states of the real world; that is, without reference to ►value judgements. Broadly, positive economics is descriptive and can either consist of statements like 'unemployment is very high' or conditional statements like 'if the economy is reflated, unemployment will fall'. Prescriptive statements, in contrast, like 'unemployment *ought* to be cut', fall into the sphere of ►normative economics. In practice, the distinction between the two is not a sharp one, because those who make what sound like prescriptive statements may reasonably claim that in fact they are implicitly making conditional statements, like 'unemployment ought to be cut if overall welfare is to be enhanced'. This has the form of a descriptive statement but is no more devoid of opinion than the first clause taken alone.

poverty The situation facing people whose material needs are least satisfied. Poverty can be defined by some *absolute* measure (earnings below some specified minimum level) or in *relative* terms (the number of the poorest 10 per cent of households, for example). Poverty exists not merely because incomes are low, but also because the needs of some low-income households are high. A single person earning £100 a week may not be in poverty, though a family of four on the same income would be. In a 1992 report the US Bureau of the Census defined the *poverty line* as $6932 for a single-person household and as $13,924 for a four-person household. The report pointed out that the number below this line was increasing. A similar trend has occurred in the UK and other ►advanced countries. The percentage of the UK population with income below half the national average doubled between 1961 and 1991.

The World Bank has estimated that 40 per cent of the world's labour has annual incomes of less than $1600. This contrasts with the average income of $17,000 received by the 8 per cent of the total who are unskilled workers in the advanced countries. The life expectancy in some Central African states is 43 years compared with 78 years in some developed countries. ►►inequality; minimum wage; social security.

poverty trap The combination of losing state-benefit entitlement and paying tax that can ensure that poor families keep very little of any extra money they earn. Under any social security system using ►means tests, as the poor earn more, they lose state benefits. For example, a poor family may lose 60p of benefit for every extra £1 it earns, and it may also pay 20p in tax on that pound. In this case the family benefits by only 20p of the extra pound. Apart from the inefficiency of suppressing the incentive for people in the poverty trap to work, concern exists over the debilitating human effects of removing from people the power to alter their own living standards. ►►income, distribution of; marginal tax rate; poverty; social security; unemployment trap.

precautionary motive The factor which causes people or firms to hold a stock of ►money to finance unforeseen expenditures. It is one of the three motives for holding money outlined by ►Keynes. A firm may know what its average pay-outs are each month; but, if these payments fluctuate, given that there are costs to being short of the cash necessary to finance them, firms will keep money in excess of what they need for the average month. The amount they keep will first depend upon the ►interest rate. This represents the cost of keeping money which would earn a return if it was invested. Secondly, it will depend upon the probability of overshooting the foreseeable expenditures – the higher the probability the more money firms will hold. Thirdly, it will depend upon the size of the firm's average spending – a big firm will keep more than a small firm. Finally, it will depend on the cost of not having cash to meet unforeseen pay-outs – the higher the cost, the more precautions a firm will take. ►liquidity preference; speculative motive; transactions demand for money.

predatory pricing Setting ►prices at very low levels with the objective of weakening or eliminating competitors or to keep out new entrants to a ►market. Since prices will be raised again once these objectives have been achieved, there is no permanent benefit to the consumer. Predatory pricing is a means of establishing or maintaining ►monopoly power.

preference shares Holders of preference shares precede the holders of ►ordinary shares, but follow ►debenture holders, in the payment of ►dividends and in the return of ►capital if the issuing company is liquidated (►liquidation). Preference shares normally entitle the holder only to a fixed rate of dividend, but participating preference shares also entitle the holder to a share of residual ►profits. Preference shares carry limited voting rights and they may be redeemable or not (►redeemable securities).

Cumulative preference shares carry forward the right to preferential dividends, if unpaid, from one year to the next. From the investor's point of view, preference shares lie between debentures and ordinary shares in terms of ►risk and ►income, while to the issuing company they permit some flexibility in distribution policy at a lower cost than debentures. Preference shares now account for a very small proportion of issues (►new-issue market), but are frequently used in the provision of ►risk capital.

preferential duty ►tariffs, import.

premium 1. The difference, where positive, between the current ►price or ►value of a ►security, or ►currency, and its issue price or ►par value. 2. A regular payment made in return for an ►insurance policy.

prepayments Payments for services such as rent and rates made in one accounting period for consumption wholly or partly in a following period and written into the balance sheet as a current ►asset.

present value The discounted value of a financial sum arising at some future period. For instance, if the *discount rate* is 10 per cent per annum, the present value this year of £110 earned next year is £100. £100 this year is equivalent to £110 next year because £100 invested at the going ➤rate of interest of 10 per cent yields £110 in one year. If there are financial flows over a number of years, the discounted sums are additive. For instance, if £110 were earned in each of two years, the present value would be: £110 earned in year two, discounted to year one, = £110/1.10; this sum is then to be discounted, again, to the base year = (£110/1.10) × 1.10 = £110/(1.10²). Finally to this sum must be added the discounted value of the sum earned in year one, that is £110/1.10. The present value, therefore, is £110/(1.10²) + £110/1.10. In general:

$$\text{Present value (PV)} = \frac{X_1}{(1+r)} + \frac{X_2}{(1+r)^2} + \frac{X_3}{(1+r)^3} + \cdots \frac{X_n}{(1+r)^n},$$

where X_n is the financial flow in year n, and r is the rate of interest (discount rate). The *net* present value is the difference between the present value of a future flow of profits arising from a project and the capital cost of the project. ➤➤investment appraisal.

price What must be given in exchange for something. Prices are usually expressed in terms of a quantity of ➤money per unit of a ➤commodity (a good or service) but in ➤barter the price of a good is what other good or goods it can be exchanged for. Price changes are the means by which the competitive process determines the allocation of resources in the ➤free-market economy. ➤➤price system; price theory; shadow price.

price discrimination The selling of the same commodity to different buyers at different prices. Several conditions must prevail for it to be profitable. First, there must be a separation between markets that does not allow buyers in one to resell the item in another (no ➤arbitrage must be possible). Secondly, the seller must possess some degree of monopoly power (➤monopoly) in at least one market for, under competitive conditions, prices will be driven down to the level of costs in all markets. Thirdly, buyers in different markets must have a different level and elasticity of demand for the good. The monopolist who discriminates will set output for each market where ➤marginal cost is equal to the ➤marginal revenue in that market. Sales will be at a higher price in markets where elasticity is generally low than where it is high. The monopolist, in effect, takes advantage of the fact that in one market consumers are prepared to pay more for his item than in the other, without losing sales in the other market. In *perfect price discrimination* the monopolist charges a different price to every individual consumer and effectively has a sales revenue equivalent to the area under the ➤demand curve for his product.

price–earnings (P/E) ratio The quoted price of an ➤ordinary share divided by the most recent year's ➤earnings per share. The P/E ratio is thus the reciprocal of the earnings ➤yield and a measure of the price that has to be paid for a given income from an ➤equity share. A company whose 25p ordinary shares were quoted at £1.00 on the ►stock exchange and which, in the previous year, had earnings of 10p per share, would have a P/E ratio of 10 to 1, i.e. the price of every penny in earnings would be 10 pence, or the earnings yield would be 10 per cent. The price of earnings will vary with the stock market's assessment of the growth potential involved. Thus a company with good growth prospects might have a P/E of 15/1 or more, but a company with a poor record might have a P/E ratio of considerably less than that.

price elasticity of demand ►elasticity.

price elasticity of supply ►elasticity.

price index ►index number.

price level, average A term used in ►macroeconomics to refer to a base from which changes in the exchange value of ►money can be measured (►index number). It is a useful concept, but not literally calculable: an ►average of the unit ►prices of all goods and services on offer in the economy would, in itself, be a meaningless number.

price maintenance ►resale price maintenance.

price mechanism ►price system.

price regulation A form of regulation, common for ►public utilities in the United Kingdom, in which the prices of the supplier are not allowed to rise above a certain level. The regulation is designed to prevent the abuse of a ►monopoly position. UK price regulation has applied to telephone, gas, electricity and water providers. In each case the design has shared certain common features: (a) allowed price rises are set out for a few years in advance, typically four or five; (b) there is a *review* at the end of each period, at which the regime governing the next period is decided; (c) allowed price rises are specified relative to the ►retail price index, and might be RPI minus 4.5 per cent each year, for example. (This protects the regulated firm against ►inflation.) Under price regulation, if firms can keep their costs low they can earn big profits. This gives them an incentive to be efficient that does not exist under ►rate-of-return regulation. But it has been suggested that, in each periodic review, the regulator looks at the rate of return to decide what new price formula should be applied, thus reducing the difference between the two types of scheme. ►►Averch–Johnson effect; monopoly; natural monopoly; regulation.

price schedule ►cost schedule.

price support A system of agricultural support by which market prices are fixed at above ►free-market levels and the government buys unsold surpluses, thus supporting the price and raising farmers' incomes. ►Common Agricultural Policy.

price system The mechanism which sends prices up when ►demand is in excess and prices down when ➤supply is in excess (➤resource allocation). The mechanism referred to is not some coordinated control from a central authority, but relies on the disparate decisions made by independent agents; it is the mechanism which makes a butcher reduce the price of a leg of lamb he is unable to sell, or an ice-cream salesman raise the price of cornets on a hot day. It is usually assumed that one price eventually settles in each market until some disturbance in costs or demand occurs (➤equilibrium). The importance of the price system is (a) that it serves as a means of rationing limited supplies among consumers, and (b) that it signals to producers where money is to be made and thus what they ought to be producing. ➤➤comparative static equilibrium analysis; economic efficiency.

price theory The area of economics concerned with the determination of prices in individual markets. It is an area of ➤microeconomics and is not directly connected to the study of ➤inflation. The two components of price theory are the ➤demand side and the ➤supply side; it is the interaction of the two that determines ➤equilibrium output and price in any market. On the demand side, the theory of demand (➤➤demand, theory of) explains consumer behaviour in terms of rational agents maximizing ➤utility. On the supply side, various alternative market structures are investigated: ➤perfect competition; ➤monopolistic competition; ➤oligopoly; and ➤monopoly. There are also alternative theories of the behaviour of firms which do not assume that profit maximization is the sole goal of producers (➤behavioural theory of the firm). ➤➤firm, theory of the; Marshall, A.; resource allocation.

prices and incomes policy A policy of restraining price or wage increases by regulated limits on the increases that are allowed. The persistent upward trend in prices during the post-war period led the ➤Organization for Economic Cooperation and Development to recommend incomes policy as a tool of economic management in 1962. In most developed countries, it was used in some form or another to counter the problem of ➤stagflation that emerged in the 1970s. Sometimes it was used in conjunction with price controls.

In the UK, some sort of incomes policy was in force almost the whole time between 1965 and 1979. For the first few years it was legally enforced, but under the Labour government of 1974 to 1979 pay increases were limited by voluntary agreement of the unions. In the 1980s price and incomes controls were abandoned in favour of a free-market approach.

Limiting wage increases is seen as a means of reducing the problem of ➤inflation associated with a given level of ➤unemployment. The difficulty faced by those trying to implement incomes policy is that it distorts the market for labour. Pressure for pay rises can also build up at the end of a period of controls, as the collapse of the pay policy of the late 1970s amid strikes and labour unrest testified. The long-term effectiveness of limiting increases in the prices of goods in the shops is to be doubted. The problem with price freezes is that of empty shelves. Either producers reduce the goods they sell or consumers buy up everything available as the prices of things no longer adequately ration the supply. ➤➤price control; repressed inflation.

pricing policy The method used by firms for determining their prices. In this area, there appears to be a discrepancy between the suggestions of theory and the observed practice of firms.
(a) In theory, firms in ➤perfect competition take the market price as given – which will equal the marginal cost of production – without being able to influence that price. A ➤monopoly or any firm in ➤monopolistic competition first determines its output and only then sets a price at the level that just sells the output chosen.
(b) In practice, firms appear to use 'rules of thumb' rather than accurate assessments of ➤marginal revenue and costs. ➤Cost-plus pricing, for example, involves charging the average cost of producing an item, plus a profit margin, the size of which is loosely determined by market conditions.

Much debate on pricing policy has surrounded the appropriate policy for ➤nationalized industries; in particular whether they should attempt to emulate the ➤marginal-cost pricing of perfect competition (➤➤Hotelling, H.; peak pricing; menu costs).

primary market ➤new-issue market.

prime costs Strictly, ➤variable costs plus administrative and other ➤fixed costs that can be avoided in the short or long term if there is no output, even while the firm remains in business. Often used loosely as a synonym for variable costs. ➤➤supplementary costs.

prime rate (US) The ➤rate of interest charged by ➤commercial banks to first-class-risk corporate borrowers for short-term ➤loans. The prime rate is the basis of the whole structure of commercial interest rates in the USA.

principal–agent problem The problem that arises in many spheres of economic activity, when one person, the principal, hires an agent to perform tasks on his behalf but cannot ensure that the agent performs them in exactly the way the principal would like. The efforts of the agent are impossible or expensive to monitor and the incentives of the agent differ from those of the principal. It does not arise if an enforceable ➤contract can be drawn up to specify all the duties of the agent (➤incomplete contract). Examples of the problem include the management of assets on behalf of investors; the management of companies on behalf of shareholders by executives; and the running of public services by private firms under ➤regulation by government authorities. The principal–agent relationship is one which is characterized by ➤asymmetric information. ➤➤moral hazard.

prior charges ➤Debenture and ➤preference shareholders have a prior claim over ➤ordinary shareholders to ➤profits or ➤capital repayments. The amount of these claims is known as prior charges on the company.

prisoner's dilemma A situation in which it pays each of several economic agents individually to behave in a particular way, even though it would pay them as a group to behave in some other way. The prisoner's dilemma is a classic and fundamental concept in ►game theory. It is best exemplified by the story from which it derives its name: A sheriff picks up two suspected criminals and puts them in separate cells. He gives each the chance to confess to having committed the crime with the other, and tells them their fate as follows:
(a) If you don't confess and your partner doesn't confess, you will get three years in gaol.
(b) If you confess and your partner confesses, you will get four years in gaol.
(c) If your partner confesses and you don't, you will get twelve years in gaol.
(d) If your partner doesn't confess and you do, you will get two years in gaol.

| | | Criminal 2 | |
		Confess	Don't confess
Criminal 1	*Confess*	4,4	2,12
	Don't confess	12,2	3,3

These results are summarized in the table, where the left-hand number in each pair is criminal 1's sentence, and the right-hand number is criminal 2's. Given these four choices, the optimal one is for them not to confess and get three years each. However, if they each believed the other was to behave in this way, it would pay them to confess in the hope of getting two years. Indeed, scrutiny of the choices shows that if one believes his partner is going to confess, he ought to confess also (avoiding the twelve years); and if one believes his partner is not going to confess, he still ought to confess in order to get two years instead of three. This compelling logic will drive both criminals to confess unless they genuinely have as much concern for each other as they do for themselves.

Although it recurs in many contexts, the prisoner's dilemma is usually seen as a way of characterizing ►oligopoly. Here it may pay firms to collude and jointly act as a monopolist, but it will pay individual firms to cheat on the colluding deal and produce more than they agreed to. ►►Nash equilibrium; repeated game; tit-for-tat.

private company A type of business organization that permits a limited number of shareholders to enjoy ►limited liability and to be taxed as a company. Unlike the ►public company, the only other incorporated form of business in the UK, a private company may not offer ►shares for public subscription; but unlike a ►partnership, and if it requires the protection of limited liability, it is obliged to file accounts. Smaller private companies are exempted from certain of the so-called *disclosure requirements* (►company law). At the end of 1996 the number of private companies registered in Britain was 1,024,700, though probably about 50 per cent of these were virtually inactive, while some of them were ➤subsidiaries of larger ➤enterprises. ➤➤company law.

private enterprise Economic activity in the private as distinct from the public sector (➤public enterprise). ➤➤capitalism; mixed economy.

private equity ➤risk capital.

private finance initiative (PFI) The regulations set by the British government which are designed to encourage the private sector to design, finance, build and operate assets providing services to and for the public sector. The PFI was launched in 1992. It was open to government departments to use the PFI as a means of ➤contracting out. Any ➤capital which was provided by the private supplier would not count as government borrowing (➤PSBR). In order to induce private providers, the public sector would have to sign contracts with them for the purchase of services from them once the assets were constructed. The Treasury has always insisted that such contracts cannot be signed, unless a sizeable amount of risk is borne by the private provider. The PFI remains an important policy initiative, designed to limit the problems of the public sector's inability to finance capital spending effectively, and in the belief the private sector can manage assets more effectively. ➤➤resource accounting.

private net product A term first used by ➤Pigou for the net ➤national income or product to distinguish it from the ➤social net product.

private sector That part of the economy in which economic activity is carried on by ➤private enterprise as distinct from the ➤public sector. The private sector includes the ➤personal sector and the corporate sector.

privatization Principally, the sale of government-owned ➤equity in ➤nationalized industries or other commercial enterprises to private investors, with or without the loss of government control in these organizations. Since 1981 shares in the following among other enterprises have been sold by the UK government: British Aerospace, Amersham International, Cable & Wireless, National Freight Corporation, Britoil, British Coal, Enterprise Oil, Associated British Ports, Jaguar Cars, Sealink, British Gas, British Telecom, British Airways, British Shipbuilders, British Steel, British Airports Authority, Railtrack, Rolls-Royce, the electricity boards and the regional water authorities. UK government revenue from sales of equity in state-owned enterprises rose from £377 million in 1979/80 to £7.1 billion in 1988/89, though it fell back to £2.4 billion in 1995/96 as fewer enterprises were available for sale. (➤public-sector financial deficit.) Similar policies are being pursued in many other countries world-wide.

Other types of privatization may take the form of deregulation of a state-supported ➤cartel or the subcontracting to the private sector of work previously carried out by state employees. Where public utilities have been privatized, leaving them in a monopoly position, new forms of ►regulation have been introduced. ►►contracting out; natural monopoly.

probability The average number of times an event occurs as a proportion of the number of times it could occur. In six throws of a die, a six could occur up to six times. On average, however, it will be thrown only once. The probability of a six in any given throw is, therefore, one in six. All probabilities take a value from zero to one. Probability is important in several areas of economics. There is a whole theory associated with consumers and ►risk (►expected utility), and in the economics of ►finance the notion of risk is important in explaining asset prices (►capital asset pricing model). In ►econometrics, probability theory underlies the statistical tests used to ascertain the significance of the results derived from ►empirical testing.

There are two major ways of viewing probability. One is that it represents the random element of a process. The other, more associated with the Bayesian school (►Baye's theorem), is that it represents a degree of ignorance about a process. In this view, when we ascribe a probability to something we do so given a certain level of knowledge about it. The probability we specify says as much about our knowledge of the event as it does about the event itself.

producer good A ►commodity used in the production of other goods and services as distinct from final or consumer goods. Whether or not a good is a producer or consumer good will depend not upon the good but upon the use to which it is put. For example, a pencil bought for use in a drawing-office is a producer good but one bought for a child is a consumer good. Producer goods are also known as intermediate goods.

producer's surplus The excess of the revenue received by a supplier of a ►commodity over the minimum amount he would be willing to accept to maintain the same level of supply. It is a similar concept to ►consumer surplus. (See diagram opposite.) ►►economic rent; quasi-rent.

product differentiation ►differentiation, product.

production, census of In the UK, the survey of output that has been carried out annually since 1970; prior to that year, it was taken at five-year intervals. The census covers all firms in manufacturing, construction, utilities and extraction industries employing twenty people or more. Although still referred to as a census, sampling techniques (►random sample) are used for firms employing fewer than 100 people. The results of the census are used in compiling national accounts (►social accounting), input–output tabulations (►input–output analysis) and the weights used in calculating the index of production and producer price index numbers. ►►index number.

production, factors of ►factors of production.

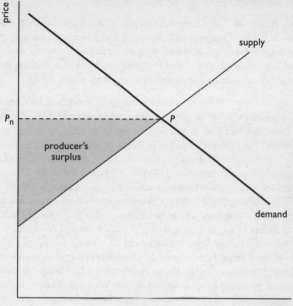

production function The mathematical relationship between output of a firm or economy and the inputs (▸factors of production) used to produce that output. In mathematical notation it is written $q = f(L, C, t \ldots)$ where q is the dependent ▸variable (output) and $L, C, t \ldots$ etc. are independent variables (inputs). The amount of inputs, e.g. labour, capital, raw materials, etc., required to produce a given output depends on technology and this will be reflected in the form of the function. For instance, it may be linear (▸linear relationship) or non-linear. An example of the latter is the ▸Cobb–Douglas function. A production function of the form $q = aL^{\beta} \cdot C^{1-\beta}$ describes a technology with *constant returns to scale*: that is, if inputs are increased by x, output is increased by x. Similarly, a function may exhibit *increasing returns to scale* (e.g. $q = aC.L$, in which if inputs are, for instance, doubled, output increases by $2 \times 2 = 4$ times), and *diminishing returns to scale* (e.g. $q = aC^{1/3} L^{1/3}$, in which, if inputs are increased by, for instance, 8 times, output increases by only 4 times). The above functions are termed homogeneous of degree n; a given increase (x) in each of the inputs (independent variables) increases output (dependent variable) by x^n. If n is greater than 1, the function reflects *increasing returns to scale*; if it is less than 1, *diminishing returns to scale*; if it is equal to 1, *constant returns to scale*. ▸▸homogeneous in degree n.

production possibility curve ➤transformation curve.

production, theory of The economic analysis of the transformation through a ➤production function of ➤inputs such as ➤labour and ➤capital into outputs. Production possibilities (➤➤isoquant; transformation curve) will depend on technology, the mix and level of factor prices and marginal productivities, and the level and price of output demanded. ➤➤economies of scale; firm, theory of the.

productivity The relationship between the output of goods and services and the inputs of resources (➤factors of production) used to produce them. Productivity is usually measured by ratios of changes in inputs to changes in outputs using ➤index numbers. For example, changes in labour productivity, the most common measure, are measured by an index of man-hours divided into an index of output. If the production index stands at 150 (1990 = 100) and the index of man-hours worked stands at 125, then the labour productivity index stands at 120, i.e. labour productivity has increased by 20 per cent over 1990 levels. This is known as a *partial productivity index*, and it does not, in fact, measure changes in the productivity of labour alone unless inputs of land and capital have remained constant.

The calculation of *total factor productivity* is difficult in practice since the proportions of the different factor inputs do not remain constant over time and their individual contribution to output change is difficult to disentangle. Comparisons between labour productivity in different sectors of the economy, for example between ➤capital-intensive manufacturing and ➤labour-intensive services, need to be interpreted with care for the same reason. Another problem in productivity calculations is that the quality of unit inputs may vary; for example, the use of more highly trained labour may lead to higher output without any increase in the number of man-hours. Since changes in productivity are affected by the level of capacity utilization, the underlying trend of productivity growth may be very different from that indicated by short-term movements in productivity indexes. In the long run productivity advance is the main cause of increases in real ➤per capita income. (The measures mentioned relate to average productivity; marginal productivity is the change in output caused by an increase or decrease of one unit of the factors of production.)

profit 1. The residual return to the ➤entrepreneur. In traditional economic theory, profit does not include any of the return to ➤land, ➤labour or ➤capital (the ➤factors of production), but is the surplus remaining after the full ➤opportunity costs of these factors have been met, formally total sales revenue minus total costs. Two types of profit are distinguished in economics. *Normal profit* is the opportunity cost of the entrepreneur, i.e. the minimum amount necessary to attract him to an activity or to induce him to remain in it. *Super-normal profit* or *economic profit* is any profit over and above normal profit. Super-normal profit will be earned only in the ➤short run and is a return to ➤monopoly power, which, unless there are ➤barriers to entry, will be eroded by new entrants. ➤➤economic rent.

2. In the accounting sense of the term, *net profit* (before tax) is the residual after deduction of all ►money costs, i.e. sales revenue minus wages, salaries, rent, fuel and raw materials etc., ►interest on ►loans and ►depreciation. Net profit after tax is after deduction of ►corporation tax or, in the case of a ►sole proprietorship or ►partnership, ►income tax. (However, ►assessable profits.) *Gross profit* is net profit before depreciation and interest.

Accounting profit and economic profit will be the same only where all the factors of production have been credited with their full opportunity costs. The reported profits of quoted companies (►public company) consist mainly of the return on capital for the shareholders which is not profit in the economic sense of the term. If a company is receiving a subsidized loan from the government, for example, or is paying ►rent below the market rate because it has a long leasehold interest, it would also be necessary for the economist to deduct full ►imputed costs for these returns to factors of production, rather than simply the actual money outlays from revenue in arriving at profit. A firm may, therefore, be making an accounting profit while operating at an economic loss.

profit, falling rate of The early classical economists (►classical economics) believed that it was a feature of the economic system for the general rate of ►profit to decline. ►Adam Smith argued that ►capital accumulation took place at a faster rate than the growth of total output. Although the absolute level of profits rose, competition lowered the ►rate of return on capital. For ►Ricardo, the decline of the general rate of profit was induced by the decline in the marginal productivity of ►land, to which all profits were linked. ►Marx took up ideas similar to Smith's, and predicted a fall in the rate of profit because of an intensification of competition between capitalists (►capitalism). There would follow, he concluded, a strong pressure to reduce real wages (►real terms).

profit-and-loss account ►double-entry bookkeeping.

profit-related pay (PRP) ►employee share-ownership schemes.

profit-sharing The name given to describe any scheme under which workers in a firm receive a remuneration which is explicitly conditional upon the future ►profits of the firm. Typical profit-sharing schemes would give workers a profit-related bonus at the end of the year, or would pay workers an amount based on a formula in which profit was a component. Two primary motivations underlie arguments for profit-sharing. First is the desire for workers' wages to be flexible and reflect the performance of their company. If remuneration automatically falls when profits fall, the need for redundancies will be minimized. The second motivation is the desire for workers to identify their interests with those of their employer – to feel that they have a personal stake in the success of the company. Against profit-sharing, it can be argued that workers desire stable ►income and that any risk of company failure should be borne by the shareholders. Secondly, that in a properly functioning free ►labour market, wages would be flexible anyway. ►►employee share-ownership schemes.

profit-taking The sale of ►shares on the ►stock exchange in order to realize ►capital appreciation. When share prices rise and then fall back again as sellers appear, including those who bought the shares in the expectation that the price would rise, the fall-off in prices is said to be the result of profit-taking. ►►stag.

progressive tax A ►tax which takes an increasing proportion of ►income as income rises.

promissory note A legal document between a lender and a borrower whereby the latter agrees to certain conditions for the repayment of the sum of money borrowed. When one borrows from a ►commercial bank, one signs a promissory note. Particular forms of promissory notes, known as *commercial paper* can be bought and sold. They are usually issued by large corporations, but in some countries, for example Spain and Japan, promissory notes are a common form of ►small business finance.

propensity to import A relationship between ►income and ►import levels. The ►demand of a ►household for foreign goods depends on its income as does its demand for domestically produced goods. Similarly, we would expect firms' demands for foreign goods – raw materials, machine tools, components, etc. – to depend on their output. The whole economy's demand for imports thus depends on ►national income.
(a) *The average propensity to import*: the ratio of the total value of imports to national income. It is the proportion of national income spent on imports.
(b) *The marginal propensity to import*: the proportion of an increase in national income which is spent on imports. For instance, if national income increased by £100, and imports increased by £20, then the marginal propensity to import would be 20/100 = 1/5. The marginal propensity to import is a useful concept in two ways. First, if it can be accurately measured and it is relatively constant over time, it can be used to predict the increase in imports which will result from an increase in income. To continue the above example, if the marginal propensity to import is estimated as 1/5 and national income is expected to increase by £10 billion, we can predict that imports will increase by £2 billion, and this may be very useful from the point of view of control of the economy and the ►balance of payments. Secondly, the marginal propensity to import determines, among other things, the value of the ►multiplier, and an estimate of it will therefore be required to estimate the effects on national income of a change in ►investment, government expenditure (►budget), exports or ►taxation.
Though, in the short run, the average and marginal propensities to import may be taken as relatively constant, it must be remembered that they reflect demands for foreign goods from firms and households, and are therefore influenced by (a)

relative prices of foreign and domestic goods, (b) the willingness of domestic agents to borrow from abroad to finance their spending.

propensity to save ➤average propensity to save.

property bond ➤bond.

proportional tax A ➤tax which is levied at the same rate at all ➤income levels. Hence it is intermediate between a ➤progressive tax and a ➤regressive tax.

proprietorship ➤sole proprietorship.

protection The imposition of ➤tariffs, ➤quotas or other devices (➤non-tariff barriers) to restrict the inflow of ➤imports. Arguments in favour of protectionism and against ➤free trade have their origin in the earliest periods of economic discussion (➤mercantilism). The arguments take many forms. Domestic industries, especially agriculture, must be maintained at a high level in case foreign sources are cut off during a war. Key industries which have a significant defence role should be protected to avoid reliance on a foreign supplier. In conditions of ➤excess capacity, protection increases employment by switching demand away from foreign to domestic production, and, through an increase in the surplus on the ➤balance of payments, enables aggregate ➤income to be raised through the ➤multiplier effect. Protection also enables new industries to develop to an optimum size – the ➤infant-industry argument. Protection can be used as a counter to ➤dumping (➤➤contingent protection) and as a retaliatory measure against other countries' restrictions. The case for protection for the ➤developing countries was put forward by R. D. Prebisch (1901 – 86). The developing countries had experienced a long-run decline in their ➤terms of trade. Their demand for imported manufactures grew much more rapidly as their ➤real incomes rose than do the advanced countries' demand for their exports, with a consequent pressure on their balance of payments. Protection would improve their terms of trade by causing a reduction in the price of their imported manufactures arising from their reduced demand, and it could also be used as a means for allocating the limited supply of ➤foreign exchange. Protection has also been proposed as a means by which the ➤advanced countries could prevent a fall in the real incomes of their unskilled labour occasioned by low-cost imports from the developing countries (➤➤income, distribution of). ➤➤barriers to entry; customs union; General Agreement on Tariffs and Trade.

PRP Profit-related pay (➤employee share-ownership schemes).

prudential regulation ➤capital adequacy.

PSBR ➤public-sector borrowing requirement.

PSFD ➤public-sector financial deficit.

public-choice theory The area of ➤welfare economics concerned with the ways in which society can and should make decisions. For ➤economic efficiency, it is important that there is an appropriate level of provision of ►public goods, and it is appropriate that those who value them most should pay most towards them. It is not possible for individual consumers to make decisions on how much defence, for example, to consume. At the same time, it is not easy to turn everybody's individual preferences for defence into a single figure for society as a whole, or to charge people for defence in proportion to their strength of preference (►free-rider problem). The concern of public-choice theory is how different alternatives should be ranked, and how voting systems or other mechanisms can be devised to obtain honest reflections of people's desires. ►►Buchanan, J.; impossibility theorem; paradox of voting; social-welfare function; welfare economics.

public company An incorporated business enterprise with limited liability which is not a ►private company. A public company may be quoted or unquoted (►quotation). Under the 1985 Companies Act in the UK, the ►Memorandum of Association of a public company must state that it is a 'public limited company' or use the abbreviation 'plc'; there must be at least two subscribers, and the nominal share capital must be at least £50,000. At the end of 1996 11,500 public companies were registered in Great Britain. ►►company law.

public debt ►national debt.

public enterprise Economic activity in the market carried on by state-owned or controlled ►enterprises. ►►nationalized industries.

public expenditure Spending by general government (►public sector). Final consumption of goods and services by the public sector accounted for over 23 per cent of the UK ►gross domestic product at market prices in 1996/97; but, if all expenditure, including debt interest, ►transfer payments, and capital grants (but not capital formation by public corporations), is included, public expenditure accounted for 41 per cent of GDP, down from 49 per cent in 1974/75. The control of public expenditure has traditionally involved the publication of forward plans, including those for the next four years, preceded by intensive activity by departments and the EDX Committee a Cabinet committee that reviews expenditure plans. The formal request to Parliament for funds is in the ►supply services estimates presented at the time of the ►budget. At the end of the financial year, *Appropriation Accounts* are prepared by the Comptroller and Auditor-General which show actual expenditure. During the preparation of the appropriation accounts the Public Accounts Committee and the National Audit Office attempt to verify that the funds have been used honestly and effectively. The system of public accounts is changing with the introduction of ►resource accounting. ►►control total; GGE(X).

public finance A branch of economics concerned with the identification and appraisal of the means and effects of government financial policies. It attempts to analyse the effects of government ►taxation and expenditure on the economic situations of individuals and institutions, and to examine their impact on the economy as a whole. It is also concerned with examining the effectiveness of policy measures directed at certain objectives, and with developing techniques and procedures by which that effectiveness can be increased. ➤budget; cost–benefit analysis; fiscal policy.

public goods Commodities the consumption of which has to be decided by society as a whole, rather than by each individual. Public goods have three characteristics. The first is that they yield *non-rivalrous* consumption: one person's use of them does not deprive others from using them. The second is that they are *non-excludable* – if one person consumes them it is impossible to restrict others from consuming them: public television is non-excludable; although, if devices are made for scrambling television pictures, except to those who own picture decoding cards, television becomes an excludable service. Thirdly, public goods are often *non-rejectable* – individuals cannot abstain from their consumption even if they want to. National defence is a public good of this sort, although television is not. Non-excludability and non-rejectability mean that no *market* can exist and provision must be made by government, financed by ➤taxation.

Many items are partly public and partly private goods. A developed patent system, for example, has public-good properties, benefiting not only the community as a whole, but especially inventors who take out patents. ➤impossibility theorem; paradox of voting; ➤externalities.

public ownership ➤nationalized industries.

public sector Comprises central government and local authorities (*general government*), together with the nationalized industries or public corporations. *Central government* includes all those departments and other bodies for whose activities a minister of the Crown or other responsible person is accountable to Parliament. ➤privatization.

public-sector borrowing requirement (PSBR) The excess of public-sector spending over its receipts. The PSBR was adopted as a specific target of UK government policy in 1980. It was seen as important as a measure of the government's fiscal stance (➤fiscal policy), influencing ➤aggregate demand, and as a measure of the burden created for future generations – it is future generations that will have to pay back the debt created, or at least service the interest payments on it. However, it became apparent in 1983 that the PSBR is limited in both of these roles, because by financing current spending through the sales of assets (➤privatization), the government can implicitly relax the fiscal stance and worsen its future financial position (through the loss of nationalized industry profits) without increasing the PSBR.

The PSBR can be financed in two ways: by the printing of ➤money (or, more formally, the sale of liquid assets (➤liquidity) to the banking private sector), or by borrowing. If it is financed by the *printing of money*, it causes an increase in

➤money supply and this will lead to either a real increase or a purely inflationary (➤➤inflation) increase, depending on the state of the economy at the time. If it is financed by *borrowing*, a high PSBR is likely to drive ➤interest rates up or, in an ➤open economy, drive the ➤exchange rate up (as ➤capital from abroad is lent to the government) (➤crowding-out).

Confusion surrounds the PSBR because the way it is financed determines its economic effects: an increase in the money supply causes, at least in the short term, low interest rates, and probably a drop in the exchange rate. This is the opposite of the expected results of an increase in borrowing. The PSBR is a *flow* concept, in contrast to the ➤national debt, which is the cumulated ➤stock of all past PSBRs. ➤➤medium-term financial strategy; public-sector financial deficit.

public-sector financial deficit (PSFD) The excess of ➤public-sector spending over ➤taxation revenues and other receipts. It differs from the ➤public-sector borrowing requirement in that it includes the proceeds of capital transactions like the sale of assets (➤privatization).

public utility An industry supplying basic public services to the market and possibly enjoying ➤monopoly power. Usually, electricity, gas, telephones, postal services, water supply and rail and often other forms of transport are regarded as public utilities. These services all require specialized capital equipment and elaborate organization. ➤➤natural monopolies; regulation.

pump priming The injection of small amounts of government spending into a depressed economy with the aim of boosting business confidence and encouraging larger-scale private-sector investment. It was the policy pursued by Roosevelt in the United States during the 1930s before ➤Keynesian economics was accepted by policy-makers. ➤➤multiplier.

purchasing-power parity (PPP) An ➤exchange rate between two currencies such that the same basket of goods and services could be bought in each country if the cost were converted at that exchange rate. For instance, if a loaf of bread cost £1 in the UK and $2 in the USA the purchasing-power parity exchange rate would be £1 to $2. Market exchange rates are determined by a mix of forces and can fluctuate considerably. This makes accurate comparisons of international economies using market exchange rates difficult. The use of purchasing-power parity is a preferred alternative, although not without its own problems of measurement. The World Bank (➤International Bank for Reconstruction and Development) published a report in 1994 in which it ranked countries by ➤gross national product per capita using this method and the OECD (➤Organization for Economic Cooperation and Development) also publishes comparable international economic data based on PPP.

purchasing-power parity theory A theory which states that the ➤exchange rate between one ➤currency and another is in ➤equilibrium when their domestic purchasing powers at that rate of exchange are equivalent. For example, the rate of exchange of £1 = $1.70 would be in equilibrium if £1 will buy the same goods in the UK as $1.70 will buy in the USA. If this holds true, purchasing-power parity exists. The theory has its source in the mercantilist (►mercantilism) writings of the seventeenth century, but it came into prominence in 1916 through the writings of the Swedish economist, Gustav Cassel (1866–1945). The basic mechanism implied by the theory is that, given complete freedom of action, if $1.70 buys more in the USA than £1 does in the UK, it would pay to convert pounds into dollars and buy from the USA rather than in the UK. The switch in demand would raise prices in the USA and lower them in the UK, and at the same time lower the UK exchange rate until equilibrium and parity were re-established. Cassel interpreted the theory in terms of changes in, rather than absolute levels of, prices and exchange rates. He argued that the falls in the ►foreign-exchange markets in the post-war period were a result of ►inflation due to unbalanced ►budgets increasing the quantity of ►money. In practice, the theory has little validity because exchange rates, which are determined by the ►demand and ►supply of currency in the foreign-exchange markets, are related to such forces as ►balance of payments disequilibria, ►capital transactions, ►speculation and government policy. Many goods and ►services do not enter into international trade, and so their relative prices are not taken into account in the determination of the exchange rate. ►►index-number problem; Mises, L. E. von; real exchange rate.

pure strategy ►mixed strategy.

put option ►option.

pyramiding ►holding company.

Q

***q* theory** A theory of ►investment behaviour which suggests that firms invest as long as the value of their ►shares exceeds the replacement cost of the physical assets of the firm. Developed by ►Tobin, *q* theory is attractive because it encompasses other theories of investment in a simple framework. The *q* referred to is the ratio of two numbers. The first is the value of a firm to its shareholders. This is equivalent to the expected future profits of the firm. The second number is the replacement cost of the assets of the firm, machines, buildings, etc. If the first exceeds the second (i.e. *q* is greater than one) the firm should want to expand as the profits it expects to make from its assets are greater than the cost of its assets. If *q* is less than one, the shares of the firm are worth less than the assets and it will pay the firm to engage in ►divestment to sell the assets rather than try to use them. What should happen is that firms invest or divest until *q* is approximately equal to one.

quality adjusted life years (*qalys*) A calculation of benefit to assist in determining the optimum allocation of resources in medicine. In considering the outcome of any particular medical procedure consideration is given not only to the number of years life is prolonged but also its quality. The costs of alternative procedures are compared with their *qalys* and other benefits which are expected to be gained from the different procedures (►►cost–benefit analysis) to help to choose the preferred option. The use of *qalys* does not imply that other aspects of decision-making in medicine are not included in assessment, such as the question of, for instance, the need for procedures to be seen to be equitable between different classes of people. ►death rate.

quantitative restrictions ►quotas.

quantity rationing The name given to one of four states of an economy that can exist when ►excess demand or ►excess supply persist in the ►labour market or in the markets for goods and services. Quantity rationing is an area of ►macroeconomics in the tradition of ►Keynes (►Keynesian economics). It focuses on the study of ►disequilibrium, in contrast to ►neo-classical economics or ►new classical economics (►economic doctrines) which are predominantly concerned with the behaviour of economies in which all markets clear. In quantity-rationing theory, in both the labour market (where firms buy, and households sell) and the goods market (where households buy, and firms sell) prices are not flexible. The wage level should adjust to clear the labour market, and the price level to clear the goods market. If wages or prices are sticky in the short run, disequilibrium can arise. This leaves either buyers or sellers rationed in how much they can trade. Once quantity constraints apply in markets, the effectiveness of price signals can be undermined. Four different regimes arise in the following situations:

(a) ►repressed inflation: excess demand exists in both the labour and good markets (buyers are rationed in both)

(b) ►Keynesian unemployment: excess supply exists in both the labour and goods markets (sellers are rationed in both. They don't sell everything they would like to sell)

(c) ►classical unemployment: excess supply exists in the labour market, and excess demand in the goods market

(d) ►underconsumption: excess demand exists in the labour market, and excess supply exists in the goods market

Despite the assumption that prices and wages are sticky in the short run, the most important implication of quantity rationing is that even if prices are flexible in the long run, under Keynesian unemployment, there will be little or no tendency for the economy to move towards equilibrium. This contrasts with other economic doctrines which hold that as long as prices and wages are flexible, all markets clear eventually.

quantity theory of money The theory that changes in the ►money supply have a direct influence on prices, and nothing else. The theory is derived from the identity $MV = PT$ (called the ►Fisher equation) where M is the stock of money, V the velocity with which the money circulates (►velocity of circulation); P is the average ►price level; and T the number of transactions. All this equation says is that the amount of money spent equals the amount of money used. It is not a theory, it is a truism. The theory itself has two key elements. (a) That the velocity with which money circulates is stable, at least in the short term, and (b) that the number of transactions (which is closely related to the level of physical output) is fixed by the tastes of individuals, and the real behaviour of firms in equilibrium. In this case, increases in M can only lead to increases in P, that is money supply increases cause ►inflation. The theory provided the basis for ►macroeconomics prior to ►J. M. Keynes's *General Theory*, and had a plausibility about it in the eyes of early proponents of ►neo-classical economics, who strongly believed in the power of markets to settle at equilibrium points. It was largely superseded by the ►Keynesian economics, under which both elements of the theory came under attack. Increases in M were held to lead to falls in V. And, in some circumstances, increases in real income. However, in the 1960s the quantity theory re-emerged in a more sophisticated form, through the work of ►M. Friedman. He accepted the Keynesian view that V could alter when M altered, but said that it did so only in stable and predictable ways. On the second postulate, whereas Keynes said that unemployment could exist at an equilibrium of the national economy, and therefore an increase in the money supply could increase real output, Friedman although admitting unemployment could persist held that this was caused by structural factors in the economy (►unemployment, natural rate of) and could not be influenced by ►aggregate demand measures, at least not for very long. ►►economic doctrines, monetarism.

quartile ►percentile.

quasi-money ►near money.

quasi-rent A term applied by ►A. Marshall to the earnings of capital, the supply of which is fixed in the short run. It is the excess made in the short run by a firm from the difference between the selling price and the ►prime cost of the product. For example, suppose that a firm can make pens at a cost of 10 pence in labour and raw materials, and it can sell them at 40 pence. A quasi-rent of 30 pence is earned. This is not, however, the profit of the firm, because there are costs of fixed inputs which have to be covered by sales, even though they don't add to the cost of making extra pens. A loss-making firm can earn quasi-rents.

Quasi-rent is analagous to ►economic rent, because it represents a return in excess of that necessary to keep the firm in production – whenever price exceeds avoidable costs. It differs from economic rent, however, in that it is a temporary phenomenon. It can exist because in the short run competing firms do not have time to enter an industry; and firms do not have time to exit an industry either, and may have irretrievable ►sunk costs. ►barriers to exit.

Quesnay, François (1694–1774) A surgeon by profession. Quesnay held the post of secretary of the French Academy of Surgery and edited its official journal. He became physician to Madame de Pompadour. His major economic works appeared in various articles in the *Encyclopédie* in 1756 and in 1757, and in the *Journal de l'agriculture, du commerce et des finances* in 1765 and in 1767. The *Tableau économique* and *Maximes*, a commentary on the *Tableau*, set out three classes of society, and showed how transactions flowed between them. The three classes were (a) landowners, (b) farmers, and (c) others, called the 'sterile class'. Only the agricultural sector produced any surplus value, the rest only reproducing what it consumed. (►Marx, K.) He anticipated ►Malthus's fear of underconsumption arising from excessive ►savings. Net ►income would be reduced if the flows in the *Tableau* were interrupted by delays in spending. This was the first attempt to construct a ►macroeconomic input–output ►model of the economy (►input–output analysis). In fact, progress in this field had to wait the application of ►matrix algebra and computerization (►Leontief, W.W.). Quesnay suggested a single tax, '*l'impôt unique*', on the net income from land, arguing that the nation would thereby save tax-collecting costs. Only agriculture yielded a surplus, and therefore ultimately it bore all taxes anyway (►Mill, J. S.). He was a central figure in the group of economists called the Physiocrats, who flourished in France between 1760 and 1770.

quotas In ►international trade the quantitative limits placed on the importation of specified ➤commodities. The ➤protection afforded by quotas is more certain than can be obtained by raising import ➤tariffs as the effect of the latter will depend on the price ➤elasticities of the imported commodities. Quotas, like tariffs, can also be used to favour a preferred source of supply (➤➤General Agreement on Tariffs and Trade; imports). The term also applies to quantitative restrictions on production which may be set by ➤cartels or colluding oligopolists (➤collusion; oligopoly).

quotation The privilege granted to the issuer of a ➤security by a ➤stock exchange of placing the price of that security on the official list. A quoted security is for this reason referred to as a ➤listed security. Only public companies fulfilling certain requirements designed to safeguard the investing public are granted quotations. Lesser standards apply in the ➤unlisted securities markets, but companies for which ➤market makers post prices in these markets are not properly described as *quoted companies*; in the UK this term is reserved for those on the official list of a recognized ➤stock exchange.

quoted company ➤quotation.

R

R & D ➤research and development.

Radcliffe Report The Committee on the Working of the Monetary System was set up in May 1957, under the chairmanship of Lord Radcliffe, with wide terms of reference. It published its report in August 1959. The report received considerable critical acclaim for the high standard of its description of the UK financial system and its institutions. At the same time, however, it gave rise to some criticism that the report had not given sufficient weight to the importance of regulating the quantity of money (➤monetary policy) as part of economic and financial policy. The Radcliffe Report concluded that monetary policy should give priority to controlling the ➤liquidity of the monetary system, and not the quantity of money in the system: 'Rejecting from among such measures [i.e. monetary measures to control ➤inflation] any restriction of the supply of money, we advocate measures to strike more directly and rapidly at the liquidity of spenders. We regard a combination of controls of ➤capital issues, bank advances and ➤consumer credit as being most likely to serve this purpose.' Reasons for taking this view were the 'theoretical difficulties' of identifying 'the supply of money' and the 'Haziness that lies in the impossibility of limiting' the income ➤velocity of circulation. Nevertheless, the report did not dismiss the quantity of money as unimportant, but rather believed that given proper control of liquidity it would look after itself. In external policy, the report was in favour of fixed ➤exchange rates. 'It would be more difficult, if there were no fixed rate to be defended, to keep domestic costs in line with costs abroad, and the need to devalue might result from the very ease with which the external value of the currency could be adjusted.'

Ramsey pricing ➤inverse elasticity rule.

random sample A ➤sample in which every member of the ➤population (*simple random sample*) or some subset of the population (➤stratified sample) being tested has an equal chance of being included in the sample. The purpose of sampling is to be able to infer, from the sample taken, the attributes of the population as a whole. Only if the sample is random can the ➤probability be calculated that a sampled attribute applies to the population as a whole. ➤➤quota sample.

random walk The path of a variable over time that exhibits no predictable pattern at all. For example, if a price, p, moves in a random walk, the value of p in any period will be equal to the value of p in the period before, plus or minus some random variable. That random variable is normally distributed with a constant

➤variance and is entirely independent of the value of p. To predict the value of p tomorrow, we can do no better than look at its value today. Certain variables, such as share prices, are held to follow a random walk because, if anyone could predict that prices were going to rise tomorrow, they would buy shares today in order to sell them tomorrow at the higher price. They would go on buying them until today's price had been driven up so high that it was no longer expected that prices would rise tomorrow. The only thing that will affect the price of a share is news about the firm which could not have been anticipated, and is thus random. ➤➤efficient markets hypothesis; rational expectations.

rate of interest The proportion of a sum of money that is paid over a specified period of time in payment for its loan. It is the price a borrower has to pay to enjoy the use of cash which he does not own, and the return a lender enjoys for deferring his consumption or parting with liquidity. The rate of interest is a price that can be analysed in the normal framework of ➤demand and ➤supply analysis. It may be seen as a price in two different markets:
(a) The market for ➤investment funds. It equalizes the *demand* for such funds, which is for investment, and the *supply*, which is ➤saving. If investors believe that they can earn a return of 10 per cent on borrowed money by building a factory, and the rate of interest is 5 per cent, they will demand all the funds that are available, indeed will eventually offer more than 5 per cent to obtain cash which will earn them a profit at any rate up to 10 per cent. Savers, on the other hand, have a rate of ➤time preference reflecting the compensation they require for putting money aside for the future and not spending it in the present. If they need only 4 per cent to be induced to save, and the rate of interest is 8 per cent, there will be so much money put into savings that the rate will be driven down. The rate of interest thus adjusts to ensure that investment equals saving, with saving reflecting the weight people attach to current consumption over future consumption, and investment the amount of extra future production that can be expected to result from building new plant and machinery.
(b) The market for liquid assets (➤liquidity). Firms and consumers may prefer their assets to be in a readily available form – they would prefer money worth £1 million to a factory worth the same. However, most borrowers will need cash for long-term use, and will need the certainty that they won't have to pay it back at short notice. Thus, to compensate people for giving up ready access to the money they lend (their loss of liquidity), interest is paid. This means that the interest rate has an important influence on the demand for money, and on very liquid assets.
    The interest rate is thus affected by ➤liquidity preference and ➤time preference. ➤Keynes introduced the idea of its importance in the demand for money and emphasized it in this role. Classical economists ignored liquidity preference, believing it to be in the market for investment that the rate of interest was determined. The problem of bringing the money market and the investment market to equilibrium with one price was at the heart of Keynesian economics. It would

be surprising if a satisfactory equilibrium was achieved in both markets simultaneously. In simple theory, only one interest rate should prevail in the economy – if, for example, one building society offers a lower return than another, investors would move their cash from the first until it has so little money that it is forced to raise its rate (►arbitrage). However, for two main reasons, many rates prevail at any one time. The first is that ►financial intermediaries charge for their services by adding to the interest rate they charge borrowers or subtracting from the rate they pay lenders. This means there is an interest-rate differential: lenders get less than borrowers pay if a financial intermediary arranges the loan. The second is that interest rates also carry a risk premium: those lending money will want a higher-than-market rate of return if their investment has an uncertain return (►risk). ►►capital asset pricing model; interest, abstinence theory of; interest, classical theory of; interest, natural rate of; interest, productivity theories of; interest, time preference theory of; liquidity trap; term structure of interest rates.

rate of return Usually, net ►profit after ►depreciation as a percentage of average ►capital employed in a business. This is the return on capital employed, often abbreviated as ROCE. One of a number of ►financial ratios used to measure the efficiency of a business as a whole, or of particular ►investment projects. The rate of return may be calculated using profit before or after ►tax, and there are a number of other variations of the concept. Profit may be defined as net of tax but not of depreciation and interest, i.e. profits available for ►equity shareholders, or as operating profit, i.e. to exclude investment income and ►capital gains. Capital employed may be defined to exclude ►loan capital, in which case the return measured is that on equity capital; sometimes ►working capital is excluded. The use of simple rates of return in the analysis of alternative investment projects is open to the serious criticism that it does not take account of the timing of capital outlays and earnings, and hence does not allow for the time value of money (►investment appraisal). Strictly speaking, the rate of return on capital employed in a business does not measure the return to capital alone or the efficiency of the use of ►resources by that business, since the returns to each of the ►factors of production cannot be separated out. However, in normal circumstances a firm which is earning a long-term rate of return lower than its cost of capital (►capital, cost of) could be said to be using resources inefficiently.

rate-of-return regulation A form of ►regulation, common for ►public utilities in the USA, under which firms are prevented from earning too high a ►rate of return. Under such a regime, price rises are capped to levels at which the target rate of return will be exceeded. This price will invariably be lower than the price which a profit-maximizing monopolist would charge. ►►Averch–Johnson effect; price regulation.

rate of technical substitution (RTS) The increase in production of one commodity an economy can achieve by cutting the production of another commodity by one unit. If a country could transfer resources from making one spoon to make two forks, the rate of technical substitution between spoons and forks is two. The rate of technical substitution between commodity A and B usually diminishes as production of A increases. If, at production of twenty aircraft and twenty million loaves of bread, society can produce a million loaves with equal ease to one aircraft, at production of thirty aircraft and ten million loaves, the production of one aircraft will require a much larger sacrifice in terms of loaves. Graphically, the RTS is the slope of the ►transformation curve. Mathematically, it is the ratio of the ►marginal products of producing two items. ►►economic efficiency; marginal rate of substitution.

rates ►local taxation.

rational expectations The assumption that the behaviour of economic agents is based on an understanding of the economy, and a forecast of future events, that are not systematically falsified by actual economic events. Nobody can predict the future with perfect foresight because unforeseen, random happenings are bound to occur. However, someone with rational expectations will construct their expectations so that on average they are correct; that is, they will be wrong only because of random, non-systematic errors. The disadvantage of other ways in which individuals may be assumed to predict the future is that they allow them to make systematic errors. ►Adaptive expectations, for example, postulate that individuals predict next year's price inflation on the basis of last year's, and the rate of change up to last year. At a time of increasing inflation, their expectation will perpetually lag behind the actual inflation rate – but despite this, under the hypothesis of adaptive expectations, everybody carries on using this predictive method although it produces biased forecasts.

The theory of rational expectations has stimulated debate in economics because it has controversial implications. The first is that it appears to demolish any case for government policy aimed at stimulating demand in the economy: if the government expands the money supply by 5 per cent, everybody will believe that prices will rise as a consequence. This will make them add 5 per cent to their wage demands or prices and a 5 per cent price inflation occurs without there being any positive effect on output or employment. (►policy ineffectiveness theorem.) The second is that markets behave efficiently (►efficient markets hypothesis). The price of the shares of a company reflects the profits the company is expected to make. If expectations are rational, the price at any point in time is based on expectations which have taken into consideration all possible information about the company. This has two consequences. The first consequence is that if some 'news' arrives that indicates the company's fortunes are likely to change, that information will cause the price to change immediately. Secondly, however, as the 'news' that arrives can reflect only random, not systematic, events, the price of the company's shares must follow a random path (►random walk).

The interesting implications of rational expectations should not necessarily make them appear a plausible description of men's behaviour. Nevertheless, like ➤perfect competition in ➤microeconomics, rational expectations provide a model of an extreme form of human behaviour that provides a benchmark against which the behaviour of people in the real world can be judged. Moreover, in the very long term, the hypothesis that systematic forecasting errors are not made appears by no means implausible. ➤➤expectations; Lucas critique; new classical economics.

Rawls, John American political theorist, whose main work, *A Theory of Justice* in 1971, outlined a basis for ranking social outcomes – an implicit ➤social-welfare function. His notion was that social welfare should simply be defined in terms of the welfare of the least well off – a so-called ➤maximin approach. The welfare of the rest of the population should only be treated as a tie-breaking rule, for ranking different outcomes that were irrelevant to the least well off. A simple caricature of the Rawlsian position has been widely quoted in ➤public-choice theory as one potential basis for judging the desirable and undesirable.

real balance effect ➤Pigou, A. C.

real business cycle theory The argument that the ➤business cycle is caused not by fluctuations in ➤aggregate demand, but by random shocks in the conditions under which producers supply their products (➤supply-side economics). This account was born of the oil crises of the 1970s, when world oil prices rose dramatically, leading to recession. The kinds of supply shocks discussed are wars, weather disturbances, new technological developments and new social developments.

real exchange rate An ➤exchange rate between two currencies calculated by valuing a given basket of goods and services in terms of the two currencies and dividing the two resulting sums. Suppose there is a 10 per cent increase in prices in Britain, no ➤inflation in Germany, and a 10 per cent depreciation of the British currency against the deutschmark; then the real exchange rate between the pound and the deutschmark is constant. ➤➤purchasing power parity.

real income ➤real terms.

real terms A ➤money value adjusted for changes in ➤prices. The nominal value of the ➤national income may rise by 10 per cent over a year with a similar increase in personal expenditure, but if consumer prices have risen by 8 per cent the quantity of goods and services that are purchased by the consumer will have increased only by about 2 per cent. Thus to convert money values to *constant prices* or real terms it is necessary to deflate (➤deflation) data at current prices by an appropriate ➤index number. In the same way money wages or other forms of income can be adjusted to *real wages* or *real income* to allow for changes in the purchasing power of earnings. ➤➤money illusion.

real wages ➤real terms.

receiver ➤bankruptcy.

recession An imprecise term given to a sharp slowdown in the rate of economic growth or a modest decline in economic activity, as distinct from a slump or ➤depression which is a more severe and prolonged downturn. Recessions are a feature of the ➤business cycle. Two successive declines in seasonally adjusted (➤seasonal adjustment), quarterly, real ➤gross domestic product would constitute a recession.

reciprocal demand ➤equation of international demand.

reciprocity The practice, sometimes called a 'fair trade' or 'beggar-my-neighbour' policy, by which governments extend to each other similar concessions or restrictions in trade. It is reflected in US trade policy in the Reciprocal Trade Agreements Acts of 1934, the Trade Expansion Act of 1962, which made possible the Kennedy round of trade negotiations under the ➤General Agreement on Tariffs and Trade, and the Trade Act of 1974.

recognized investment exchanges (RIEs) ➤Financial Services Act 1986.

recursive model A system of equations in which ➤endogenous variables in one equation appear as ➤exogenous variables in others, but in which there are no subsets of equations which each cross-refer to endogenous variables. For example, the following two-equation system is recursive:

$$a = f_1(z)$$
$$b = f_2(a)$$

while the following system is not:

$$a = f_1(b)$$
$$b = f_2(a)$$

The significance of the recursive model is the ease with which it can be solved in terms of exogenous variables: values for all the endogenous variables can be found straightforwardly if the equations are solved in the right order.

redeemable securities ➤Stock or ➤bonds that are repayable at their ➤par value at a certain date, dates or specified eventuality. Most fixed-interest ➤securities are redeemable, though ➤consols bear no redemption date. ➤Ordinary shares and some ➤preference shares are irredeemable. ➤➤redemption date.

redemption date The date at which a ➤loan will be repaid or release given from other obligations. ➤➤redeemable securities.

redemption yield ➤yield.

reducing balance A means of recording ➤depreciation expenses in which the original ➤cost of an ➤asset is 'written down' by a fixed fraction each year. In this way, the amount of depreciation allowed falls each year: e.g. a machine costing £500 could be written down by 20 per cent per annum, i.e. £100 in the first year and then 20 per cent on its written-down value of £400, i.e. £80 in the following year, and so on. A rate can be chosen to write down an asset to an expected residual value in a chosen period of years, e.g. five years and £50, which in our example would require an annual depreciation rate of about 37 per cent. Although the reducing-balance system gives a lighter depreciation charge in later years when maintenance and repair costs as well as risk of ➤obsolescence may be higher (as opposed to the straight-line method, where equal depreciation is charged every year), it is unlikely to accord very closely with actual depreciation. However, the taxation authorities in Britain and other countries base ➤tax allowances for certain ➤capital investment on a reducing balance (➤capital allowances).

reflation A ➤macroeconomic policy of increasing ➤aggregate demand in the economy in order to reduce unemployment. The argument for reflation can most clearly be seen in terms of ➤Keynesian interpretations of the economy. When a ➤deflationary gap exists, unemployment exists, indicating that there is spare capacity in the economy. Additional demand leads to a rise in spending, itself boosted by the ➤multiplier, with a consequential rise in the number employed. Criticisms have been made of reflation as a policy prescription, however, often associated with the doctrine of ➤monetarism. The argument is as follows: the reflation is generated by either printing money or by increased borrowing (➤public-sector borrowing requirement). If it is through printing money, no non-monetary variables can change. The level of aggregate demand rises; prices rise; more labour is sought to produce the extra demand, so wages rise; at the end of the process real wages (➤real terms) are constant, as are all relative prices. Nothing changes except the absolute price level. If, on the other hand, the reflation is financed by borrowing, every pound the government borrows the private sector lends, and thus for every extra pound of government spending there is a pound less of private spending: this is called ➤crowding out, and it occurs because, when the government borrowing increases, ➤interest rates rise, squeezing private investment (➤➤classical economics). These criticisms rely on a belief that market forces work effectively and that unemployment is at its natural rate (➤unemployment, natural rate of), suggesting that a deflationary gap could never exist. They also imply that private investment is highly responsive to interest-rate changes and that interest rates themselves are highly sensitive to changes in the supply of government bonds. ➤➤Keynesian unemployment.

regional policy The framework for measures taken in the attempt to reduce disparities between economic development in general and ➤unemployment in particular among different parts of the country. All countries have prosperous and depressed regions, though in some the disparities are greater than in others. In most cases depressed areas result from the decline of once important industries or other economic activities, for example mining and shipbuilding in the UK. Governments have attempted to restore prosperity by creating incentives for new industry to move into these areas and by improvements in local ➤infrastructure, though these policies have had only limited success. More recently attention has shifted towards the scope for stimulating self-regeneration capacity by the promotion of ➤small business. ➤assisted areas.

Registrar of Restrictive Practices ➤Restrictive Trade Practices Acts.

regression analysis A mathematical technique for estimating the ➤parameters of an equation from sets of data of the independent and dependent ➤variables. For instance, in the demand equation $q = aY + bP + c$, in which q = quantity bought of a good, Y = income and P = price, the parameters a, b and c can be estimated, provided there is a sufficient number of actual observations of the variables, q, Y and P. Regression analysis finds the values of a, b and c, which when substituted in the expression $aY + bP + c$ yields the least error in estimating q. Regression analysis is widely used in ➤econometrics. ➤➤auto-correlation; beta; dummy variable; heteroscedasticity; latent variable, least-squares regression; multicollinearity.

regression model ➤regression analysis.

regressive tax A ➤tax which takes a decreasing proportion of ➤income as income rises.

regulation The supervision and control of the economic activities of ➤private enterprise by government in the interest of economic efficiency, fairness, health and safety. Regulation has a long history, pre-dating the industrial revolution, and takes many different forms. ➤Externalities such as noise and pollution have made it necessary (among other reasons) to regulate road and air transport. The temptation for producers to collude (➤oligopoly), or exploit other instances of ➤monopoly power also require intervention (➤competition policy). More recently, economists have been mostly interested in the regulation of private ➤natural monopolies, such as utilities. This has become the predominant model of ensuring the public interest, replacing public ownership (➤nationalized industries). The choice between different regulatory regimes – ➤price regulation, ➤rate of return regulation or sometimes ➤yardstick competition – are all different approaches to the task. The system of regulation of financial services has also been under recent review. There has also been recent interest in the justification for and consequences of a broader range of regulatory instruments. These other forms of regulation include: measures to safeguard the rights of employees (for example the Employment Protection Acts); to regulate the trade unions; the financial system; personal privacy (the Data Protection Act); the Health and Safety at Work Act; fishing rights; the ➤Consumer Credit Act; town and country planning; food and drugs; industrial training; the licensing of street traders and taxi-cabs.

Regulation may be imposed simply by enacting laws and leaving their supervision to the normal processes of the law, by setting up special regulatory agencies or by encouraging self-regulation by recognizing, and in some cases delegating powers to, voluntary bodies. Except where regulation is necessary to prevent the abuse of monopoly power, in the interests of preserving health and safety or to correct ►externalities or other instances of ►market failure, and even then, there is a risk that the ►compliance costs and other costs of regulation may exceed the ►social benefits. These other costs include administration costs in government or regulatory agencies and what economists call *excess burdens*. Excess burdens are costs imposed on society as a whole through regulatory obstruction of the workings of markets, e.g. by the creation of ►barriers to entry and reduction in competition and ►innovation. The measurement of excess burdens is necessarily imprecise. Attempts have been made to measure consumer prices and innovative activity before and after deregulation, which indicate that these costs may be substantial. The rapid growth of regulation since the Second World War has led to increasing concern about the costs of regulation and a call for the reform and even abolition of regulatory requirements, i.e. ►deregulation. There has in fact been some deregulation, but new demands for regulation arise all the time. ►►free trade; regulatory capture.

Regulations of the European Union ►Directives of the European Union.

regulatory capture The situation that occurs when regulators advocate the interests of the producers they are intended to regulate. ►►regulation.

re-intermediation ►disintermediation.

relative-income hypothesis A theory of ►consumption and ►saving which suggests that individuals are more concerned with their consumption relative to other people's than they are with their absolute living standard. If everybody wants to 'keep up with the Joneses' in their consumption, the poor will spend a higher proportion of their income than the rich. This is observed to be the case. However, as society as a whole gets richer, no one will feel able to consume less, because everybody will also be getting richer. This too is observed. The relative-income hypothesis, developed by James Duesenberry, is an alternative, and rather less widely accepted theory for reconciling the ►time series and ►cross-section evidence on consumption within different countries, compared to the ►permanent-income hypothesis and the ►life-cycle hypothesis. Nevertheless, the insight that relative income matters to utility is not to be disregarded. Most people would consider that someone today on the average ►real income of 1930 would genuinely be poorer than his 1930s' counterpart, if only because certain types of important social interaction (such as joining in office chat) require possession of the means to share experiences (such as having a TV to watch, and videos to discuss). ►►consumption function.

rent 1. The income accruing to the owner for the services of a ►durable good such as a piece of land, property or a computer. (➤Ricardo, D.) **2.** ➤economic rent.

rent-seeking behaviour Behaviour which improves the welfare of someone at the expense of the welfare of someone else. The most extreme example of rent-seeking behaviour is that of a protection racket, in which one group betters themselves without creating any welfare-enhancing output at all. Not all examples are criminal, however: the behaviour of labour or management when they put more effort into increasing their share of ➤turnover, rather than into increasing the total volume of turnover, can be described as rent-seeking.

rentier Someone who receives his income in the form of ➤interest and ➤dividends rather than in wages or salary and who does not otherwise participate in the process of production. A provider of ➤capital and person of independent means.

repeated games A strategic interaction between a small number of players that occurs in the same form many times. The distinguishing features of repeated games are that the players can learn about the strategies of the other players by looking at what they do in earlier rounds, and that the players can punish or reward cooperative behaviour in early rounds by adopting certain strategies in later rounds, substantially changing the nature of the game. This is of more significance in games that go on being repeated indefinitely than those that are played a known, finite number of times. ➤➤game theory; prisoner's dilemma; tit-for-tat.

replacement-cost accounting ➤inflation accounting.

replacement rate ➤unemployment trap.

repo Sale and repurchase agreement under which funds are borrowed through the sale of short-term securities (➤money market) on condition that the instruments are repurchased at a given date. Used between ➤central banks and the money market as part of ➤open-market operations. First developed in the United States, repos are also widely used as a borrowing method by large corporations, banks and non-banking institutions. ➤➤gilt repo.

repressed inflation The state of a set of markets or an economy in which there is persistent ➤excess demand for goods and services. If prices are below their market-clearing levels, demand will outweigh the available supply; this should drive prices up, causing ➤inflation. If, however, prices are prevented from rising, for example, because of price controls (➤prices and incomes policy), the inflation can be prevented but consumers will not be able to obtain as much of things as they want. Features of markets suffering repressed inflation will thus be queues, explicit state rationing, constant shortages or black markets.

While the term repressed inflation can be used to refer to a state of any set of markets in which excess demand is not removed by price increases, more specifically it is one of four forms of ➤quantity rationing in the macroeconomy; the others are ►Keynesian unemployment, ►classical unemployment and ►underconsumption. In terms of these models of the economy, repressed inflation is one in which buyers in both the labour and goods markets are rationed: households cannot get the goods they want and firms the labour they want. It can be cured by freeing prices and wages and letting them rise, so that they meet equilibrium prices, or by cutting aggregate demand so that the equilibrium price in each market moves down to the level of the actual price. ►►planned economy.

resale price maintenance (RPM) The practice whereby a manufacturer requires the distributors of his product to resell at certain ►prices, or at not less than minimum prices, which he has set for his products. There have been a number of UK governmental inquiries into the practice to determine whether or not it was in the public interest. The arguments in favour were that price-fixing set ►profit margins which ensured fair returns, both to the manufacturer and to the distributors for their services, and that no government had the right without very good reason to interfere with the freedom of private citizens to make contracts. In 1955 the ►Monopolies and Mergers Commission's report *Collective Discrimination – A Report on Exclusive Dealing, Aggregated Rebates and Other Discriminatory Trade Practices* recommended that RPM, collectively enforced by manufacturers, should be made illegal, although individual manufacturers should be permitted to continue the practice. The report served as the basis for the ►Restrictive Trade Practices Act of 1956. This Act specifically prohibited the collective enforcement of RPM and set up the Restrictive Practices Court to decide each individual case on its merits. Restrictive agreements had to be registered. The manufacturer could, under the Act, take a price-cutting retailer to court, even if there was no explicit contract between them, and the court could issue an injunction restraining the retailer. In 1964 the Resale Prices Act was passed under which all resale price agreements were assumed to be against the public interest unless it could be proved otherwise to the court. ►►Competition Act; Fair Trading Act; vertical restraints.

research and development (R & D) Activity which includes: (a) basic or pure research intended to increase knowledge without any particular application in view, such as research into the properties of materials; (b) applied research directed at a particular objective, for example searching for a new material for a product; (c) experimental or development work on new inventions or the improvement of existing products and processes. All three types of R & D are carried out by government research laboratories, universities, research institutes and company research establishments. About 2 per cent of the employed ►labour force is engaged in R & D work in the United States and about half that percentage in Europe. However, these figures relate to professional, recorded R & D workers only; a substantial amount of research and development is carried on by amateurs and in small firms which goes unrecorded. R & D activity is important because of its role in defence policy and in commercial ►innovation. While it is the case that some countries may have an interest in avoiding the costs of R & D, while enjoying the benefits of other countries' investments in it (►free-rider problem), academics in the area surmise that a minimum national investment in R & D is necessary even to adopt or replicate other nations' technology. That basic minimum may be seen as an 'entry-ticket' to the modern world.

reserve asset ratio ►credit control.

reserve currency A ►currency which governments and international institutions are willing to hold in their ►gold and foreign-exchange reserves and which finances a significant proportion of ►international trade. These two conditions normally require that (a) the value of the currency must be stable in relation to other currencies, (b) the currency is that of a country which holds an important share of world trade, (c) there exists an efficient ►foreign-exchange market in which the currency may be exchanged for other currencies, and (d) the currency is convertible (►convertibility). The major reserve currency is the US dollar which accounts for over 50 per cent of the total, followed by the ►European Currency Unit, the German deutschmark, the Japanese yen and UK sterling. ►►international liquidity.

reserve ratio ►reserve requirement.

reserve requirement 1. An obligation on a ►bank or other ► financial intermediary to maintain a specified proportion of total assets in ►liquid form. These can be designed to ensure solvency of banks (►capital adequacy) or they can be used as a device for helping limit the creation of credit. 2. (US) Legal reserves that member banks in the ►Federal Reserve System are required to maintain at their Federal Reserve Bank. The reserves are related to ►deposits and the *reserve ratios* vary according to the type of deposit. By raising or lowering reserve requirements, the Fed can tighten or loosen bank credit.

resource accounting The initiative launched in the UK ►budget of November 1993, designed to recast the accounting practices of the public sector. The goal is for government departments to produce information not just on the basis of the ►cash flow passing through their books, but also on the basis of the resources. The most important distinction between the two relates to ►capital assets, which incur a large cash flow in one year, but not such a large real flow of resources. The hope is that the bulk of such assets in the public sector can be valued, in order that an annual charge can be levied for the ►cost of capital incurred by the department. In managing resources, that should give a greater incentive for efficient management of current and future cash. ►►public expenditure; private finance initiative.

resource allocation The assignment of a role to scarce resources (►►factors of production) in the economy to the production of outputs. The fact of ►scarcity leads to the need for allocation. As this allocation of scarce inputs determines the composition and size of an economy's output, each possible bundle of goods and services produced by an economy constitutes an allocation of resources. Each allocation therefore can be defined in two ways: either by the use made of inputs or by the mix of total output. In a world consisting of only two goods, say milk and honey, each allocation may be represented by a point on a graph with output of one of the commodities on each axis. In such an economy, if no more milk can be produced without a fall in the output of honey, the allocation is efficient and lies on the ►transformation curve of the economy. If the combination lies within that curve, resources are used inefficiently because by, say, swapping some of the beekeepers assigned to tending dairy cows with some of the farmers assigned to beekeeping, production of both milk and honey can be increased. Economics may be said to be about the allocation of scarce resources. It is concerned with the optimum allocation of those resources to the production of goods and services required by society and determined through the ►price system. ►►economic efficiency; market forces.

resources Scarce inputs that can yield ►utility through production or provision of goods and services (►depletion theory; factors of production; natural resources; production function; resource allocation).

restriction, exchange ►exchange control.

Restrictive Practices Court ►Restrictive Trade Practices Acts.

Restrictive Trade Practices Acts The UK Act of 1956, based on the recommendations of the ►Monopolies and Mergers Commission's 1955 report on *Collective Discrimination – A Report on Exclusive Dealing, Aggregated Rebates and Other Discriminatory Trade Practices*. This Act required the registration of all agreements between two or more firms, whether buyers or sellers, which contain restrictions on ►prices, quantities or quality of goods traded or on channels of distribution. It set up a Restrictive Practices Court, serviced by five judges and up to ten laymen and a Registrar of Restrictive Trading Agreements. The court was required by the Act to assume that each agreement is against the public interest unless it could be shown to have advantages on reference to seven explicit factors: (a) that the restriction is necessary for public safety; (b) that it confers specific and substantial benefits or advantages on consumers; (c) that it neutralizes monopolistic or restrictive activities of others; (d) that it is necessary in order to be able to negotiate fair terms with strong buyers or sellers; (e) that removal of the agreement would lead to significant regional ►unemployment; (f) that removal would reduce ►export earnings; and (g) that it is necessary to support other restrictive practices which are in the public interest. Under the 1956 Act only agreements of 'no substantial economic significance' could be exempted from appearing before the court, and even this could be achieved only by their removal from the register. In 1968 a second Restrictive Trade Practices Act was passed by which agreements could be exempted from court proceedings as a result of a

Board of Trade directive. The Act also gave the Board of Trade (now the Department of Trade and Industry) powers to call certain information agreements for registration which were excluded from the previous Act. The functions of the Registrar of Restrictive Trading Agreements were taken over by the Director-General of Fair Trading under the ►Fair Trading Act 1973, which also extended the scope of the legislation to include commercial services. The Restrictive Trade Practices Act of 1976 consolidated previous legislation. ►►Competition Act; resale ►price maintenance; vertical restraints.

retail banking ►wholesale banking.

retail prices index An index (►index number) of the prices of goods and services purchased by consumers to measure the rate of ►inflation or the cost of living. The weights used in the index are revised annually and are based on the proportion of ►household expenditure spent on each item, information on which is obtained in the UK from the Family Expenditure Survey. The prices of these items are collected, and the index updated, monthly. Changes in the index have an important effect on the economy because they may influence wage and salary awards and may affect the value of index-linked assets and pensions. ►►indexation; harmonized indices of consumer prices.

retail trade The final link in the chain of distribution from the manufacturer to the final consumer. The economic functions of the retailer are to hold stocks at a location convenient to the consumer so as to provide him with choice, guidance and after-sales service and, where appropriate, credit facilities (►consumer credit). In providing these services, the retailer adds value to the goods he purchases from the wholesaler or direct from the manufacturer (►value added). There were 221,000 retail businesses registered for ►value-added tax at the end of 1994 in the UK (not all retailers need to register for VAT) but the number of small retailers has fallen substantially since 1950, mainly as a result of competition from the large multiple retailers which enjoy ►economies of scale in operation and in purchasing from their suppliers (►countervailing power).

retained earnings Undistributed ►profits. ►►self-financing.

retentions Undistributed profits. ►►self-financing.

return on capital employed ►►rate of return.

return on investment (ROI) ►►rate of return.

returns to scale The proportionate increase in output resulting from proportionate increases in all inputs. If the number of workers, raw materials and machines used by a firm are all doubled, three situations can result: *decreasing returns to scale* would hold if output less than doubled; *constant returns to scale* would exist if output exactly doubled; and *increasing returns to scale* would hold if output more than doubled. Decreasing returns to scale should not be confused with the law of revaluation

>diminishing returns which traces the response of output to an increase in one individual input with all others held constant. >>economies of scale; production function.

revaluation >devaluation; exchange rate.

revealed preference An approach to demand theory which derives the traditional laws of demand using only information on the choices the consumer makes in different price and income situations coupled with the assumption that such choices are made rationally. It can be seen as a third approach to consumer behaviour, in contrast to the cardinal approach (>marginal utility), which requires there to be an absolute, single, measure of utility, and the >ordinal utility approach (based on >indifference-curve analysis), which requires there to be some measure of relative utility, albeit one that does not require actual magnitudes of utility to be ascribed to bundles of commodities.

The revealed-preference approach holds that only two types of information are theoretically necessary to predict the behaviour of consumers and derive the laws of demand. The first is the observed spending of a consumer in different price–income situations – this reveals which bundles of commodities are preferred to others. The second is the assumption that the consumer's behaviour accords to certain axioms of 'rationality' – to predict how someone will spend their money, we must know that they will not behave erratically (>transitivity). It can be shown that, if such information were available in full, an indifference map could be constructed for the consumer. Implicitly, therefore, the approach does construct at least a partial indifference map of the form used in indifference-curve theory and should best be seen as an alternative expression of this theory rather than a replacement for it. >>demand, theory of; Samuelson, P. A.

revenue reserves >company reserves.

reverse take-over The acquisition or >take-over of a public company by a private company. Often also used to refer to the acquisition of a company by another, smaller, one.

reverse yield gap >yield gap.

Ricardian equivalence The idea originally expounded by >Ricardo, and more recently by Robert Barro, that government deficits do not matter because private citizens anticipate the fact that any borrowing now has to be repaid later, and thus increase their saving with that in mind. The essence of the proposition is that individuals can unravel the effect of government policy. If the government consumes more and borrows the money to do so, and if the private sector did not want overall consumption to rise, the private sector would save more now so that when the debts had to be repaid, the money was available. The government might as well have taxed people rather than borrow the money. Ricardian equivalence can be seen as part of a thread of economic thinking which holds that only decisions

360

about real variables – like consumption and production – matter; and that decisions about financing will, in perfectly functioning markets, never have an effect. ➤crowding-out; deficit financing; Modigliani – Miller theorem.

Ricardo, David (1772 – 1823) The son of Jewish parents who were connected with the ➤money market, first in the Netherlands and later in London, Ricardo had little formal education. At the early age of fourteen, however, he was already working in the money market himself. It was James Mill (the father of ➤J. S. Mill) who persuaded Ricardo, himself diffident about his own abilities, to write. Nevertheless, Ricardo succeeded in making a fortune on the ➤stock exchange, sufficient for him to be able to retire at forty-two. Not surprisingly, many of his earlier publications were concerned with money and banking. In 1810 he published a pamphlet on *The High Price of Bullion, a Proof of the Depreciation of Bank Notes*; in 1811 appeared the *Reply to Mr Bosanquet's Practical Observations on the Report of the Bullion Committee*; and in 1816 *Proposals for an Economical and Secure Currency*. However, his work on monetary economics did not have the originality or exert the influence comparable to his studies in other branches of economics. In 1815 he published his *Essay on the Influence of the Low Price of Corn on the Profits of Stock*, which was the prototype for his most important work. This first appeared in 1817 under the title of *The Principles of Political Economy and Taxation*, a work which was to dominate English ➤classical economics for the following half-century. In his *Principles* Ricardo was basically concerned 'to determine the laws which regulate the distribution (between the different classes of landowners, capitalists and labour) of the produce of industry'. His approach was to construct a theoretical ➤model which abstracted from the complexities of an actual economy so as to attempt to reveal the major important influences at work within it. His economy was predominantly agricultural. With ➤demand rising as a result of increasing ➤population, and a level of subsistence which tended, by custom, to rise also over time, more and more less-fertile ➤land had to be brought into cultivation. The return (in terms of the output of corn) of each further addition of ➤capital and ➤labour to more land fell (➤diminishing returns, law of). This process continued until it was no longer considered sufficiently profitable to bring any additional plots of land under cultivation. However, ➤opportunity costs and ➤profits must be the same on all land, whether or not it was marginal. Labour cost the same wherever it was applied. If profits were higher at one place than at another, it would encourage capital to be invested at the place of high return, until by the process of diminishing returns, profit fell into line with profits elsewhere. Therefore, as costs and profits were the same throughout, a surplus was earned on the non-marginal land, and this was ➤rent (shaded in the diagram).

The consequence of this was that, as the population expanded and more less-fertile land was brought into cultivation, profits became squeezed between the increasing proportion of total output which went in rent and the basic minimum level of subsistence allocated to the wages of labour. Ricardo assumed that prices were determined principally by the quantity of labour used during production (►value, theories of). However, he recognized that capital costs did nevertheless also have an influence on prices and that the effect of a rise in wages on relative prices depended on the proportion of these two ►factors of production in the various ►commodities. With a rise in wages, ►capital-intensive goods became cheaper relative to ►labour-intensive goods, with a consequent shift in the demand and output in favour of the former (►Ricardo effect).

In the theory of ►international trade Ricardo stated explicitly for the first time the law of comparative costs. This law can best be illustrated by means of the example of two countries (A and B) producing two commodities (say cloth and wine). If the relative cost of cloth to wine is the same in both countries, then no trade will take place because there is no gain to be had by exchanging wine (or cloth) for cloth (or wine) produced abroad for that produced at home. Trade will take place where cost differences exist. These can be of two kinds. First, if wine is cheap in A and cloth in B, A will specialize in wine and B in cloth, and exchange will take place to their mutual advantage. Secondly, the law of comparative costs states the condition under which trade will take place, even though both commodities may be produced more cheaply in one country than another.

Man-hours per unit of output

Country	Wine	Cloth
A	120	100
B	80	90

Country *B* exports one unit of wine to *A*, and imports in exchange 120/100 units of cloth. If Country *B* had devoted the eighty man-hours employed in making wine for exports to making cloth instead, it would have produced only 80/90 units of cloth. Country *B* therefore gains from trade by the difference ((120/100) – (80/90)) units of cloth. As long as *B* can exchange wine for cloth at a rate higher than 80/90, it will therefore gain from the trade. If Country *A* exports a unit of cloth to Country *B*, it will obtain in exchange 90/80 units of wine. If the hundred man-hours required by *A* to produce a unit of cloth had been devoted to the home production of wine, only 100/120 units of wine would be obtained. The gain from trade therefore is ((90/80) – (100/120)) units of wine. Provided therefore *A* can exchange cloth for wine at a rate higher than 100/120, it will gain from the trade. Within the range of exchange of wine for cloth of 120/100 and 80/90 both countries therefore benefit.

The law of comparative costs survives as an important part of the theory of international trade today. Otherwise Ricardo's main contribution is the analytical approach of theoretical model building which has contributed substantially to economists' methodological tool-kits. ➤equation of international demand; Heckscher–Ohlin principle; Ricardian equivalence.

Ricardo effect The idea, supported by ➤von Hayek that, if the ➤prices which firms received for their outputs increased more than the ➤opportunity costs of their raw materials and wages, the average rate of ➤profit on ➤capital employed per year increased more for those firms with a short than for those with a long turnover period. This can best be illustrated by a simple arithmetical example. If the rate of profit per year is 5 per cent, £100 of capital will yield £105 in one year and £110 in two years (approximately, ignoring ➤compound interest). If output prices rise by, say, 1 per cent, the ➤yield rises to £6 for one year and to £11 in two years. The rate of profit, therefore, rises to 6 per cent per annum for the capital which can be turned over in one year, but only to 5½ per cent per annum for capital with a two-year turnover period. Consequently, in a boom, when ➤commodity prices rise faster than wages, firms are discouraged from investing in capital goods' industries because of the long production time required. This reaction is called the Ricardo effect because of its affinity to Ricardo's argument that, if ➤real wages fall, firms tend to substitute ➤labour for machinery. This conclusion contrasted sharply with ➤Keynes's views based on the principle of the accelerator (➤acceleration principle).

RIE Recognized investment exchange (➤Financial Services Act 1986).

rights issue An offer of new ➤shares to existing shareholders. A company will offer the 'rights' in a certain proportion to existing holdings, depending upon the amount of new ➤equity capital it wishes to raise. Thus, in a 'one for one rights issue', each shareholder would be offered a number of new shares equal to the number he already holds. To ensure that the issue is taken up, the new shares are typically offered at well below the market price of the existing shares. The choice of the discount below the ruling price is not as critical in normal circumstances as is often supposed, because when the rights issue is announced the market price of the shares will adjust to the market's view of the value of the rights price. Rights issues are a relatively cheap way of raising ➤capital for a quoted company since the costs of preparing a brochure, ➤underwriting commission or press advertising involved in a new issue are avoided. Moreover, because existing shareholders are given the right of first refusal on them, they ensure that companies cannot issue new shares at a price that effectively reduces the value of existing shares. ➤➤new-issue market.

risk A state in which the number of possible future events exceeds the number of events that will actually occur, and some measure of ➤probability can be attached to them. This definition distinguishes risk from ➤uncertainty, in which the probabilities are unknown. A gambler, for example, faces risk because he could either be very much richer tomorrow than he is today or (more likely) slightly poorer, depending on whether a roulette wheel spins the ball into the right hole – and he knows the odds of the roulette wheel. ➤➤Bernoulli's hypothesis; probability.

It is normally assumed that economic agents dislike risk (➤➤risk aversion) and in the market for financial assets the riskier an asset, the higher the expected return investors will require of it (➤➤expected utility; portfolio theory).

risk assessment A measure of the risks of a course of action, and the costs and benefits of reducing those risks. Risk assessment has been promoted as a means of preventing economic activity which creates more dangers than are reasonable. But perhaps more importantly, it can prevent the error of creating 'too much safety' – the imposition of costly safety mechanisms that reduce risks less than is worthwhile, given the cost. Economists argue that it is not worth investing millions of pounds in, say, a rail safety system, if it is expected to save one life a year, if the money could have saved more lives invested elsewhere. ➤➤cost–benefit analysis; quality-adjusted life years.

risk aversion The placing of a higher value on a prospect arriving with certainty than on an uncertain prospect which has the same expected outcome, but with some ➤risk or ➤uncertainty attached. If you would prefer to be given £10 with certainty than to have a 50 per cent chance of £15 and a 50 per cent chance of £5 (which gives an average of £10) then you are risk-averse. Economists normally assume that consumers are risk-averse on account of ►diminishing marginal utility. The displeasure of losing £5 outweighs the pleasure of winning an extra £5 because the richer we are, the less we probably value £5 (►►Bernoulli's hypothesis). Risk aversion explains why people normally insure against disaster. Gambling, on the other hand, is risk-loving behaviour; people at casinos on average pay out more than they win back. ►►Allais, Maurice; expected utility.

risk capital Medium- and long-term funds invested in enterprises particularly subject to ►risk, as in new ventures. Sometimes used as a synonym for ►equity capital, it is also used instead of the term *venture capital*, a somewhat more precise term meaning equity and ►loan capital provided for a new or ►small business undertaking by persons other than the proprietors. Neither term is unambiguous, since all capital except that secured by fixed assets is at risk. Venture capital is provided by private investors, sometimes known as *business angels*, and by a number of specialized venture-capital institutions of which there are over 120 in the UK, some owned by banks or other financial institutions (*captives*). In the United States the term 'venture capital' is restricted to seed or development capital for new or young enterprises and does not include capital for ►management buy-outs, as in the UK. In the USA, venture capital plus capital for buy-outs (known there as *leveraged buy-outs*) is known as *private equity*.

Robbins, Lionel, Baron Robbins of Clare Market (1898–1984) Lord Robbins became a lecturer at the London School of Economics after graduating there. After a brief period as a lecturer at New College, Oxford, in 1924, and again from 1927 to 1929, he was appointed in 1929 to the Chair of Economics at the London School of Economics, a position he held until 1961. During the Second World War he was, from 1941 to 1945, Director of the Economics section of the Cabinet Office. In 1961 he became chairman of the *Financial Times* newspaper. He chaired the Committee on Higher Education. An economist in the tradition of the English ►classical school, in *An Essay on the Nature and Significance of Economic Science*, which appeared in 1932, he defined economics as 'a science which studies human behaviour as a relation between ends and scarce means which have alternative uses'. Economic analysis should beware of including propositions based on value judgements; that is, it should be a scientific logical process without ethical or moral overtones. (►normative economics; positive economics.) His other publications include *The Great Depression* (1934), *Economic Planning and International Order* (1937), *The Economic Problem in Peace and War* (1947), *The Economist in the Twentieth Century* (1956), *Robert Torrens and the Evolution of Classical Economics* (1958), *Politics and Economics* (1963), *The Evolution of Modern Economic Theory* (1970) and *Autobiography of an Economist* (1971).

Robinson, Joan Violet (1903–83) Educated at Girton College, Professor Robinson took up a post as assistant lecturer at Cambridge University in 1931, becoming reader in 1949. She was elected to the Chair of Economics in 1965 on the retirement of her husband, Professor Sir E. A. G. Robinson, and remained in this post until 1971. Economic theorists in the 1920s were much concerned with the problem of the meaning of a theory of ►value based on ►perfect competition. In particular, it was felt of doubtful validity to assume a situation in which there were so many firms supplying a ►commodity that none of them individually could affect the ►price – in face of the existence of the economies of large-scale output, Professor Robinson broke out of the analytical framework of perfect competition and built up her analysis on the basis of firms in 'imperfect competition' (►►monopolistic competition). Each firm had a ►monopoly in its products which was based on the preferences of consumers (►►consumer preference), in spite of the existence of very close substitutes produced by other firms. (►►Chamberlin, who developed similar ideas simultaneously and independently.) These ideas were set out in her book *Economics of Imperfect Competition*, published in 1933. Her other published works include *An Essay on Marxian Economics* (1942), *Accumulation of Capital* (1956), *Essays on the Theory of Economic Growth* (1963), *Collected Economic Papers* (3 vols, 1951, 1960 and 1965), *Economics: An Awkward Corner* (1966), *Freedom and Necessity* (1970), *Economic Heresies* (1971), *Contributions to Modern Economics* (1978) and *Aspects of Development and Underdevelopment* (1979). Government economic controls are confined to the regulation of aggregate effective ►demand, and the allocation of the country's economic ►resources is left to ►free-market competition. There is, however, no more reason to suppose that competition efficiently allocates available resources, given the political and social aims of society, better than it can regulate ►aggregate demand. Professor Robinson played a dominant role in the ►Cambridge school of economic thought, with the development of post-Keynesian ►macroeconomics linked to the early classical period of ►Ricardo and ►Marx (►capital re-switching).

Robinson – Patman Act ►anti-trust.

ROCE ►rate of return.

ROI Return on investment (►rate of return).

roll-over ►corporation tax.

Rostow, Walt Whitman (b. 1916) Educated at Yale, and at Oxford as a Rhodes Scholar, Rostow served during the Second World War in the Office of Strategic Services, and was the assistant chief of the Division of German – Austrian Economic affairs of the US Department of State from 1945 to 1946. He was Pitt Professor of American History at Cambridge University for 1949–50, and Professor of Economic History of Massachusetts Institute of Technology from 1950 to 1965. Since 1969 he has been Professor of Economics and History at the University of Texas. He was appointed special assistant to the President in 1966. His major publications include *Essays on the British Economy of the Nineteenth Century* (1948), *The Processes of Economic Growth* (1952), *The Growth and Fluctuations* *of the British Economy 1790–1850* (1953), *Stages of Economic Growth* (1960), *Politics and the Stages of Growth* (1971), *How It All Began – Origins of the Modern Economy* (1975), *Why the Poor Get Richer and the Rich Slow Down* (1980) and *British Trade Fluctuations 1868–1896* (1981). He postulated that societies passed through five stages of economic development: (a) the traditional society; (b) the pre-conditions for take-off; (c) the take-off, when growth becomes a normal feature of the economy; (d) the drive to maturity; and, some sixty years after take-off begins, (e) maturity, reached in the age of high mass ➤consumption. ➤➤economic growth, stages of; growth theory.

'roundabout methods of production' ➤Böhm-Bawerk, E. von; capital.

rounding error The discrepancy that sometimes arises when numbers are shown to fewer digits than those in which they were calculated. When suppressing a decimal place it is usual to round down when a number is below 0.5 and to round up when it is above 0.5. The same principle applies to the rounding of whole numbers. For example, the following numbers total 6.68 to two decimal places or 6.7 to one decimal place. If each is rounded to the nearest whole number the total of 7 is still retained, although the rounded numbers add to 8.

1.64	2
1.66	2
1.69	2
1.69	2
6.68	8

RPI minus X ➤price regulation.

RPIX ➤underlying inflation.

RPM ➤resale price maintenance.

r-squared ➤multiple correlation coefficient.

RTS ➤rate of technical substitution.

S

saddle point 1. A combination of values of the ➤independent variables in a function such that the resulting value of the function is a maximum in one dimension and a minimum in another. Imagine a function $Y = f(X,Z)$. If Y rises then falls as X rises, and if it falls then rises as Z rises, the function could have a saddle point where it is at its peak with regard to X and its trough with regard to Z. 2. An ➤equilibrium which is stable (➤stability analysis) in some directions, but not in others. For example, we can ask whether there is a tendency for the price in an industry to converge towards the equilibrium price. If it is true that it converges only when it starts at certain levels, but it does not converge if it starts from other points, the equilibrium is known as a saddle point.

sales promotion ➤advertising.

sales tax A tax levied as a proportion of the retail ➤price of a ➤commodity at the point of sale. An indirect tax (➤direct taxation), the term is sometimes used to refer to all taxes on expenditure, i.e. to include ➤value-added tax, which is levied at all levels of production and distribution. There are no single-stage sales taxes as such in the UK, though they are levied in the United States and some other countries. Sales taxes may be general, i.e. levied on all sales, or targeted, i.e. levied on a selective basis. ➤➤fiscal neutrality; taxation.

sample The study of a few members of a ➤population for the purpose of identifying attributes applicable to the population as a whole. The advantage of sampling is that it is cheaper than a study covering the entire population, Moreover, testing the entire population may be impractical; for example, when the test procedures are destructive (e.g. food-tasting). Provided that the sampling procedures are properly designed, the margin of error in the estimates may be calculated and the degree to which the error may be reduced by increasing the sample size. ➤➤quota sample; random sample; stratified sample.

Samuelson, Paul Anthony (b. 1915) Professor Samuelson was appointed to the Chair of Economics at Massachusetts Institute of Technology in 1947. He served in the US Treasury for seven years after the end of the Second World War. In 1970 he received the ➤Nobel Prize in Economics. His publications include *Foundations of Economic Analysis* (1947), *Economics* (1948) and *Linear Programming and Economic Analysis* (with R. Dorfman and ➤Solow, R. M.) (1958). Samuelson developed the ➤Heckscher–Ohlin principle by showing how an increase in the ➤price of a ➤commodity can raise the ➤income of the ➤factor of production which is used most intensively in producing it (►capital-intensive). This led to his formulating the *factor price equalization theorem*, which states the conditions under which, as ►free trade in commodities narrows differences in commodity prices between countries, in so doing the prices (incomes) of factors of production are also brought into line. In other words, free trade is a substitute for the free mobility of factors of production. Professor Samuelson has made important contributions to the development of mathematical economics, general ►equilibrium theory and the theory of ►consumer behaviour. To free the last from what he considered to be the constraint of the traditional concept of ►utility, he invented ►revealed preference. In macroeconomic theory (►macroeconomics), he was, in an article in 1939, the first to formulate the interaction between the accelerator and the multiplier. He was a leading figure on the side of ►neo-classical economics in the debate with the ►Cambridge school regarding the integration of classical (►classical economics) microeconomics and modern macroeconomics in growth theory (►accelerator – multiplier model; social-welfare function; turnpike theorem).

satisficing Behaviour which attempts to achieve some minimum level of a particular ►variable, but which does not strive to achieve its maximum possible value. The most common application of the concept in economics is in the ►behavioural theory of the firm, which, unlike traditional accounts, postulates that producers do not treat ►profit as a goal to be maximized, but as a constraint. Under these theories, although at least a critical level of profit must be achieved by firms, thereafter priority is attached to the attainment of other goals. ►►bounded rationality; optimum; Simon, H. A.

saturation point A level beyond which the *relative* absorption of a product or service is not expected to increase. It is defined in terms of a ratio, e.g. ownership of videos per household or per hundred persons. Once the saturation point is reached, the growth of demand slows down to levels determined by population growth and replacement, although in some cases predictions of saturation points have been falsified by the emergence of multiple ownership, e.g. of cars and television sets. ►►logistic curve; market share.

saving ►Income not spent. At the end of any period, saving is equal to income in that period minus ►consumption, and could be negative if expenditure exceeds income (►dissaving). Note that paying off debt is a form of saving in the economic sense of the term. Saving can occur in the ►public sector when tax revenues exceed final consumption by government plus ►transfer payments and ►subsidies and in the company sector where ►profits are not distributed (►self-financing) as well as in the ►household, though typically the public sector is a net borrower (►public-sector borrowing requirement) while the personal sector and industrial and commercial companies are net lenders.

For the economy as a whole, if total saving is equal to total ►investment, then expenditure by firms and individuals will be in ➤equilibrium (for simplicity we ignore the public sector and foreign trade); if saving exceeds investment then expenditure from wages, salaries and dividends will not return to firms in the form of payments for goods and services (including investment goods) and output would have to fall, thus reducing incomes and bringing saving and investment into balance (➤circular flow of income). What determines the level of saving is, therefore, important in ➤macroeconomics. There are several interpretations of this problem: one is that saving will be a function of the level of income (➤consumption function) (this assumption underlies the mechanism of ➤income determination just outlined), another is that changes in savings will be used to maintain a steady rate of consumption (➤permanent-income hypothesis). ➤➤savings ratio.

savings and loan (S & L) associations (US) ➤savings bank.

savings bank A bank which accepts ➤interest-bearing ➤deposits of small amounts. The earliest savings banks were established in the private sector but later were set up or supported by governments, to encourage individual ➤savings. In the UK there is a ➤National Savings Bank, and the ➤building societies share the basic objectives of savings banks elsewhere. In the United States, savings banks are also called thrift institutions or *savings and loan (S & L) associations*, many of which are ➤mutual companies.

savings certificates ➤National Savings certificates.

savings function ➤savings ratio.

savings ratio The proportion of income which is saved, usually expressed for household savings as a percentage of total household ➤disposable income. It may be calculated gross or net. In the latter case a deduction is made for the ➤depreciation of household fixed assets. The savings ratio in the UK increased from an average of about 2 per cent in the late 1940s and early 1950s to around 8–10 per cent in the 1960s. It peaked at 15 per cent in 1980, fell to 5.4 per cent in 1988 and by 1996 had returned to about 11 per cent. The savings ratio differs significantly between countries as well as over time. The ratio will depend on: the proportion of old people in the ➤population, as young people have more incentive and greater means to save; the rate of ➤inflation, as expectations of rising prices encourage people to spend or invest in fixed assets; the tax regime which in the UK, for instance, has given financial incentives to borrow (negative saving) for house purchase. The *savings function* gives the relationship between aggregate savings, which include non-personal savings, and ➤income and is the inverse of the ➤consumption function.

Say, Jean-Baptiste (1767–1832) A practical businessman, Say developed an interest in economics and began lecturing in the subject in 1816. In 1819 he was appointed to the Chair of Industrial Economy at the Conservatoire National des Arts et Métiers. In 1831 he was appointed Professor of Political Economy at the

Collège de France. His most important published works are *Traité d'économie politique*, which appeared in 1803, and *Cours complet d'économie politique pratique*, which was published in 1829. Although he can claim some credit for the introduction of the concept of an ➤entrepreneur into economic theory, and also the division of the fundamental ➤factors of production into three – ➤land, ➤labour and ➤capital – his fame and notoriety spring from his '*loi des débouchés*', or 'law of markets'. It is probable that his 'law' would not figure so prominently in economics today had not ➤Keynes accused the ➤classical school of being gravely misled by accepting it as the pivot of their macroeconomic theory (➤macroeconomics). According to Keynes, the law said that the sum of the values of all ➤commodities produced was equivalent (always) to the sum of the values of all commodities bought. By definition, therefore, there could be no underutilization of ➤resources; 'supply created its own demand'. However, there is some considerable doubt about what Say actually meant. Several versions have been put forward; some are incontrovertible platitudes, such as in barter a seller must also be a buyer, and if a good is sold somebody must have bought it. Probably the most meaningful interpretation is that of Keynes, but only as a condition which must be satisfied for ➤equilibrium to exist. ➤➤Walras, M. E. L.

Say's law of markets ➤Say, J.-B.

scarce currency ➤hard currency.

scarcity A situation in which the needs and wants of an individual or group of individuals exceed the resources available to satisfy them. In the presence of scarcity, choices have to be made between those wants which can be satisfied and those which cannot be; the available resources must in some way be rationed, either through price or some central distribution system. In the absence of scarcity, no difficult choices would need to be made, no prices would need to be attached to anything, and the study of economics would be rendered entirely unnecessary. As the economist uses the term, scarcity is present in any society in which there is anyone whose desires are not all completely satisfied; it is not a concept of any more relevance to a poor society where want and deprivation are rife than a rich one, where even a scarcity of Rolls-Royces is considered a shortcoming worthy of attention. ➤➤price system; resource allocation; resources.

Schedule D ➤income tax.

Schedule E ➤income tax.

Schengen Treaty A treaty signed at Schengen, Luxembourg, between Belgium, France, Germany, Luxembourg and the Netherlands in June 1990. Austria, Greece, Italy, Portugal and Spain have since also become parties to the agreement. The member countries agreed to abolish customs and immigration border controls at their common frontiers; to establish a common list of countries whose nationals would require visas for entry; and to grant their police the right of pursuit across their common frontiers. At the same time they promised to tighten controls on their external frontiers. In the event Austria, Italy and Greece delayed implementation of the treaty until 1997. ➤➤European Union.

Schultz, Theodore W. (b. 1902) After graduation in economics at the South Dakota State College, Professor Schultz obtained a Ph.D. at the University of Wisconsin. In 1943 he accepted a Chair in Economics at the University of Chicago where he remained until his retirement in 1974. He was awarded the ➤Nobel Prize in Economics in 1979 (jointly with Lewis). His major publications include *Agriculture in an Unstable Economy* (1945), *The Economic Organisation of Agriculture* (1953), *The Economic Value of Education* (1963), *Transforming Traditional Agriculture* (1964), *Economic Crises in World Agriculture* (1965), *Economic Growth and Agriculture* (1968) and *Investment in Human Capital: The Role of Education and Research* (1971). Professor Schultz developed the ideas of human-capital theory in his work on the economics of education and made major contributions to the analysis of agriculture in ➤developing countries. He highlighted the distortion of policy in taxation and trade which biases development against agriculture, condemning the sector to subsistence farming.

Schumacher, Ernst Friedrich (1911–77) ➤intermediate technology.

Schumpeter, Joseph Alois (1883–1950) In 1919 Schumpeter was appointed Professor of Economics at Czernowitz, subsequently moving to Graz. He was appointed Minister of Finance in the Austrian Republic for a short period after the First World War. From 1925 until 1932 he held the Chair of Public Finance at Bonn. From 1932 until his death he was at Harvard University. His major publications include *Theory of Economic Development* (1912), *Business Cycles* (1939), *Capitalism, Socialism and Democracy* (1942) and *History of Economic Analysis*, which appeared posthumously and unfinished in 1954. He built up a theory of the ➤business cycle which was based on three time periods, (a) short, (b) medium and (c) long, to each of which he attributed different causes. He tested his theory against actual fluctuations from the eighteenth to the twentieth century. Although it was reasonably successful, he was doubtful of the predictive efficiency of his theory for future periods. He attempted to work out a theory of economic growth and fluctuation around an explicit recognition of the contribution of technical ➤innovation. He tried to argue that, without the latter, an economy would reach a static ➤equilibrium position of a 'circular flow' of goods with no net growth. He emphasized the evolutionary nature of the capitalist system (➤capitalism). He argued that under ➤monopoly capitalism, firms would place less emphasis on ➤price competition, but would increasingly compete in technical and organizational innovation, thus sending 'gales of creative destruction' through the economic system. He predicted that capitalism would evolve gradually into socialism. ➤➤Kondratieff cycle.

screening The use of a mechanism that allows someone to judge the characteristics second best, theory of

of someone or something even though they cannot see those characteristics directly. In situations of ►asymmetric information, one party to a transaction may wish to know about some feature of the other party – for example, how hard-working they are – which cannot easily be judged before employing them. A screening device is one that can be observed directly, and correlates with the unobservable characteristics. For example, if hard-working people enjoy school and spend many years there, and lazy people hate it and leave as soon as possible, the number of years spent at school may provide a device for screening hard-working from lazy people. However, the device can work only as long as the extra pay that hard-working people get is not so attractive to lazy people that they do choose to suffer spending time at school anyway. This is known as the ►incentive compatibility condition. ►►signalling.

scrip issue An issue of new ►shares to shareholders in proportion to their existing holdings made, as distinct from a ►rights issue, without charge. A scrip or bonus issue does not raise new ►capital. It is merely an adjustment to the capital structure which capitalizes reserves, usually consisting of past ►profits. The word 'scrip' is an abbreviation of 'subscription certificate'. ►►capitalization.

SDR ►special drawing rights.

SEAQ Stock Exchange Automated Quotation (►stock exchange).

seasonal adjustment The elimination from a ►time series of fluctuations that exhibit a regular pattern at a particular time during the course of a year which are similar from one year to another. For instance, unemployment rises in the winter months because of the interruption of work by winter weather conditions. From a study of a series of winter periods, the percentage effect this has on the numbers unemployed may be estimated and the time series of unemployment statistics may be offset by this percentage. The resultant, adjusted, series gives a clearer picture of the underlying trend in unemployment. ►►moving average.

seasonal unemployment ►Unemployment which varies with the season as in the construction, tourist and agricultural sectors. ►►seasonal adjustment.

second best, theory of A theory formulated by R. G. Lipsey and K. Lancaster in *The General Theory of Second Best* (1956), which says that, in the absence of being able to attain all the conditions necessary for the existence of the most desirable possible economic situation, the second-best position is not necessarily one in which the remaining conditions will hold. In an efficient economy, for example, price will equal ►marginal cost in all industries. This will ensure that no consumer who values a commodity more than it costs society to produce will be deterred from buying it (►marginal-cost pricing). If in one industry, however, price is higher than marginal cost, the theory of the second best suggests that it is not efficient for price to be equal to marginal cost in all the other industries for this would encourage too much consumption of those items relative to the more highly priced one. In the second-best world, all other items would be taxed so that everything was priced in excess of marginal cost, and consumers would allocate their budgets almost identically to the way they would in a world of full marginal-cost pricing. ➤➤welfare economics.

secondary bank A financial institution which accepts deposits and makes loans but which has relatively few branches (in the UK) and therefore does not play a major role in the payments system as far as the general public is concerned. Included in the term are the ➤merchant banks, and other money-market banks, the British ➤overseas banks, consortium banks, and some ➤finance houses. There was a secondary banking crisis in 1973 when a number of minor banks (mainly deposit-taking finance houses and other institutions heavily lent to the property sector) got into difficulties when ➤monetary policy was tightened following the oil crisis. ➤➤banking.

secondary market A ➤market in which ➤assets are resold and purchased, as distinct from a primary market in which assets are sold for the first time. The ➤stock exchange is a secondary market in which financial ➤securities are traded, although it is also a primary market where these securities are issued for the first time (➤new-issue market). Another example is the secondary ➤mortgage market in the USA, where holders of mortgages who need funds can dispose of their holding before maturity. Secondary markets are typically larger than primary markets and perform an important function, since purchasers of new issues of securities would be reluctant to purchase and would offer a lower price for them (a bigger ➤discount) unless they were confident that they could, if necessary, dispose of them in the secondary market.

secular trend A long-term directional movement in the trend of an economic ➤time series, as distinct from effects generated by the fluctuations of the ➤business cycle or seasonality (➤seasonal adjustment). Such movements could, for instance, be due to changes in tastes or technology, or the contraction of an industry due to the growth of overseas competitors.

securities 1. In the widest sense, documents giving title to property or claims on ➤income which may be lodged, e.g. as security for a ➤bank loan. **2**. Income-yielding and other paper traded on the ➤stock exchange or in ➤secondary markets. Usually a synonym for ➤stocks and ➤shares. An essential characteristic of a security is that it is saleable. The main types of security are: (a) *fixed interest*: ➤debentures, ➤preference shares, stocks and ➤bonds (including all ➤government securities and local authority securities); sometimes a distinction is made between ➤gilt-edged securities and other fixed-interest securities, though in both cases the holder normally receives a predetermined and unchanging rate of interest on the ➤nominal value of the stock, which is what is meant by fixed interest; (b) *variable interest*: ➤ordinary shares; (c) *other*: ➤bills of exchange, ➤assurance policies,

➤warrants. Securities may be ➤redeemable or ➤irredeemable, quoted or unquoted (➤quotation). ➤➤bond; equities; gilt-edged securities.

Securities and Investments Board (SIB) ➤Financial Services Act 1986.

securitization The substitution of ➤securities for ➤loans. Banks and other ➤financial intermediaries, for example, have packaged house mortgages and (in the United States) ➤credit card loans in this way so that borrowers continue to pay interest which is received by the investor in the security representing the underlying loans. Securitization converts inflexible assets such as long-term bank loans into readily saleable paper.

Select Committee on Estimates A select committee of the British House of Commons, whose purpose is to investigate whichever of the ➤estimates of projected government expenditure it thinks should be examined. Its purpose is essentially to find if any economies may be achieved consistent with the policies implied in the estimates.

self-assessment Method of assessing income-tax liability by letting individuals calculate and declare their income at the year end, and then pay whatever has not been deducted from their wages during the year. It is used in the United States and is being adopted in the UK. From 1996/97 ➤income tax payers may opt to calculate their own tax liability and make provisional payments on 31 January and 31 July. Penalties will be charged for late returns. Persons whose whole income is taxed under the ➤pay-as-you-earn system will not be affected. Under the new system, the ➤self-employed will be assessed on their income on a current-year basis, after a transition system, and no longer on the preceding-year basis which gave rise to considerable complications. Self-assessment was introduced for ➤corporation tax in 1993.

self-employed Working on his or her own account. The number of self-employed persons in the UK is estimated to have risen from 1.9 million in 1979 to 3.3 million in 1996 and now accounts for 12.7 per cent of the ➤labour force. A self-employed person may be a proprietor of an unincorporated business either with or without employees.

self-financing Generating ➤capital from ➤income. A firm which is self-financing is generating its ➤investment funds from internal sources, i.e. the ploughing back of retained ➤profits (or retentions), and ➤depreciation, as opposed to external borrowing, A quoted company has the choice of financing fixed-capital formation or increasing its stocks and work in progress or acquiring other companies or ➤shares in them, either by borrowing on the ➤stock exchange (or from other sources, including banks) or by using undistributed income. If it borrows, it will have to pay ➤interest or ➤dividends and issuing costs on new issues. If it uses undistributed income, it is choosing to pay its ordinary shareholders a lower dividend, i.e. to distribute less of its income. Unquoted companies do not have the alternative of new issues of shares, although they may take further ➤equity from private sources and borrow from other sources. In fact, the bulk of capital expenditure is financed from internal sources. Of total sources of funds of UK industrial and commercial companies over 70 per cent in recent years has been provided from internal sources. The remainder comes from ➤new issues, ➤bank loans, ➤mortgages, inward investment (➤foreign investment) and capital transfers.

self-financing ratio ➤Investment funds derived from undistributed ➤income as a proportion of total investment funds in any accounting period. ➤➤self-financing.

self-liquidating A term used to describe a low-risk financial transaction or ➤loan which incorporates a procedure for simultaneous termination and clearing indebtedness. A ➤hire-purchase transaction is self-liquidating in that regular payments culminate in a final instalment which clears the ➤debt. More generally, the term is applied to any form of finance to fill a temporary shortfall of funds, e.g. ➤bills of exchange, or a bridging loan by a bank to a customer in the process of selling one house and buying another.

selling costs ➤Opportunity costs incurred in ➤marketing and distributing a product, including the costs of advertising, sales promotion, packaging and sales staff.

Selten, Reinhard (b. 1930) A German economist, who has specialized in ➤game theory, and jointly won the ➤Nobel Prize for Economics in 1994. Selten has been one of the economists most concerned with defining the characteristics of an ➤equilibrium in a game. ➤Nash, J., a fellow prize-winner, had developed one such equilibrium (➤Nash equilibrium), but Selten was the first to refine the concept for analysing dynamic situations. One problem with Nash's equilibrium concept had been its inclusion of intuitively unsatisfactory strategic combinations. In particular, if one party to a game makes an untenable threat to the other; and the other is deterred by that threat from some course of action, it is a Nash equilibrium even if the threat was unlikely to be carried out. That did not seem a likely outcome to an interaction. Selten introduced the refined notion of *sub-game perfection*, which essentially counted only those Nash equilibria which would also be Nash in each and every segment of a game taken on its own. In effect, only credible threats should be taken into account. He also devised the notion of the *trembling hand* equilibrium, which is a Nash equilibrium which still holds, even if the players assume one of the players may have a 'trembling hand', and make a mistake as to which rational strategy to follow.

Senior, Nassau William (1790–1864) Educated at Oxford University, Senior was called to the Bar in 1819 and became a Master in Chancery in 1836. In 1825 he was appointed the first Drummond Professor of Political Economy at Oxford. He held this position twice, the first time until 1830 and the second from 1847 to 1852. He served on many Royal Commissions. His major work on economics was an *Outline of the Science of Political Economy*, which appeared in 1836. He is remembered mainly for his abstinence theory of ➤interest. Interest was a reward for abstaining from the unproductive use of ➤savings. The creation of new capital involved a sacrifice. A positive return must therefore be expected to make the sacrifice worth while. Senior can be regarded as one of the first pure theorists in economics. He attempted to elaborate economic theory on the basis of deductions from elementary propositions.

separation of ownership from control The situation where the owners of a corporation do not actively participate in its management. In its earliest form, business was owned and managed by the same people. Economic and technological development led to the advent of the joint-stock company in the seventeenth century to meet the need for larger amounts of ➤capital. This began the process of the separation of ownership from control that continued with the introduction of ➤limited liability for both ➤public companies and ➤private companies, and the gradual emergence of the modern giant corporation in which none of the directors or managers has more than a minority financial interest. This process has given rise to the possibility that the interests of those who control business and those who own it may conflict, a subject of continuing controversy among economists since the publication of *The Modern Corporation and Private Property* by A. A. Berle and G. C. Means in 1932. ➤firm, theory of the; Galbraith, J. K.; moral hazard; principal–agent problem.

SEQUENCE ➤stock exchange.

serial correlation ➤auto-correlation.

Serra, Antonio (15?–16?) A Neapolitan writer in the mercantilist tradition (➤mercantilism), who was the first to analyse and fully use the concept of the balance of trade, both visible and invisible. He explained how the shortage of precious metals in the Neapolitan kingdom was a result of a deficit on the ➤balance of payments. In so doing, he rejected the idea, current at the time, that the ➤scarcity of money was due to the unfavourable ➤exchange rate. The solution was to be found in the encouragement of ➤exports.

services Intangible, non-transferable economic goods as distinct from physical ➤commodities. Services are difficult to define unambiguously. The output of some services from, for example, a bank may take a physical form (a cheque or bank statement); while, although many services are consumed at the point of sale and are not, therefore, transferable (for example a concert or a haircut), a service in which knowledge is imparted (for example a medical consultation or tax advice) may be freely transferable from one consumer to another. The intangible nature of much of the output of the service sector creates difficulties in the calculation of unit ➤productivity. Generally speaking, the service sector of the economy is more ➤labour-intensive than the manufacturing sector, but even this generalization is misleading because with computerization and the development of telecommunications, automated warehouses, special-purpose buildings and other plant and equipment, much of the service sector now employs more ►capital per worker than manufacturing industry. The service sector also contributes proportionately less to exports than manufacturing, but ►invisible exports are of growing importance and world trade in services is growing slightly faster than world trade in physical commodities. Some parts of the service sector and that sector as a whole, on average, have lower levels of ►concentration than the manufacturing or extractive industries, but some (for example ►banking) are highly concentrated in the UK. Parts of the sector, notably distribution, banking, business services and communications, have been growing very rapidly in the past decade. The relative decline of agriculture and manufacturing has given rise to fears of ►deindustrialization, though these fears are probably misplaced, since the growth of services has been characteristic of all the ►advanced countries and the exceptional relative (and absolute) decline of the manufacturing sector in Britain to some extent, at least, reflects the growth of the North Sea oil industry. ►►Baumol effect; Petty, Sir William.

servicing debt ►debt.

shadow economy ►black economy.

shadow price The ►opportunity cost to a society of engaging in some economic activity. It is a concept applied to situations where actual prices cannot be charged, or where actual prices charged do not reflect the real sacrifice made when some activity is pursued. In a perfectly functioning economy, market prices will be equal to ►marginal cost (►perfect competition), which itself represents the true cost to society of producing one extra unit of a commodity; it is equivalent to the value of the items that could have been made as alternatives to the last unit of the commodity produced, with the same resources. In the competitive economy, therefore, the market price of an item is equal to the opportunity cost of producing that item. In an economy which does not function perfectly, however, this is not so. Suppose there is unemployed labour in the economy: the cost of using that labour to society is virtually zero – by employing it no sacrifice is made in terms of other goods produced. The shadow price of labour is zero, even though the workers, if employed, would have to be paid a wage. Alternatively suppose that there is an ►excess demand for labour; at the going wage rate, labour is in short supply. In this case, employing a worker may cost a firm only the going wage, but the cost to society of that firm employing that worker is the production the worker could have produced in an alternative occupation: this will be worth more than the wage rate if labour is in excess demand. The shadow price of labour in this case is higher than the wage rate. In effect, it reflects the benefit that would result from relaxing the constrained supply of workers by one unit.

More generally, shadow prices are used in valuing any item which is implicitly rationed or constrained in some way. Shadow prices can be derived using ►linear programming techniques, and can be used in social ►cost–benefit analysis, which attempts to achieve an optimal ►resource allocation in the absence of an effective ►price system.

share One of a number of equal portions in the nominal ►capital of a company entitling the owner to a proportion of distributed ►profits and of residual ►value if the company goes into ►liquidation; a form of ►security. Shares may be fully ►paid-up or partly paid, ►voting or non-voting (sometimes called 'A' shares). ►►bearer bonds; ordinary shares; preference shares; stocks.

share certificate A document showing ownership of ►shares in a company. ►►CREST; transfer deed.

share indices ►Index numbers indicating changes in the average prices of ►shares on the ►stock exchange. The indices are constructed by taking a selection of shares and 'weighting' (►weighted average) the percentage changes in prices together as an indication of aggregate movements in share prices. Roughly speaking, a share index shows percentage changes in the ►market value of a ►portfolio compared with its ►value in the base year of the index. Index numbers are published by several daily papers and weekly journals. ►►*Financial Times* share indices.

share options ►option.

shareholders' interest ►balance sheet.

Sharpe, William (b. 1934) An economist at Stanford University in California, William Sharpe, was a pioneer of the ►capital asset pricing model, from his 1964 article 'Capital Asset Prices: A Theory of Market Equilibrium under Conditions of Risk'. He jointly won the ►Nobel Prize *for* Economics in 1990 for that achievement, which built upon the foundations laid in ►portfolio theory by one of his fellow winners, ►Markowitz, H. ►►envelope theorem.

Sherman Act ►anti-trust.

shock therapy ►transition, economies in.

short-dated securities ►dated securities.

short run A period of time in which only some ►variables change or economic processes work. It is a concept which can strictly be defined only in the particular context in which it is applied, because its meaning depends on which variables or processes the user of the term has in mind as flexible. Its most common use is in the theory of the firm (►firm, theory of the), where it is defined as the period in which the quantity of certain ►factors of production employed (for example, plant and machinery) is fixed and only, say, the number of workers hired can be changed. The specific period of time being referred to as the 'short run' also varies with every application of the term, because, for example, it takes different amounts

of time to build the plant and machinery for different industries. ➤impact effect;
long run; Marshall, A.

short-run cost curves A graphical representation of the relationship between the
output of a firm and the cost of producing that output with the firm's given level
of fixed assets. For example, a record company may have one plant capable of
producing anything between no records and 1 million. The short-run cost curve
shows how much it would cost to make any number of records with that plant,
taking into account the extra labour and raw materials that would be required to
produce a given quantity (➤firm, theory of the). In contrast, the *long-run cost
curve* would depict how much each number of records would cost if the number
and size of the plants of the record company were allowed to alter. There is,
therefore, one short-run cost curve for every number of plants and level of plant
size. The long-run cost curve joins the average short-run curves tangentially.

Any short-run cost curve can be broken down into two elements. First, short-run
fixed costs: the payments incurred independently of the level of production. Second,
short-run *variable costs*: like raw materials and labour costs which vary with the
level of output. The sum of these produces short-run total *costs*. This cost function
may be depicted as an average cost curve (in which case it is generally assumed
that as production rises it falls to a minimum, and then rises). ➤marginal analysis.

short-term capital ➤business finance.

short-term gains ➤capital gains.

SIB Securities and Investments Board. ➤Financial Services Act 1986.

SIC ➤Standard Industrial Classification.

signalling The use of a mechanism by which someone indicates to someone else
that they have certain characteristics, even though these characteristics are not
directly observable. A signal is the converse of a screen (➤screening). Advertising
is seen as signalling the quality of a product to consumers, because it is only those
firms who have faith in their product, and who think it will be in production for
many years, who will find it worth engaging in expensive advertising. The
engagement ring is a signal of commitment to the fiancée, for, as long as it is
expensive enough, it would not pay the man to buy the ring unless he was serious
about getting married. Economists have been increasingly inclined to explain
economic and non-economic phenomena as signals. ➤asymmetric information.

Simon, Herbert A. (b. 1916) A graduate of the University of Chicago, Professor
Simon held the post of Director of Administrative Measurement Studies at the
Bureau of Public Administration of the University of California from 1939 to
1942, in which year he moved to the Illinois Institute of Technology, becoming
a Professor of Political Science there in 1947. In 1949 Professor Simon was
appointed Professor of Administration and Psychology at the Carnegie Mellon

380

University, becoming Professor of Computer Science and Psychology in 1955. He was awarded the ►Nobel Prize in Economics in 1978. His major publications include *Administrative Behaviour* (1947), *Public Administration* (1950), *Organisations* (1958), *The New Science of Management Decisions* (1960), *The Shape of Automation for Men and Management* (1965), *Models of Discovery* (1977) and *Models of Bounded Rationality and Other Topics in Economics* (1982). Simon argued that the central assumption in economic theory of a rational 'economic man', who maximizes benefits and minimizes costs, is unrealistic. Any decision faced by an individual, in a household or in a firm, is bounded by uncertainties and ignorance. Individuals 'satisfice' (►satisficing). They adjust their behaviour and ambitions continually in the light of experience.

simple interest ►compound interest.

simple random sample ►random sample.

simulation The construction of a ►model which describes mathematically the structure and processes of a real-world situation to be studied and the inputting of values of ►variables in the model in order to generate appropriate out-turns. The model enables the results of a process to be simulated without the need to test the process in an actual situation. ►►Monte Carlo method; operations research.

Single European Act The Act which was passed into law by, and became effective in, each member state of the ►European Union in 1987. By this Act each state agreed to the setting-up of a single market throughout the European Union by 1992. The programme involved the abolition of exchange controls, the recognition of qualifications, the abolition of restrictions on internal transport (►cabotage), liberalization of the market in air services, public procurement tendering, life insurance and banking services, and the abolition of frontier controls (►Schengen Treaty). The Act also widened the application of qualified majority decision-making in the Community. The Commission monitors competition to ensure that no enterprise acts in such a way as to restrict the free movement of goods and services in the Community or to exploit a dominant market position (►competition policy). The Act also widened the areas in which decisions could be made by majority, as opposed to unanimous, vote. A number of areas, such as taxation, still required a unanimous decision from member states for any policy changes to be made. ►►single market.

single market 1. The name given to the objective of the then European Community's (►European Union) 1985 initiative to foster free trade in goods, services and capital within Europe. The idea is to limit the degree to which technical, fiscal and physical barriers limit the flow of commodities across borders. The initiative aimed to create a single market by 1 January 1993; in reality, the programme consists of 286 measures that are still being introduced. The single-market programme does not aim to remove all the factors that inhibit trade: some natural barriers, such as differences in national tastes, will obviously remain. In this regard, the phrase single market is not used in its strict economic sense. **2.** A trading zone in which roughly homogeneous items are traded in roughly uniform conditions of supply and demand. It is likely that in a single market the ►law of one price will prevail. ►►market.

sinking fund ►amortization.

Sismondi, Jean Charles Léonard Simonde de (1773–1842) A Swiss historian and economist, who after a period in exile in England began lecturing at Geneva Academy in 1809 on history and economics. His economic works include *Richesse commerciale* (1803), *Nouveaux principes d'économie politique* (1819) and *Études sur l'économie politique* (1837). Sismondi argued against the doctrine of ►*laissez-faire* in favour of state intervention. He recommended ►unemployment and sickness benefits, and pension schemes for workers. With ►Malthus, he attacked ►Ricardo for not recognizing the possibility of economic crisis developing from underconsumption. He tried to emphasize the dynamic nature of the economic process, compared with the comparative statics of Ricardo (►comparative static equilibrium analysis), and was the first to use sequence analysis as an analytical device. Increased output in one period, he argued, is faced with a level of ►income generated by a lower level of output in the previous period. Total demand falls short of the available supply. Lags in the economic system, therefore, could give rise to underconsumption.

size distribution of firms ►concentration ratio.

Slutsky, Eugen (1880–1948) Slutsky was appointed a professor at Kiev University in 1918, where he remained until 1926. In 1934 he accepted a post at the Mathematics Institute of the Academy of Sciences of the USSR, where he remained until his death. He published an article in the Italian journal *Giornale degli economisti* in 1915 on consumer behaviour in which he showed how the concept of ►ordinal utility could be used to build a theory of consumer behaviour of the same scope as that of ►Marshall, but without the underlying assumption of the measurability of ►utility. However, the article lay unnoticed until ►Hicks and R. G. D. Allen rediscovered it in 1934. In his book *Value and Capital*, Hicks applied Slutsky's name to the mathematical formulae which illustrate how a consumer would react to ►price and ►income changes (►consumer behaviour; Pareto, V. F. D.). Slutsky did little further work in economic theory, but made important contributions to statistics and ►probability theory which are of relevance to economics. He emphasized the danger of assuming causes for observed fluctuations in ►time series by showing how regular cycles could be generated in the derivation of ►moving averages from a series, even though the latter was made up of random numbers. He also made important advances in the study of ►autocorrelation.

small and medium enterprises (SME) ►small business.

small business A firm, managed in a personalized way by its owners or part-owners, which has only a small share of its market and is not sufficiently large to have access to the ►stock exchange in raising ►capital. Given that *small and medium enterprises* (SME) typically have little recourse to institutional sources of finance other than the ►commercial banks and rely heavily upon the personal savings of the proprietors, their families and friends, the long-term growth in ►taxation on income and wealth is believed by some economists to have inhibited the growth of the small-firm sector. SMEs play an important role in the economy, in a dynamic as well as a static sense, and create a disproportionate share of new jobs. A few SMEs grow to challenge existing large firms (cf. ►Schumpeter, J. A.'s 'gale of creative destruction'), change and renewal being an essential feature of the ►free-market economy. It is estimated that in 1986 all but 11,500 of the 2.5 million business ►enterprises in the UK employed fewer than 200 persons. Enterprises employing less than 100 persons account for about 50 per cent of non-government employment. Most small businesses are ►sole proprietorships and ►partnerships, but the vast majority of Britain's active 400,000 or so ►private companies are small firms. ►►enterprise; entrepreneur; establishment; self-employed.

SME ►small business.

Smith, Adam (1723–90) A Scotsman brought up by his mother at Kirkcaldy, he became a student under Francis Hutcheson at Glasgow University at the age of fourteen and won a scholarship to Oxford, where he spent six years until 1746. He lectured at Edinburgh University from 1748 to 1751. From 1751 until 1763 he was at Glasgow, first in the Chair of Logic and a year later the Chair of Moral Philosophy, which he took over from Hutcheson. From 1764 to 1766 he toured France as tutor to the Duke of Buccleuch. His major work on economics, *An Inquiry into the Nature and Causes of the Wealth of Nations*, appeared in 1776. This work of Adam Smith became the foundation upon which was constructed the whole subsequent tradition of English ►classical economics, which can be traced from ►Ricardo through ►Marshall to ►Pigou. Smith was primarily concerned with the factors which led to increased ►wealth in a community and he rejected the ►Physiocrats' view of the pre-eminent position of agriculture, recognizing the parallel contribution of manufacturing industry. He began his analysis by means of a sketch of a primitive society of hunters. If it cost twice the labour to kill a beaver as it does a deer, one beaver would exchange for two deer. ►Labour was the fundamental measure of ►value, though actual ►prices of ►commodities were determined by ►supply and ►demand on the ►market (►Ricardo and Marx). There were two elements in the problem of increasing wealth: (a) the skill of the ►labour force and (b) the proportion of productive to unproductive labour. (According to Smith, the ►service industries did not contribute to real wealth.) The key to (a) was the ►division of labour. To illustrate his point, he quoted the example of the manufacture of pins. If one man were set the task of carrying out all the operations of pin manufacture – drawing the wire, cutting, head-fitting and sharpening – his output would be minimal. If, however, each man specialized in a single operation only, output would be increased a hundredfold. The size of the output need only be limited by the size of its market. The key to (b) was the accumulation of ➤capital. Not only did this enable plant and machinery to be created to assist labour, but it also enabled labour to be employed. Capital for the latter was the wages fund (➤wage-fund theory). The workers must be fed and clothed during the period of production in advance of the ➤income earned from their own efforts. Smith believed that the economic system was harmonious and required the minimum of government interference (➤'laissez-faire'). Although each individual was motivated by self-interest, they each acted for the good of the whole, guided by a 'hidden hand' (➤'invisible hand') made possible by the free play of competition (➤Mandeville, B. de). Free competition was the essential ingredient of the efficient economy. However, from his *Wealth of Nations* it is clear that not only did his scholarship range widely over the fields of history and contemporary business, but that, at the same time, he was a very practical man. He was quite aware, for instance, of the forces which were at work to limit competition: 'People of the same trade seldom meet together even for merriment and diversion, but the conversation ends in a conspiracy against the public, or on some contrivance to raise prices' (Book One, chapter X, part 2). In his discussions of ➤public finance, he laid down four principles of ➤taxation: (a) equality (taxes proportionate to ability to pay), (b) certainty, (c) convenience and (d) economy. ➤➤Hume, D.

Smithsonian Agreement An agreement concluded in December 1971 between the 'Group of Ten' of the ➤International Monetary Fund at the Smithsonian Institute, Washington. Under the agreement, the major currencies were restored to fixed parities but with a wider margin, ±2.25 per cent of permitted fluctuation around their par values. The dollar was effectively devalued by about 8 per cent and the dollar price of gold increased to $38 per oz. Sterling was set at $2.6057 (➤exchange rate).

Smithsonian parities ➤Smithsonian Agreement.

social accounting The presentation of the ➤national income and expenditure accounts in a form showing the transactions during a given period between the different sectors of the economy. The tabulations are set out in the form of a ➤matrix showing the source of ➤inputs of each sector or part of sector and the distribution of their outputs. The production sector, for instance, shows for an industry how much of its inputs were bought from other home industries, how much it imported and how much it spent on wages, salaries and ➤dividends. At the same time, it shows how much of its output it sold to other industries, how much it exported and how much was consumed by private individuals or the government sector. These transactions of the producers' sector are counterbalanced by corresponding transactions of the other sectors. For instance, the personal sector shows the value and sources of ➤incomes earned from the producers' sector and others, as well as the way these incomes are saved or spent on the outputs of the various industries or on ➤imports. ➤➤input–output analysis; Leontief, W. W.

social benefits The total increase in the welfare of society from an economic action. In effect, it is the sum of two benefits: (a) the benefit to the agent performing the action, for example the ➤producer's surplus or ➤profit made; (b) the benefit accruing to society as a result of the action, for example an increase in tax revenues (➤externalities). The phrase is sometimes used to describe the second of these on its own. ➤➤social welfare.

social capital The total stock of a society's productive assets, including those that allow the manufacture of the marketable outputs that create private-sector profits, *and* those that create non-marketed outputs, such as defence and education. ➤➤capital.

Social Charter A Social Charter and Social Action Programme was drafted by the Social Affairs Commissioner of the then European Community (➤European Union) in 1989 for discussion by the member states. The programme included (a) health and safety at work; (b) freedom of movement of workers throughout the Community; (c) equality of opportunity; (d) part-time and temporary work; (e) contractual conditions of employment; (f) management consultation of employees; (g) social security; and (h) immigrant workers. A separate protocol to the Maastricht Treaty (➤European Monetary Union) on social policy was adopted by eleven member states in 1991, the UK not being a signatory.

social cost The total cost to society of an economic activity. It is the sum of the ➤opportunity costs of the ➤resources used by the agent carrying out the activity plus any additional costs imposed on society from the activity. For example, when people drive their cars they incur the private cost of petrol and wear and tear on the vehicle, but the social cost of them driving also adds wear and tear on the roads, and the congestion and pollution they cause, which they do not pay for directly. By taxation, social costs can be incorporated into private costs so that market prices properly represent the true costs to the community. ➤➤externalities; Pigou, A. C.; shadow price.

social net product The difference between the ➤social benefits and the ➤social cost arising from the use of some ➤factor of production or from some form of economic activity.

social overhead capital ➤infrastructure.

social security A system of government-financed income transfers designed to effect a distribution of income considered desirable. The main component of most social-security systems is welfare benefits, given to those in ➤poverty. This can be done in two ways: (a) by identifying groups that are likely to be poor, and giving benefits to them (e.g. the unemployed, the elderly and the disabled) irrespective of their actual income; (b) by identifying, through ➤means tests, people who are poor. The second of these approaches is a less expensive method of eradicating poverty, but leads to the problem of the ➤poverty trap. ➤National Insurance. ➤life-cycle hypothesis; minimum-wage laws.

social welfare The total well-being of a community. It is not measurable because it is not possible to sum the benefits or ➤utilities enjoyed by the individuals composing the community. It is possible, however, for the community to judge whether it prefers one situation to another. ➤compensation principle; indifference-curve analysis; Pigou, A. C.; social-welfare function; welfare economics.

social-welfare function An expression of society's taste for different economic states. The analysis of society's optimal behaviour is analogous to ➤indifference-curve analysis for individuals. Just as the individual's taste can be defined by his or her ranking of different combinations of commodities, social priorities can be defined by a list of preferences of alternative national combinations of commodities. (Just as for the individual, such a list would never in practice approach a complete ordering of every possible allocation, but in theory there is no reason for this limitation to be imposed.) The comparison between individual and social-welfare functions can be taken no further, however; for, whereas any bundle of commodities is assumed uniquely to define a level of ➤utility for an individual, it does not do so for society, because each bundle can be distributed between individuals in different ways. Each alternative distribution will produce a different level of total welfare unless all individuals are identical and their interests are all considered of equal importance. In short, the individual only has to decide how much of each commodity to consume. Society has to choose how much of each commodity should be produced, *and* how it should be distributed. For this reason, unlike the individual's utility function, which is expressed in terms of commodity quantities, the social-welfare function is usually expressed in terms of the utility of the members of society. The function may, for example, be the simple sum of all individual preferences or it might attach a high weighting to the preferences of a particular group of citizens and a low weight to the rest. ➤Value judgements must be made; but the procedure can be applied to derive the consequences of such judgements.

The importance of the social-welfare function is that it provides a criterion for choosing between different economically efficient (➤economic efficiency) states and it can do so with more flexibility than ➤Pareto optimality or the ➤compensation principle criteria. Suppose moving from an efficient allocation, A, to another efficient allocation, B, makes one person better off and another worse off; the social-welfare function can be used to determine which of A and B is to be preferred. There are two approaches to the derivation of the welfare function. The first is that it can be imposed on society. Each individual has a social-welfare function representing their own ranking of different allocations of resources, and the charge of producing one for society as a whole could be assigned to government. The second approach is to devise a constitution or voting system which can turn the rankings of each individual into a single social ranking. To find such a constitution which can guarantee to provide consistent and decisive results is, however, not possible, as Kenneth Arrow shows in the ➤impossibility theorem. It is this issue which has dominated discussion of social-welfare functions in economic literature. ➤➤welfare economics.

socialism A social and economic system in which the means of production are collectively owned and equality is given a high priority. There are various forms of socialism from ➤Marxism to the social-democrat systems in Western Europe, but all share a belief in the necessity for collective intervention in economic affairs. ➤➤planned economy; state planning.

soft currency A ➤currency whose ➤exchange rate is tending to fall because of persistent ➤balance of payments deficits or because of the building up of speculative selling of the currency in expectation of a change in its exchange rate. Governments are unwilling to hold a soft currency in their foreign-exchange reserves. ➤reserve currency.

soft loan A ➤loan bearing either no ➤rate of interest, or an interest rate which is below the true cost of the ➤capital lent. It is the policy of the ➤International Bank for Reconstruction and Development working through its affiliate, the ➤International Development Association, to give 'soft' loans to ➤developing countries for long-term capital projects.

sole proprietorship, sole trader An unincorporated business owned by one person which may or may not have employees. The majority of small firms are sole traders or ➤partnerships. ➤➤company law; self-employed.

Solow, Robert M. (b. 1924) Having been educated at Harvard University, from which he also received his Ph.D. in 1951, Solow remained in Cambridge, Massachusetts, taking a position at MIT, where, with the exception of those periods spent visiting academic institutions abroad, he has remained since. He received the ➤Nobel Prize in Economics in 1987. His major works include *Linear Programming and Economic Analysis* (with R. Dorfman and Paul ➤Samuelson; 1958); *Capital Theory and the Rate of Return* (1963), *The Nature and Sources of Unemployment in the US* (1964) and *Growth Theory: An Exposition* (1970). He has also published numerous articles on ➤depletion theory, including 'The Economics of Resources or the Resources of Economics' in the *American Economic Review* in 1974. He has played a dominant role in debates on ➤growth theory, developing a standard growth model that contrasted in its assumptions with that of the ➤Harrod–Domar model. He has also questioned the effectiveness of ➤market forces in clearing the labour market. ➤➤capital re-switching.

sources and uses of funds An accounting statement describing the ➤capital flows sow's ear effect

of a business. Sources of funds are ►profits from trading operations, ►depreciation provisions, sales of ►assets and borrowing, including capital issues. Uses of funds are purchase of fixed or financial assets (including ►cash), and distribution of ►income. ►►self-financing.

sow's ear effect The inability of a country to raise its ►productivity or per capita ►gross domestic product relative to other countries of comparable development in spite of policy adjustments in ►macroeconomic variables (e.g. the ►exchange rate or ►rate of interest) because of deficiencies on the supply side of the economy such as, for instance, an inadequately educated labour force (►supply-side economics). The term refers to the old saying 'You can't make a silk purse out of a sow's ear'. ►►convergence; institutional economics.

special drawing rights (SDRs) The instruments for financing international trade after the Second World War were predominantly the ►reserve currencies, such as dollars and sterling, and gold. Dependence on the latter, as ►Keynes pointed out, was an anachronism which had been successfully terminated as far as domestic economies were concerned. The problem of depending on the former was that the supply of these currencies was regulated by their countries' ►balance of payments deficits or surpluses. The deficit on the US balance of payments had been an important source of the flow of ►liquidity into ►central bank reserves. The difficulty was that persistent deficits led to doubts about the maintenance of the currency's ►exchange rate and made central banks less willing to hold dollars. This problem came to a head in August 1971, when the US government imposed various measures to correct its balance-of-payments deficit. In December 1971 the dollar was devalued by about 10 per cent.

Keynes had put forward the idea of an international currency, to be called ►Bancor, regulated by a central institution (►Keynes Plan). This idea was turned down then for fear that the creation of liquidity would generate ►inflation. In 1969 the 'Group of Ten' (►International Monetary Fund) agreed to establish SDRs, which are similar in principle to Keynes's original idea, and their agreement was ratified by the IMF. The SDR was linked to gold and equivalent to $1 US at the gold rate of exchange of $35 per oz. Until December 1971 an SDR was equivalent to $1; but, with the effective devaluation of the dollar following the ►Smithsonian Agreement, the rate became 1 SDR = $1.08571. With the subsequent breakdown of the fixed-parity system, the IMF valued the SDR in terms of a 'basket' of sixteen currencies, so that, as from July 1974, the rate in relation to the dollar 'floated'. By 1996 SDR 30 billion had been created. These sums are distributed to each member country in proportion to its IMF quota. In 1981 the SDR was simplified to a weighted ►average of US dollars (42 per cent), German deutschmarks (19 per cent), French francs, Japanese yen and UK sterling (13 per cent each). The weights reflect the importance of each country in world trade. Accordingly, these weights are revised periodically. In 1997 they were US dollars

(39 per cent), German deutschmarks (21 per cent), Japanese yen (18 per cent), French francs and UK sterling (11 per cent each).

specialization ➤division of labour.

specie points The limits between which the ➤exchange rate between two ➤currencies on the ➤gold standard fluctuated. For instance, before the First World War the same amount of gold could be bought in London for £1 and in New York for $4.87, and therefore the par rate of exchange was £1 for $4.87. If the pound fetched less than $4.87 in London, it would pay a merchant to ship gold to the USA to settle his debts provided the cost of freight and insurance were less than the difference between the par rate and the London rate. Therefore, in practice the rate never fell by an amount more than the cost of shipment. Similar forces applied in reverse to prevent the rate rising by an amount in excess of the cost of shipment.

specific tax ➤tax, specific.

speculation Buying and selling with a view to buying and selling at a ➤profit later when ➤prices have changed. ➤➤arbitrage; bear; bull; stag.

speculative bubble A deviation between the price of an ➤asset in the market, and the price justified by the inherent ➤value of the asset, sustained by a belief on the part of buyers that they will be able to sell at an inflated price. The interesting thing about a bubble is that, as long as everyone believes in it, the bubble need not burst. The price can indefinitely deviate from fundamental value. While some have suggested bubbles are a sign of irrationality in the financial markets, creating more variability in the price of assets than is merited by fundamental swings in values, attempts have been made to account for them as rational phenomena.

speculative motive The reason which causes people or firms to hold a stock of ➤money in the belief that a capital gain or the avoidance of a loss can be achieved by so doing. It is one of three motives for holding money outlined by ➤Keynes. When the price of bonds falls, the attraction of holding them increases; this is because people will expect their price to rise again, and anyone owning them when this happens will make a capital gain. People will tend to buy bonds when their price is low, and will thus hold little money. When the price of bonds is high, on the other hand, they will believe their price could fall and hold more money. The amount of money held under this motive thus varies with the price of bonds; as the ➤rate of interest varies inversely with the bond price, the speculative motive for money varies inversely with interest rates. ➤➤liquidity preference; liquidity trap; portfolio theory; precautionary motive; transactions motive.

spillover effect ➤externalities.

spot market A ➤market in which goods or ➤securities are traded for immediate delivery, as distinct from a ➤forward market. 'Spot' in this context means 'immediately effective', so that *spot price* is the price for immediate delivery.

spot price ➤spot market.

spot sterling ➤forward exchange market.

Sraffa, Piero (1898–1983) Sraffa was a Turin-born socialist who came to Britain in the 1920s and settled in Cambridge. He had a reclusive nature, but was broad in his intellectual company, mixing with ➤Keynes and the philosopher Ludwig Wittgenstein. His three main works were an article in the *Economic Journal* in 1926, 'The Laws of Returns under Competitive Conditions'; the eleven-volume *Works and Correspondence of David Ricardo* (which he edited), began in 1930 and finished in 1971 (although most of the substance was published in the 1950s); and *Production of Commodities by Means of Commodities* in 1960.

His primary preoccupation in the 1920s was to expose the flaws in the theory of the firm (➤firm, theory of the) of ➤Marshall. He inspired others to develop theories of production which were not embedded in ➤perfect competition, which he did not think adequately reflected the true state of capitalist society. His 1960 book was a contribution to the perennial problem of finding an invariable measure of value (➤value, theories of). He presented a model in which prices of goods reflected costs of production, a return to a notion of value reminiscent of ➤classical economics. These prices would be determined by technology and stated in terms of a standard commodity, a composite of the commodities used in what is assumed to be equal proportions in the production of everything. In this, the Sraffa model can be said to adopt the assumptions and derive the conclusions of the ➤non-substitution theorem.

Some of his results derive from a particular assumption that the ratio of investment to profits is an ➤exogenous variable, which has led some to conclude that Sraffa's model is a special case of a more general model of economic activity attributable to John von Neumann. ➤➤Ricardo, D.

SRO Self-regulating organization (➤Financial Services Act 1986).

stability analysis The study of the behaviour of ➤variables in ➤disequilibrium to see whether they have a tendency to converge on an ➤equilibrium level (➤dynamics). Most equilibria considered in economics are stable, but models have been developed which are unstable. ➤➤cobweb model; Harrod–Domar model.

stability and growth pact Agreement among members of the ➤European Union, that those entering ➤Economic and Monetary Union, will comply with strict rules on controlling fiscal deficits. The agreement was reached in Dublin in December 1996. It elaborated on provisions in the ➤Maastricht Treaty, which set out the principle of fiscal austerity.

stabilization policy 1. Government action aimed at reducing fluctuations in ➤national income. Such policy – to expand demand when ➤unemployment exists and reduce demand when ➤inflation threatens became the norm after the Second World War in all Western economies, and the low rates of unemployment prevailing during the 1950s coupled with high rates of economic growth were seen as a testimony to its success. In the 1960s, however, the UK faced difficulties sustaining a stabilization policy, with a ►stop–go cycle by which ►reflation occurred, the economy would 'overheat' and then a rapid ►deflation would be necessary. In the 1970s ►stagflation developed, and the traditional-style stabilization policy became obsolete. In the 1980s it was replaced in the UK by an explicit non-stabilizing policy in the form of the *medium-term financial strategy*.

Stabilization policy fell out of favour for two main reasons. First, there are immense practical difficulties in implementing it, primarily because of a lack of sufficient information. All that is known about the economy is how it was behaving several months ago, but actions have to be taken several months in advance. The problem has been likened to attempts at controlling the temperature of water coming out of a shower when any twist of the hot or cold tap takes half a minute to affect the temperature of that coming out of the nozzle. Secondly, it is argued that the temptation to attempt to keep unemployment below its market level (►unemployment, natural rate of) inevitably causes ever-accelerating inflation. Instead, it is suggested, if the equilibrium level of unemployment is too high, measures affecting the supply of labour, rather than demand, are necessary (►supply-side economics). Despite the criticisms, stabilization to some extent exists in all economies: built-in stabilizing factors (►built-in stabilizers) (for example, in recession, unemployment benefits paid out rise, causing an increase in government spending) will never be removed. Moreover, most economists allow that moderate ►reflation at times of recession can be justified. What is rarely attempted is the fine-tuning of the economy that occurred in earlier decades. ►►fiscal policy; monetary policy.

2. The action of government or trade associations to stabilize the price of certain commodities. By holding stocks of the item in question, the authorities can, at least temporarily, affect demand and supply in the market and maintain a constant price. ►►international commodity agreements.

stag A speculator (►speculation) who subscribes to new issues in the expectation of selling his allotment of ►securities at a profit when dealings in them begin. ►►new-issue market.

stagflation The simultaneous existence of ►unemployment and ►inflation. In the early post-war era, it was believed that stagflation would never occur. Either there would be an ►inflationary gap or a ►deflationary gap, with inflation or unemployment respectively; but never the two together. In the 1970s the problem emerged, largely as the natural rate of unemployment (►unemployment, natural rate of) rose with strong wage pressure. The idea that there cannot be ►Keynesian unemployment at the same time as inflation is still credible.

stamp duty A form of indirect taxation (►direct taxation) which involves the fixing of prepaid stamps to legal and commercial documents. The tax may be ad valorem (►tax, ad valorem), as on the conveyancing of property, or specific (►tax, specific), as on declarations of trust. Compliance is enhanced by the fact that specified documents are invalid in law unless stamped. Stamp duty is a very ancient form of taxation but is now of diminishing importance.

standard deviation A measure of the spread of a series of values of a ►variable around its mean (►average). It is defined as the square root of the ►variance. The formula for the standard deviation is:

$$\sigma = \sqrt{\frac{1}{n} \sum_{i=1}^{n} (x_i - \bar{x})^2}$$

where x_i is the ith value, $\bar{x}$ is the mean and n is the number of observations.

Standard Industrial Classification (SIC) A categorization of economic activity used in compiling and presenting official statistics. It consists of *Minimum List Headings* grouped into *Order Numbers*. First introduced in 1948 and revised in 1958, 1968 and 1980, the British SIC system follows the same principles as the International Standard Industrial Classification (ISIC) issued by the United Nations and the NACE (*Nomenclature des Activités établies dans les Communautés Européennes*) system used by the ►European Union.

standard of living The quantity of goods and ►services consumed by an individual or a household. A general measure of standard of living made for comparisons between countries or between different time periods is ►gross national income per head of population. ►externalities; income, distribution of; poverty; retail prices index.

State Earnings-Related Pensions Scheme (SERPS) ►National Insurance.

state planning The regulation of any sector or sphere of an economy by public administrators rather than the ►price system. If state planning is comprehensive, a ►planned economy is said to exist. In many countries, however, there is partial planning, that can take one of two broad forms. The first is very detailed planning in certain key sectors of an economy. For example, the UK National Health Service is controlled by administrators rather than prices: queues ration the supply of certain operations, and the wages and activity of health workers are determined by the administrators, albeit after consideration of where demand is greatest and what supply of labour is available. The second common type of state planning covers virtually all sectors of the economy, but only in a very limited way, with production targets, performance monitoring and some state subsidies, and in the form of a national plan. ►►input–output analysis; nationalized industries; transition, economies in.

static equilibrium ►Equilibrium in which the relevant ►variables do not change over time (in contrast to dynamic equilibrium in which the variables change over time). ►►balanced growth.

statistical inference The method of discovering information about a statistical population by sampling procedures (►sample).

steady-state growth A feature of an economy in which all variables grow (or contract) at a constant rate: for example, population may rise at 3 per cent a year, national income at 4 per cent and the capital stock at 5 per cent. If these rates are maintained indefinitely, steady-state growth exists. It is distinct from ►balanced growth in which all variables grow at the *same* constant rate. Steady-state growth is an ►equilibrium concept, and much of ►growth theory has been concerned with whether it is likely to be achieved. ►►economic growth; Harrod–Domar model.

Stigler, George Joseph (1911–91) Professor Stigler graduated from the University of Washington in 1931 and, after a year at the Northwestern University, obtained his Ph.D. at the University of Chicago. In 1936 he was appointed Assistant Professor in Economics at Iowa State University and in 1938 moved to the University of Minnesota. In 1947 he was appointed to the Chair of Economics at Columbia University, where he stayed until 1959, in which year he returned to the University of Chicago as Professor of American Institutions. Professor Stigler was awarded the ►Nobel Prize in Economics in 1982. His publications include *Production and Distribution Theories* (1941), *The Theory of Prices* (1942), *Five Lectures on Economic Problems* (1948), *Capital and Rates of Return in Manufacturing Industries* (1963), *Essays in the History of Economics* (1965), *The Organisation of Industry* (1968), *Domestic Servants in the USA* (1974), *The Citizen and the State: Essays on Regulation* (1975), *Demand and Supply of Scientific Personnel* (1975) and *The Economist as Preacher* (1982). Professor Stigler analysed the cost of obtaining economic information by firms faced with a range of prices offered by competitive suppliers. He contributed to the analysis of ►unemployment, pointing up the need for workers to devote time to look for the highest available pay rates for the work and conditions they require. He advocated a more empirical approach to the study of government ►regulation and demonstrated that often regulations set for the benefit of consumers will rather turn out in practice to benefit producers.

stochastic process A process subject to random influences (►probability; random sample). For instance, a dependent ►variable may be determined by an independent variable x plus a random element, so that the process generating y is not fully determined by x and predictable by x. The process is stochastic because the value of y depends partially on chance.

stock 1. A particular type of ►security, usually quoted in units of £100 value rather than in units of proportion of total ►capital, as in ►shares. Stock, or stocks and shares, have now become synonymous with securities, and the original distinction between shares and stock has become blurred. The term stock, however, is now coming to mean exclusively a fixed-interest security, i.e. loan stock in a company or local or central government stock. **2**. An accumulation of a

➤commodity. ➤➤inventory.   **3.** (US) A share in the ownership of a company, i.e. equity.

stock appreciation Increase in the value of stock (➤inventories) resulting from an increase in market prices.

stock exchange A ➤market in which ➤securities are bought and sold. There are stock exchanges in most capital cities, as well as in the larger provincial cities, in many countries. The largest in terms of ➤market capitalization is the ➤New York Stock Exchange, followed by London. Other important markets include the ➤Tokyo Stock Exchange, ➤NASDAQ (➤over-the-counter market), and the Association of Exchanges of the Federal Republic of Germany (*Deutsche Börse*). Continental European exchanges are often referred to as *bourses* (Fr.). The economic importance of stock exchanges is that they facilitate ➤saving and ➤investment, first by making it possible for investors to dispose of securities quickly if they wish to do so, and secondly in channelling savings into productive investment. Ready marketability requires that new issues (➤new-issue market) should be made or backed by reputable borrowers or institutions, that information should be available on existing securities, and that there should be both a legal framework and market rules to prevent fraud and sharp practice (➤Financial Services Act 1986). Stock exchanges have their own rules and conventions, but their functioning depends also on the existence of company and other law and ➤financial intermediaries, such as the ➤issuing houses. In recent years stock exchanges have been deregulated (➤deregulation) and many trading floors have given way to electronic trading systems. Trading in many ➤securities is now a global market (➤globalization).

The British Stock Exchange, founded in 1773, developed from informal exchanges in coffee houses in the City of London. The London Stock Exchange's official title is *The International Stock Exchange*. It is managed by a council of member firms. Members are formed into a declining number of firms now including major ➤merchant banks, the ➤clearing banks and other financial intermediaries, many of which are foreign-owned. Business is still conducted by word of mouth, but the traditional trading floor where broker–dealers gathered to buy and sell closed following the ➤Big Bang. The bulk of business is conducted between members by telephone and, for small transactions, dealing can be carried out automatically by electronic means. (➤➤CREST.) The Stock Exchange Automated Quotation (SEAQ) service allows ➤market makers and others to see competing quotations on their screens and ➤stockbrokers to select the best bid/offer for their clients. A new system, Stock Exchange Trading System (SETS), based on the SEQUENCE platform, allows electronic matching of buy and sell orders.

Stock Exchange Automated Quotation (SEAQ) ➤stock exchange.

stock-sales ratio ➤inventories; turnover.

stock split An issue of new ➤shares to shareholders without increasing total

➤capital. The object of a stock split is to reduce the average quoted price of shares to promote their marketability.

stock turnover ➤inventories; turnover.

stockbroker A member of the ➤stock exchange, who buys and sells ➤shares on his own account, or for non-members, in return for a ➤commission on the ➤price of the shares. ➤broker; market maker.

Stone, Sir J. Richard (1913–91) One of Britain's most eminent economists, Sir Richard Stone started his career at Cambridge University as an undergraduate, obtained a D.Sc., and became a Fellow and eventually Emeritus Professor there. His academic life was interrupted by a period in the statistical section of the Office of the War Cabinet between 1940 and 1945, and he held visiting posts at different institutions around the world, including Princeton's Center for Advanced Study. He was awarded the ➤Nobel Prize in Economics in 1984. He has written widely on the measurement of national accounts data and econometric analysis of consumer demand. He wrote several books on the subject, including *National Income and Expenditure* (with ➤Meade; 1944), *The Role of Measurement in Economics* (1951) and *The Measurement of Consumers' Expenditure and Behaviour in the United Kingdom 1920–1938* (with D. A. Rowe et al.; 1954), and many articles, including 'Linear Expenditure Systems and Demand Analysis' in the *Economic Journal* in 1954. One of his main contributions is to have laid the foundation of ➤national income accounting. He also bridged the gulf between the theory of consumer demand (➤demand, theory of) and ➤empirical testing of the subject with what is known as the linear expenditure system. He saw that, by making various assumptions, a tractable system of equations could be used to estimate consumer demands for different groups of commodities more reliably than by estimating the demand for each group in isolation.

stop–go A phrase used to describe the attempted management of ➤aggregate demand in the UK during the post-war period and particularly in the 1960s as the period of fixed ➤exchange rates drew to a close. The exchange rate came under pressure during periods of rising economic activity, but as ➤fiscal policy and ➤monetary policy were applied to reduce aggregate demand and improve the ➤balance of payments it soon became necessary to stimulate the economy again to counteract ➤recession. The stop–go cycle tended to amplify movements in the ➤business cycle.

stratified sample A method of sampling (➤random sample) which is used when the population to be sampled is not homogeneous and the nature of the population's heterogeneity is pertinent to the characteristic of the population about which information is sought. Suppose we wish to find out the percentage of households (the population) which owns dish-washers. Households are not homogeneous; they may be classified into subgroups or strata by, for instance, social group, or income level and, moreover, these subgroups are likely to differ in their ownership of consumer durables, such as dish-washers. Rather than take a random sample of the whole population of households, this is first subdivided into the appropriate categories or strata and random samples taken from each. If the population is heterogeneous a stratified sample will give more accurate results than a simple random sample of the same size.

structural budget deficit A measure of the level of government borrowing, after the effects of the ►business cycle have been taken into account. It is what the level of borrowing would be if the year in question were a year without ►recession or boom. It is the government's budget deficit in a year in which the ►output gap is zero. As there can be no precise measure of the output gap, there can be no precise measure of the structural budget deficit. Estimates for the UK were first provided in the budget of 1997. The ►Organization for Economic Cooperation and Development produces estimates for its member countries. ►public-sector borrowing requirement; built-in stabilizers.

structural impediments initiative An agreement reached in 1990 between the USA and Japan with the long-term aim of reducing the US ►balance of payments deficit in trade with Japan. Under the agreement Japan promised a level of public expenditure of 430,000 yen over ten years, to improve procedures for adopting patents, to tighten anti-►monopoly regulations and eliminate collusive business practices, to reduce high land prices which inhibit the setting-up of new businesses, and to reform land taxes. The USA agreed to reduce its budget deficit and to encourage private ►savings, to ensure that investment rules and practices in the USA did not discriminate against Japanese investors, to improve export promotion, and to consider metrication. Progress in achieving these aims will be reviewed at future meetings over a number of years. ►►international trade.

structural unemployment ►Unemployment arising from changes in ►demand or ►technology which lead to an oversupply of labour with particular skills or in particular locations. Structural unemployment does not result from an overall deficiency of demand and therefore cannot be cured by ►reflation, but only by retraining or relocation of the affected work-force, some of which may find work at low wages in unskilled occupations (►classical unemployment). Structural unemployment is distinct from ►frictional unemployment, which is essentially a short-term phenomenon.

stylized fact A broad generalization, true in essence, though perhaps not in detail. It is perhaps the most important, and least acknowledged, form of ►empirical testing in economics. Economic ►models are judged by their ability to account for real-world phenomena. While some models attempt to capture the detail of a situation, or apply precise estimates of ►parameter values, and are tested using ►econometrics, many models are designed simply to explain behaviour at its simplest, and can be judged only against the broad truth, rather than the detail.

An example of stylized fact is the following: 'the profit rate – the level of profits in the economy, relative to the value of the capital stock – is constant in the long run'. This is a fact which traditional models of growth are held to explain. ►growth theory.

subsidiaries Companies legally controlled by other companies. Although a shareholding of less than 50 per cent may be sufficient to control a company effectively, it is not correctly described as a subsidiary unless between 50 and 100 per cent of the ►shares are owned by another. Companies may choose to retain subsidiaries rather than to integrate them fully into their own organizations for a variety of reasons, e.g. the desire to allow local participation, a wish to conceal a business connection or to avoid the cost and complication of integrating an acquired company. ►►holding company.

subsidiarity The notion that political authority should vest in the most local jurisdiction possible. Under subsidiarity, problems that affect only a town should be decided by the town, those that extend beyond the town should be decided by the county, and those that extend beyond the county should be handled nationally. The twin precepts of subsidiarity are that everyone who is affected by an issue should be in the jurisdiction with responsibility for it; and that as few people as possible not affected by an issue should be in the jurisdiction responsible for it. ►►public-choice theory.

subsidy Government grants to suppliers of goods and services. A subsidy may be intended to keep prices down (i.e. to raise ►real incomes of buyers), to maintain incomes of producers (for example farmers) or to maintain a service or employment (for example subsidies to British Rail or the Rover Group). An essential characteristic of a subsidy, as distinct from a ►transfer payment, is that it has the object of keeping prices below the ►factor cost of production. Subsidies, by distorting market ►prices and ►opportunity costs, may lead to a misallocation of resources, although they may be justified in certain circumstances (for example to correct for ►externalities) and may be used instead of ►tariffs to protect new industry (►infant-industry argument) where not banned by international agreements. It may be possible to achieve the objectives of subsidies by alternative means which have less distorting effects, for example by direct income support through the ►taxation system. ►►cross-subsidy.

subsistence theory of wages ►wage-fund theory.

substitutes Products which at least partly satisfy the same needs of consumers. Products are defined as substitutes in terms of cross-price effects between them. If, when the price of cassettes goes up, sales of compact discs rise, compact discs are said to be a substitute for cassettes, because consumers can to some extent satisfy the need served by cassettes with compact discs. This account is complicated by the fact that, when the price of an item changes, it affects both the ►real income substitution effect

of consumers and the relative prices of different commodities. Strictly, one product is a substitute for another if it enjoys increased demand when the other's price rises *and* the consumer's income is raised just enough to compensate for the drop in living standards caused. One product is a *gross substitute* for another if it enjoys an increase in demand when the price of the other rises and no compensation is made.

Substitution is not a relationship that only holds between individual commodities – groups of commodities can also be substitutes for each other. Benson & Hedges cigarettes may be a substitute for Marlboro; while cigarettes in general may be a substitute for alcoholic drink. Both together may be a weak substitute for restaurant meals. Substitution (but not gross substitution) is a symmetric relationship: if apples are a substitute for bananas, bananas are a substitute for apples. ➤complementary goods; cross-price elasticity of demand.

substitution effect The rate at which consumers switch spending to or from a commodity when its relative price changes but the total ➤utility of consumers is left constant (➤cross-price elasticity of demand). The substitution effect measures how much consumers would switch their spending away from or towards an item whose price had changed, if the resultant change in purchasing power were offset by a compensating transfer of income that would allow them to maintain their total utility (enough to keep them on their ➤indifference curve). It thus isolates the impact of a change in relative prices from the ➤income effect. In terms of ➤indifference-curve analysis, the substitution effect represents a swivel of the budget line around a single indifference curve while the income effect represents a parallel shift of the budget line on to a new indifference curve.

The substitution effect is always negative: consumers always switch spending away from items whose prices rise as they attempt to shield their living standards from the impact. If the price of butter rises by 10 per cent, no great loss is incurred by the consumer who can switch to margarine. The substitution effect is not a concept unique to consumer theory. It arises in many areas of economic analysis including, for example, the demand for ➤labour and ➤capital by firms. ➤giffen good; inferior good; substitutes.

'sun-spot' theory ➤Jevons, W. S.

sunk costs ➤Opportunity costs incurred in the past which are irretrievable and therefore not relevant to current decisions; in ➤Jevons's famous phrase 'bygones are for ever bygones'. For example, a small bakery might buy an oven at a fixed cost, but which it could sell at some future date should it want to. It also might pay out a large amount in advertising its services. However, this latter cost could not be recovered later on – once paid for, the advertising has gone, whether or not the promotion is successful. Sunk costs represent a ➤barrier to entry in an industry because they scare potential entrants from entering – should they fail, they would have wasted all the sunk costs. ➤contestability.

superneutrality of money The inability of changes in the growth rate of the ➤money stock in an economy to affect any ➤variable except the rate of ➤inflation. Money is *neutral* (➤neutrality of money) if the *level* of the money supply only affects the level of prices, but no real variables, such as output. It is *superneutral* if only the *rate* at which that level changes affects the level of prices and no real variables.

super-normal profit ➤profit.

supplementary costs A now little-used synonym for ➤fixed costs or ➤overheads.

supply The quantity of a good (or service) available for sale at any specified ➤price. Supply is determined by a number of influences. The first is price itself: the higher the price, the more profitable it is, other things being equal, for producers to sell a good and the more they will attempt to sell. The second is the cost of inputs: the lower are costs, the more profitable it is to sell a good at a given price and more will be offered for sale. The third is the price of other goods: when the price of other goods rises, the supplier of a good may find it advantageous to switch his production to the supply of the newly high-priced goods rather than stay in the relatively less profitable industry, where supply will fall. It should be noted that supply is *planned* supply, not necessarily what is actually sold. The latter depends on ➤equilibrium in the market. The conditions of supply constitute but one aspect of the determination of the quantities sold and market price, the other being the conditions of ➤demand. ➤➤firm, theory of the; Marshall, A.

supply curve A graphical representation of the quantity of a good or service supplied at different price levels. With ➤price on the vertical axis and quantity supplied on the horizontal axis, supply curves normally slope upwards for two reasons: (a) higher prices allow profits to be made at higher levels of production for firms already in the market; (b) if profits are made, new entrants are attracted into a market.

➤Supply curves can be drawn for the ➤short run and the ➤long run. In the short term, new firms do not have time to enter a market and higher output results only from an increase in production by market incumbents. In the long term, however, new entry occurs. The long-run supply curve links demand–supply equilibrium points on these short-run curves, which (as shown in the diagram below) will be steeper than the long-run curve. ➤➤firm, theory of the.

supply services An item in the British ➤budget and government accounts consisting of expenditures which are estimated annually and voted in Parliament. It includes expenditure by government departments, such as Defence, Agriculture, including ➤subsidies, the National Health Service, etc.

supply-side economics The study of the factors affecting and the policies appropriate for influencing the real economy, that is, the physical behaviour of economic agents, and its response to changes in the structure of relative ➤prices rather than

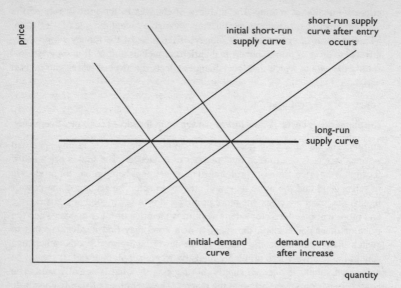

nominal prices. Supply-side economics is roughly based on a positive and negative thesis. On the *negative* side, supply-side economists tend to deny a role to a ➤stabilization policy. Because, they believe, economic agents are only concerned with their real income and because markets have a tendency to clear at their ➤equilibrium levels, an artificial increase in ➤aggregate demand cannot achieve anything. When demand is boosted, the price of all goods rises and, out of a desire to feed the extra demand, more labour will be sought, requiring an increase in wages. Out of all this, nothing changes in real terms: ➤real wages are the same as they were, as are relative prices; all economic agents behave in the same way as they did before, even though the absolute price level might have changed, and possibly some temporary aberration from market equilibria occurred. The *positive* views of such economists relate to the policies that they believe can be effective in influencing the performance of an economy. Anything that attempts to influence the supply of ➤labour or the supply of goods can be called a supply-side measure. Such policies could include: (a) cutting taxes to improve incentives (affecting people's personal trade-off between going out to work and staying at home); (b) heavily legislating against ➤monopoly in order to encourage free competition, low prices and incentives to be efficient; (c) diminishing the ability of trade unions to inhibit the workings of a free labour market; (d) restricting the growth of the ➤money supply to control ➤inflation, improve economic stability and encourage investment; (e) measures to increase the mobility of labour (➤labour, mobility of); (f) cutting the benefits available to those out of work to improve their incentive to take on work (►unemployment trap).

It would be wrong, however, to believe that supply-side measures are only the concern of free-market economists. State interference in the economy can be classed as on the supply side, and measures of this sort might include: (g) increases in spending on education to retrain employees; (h) the introduction of ►profit-sharing as a means of removing industrial conflict, (i) the establishment of a state investment bank for subsidizing high-risk, new-technology firms. In general, supply-side measures can be justified in terms of the findings of ►microeconomics, which is concerned with the behaviour of individual workers and firms rather than with the behaviour of economic aggregates (►►macroeconomics). Free-market supply-side economics emerged as a body of thought in the early 1980s as a doctrine complementary to ►monetarism, which first provided a macroeconomic case against demand-management; it was strengthened by the theoretical revolution that arrived in the form of ►rational expectations. ►►Laffer curve; sow's ear effect.

support ratio ►►dependency ratio.

surplus value ►Marx, K.

sustainable development The notion that economic development should proceed at a pace and in a manner which will conserve the environment and depletable natural resources. In its extreme form (steady state growth) human ►population would be stabilized and renewable resources only would be employed. ►environmental economics.

swap A transaction in which ►securities of a certain value are sold to a buyer in exchange for the purchase from the buyer of securities having the same value, the purpose being to obtain an improvement, in the eyes of either of the parties, in the quality of the security, or to anticipate a change in ►yield. ►Currency as well as securities are swapped in this way.

T

'*tableau économique*' The table with which ►Quesnay analysed the circulation of ►wealth in the economy by setting out the different classes of society. The table showed how the '*produit net*' produced by the agricultural sector circulated between the owners of the ►land, the tenant farmers and other classes such as artisans and merchants. Only agriculture produced any net additions to wealth; all other activities were 'sterile'. The table showed, too, how output is annually reproduced. The sterile classes were essential in that they created the necessary demand for the agricultural sector. ►►Cantillon, R.; Leontief, W. W.; Physiocrats.

take-off in economic development ►economic growth, stages of.

take-over The acquisition of one company by another. Take-overs are sometimes financed by paying ►cash at an offer ►price in excess of the ►market price of the ►shares, but, more frequently for large acquisitions, by the exchange of shares or loan ►stock, possibly with some cash adjustment, issued by the acquiring company for the shares of the acquired company. The term 'take-over' is normally used to imply that the acquisition is made on the initiative of the acquirer and often without the full agreement of the acquired company; as distinct from a ►merger. ►►Monopolies and Mergers Commission; reverse take-over.

Take-Over Panel (UK) A committee responsible for supervising compliance with the City Code on Take-Overs and Mergers, a non-statutory code issued in 1968 and revised subsequently. The code is intended to protect the interests of ►shareholders (►mergers). One requirement of the code is that any company acquiring 30 per cent or more of the ►shares in a quoted company (►quotation) must make a full bid at a price not lower than the highest price paid for its shareholding.

tap issue An issue of ►treasury bills to government departments and others at a fixed ►price and without going through the ►market; as distinct from a tender issue (►tenders).

tariffs, import Taxes imposed on commodity ►imports. They may be levied on an ad valorem basis, i.e. as a certain percentage of ►value, or on a specific basis, i.e. as an amount per unit. Their purpose may be solely for raising revenue, in which case the home-produced product corresponding to the import would bear an equivalent compensatory tax. However, import duties are generally applied for the purpose of carrying out a particular economic policy, and in this context may be used to serve many functions:

(a) To reduce the overall level of imports by making them more expensive relative to their home-produced ►substitutes, with the aim of eliminating a ►balance of payments deficit. ►►devaluation.

(b) To counter the practice of ►dumping by raising the import price of the dumped commodity to its economic level.

(c) To retaliate against restrictive measures imposed by other countries (►reciprocity).

(d) To protect a new industry until it is sufficiently well established to compete with the more developed industries of other countries (►infant-industry argument).

(e) To protect 'key' industries, such as agriculture, without which the economy would be vulnerable in time of war.

For instance, in respect of members compared with non-members of a ►common market tariffs are preferential. It is an accepted principle under the ►most-favoured nation clause of the ►General Agreement on Tariffs and Trade that tariffs should be non-discriminating and any concessions agreed between two or more countries should automatically be extended to all. It has, however, been accepted that this principle may be waived in the interests of the ►developing countries. Significant progress has been made through the GATT in the reduction of tariff levels by means of a series of negotiations, of which the ►Uruguay round of trade negotiations was the latest (►generalized system of preferences; World Trade Organization).

tatonnement process The 'tatonnement' (or 'groping') process was suggested by ►Walras to illustrate that equilibrium in perfect markets (►perfect competition) can be attained at a particular set of prices no matter what the original disequilibrium position of the markets and the route by which prices move before reaching equilibrium. Buyers and sellers make known their prices in the first round. In the second round, buyers and sellers increase their published prices, where there is excess demand, reduce them where there is a shortfall in demand and keep them the same where demand and supply are in balance. The process continues until there is a balance of demand and supply in all markets. At this stage, actual transactions take place; no trade is done until equilibrium is reached. ►►price system.

Taussig, Frank William (1859–1940) Apart from a period from 1917 to 1919 when he was chairman of the US Tariffs Commission, Taussig spent his whole career at Harvard University. His works on economics include *Tariff History of the United States* (1888), *Wages and Capital* (1896), a textbook, *Principles of Economics* (1911) and *International Trade* (1927). An economist in the tradition of ►Ricardo and ►Marshall, he attempted to relate his theory to established statistical data.

tax ►taxation.

tax, ad valorem An indirect tax (►taxation) which is expressed as a proportion tax, 'cascade'

of the ➤price of a ➤commodity – hence it is 'by value'. ➤value-added tax is an ad valorem tax. ➤➤sales tax.

tax, 'cascade' ➤turnover tax.

tax, progressive ➤progressive tax.

tax, proportional ➤proportional tax.

tax, regressive ➤regressive tax.

tax, specific A tax (➤taxation) of an absolute amount levied per unit of a ➤commodity sold or produced. Examples are ➤stamp duty and ➤excise duties. An indirect tax (➤direct taxation), not to be confused with a ➤tax, ad valorem. Where tax rates are applied at very high rates on a commodity – like cigarettes, in the UK – specific duties do not unduly penalize higher quality brands of the commodity, which cost a little more before tax, but would be hugely more expensive after tax if an ad valorem duty was applied.

tax tolerance The willingness or ability of a population to support high or increasing levels of taxation. Tax tolerance – and its inverse, tax resistance – has become a fashionable topic among economists interested in ➤public-choice theory. It is argued that the public have rebelled against the desires of political leaders to raise extra revenue, and the resistance has been shown in the election of governments committed to lower taxation; the growth of the ➤black economy; and specific voter initiatives such as *Proposition 13* in California in 1978, to limit the authority of the state government to levy local property taxes. It has been argued that the growth of government budget deficits (➤public-sector borrowing requirement) has been caused by the inability of governments to curb spending growth, and the unwillingness of populations to pay higher taxes. ➤➤Buchanan, James McGill; hypothecation.

tax, turnover ➤turnover tax.

tax and price index An ➤index number which measures the percentage change in gross income required by taxpaying individuals to maintain their real disposable income (➤real terms). The index takes into account the movement in the ➤retail prices index and changes in ➤direct taxation and employee National Insurance contributions.

tax avoidance Arranging one's financial affairs within the law so as to minimize taxation ➤liabilities, as opposed to *tax evasion*, which is failing to meet actual tax liabilities through, e.g., not declaring ➤income or ➤profit.

tax base The quantity or coverage of what is taxed. The tax base for ➤income tax is the assessed incomes of the whole population. The tax base for ➤value-added tax does not include sales of most foods, books and financial services.

taxation, incidence of

tax burden The amount of ➤money which an individual, institution or group must pay in ➤tax. It should include all costs to the taxpayer which he incurs in paying the tax, e.g. the net-of-tax cost of employing an accountant to complete a tax form, as well as the tax itself. (➤➤compliance cost.) In most policy discussion, the tax burden is taken as the proportion of ➤gross domestic product levied by the government in taxation.

tax equalization account ➤company reserves.

tax evasion ➤tax avoidance. ➤➤black economy.

tax expenditures The costs of tax allowances and reliefs. It has been argued that tax allowances are similar to ➤subsidies and may be seen as a form of ➤public expenditure. However, tax expenditures can never be more than estimates since it cannot be assumed that the ➤tax base would remain unaltered if the allowances were abolished. There is a wide range of allowances and reliefs, most of which probably lead to the loss of some revenue and all of which complicate the administration of the tax system and raise ➤compliance costs. UK tax expenditure estimates for 1996/97 include the following: married couple's allowance, £2800 million; capital allowances against ➤corporation tax and ➤income tax, £18,600 million and ➤mortgage interest relief, £2400 million. Tax allowances and reliefs necessitate higher rates of tax than would otherwise be necessary and lead to distortions in factor markets (➤factors of production) and probably also to higher ➤tax avoidance, and there is increasing interest in reducing them.

tax impact ➤taxation, incidence of.

tax yield The amount of ➤money which results when the rate of ➤tax is applied to the money value of the ➤tax base, minus the costs of collecting the tax.

taxation A compulsory transfer of ➤money (or occasionally of goods and ➤services) from private individuals, institutions or groups to the government. It may be levied upon ➤wealth or ➤income, or in the form of a surcharge on ➤prices. In the first case, it would be called a ➤direct tax; in the latter, an *indirect tax*. Taxation is one of the principal means by which a government finances its expenditure. While it seems obvious what is tax and what is not, there is an awkward boundary. The TV licence is effectively a tax; but are contributions to the ➤State Earnings-Related Pension Scheme? And would compulsory saving to purchase, say, a pension, not be equivalent in spirit to taxation? or, if the government were to apply high prices to the output of ➤nationalized industries, in order to raise revenue? ➤➤air passenger duty; capital gains; corporation tax; hypothecation; income tax; inheritance tax; insurance premium tax; local taxation; public goods; sales tax; self-assessment; stamp duty; tax, specific; tax expenditures; unit tax; value-added tax.

taxation, incidence of The ultimate distribution of the burden of a tax. The initial *tax impact*, or formal incidence of an ➤excise duty on tobacco, for example, may be on the importer or wholesaler who has to pay over the tax to the authorities, but he is likely to pass on some or all of the tax in the form of higher prices to the retailer and the consumer. Whether or not a tax is wholly shifted forward will depend upon the price ➤elasticity of demand and supply for tobacco. If the consumer does not reduce his purchases following the increase in price, he will bear the whole of the tax. If he does reduce his purchases, the wholesaler and the retailer will also be worse off and will be bearing part of the tax. There are two general rules of incidence. In general, a tax on any company must be paid by its shareholders, its employees or its customers. The company itself does not pay tax. And secondly, in the very long term, tax ends up being borne by people in proportion to their ability to transfer the inputs they provide to an economy, or their consumption, from one jurisdiction to another. If capital can move anywhere, governments will find themselves unable to capture revenue from providers of capital. On this account, jurisdictions with high taxes on capital, will simply have less capital, and capital will thus earn high pre-tax returns.

technical analysis ➤chartist.

technical substitution, rate of ➤rate of technical substitution.

technology The sum of knowledge of the means and methods of producing goods and services. Technology is not merely applied science, because it often runs ahead of science – things are often done without precise knowledge of how or why they are done except that they are effective. Early technology – craft skill – was almost entirely of this sort. Modern technology is increasingly science-based, however, and, rather than relying on acquired skill, is easily communicable by demonstration and printed material to those qualified to receive it. It also includes methods of organization as well as physical technique. Technological change and the diffusion of technology are important in economics because new methods, including those embodied in ➤investment, play an important part in theories of ➤economic growth. There is, however, some controversy about the extent to which technological development is an autonomous factor in economic growth. Because it is so difficult to measure there is also room for doubt about whether or not technological change is, or has recently been, accelerating. ➤endogenous growth theory. ➤➤research and development.

tenders Offers to supply at a fixed ➤price. A ➤discount house tendering for an issue of ➤treasury bills, for example, will offer to take up so many bills at a certain price. ➤➤contracting out.

term loan A bank advance for a specific period (normally three to ten years) repaid, with ➤interest, usually by regular periodical payments. Term loans are common practice in the US commercial banking system for business finance, and for larger borrowings the ➤loan may be syndicated, i.e. the provision of funds and the interest earned are shared between several banks. Similar facilities are available in Britain, mainly from the ►commercial banks or other institutions, but ►overdrafts are still a common form of ►bank loan, and may be a cheaper form of finance. Unlike an overdraft, the interest of a term loan is fixed and the loan cannot be recalled in advance of its maturity date.

term structure of interest rates The relationship between the interest rate paid on a ►bond and the number of years there are until the bond is repaid. Suppose, for simplicity, bonds are held for either one year or two years. People wanting to invest for two years can do so either by buying a two-year bond or by buying a one-year bond now and then buying a new one when that one expires. The term structure compares the annual yield on each type of bond. It is affected by a number of factors. Most important, if interest rates are expected to rise next year, the two-year bond will have to offer a higher annual return than the one-year bond. Otherwise everyone would sell two-year bonds and hold a one-year bond this year and a higher-yielding one-year bond next year. (►►yield curve.) ►Inflation expectations also determine the term structure (►credibility). In general, if ►fiscal policy and ►monetary policy are 'tight', i.e. tending to have a deflationary effect (►deflation), then long-term rates will be lower than usual, relative to short-term rates. ►►yield curve.

terms of trade The ratio of the index of ►export prices to the index of ►import prices. An improvement in the terms of trade follows if export prices rise more quickly than import prices (or fall more slowly than import prices). ►►United Nations Conference on Trade and Industry.

theories of value ►value, theories of.

theory of distribution ►distribution, theory of.

theory of games ►game theory.

theory of income determination ►income determination, theory of.

theory of production ►production, theory of.

theory of second best ►second best, theory of.

theory of the firm ►firm, theory of the.

Third World A synonym for ►developing countries.

Thornton, William Thomas (1813–80) ►wage-fund theory.

Thünen, Johann Heinrich von (1783–1850) A member of the landowning Prussian class of Junkers, after completing his education at agricultural college he attended the University of Göttingen. For the remainder of his life he farmed his estate at Mecklenburg. The first volume of his work *Der isolierte Staat in Beziehung auf Landwirtschaft und Nationalökonomie* was published in 1826, and part one of volume two in 1850. The rest of volume two and volume three appeared in 1863. He used his farm as a source of facts for his theoretical work in agricultural economics. He built a theoretical ►model which he used to find the important factors that determined the most profitable location of various branches of agriculture in relation to their sources of ►demand. In so doing, he devised a theory of ►rent similar to that of ►Ricardo. He set out a theory of ►distribution based on marginal productivity, using ►calculus, which was considerably ahead of his own time, and he could be considered one of the founders of ►marginal analysis. ►►location theory.

tie-in sales Sales of a product that have a condition that some other item will be purchased at the same time. An example would be the condition that in order to subscribe to the services of a telephone utility, you have also to rent or buy one of their telephones. It is an example of a ►vertical restraint. ►►full-line forcing.

tied loan A ►loan made on condition that certain purchases are made from the lender. In the brewing industry tied loans are made to pubs and clubs for fitting out bars and restaurants on the understanding that beer is supplied by the brewer making the loan. In foreign aid loans are made on favourable terms on condition that capital equipment or services are purchased from the lending country.

tight money ►dear money.

time deposit (US) Money in a bank account for which the bank may require notice of withdrawal, usually of up to three months. ►►deposit account.

time inconsistency A change in preferences that occurs quite predictably after a certain situation has been arrived at. For example, a government that wants to deter the taking of hostages, may say that it will never negotiate with hostage-takers; but it finds that once a hostage has been taken it pays to negotiate, whatever its preference beforehand. Or a government that wants to encourage investment and is thus willing to promise tax concessions to firms opening new plants finds that once the new plants are open it would prefer to remove the tax concessions.

Unless they can commit themselves to the original course of action, the existence of time-inconsistent preferences can prevent certain measures of government, or other economic agents, being credible. Whenever agents lay out ►sunk costs, it is possible that their options will change and they will exhibit time inconsistency. The problem has been analysed in ►game theory. ►►principal–agent problem.

time preference The amount by which consumers value immediate ►consumption in preference to deferred or postponed consumption. Suppose an individual has £1; he can either spend it now, or put it aside and spend it next year. The rate of time preference of that consumer is the amount of money necessary so as just to persuade him to save the pound. If he thinks he will be doing very well next year and has no need to save, or out of fear of nuclear war believes the world will no longer exist next year, he will require a large amount of compensation to persuade him not to spend the pound. If on the other hand he believes he is perfectly well off at the moment and conditions are unlikely to change much, he may think a rather small amount of compensation makes saving worth while.

Several factors affect the time preference of consumers. The first is the level of consumption they enjoy in the present. Other things being equal, the more consumption there is now, the lower the compensation needed for ►saving. As saving implies a fall in current consumption, the more that is saved, the higher the required level of compensation. As a corollary of this, the second factor is the level of consumption expected to be enjoyed in the future. If great wealth is expected tomorrow, a lot of reward will be needed to induce saving today. Again, as saving today implies higher consumption in the future, the more that is saved, the higher the required level of compensation. The third factor is the risk the consumer attaches to the arrival of the future: if tomorrow is unlikely to come, huge compensation is needed to cause saving. Finally, consumer taste will influence the time-preference rate – some people may believe that they can only enjoy spending money when they are young: others might believe the reverse.

The market ►rate of interest expresses the amount a consumer will actually be compensated for saving, and rational consumers will save enough for their time-preference rate to equal the interest rate. If the interest rate exceeds their time-preference rate, they should save more, raising their time-preference rate until it is equal to the market interest rate. The reverse would be true if their time-preference rate exceeded the interest rate. If the interest rate is lower than their time-preference rate even when they are saving nothing, it is rational for them to borrow money and pay interest on it; this raises current consumption and lowers future consumption and thus lowers their time-preference rate. Optimal consumption through time can be analysed with the help of ►indifference curves, depicting the bundles of consumption today and in the future between which the consumer is indifferent. ►►Fisher, I.; marginal utility of money.

time series The values of a particular ►variable at consecutive periods of time.

time-series analysis The application of statistical methods to find explanations of movements of ►variables over time. ►►cross-section analysis.

times covered ►dividend cover.

Tinbergen, Jan (1903–94) A Dutch economist, from the Netherlands School of Economics in Rotterdam, Tinbergen jointly won, with ►Frisch, R., the first ►Nobel Prize in Economics in 1969, 'for having developed and applied dynamic models for the analysis of economic processes'. He spent ten years as director of the Netherlands Central Planning Bureau, where he formulated some important ideas on the conduct of economic policy. He is associated with the central principle that there must be as many instruments as there are targets of policy.

tit-for-tat A strategy in a repeated ►prisoner's dilemma game (►repeated game) by which a player agrees to be cooperative in the first round of the game, and for each subsequent round to do whatever the other player did the round before. The strategy has been shown empirically to be effective when the prisoner's dilemma is repeated a large number of times, or when it continues for an unknown number of rounds. Its importance in ►game theory is to have shown that there are circumstances when the cooperative outcome can be sustained in situations which are structurally similar to the prisoner's dilemma. It is not, however, a ►dominant strategy.

Tobin, James (b. 1918) Professor Tobin studied at Harvard University, obtaining his Ph.D. in 1947. He moved to Yale in 1950 and was appointed Sterling Professor of Economics. He was awarded the ►Nobel Prize in Economics in 1981. Professor Tobin's major published works include *Liquidity Preference as Behaviour towards Risk* (1958), *National Economic Policy* (1966), *Financial Markets and Economic Activity* (1967), *Essays in Economics: Macroeconomics* (1971), *Economics, One Decade Older* (1974), *Essays in Economics: Consumption and Econometrics* (1975), *Asset Accumulation and Economic Activity* (1980) and *Essays in Economics: Theory and Policy* (1982). Professor Tobin has made important contributions to the theory of finance through his analysis of the demand for financial assets (►liquidity preference). He criticized ►monetarism for its narrow emphasis on money. There is a range of financial assets which investors may be willing to hold in their portfolios, not only money but bonds and equities. Moreover, their preferences are determined by their weighing up the rates of return and capital-gains prospects, against the risks. Professor Tobin explored the links between the mix of financial portfolios and the real assets of firms to show how government and central bank policy impinge on real ►gross national product and employment. He has also contributed to the theory of ►econometrics: Tobit, a statistical analytical technique for the estimation of variables subject to ►probability, was named after him. ►►*q* theory; Tobin tax.

Tobin tax A tax on ►foreign exchange transactions originally proposed by Professor James ►Tobin. It has been estimated that in 1995 world foreign exchange transactions reached over $260,000 billion on an annual basis. Concern has been expressed that the high proportion of this which is of a short-time nature could lead to serious instability in ►exchange rates because of the speed with which it could switch from one economic region to another. It has been suggested that a tax would not only help to control these flows but also be a useful source of revenue.

Tokyo round of trade negotiations The seventh round of trade negotiations under the auspices of the ►General Agreement on Tariffs and Trade. These negotiations began in 1974, after the passing in the United States of the Trade Act, which gave the President powers to negotiate. The negotiations were concluded at the end of 1979. Agreement was reached on the following matters:

(a) The major developed countries agreed to reduce their tariffs (➤tariffs, import) by, on the average, one-third over a period ending on 1 January 1987.

(b) A new code of conduct was drawn up covering customs-valuation procedures, barriers caused by technical specifications, import licences and government procurement policies. For instance, the American Selling Price system was abolished. Under this system the United States revalued imports of chemicals to the higher level of that charged by US domestic producers and then calculated the import duty on this higher figure.

(c) A new code was also agreed concerning the application of ➤countervailing duties. These duties may only be applied when it can be demonstrated that material injury is being caused to the domestic producers of a commodity because of the importation of that commodity from a subsidized overseas source. ➤contingent protection; dumping. ➤➤Uruguay round of trade negotiations.

Tokyo Stock Exchange The ➤securities market in Tokyo. It is one of the world's largest and is one of the three central Japanese ➤stock exchanges; Osaka and Nagoya are the other two. There are also five regional exchanges in Japan, though Tokyo, which unlike London still has a trading floor, accounts for well over 80 per cent of all transactions. Non-Japanese dealing firms were permitted to become members of the exchange in 1986. There is also an ➤over-the-counter market.

total factor productivity ➤productivity.

tournament theory The piece of economic thinking that suggests rewards can usefully be based upon the relative performance of economic agents, rather than on their absolute performance. It is sometimes used to explain behaviour observed in the ➤labour market, where patterns of reward are often more subtle than traditional theories (➤marginal productivity theory of wages) would suggest. In particular, those accounts argue there should be a close relationship between the value of the output of a worker, and the wage the worker receives. In practice the ➤productivity of workers varies, and companies find it hard to observe the individual output of every worker. Instead, it is argued, companies can rank workers and pay them on their relative standing. That gives them each an incentive to perform well, but does not require as detailed a profile of everybody's performance. Because workers are effectively competing against each other, they are in a tournament. The approach can also be applied to the ➤regulation of ➤monopoly utilities, where it becomes ➤yardstick competition. It is one of many pieces of economic thinking that attempts to justify and explain real-world behaviour on the grounds that the information facing decision-makers is incomplete. ➤➤efficiency-wage hypothesis, signalling, screening.

trade barrier A general term covering any government limitation on the free international exchange of merchandise. These barriers may take the form of, for instance, ➤tariffs, ➤quotas, ➤import deposits, restrictions on the issue of ➤import licences or stringent regulations relating to health or safety standards. ➤➤protection.

trade credit The ►credit extended by business firms to other business firms. It may occur explicitly through the issue of a ►bill of exchange, or may arise from the delay of receipts and payments for services performed. ►►factoring.

trade cycle ►business cycle.

trade discount The percentage below the published retail ►price at which a manufacturer sells to his distributors (wholesale or retail) or at which a wholesaler sells his goods to a retailer. In addition, further discounts are sometimes given on a scale related to the quantities of the goods taken. A *'concealed' discount* is one granted by a manufacturer or wholesaler to favoured customers and not made publicly known to prevent accusations of unfair trading. ►►resale price maintenance.

trade diversion and trade creation ►customs union.

trade gap The excess of the value of ►imports of goods and services over the value of ►exports of goods and services. ►►balance of payments.

trade investments ►Shares held by one company in another; normally minority holdings in customers or suppliers.

trading currency Currency in which ►international trade is invoiced. ►►reserve currency.

transactions costs The costs associated with the process of buying and selling. These are small frictions in the economic sphere that often explain why the price system does not operate perfectly. Transactions costs may affect decisions by an organization to make or buy (►contracting out) and the study of transactions-costs economics, associated notably with Oliver Williamson, has implications for a wide range of issues affecting ►industrial organization, including ►competition policy. ►►Coase, R.; menu costs.

transactions demand for money The holding of cash by people or firms to finance foreseeable expenditures. When people are paid, they probably put their salary into a bank account, from which they can spend it very easily, using cheques or cash taken from a machine. If they wanted to, however, instead of putting it in the bank's current account, they could invest it in, say, government bonds, which would pay interest. People, however, keep much of their money in easy-access, low-return accounts. This is the transactions demand for money.

The transactions demand depends on three factors. First, the volume and pattern of transactions to be financed. A rich man requires more ready cash than a poor man, because he spends more. The pattern of transactions matters too: if spending and income were £20 a day, virtually no money would be kept for transactions, but if spending were £20 a day and income £140 a week, for the first six days of the week a positive balance would be kept. Secondly, the rate of interest has an effect, because it represents the sacrifice made from not investing money. The third factor is the cost of making transactions in interest-bearing assets: the brokerage fees, costs of acquiring information, etc.

The foregoing applies equally to the corporate demand for money. It is generally believed that the transactions demand relates to the function of money as a medium of exchange (►money), and, of the various possible definitions of money supply, the most relevant to this demand is a 'narrow' one, of very liquid assets (►►money supply). Although it was seen as the only possible reason for holding money by classical economists, it was ►Keynes who introduced the idea that the interest rate might be important in determining the demand for money, and outlined other motives for holding cash too. ►►precautionary motive; speculative motive; Tobin, J.

transactions motive The factor which causes people or firms to hold a stock of money to finance their foreseeable expenditures. It is one of three motives for holding money outlined by Keynes. ►►precautionary motive; speculative motive; transactions demand for money.

transfer costs The total ►opportunity costs of moving goods or materials from one place to another including loading/unloading costs and administrative costs as well as transport costs.

transfer deed A legal document by which ownership of ►securities is transferred from the seller to the buyer. In Britain it is no longer necessary for both parties to sign such a document when disposing of a share. The seller gives his authority to the issuer of the security to remove his name from the records while the buyer's ►broker simply informs the issuer of the purchaser's name. ►►CREST.

transfer earnings The minimum payment necessary to keep a ►factor of production in its existing use and deter movement to other employment. Earnings in excess of transfer earnings are ►economic rent.

transfer payments Grants or other payments not made in return for a productive service, for example pensions, unemployment benefits (►jobseeker's allowance) and other forms of income support, including charitable donations by companies. Transfer payments are a form of income redistribution, not a return to the ►factors of production. ►Social security cost the UK government £96.6 billion in 1996/97, the vast bulk of transfer payments in the country. ►Subsidies which are paid by government to producers are not counted as transfer payments.

transfer pricing Internal (as distinct from ►market) prices used in large organizations for transactions between semi-autonomous divisions. A ►multinational corporation, for example, will have to set transfer prices for the supply of components from one subsidiary to another. Transfer prices between subsidiaries acting as profit centres may approximate to market prices or they may be set above or below them so as to minimize the payment of ►tariffs or to shift ►profit from a high-►taxation country to a low-taxation country.

transformation curve (production possibility curve) A graphical representation of the maximum amount of one good or service that an economy can produce by reducing production of a second good or service and transferring the resources saved to the production of the first good. For example, an economy might be capable of producing fifty battleships if it produces no food, or no battleships if it produces a million tons of food. Either of these combinations would be a point on the transformation curve, which can be plotted on a graph with the number of battleships produced on one axis and the amount of food on the other. It traces the number of tons of food that can be made using the resources required for any given level of battleship production.

A transformation curve is normally assumed to be concave to (i.e. bulge away from) the origin. This is because the ►rate of technical substitution declines the more of a commodity that is produced: a large amount of food can be made for the sacrifice of one battleship if no food is being made to start with, because the best fields can be used and the people good at farming but poor at battleship building can be transferred to farming productively. However, suppose that only one battleship is being built and the rest of the economy is geared to food production; transferring resources from the battleship to food will have hardly any effect on food output. Thus, the rate at which battleships can be transformed into food declines as food production rises. ►►economic efficiency.

transition, economies in Countries in transition from a ►planned economy to a ►free-market economy. Specifically refers to Russia and the members of the former Soviet Union and other Communist states in Eastern and Central Europe. The process began in October 1989 with the opening of the Berlin Wall between East and West Germany. The countries in transition, unlike ►developing countries, have highly educated populations, substantial, though generally run-down, ►infra-structure and large manufacturing sectors. The economies are dominated by heavily indebted state enterprises with low ►productivity and generally uncompetitive products and services. Most are characterized by high ►inflation and ►unemploy-ment and ►balance of payments deficits. Output is still generally below 1989 levels, partly because of the disruption of trade patterns between these countries. The countries most advanced in the process of transition include Poland, Hungary and the Czech and Slovak Republics, which have negotiated special relationships with the ►European Union and aspire to membership.

The economic policies being pursued by countries in transition vary and are controversial. These policies have been heavily influenced by the international institutions and ►Organization for Economic Cooperation and Development member states which are providing them with financial ►aid and technical assist-ance. Some economists have advocated *shock therapy* to free prices from controls, removal of ►subsidies, convertibility of currencies, rapid ►privatization of State enterprises, and stringent ►monetary policy. Others advocate a more gradualist approach which would focus more on the development of appropriate institutions first (such as property rights and the banking system ►institutional economics). The gradualists argue that the shock approach will be politically disruptive and ineffective until institutions develop to allow market forces to work.

transitivity A characteristic of rational preferences which holds that if a combination of goods, *A*, is preferred to another combination, *B*, and *B* is preferred to a third combination, *C*, then *A* must be preferred to *C*. Transitivity is also assumed to hold for the indifference relation between combinations of goods. ►indifference-curve analysis; paradox of voting.

transmission mechanism The process by which changes in the money supply – or changes in the ►rate of interest on short-term assets – affect the level of ►aggregate demand. There are different ways in which the mechanism can operate. First, with extra cash (or lower interest rates) people may choose to spend more and save less. Second, and more indirectly, with extra cash, people may buy more ►bonds, as a means of storing their new wealth. (Or, with lower short-term interest rates, people will buy more long-term bonds as a substitute.) This increase in the demand for bonds will push their prices up and interest rates down and this will stimulate new ►investment. ►Monetarism concentrates on the more direct process, while ►Keynesian economics has tended to play down the power of money, believing that its effects work only through the second, indirect mechanism. In an ►open economy, the transmission mechanism can also operate through the ►exchange rate. An increase in ►money supply, or a reduction in interest rates, tends to lead to a ►depreciation of the exchange rate, and promote exports.

transnational corporation ►multinational firm.

Treasury The UK Ministry of Finance. Managed on a day-to-day basis by the Chancellor of the ►Exchequer, though the First Lord of the Treasury is the Prime Minister, this department coordinates national economic policy (including ►monetary policy), and controls ►public expenditure. Some of its functions passed to the Department of Economic Affairs when it was set up in 1964, but returned to it in 1969 when the DEA was closed. Also, prior to the establishment of the Civil Service Department in 1970, the Treasury was responsible for the management of the Civil Service, but this role is now performed by the Management and Personnel Office in the Cabinet Office.

treasury bills Instruments for short-term borrowing by the government. The bills are promissory notes to pay to the bearer £5000 upwards ninety-one days from the date of issue. The bills are issued by tender to the ►money market and to government departments through ►tap issues. ►Tenders are invited every week from bankers, ►discount houses and ►brokers. On the one hand, treasury bills provide the government with a highly flexible and relatively cheap means of borrowing ►money to meet its fluctuating needs for ►cash. On the other hand, the bills provide a sound ►security for dealings in the money market, and the ►Bank of England, in particular, can operate on that market by dealing in treasury bills. Since 1988 the government has also issued bills denominated and payable in ►European Currency Units (ECUs).

Treaty of Rome ►European Union.

trend growth The level of ►economic growth of an economy that is sustainable over the long term, without any tendency for the rate of ►inflation to rise or fall. It is sometimes held to be the rate at which the productive capacity of the economy – its potential for production – expands. It could equally be taken as a measure of the growth of the ►supply side. It is also interpreted as the long-term growth rate, as it assumed that in the long term, the economy must perform according to its potential. The rate is affected by growth in the labour force, and the growth in productivity, itself primarily determined by technology and social institutions. Actual growth in any year may exceed, or underperform trend growth, usually because fluctuations in ►aggregate demand affect actual ►gross domestic product more than they affect the long-term capacity of the economy to produce things. Trend growth is a useful benchmark for whether the economy is growing too quickly (►overheating) or too slowly. In the UK ►budget in 1997 the trend growth rate was officially declared to be 'between 2 and 2.75 per cent'. That is a number close to the long-term average growth rate. A similar estimate is regarded as reasonable for most highly developed economies, but it recognized that developing countries may outperform this level for a sustained period of catch-up. Trend growth is a concept more often used by policy-makers, than theoretical economists. It has largely been ignored by the different theories of growth (►growth, theories of), and should not be confused with the natural rate of growth, used in the ►Harrod–Domar model. ►output gap.

truck system ►fringe benefits.

trust 1. ►Money or property vested with an individual or group of individuals to administer in the interest of others. Trusts of this kind are usually set up to continue interests in accordance with the general instructions of the initiator and to protect them from outside interference and for tax reasons. Thus people set up trusts or appoint trustees to administer their estates after their death. Certain newspapers are administered by trusts. Banks act as trustees for a fee, and a similar service is provided by the Public Trustee, established in 1908. The term is a legal one. **2.** Financial trusts are also established for commercial purposes where particular protection is required against fraud, e.g. ►unit trusts or ►investment trusts. **3.** (US) A very large amalgamation of firms. ►►anti-trust.

Turgot, Anne Robert Jacques, Baron de l'Aulne (1727–81) Educated for the Church, he became an abbé at the Sorbonne in Paris, but then took up a career in the civil service, where he remained for the rest of his life. He was the Administrator of the District of Limoges from 1761 to 1774, when he became Secretary of State for the Navy. For a short time he held the post of Controller of Finance. His economic work appeared in *Réflexions sur la formation et la distribution des richesses*, published in 1766. In this work he gave a clear analysis of the law of ►diminishing returns. He demonstrated how more and more applications of a ►factor of production (►capital) to a constant factor (►land) will first increase then decrease the return at the margin. He was the first to equate capital accumulation with ►saving, a view which became a central feature of ►classical economics.

turnover The total sales revenue of a business.

turnover tax A ►tax levied as a proportion of the ►price of a ►commodity on each sale in the production and distribution chain; also called a *cascade tax*. Such a tax encourages ►vertical integration. Turnover taxes were widespread in Europe, for example in Germany, before the introduction of the ►value-added tax now standard throughout the ►European Union.

turnpike theorem ►optimal-growth theory.

U

unavoidable costs ➤Opportunity costs which have to be borne even if no output is produced. ➤➤fixed costs.

uncalled capital ➤Authorized capital issued to the public, but not called (➤call) and not ➤paid-up capital.

uncertainty The state in which the number of possible outcomes exceeds the number of actual outcomes and when no probabilities can be attached to each possible outcome. It differs from risk, which is defined as having measurable probabilities. Where probabilities are measurable, insurance can be taken out to cover the worst contingencies: the risk of them occurring is spread among many people or taken on by someone who can reasonably be certain to bear them. In the case of uncertainty, however, no insurance company could properly assess what premium to charge to cover bad outcomes: it is simply a possibility that has to be faced. It is the role of the entrepreneur to face each uncertainty when setting up a new company that justifies ➤profit as a reward. ➤➤risk.

UNCTAD ➤United Nations Conference on Trade and Development.

undated securities ➤Securities not bearing a ➤redemption date or ➤option, hence ➤irredeemable securities.

underconsumption ➤quantity rationing.

underdeveloped country ➤developing country.

underlying inflation The rate at which prices are rising in the economy, once the impact of erratic effects on price measurements has been removed. There is no precise definition of underlying inflation, and in the UK it is often used to label the measure used as the basis of the government's ➤inflation target. That is the measure known as *RPIX*, equivalent to the retail prices index excluding the impact of mortgage tax relief. It has been argued that a better measure of underlying inflation would also exclude the effect of changes in indirect taxation (➤direct taxation) and such a measure, *RPIY*, is compiled although not much publicized outside of the Bank of England's Inflation Report. ➤➤harmonized index of consumer prices.

undervalued currency A ➤currency whose ➤exchange rate is below either its ➤free-market level or the ➤equilibrium level which it is expected to reach in the ➤long run. Conversely, an overvalued currency may develop as a consequence of balance-of-payments deficits. ➤devaluation; revaluation; ➤➤exchange rate over-shooting.

underwriting The business of insuring against ➤risk. An underwriter in return for a ➤commission or ➤premium agrees to bear a risk or a proportion of a risk. Specifically, an underwriter is a member of ➤Lloyd's, who joins with others to underwrite the risk of damage or loss to a ship or cargo – if the ship sinks and is not recoverable he will pay a proportion of the cost of the loss to be insured – but the term is generally used to describe the basic activity of ➤insurance. An ➤issuing house also underwrites directly or indirectly a new issue of ➤shares – if the public does not take up the whole issue, the balance will be taken up by the underwriters (➤new-issue market).

unearned income ➤earned income.

unemployment The existence of a section of the labour force able and willing to work, but unable to find gainful employment. Unemployment is measured as the percentage of the total labour force out of work. Historically, it was very high in the 1930s; it fell to its lowest level in the 1950s and re-emerged as a worsening phenomenon in western economies after the oil crisis of 1973, for the first time simultaneously appearing with high inflation. In 1997 the ➤International Labour Organization expressed concern at the high levels of unemployment and under-employment that persisted in the world economy. The Organization estimated that 30 per cent of the world ➤labour force was without full-time employment. Four distinct causes of unemployment can be distinguished:

(a) ➤frictional unemployment is caused by people taking time out of work being between jobs or looking for a job

(b) ➤classical unemployment is caused by excessively high wages

(c) ➤structural unemployment refers to a mismatch of job vacancies with the supply of labour available, caused by shifts in the structure of the economy

(d) ➤Keynesian unemployment results from the existence of a deficiency of ➤aggregate demand which is simply not great enough to support full employment

A fall in wages – which should cause an increase in the ➤demand for ➤labour – merely reduces aggregate demand further because it reduces the spending power of the employed, and thus fails to clear the excess supply of workers. Much economic debate has centred on whether, in the long term, cuts in wages cannot in fact increase demand (➤➤real balance effect), and thus whether Keynesian unemployment is not just a special case of ➤classical unemployment in which workers are simply pricing themselves out of jobs.

Monetarist and neo-classical economists have tended to argue that all unemployment is either classical or voluntary (➤unemployment, natural rate of). Either, they assert, the market fails to clear because wages are artificially held too high; or, if the market does clear, the unemployed have chosen not to take a job at the going rate. However, in practice, it has been shown that at times persistent unemployment can be cured by a boost in aggregate demand. The labour market is widely recognized as being slower to adjust than any other; excess supply in this market persists in a way that it could not elsewhere, despite the high social and human costs of unemployment. In recent years attention has focused on the particular problem of ►long-term unemployment, especially among unskilled men. It is surmised that the market wage of manual workers – especially those in heavy physical occupations – has declined (►weightlessness). And that work incentives have correspondingly diminished too. ►unemployment trap. ►►claimant count; employment, full; hysteresis; labour force; labour-force survey; labour, mobility of.

unemployment, natural rate of The level of ►unemployment in an economy that is just consistent with a stable rate of ►inflation. It is the unemployment that prevails when all markets in the economy are in equilibrium, and there is no deficiency of ►aggregate demand. It can be thought of as the unemployment rate when output in the economy is just at its potential, no more and no less (►output gap). The natural rate may be non-negligible – in much of Europe it is estimated to be over 8 per cent of the ►labour force, and appears to have risen over the 1980s. The point about the natural rate is that it is not easily solvable by ►fiscal policy or ►monetary policy. It is a supply-side feature of the economy (►supply-side economics), a reflection of labour-market institutions.

The concept of the natural rate was central to the monetarist critique to the policies motivated by ►Keynesian economics (►monetarism). It arises out of the failures of policy in the 1950s and 1960s to sustain low levels of unemployment in the 1970s. Somehow, demand had to be stoked up to ever higher levels to maintain the same level of unemployment. The economy appeared to exhibit a natural tendency towards some level, and it was not possible to get that level lower by allowing higher inflation. At best, it appeared possible to get it below the natural rate temporarily, or by ever-accelerating rates of inflation. Indeed, on modern accounts, macroeconomic policy cannot even take unemployment below the natural rate at all. (►policy ineffectiveness theorem.)

Today the natural rate is accepted by academics of most ►economics doctrines, and it certainly motivates the conduct of economic policy day to day throughout the western world. Some think of the natural rate as being the correct definition of 'full employment'. To get the actual level of unemployment below it, it is argued, requires government to consider such factors as the level of benefits for the out-of-work, the ease with which workers can change jobs and the stigma attached to being out of work. The natural-rate hypothesis has increased the attention given to ►active labour-market policies. The ►Organization of Economic Cooperation and Development has stressed the need for nations to make their labour markets 'flexible'. It estimates that the UK's natural rate has fallen well below that of other European nations as a result of policies of ►deregulation of the labour market.

Because unemployment cannot be held below the natural rate without accelerating inflation, it is often called the *non-accelerating inflation rate of unemployment* (NAIRU).

unemployment trap The existence of ►social security benefits for the out-of-work that erode any incentive for the unemployed to take a job. The incentive for the unemployed to find a job can depend on (a) the generosity of state benefits, (b) the level of pay offered, (c) the tax paid on that pay. ►►poverty trap.

unfunded ►pension funds; personal pension.

uniform business rate ►local taxation.

unit banking ►branch banking.

unit cost ►average cost.

unit trust An organization which invests funds subscribed by the public in ►securities, and in return issues units which it will repurchase at any time. The units, which represent equal shares in the trust's investment ►portfolio, produce ►income and fluctuate in value according to the ►interest and ►dividends paid and the ►stock exchange prices of the underlying ►investments. The trustees which actually hold the securities are usually banks or ►insurance companies, and are distinct from the management company. The subscriber to a unit trust does not, unlike a shareholder in an ►investment trust, receive any of the ►profits of the organization managing the trust. Management derives its income from a regular service charge as a percentage of the income of the trust's investments and the difference between the (bid) price at which it buys in units and the (offer) price at which it sells them, which may include an initial charge. Unit trusts in the UK are strictly controlled by the Investment Managers' Regulatory Organization (►Financial Services Act 1986), which must give its approval to a trust before units can be offered to the public, and which sets maximum management charges and generally supervises the operation of the trusts. Unit trusts were introduced in Britain as long ago as 1930, but they have grown particularly rapidly since the late 1950s. In January 1996 unit trust holdings had funds of well over £100 billion under management. Unit trusts are directed particularly at the investor with small sums at his disposal. Units are easily purchased and resold, and risks are widely spread, it being usual for holdings of any one security to be kept below 5 per cent of the total. The investor also benefits from expert management, although the performance of the trusts varies enormously. Trusts may be fixed or flexible, i.e. their portfolio may remain the same or be altered as market conditions dictate. Some unit trusts specialize in small companies or ►blue chip shares, others in ►commodities or foreign companies or countries. Some are designed to maximize income, others ►capital growth. The latter offer the option of distributed or reinvested income, and there are also trusts incorporating life assurance which can be subscribed to by regular payments (►assurance).

United Nations Conference on Trade and Development (UNCTAD) A conference first convened in 1964 in response to a growing anxiety among ►developing countries over the difficulties they were facing in their attempts to bridge the ►standard of living gap between them and the ►advanced countries. Since then full conferences have been held every three or four years. UNCTAD IX was held in 1996. The goal was to improve prospects for developing countries' trade, and to prevent balance of payments problems acting as constraint on growth. The problem could be tackled on two fronts: through measures (a) to offset the deterioration in the terms of trade and (b) to promote their exports. The terms-of-trade approach could be through ►international commodity agreements, which would be designed to prevent primary prices from falling, and through compensatory finance arrangements. It was also suggested that the developing countries should be free to combine to discriminate against imports of manufactures from the developed countries, and at the same time the latter should give preferences (►infant-industry argument). The distaste felt by the developing countries for the ►most-favoured nation clause of the ►General Agreement on Tariffs and Trade was recognized by that institution. A new chapter to the GATT was added in 1965 on trade and development, which called for the reduction of ►tariffs and ►quotas on developing countries' exports. It became possible for preferential duties to be given to imports from developing countries without having to extend these preferences to all the contracting parties of the GATT. (►generalized system of preferences.) UNCTAD has a permanent secretariat based in Geneva and publishes regularly papers on development problems and an annual report.

universal bank A ►bank (►banking) which provides a wide range of financial services in one largely unified structure. In some continental European countries some large banks have combined the roles of ►commercial banks, ►investment banks, ►insurance and ►brokerage. Although in the distant past these functions were performed in the UK by independent organizations, they are now increasingly offered by partially integrated financial ►conglomerates.

unlisted securities market(s) (USM) **1**. Generally, the markets for shares of ►public companies not included in the Official List for the main market (or first tier) of the ►stock exchange. Most of the ►advanced countries have organized lower-tier markets or informal 'placing markets' in which unlisted shares are traded. These markets are less stringently regulated and perform an important function in providing a stepping-stone to the main markets. (►over-the-counter market; quotation.) **2**. Specifically, a market set up in 1980 by the London Stock Exchange to trade in designated unlisted securities and closed in 1996. The *Alternative Investment Market* (AIM) opened on 19 June 1995 to replace the USM and the Rule 4.2 market (in which members of the Stock Exchange were allowed to deal in unlisted shares). AIM's admission requirements are less stringent than those for the former USM and the Official List and the costs of ►flotation much lower. By September 1996 213 company shares were being traded on AIM.

unredeemable securities ➤irredeemable security.

unrequited exports ➤Exports for which there is no reverse flow of goods or finance in payment. They take place in the settlement of past ➤debts.

Uruguay round of trade negotiations The eighth round of trade negotiations of the ➤General Agreement on Tariffs and Trade (GATT) opened at Punta del Este, Uruguay in 1986. The aim, as with previous Rounds (➤Tokyo round of trade negotiations), was to reduce trade restrictions and to encourage ➤free trade on a multilateral basis. The negotiations sought to obtain agreements in the following main subject areas: (a) the reduction in trade-distorting agricultural subsidies; (b) the reduction of restrictions on ➤imports of tropical produce; (c) the reduction of ➤tariffs on industrial goods; (d) the reduction of restrictions on ➤foreign investment; (e) the review of the rules governing the origin of imports (➤certificate of origin); (f) a review of the rules governing the application of anti-dumping measures; (g) the reduction of restraints on trade in services, such as banking, insurance, transport, tourism, telecommunications (➤invisibles); (h) the international protection of intellectual property rights (e.g. patents, trademarks, copyright); (i) the review of the ➤Multi-Fibre Arrangement. The negotiations were concluded and agreement signed in 1994. Industrial tariffs in ➤developed countries were to be reduced from an average of 6.3 per cent to 3.9 per cent and the proportion of imports free of tariffs was to be increased from 20 per cent to 43 per cent. All tariffs were to be 'bound', that is never raised. The Multi-Fibre Arrangement was to be phased out. For the first time, services were to be, in principle, subject to the same multilateral trading rules as industrial products. However, agreement could not be reached on telecommunications, financial services and shipping. Under the General Agreement or Tariffs and Trade, agriculture had been excluded from many provisions which applied to other products, such as those relating to export subsidies and import quotas. The Uruguay Agreement brought agriculture into the multilateral system of trading rules. ➤Non-tariff barriers were converted into tariffs and these tariffs were to be reduced by 36 per cent over a six-year period. Countries could not impose quotas, minimum import prices, restrictive licences, or variable levies on imports. Constraints were placed on subsidies that distort trade which will become more stringent over time. Agricultural export subsidies were to be reduced. (➤Common Agricultural Policy). The ➤World Trade Organization was set up to replace GATT.

USM ➤unlisted securities market.

utilitarianism The philosophy by which the purpose of government was the maximization of the sum of ➤utility, defined in terms of pleasure and pain, in the community as a whole. It was not hedonistic (➤hedonism) in so far as pleasure could include, for instance, the satisfaction of helping others. The purpose of government was to ensure the 'greatest happiness of the greatest number'. It implied that utility could be measured and interpersonal comparisons made. Its chief advocate was ►Bentham, J.

utility The pleasure or satisfaction derived by an individual from being in a particular situation or from consuming goods or services. Utility is defined as the ultimate goal of all economic activity, but it is not a label for any particular set of pursuits such as sensual pleasure or the acquisition and use of material goods. ►Bentham described it as that which appears 'to augment or diminish the happiness of the party whose interest is in question', but this barely illuminates the issue, given that the notion of happiness used is a complex one. Some things which appear to make people unhappy, like sad films, can generate utility while other things appear to make people happy but do not. As no single measure of utility exists (►ordinal utility), it is by their choices of combinations of available commodities that consumers reveal what it is that generates utility for them. Economists ignore possible circularities in the concept and rarely argue about what consumers enjoy, taking it as a matter of psychological fact. ►►endogenous preferences; Hicks, J. R.; indifference-curve analysis; marginal utility, diminishing; Pareto, V. F. D.; Slutsky, E.

rates in the medium term, the shift from destination to origin principle has proved controversial and probably some sort of clearing mechanism to restore the balance of tax revenues will be devised.

value judgement A proposition which cannot be reduced to an arguable statement of fact but which effectively asserts that something is good or that something ought to happen. Economists usually attempt to draw a distinction between facts and value judgements, but the two often merge. For example, the statement, 'We can control inflation by cutting the money supply', is clearly arguable but not a value judgement. However, the statement 'Therefore, we ought to cut the money supply', may be a value judgement (based on the belief that inflation is an evil per se), or alternatively could be an economic judgement made on the basis of a belief that the control of inflation stimulates long-term economic growth. In practice, all statements of economists can be of two types: descriptive statements (e.g. unemployment is falling); or prescriptive (e.g. unemployment should be cut). The former should be devoid of any value judgements. The latter will always be a combination of value and economic judgement. Usually, but not always, the value judgements contained in prescriptive statements are either uncontroversial or explicit enough for the reader to make a clear assessment of them. ➤➤normative economics; positive economics; Robbins, L.

variable A number that may take different values in different situations. For instance, quantity of a good demanded will vary according to its price.

variable costs Costs which vary directly with the rate of output, e.g. ➤labour costs, raw-material costs, fuel and power. Also known as *operating costs*, *prime costs*, *on costs* or *direct costs*.

variance A measure of the degree of dispersion of a series of numbers around their mean (➤average). The larger the variance the greater the spread of the series around its mean. The formula is as follows:

$$\text{Variance} = \sigma^2 = \frac{1}{N} \sum_{i=1}^{N} (x_i - \bar{x})^2$$

where $\bar{x}$ is the mean (➤average), x_i is the value of the ith item and N is the number of items in the series. For example, consider the two series (a) 8, 10, 12 and (b) 2, 10, 18. The mean of both (a) and (b) is 10. The variance of (a) is $[(-2)^2 + (2)^2]/3 = 2.67$. The variance of (b) is $[(-8)^2 + (8)^2]/3 = 42.67$. The variance of (b) is greater than (a), reflecting the wider spread of the (b) series. ➤➤standard deviation.

VAT value-added tax.

Veblen, Thorstein Bunde (1857–1929) ➤conspicuous consumption; institutional economics.

vector A set of numbers (elements) arranged as a row or a column. For instance,

[1, 5, 8] is a row vector, and $\begin{bmatrix} 1 \\ 5 \\ 8 \end{bmatrix}$ is a column vector. A vector of n elements is referred to as n-dimensional. The above vectors, therefore are three-dimensional. The *null vector* has all its elements equal to zero. A *unit vector* is a vector with one element equal to unity and the rest all equal to zero. There are, therefore, n unit vectors possible for an n-dimensional vector. There is an algebra for vectors, with appropriate rules for addition and multiplication. ➤matrix.

velocity of circulation The speed with which the money in an economy circulates. Each £10 note that exists is used many times, and each time it is used a transaction of value £10 occurs. It is possible to imagine two economies, one with twice as much money in it as the other, but where on average the money is used half the number of times. The total value of all transactions in each economy would be the same, because it equals the value of the stock of money multiplied by the velocity with which it circulates. The income velocity equals the money value of ➤national income divided by the stock of money in the economy.

The velocity of circulation is related to the demand for money (➤money, demand for): if people hold cash, it circulates slowly. If, on the other hand, they do not wish to hold cash, they dispose of money holdings and the circulation of money increases. The velocity of money is central to the debate between ➤monetarism and ➤Keynesian economics. Monetarists hold that ➤interest rates do not much affect the demand for money or its velocity. They claim that institutional factors, such as the frequency with which people are paid or the number of people who have bank accounts, affect it and these factors are unlikely to change in the short term. Keynesians on the other hand believe that the velocity of money varies substantially with the interest rate. Under both doctrines, however, a higher than expected ➤inflation rate would increase the velocity. This is seen in an extreme form in an economy enduring ➤hyperinflation, in which anyone holding money is holding a depreciating asset; everybody attempts to rid themselves of cash and acquire goods whose value is stable. ➤neutrality of money.

venture capital ➤risk capital.

venture capital trust (VCT) Qualifying ➤investment trusts holding at least 70 per cent of their investments in unlisted companies (➤unlisted securities market(s)). Individual investors receive ➤income tax relief at 20 per cent when new ➤ordinary shares in the VCTs are subscribed for up to a limit of £100,000 in the amount subscribed. VCTs are exempt from tax on their ➤capital gains, as are shareholders on disposal of their shares in the VCT.

vertical integration The extent to which successive stages in production and distribution are placed under the control of a single ➤enterprise. Oil companies which own oilfields, tankers, refineries and filling stations exhibit a high degree of vertical integration. Firms move to integrate, either forwards towards retailing or backwards towards sources of raw materials, in order to eliminate the profit margins of intermediaries or to secure sources of supply or markets.

vertical restraints Restrictions or conditions imposed on the seller or buyer of an item. Common restraints are ➤resale price maintenance and ➤tie-in sales. They are usually either structured to extend a ➤natural monopoly in one market to a more competitive market (e.g. when national telephone operators demand that customers obtain their telephone handset from them); or they are designed to affect the retail conditions in which a product is sold (e.g. when perfume makers refuse to supply down-market stores with their produce). Competition authorities have been concerned to limit the application of these restrictions, although more recently it has been argued that in most cases vertical restraints are as much against the producer's interest as the public interest where they are against the public interest at all. ➤Chicago school.

Vickrey, William (1914–96) A Canadian-born economist, who was based at Columbia University in New York, William Vickrey was a joint winner of the ➤Nobel Prize just days before his death. His most enduring legacy will be the design of auction named after him (➤auction). It was just one example of his interest in designing economic mechanisms for overcoming the problems associated with ➤asymmetric information (in that case, the fact that the seller of an item does not know the true value placed on it by potential buyers). The main design feature of his auction was the fact it gave potential buyers the incentive to tell the truth about how much they value the item being sold. Other economists have designed similar mechanisms for other contexts. ➤incentive compatibility.

Viner, Jacob (1892 1970) ➤customs union.

visible balance The ➤balance of payments in ➤visible trade (➤imports and ➤exports of merchandise).

visible trade ➤International trade in merchandise, ➤imports and ➤exports. ➤invisible.

voluntary export restraints (VER) An agreement to restrict the number of ➤exports in a particular sector that one country makes to another. VERs are beyond the terms of the ➤General Agreement on Tariffs and Trade and grew in the 1980s as tariffs generally fell.

voting shares ➤Equity shares entitling holders to vote in the election of directors of a company. Normally all ➤ordinary shares are voting shares, but sometimes a company may create a class of non-voting ordinary shares if the holders of the equity wish to raise more equity capital but exclude the possibility of losing control of the business. ➤preference shares are rarely, and ➤debenture shares never, voting shares.

W

wage drift The difference between wage rates set by national agreements and the total earnings received by workers, which includes overtime pay, special bonuses and commissions. If wage negotiations take place between union leaders and management bodies at a national level, whatever the outcome of those negotiations in certain areas of the country, the wage agreed may not be high enough to attract all the workers demanded. In this case, local employers will attempt to entice workers with side payments that do not directly infringe national agreements. Such payments are difficult to monitor and control, and thus undermine attempts to run a ➤prices and incomes policy, but they are defended as necessary if the labour market is to work freely. If wage drift could lead to cuts in pay as well as increases, it would be a more economically efficient means of introducing pay flexibility. As it happens, though, wage drift has the consequence of making a nationally agreed pay rate the bare minimum anyone receives, with 'top ups' the norm. ➤bargaining theory of wages.

wage-fund theory The idea that ➤Adam Smith took over from the ➤Physiocrats, that wages are advanced to workers in anticipation of the sale of their output. Wages could not be increased unless the ➤capital destined to pay them was increased. Capital, in turn, was determined by ➤savings. The ➤classical school developed its theory of wages around these ideas. In the short run, there was a given number of workers and a given amount of savings to pay their wages. The two together determined the average wage. In the long run, the supply of ➤labour was related to the minimum of subsistence needed to sustain the ➤labour force. (This subsistence level was not simply physiological; it was related to a ➤standard of living accepted by custom.) If the wage rate rose above this, the ➤population increased; if it fell below, it contracted. In the long run, the level of the demand for labour was determined by the size of the wage fund, and this, in turn, by the level of savings. This meant that, as ➤J. S. Mill put it, 'the demand for ➤commodities is not the demand for labour'. If you increased ➤consumption you reduced savings and therefore the wage fund. ➤productivity did not influence ➤real wages, what mattered was the level of ➤profits, for savings depended on profits. The argument assumed that savings flowed into fixed capital and variable (wage) capital in equal proportions so that what ➤Marx called the organic composition of capital remained constant. ➤Ricardo worried about this point in his analysis of the effect of machinery on employment. Investment bypassed the wage fund and the demand for labour was reduced. W. T. Thornton criticized the wage-fund doctrine on the grounds that wages were determined by ➤supply and ➤demand in the market. J. S. Mill accepted some of Thornton's points and admitted that the wage-fund idea might be more appropriate in the context of a discontinuous production process (akin to seed-time to harvest) rather than a continuous flow of output, which was the true state of affairs. There was some popular confusion at the time, because it was thought the economists meant there existed a definite fund available for wages so that there was no hope of workers obtaining higher average earnings.

wage rates ➤earnings.

Wall Street (US) ➤New York Stock Exchange.

Walras, Marie Esprit Léon (1834–1910) A mining engineer by training, Walras accepted the offer of a newly created Chair of Economics in the Faculty of Law at Lausanne in 1870. He held this post until he was succeeded by ➤Pareto upon his retirement in 1892. His publications include *Éléments d'économie politique pure* (1874–7), *Études d'économie sociale* (1896) and *Études d'économie politique appliquée* (1898). One of the three economists to propound a ➤marginal utility theory in the 1870s, he set out the theory of diminishing marginal utility and showed how ➤prices at which ➤commodities exchanged are determined by the relative marginal utilities of the people taking part in the transaction (➤➤Gossen, H. H.; Jevons, W. S.; Menger, C.). He also constructed a mathematical ➤model of ➤general equilibrium as a system of simultaneous equations in which he tried to show that all prices and quantities are uniquely determined. This is regarded as one of the foremost achievements in mathematical economics, of which Walras is considered the founder. ➤➤Arrow, K. J.

warranted rate of growth ➤growth theory; Harrod–Domar model.

warrants ➤Securities giving the holder a right to subscribe to a ➤share or a ➤bond at a given price and from a certain date. Warrants, which are commonly issued 'free' alongside the shares of new ➤investment trusts when launched, and carry no income or other rights to ➤equity, immediately trade separately on the ➤stock exchange, but at a price lower than the associated share or bond. This provides the investor in warrants with an element of ➤gearing since, if the associated share or bond price ultimately rises above the subscription price it will have a value corresponding to the difference between the subscription price at which the warrant rights may be exercised and the market price of the share or bond. Similar to an ➤option.

Wassenaar Arrangement ➤Coordinating Committee for Multilateral Controls.

wasting assets ➤Assets with strictly limited, though not necessarily determinate, lives, e.g. a mine, timber lands or a property on lease. Wasting assets have many of the characteristics of ➤current assets, but they are normally included under fixed assets.

watering, stock The issue of the nominal capital of a company in return for less than its money value, thus overstating the capital of the company and reducing its apparent return on capital (►rate of return).

wealth A stock of assets held by any economic unit that yields, or has the potential for yielding, income in some form. Wealth can take a multitude of forms: cash, bank deposits, loans or shares are all financial assets. Diamonds, factories and houses are examples of physical assets. To these should be added human wealth, which consists of the earnings potential of individuals (►human capital). These forms of wealth can be divided into those that constitute a liability to another economic agent, like loans; and those that do not, like physical assets. For the community as a whole, it is only really the latter which constitute net wealth, just as in a family, if a brother owes his sister £100, it comprises part of the sister's wealth but not that of the family as a whole. ►►Ricardian equivalence.

In perfect markets, assets should be priced at the ►present value of the future income they are expected to earn. However, the notion of income is general and would include, for example, the pleasure the owners of a picture would derive from its display (►income). The bulk of most individuals' wealth is held in the form of a house or accumulated assets invested in a pension fund. ►personal pension.

weighted average An ►average in which each item in the series being averaged is multiplied by a 'weight' relevant to its importance, the result summed and the total divided by the sum of the weights. For instance, suppose the price of meat has risen by 10 per cent and of vegetables by 20 per cent, the average rise is 15 per cent, being the arithmetic mean of 10 and 20. This could be misleading if we were considering the effect of the price increases on a particular household. The above mean assumes that the household regards meat and vegetables as equally important. If, however, the household spends £10 on vegetables for every £25 on meat, a more accurate representation of the average price change would be a weighted average, i.e. $[(10\% \times 25) + (20\% \times 10)]/(25 + 10) = 450/35 = 12.9\%$. In the example the weights are 25 (for meat) and 10 (for vegetables), so that the result is more in keeping with the importance the household attaches to meat in its budget. At the extreme, if no vegetables were bought at all, the 'vegetable' weight would be zero. ►►index number.

weights ►weighted average.

weightlessness The term used to describe the decreasing material component in the value of world output. The decline of heavy industry (►de-industrialization) and the relative growth of the services industries in richer countries (►economic growth, theories of) account for the decline in physical ►value added. In particular, it is argued, more value derives from 'knowledge-based' industries. The software for a computer game is the more important component of its value, and the resources for writing the software are those which are most scarce, as opposed to those deployed in the manufacture of the consol on which the game is played. One important consequence of weightlessness is the potential for activity and value to flow across national boundaries without incurring a burden of transport costs; another is the tendency for workers whose main attribute in the ►labour market is physical strength, to suffer a relative decline in attainable income. ►globalization.

welfare economics The study of the social desirability of alternative arrangements of economic activities and allocations of ►resources. It is, in effect, the analysis of the optimal behaviour of individual consumers at the level of society as a whole. Just as, at the level of the individual, there is a need for a subjective ranking of bundles of goods dependent on the consumer's taste (►►indifference-curve analysis), at the level of a society there is a need for a ranking of economic states, and this will usually rely on subjective or ►normative criteria: judgements of taste about how society should look. Carrying the methods of indifference analysis from individuals to groups of individuals is not straightforward, however (►►social-welfare function), and thus welfare economics is a broader subject than the theory of demand (►demand, theory of).

The study of welfare economics consists of the following: first, the determination of efficient states in which no individual can be made better off without an offsetting loss to another individual (►economic efficiency); secondly, the choice between the many efficient states that can exist, either through a decision imposed by a dictator, or through democratically determined decisions (►►impossibility theorem; social welfare; social-welfare function); thirdly, coverage of a number of other smaller topics like the optimal provision of ►public goods, ►externalities, and the theory of the second best (►second best, theory of). All these topics share the common aim of helping to show when it is desirable to move from one economic state to another. ►►compensation principle; cost–benefit analysis; Pigou, A. C.

welfare to work ►►active labour-market policies.

wholesale banking The making of loans or acceptance of deposits on a large scale between banks and other financial institutions, especially in the ►inter-bank market. As distinct from *retail banking*, a term for the business of the ►commercial banks carried out with customers of their branches.

wholesale markets Generally a ►market in which goods or services are bought and sold on a large scale among professionals. The *financial wholesale markets* ('the financial markets') include the ►money market, the ►foreign-exchange market and the ►stock exchange.

Wicksell, Knut (1851–1926) Educated at Uppsala University in Sweden, where he studied mathematics and philosophy, Wicksell was appointed to the Chair of Economics at Lund in 1904, a post he held until 1916. His major publications include *Über Wert, Kapital und Rente* (1893) and *Geldzins und Güterpreise* (1898).

A synthesis of his work was published in 1901 and 1906 with the English title of *Lectures on Political Economy*. He assimilated the ➤general equilibrium analysis of ➤Walras with the work of ➤Böhm-Bawerk and worked out a theory of ➤distribution based on the new ➤marginal analysis of ➤Jevons, ➤Walras and ➤Menger. In addition, he had a significant influence on monetary theory. He pointed out that high ➤rates of interest often coincided with high prices, which was contrary to what current theory predicted. He drew attention to the significance of the relative level of interest rates rather than their absolute level. Prices were related to the difference between changes in the real or natural rate of ➤interest (which was determined by the expected rate of ➤profits) and the money rate. The ➤central bank had an important influence over the price level through its operations on the discount rate (➤bank rate). These theories were incorporated into his theory of the ➤business cycle. ➤➤interest, natural rate of; Wicksell effect, price.

Wicksell effect, price A phenomenon noted by ➤Wicksell in discussing the derivation of ➤factor prices from the value of ➤marginal products. He pointed out that in equilibrium the rate of interest would be greater than the value of the marginal product of capital. This is because the whole of the existing stock of capital is revalued when rates of interest change (➤capital re-switching).

Wieser, Friedrich von (1851–1926) Wieser succeeded ➤Menger in the Chair of Economics at Vienna University in 1903 after a period at Prague University. His most important works include *Über den Ursprung und die Hauptgesetze des Wirtschaftlichen Wertes* (1884), *Der natürliche Wert* (1889) and *Theorie der gesellschaftlichen Wirtschaft* (1914). He developed a law of costs which became known later as the principle of ➤opportunity cost. ➤factors of production would be distributed by competition such that, in ➤equilibrium, the value of their marginal outputs would be equal. The costs of production of any ➤commodity reflect the competing claims in other uses for the services of the factors needed to produce it. The law became an important element in the theory of ➤resource allocation (➤➤economic efficiency).

Williamson, Oliver ➤transaction costs.

windfall tax Specifically, a once and for all direct tax (➤direct taxation) on privatized (➤privatization) utility companies imposed by the UK government in 1997.

Generally, any tax imposed on persons or organizations deemed to have benefited from external events outside the normal course of their economic activities. The justification is generally made on the grounds that the taxpayers have benefited unfairly from gains that are due to society as a whole. The UK tax was justified on the grounds that shareholders benefited from state assets being sold below their value. There are precedents; for example the US government imposed a special tax on oil companies following the sudden increase in oil prices by the ➤Organization of Petroleum Exporting Countries in the 1970s. In 1981 the UK government imposed a special levy on bank deposits, partly on the grounds that the banks were largely exempt from ➤valued-added tax. Increases in land prices following the grant of planning permission have also been taxed.

Windfall taxes are highly controversial. It is usually difficult to design taxes which will, in fact, extract from the ultimate beneficiaries revenue proportionate to the gains made. This is both because of the usual problem of establishing incidence (➤taxation, incidence of) and for other reasons: for example, in the case of the UK windfall tax, many beneficiaries would have sold their shares in utilities before plans for the tax were announced. A theoretical justification for windfall taxes is that they are unlikely to distort behaviour or resource allocation because they are once and for all. (➤life-cycle hypothesis.) They may also be argued to promote 'social justice' in a rough and ready way, even though they breach the convention that taxes should not be imposed retrospectively.

winding up ➤liquidation.

window dressing Financial adjustments made solely for the purpose of accounting presentation, normally at the time of auditing of company accounts. An example is the sale of ➤securities so as to show large holdings of cash at the ➤balance sheet date, only to repurchase them immediately afterwards.

withholding tax ➤Taxation deducted from payments to non-residents. Withholding taxes are usually in the form of a standard rate of ➤income tax applied to ➤dividends or other payments by companies and are often reclaimable against tax liabilities in the country of residence of the recipient under a double-taxation agreement.

workers' participation ➤industrial democracy.

workfare Programmes that make the receipt of unemployment-related benefits conditional upon participation in some local work scheme. Workfare, an example of an ➤active labour-market policy, can reduce ➤long-term unemployment. This is partly because participation in any kind of work, has been shown to improve labour-market prospects of the unemployed (countering ➤hysteresis); and also because it encourages benefit claimants who do have viable options to work to take them. The relative weight of the 'carrot and stick' elements can be tailored scheme by scheme. In the UK workfare approaches have been piloted in *project work*. Explicit workfare has been superseded by the adoption of a broader programme of *welfare-to-work* measures, often with elements of workfare embodied in them.

working capital That part of current ➤assets financed from long-term funds. ➤➤current ratio.

World Bank Group ➤International Bank for Reconstruction and Development; International Development Association; International Finance Corporation; Multilateral Investment Guarantee Agency.

World Trade Organization The World Trade Organization was set up in Geneva in 1995 following the conclusion of the ►Uruguay round of trade negotiations. It replaced the ►General Agreement on Tariffs and Trade (GATT). The WTO is charged with the further development of and the policing of the multilateral trading system along the principles followed by the eight rounds of trade negotiations concluded under its predecessor. It provides the resources and the legal status for the resolution of trade disputes through independent disputes panels. A member may appeal to the WTO Appeals Tribunal but must accept its ruling. The failure of a member country to accept the WTO ruling would subject it to trade sanctions. In 1996 there were 122 member states. In 1997 agreement was reached for the liberalization of the telecommunications market world-wide with effect from 1998, which had not been achieved, as planned, under the Uruguay round.

writing-down allowance ►capital allowances.

X

***X*-efficiency** The effectiveness of a firm's management in minimizing the cost of producing a given output or maximizing the output produced by a given set of inputs. There is often a discrepancy between the efficient behaviour of firms as implied by economic theory and their observed behaviour in practice. This is frequently a result of a lack of the competitive pressures assumed. It was called *X*-efficiency by H. Liebenstein in 1966. ►firm, theory of the.

Y

Yaoundé Convention ➤Lomé Convention.

yardstick competition A device used in the ➤regulation of an industry, dominated by a number of regional ➤monopoly producers. Although the companies do not compete with each other directly, the regulator can use the performance of all the local monopolies as a benchmark for judging each of them. For example, in deciding what level of costs is a reasonable level to be reflected in the price (➤➤price regulation), a regulator can take the average cost of the companies. Those who can achieve lower costs would then be able to make larger profits than the others. This gives the companies an incentive to cut costs, while allowing the regulator a firm basis for deciding what can reasonably be expected of a producer. ➤➤tournament theory.

yield The ➤income from a ➤security as a proportion of its current market price. Thus, the *dividend yield* is the current ➤dividend as a percentage of the market price of a security. The *earnings yield* is a theoretical figure, based on the last dividend paid as a percentage of the current market price. The *redemption yield* is normally applied only to fixed-interest securities, and is the interest payment over the remaining life of the security, plus or minus the difference between the purchase price and the redemption value, i.e. it is the earnings yield adjusted to take account of any ➤capital gain or loss to redemption. With fixed-interest securities, the nominal interest, or ➤coupon, is unlikely to be the same as the actual yield. An ➤irredeemable security in the form of a government bond having a flat yield of 3 per cent with a ➤par value of £100, but a market price of £50, provides an earnings yield of 6 per cent. The earnings yield will fluctuate with the price of the security, rising as security prices fall, and vice versa. ➤➤gilt-edged securities.

yield curve A graphical representation of the relationship between the annual return on an asset and the number of years the asset has before expiring. Longer-term assets usually offer some premium over short-term ones and yield curves thus typically slope upwards. This effect is more pronounced if short-term interest rates are expected to rise. ➤➤term structure of interest rates.

yield gap The ➤yield on ➤ordinary shares minus the yield on ➤gilt-edged securities, e.g. 2½ per cent irredeemable ➤consols. If the latter exceeds the former, it is called the *reverse yield gap*.

Z

zero-sum game A game (➤game theory) in which one player's gain is equal to other players' losses, whatever strategy is chosen. The players can only compete for slices of a fixed cake; there are no opportunities of overall gain through collusion. The sum of gains will always equal the sum of losses, the whole summing to zero. ➤bilateral monopoly.